Encyclopedia of Decision Making and Decision Support Technologies

Frédéric Adam
University College Cork, Ireland

Patrick Humphreys
London School of Economics and Political Science, UK

Volume I
A–Im

Information Science
REFERENCE

INFORMATION SCIENCE REFERENCE
Hershey · New York

Acquisitions Editor:	Kristin Klinger
Development Editor:	Kristin Roth
Senior Managing Editor:	Jennifer Neidig
Managing Editor:	Sara Reed
Assistant Managing Editor:	Carole Coulson,
Copy Editor:	Joy Langel, Jeannie Porter, Holly J. Powell, Shanelle Ramelb
Typesetter:	Lindsay Bergman, Carole Coulson
Cover Design:	Lisa Tosheff
Printed at:	Yurchak Printing Inc.

Published in the United States of America by
Information Science Reference (an imprint of IGI Global)
701 E. Chocolate Avenue, Suite 200
Hershey PA 17033
Tel: 717-533-8845
Fax: 717-533-8661
E-mail: cust@igi-global.com
Web site: http://www.igi-global.com/reference

and in the United Kingdom by
Information Science Reference (an imprint of IGI Global)
3 Henrietta Street
Covent Garden
London WC2E 8LU
Tel: 44 20 7240 0856
Fax: 44 20 7379 0609
Web site: http://www.eurospanonline.com

Copyright © 2008 by IGI Global. All rights reserved. No part of this publication may be reproduced, stored or distributed in any form or by any means, electronic or mechanical, including photocopying, without written permission from the publisher.

Product or company names used in this set are for identification purposes only. Inclusion of the names of the products or companies does not indicate a claim of ownership by IGI Global of the trademark or registered trademark.

Library of Congress Cataloging-in-Publication Data

Encyclopedia of decision making and decision support technologies / Frederic Adam and Patrick Humphreys, editors.
  p. cm.
  Summary: "This book presents a critical mass of research on the most up-to-date research on human and computer support of managerial decision making, including discussion on support of operational, tactical, and strategic decisions, human vs. computer system support structure, individual and group decision making, and multi-criteria decision making"--Provided by publisher.
  ISBN-13: 978-1-59904-843-7
  ISBN-13: 978-1-59904-844-4
  1. Decision support systems. 2. Decision making--Encyclopedias. 3. Decision making--Data processing. I. Adam, Frédéric. II. Humphreys, Patrick.
  HD30.213.E527 2008
  658.4'03--dc22
                                2007047369

British Cataloguing in Publication Data
A Cataloguing in Publication record for this book is available from the British Library.

All work contributed to this encyclopedia set is original material. The views expressed in this encyclopedia set are those of the authors, but not necessarily of the publisher.

> *If a library purchased a print copy of this publication, please go to http://www.igi-global.com/agreement for information on activating the library's complimentary electronic access to this publication.*

This encyclopedia is dedicated in memory of Ward Edwards and Oleg Larichev, two great pioneers of our discipline

Editorial Advisory Board

David Arnott
Monash University, Australia

Frada Burstein
Monash University, Australia

Sven Carlsson
Lund University, Sweden

Georgios Doukidis
Athens University of Economics and Business, Greece

Eleanor Doyle
University College Cork, Ireland

Peter Gelleri
Budapest University of Technology and Economics, Hungary

Zita Paprika
Corvinus University of Budapest, Hungary

David Paradice
Florida State University, USA

Jean-Charles Pomerol
University Pierre et Marie Curie (Paris 6), France

Dan Power
*University of Northern Iowa, USA
DSS Resources.com*

List of Contributors

Adam, **Frédéric** / *University College Cork, Ireland* 426, 922, 930, 950
Aickelin, **Uwe** / *University of Nottingham, UK* 554, 645
Angulo Meza, **Lidia** / *Federal Fluminense University, Brazil* 709
Antunes, **Luis** / *GUESS/LabMAg/Universidade de Lisboa, Portugal* 716
Ashikhmin, **Ilya** / *Cork Constraint Computation Centre – University College Cork, Ireland* 514
Averweg, **Udo Richard** / *eThekwini Municipality and University of KwaZulu-Natal, South Africa* 218
Balsa, **João** / *GUESS/LabMAg/Universidade de Lisboa, Portugal* 716
Barbosa Diniz, **Viviane** / *Federal University of Rio de Janeiro, Brazil* 184
Beuschel, **Werner** / *Brandenburg University of Applied Sciences, Germany* 116
Beynon, **Malcolm J.** / *Cardiff University, UK* 76, 278, 382, 743, 751, 783
Bittmann, **Ran M.** / *Graduate School of Business Administration – Bar-Ilan University, Israel* 296
Borges, **Marcos R. S.** / *Federal University of Rio de Janeiro, Brazil* 184, 434
Brena, **Ramon** / *Centro de Sistemas Inteligentes – Tecnológico de Monterrey, Mexico* 489
Brézillon, **Patrick** / *University Paris 6, France & Université Pierre et Marie Curie, France* 102, 426
Brown, **Rex** / *George Mason University, USA* 141
Bruha, **Ivan** / *McMaster University, Canada* 176
Burstein, **F.** / *Monash University, Australia* 638
Butler, **Tom** / *University College Cork, Ireland* 466
Canós, **José H.** / *Technical University of Valencia, Spain* 184
Captivo, **Maria Eugénia** / *Universidade de Lisboa, Portugal* 53
Carlsson, **Sven A.** / *Lund University, Sweden* 38, 848
Carton, **Fergal** / *University College Cork, Ireland* 443
Casado Lumbreras, **Cristina** / *Universidad Complutense de Madrid, Spain* 482
Celia, **Helen** / *University of Leeds, UK* 645
Cervantes, **Francisco** / *Universidad Nacional Autónoma de México, Mexico* 455, 680
Chakraborty, **Chandana** / *Montclair State University, USA* 29
Chen, **Qiyang** / *Montclair State University, USA* 124, 236
Chen, **Zhen** / *Liverpool John Moores University, UK* 253, 958
Chesñevar, **Carlos** / *Universidad Nacional del Sur, Argentina* 489
Chugunov, **N.** / *Institute for Systems Analysis – Russian Academy of Sciences, Russia* 732
Churilov, **Leonid** / *Monash University, Australia* 245, 496
Clegg, **Chris** / *University of Leeds, UK* 645
Clímaco, **João Carlos Namorado** / *Coimbra University, Portugal & INESC Coimbra, Portugal* 53, 709
Coelho, **Helder** / *GUESS/LabMAg/Universidade de Lisboa, Portugal* 716
Coffey, **Seamus** / *University College Cork, Ireland* 402
Colomo Palacios, **Ricardo** / *Universidad Carlos III, Spain* 46, 482
Cowie, **J.** / *University of Stirling, UK* 638

Crichton, Susan / *University of Calgary, Canada*... 865
Csáki, Csaba / *University College Cork, Ireland* 653
Cunningham, Joe / *University College Cork, Ireland* 356
Dargam, Fátima C.C. / *SimTech Simulation Technology – Graz, Austria & ILTC, Instituto Doris Aragon – Rio de Janiero, Brazil* 374
Davis, Robert A. / *Texas State University – San Marcos, USA* 286
DeLuca, Dorrie / *University of Delaware, USA* 790
Deokar, Amit V. / *Dakota State University, USA* 61, 272
Dolgui, A. / *Ecole Nationale Supérieure des Mines de Saint-Etienne, France* 155, 165
Donati, A. / *ESA/ESOC, Germany* 391
Doyle, Liam / *Waterford Institute of Technology, Ireland* 814
El-Gayar, Omar F. / *Dakota State University, USA* 61, 272
Elfvengren, Kalle / *Lappeenranta University of Technology, Finland* 822
Fernandes, Sérgio / *Instituto Politécnico de Setúbal, Portugal* 53
Findlay, John / *Zing Technologies, Australia* 856
Finnegan, Pat / *University College Cork, Ireland* 882
Fitzgerald, Robert / *University of Canberra, Australia* 856
Forgionne, Guisseppi / *University of Maryland, Baltimore County, USA* 320, 329, 455, 680, 892, 939
Furems, Eugenia / *Russian Academy of Sciences, Russia* 514
Gachet, Alexandre / *University of Hawaii at Manoa, USA* 93
García Crespo, Ángel / *Universidad Carlos III, Spain* 46
García de la Cerda, Osvaldo / *Universidad de Santiago de Chile, Chile* 612
Gawinecki, Maciej / *Systems Research Institute of the Polish Academy of Sciences, Poland* 798
Gelbard, Roy M. / *Graduate School of Business Administration – Bar-Ilan University, Israel* 296
Gelman, Ovsei / *Universidad Nacional Autónoma de México, Mexico* 455, 680
Gomes, José Orlando / *Federal University of Rio de Janeiro, Brazil* 184, 434
Gómez Berbís, Juan Miguel / *Universidad Carlos III, Spain* 46, 482
Grundstein, Michel / *Dauphine University, France* 584
Gudes, Ori / *Ben-Gurion University of the Negev, Israel* 969
Guschinskaya, O. / *Ecole Nationale Supérieure des Mines de Saint-Etienne, France* 155
Guschinsky, N. / *United Institute of Informatics Problems, Belarus* 155, 165
Han, Jung Hoon / *University of Queensland, Australia* 691
Handzic, Meliha / *Sarajevo School of Science and Technology, Bosnia and Herzegovina* 134
Hayes, Jeremy / *University College Cork, Ireland* 882
Holsapple, C. W. / *University of Kentucky, USA* 837
Hong, Ju / *Beijing Institute of Civil Engineering and Architecture, China* 958
Humphreys, Patrick / *London School of Economics and Political Science, UK* 148, 225
Iafrate, Fernando / *Euro Disney SCA, France* 584
Índio dos Reis, Marcelo / *Federal University of Rio de Janeiro, Brazil* 434
Januszewski, Arkadiusz / *University of Technology and Life Sciences in Bydgoszcz, Poland* 1, 628
Jones, James D. / *Center for Advanced Intelligent Sytems, Texas Tech University, USA & Computer Science, Angelo State University, USA* 576, 593
Kale, Hrishikesh S. / *K.K.Wagh Institute of Engineering Education & Research, India* 539
Khan, Khaled M. / *Qatar University, Qatar* 211
Kivijärvi, Hannu / *Helsinki School of Economics, Finland* 200, 822
Klein, Michel R. / *Information Systems and Decision Science, HEC School of Management, France* 565
Kortelainen, Samuli / *Lappeenranta University of Technology, Finland* 822
Kouamou, G. / *National High School of Engineering, Cameroon* 368
Lee, Sang Ho / *Hanbat National University, South Korea* 691

Levin, G. / *United Institute of Informatics Problems, Belarus* 155, 165
Li, Aihua / *Montclair State University, USA* 410
Li, Heng / *The Hong Kong Polytechnic University, China* 253, 958
Lin, Chad / *Curtin University of Technology, Australia* 807
Lin, Koong / *Tainan National University of the Arts, Taiwan* 807
Lu, June / *University of Houston – Victoria, USA* 236
Lumsden, Joanna / *National Research Council of Canada, Canada* 618
Madritsch, Thomas / *University for Applied Sciences, Kufstein Tirol, Austria & University for Health Sciences, Medical Informatics and Technology, Austria* 84
May, Michael / *University of Applied Sciences, FHTW, Germany* 84
McAvoy, John / *University College Cork, Ireland* 466
McElroy, Todd / *Appalachian State University, USA* 757
Meredith, Rob / *Monash University, Australia* 474
Mora, Manuel / *Autonomous University of Aguascalientes, Mexico* 320, 455, 680
Morantz, Brad / *Science Applications International Corporation, USA* 661
Mustamil, Norizah / *Curtin University of Technology, Australia* 313
Neiger, Dina / *Monash University, Australia* 245, 496
Niezette, M. / *VEGA IT, Germany* 391
Nunes, I. L. / *Universidade Nova Lisboa, Portugal* 528
O'Donnell, Peter / *Monash University, Australia* 474
Ochoa, Sergio F. / *Universidad de Chile, Chile* 69
Orellana Muermann, Renato / *CIGAR Ltda., Chile* 612
Ostermann, Herwig / *University for Health Sciences, Medical Informatics and Technology, Austria* 84
Ouyang, Huanyu / *The People's Hospital of Jiangxi Provence, China* 29
Pankowska, Malgorzata / *Karol Adamiecki University of Economics in Katowice, Poland* 798
Paradice, David / *Florida State University, USA* 192, 286
Pendegraft, Norman / *University of Idaho, USA* 306
Pereira, R. Marques / *Università degli Studi di Trento, Italy* 391
Peters, Georg / *Munich University of Applied Sciences, Germany* 901
Petrovsky, Alexey / *Institute for Systems Analysis – Russian Academy of Sciences, Russia* 418, 514
Pettang, C. / *National High School of Engineering, Cameroon* 368
Phillips-Wren, Gloria E. / *Loyola College in Maryland, USA* 320, 505
Piirainen, Kalle / *Lappeenranta University of Technology, Finland* 822
Pino, José A. / *Universidad de Chile, Chile* 69
Pomerol, Jean-Charles / *Université Pierre et Marie Curie, France* 102, 426, 922, 930
Power, Bernadette / *University College Cork, Ireland* 766
Power, Daniel J. / *University of Northern Iowa, USA* 232
Quaddus, Mohammed / *Curtin University of Technology, Australia* 313
Rahimi, Shahram / *Southern Illinois University, USA* 798
Respício, Ana / *Operations Research Center/GUESS/Universidade de Lisboa, Portugal* 716
Ribeiro, R. A. / *UNINOVA – CA3, Portugal* 391, 528
Rine, David C. / *George Mason University, USA* 339
Rosenthal-Sabroux, Camille / *Dauphine University, France* 584
Rounds, Mark / *University of Idaho, USA* 306
Russell, Stephen / *University of Maryland, Baltimore County, USA* 329, 892, 939
Ryan, Geraldine / *University College Cork, Ireland* 402, 724, 776
Sammon, David / *University College Cork, Ireland* 348, 910, 916
Saygin, Omur / *Izmir Institute of Technology, Turkey* 699
Scheuerer, Stephan / *Fraunhofer Center for Applied Research on Technologies for the Logistics Service Industries ATL, Germany* 604

Schlueter Langdon, Chris / *Center for Telecom Management, University of Southern California, USA*...668
Serra, P. / *UNINOVA – CA3, Portugal*...391
Shepelyov, G. / *Institute for Systems Analysis – Russian Academy of Sciences, Russia*...732
Shinnick, Edward / *University College Cork, Ireland*...724, 776
Siebers, Peer-Olaf / *University of Nottingham, UK*...554, 645
Soares de Mello, João Carlos / *Federal Fluminense University, Brazil*...709
Sprague, Ralph / *University of Hawaii at Manoa, USA*...93
Stanek, Stanislaw / *Karol Adamiecki University of Economics in Katowice, Poland*...798
Staudinger, Roland / *University for Health Sciences, Medical Informatics and Technology, Austria*...84
Steel, R. / *VEGA IT, Germany*...391
Sternin, Michael / *Institute for Systems Analysis – Russian Academy of Sciences, Russia*...514, 732
Strand, Mattias / *University of Skövde, Sweden*...848
Sun, Szu-Li / *The University of Reading, UK*...253
Tuominen, Markku / *Lappeenranta University of Technology, Finland*...200, 822
Valacich, Joseph S. / *Washington State University, USA*...790
Vasant, Pandian / *Universiti Teknologi Petronas, Malaysia*...539
Wang, Dajin / *Montclair State University, USA*...410
Wang, John / *Montclair State University, USA*...29, 124, 236, 410
Whalen, Thomas / *Georgia State University, USA*...661
Wood, Margaret W. / *George Mason University, USA*...339
Woodworth, Simon / *University College Cork, Ireland*...356
Xu, Qian / *Liverpool John Moores University, UK*...253, 958
Yaniv, Hanan / *University of Calgary, Canada*...865, 872
Yao, James / *Montclair State University, USA*...124, 236
Yigitcanlar, Tan / *Queensland University of Technology, Australia*...691, 699, 969
Zaraté, Pascale / *Université de Toulouse – INPT – IRIT, France*...109
Zhang, G. Peter / *Georgia State University, USA*...661
Zoltay Paprika, Zita / *Corvinus University of Budapest, Hungary*...20

Contents
by Volume

VOLUME I

Activity-Based Costing System for a Small Manufacturing Company: A Case Study /
Arkadiusz Januszewski, University of Technology and Life Sciences in Bydgoszcz, Poland 1

Analysis and Intuition in Strategic Decision Making: The Case of California /
Zita Zoltay Paprika, Corvinus University of Budapest, Hungary 20

Analytic Hierarchy Process: Structuring, Measurement, and Synthesis, The /
*John Wang, Montclair State University, USA; Chandana Chakraborty, Montclair State University, USA;
and Huanyu Ouyang, The People's Hospital of Jianxi Provence, China* 29

Attention-Based View on DSS, An / *Sven A. Carlsson, Lund University, Sweden*................................... 38

Balanced Scorecard Concepts, Technology, and Applications / *Ricardo Colomo Palacios,
Universidad Carlos III, Spain; Juan Miguel Gómez Berbís, Universidad Carlos III, Spain;
and Ángel García Crespo, Universidad Carlos III, Spain*.. 46

Bi-Criteria DSS Dedicated to Location Problems, A / *Maria Eugénia Captivo, Universidade de Lisboa,
Portugal; João Carlos Namorado Clímaco, Coimbra University & INESC Coimbra, Portugal;
and Sérgio Fernandes, Instituto Politécnico de Setúbal, Portugal*... 53

Business Process Management Systems for Supporting Individual and Group Decision Making /
Amit V. Deokar, Dakota State University, USA and Omar F. El-Gayar, Dakota State University, USA............ 61

Challenges for Decision Support in Urban Disaster Scenarios / *Sergio F. Ochoa, Universidad de Chile,
Chile and José A. Pino, Universidad de Chile, Chile*.. 69

Classification and Ranking Belief Simplex / *Malcolm J. Beynon, Cardiff University, UK*........................... 76

Computer Aided Facility Management (CAFM) as a New Branch of Decision Making Technologies
Support in the Field of Facility Management / *Thomas Madritsch, University for Applied Sciences
Kufstein Tirol, Austria, Univeristy for Health Sciences, Medical Informatics and Technology, Austria;
Michael May, University of Applied Sciences, FHTW, Germany; Herwig Ostermann, Univeristy for
Health Sciences, Medical Informatics and Technology, Austria; and Roland Staudinger, Univeristy for
Health Sciences, Medical Informatics and Technology, Austria*... 84

Context in Decision Support Systems Development / *Alexandre Gachet, University of Hawaii at Manoa, USA and Ralph Sprague, University of Hawaii at Manoa, USA* 93

Contextualization in Decision Making and Decision Support / *Patrick Brézillon, University Paris 6, France & Université Pierre et Marie Curie, France and Jean-Charles Pomerol, Université Pierre et Marie Curie, France* 102

Cooperative Decision Support Systems / *Pascale Zaraté, Université de Toulouse – INPT – IRIT, France* 109

Dashboards for Management / *Werner Beuschel, Brandenburg University of Applied Sciences, Germany* 116

Data Warehousing for Decision Support / *John Wang, Montclair State University, USA; James Yao, Montclair State University, USA; and Qiyang Chen, Montclair State University, USA* 124

Debiasing Decision Makers Through Knowledge Management / *Meliha Handzic, Sarajevo School of Science and Technology, Bosnia and Herzegovina* 134

Decision Aiding Research Needs / *Rex Brown, George Mason University, USA* 141

Decision Hedgehog: Group Communication and Decision Support, The / *Patrick Humphreys, London School of Economics and Political Science, UK* 148

Decision Making and Support Tools for Design of Machining Systems / *A. Dolgui, Ecole Nationale Supérieure des Mines de Saint-Etienne, France; O. Guschinskaya, Ecole Nationale Supérieure des Mines de Saint-Etienne, France; N. Guschinsky, United Institute of Informatics Problems, Belarus; and G. Levin, United Institute of Informatics Problems, Belarus* 155

Decision-Making and Support Tools for Design of Transmission Systems / *A. Dolgui, Ecole Nationale Supérieure des Mines de Saint-Etienne, France; N. Guschinsky, United Institute of Informatics Problems, Belarus; and G. Levin, United Institute of Informatics Problems, Belarus* 165

Decision Making by a Multiple-Rule Classifier: The Role of Rule Qualities / *Ivan Bruha, McMaster University, Canada* 176

Decision Making Support in Emergency Response / *Viviane Barbosa Diniz, Federal University of Rio de Janeiro, Brazil; Marcos R. S. Borges, Federal University of Rio de Janeiro, Brazil; José Orlando Gomes, Federal University of Rio de Janeiro, Brazil; and José H. Canós, Technical University of Valencia, Spain* 184

Decision Support and Problem Formulation Activity / *David Paradice, Florida State University, USA* 192

Decision Support System for Evaluation of Investments in a Computer-Integrated Production System, A / *Hannu Kivijärvi, Helsinki School of Economics, Finland and Markku Tuominen, Lappeenranta University of Technology, Finland* 200

Decision Support System for Selecting Secure Web Services, A / *Khaled M. Khan, Qatar University, Qatar* 211

Decision Support Systems and Decision-Making Processes / *Udo Richard Averweg, eThekwini Municipality and University of KwaZulu-Natal, South Africa* 218

Decision Support Systems and Representation Levels in the Decision Spine / *Patrick Humphreys, London School of Economics and Political Science, UK* 225

Decision Support Systems Concept / *Daniel J. Power, University of Northern Iowa, USA* 232

Development and Design Methodologies in DWM / *James Yao, Montclair State University, USA; John Wang, Montclair State University, USA; Qiyang Chen, Montclair State University, USA; and June Lu, University of Houston – Victoria, USA* 236

Diagrammatic Decision-Support Modeling Tools in the Context of Supply Chain Management / *Dina Neiger, Monash University, Australia and Leonid Churilov, Monash University, Australia* 245

Disaster-Oriented Assessment of Urban Clusters for Locating Production Systems in China, The / *Zhen Chen, Liverpool John Moores University, UK; Heng Li, The Hong Kong Polytechnic University, China; Qian Xu, Liverpool John Moores University, UK; and Szu-Li Sun, The University of Reading, UK* 253

Distributed Model Management: Current Status and Future Directions / *Omar F. El-Gayar, Dakota State University, USA and Amit V. Deokar, Dakota State University, USA* 272

DS/AHP / *Malcolm J. Beynon, Cardiff University, UK* 278

DSS and Multiple Perspectives of Complex Problems / *David Paradice, Florida State University, USA and Robert A. Davis, Texas State University – San Marcos, USA* 286

DSS Using Visualization of Multi-Algorithms Voting / *Ran M. Bittmann, Graduate School of Business, Bar-Ilan University, Israel and Roy M. Gelbard, Graduate School of Business, Bar-Ilan University, Israel* 296

Dynamic System Simulation for Decision Support / *Norman Pendegraft, University of Idaho, USA and Mark Rounds, University of Idaho, USA* 306

Ethical Decision Making: A Critical Assessment and an Integrated Model / *Norizah Mustamil, Curtin University of Technology, Australia and Mohammed Quaddus, Curtin University of Technology, Australia* 313

Evaluation of Decision-Making Support Systems / *Gloria E. Phillips-Wren, Loyola College in Maryland, USA; Manuel Mora, Autonomous University of Aguascalientes, Mexico; and Guisseppi Forgionne, University of Maryland, Baltimore County, USA* 320

Evaluation of Decision-Making Support Systems Functionality, The / *Guisseppi Forgionne, University of Maryland, Baltimore County, USA and Stephen Russell, University of Maryland, Baltimore County, USA* 329

Exploring the Risks That Affect Community College Decision Makers / *Margaret W. Wood, George Mason University, USA and David C. Rine, George Mason University, USA* 339

Extended Model of Decision Making: A Devil's Advocate Workshop, An / *David Sammon, University College Cork, Ireland* 348

Facilitation of Supply Chain Decision Processes in SMEs, Using Information Systems / *Simon Woodworth, University College Cork, Ireland and Joe Cunningham, University College Cork, Ireland* 356

Federative Approach of Decision-Making Aid in Urban Development, A / *G. Kouamou, National High School of Engineering, Cameroon and C. Pettang, National High School of Engineering, Cameroon* 368

Finite-Base Revision Supporting Knowledge Management and Decision Making / *Fátima C.C. Dargam, SimTech Simulation Technology – Graz, Austria & ILTC, Instituto Doris Aragon – Rio de Janeiro, Brazil* 374

Fuzzy Decision Trees / *Malcolm J. Beynon, Cardiff University, UK* 382

Fuzzy Thermal Alarm System for Venus Express / *P. Serra, UNINOVA – CA3, Portugal; R. A. Ribeiro, UNINOVA – CA3, Portugal; R. Marques Pereira, Università degli Studi di Trento, Italy; R. Steel, VEGA IT, Germany; M. Niezette, VEGA IT, Germany; and A. Donati, ESA / ESOC, Germany* 391

Games of Strategy / *Geraldine Ryan, University College Cork, Ireland and Seamus Coffey, University College Cork, Ireland* 402

Goal Programming and Its Variants / *John Wang, Montclair State University, USA; Dajin Wang, Montclair State University, USA; and Aihua Li, Montclair State University, USA* 410

Group Verbal Decision Analysis / *Alexey Petrovsky, Insitute for Systems Analysis – Russian Academy of Sciences, Russia* 418

How Groupware Systems Can Change How an Organisation Makes Decisions: A Case Study in the Publishing Industry / *Frédéric Adam, University College Cork, Ireland; Jean-Charles Pomerol, Université Pierre et Marie Curie, France; and Patrick Brézillon, Université Pierre et Marie Curie, France* 426

Identifying Resilient Actions in Decision Making During Emergencies / *Marcelo Índio dos Reis, Federal University of Rio de Janeiro, Brazil; Marcos R. S. Borges, Federal University of Rio de Janeiro, Brazil; and José Orlando Gomes, Federal University of Rio de Janeiro, Brazil* 434

Impact on Decsion Making of Centralisation in a Multi-National Manfacturing Company: The Materials Purchasing Function, The / *Fergal Carton, University College Cork, Ireland* 443

Implementation of Large-Scale Decision-Making Support Systems: Problems, Findings, and Challenges, The / *Manuel Mora, Autonomous University of Aguascalientes, Mexico; Ovsei Gelman, Universidad Nacional Autónoma de México, Mexico; Guisseppi Forgionne, University of Maryland, Baltimore County, USA; and Francisco Cervantes, Universidad Nacional Autónoma de México, Mexico* 455

VOLUME II

Ineffective Decision Making in Adopting an Agile Software Development Methodology / *John McAvoy, University College Cork, Ireland and Tom Butler, University College Cork, Ireland* 466

Influence Diagrams as a Tool for Decision Support System Design / *Peter O'Donnell, Monash University, Australia and Rob Meredith, Monash University, Australia* 474

Influence of Emotions in Making Hard Decisions in Organizational Contexts, The / *Cristina Casado Lumbreras, Universidad Complutense de Madrid, Spain; Ricardo Colomo Palacios, Universidad Carlos III de Madrid, Spain; and Juan Miguel Gómez Berbís, Universidad Carlos III de Madrid, Spain* 482

Information Distribution Decisions Supported by Argumentation / *Ramon Brena, Centro de Sistemas Inteligentes – Tecnológico de Monterrey, Mexico and Carlos Chesñevar, Universidad Nacional del Sur, Argentina* 489

Integration of Diagrammatic Business Modeling Tools / *Dina Neiger, Monash University, Australia and Leonid Churilov, Monash University, Australia* 496

Intelligent Agents in Decision Support Systems / *Gloria E. Phillips-Wren, Loyola College in Maryland, USA* 505

Intelligent DSS Under Verbal Decision Analysis / *Ilya Ashikhmin, Cork Constraint Computation Centre – University College Cork, Ireland; Eugenia Furems, Russian Academy of Sciences, Russia; Alexey Petrovsky, Institute for Systems Analysis – Russian Academy of Sciences, Russia; and Michael Sternin, Institute for Systems Analysis – Russian Academy of Sciences, Russia* 514

Interfaces Usability for Monitoring Systems / *R. A. Ribeiro, UNINOVA – CA3, Portugal and I. L. Nunes, Universidade Nova Lisboa, Portugal* 528

Introduction to Fuzzy Logic and Fuzzy Linear Programming / *Pandian Vasant, Universiti Teknologi Petronas, Malaysia and Hrishikesh S. Kale, K.K.Wagh Institute of Engineering Education & Research, India* 539

Introduction to Multi-Agent Simulation / *Peer-Olaf Siebers, University of Nottingham, UK and Uwe Aickelin, University of Nottingham, UK* 554

Knowledge Based DSS / *Michel R. Klein, Information Systems and Decision Science, HEC School of Management, France* 565

Knowledge Representation to Empower Expert Systems / *James D. Jones, Center for Advanced Intelligent Systems, Texas Tech University, USA & Computer Science, Angelo State University, USA* 576

Knowledge Worker Desktop Model (KWDM) Applied to Decision Support System, A / *Camille Rosenthal-Sabroux, Dauphine University, France; Michel Grundstein, Dauphine University, France; and Fernando Iafrate, Euro Disney SCA, France* 584

Logic Programming Languages for Expert Systems / *James D. Jones, Center for Advanced Intelligent Systems, Texas Tech University, USA & Computer Science, Angelo State University, USA* 593

Metaheuristics: Heuristic Techniques for Combinatorial Optimization Problems / *Stephan Scheuerer, Fraunhofer Center for Applied Research on Technologies for the Logistics Service Industries ATL, Germany* 604

Metasystemic Re-Engineering: An Organizational Intervention / *Osvaldo García de la Cerda, Universidad de Santiago de Chile, Chile and Renato Orellana Muermann, CIGAR Ltda., Chile* 612

Method for Systematic Artifact Selection Decision Making, A / *Joanna Lumsden, National Research Council of Canada, Canada* 618

Method of Appraising Needs and Possibilities of Activity-Based Costing Implementation, The / *Arkadiusz Januszewski, University of Technology and Life Sciences in Bydgoszcz, Poland* 628

Mobile Decision Support for Time-Critical Decision Making / *F. Burstein, Monash University, Australia and J. Cowie, University of Stirling, UK* 638

Multi-Agent Simulation and Management Practices / *Peer-Olaf Siebers, University of Nottingham, UK; Uwe Aickelin, University of Nottingham, UK; Helen Celia, University of Leeds, UK; and Chris Clegg, University of Leeds, UK* 645

Mythical Decision Maker: Models of Roles in Decision Making, The / *Csaba Csáki, University College Cork, Ireland* 653

Neural Network Time Series Forecasting Using Recency Weighting / *Brad Morantz, Science Applications International Corporation, USA; Thomas Whalen, Georgia State University, USA; and G. Peter Zhang, Georgia State University, USA* 661

Next Generation Analytics and Dynamic Decision Support: AutoMarketSIM and Vehicle Sales Decay Navigation / *Chris Schlueter Langdon, Center for Telecom Management, University of Southern California, USA* 668

On Frameworks and Architectures for Intelligent Decision-Making Support Systems / *Manuel Mora, Autonomous University of Aguascalientes, Mexico; Francisco Cervantes, Universidad Nacional Autónoma de México, Mexico; Guisseppi Forgionne, University of Maryland, Baltimore County, USA; and Ovsei Gelman, Universidad Nacional Autónoma de México, Mexico* 680

Online Environmental Information Systems / *Tan Yigitcanlar, Queensland University of Technology, Australia; Jung Hoon Han, University of Queensland, Australia; and Sang Ho Lee, Hanbat National University, South Korea* 691

Online Urban Information Systems / *Tan Yigitcanlar, Queensland University of Technology, Australia and Omur Saygin, Izmir Institute of Technology, Turkey* 699

Performance Measurement: From DEA to MOLP / *João Carlos Namorado Climaco, Coimbra University, Portugal & INESC Coimbra, Portugal; João Carlos Soares de Mello, Federal Fluminense University, Brazil; and Lidia Angulo Meza, Federal Fluminense University, Brazil* 709

Policy Decision Support Through Social Simulation / *Luis Antunes, GUESS/LabMAg/Universidade de Lisboa, Portugal; Ana Respício, Operations Research Center/GUESS/Universidade de Lisboa, Portugal; João Balsa, GUESS/LabMAg/Universidade de Lisboa, Portugal; and Helder Coelho, GUESS/LabMAg/Universidade de Lisboa, Portugal,* 716

Power of Incentives in Decision Making, The / *Geraldine Ryan, University College Cork, Ireland and Edward Shinnick, University College Cork, Ireland* 724

Probabilistic Methods for Uncertainty Quantification / *N. Chugunov, Institute for Systems Analysis – Russian Academy of Sciences, Russia; G. Shepelyov, Institute for Systems Analysis – Russian Academy of Sciences, Russia; and Michael Sternin, Institute for Systems Analysis – Russian Academy of Sciences, Russia* 732

PROMETHEE / *Malcolm J. Beynon, Cardiff University, UK* 743

Qualitative Comparative Analysis / *Malcolm J. Beynon, Cardiff University, UK* 751

Rational Decision Making, Dual Processes, and Framing: Current Thoughts and Perspectives / *Todd McElroy, Appalachian State University, USA* 757

Real Options Reasoning as a Tool for Managerial Decision Making / *Bernadette Power, University College Cork, Ireland* 766

Role of Information in Decision Making, The / *Edward Shinnick, University College Cork, Ireland and Geraldine Ryan, University College Cork, Ireland* 776

Rough Set Theory / *Malcolm J. Beynon, Cardiff University, UK* 783

Situational Synchronicity for Decision Support / *Dorrie DeLuca, University of Delaware, USA and Joseph S. Valacich, Washington State University, USA* 790

Software Agents / *Stanislaw Stanek, Karol Adamiecki University of Economics in Katowice, Poland; Maciej Gawinecki, Systems Research Institute of the Polish Academy of Sciences, Poland; Malgorzata Pankowska, Karol Adamiecki University of Economics in Katowice, Poland; and Shahram Rahimi, Southern Illinois University, USA* 798

Study of Information Requirement Determination Process of an Executive Information System, A / *Chad Lin, Curtin University of Technology, Australia and Koong Lin, Tainan National University of the Arts, Taiwan* 807

Supply Chain Information Systems and Decision Support / *Liam Doyle, Waterford Institute of Technology, Ireland* 814

Support System for the Strategic Scenario Process, A / *Hannu Kivijärvi, Helsinki School of Economics, Finland; Kalle Piirainen, Lappeenranta University of Technology, Finland; Markku Tuominen, Lappeenranta University of Technology, Finland; Samuli Kortelainen, Lappeenranta University of Technology, Finland; and Kalle Elfvengren, Lappeenranta University of Technology, Finland* 822

Supporting Decisional Episodes / *C. W. Holsapple, University of Kentucky, USA* 837

Syndicate Date Suppliers: Their Business Environment, the Industry, and Their Core Business Process / *Mattias Strand, University of Skövde, Sweden and Sven A. Carlsson, Lund University, Sweden* 848

Team Learning Systems as a Collaborative Technology for Rapid Knowledge Creation / *Robert Fitzgerald, University of Canberra, Australia and John Findlay, Zing Techologies, Australia* 856

ThinkClick: A Case Study of a Large Group Decision Supporrt System (LGDSS) / *Hanan Yaniv, University of Calgary, Canada and Susan Crichton, University of Calgary, Canada* 865

ThinkTeam: GDSS Methodology and Technology as a Collaborative Learning Task / *Hanan Yaniv, University of Calgary, Canada* 872

Towards a Framework for Assisting Decision-Makers Assess the Potential of E-Business Models / *Pat Finnegan, University College Cork, Ireland and Jeremy Hayes, University College Cork, Ireland* 882

Unambiguous Goal Seeking Through Mathematical Modeling / *Guisseppi Forgionne, University of Maryland, Baltimore County, USA and Stephen Russell, University of Maryland, Baltimore County, USA* 892

Uncertainty and Vagueness Concepts in Decision Making / *Georg Peters, Munich University of Applied Sciences, Germany* 901

Understanding Non-Decision Making / *David Sammon, University College Cork, Ireland* 910

Understanding Sense-Making / *David Sammon, University College Cork, Ireland* 916

Understanding the Influence of Context on Organisational Decision Making / *Frédéric Adam, University College Cork, Ireland and Jean-Charles Pomerol, Université Pierre et Marie Curie, France* 922

Understanding the Legacy of Herbert Simon to Decision Support Systems / *Jean-Charles Pomerol, Université Pierre et Marie Curie, France and Frédéric Adam, University College Cork, Ireland* 930

Use of Simulation as an Experimental Methodology for DMSS Research, The / *Guisseppi Forgionne, University of Maryland, Baltimore County, USA and Stephen Russell, University of Maryland, Baltimore County, USA* 939

Using Network Analysis for Understanding How Decisions are Made / *Frédéric Adam, University College Cork, Ireland* 950

Web-Based Decision Support for Knowledge Sharing and Management in Intelligence Buildings Assessment / *Zhen Chen, Liverpool John Moores University, UK; Ju Hong, Beijing Institute of Civil Engineering and Architecture, China; Heng Li, The Hong Kong Polytechnic University, China; and Qian Xu, Liverpool John Moores University, UK* 958

Web-Based Public Participatory GIS / *Tan Yigitcanlar, Queensland University of Technology, Australia and Ori Gudes, Ben-Gurion University of the Negev, Israel* 969

Contents
by Keyword

Activity-Based Costing Implementation
Method of Appraising Needs and Possibilities of Activity-Based Costing Implementation, The /
Arkadiusz Januszewski, University of Technology and Life Sciences in Bydgoszcz, Poland 628

Activity-Based Costing Systems
Activity-Based Costing System for a Small Manufacturing Company: A Case Study /
Arkadiusz Januszewski, University of Technology and Life Sciences in Bydgoszcz, Poland 1

Adoption Decisions
Ineffective Decision Making in Adopting an Agile Software Development Methodology / *John McAvoy,
University College Cork, Ireland and Tom Butler, University College Cork, Ireland* 466

AHP / Multi-Criteria
Analytic Hierarchy Process: Structuring, Measurement, and Synthesis, The /
*John Wang, Montclair State University, USA; Chandana Chakraborty, Montclair State University, USA;
and Huanyu Ouyang, The People's Hospital of Jianxi Provence, China* 29

Attention-Based View
Attention-Based View on DSS, An / *Sven A. Carlsson, Lund University, Sweden* 38

Balance Scorecard
Balanced Scorecard Concepts, Technology, and Applications / *Ricardo Colomo Palacios,
Universidad Carlos III, Spain; Juan Miguel Gómez Berbís, Universidad Carlos III, Spain;
and Ángel García Crespo, Universidad Carlos III, Spain* 46

Business Intelligence Analytics
Next Generation Analytics and Dynamic Decision Support: AutoMarketSIM and Vehicle Sales Decay
Navigation / *Chris Schlueter Langdon, Center for Telecom Management, University of Southern
California, USA* 668

Business Process Management Systems
Business Process Management Systems for Supporting Individual and Group Decision Making /
Amit V. Deokar, Dakota State University, USA and Omar F. El-Gayar, Dakota State University, USA 61

CaRBS
Classification and Ranking Belief Simplex / *Malcolm J. Beynon, Cardiff University, UK*...............76

Centralisation of Decision Making
Impact on Decsion Making of Centralisation in a Multi-National Manfacturing Company:
The Materials Purchasing Function, The / *Fergal Carton, University College Cork, Ireland*.................434

Classification of DSS
Decision Support Systems Concept / *Daniel J. Power, University of Northern Iowa, USA*.....................232

CLEHES
Metasystemic Re-Engineering: An Organizational Intervention / *Osvaldo García de la Cerda, Universidad de Santiago de Chile, Chile and Renato Orellana Muermann, CIGAR Ltda., Chile*................612

Collaboration
Team Learning Systems as a Collaborative Technology for Rapid Knowledge Creation / *Robert Fitzgerald, University of Canberra, Australia and John Findlay, Zing Techologies, Australia*....................856

Collaborative Decision Making
Cooperative Decision Support Systems / *Pascale Zaraté, Université de Toulouse – INPT – IRIT, France*.......109

Complex Decision Making
DSS and Multiple Perspectives of Complex Problems / *David Paradice, Florida State University, USA and Robert A. Davis, Texas State University – San Marcos, USA*.................286

Context in Decision Making
Understanding the Influence of Context on Organisational Decision Making / *Frédéric Adam, University College Cork, Ireland and Jean-Charles Pomerol, Université Pierre et Marie Curie, France*........922

Contextualization for Decision Making
Contextualization in Decision Making and Decision Support / *Patrick Brézillon, University Paris 6, France & Université Pierre et Marie Curie, France and Jean-Charles Pomerol, Université Pierre et Marie Curie, France* 102

Data Warehousing
Data Warehousing for Decision Support / *John Wang, Montclair State University, USA; James Yao, Montclair State University, USA; and Qiyang Chen, Montclair State University, USA*...................124

Data Warehousing Design and Development
Development and Design Methodologies in DWM / *James Yao, Montclair State University, USA; John Wang, Montclair State University, USA; Qiyang Chen, Montclair State University, USA; and June Lu, University of Houston – Victoria, USA* 236

Debiasing and Decision Making
Debiasing Decision Makers Through Knowledge Management / *Meliha Handzic, Sarajevo School of Science and Technology, Bosnia and Herzegovina*...................134

Decision Makers
Mythical Decision Maker: Models of Roles in Decision Making, The / *Csaba Csáki, University College Cork, Ireland*..653

Decision Making and Decision Support Concepts
Decision Support Systems and Decision-Making Processes / *Udo Richard Averweg, eThekwini Municipality and University of KwaZulu-Natal, South Africa*...218

Decision Making Support System Evaluation
Evaluation of Decision Making Support Systems / *Gloria E. Phillips-Wren, Loyola College in Maryland, USA, Manuel Mora, Autonomous University of Aguascalientes, Mexico, and Guisseppi Forgionne, University of Maryland – Baltimore County, USA*...320

Decisional Episodes
Supporting Decisional Episodes / *C. W. Holsapple, University of Kentucky, USA*..........................837

Decision-Hedgehog
Decision Hedgehog: Group Communication and Decision Support, The / *Patrick Humphreys, London School of Economics and Political Science, UK*..148

Diagramming for Supply Chain Management
Integration of Diagrammatic Business Modeling Tools / *Dina Neiger, Monash University, Australia and Leonid Churilov, Monash University, Australia*..496

Diagramming for Supply Chain Management
Diagrammatic Decision-Support Modeling Tools in the Context of Supply Chain Management / *Dina Neiger, Monash University, Australia and Leonid Churilov, Monash University, Australia*...................245

Digital Dashboards
Dashboards for Management / *Werner Beuschel, Brandenburg University of Applied Sciences, Germany*.......116

Distributed Model Management
Distributed Model Management: Current Status and Future Directions / *Omar F. El-Gayar, Dakota State University, USA and Amit V. Deokar, Dakota State University, USA*.....................................272

DS / AHP
DS/AHP / *Malcolm J. Beynon, Cardiff University, UK*..278

DSS Development
Context in Decision Support Systems Development / *Alexandre Gachet, University of Hawaii at Manoa, USA and Ralph Sprague, University of Hawaii at Manoa, USA*..93

Emergency
Decision Making Support in Emergency Response / *Viviane Barbosa Diniz, Federal University of Rio de Janeiro, Brazil; Marcos R. S. Borges, Federal University of Rio de Janeiro, Brazil; José Orlando Gomes, Federal University of Rio de Janeiro, Brazil; and José H. Canós, Technical University of Valencia, Spain*..184

Emergency Management

Challenges for Decision Support in Urban Disaster Scenarios / *Sergio F. Ochoa, Universidad de Chile, Chile and José A. Pino, Universidad de Chile, Chile* 69

Emergency Response

Identifying Resilient Actions in Decision Making During Emergencies / *Marcelo Índio dos Reis, Federal University of Rio de Janeiro, Brazil; Marcos R. S. Borges, Federal University of Rio de Janeiro, Brazil; and José Orlando Gomes, Federal University of Rio de Janeiro, Brazil* 457

Emotions in Decision Making

Influence of Emotions in Making Hard Decisions in Organizational Contexts, The / *Cristina Casado Lumbreras, Universidad Complutense de Madrid, Spain; Ricardo Colomo Palacios, Universidad Carlos III de Madrid, Spain; and Juan Miguel Gómez Berbís, Universidad Carlos III de Madrid, Spain* 482

Equivocality in Decision Making

Finite-Base Revision Supporting Knowledge Management and Decision Making / *Fátima C.C. Dargam, SimTech Simulation Technology – Graz, Austria & ILTC, Instituto Doris Aragon – Rio de Janeiro, Brazil* 374

Ethical Decision Making

Ethical Decision Making: A Critical Assessment and an Integrated Model / *Norizah Mustamil, Curtin University of Technology, Australia and Mohammed Quaddus, Curtin University of Technology, Australia* 313

Evaluation of DMSS

Evaluation of Decision-Making Support Systems / *Gloria E. Phillips-Wren, Loyola College in Maryland, USA; Manuel Mora, Autonomous University of Aguascalientes, Mexico; and Guisseppi Forgionne, University of Maryland, Baltimore County, USA* 329

Executive Information Systems (EIS)

Study of Information Requirement Determination Process of an Executive Information System, A / *Chad Lin, Curtin University of Technology, Australia and Koong Lin, Tainan National University of the Arts, Taiwan* 807

Facility Management

Computer Aided Facility Management (CAFM) as a New Branch of Decision Making Technologies Support in the Field of Facility Management / *Thomas Madritsch, University for Applied Sciences Kufstein Tirol, Austria, Univeristy for Health Sciences, Medical Informatics and Technology, Austria; Michael May, University of Applied Sciences, FHTW, Germany; Herwig Ostermann, Univeristy for Health Sciences, Medical Informatics and Technology, Austria; and Roland Staudinger, Univeristy for Health Sciences, Medical Informatics and Technology, Austria* 84

Forecasting (DSS for)

Neural Network Time Series Forecasting Using Recency Weighting / *Brad Morantz, Science Applications International Corporation, USA; Thomas Whalen, Georgia State University, USA; and G. Peter Zhang, Georgia State University, USA* 661

Framing-Effect
Rational Decision Making, Dual Processes, and Framing: Current Thoughts and Perspectives / *Todd McElroy, Appalachian State University, USA* 757

Fuzzy Decision Trees
Fuzzy Decision Trees / *Malcolm J. Beynon, Cardiff University, UK* 382

Fuzzy Inference Systems
Fuzzy Thermal Alarm System for Venus Express / *P. Serra, UNINOVA – CA3, Portugal; R. A. Ribeiro, UNINOVA – CA3, Portugal; R. Marques Pereira, Università degli Studi di Trento, Italy; R. Steel, VEGA IT, Germany; M. Niezette, VEGA IT, Germany; and A. Donati, ESA / ESOC, Germany* 391

Fuzzy Linear Programming
Introduction to Fuzzy Logic and Fuzzy Linear Programming / *Pandian Vasant, Universiti Teknologi Petronas, Malaysia and Hrishikesh S. Kale, K.K.Wagh Institute of Engineering Education & Research, India* 539

Game Theory
Games of Strategy / *Geraldine Ryan, University College Cork, Ireland and Seamus Coffey, University College Cork, Ireland* 402

Goal Programming
Goal Programming and Its Variants / *John Wang, Montclair State University, USA; Dajin Wang, Montclair State University, USA; and Aihua Li, Montclair State University, USA* 410

Goal Seeking
Unambiguous Goal Seeking Through Mathematical Modeling / *Guisseppi Forgionne, University of Maryland, Baltimore County, USA and Stephen Russell, University of Maryland, Baltimore County, USA* 892

Group Decision Support Systems
ThinkTeam: GDSS Methodology and Technology as a Collaborative Learning Task / *Hanan Yaniv, University of Calgary, Canada* 872

Group Decision Support Systems for Large Groups
ThinkClick: A Case Study of a Large Group Decision Supporrt System (LGDSS) / *Hanan Yaniv, University of Calgary, Canada and Susan Crichton, University of Calgary, Canada* 865

Group Verbal Decision Analysis
Group Verbal Decision Analysis / *Alexey Petrovsky, Insitute for Systems Analysis – Russian Academy of Sciences, Russia* 418

Groupware
How Groupware Systems Can Change How an Organisation Makes Decisions: A Case Study in the Publishing Industry / *Frédéric Adam, University College Cork, Ireland; Jean-Charles Pomerol, Université Pierre et Marie Curie, France; and Patrick Brézillon, Université Pierre et Marie Curie, France* 426

Heuristics for Decision Support
Metaheuristics: Heuristic Techniques for Combinatorial Optimization Problems / *Stephan Scheuerer, Fraunhofer Center for Applied Research on Technologies for the Logistics Service Industries ATL, Germany* 604

iDMSS
On Frameworks and Architectures for Intelligent Decision-Making Support Systems / *Manuel Mora, Autonomous University of Aguascalientes, Mexico; Francisco Cervantes, Universidad Nacional Autónoma de México, Mexico; Guisseppi Forgionne, University of Maryland, Baltimore County, USA; and Ovsei Gelman, Universidad Nacional Autónoma de México, Mexico* 680

Incentives
Power of Incentives in Decision Making, The / *Geraldine Ryan, University College Cork, Ireland and Edward Shinnick, University College Cork, Ireland* 724

Influence Diagrams
Influence Diagrams as a Tool for Decision Support System Design / *Peter O'Donnell, Monash University, Australia and Rob Meredith, Monash University, Australia* 474

Information (Role of)
Role of Information in Decision Making, The / *Edward Shinnick, University College Cork, Ireland and Geraldine Ryan, University College Cork, Ireland* 776

Intelligent Agents
Intelligent Agents in Decision Support Systems / *Gloria E. Phillips-Wren, Loyola College in Maryland, USA* 505

Investment Evaluation (a DSS for)
Decision Support System for Evaluation of Investments in a Computer-Integrated Production System, A / *Hannu Kivijärvi, Helsinki School of Economics, Finland and Markku Tuominen, Lappeenranta University of Technology, Finland* 200

Knowledge Management
Information Distribution Decisions Supported by Argumentation / *Ramon Brena, Centro de Sistemas Inteligentes – Tecnológico de Monterrey, Mexico and Carlos Chesñevar, Universidad Nacional del Sur, Argentina* 489

Knowledge Representation
Knowledge Representation to Empower Expert Systems / *James D. Jones, Center for Advanced Intelligent Systems, Texas Tech University, USA & Computer Science, Angelo State University, USA* 576

Knowledge Worker Desktop's Model (KWDM)
Knowledge Worker Desktop Model (KWDM) Applied to Decision Support System, A / *Camille Rosenthal-Sabroux, Dauphine University, France; Michel Grundstein, Dauphine University, France; and Fernando Iafrate, Euro Disney SCA, France* 584

Knowledge-Based DSS
Knowledge Based DSS / *Michel R. Klein, Information Systems and Decision Science, HEC School of Management, France* 565

Large-Scale Decision-Making Support Systems
Implementation of Large-Scale Decision-Making Support Systems: Problems, Findings, and Challenges, The / *Manuel Mora, Autonomous University of Aguascalientes, Mexico; Ovsei Gelman, Universidad Nacional Autónoma de México, Mexico; Guisseppi Forgionne, University of Maryland, Baltimore County, USA; and Francisco Cervantes, Universidad Nacional Autónoma de México, Mexico* 446

Levels of Representation of Decision Problems
Decision Support Systems and Representation Levels in the Decision Spine / *Patrick Humphreys, London School of Economics and Political Science, UK* 225

Location Analysis
Bi-Criteria DSS Dedicated to Location Problems, A / *Maria Eugénia Captivo, Universidade de Lisboa, Portugal; João Carlos Namorado Clímaco, Coimbra University & INESC Coimbra, Portugal; and Sérgio Fernandes, Instituto Politécnico de Setúbal, Portugal*..53

Location DSS
Disaster-Oriented Assessment of Urban Clusters for Locating Production Systems in China, The / *Zhen Chen, Liverpool John Moores University, UK; Heng Li, The Hong Kong Polytechnic University, China; Qian Xu, Liverpool John Moores University, UK; and Szu-Li Sun, The University of Reading, UK*..........253

Logic Programming Languages
Logic Programming Languages for Expert Systems / *James D. Jones, Center for Advanced Intelligent Systems, Texas Tech University, USA & Computer Science, Angelo State University, USA*..............................593

Methods for Decision Support
Method for Systematic Artifact Selection Decision Making, A / *Joanna Lumsden, National Research Council of Canada, Canada* 618

Mobile Decision Support for Time-Critical Decision Making
Mobile Decision Support for Time-Critical Decision Making / *F. Burstein, Monash University, Australia and J. Cowie, University of Stirling, UK* 638

Models
Towards a Framework for Assisting Decision-Makers Assess the Potential of E-Business Models / *Pat Finnegan, University College Cork, Ireland and Jeremy Hayes, University College Cork, Ireland*........882

Multicriteria DEA
Performance Measurement: From DEA to MOLP / *João Carlos Namorado Clímaco, Coimbra University, Portugal & INESC Coimbra, Portugal; João Carlos Soares de Mello, Federal Fluminense University, Brazil; and Lidia Angulo Meza, Federal Fluminense University, Brazil* 709

Multi-Agent Simulation
Introduction to Multi-Agent Simulation / *Peer-Olaf Siebers, University of Nottingham, UK and Uwe Aickelin, University of Nottingham, UK* 554

Multi-Agent Simulation and Modeling
Multi-Agent Simulation and Management Practices / *Peer-Olaf Siebers, University of Nottingham, UK; Uwe Aickelin, University of Nottingham, UK; Helen Celia, University of Leeds, UK; and Chris Clegg, University of Leeds, UK* 645

Network Analysis
Using Network Analysis for Understanding How Decisions are Made / *Frédéric Adam, University College Cork, Ireland* 950

Non-Decision Making
Understanding Non-Decision Making / *David Sammon, University College Cork, Ireland* 910

Online Environmental Information Systems
Online Environmental Information Systems / *Tan Yigitcanlar, Queensland University of Technology, Australia; Jung Hoon Han, University of Queensland, Australia; and Sang Ho Lee, Hanbat National University, South Korea* 691

Online Urban Information Systems
Online Urban Information Systems / *Tan Yigitcanlar, Queensland University of Technology, Australia and Omur Saygin, Izmir Institute of Technology, Turkey* 699

Organisational Self-Assessment
Extended Model of Decision Making: A Devil's Advocate Workshop, An / *David Sammon, University College Cork, Ireland* 348

Problem Formulation
Decision Support and Problem Formulation Activity / *David Paradice, Florida State University, USA* 192

PROMETHEE
PROMETHEE / *Malcolm J. Beynon, Cardiff University, UK* 743

Qualitative Comparative Analysis
Qualitative Comparative Analysis / *Malcolm J. Beynon, Cardiff University, UK* 751

Real Options Reasoning
Real Options Reasoning as a Tool for Managerial Decision Making / *Bernadette Power, University College Cork, Ireland* 766

Research Needs for Decision Support
Decision Aiding Research Needs / *Rex Brown, George Mason University, USA* 141

Risks in Decision Making
Exploring the Risks That Affect Community College Decision Makers / *Margaret W. Wood, George Mason University, USA and David C. Rine, George Mason University, USA*..339

Rough Set Theory
Rough Set Theory / *Malcolm J. Beynon, Cardiff University, UK*..783

Rule Quality
Decision Making by a Multiple-Rule Classifier: The Role of Rule Qualities / *Ivan Bruha, McMaster University, Canada* 176

Security Aware Web Services
Decision Support System for Selecting Secure Web Services, A / *Khaled M. Khan, Qatar University, Qatar*..211

Sense-Making
Understanding Sense-Making / *David Sammon, University College Cork, Ireland* 916

Simon, Herbert
Understanding the Legacy of Herbert Simon to Decision Support Systems / *Jean-Charles Pomerol, Université Pierre et Marie Curie, France and Frédéric Adam, University College Cork, Ireland* 930

Simulation
Use of Simulation as an Experimental Methodology for DMSS Research, The / *Guisseppi Forgionne, University of Maryland, Baltimore County, USA and Stephen Russell, University of Maryland, Baltimore County, USA* 939

Social Simulation for Policy Decisions
Policy Decision Support Through Social Simulation / *Luis Antunes, GUESS/LabMAg/Universidade de Lisboa, Portugal; Ana Respício, Operations Research Center/GUESS/Universidade de Lisboa, Portugal; João Balsa, GUESS/LabMAg/Universidade de Lisboa, Portugal; and Helder Coelho, GUESS/LabMAg/Universidade de Lisboa, Portugal*..716

Software Agents
Software Agents / *Stanislaw Stanek, Karol Adamiecki University of Economics in Katowice, Poland; Maciej Gawinecki, Systems Research Institute of the Polish Academy of Sciences, Poland; Malgorzata Pankowska, Karol Adamiecki University of Economics in Katowice, Poland; and Shahram Rahimi, Southern Illinois University, USA* 798

Strategic Decision Making
Analysis and Intuition in Strategic Decision Making: The Case of California / *Zita Zoltay Paprika, Corvinus University of Budapest, Hungary* 20

Strategic Decision Making (a DSS for)
Support System for the Strategic Scenario Process, A / *Hannu Kivijärvi, Helsinki School of Economics, Finland; Kalle Piirainen, Lappeenranta University of Technology, Finland; Markku Tuominen, Lappeenranta University of Technology, Finland; Samuli Kortelainen, Lappeenranta University of Technology, Finland; and Kalle Elfvengren, Lappeenranta University of Technology, Finland* 822

Supply Chain Information and Decision Systems
Supply Chain Information Systems and Decision Support / *Liam Doyle, Waterford Institute of Technology, Ireland* 814

Suppy Chain Management Decisions
Facilitation of Supply Chain Decision Processes in SMEs, Using Information Systems / *Simon Woodworth, University College Cork, Ireland and Joe Cunningham, University College Cork, Ireland* 356

Synchronicity
Situational Synchronicity for Decision Support / *Dorrie DeLuca, University of Delaware, USA and Joseph S. Valacich, Washington State University, USA* 790

Syndicate Data
Syndicate Date Suppliers: Their Business Environment, the Industry, and Their Core Business Process / *Mattias Strand, University of Skövde, Sweden and Sven A. Carlsson, Lund University, Sweden* 848

System Dynamics
Dynamic System Simulation for Decision Support / *Norman Pendegraft, University of Idaho, USA and Mark Rounds, University of Idaho, USA* 306

Tools for Decision Support
Decision Making and Support Tools for Design of Machining Systems / *A. Dolgui, Ecole Nationale Supérieure des Mines de Saint-Etienne, France; O. Guschinskaya, Ecole Nationale Supérieure des Mines de Saint-Etienne, France; N. Guschinsky, United Institute of Informatics Problems, Belarus; and G. Levin, United Institute of Informatics Problems, Belarus* 155

Tools for Decision Support
Decision-Making and Support Tools for Design of Transmission Systems / *A. Dolgui, Ecole Nationale Supérieure des Mines de Saint-Etienne, France; N. Guschinsky, United Institute of Informatics Problems, Belarus; and G. Levin, United Institute of Informatics Problems, Belarus* 165

Uncertainty in Decision Making
Uncertainty and Vagueness Concepts in Decision Making / *Georg Peters, Munich University of Applied Sciences, Germany* 901

Uncertainty Quantification and Propagation
Probabilistic Methods for Uncertainty Quantification / *N. Chugunov, Institute for Systems Analysis – Russian Academy of Sciences, Russia; G. Shepelyov, Institute for Systems Analysis – Russian Academy of Sciences, Russia; and Michael Sternin, Institute for Systems Analysis – Russian Academy of Sciences, Russia* 732

Urban Development Decision Making

Federative Approach of Decision-Making Aid in Urban Development, A / *G. Kouamou, National High School of Engineering, Cameroon and C. Pettang, National High School of Engineering, Cameroon* 368

User-Friendly Interfaces

Interfaces Usability for Monitoring Systems / *R. A. Ribeiro, UNINOVA – CA3, Portugal and I. L. Nunes, Universidade Nova Lisboa, Portugal* 528

Verbal Decision Analysis

Intelligent DSS Under Verbal Decision Analysis / *Ilya Ashikhmin, Cork Constraint Computation Centre – University College Cork, Ireland; Eugenia Furems, Russian Academy of Sciences, Russia; Alexey Petrovsky, Institute for Systems Analysis – Russian Academy of Sciences, Russia; and Michael Sternin, Institute for Systems Analysis – Russian Academy of Sciences, Russia*...............514

Visualisation Tools for Decision Making

DSS Using Visualization of Multi-Algorithms Voting / *Ran M. Bittmann, Gradutate School of Business, Bar-Ilan University, Israel and Roy M. Gelbard, Graduate School of Business, Bar-Ilan University, Israel* 296

Visualisation in DSS

Web-Based Decision Support for Knowledge Sharing and Management in Intelligence Buildings Assessment / *Zhen Chen, Liverpool John Moores University, UK; Ju Hong, Beijing Institute of Civil Engineering and Architecture, China; Heng Li, The Hong Kong Polytechnic University, China; and Qian Xu, Liverpool John Moores University, UK*...............958

Web-Based GIS

Web-Based Public Participatory GIS / *Tan Yigitcanlar, Queensland University of Technology, Australia and Ori Gudes, Ben-Gurion University of the Negev, Israel*...............969

Foreword

The compilation work undertaken by Frédéric Adam and Patrick Humphreys is destined to have a lasting impact on the discipline of decision support in that it provides a comprehensive survey of the decision making domain, from theory to applications.

This encyclopaedia features more than 100 articles written by over one hundred and fifty researchers from 25 countries. One remarkable feature of this work is that for the first time, a broad range of key topics, covering the theoretical bases and important concepts of the domain are presented in a very pedagogical form and in one single book to students and practitioners. At the same time, many applications of the practice of decision making in the business world are presented (multi-criteria decision making, balanced scorecard, influence diagrams…). The tools of the trade of decision support are therefore described in the context of their managerial applications, for instance, urban planning, facility management, disaster planning and recovery, etc.

Finally and crucially, the practice of decision support cannot be fully and effectively achieved without the seamless integration of information systems in the organisations they are designed to serve. Thus, numerous articles have been included that deal with leading edge intelligent DSS applications, including data warehousing, workflow automation, knowledge management, group communication and decision support, amongst others, all extremely important aspects of the cooperative work that underlies all modern organisations.

In the end, one must thank the authors and editors for undertaking this significant venture towards making available to students and managers the requisite tools, both conceptual and practical, for effective decision support. It is without doubt that readers can leverage the material presented in this encyclopaedia for the sustained benefit of their organisations. It is worth restating, in unambiguous terms, that modern management in competitive environments cannot be successful without a finely-tuned and well integrated infrastructure of information and decision support systems. It is one fundamental quality of this book that it provides a demonstration of this reality and also provides the means to concretely tackle it. Let's hope that this ensures the success which this venture deserves.

Jean-Charles POMEROL
President,
Université Pierre et Marie Curie, Paris, France

Preface

The field of decision support systems is one of the most enduring in the information systems domain, having emerged in the 1960s, at the beginning of the history of information systems as an area of research, from the pioneering work of Simon, Keen, and Scott Morton amongst many others. Through five decades, this field has continued to attract considerable and increasing attention from researchers and practitioners, under a range of banners.

Back in 1991, Teng and Galletta (1991) conducted a survey of IS researchers which showed 32% of respondents listed DSS as their area of research, with a further 22% listing artificial intelligence and 21% database management systems. These three areas, which totalled 281 mentions out of 845 valid responses, were actually the top 3 IS research areas listed by Teng and Galletta. In more recent times, Arnott and Pervan's (2006) comprehensive review of the DSS field yielded 1093 research papers published from 1990 to 2004 in 14 major journals, the key journals in a broadly defined IS research area. These papers represented 15.2% of all papers published in the 14 journals.

These statistics present a view of DSS as a core area of the IS domain and one with a dynamism well illustrated by the strength of such international groupings as the AIS Special Interest Group on Decision Support, Knowledge and Data Management Systems (SIG DSS), the Working Group 8.3 of the International Federation for Information Processing (IFIP) on DSS and the EURO Working Group on DSS (EWG DSS). Needless to say, researchers from these groupings form a large proportion of the contributors to this encyclopedia. Nertheless, as evidenced by the wide scope of the contibutions presented in the encyclopaedia, and the range of backgrounds and expertise of their authors, the area of DSS can now successfully claim to integrate groundings from a wide range of disciplines, ranging from Operations Research, to Management and to Social Psychology, with excellent, insightful and sometimes fascinating results.

Notwithstanding the debates about the best vehicle to study the way organisations work and what kind of systems to develop to support their needs, as illustrated in Morgan's (1986) superb *Images of Organisations*, we stand firm in our belief that thinking of organisations as decision making entities and the systems to support them as decision support system is a perspective that has served our discipline very well. Though no perspective should ever be adopted in an exclusive fashion and to the detriment of other equally valid perspectives, we will continue to preach the wide adoption of decisions and decision support artefacts as objects of study, now and in the future. In passing, we will smile knowingly when colleagues greet us with their usual joke: "*But DSS is dead at the stage!*" or "*DSS! It's just like flogging a dead horse!!*" As this encyclopaedia illustrates, the DSS horse is not only alive and well, it is prancing around the field; or has it even jumped the fence to conquer new pastures.

However, the success of the DSS field is also one of its weaknesses: as the area has grown and knowledge from an increasing number of domains is brought to bear on the problems that must be studied, it becomes increasingly difficult to maintain a complete vision of DSS and all its latest developments. Already, it is arguably the case that a researcher would struggle to keep a handle on all requisite knowledge to be able to understand or review all the DSSs papers produced in a year. For instance, it becomes difficult to keep pace with developments in Multi-Criteria Decision Making or in the modelling of uncertainty on the one hand, as well as with our increased understanding of the role of emotions in human decision making or with the lastest ideas of how to study Recognition-Primed Decision Making. Furthermore, for students of DSS, young researchers and practitioners who want to train themselves to be worthy of the *DSS specialists* label, it is increasingly difficult to know what to learn and what skills to practice.

This encyclopaedia project is born out of these observations that the diversity in our domain requires a source of information that does justice to the growth of DSS in recent years, offers the theoretical basis for researching and developing DSSs and provides visibility on the topics where research should be directed in the future. Of course, no single book can meet all the requirements for such an ambitious a target, but we hope that this encyclopaedia of *Decision Making and Decision Support Technologies* will contribute to the formalisation of the DSS area in its current, diversified form. Repository of formal DSS knowledge, reference for the research carried out to date, instructional manual, springboard for future research, this book should help students, researchers, consultants and managers alike in their learning and experimentation with DSS concepts and artefacts.

In sourcing the material hereby presented, we have appealed to a broad range of constituencies of researchers and practitioners worldwide both within the specialised groups which explicitly work on DSS and in the wider IS community. Response was excellent from this all quarters. This led to the submission of over 200 proposals from which, after a lengthy reviewing process, 110 entries were selected and finalised. In classifying the material and to facilitate browsing through the 110 entries, we have relied on the authors of the contributions to provide each a keyword which best captured the essence of their contributions. These keywords were used to create the thematic table of contents (see Contents by Keyword) which was added to this encyclopedia in addition to the alphabetical table of contents of the paper titles. It is proposed that this provides a straightforward way to navigate the 1000 or so pages of the two volumes of this encyclopedia, either in leisurely fashion, following no particular sequence, or in a more orderly fashion, to meet a specific research, learning or teaching need. The Key Terms listed at the end of each contribution, compiled by each contributor, should also be an extremely valuable resource as they represent over a thousand terms and definitions pertaining to our discipline which students may be finding difficult to grasp and for which there may be no obvious source of a recent definition. Definitions, of course, can be difficult to agree upon, but the whole point of this broadly contributed compilation effort is precisely to offer a broad spectrum of perspectives on DSS topics, such that the glossary featuring in these pages should be a true representation of what DSS researchers around the world think is important in the area.

In concluding this preface, let us wish that these volumes represent an authentic, fresh and useful book (in the words of one of our editorial board members) that adds value to the domain, solves the problem of finding clear sources of information for the DSS researchers of the future and provides fresh impetus to pursue the study and development of DSS artefacts that support people and organisations as they make their decisions.

Frédéric Adam and Patrick Humphreys
Cork and London, December 2007

REFERENCES

Arnott, D., & Pervan, G. (2006). Eight key issues for the decision support systems discipline. In Adam, Brezillon, Carlsson, & Humphreys (Eds.), *Creativity and innovation in decision making and decision support*. London: Decision Support Press.

Morgan, G. (1986). *Images of organisations*. London: Sage Publications.

Teng, J., & Galletta, D. (1991). MIS research directions: A survey of researchers' views, *Database*, Winter/Spring, 53-62.

Acknowledgment

The completion of a project of this size (moderate in comparison to building the Pyramids in Egypt, but substantial enough for two overworked academics), requires the carefully-planned collaboration of many people. We are particularly grateful to the following individuals:

For their willingness to engage in the process of writing rich and valuable contributions to this encyclopaedia, we are very grateful to the 161 contributors whose work is presented here. Obviously, the success of such a venture as this one is entirely dependent on the work carried out by our contributors, who made sure that this project would not turned into just another encyclopaedia.

Most contributors also turned into reviewers when it was required (all proposed entries were reviewed at least twice so we needed many reviewers). Also involved in the reviewing process were: Margaret Healy and Ciara Heavin (University College Cork, Ireland), John Artz (The George Washington University, Washington DC), Lucia Garcia (London School of Economics, London), Seamus Hill (University College Galway, Ireland) and Peter Tatray (Agrementa Consulting AB, Sweden).

The preparation of the encyclopedia, especially the formatting of the papers, involved substantial work. This was carried out by Marie Escudie, from the Ecole Supérieure d'Agronomie de Montpellier (France), during her visit to UCC in the Summer of 2007. The successful completion of the project rested largely on her shoulders during this time and she deserves special thanks for her efforts and the professionalism she displayed in preparing the final submission. Aude Montovert, from the Ecole d'Ingénieurs de Purpan (Toulouse, France) also deserves our sincere thanks for her work on the indexes.

Other colleagues deserves our thanks for the rich discussions we have had with them over the years, particularly those on our editorial advisory noard and, more generally, the members of the Working Group 8.3 of the International Federation for Information Processing (IFIP) on DSS, the AIS Special Interest Group on Decision Support, Knowledge and Data Management Systems (SIG DSS), and the EURO Working Group on DSS (EWG DSS), many of whom were also contributors or reviewers on this project.

The support team at IGI Global and in particular, Kristin Roth, our managing development editor, deserve a special mention. Kristin's patience with missed deadlines and kindness when things didn't go well, are only equalled by the speed and accuracy with which she can reply to a question, despite time differences between the States and Europe. Also, in the final stages of the production of these volumes, Jamie Sue Snavely, our Production Managing Editor, managed to keep the whole process on schedule, despite some ultimate hurdles.

About the Editors

Frédéric Adam is a senior lecturer in the Business Information Systems Group at University College Cork, Ireland and visiting research fellow in the Institute of Social Psychology, London School of Economics. He holds PhDs from the National University of Ireland and Université Paris VI (France). His research has been published in international journals including the *Journal of Strategic Information Systems, Decision Support Systems*, and the *Journal of Information Technology*. He is the editor-in-chief of the *Journal of Decision Systems* and the co-author of *The Enterprise Resource Planning Decade: Lessons Learnt and Issues for the Future* (IGI Global, 2004). He is also vice-chair of the Working Group 8.3 on DSSs of the International Federation for Information processing (IFIP) since 2004.

Patrick Humphreys is Head of the Institute of Social Psychology at the London School of Economics and Political Science and co-director of the London Multimedia Lab for Audiovisual Composition and Communication, where he directs the project "Creative Partnerships: Pathways to Value" for the Arts Council England. He also leads the LSE team on the EU Framework 6 Project "Incas: Intellectual Capital Statement for Europe". He has both research and practical expertise in innovative and creative decision-making, decision support systems, and enhancement of resources for health, culture, development, and networking. He has been involved in initiatives involving organizational transformation and sector development in many countries. He has been involved in initiatives involving organizational transformation and sector development in many countries. He is chair of IFIP WG8.3. In 2006 he was programme chair for the IFIP WG8.3 Conference on Creativity and Innovation in Decision Making and Decision Support and was a sponsor of the workshop "Live dialogues between different individuals and alternative urban models in the Pearl River Delta" coordinated in China by Vitamin Creative Space.

Activity-Based Costing System for a Small Manufacturing Company: A Case Study

Arkadiusz Januszewski
University of Technology and Life Sciences in Bydgoszcz, Poland

INTRODUCTION

The selection of the right cost calculation method is of critical importance when it comes to determining the real product profitability (as well as clients and other calculation objects). Traditional cost calculation methods often provide false information. The literature offers many examples of big companies that have given up traditional methods and applied a new method: **activity-based costing** (ABC). They discovered that many products that are manufactured generate losses and not profits. Managers, based on incorrect calculations, mistakenly believed in the profitability of each product. Turney (1991) reports on an example of an American manufacturer of over 4,000 different integrated circuits. The cost calculation with the allocation of direct production costs as machinery-hour markup demonstrated a profit margin of over 26% for each product. Implementing ABC showed that the production of more than half of the products was not profitable, and having factored in additional sales and management costs (which accounted for about 40% of the total costs), it was as much as over 75%.

Similarly, there are also numerous examples of when not all customers render benefits: Some of them cause losses as well. A typical example reported by Kaplan (1989) involves a Swedish company Kanthal, a manufacturer of heating pipes. Implementing **ABC** revealed great differences in the profitability of respective clients of Kanthal. It appeared that 20% of the most profitable clients generated 225% of the total profit, 70% of other clients were found on the border of profitability, and 10% of the least profitable clients generated a loss that accounted for 125% of the profit reported at the end of the accounting period. Kanthal made a detailed analysis of causes of losses for the least profitable clients and took adequate measures, which in the following year enhanced the results of the company considerably.

Polish literature gives an example of a distribution company representing the FMCG business (fast-moving consumer goods), which as a result of implementing **ABC** learned that as much as 23% of the clients generated PLN 374,000 of the profit for the company, another 57% of the clients were found on the border of profitability, and the last group of 29% of the clients generated losses of PLN 540,000, thus resulting in the profitability ratio calculated for the entire company showing a negative value (Zieliński, 2005).

The investigations reported by the present author demonstrate that the problem of a false picture of profitability of products and clients concerns also smaller companies. Examples representing SMEs (small and medium-sized enterprises) revealed that calculations made using the ABC method provided quite different results of unit costs (and as a result profitability) of products than the results obtained with traditional methods. With a foodstuffs manufacturer the **ABC** implementation showed that only 37% of the products were profitable, 10% of the products were found on the border of profitability, and as much as 53% generated losses. In the case of many products, the profitability calculated with a traditional as well as with the **ABC** method differed considerably (Januszewski, 2006b). In yet another small trading enterprise researched by the present author it was demonstrated that 20 of 392 clients (5%) generated a contribution margin (CM) at the total amount of PLN 500,000. Another 100 of them (25%) yielded PLN 500,000. It also turned out that almost 66% of the clients did not contribute any profit and 12.5% caused losses (Januszewski, 2006a).

In the opinion of the present author, small enterprises are equally, if not more, exposed to hazards as a result of cooperation with unprofitable clients and manufacturing unprofitable products. Market competition drives companies to a search for new clients. On the one hand, small and medium-sized entities often accept any client that would be willing to acquire their products, commodities, and articles. On the other hand, they use simple accounting systems and cost calculations that do not allow a thorough and true determination of product manufacture costs or costs of serving the client or supplier. As a result, it does not allow them to assess if a customer or supplier is ultimately profitable or not.

One shall also add that SMEs less frequently than big companies implement cost calculation for their activities (as well as other advanced systems), which coincides with the results of research carried out in Great Britain in 1999 by Innes, Mitchell, and Sinclair (2000). It is often a result of no awareness of a potential distortion of costs calculated with traditional methods, a lack of adequately qualified staff, and a belief that advanced methods are addressed to big companies and a small enterprise does not need them.

The intention of the present author is to demonstrate that the application of cost calculation for activities of small and medium-sized enterprises is not difficult and that it is worth implementing. A small company manufacturing liquid cleaning products will be used as an example. The article will show how to develop the **ABC** system and will give results of product and client profitability. Other examples of the **ABC** models for small-sized enterprises are also presented by Hicks (2002).

BACKGROUND

Origin of the ABC

For the last few dozen years, the following company operation phenomena have been observed:

- The automation of production processes has meant the demand for unskilled workers is decreasing while the demand for specialists is increasing.
- The importance of secondary processes, going around production, is increasing (inspection, supervision, sale, marketing processes, etc.).
- Firms are outsourcing many services (e.g., tax advising).

Cokins (2001, p. 5-6) states,

over the last few decades organizations have been increasingly offering a greater variety of products and services as well as using more types of distribution and sales channels. In addition, organizations have been servicing more and different types of clients. Introducing greater variation and diversity (i.e., heterogeneity) into an organization creates complexity, and increasingly complexity results in more overhead expenses to manage it.

As a result of these phenomena, there occurred a complete change in the cost structure of company operations. Research results published in 1985 show that for 100 years in American industry, common costs (indirect costs) had been continually growing from 40% to 75% of the entire costs, while participation of direct costs of labour had been diminishing from 55% to 25% of the entire costs (Kaplan, 1990). According to Cokins, Stratton, and Helbling (1993, p. 2), "As businesses have become more complex, the elements of costs are replacing the direct costs of touch-laborers and purchase materials."

Here it is highly probable that the use of traditional methods of cost calculation will result in a distortion of unit costs of the products. Traditional cost allocation methods work only when the following apply (Cokins, 1996):

- Few very similar products or services are produced.
- Overheads are low.
- Production and conversion processes are homogenous.
- Customers, customer demands, and marketing channels are homogenous.
- Selling, distribution, and administration costs are low.

The change in the cost structure in organizations has become one of the main reasons for the criticism of the traditional cost accounting systems and their usefulness in the evaluation of products and services profitability.

As an answer, by the end of the 1980s, a new cost-calculating method, activity-based costing, was proposed (Cooper & Kaplan, 1988; Johnson & Kaplan, 1987; Kaplan, 1988). According to Kaplan and Cooper (1997), there exist two simple rules to be used when searching for a potential applicable use of ABC systems:

- **The principle of Willy Sutton:** The share of indirect costs in all the costs is high.
- **The principle of high diversity:** There are a lot of different products, clients, suppliers, processes, and so forth.

One shall stress again that these requirements are met in a growing number of companies as the increasing competition makes them flexible in meeting diverse client needs and calls for factoring in different conditions of cooperation with partners on the market.

Definition of Activity-Based Costing

According to the Consortium for Advanced Manufacturing-International (CAM-I, 2000, p.2), **activity-based costing** is a methodology that measures the cost and performances of cost objects, activities and resources. Cost objects consume activities and activities consume resources. Resources costs are assigned to activities based on their use of those resources, and activity costs are reassigned to cost objects (outputs) based on the cost objects' proportional use of those activities.

ABC theory contends that many important cost categories vary in design, mixture, and range of product and company customers. To calculate the product cost, ABC focuses on activities. The activities are what people and equipment do to satisfy customer needs. The company is seen as the system of activities to produce goods and to deliver them to customers. **ABC** analyzes all activities that exist to support production and deliver goods and services. The activities are the real reasons of resource consumption such as human work, materials, machines, production, and office space. In the **ABC model**, the main object of calculation, instead of products, becomes action, operation, or otherwise activity. The product itself consumes such a portion of activities, which serves to produce and to deliver it to the market. Indirect costs are traced from activities to products based on product demands for those activities during a production process and a delivering process. So, costs are credited to products on the base of the real utilization of resources. To assign the costs of resources to activities we use resource drivers, and to assign costs of activities to cost objects (products, clients), we use activity drivers.

Cokins (1996, p. 40) says, "In a narrow sense, **activity-based costing** can be considered the mathematics used to reassign costs accurately to cost objects, that is, outputs, products, services, customer. Its primary purpose is for **profitability analysis**." In that sense, ABC will be understood and applies to build the ABC system for a small-sized company, described further.

ABC as a Springboard for Making Long-Term Decisions

ABC provides credible information on the costs and profitability of products and clients. This information is a springboard for decision making on the development of product portfolios and cooperation with clients. These decisions are long term and should be made based on the long-term **profitability analysis**. One shall therefore factor in both the product life cycle and the client life cycle. Calculating the profitability according to the ABC cannot be, therefore, a single exercise. It is meaningful over a longer period only once the evolution of customers' behaviour patterns has been observed. Only then can the ABC analysis lead to final decisions.

Yet another factor to be considered when making decisions on further manufacturing or giving up the manufacturing of a given product is the division into variable and fixed costs. If, according to the ABC, a given product shows to be unprofitable, it does not necessarily mean that giving up its production will be a good decision as one has to remember that fixed costs assigned to that product will not disappear automatically once its production is given up. The fixed costs are transferred to other products and thus decrease their profitability. The decision on giving up the product will be justifiable only when canceling a given product can reduce fixed costs (e.g., by selling production machinery, reduction of employment, etc.) or when we can involve resources generating costs into the production of other goods that are profitable. In other words, we should be able, thanks to the released resources, to increase the production and sales of profitable goods. Before giving up the unprofitable products, one should consider other possibilities, such as product price increase, launching replacements, product redesigning, and production process enhancement (Kaplan & Cooper, 1998). The same is true for clients. Identifying no profitability from a given client does not necessarily mean a need to give up the cooperation with this client. Contemporary marketing concepts call for a creation of lasting relationships with clients. So, one should, first of all, take actions that would result in such a change in cooperation rules that would lead to a reduction of service costs. It obviously requires investigating the reasons for no profitability and making an attempt at their elimination. Unprofitable clients are most frequently the ones who often buy low quantities or those who require special service (e.g., special packaging, specific delivery terms). Such requirements of the clients result in high costs of client service and, as a result, in a low profitability. The information obtained thanks to the ABC can be used to define new methods of cooperation with clients (e.g., automation of order processing) and be a major argument when negotiating new pricing rules (e.g., higher prices for low quantities and nonstandard orders and discounts for large quantities). Examples of such actions taken by Procter & Gamble and the already mentioned company of Kanthal are reported by Kaplan and Cooper (1998).

GENERAL ARCHITECTURE OF THE ABC SYSTEM FOR SMES

An information system that uses activity-based costing will be considered an **activity-based information system** (**ABIS**). The conceptual architecture of ABIS consists of three layers (Januszewski, 2003; Figure 1):

- The supplying layer (source data for ABC model)
- The calculating layer (according to the ABC method)
- The presentation layer (reporting and analytical tools)

The second layer is the basic layer, specific to ABIS. Here the ABC model is defined and necessary computations are performed: The costs of resources are assigned to activities and costs of activities are assigned to cost objects. The **ABC model** usually consists of three modules: the resources module, the activities module, and the cost objects module. The first-layer task is to deliver data into the ABC model. It encompasses all data sets in an organization, which are necessary for calculations using the ABC method. The sources of data for ABC are included in the transactional information system databases. For the data that are not recorded, ways to measure or estimate them have to be proposed. Cost data are acquired either from the general ledger of the bookkeeping system or directly from the subsystems like the payroll, inventory, fixed-assets, and manufacturing systems. Sales data usually come from the invoicing system. The quantities of activity drivers are also often recorded in the database of a transactional information system. The main task of the third layer is to report and analyze the information with the use of spreadsheets

Figure 1. Data flow and architecture in the ABC system for small and medium-sized companies

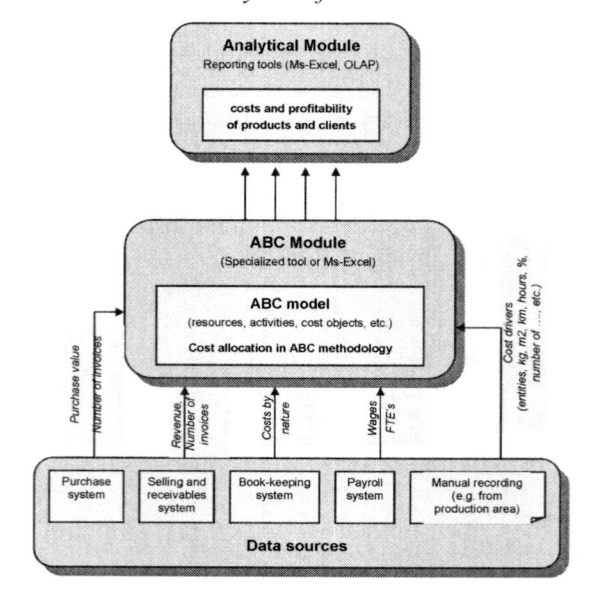

and tools such as online analytical processing (OLAP), business intelligence (BI), and so forth.

An IT system that supports ABC in a small or medium-sized manufacturing company is of less compound architecture and needs less input data than those of a big manufacturing enterprise.

Unlike in big companies, SMEs generally do not use IT systems (or they use very simples ones) for manufacturing. The working time is frequently recorded manually, and computer stock keeping takes place in the material warehouse and end-products warehouse and does not cover a detailed implementation of production processes.

ACTIVITY-BASED COSTING SYSTEM FOR A SMALL MANUFACTURING COMPANY

The Aim and Steps of the ABC Implementation Project

The company researched was established in 1989 and employed 10 people in 2005. It is a small manufacturing enterprise that produces 17 types of liquids. The production is secured by five regular chemical suppliers and three plastic packaging suppliers. The company has 110 regular clients, with ZELMER S.A. based in Rzeszów as the biggest one, whose share in the total sales accounts for almost 50%. Another 10 clients generate 30% of total sales and the other 99 clients slightly more than 20%. Before the project was launched, the company researched calculated the profitability of neither products nor clients. The only analytical information was that on sales revenues. The manager examined it thoroughly but did not know which products and which customers were profitable. The sole management-supporting systems were the goods flow (reception-dispatch) system and the accounting system. Costs by nature were the only ones posted in the general ledger (GL), making the companyís accounting system excessively simplified and thus insufficient for managerial purposes.

The main aim of the project was to implement the ABC model in the area of **profitability analysis** for numerous clients and products of the company.

The project was performed by two external consultants who analyzed the company's processes, interviewed the key personnel, and verified the information and recording systems. The **ABC implementation** took 3 months with the average week engagement of 2 days per participant.

In order to accomplish the project, the following steps were planned and performed:

- Audit of recording systems (i.e., bookkeeping system), business processes, and management procedures
- Development of the ABC model and its implementation in the environment of a stand-alone ABC software
- Preparation and inputting data for the model
- Processing the data and analysis of outcomes

The first two stages were led simultaneously and interactively. While the first framework version of the ABC model was developed without any IT tool, the other ones were created in an IT environment and brought about detailed analyses through the availability of the required data.

The estimated time burden of subsequent project stages was as follows:

- Audit and analyses 15%
- Development and implementation of the model 50%
- Preparation and input of data 25%
- Outcome figures analysis 10%

A relatively high time consumption of the data preparation and inputting stage results from a manual verification of source accounting evidence and supporting calculations in a spreadsheet, as the required data were not accessible in the recording system of the company. For example, reports on the number of invoices issued to every client were not produced in the company systems. The present author's experience acquired at previous projects shows that IT tools being in application in small and medium-sized companies very often does not support even basic managerial reporting.

Structure of the Elaborated ABC Model

In order to build the **ABC model**, the project team had to:

- Identify the objects for costing and profitability measurement purposes
- Analyze processes and activities in the domains of purchases, production, sales, distribution, marketing, finance management, and administration,
- Categorize the company's resources and their costs
- Define activities that are required by particular cost objects
- Define resources that are used up by particular activities
- Decide on how to assign costs of resources to activities and costs of activities to costs objects

The critical analysis of trial balances of cost and revenue accounts from the bookkeeping system, revision of purchases and sales reports, as well as personal interviews were applied as distinguished methods in managing the project.

The overall structure of the model is shown in Figure 2. The model consists of four parts. Each includes costs classified as follows:

1. Costs by nature (53 accounts; seven groups)
2. Costs according to resources (19 kinds of resources in seven groups)
3. Costs according to activities (24 activities in five processes)
4. Costs according to cost objects (17 products, 110 clients and infrastructure object)

The model elements are joined with so-called costs flow paths defined as over 1,500. They depict flows of costs by nature to respective resources and further through activities to products and customers.

Cost Calculation

The model cost calculation involves five stages. At the first stage, the costs by nature are assigned to respective resources; assigning is applied according to value (e.g., depreciation cost is assigned to the production building directly) or allocation keys such as square meters (e.g., heating energy costs are allocated among the production building and office space proportionally according to the area). After the first stage of cost calculation, each kind of resource defined has all of its related costs. Table 1 demonstrates costs by nature assigned to the production building.

At the second stage, the resource costs are assigned to activities at the performance of which they are consumed. Figure 3 presents sample production-building costs allocated to activities performed. Square meter (m^2) is used as the resource cost driver.

Figure 2. General structure of the ABC model developed for the company researched

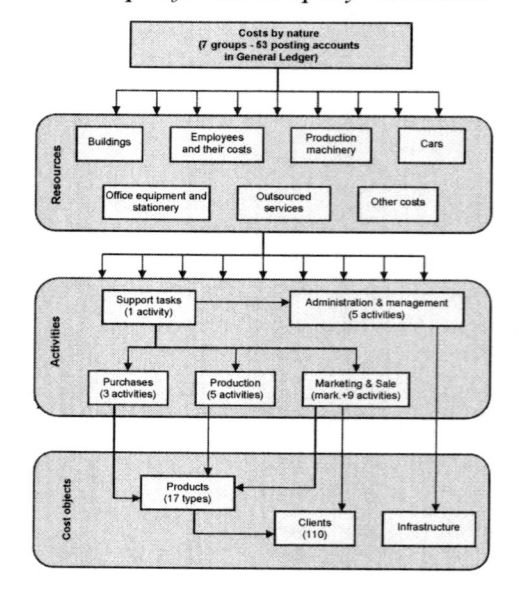

Activity-Based Costing System for a Small Manufacturing Company

Table 1. Costs by nature assigned to the production building

Cost by nature	Value in PLN
Electrical energy	110
Heating energy	2,297
Deprecation of fixed assets	815
Perpetual land usufruct depreciation	55
Business rates	2,071
Perpetual land usufruct charges	918
Property insurance	144
Other repair services	4,263
Public utilities, rubbish collection	1,003
Public utilities, water and waste water	91
Total	11,767

Figure 3. Production-building costs allocated to the activities performed

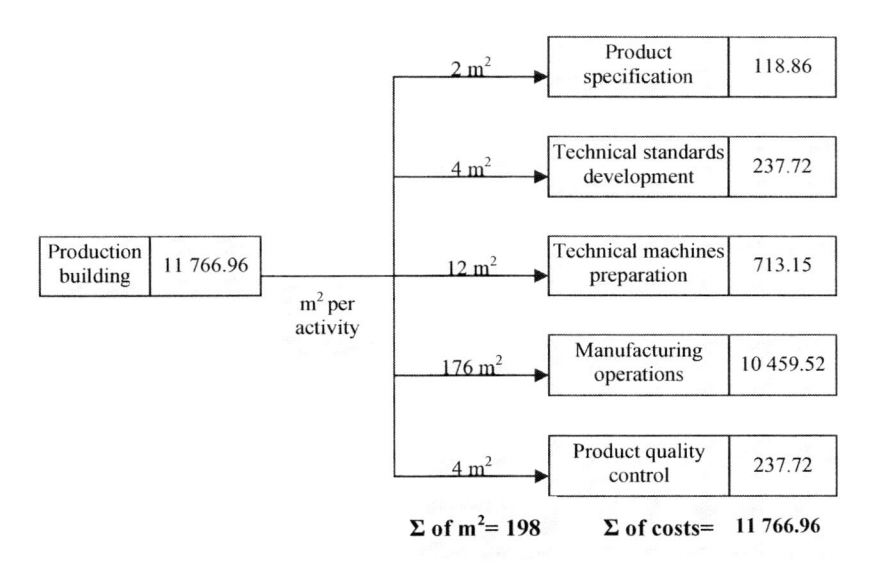

From	m²	Activity	Cost
Production building 11 766.96	2 m²	Product specification	118.86
	4 m²	Technical standards development	237.72
	12 m²	Technical machines preparation	713.15
	176 m²	Manufacturing operations	10 459.52
	4 m²	Product quality control	237.72

Σ of m² = 198   Σ of costs = 11 766.96

According to the assumptions of the ABC for activities, one should first calculate the costs of the resources of the production building per square meter:

PLN 11,766.96 : 198 m² = 59.42909 PLN/ m².

Then, for each activity, the value obtained is multiplied by the number of square meters it involves, for example, for the activity titled Manufacturing Operations, we get the following:

59.42909 PLN/ m² * 176 m² = PLN 10459.52.

Table 2 presents all the resources defined and resource cost drivers used in assigning resource cost to activities.

The third stage concerns the allocation of costs of supporting activities, such as cleaning among others, according to the square-meter allocation key. The calculations are performed the same way as before.

At the fourth stage, cost calculation for activities is made among cost objects. As given in Figure 2, supply and production activity costs are assigned to products, while the costs of all the activities connected with the sales process are assigned to clients, except for marketing costs, which are shared between products and

Table 2. Resources and resource drivers

Group of resources	Resources	Resource cost driver
Cars	Van	Percentages
	Vehicle given for use	Percentages
Employees and their costs	Salaries and wages	Number of people
	Other employee benefits	Percentages
	Mobiles	Number of mobiles
	Telecommunication	Percentages
Production machinery	Production machine	Evenly assigned (100%)
Buildings	Production building	m² per activity
	Offices	m² per activity
Office equipment and stationery	Office equipment	Percentages
	Stationery	Percentages
	Housekeeping goods	Evenly assigned
Outsourced services	Transport services	Evenly assigned (100%)
	Financial services	Percentages
	Postal Services	Percentages
	Certificates and patents	Percentages
Other costs	Court charges and stamp duties	Percentages
	Advertising	Percentages
	Other costs	Percentages

clients. The costs of administrative and management activities are traced to the infrastructure object. Figure 4 presents sample cost allocation of the activity titled Manufacturing Operations to respective products. The activity cost driver used involved liters of the cleaning liquid produced.

As before, one should first calculate the costs of the activity Manufacturing Operations according to liters of the cleaning liquid:

PLN 37,522.55 : 25,567.46 liters = 1.46759 PLN/liter.

The second step, for each product, involves multiplying the value obtained by the number of liters produced. So, for example, for products ANTY BE 75 and G 05 we obtain, respectively,

1.46759 PLN/liter * 2,424 liters = PLN 3,557.44

and

1.46759 PLN/liter * 12,326 liters = PLN 18,089.51.

The list of all the activities and activity cost drivers used in cost calculation is given in Table 3.

The last stage of cost calculation involves assigning product costs to clients. First the indirect costs calculated according to the ABC must be added with direct material costs and then unit product cost must be calculated. It covers all of the product manufacturing costs; however, it does not cover the costs related to client service and administrative and management costs. The allocation key used for the product cost distribution among clients is the unit cost multiplied by the amount of product sold to a given client. Sample product cost allocation for ANTY BE 75 to clients is given in Figure 5. The calculations are made as given before.

Figures 3 to 5 demonstrate only 32 examples of cost assigning paths (5 connections from production-

Figure 4. Manufacturing operations costs allocated to products

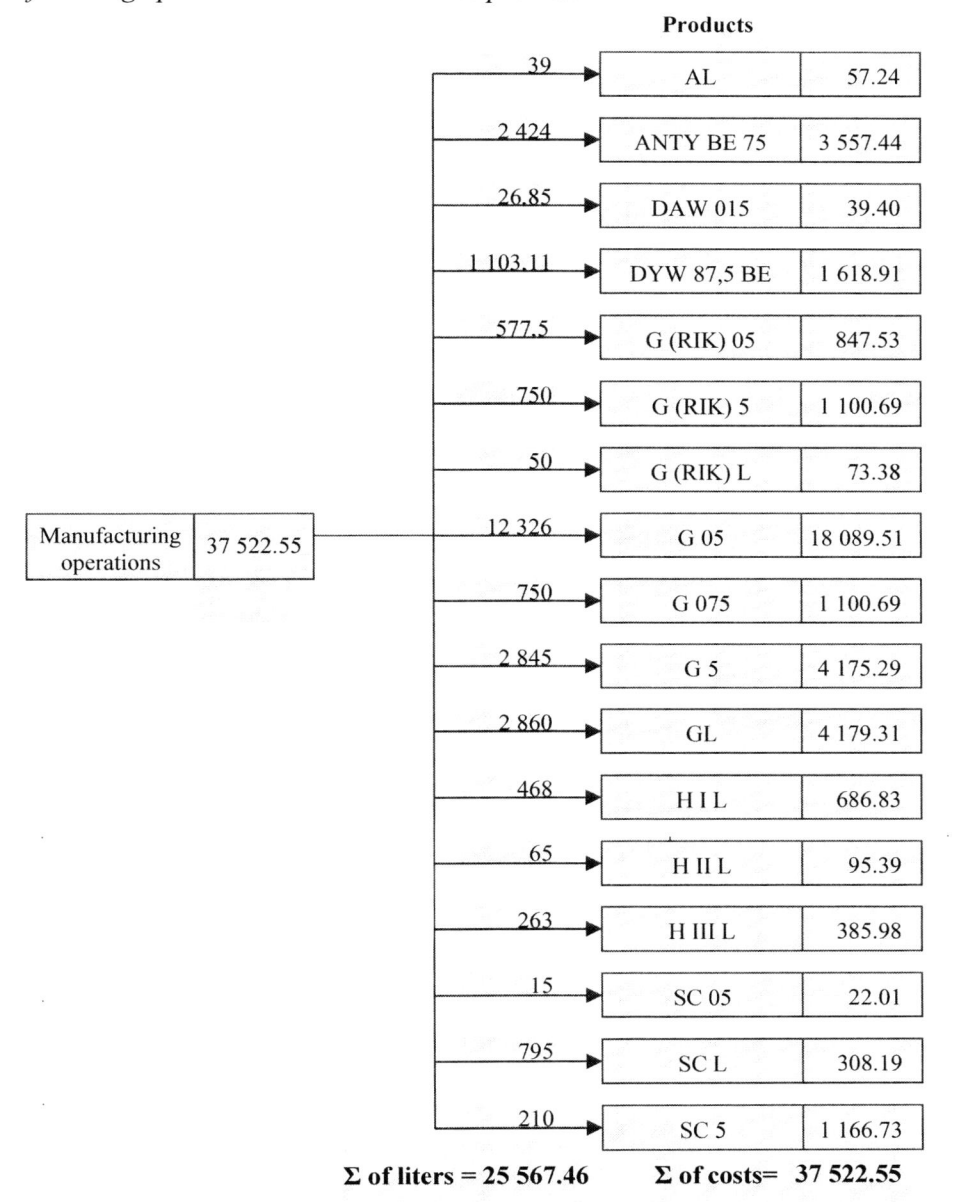

Manufacturing operations	37 522.55	→	Products	
		39 →	AL	57.24
		2 424 →	ANTY BE 75	3 557.44
		26.85 →	DAW 015	39.40
		1 103.11 →	DYW 87,5 BE	1 618.91
		577.5 →	G (RIK) 05	847.53
		750 →	G (RIK) 5	1 100.69
		50 →	G (RIK) L	73.38
		12 326 →	G 05	18 089.51
		750 →	G 075	1 100.69
		2 845 →	G 5	4 175.29
		2 860 →	GL	4 179.31
		468 →	H I L	686.83
		65 →	H II L	95.39
		263 →	H III L	385.98
		15 →	SC 05	22.01
		795 →	SC L	308.19
		210 →	SC 5	1 166.73

Σ of liters = 25 567.46   Σ of costs = 37 522.55

building resource to activities, 17 connections from manufacturing operations to products, and 5 connections from the ANTY BE 75 product to clients). The whole model involves more than 1,500 paths showing cost flows from ledger accounts through resources, activities, and products to clients, and so it is recommended to use the IT tools to support ABC modeling and to make calculations automated.

Implementing the ABC Model in OROS Modeler Environment

The next step in the project was to base the ABC model in an IT environment. An **activity-based information system** was built with the use of the ABC modeling software OROS Modeler, which is now a part of SAS ABM software package developed by SAS Institute and is said to be one of the most popular tools of the stand-alone type for ABC modeling (Miller, 1996).

Table 3. Processes and activities

Process	Activity	Activity driver
Purchases	Own transport of raw materials	Weight of product sold
	Raw materials delivery	Weight of product sold
	Storage	Weight of product sold
Production	Technical machines Preparations	Working cycles
	Manufacturing operations	Number of liters
	Product quality control	Number of controls
	Product specification	Evenly assigned
	Technical standards development and verification	Evenly assigned
Sale	Marketing	Percentages
	Sending offers to contractors	Evenly assigned
	Order processing	Number of invoices
	Phone calls	Number of invoices
	Invoicing	Number of invoices
	Sales document completing	Number of invoices
	Shipping by the courier	Number of shipments*km
	Transport of products	Number of invoices*km
	WZ and tachographs completing	Number of invoices
	Receivables processing and department collections	Number of cases*km
Administration and management	Bookkeeping	Evenly assigned
	Human resources management	Evenly assigned
	Liabilities processing	Evenly assigned
	Economic analyses	Evenly assigned
	Legal services	Evenly assigned
Supporting tasks	Cleaning and maintenance	m2 per activity

Figure 5. ANTY BE 75 product cost allocation to clients

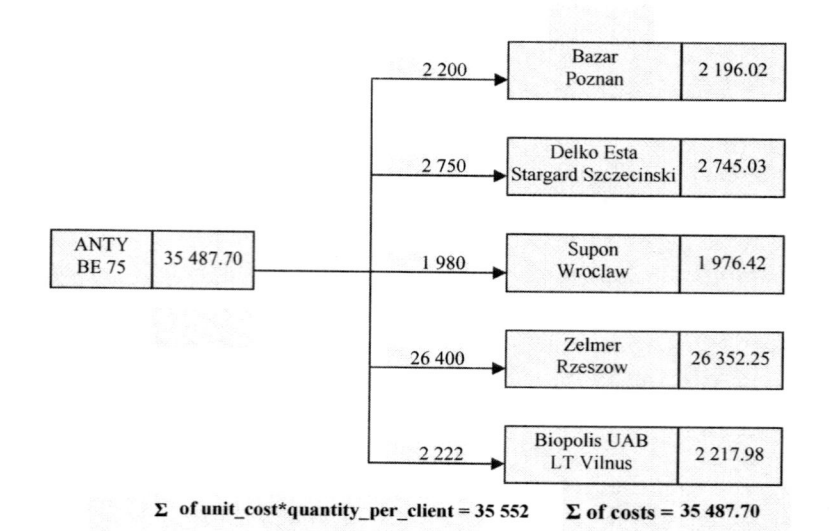

ANTY BE 75 — 35 487.70

- 2 200 → Bazar Poznan — 2 196.02
- 2 750 → Delko Esta Stargard Szczecinski — 2 745.03
- 1 980 → Supon Wroclaw — 1 976.42
- 26 400 → Zelmer Rzeszow — 26 352.25
- 2 222 → Biopolis UAB LT Vilnus — 2 217.98

Σ of unit_cost*quantity_per_client = 35 552 Σ of costs = 35 487.70

Activity-Based Costing System for a Small Manufacturing Company

Figure 6. Unit activities

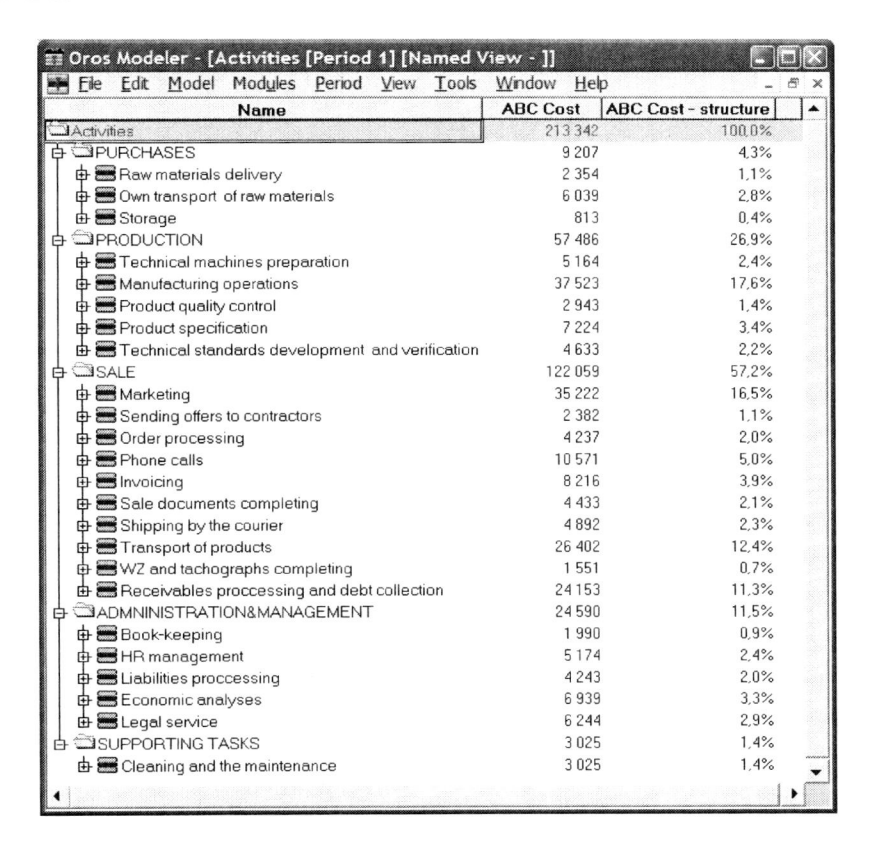

Name	ABC Cost	ABC Cost - structure
Activities	213 342	100,0%
PURCHASES	9 207	4,3%
Raw materials delivery	2 354	1,1%
Own transport of raw materials	6 039	2,8%
Storage	813	0,4%
PRODUCTION	57 486	26,9%
Technical machines preparation	5 164	2,4%
Manufacturing operations	37 523	17,6%
Product quality control	2 943	1,4%
Product specification	7 224	3,4%
Technical standards development and verification	4 633	2,2%
SALE	122 059	57,2%
Marketing	35 222	16,5%
Sending offers to contractors	2 382	1,1%
Order processing	4 237	2,0%
Phone calls	10 571	5,0%
Invoicing	8 216	3,9%
Sale documents completing	4 433	2,1%
Shipping by the courier	4 892	2,3%
Transport of products	26 402	12,4%
WZ and tachographs completing	1 551	0,7%
Receivables proccessing and debt collection	24 153	11,3%
ADMNINISTRATION&MANAGEMENT	24 590	11,5%
Book-keeping	1 990	0,9%
HR management	5 174	2,4%
Liabilities proccessing	4 243	2,0%
Economic analyses	6 939	3,3%
Legal service	6 244	2,9%
SUPPORTING TASKS	3 025	1,4%
Cleaning and the maintenance	3 025	1,4%

OROS Modeler has been taken as an example tool, and the following description is to illustrate the way the ABC model has been implemented, which is quite similar in any other stand-alone environment.

The ABC model implemented in OROS Modeler consists of three units: resources, activities, and cost objects. In the first step, cost centers (that represent groups of resources and processes, and groups of cost objects) and cost accounts (that represent particular resources, activities, or cost objects) have been introduced in each unit. Figure 6 depicts the unit Activity. The resource unit and cost-objects unit look similar.

In the next step, cost assignment paths have been defined and resource and activity drivers have been established. A cost assignment path is a procedure that links aggregated costs to target accounts. Examples of cost assignment paths with suitable drivers are given in Figures 7 and 8.

As presented in Figure 7, the resource cost driver of square meters is used for the cost allocation of office-space resources to activities. There are also visible costs by nature (electrical energy, depreciation of fixed assets, property insurance, etc.) beforehand assigned to this resource.

Figure 8 shows the activity cost driver Number of Invoices used for the cost assigning of the order-processing activity to clients. Additionally, the costs of resources (salaries and wages, office space, etc.) and costs of supporting activity Cleaning, beforehand allocated to this activity, are also available.

Let us remind you that in the case studied, the ABC method was used to calculate the profitability of the products manufactured and the profitability of the clients.

According to the ABC principles, it was assumed that the client service costs will not be factored in while determining the product profitability but only while calculating the client profitability. So, the product profitability was calculated for two levels:

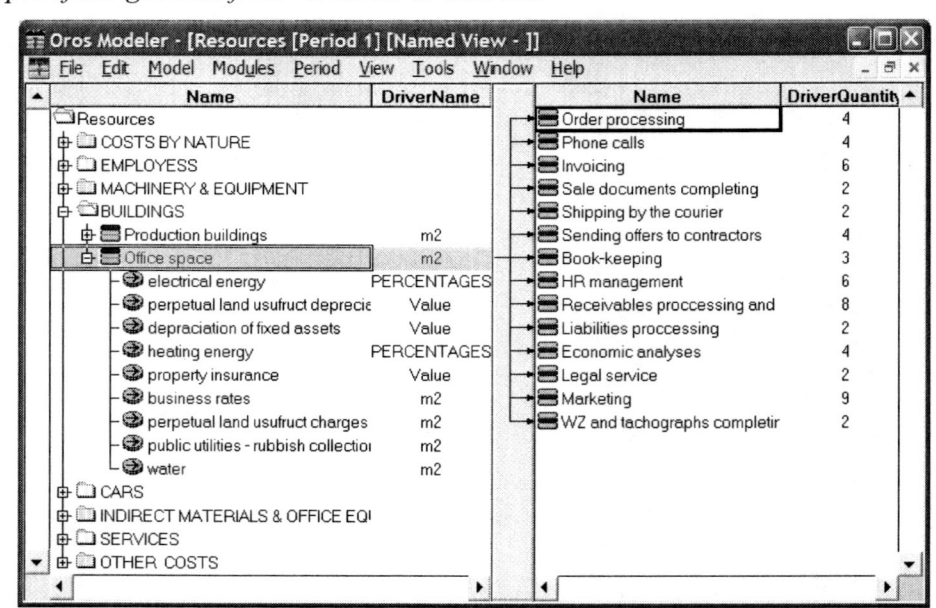

Figure 7. Example of assignments from resources to activities

Figure 8. Example of assignments from activities to cost objects

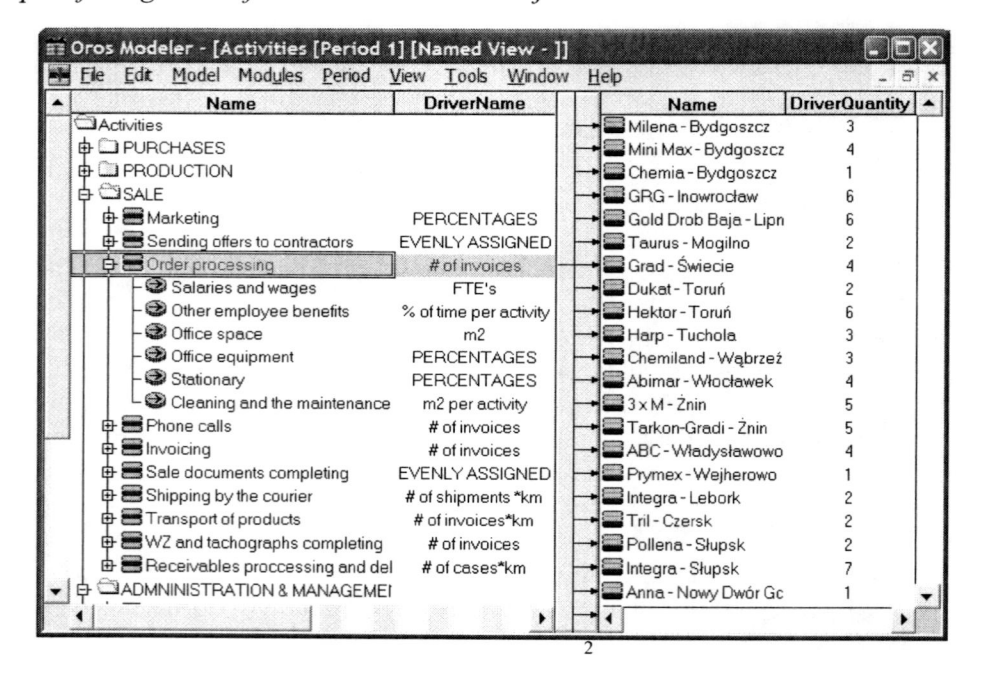

- **Contribution Margin I:** Calculated as the difference between the net value of the products sold and the costs of raw material and
- **Contribution Margin II:** Calculated as the difference between the margin of the first degree and indirect product costs (calculated according to ABC).

Compliant with the ABC method, the client profitability is calculated as the difference between the net value of sales and the total product costs (costs of raw material and indirect product costs, ABC product-related costs) and client service costs.

In the last step of the model implementation in OROS Modeler, two variants of the solution have been

Activity-Based Costing System for a Small Manufacturing Company

offered: one to calculate the product profitability and the other one to determine the client profitability. In each case, special views of profit and profitability had to be designed by including additional columns into the unit Cost Objects.

In the first version of our solution, the following columns have been added:

- Raw materials (representing standard raw material costs)
- Product_Revenue (net sales revenue generated by each product)
- Contribution Margin I (Product_Revenue - Raw materials)
- Contribution Margin I ratio (CM I/ Product_Revenue *100%)
- Contribution Margin II (CM I –ABC Product Related Costs)
- Contribution Margin II ratio (CM II/ Product_Revenue *100%)

To run properly, the model has to be provided with the following data:

1. Costs by nature
2. Resource and activity drivers
3. Net sales revenues generated by each product
4. Raw material costs for each product

The identification of resource and activity-driver figures turned out to be particularly time-consuming and challenging processes in the course of model implementation. A total of almost 20 tables have been developed, including calculation of data needed in ABC. For example, additional calculations were needed in order to establish the number of FTEs (full-time employees) for each activity. Measurement of the area on which activities are performed was also necessary. After the required data were entered into the system, information on profitability of products became available (Figure 9).

The other variant of the solution first required entering raw material costs for each product as the so-called cost element, and then assigning the product costs to the clients with the driver of unit_cost*quantity_per_client (see Figure 10, the first item below product G 5).

In the last step of defining the model, three new columns have been added:

- Client_Revenue (net sales revenue generated by each client)
- Contribution Margin (Client_Revenue – ABC_Costs)
- Contribution Margin ratio (CM/Client_Revenue*100%)

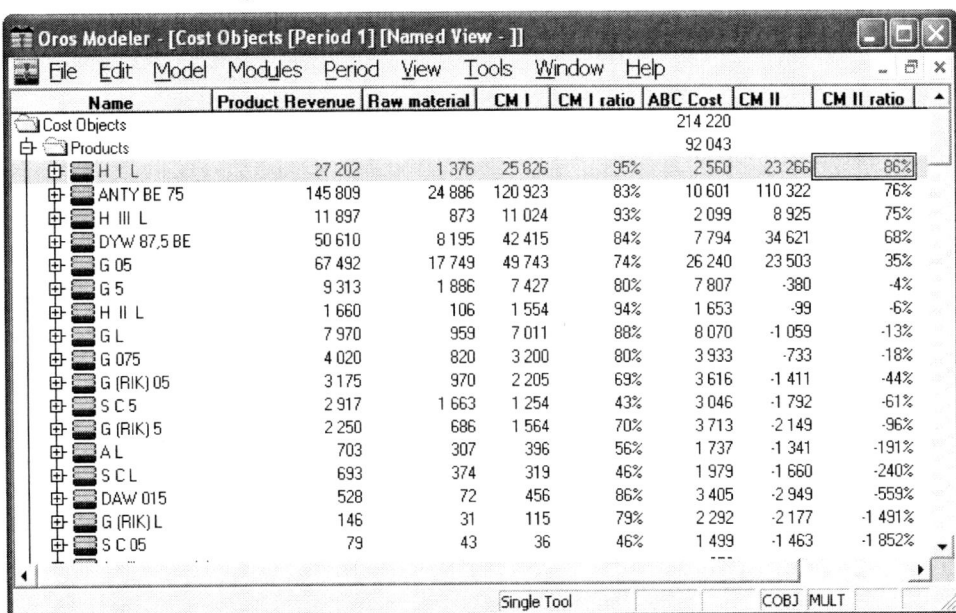

Figure 9. Product contribution margin

Name	Product Revenue	Raw material	CM I	CM I ratio	ABC Cost	CM II	CM II ratio
Cost Objects					214 220		
Products					92 043		
H I L	27 202	1 376	25 826	95%	2 560	23 266	86%
ANTY BE 75	145 809	24 886	120 923	83%	10 601	110 322	76%
H III L	11 897	873	11 024	93%	2 099	8 925	75%
DYW 87,5 BE	50 610	8 195	42 415	84%	7 794	34 621	68%
G 05	67 492	17 749	49 743	74%	26 240	23 503	35%
G 5	9 313	1 886	7 427	80%	7 807	-380	-4%
H II L	1 660	106	1 554	94%	1 653	-99	-6%
G L	7 970	959	7 011	88%	8 070	-1 059	-13%
G 075	4 020	820	3 200	80%	3 933	-733	-18%
G (RIK) 05	3 175	970	2 205	69%	3 616	-1 411	-44%
S C 5	2 917	1 663	1 254	43%	3 046	-1 792	-61%
G (RIK) 5	2 250	686	1 564	70%	3 713	-2 149	-96%
A L	703	307	396	56%	1 737	-1 341	-191%
S C L	693	374	319	46%	1 979	-1 660	-240%
DAW 015	528	72	456	86%	3 405	-2 949	-559%
G (RIK) L	146	31	115	79%	2 292	-2 177	-1 491%
S C 05	79	43	36	46%	1 499	-1 463	-1 852%

Figure 10. Example of assignments from product G 5 to clients

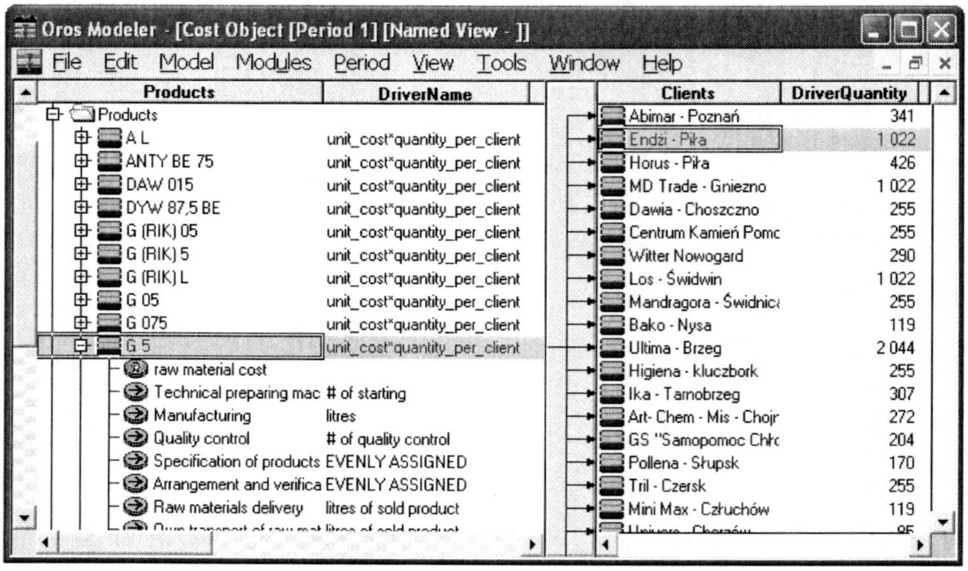

Figure 11. Client contribution margin

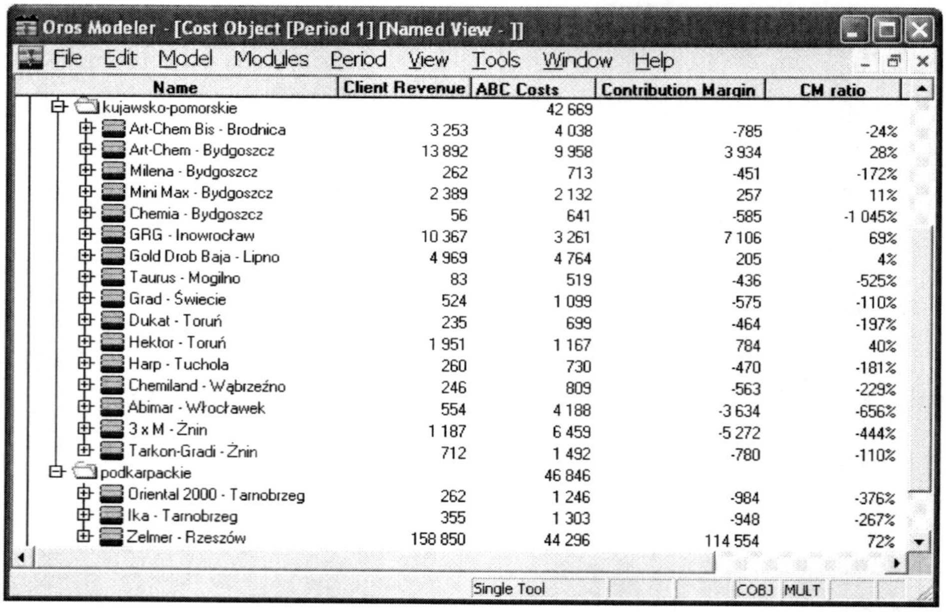

Parameter ABC_Costs included both product-related costs (raw material costs, indirect product costs) and client-related costs calculated using the ABC procedure in OROS Modeler. In order to get information on the profitability of clients, the model has to be provided with the data of net sales revenue generated by each client (Figure 11).

Outcomes of Profitability Analysis of Products and Clients

The first effect of the **ABC implementation** was to determine the structure of the company costs (without the costs of raw materials) by processes and activities (Figure 3). It turned out that the most expensive one was the sales process, absorbing over 57% of all the costs, and the production process, almost 27% of the costs. However, while considering respective activities, one can observe that the most expensive ones cover the following:

- Manufacturing: 17.6%
- Marketing: 16.5%
- Transport of products (own transport and using courier services): 14.7%
- Service and debt-collection of receivables: 11.1%

Managers were especially surprised by a high share of marketing costs as well as debt-collecting costs, which were finally found to be responsible for generating high losses by the worst clients.

If we include additionally the costs of raw materials, which in 2005 were slightly over PLN 60,000, as part of production process costs, then the cost structure will obviously be different. However, the most expensive ones will still be part of the sales process, which covers client service (Table 4).

Analyzing the product profitability, one can note that all the products show a very high CM I ratio ranging from 43% even up to 95% (Figure 6). This ratio obviously does not depend on the turnover as it can be calculated as the difference between the selling price and the unit costs of raw material divided by the selling price. As for as much as 11 out of 17 products, CM I accounts for as much as about 80%, which suggests a very high profitability of these products. More detailed information is obtained by analyzing the CM II ratio, which factors in the costs of activities leading to product manufacture (that is supply and production costs). Here, only 5 of the 17 products revealed a positive value of CM II (Figure 6). The CM II ratio for these five products remained high ranging from 35% to 86%. One can easily observe that the negative value of CM II was found for products sold in low quantities, which are products of low or very low sales (below PLN 10,000).

Let us remind you that CM II for products does not factor in any costs of client service, administration, or management. Client service costs have, however, been included in the second variant of the solution developed. Considering a high level of client service costs in the costs in total (44%), one should expect that the profitability at that level of the analysis will be much lower. Indeed, CM calculated for clients is a positive value only for 15 of the total 110 clients of the company, which means that only 15 clients build the company profit, while the other ones generate losses.

The client **profitability analysis** often uses the so-called whale curve of profitability, which shows how clients build company profit. The x-axis of the graph represents respective clients following the criterion of decreasing profit, while the vertically-axis of the graph demonstrates the cumulated profit generated by all the clients (Figure 12).

The final result of the entire client portfolio service, given at the right end of the whale curve, is almost PLN 86,000. If we assume this value as 100%, then we can read from the graph that the first 15 clients have generated over PLN 168,000 of profit, which corresponds to 196% of the value of cumulated profit generated by all the 110 clients. This value must be interpreted as a potential profit the company can make when it brings the unprofitable client-service process to the point where the manufacturer neither earns nor loses from cooperation with these clients. Interestingly, the biggest client of the company generated over 133% of the profit in that period.

Table 4. Process costs structure

Process	Costs	Structure
Purchases	9,207	3.3%
Production	118,482	42.7%
Sale	122,059	44.0%
Administration & management	24,590	8.9%
Supporting tasks	3,025	1.1%
Total	277,363	100.0%

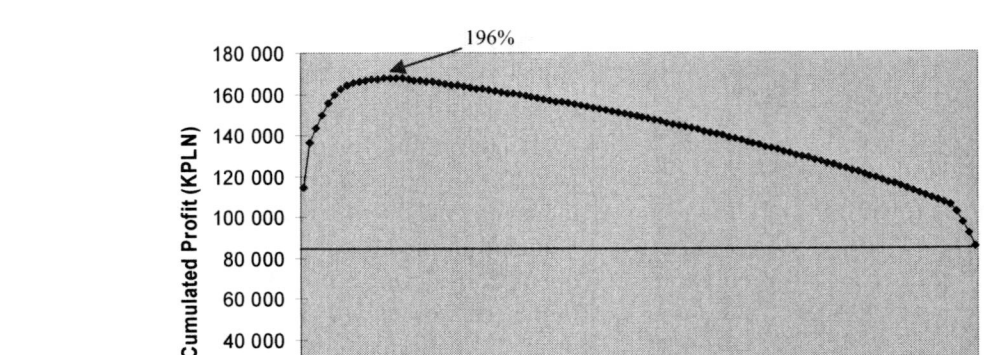

Figure 12. Client-cumulated profit

A detailed analysis demonstrated that loss was mainly incurred by the four worst clients due to high debt collection of receivables. The other loss-generating clients ordered unprofitable products and frequently placed small-quantity orders.

Decisions Made Based on the ABC Information

Based on the information received from the ABC system, adequate decisions should be made to increase the company profitability. Thorough analyses demonstrated that three highly unprofitable products generated very low revenues and were ordered by one or two clients, so it was decided that their production should be given up. Another two products that enjoyed little interest (only a few clients) were decided to be produced still, and if no sales increase should take place were to be canceled in the successive year. It was found that all the products of the first-degree contribution margin (revenues minus raw material costs) below 70% were highly unprofitable. Since all these products enjoyed the interest of several or even several dozen clients, it was decided that the prices should be increased by 10% to 20%. The analysis of the most profitable products demonstrated that they were purchased by no more than a few clients and so it was decided that promotion activities of these products should be intensified.

Taking into account a high profitability of products sold at large quantities, a decision was made to develop and to introduce a discount system promoting big orders.

Bearing in mind difficulties in gaining new clients and the fact that giving up cooperation with the client does not necessarily enhance the profitability of the company (a decrease in revenues can be greater than cost cutting), a decision was made to give up only the four worst clients who generated losses, mainly due to high debt-collection costs. As mentioned before, the amount of these costs came as quite a surprise for the managers. A thorough analysis demonstrated that in the case of three clients, they were even higher than revenues and so it was agreed that in the future debt-collection activities should be taken very cautiously in the case of low amounts of receivables.

There was also made a **profitability analysis** for client groups according to regions. It appeared that in some regions, all the clients generated losses. Another such analysis was to be made after 1 year when the effect of decisions on changes in prices and giving up unprofitable products will be visible. If the situation should not get better, it was decided that unprofitable regions would be given up and the profitable regions and foreign clients should be targeted. Currently, the company has a single foreign client only and it is a client who generates relatively high profits.

The last decision made based on the ABC information was to introduce thorough marketing-costs monitoring; the share of these costs in the total costs was relatively high. These costs in many cases resulted in no profitability of a given product.

CONCLUSION AND FURTHER RESEARCH

Managers often intuitively feel that some products and some clients do not earn profit for the company. However, they do not realize the extent of that observation. Apparently, one could expect that this comment concerns only big companies, which run diverse activities, produce many complex products, and serve many clients. A correct cost and profitability calculation is indeed in such cases a difficult task. Yet, it appears that many small enterprises carrying out simple activities do not have information on the costs and profitability either, or otherwise the information is distorted, which coincides with the results of earlier SME-sector reports of the present author as well as the case of the small company reported in the present article, in which, thanks to ABC, it was discovered that only 29% of products and 14% of the clients generated profit while the others generated losses. More thorough analysis facilitate taking a closer look at the causes of no profitability and initiating actions that would enhance profitability of the company as a whole. Decisions on canceling some products or eliminating some clients should be taken with caution bearing in mind their long-term character and their potential effect on revenues getting lower than cost cutting; variable costs are the only ones that definitely go down. So, first off all, it should be considered whether the resources released by specific product canceling or by giving up clients could be incorporated to manufacture profitable products or to serve profit-generating clients.

In the opinion of the present author, it seems justifiable to use ABC in SMEs, especially since, as shown here, it is quite an easy task that can be performed within a short time and benefits in the form of credible information on profitable and unprofitable products and clients are unquestionable. It is the information that should be the springboard for making strategic decisions on the product portfolio development and defining the rules of cooperation with clients.

To make an accurate calculation of costs, thorough ABC models must be developed and therefore ABC modeling calls for a specialized, dedicated tool. Even in small-sized companies, there are a lot of elements with mutual relationships in the ABC model. In the author's opinion, a spreadsheet would not be a sufficient tool to succeed. The final ABC model is created as a result of iteration. Changes are made much more easily with a specialized tool rather than a spreadsheet.

According to the author, further research into the ABC implementation in SMEs is most justifiable. The ABC models developed so far for such enterprises demonstrate many similarities, including a similar group of the resources used and performance of activities as well as frequently similar method of cost assignment (similar resource and activity drivers). Further research should facilitate a creation of the ABC model reference base for SMEs. Such models could be customized to specific cases easily and time effectively.

Yet another possibility of using the results of SME research would be to create a database with different parameters characteristic for the activities of such enterprises. Valuable information could be provided by investigating the relationships (correlations) between the cost structure by activities and the cost structure by resources and profitability.

REFERENCES

Cokins, G. (1996). *Activity-based cost management: Making it work.* McGraw Hill.

Cokins, G. (2001). *Activity-based cost management: An executive's guide.* New York: John Wiley & Sons, Inc.

Cokins, G., Stratton, A., & Helbling, J. (1993). *An ABC manager's primer: Straight talk on activity-based costing.* McGraw Hill.

Consortium for Advanced Manufacturing-International (CAM-I). (2000). *Glossary of activity-based management terms.*

Cooper, R., & Kaplan, R. S. (1988). Measure costs right: Make the right decisions. *Harvard Business Review, September-October,* 96-103.

Hicks, D. T. (2002). *Activity-based cost management: Making it work for small and mid-sized companies.* John Wiley & Sons, Inc.

Innes, J., Mitchell, F., & Sinclair, D. (2000). Activity-based costing in U.K.'s largest companies: A comparison of 1994 and 1999 survey results. *Management Accounting Research, 11*(3), 349-362.

Januszewski, A. (2003, June 4-6). *The model and tools for creating a decision support system with the application of activity based costing (ABC-DSS)*. Paper presented at the Sixth International Conference on Business Information Systems, Colorado Springs, CO.

Januszewski, A. (2006a). *Rachunek kosztów działań w przedsiębiorstwie handlowym: Studium przypadku*. Prace Naukowe Akademii Ekonomicznej we Wrocławiu.

Januszewski, A. (2006b). Studium przypadku: Komputerowo wspomagany model rachunku kosztów działań dla przedsiębiorstwa branży spożywczej. Część III. *Controlling i Rachunkowość Zarządcza, 2*.

Johnson, H. T., & Kaplan, R. S. (1987). *Relevance lost: The rise and fall of management accounting*. Boston: Harvard Business School Press.

Kaplan, R. S. (1988). One cost system isn't enough. *Harvard Business Review, January-February*, 61-66.

Kaplan, R. S. (1990). The four-stage model of cost system design. *Management Accounting, 71*(2).

Kaplan, R. S., & Cooper, R. (1998). *Cost & effect: Using integrated cost systems to drive profitability and performance*. Boston: Harvard Business School Press.

Miller, J. A. (1996). *Implementing activity-based management in daily operations*. John Wiley & Sons, Inc.

Turney, P. B. B. (1991). *Common cents: The ABC performance breakthrough*. Cost Technology.

Zieliński, T. (2005). Wieloryby w dystrybucji: Wykorzystanie systemów ABC/M. *Controlling i Rachunkowość Zarządcza, 11*.

KEY TERMS[1]

ABC Model: "A representation of resources costs during a time period that are consumed through activities and traced to products, services, and customers or to any other object that creates a demand for the activity to be performed."

ABC System: "A system that maintains financial and operating data on an organization's resources, activities, drivers, objects and measures. ABC models are created and maintained within this system."

Activity-Based Costing (ABC): "A methodology that measures the cost and performances of cost objects, activities and resources. Cost objects consume activities and activities consume resources. Resources costs are assigned to activities based on their use of those resources, and activity costs are reassigned to cost objects (outputs) based on the cost objects' proportional use of those activities. Activity-Based costing incorporates causal relationships between cost objects and activities and between activities and resources."

Activity-Based Information System (ABIS): An ABC system supported by information technologies. It is an information system that includes the ABC model. ABIS can by supplied by data from transactional systems, data warehouses, and other data sources. Data that are specific for ABC can be manually entered into the ABIS database. Mainly, specialized ABC modeling and reporting tools (e.g., online analytical processing or business intelligence tools) are used in ABIS.

Activity Driver: "The best single quantitative measure of the frequency and intensity of the demand placed on an activity by cost objects or other activity. It is used to assign activity costs to cost objects or to other activities."

Activity Work: "Performed by people, equipment, technologies or facilities. Activities are usually described by the 'action-verb-adjective-noun' grammar convention. Activities may occur in a linked sequence and activity-to-activity assignments may exist."

Cost Object: "Any product, service, customer, contract, project, process or other work unit for which a separate cost measurement is desired."

Process: "A series of time-based activities that are linked to complete a specific output."

Profitability Analysis: "The analysis of profit derived from cost objects with the view to improve or optimize profitability. Multiple views may be analyzed, such as market segment, customer, distribution channel, product families, products, technologies, platforms, regions, manufacturing capacity, etc."

Activity-Based Costing System for a Small Manufacturing Company

Resource Driver: "The best single quantitative measure of the frequency and intensity of the demand placed on a resource by other resources, activities, or cost objects. It is used to assign resource costs to activities, and cost objects, or to other resources."

Resources Economic: "Elements applied or used in the performance of activities or to directly support cost object. They include people, materials, supplies, equipment, technologies and facilities."

ENDNOTE

[1] Apart from Activity-Based Information System (ABIS), all terms come from Glossary of Activity-Based Management Terms published by the Consortium for Advanced Manufacturing-International (CAM-I, 2000).

Analysis and Intuition in Strategic Decision Making: The Case of California

Zita Zoltay Paprika
Corvinus University of Budapest, Hungary

INTRODUCTION

"The primary wisdom is intuition."
Ralph Waldo Emerson, American philosopher

Many management scholars believe that the process used to make strategic decisions affects the quality of those decisions. However, several authors have observed a lack of research on the strategic decision-making process. Empirical tests of factors that have been hypothesized to affect the way strategic decisions are made are notably absent (Fredrickson, 1985). This article reports the results of a study that attempts to assess the effects of decision-making circumstances, focusing mainly on the approaches applied and the managerial skills and capabilities the decision makers built on during concrete strategic decision-making procedures. The study was conducted in California between September 2005 and June 2006 and it was sponsored by a Fulbright research scholarship grant.

Strategic decisions are those that affect the direction of the firm. These major decisions concern areas such as new products and markets, product or service development, acquisitions and mergers, subsidiaries and affiliates, joint ventures, strategic alliances, finding a site for a new investment, reorganisation, and other important matters. Strategic decision making is usually conducted by the firm's top management, led by the CEO (chief executive officer) or president of the company. That is why in this research 20 top-level managers were targeted: 12 were CEOs, presidents, vice presidents, or chief financial officers (I will call them executives) while 8 were founders and majority owners of their own enterprises (they will be called entrepreneurs). Sixteen respondents were male, four were female. The average respondent has been working for 28.7 years in general, for 13.8 years for the actual company, and for 8.4 years in the current position. Sixty percent of the respondents have a graduate business degree, 60% have an undergraduate degree, seven of them have an MBA or a PhD, and two out of these seven have both an MBA and a PhD. One respondent is working on his PhD right now.

The interviews took 2½ hours on the average, varying from 2 hours up to 5 hours. During the interviews, a preliminary structured list of questions was followed. With each respondent we investigated the circumstances of four different strategic-decision cases from his or her practice. The participants could choose the cases on their own. Using this technique, a database of 80 strategic decisions could be built.

BACKGROUND

Kathleen M. Eisenhardt (1998), professor of strategy and organisation at Stanford University, found that top managers at more effective firms were able to make quick and high-quality decisions that were highly supported throughout the firm. Her studies identified four areas in which effective decision makers outperformed counterparts at less effective firms:

- Building collective intuition
- Stimulating conflict
- Maintaining a pace or schedule for decision making
- Defusing political behaviour

In my research, I focused on the role of intuition in strategic decision making. As Ashley F. Fields (2000) stated, intuition is one of the more mysterious concepts associated with the study of human capital. Classical theoreticians, from Carl Jung (1934) to Chester Barnard (1938) and Abraham Maslow (1954) have commented on the existence and value of intuition in organisational settings. Carl Jung said, "Intuition does not denote something contrary to reason, but something outside of the province of reason." It is real but it is not in our heads, and our heads cannot control it. Harold Leavitt (1975) viewed intuition as a valuable weapon to be used against the heavily analytical practices, which gave rise to his derisive term "analysis paralysis." Fascination with the subject of intuition remains alive and well in recent years too.

Intuition is usually defined as knowing or sensing something without the use of rational processes. Alternatively, it has been described as a perception of reality not known to consciousness, in which the intuition knows, but does not know how it knows. Westcott (1968) redefined intuition as a rational process, stating that it is a process in which an individual reaches a conclusion on the basis of less explicit information than is ordinarily required to reach that decision. Weston Agor (1997) argued that intuition is a built-in capacity that some of us have and some do not. In my research, I basically relied on the definition given by Martha Sinclair and Neal Ashkanasy (2000). According to these authors, intuition is a nonsequential information processing mode, which comprises both cognitive and affective elements and results in direct knowing without any use of conscious reasoning. Practically, it is an unconscious process of making decisions on the basis of experience and accumulated judgment.

Isenberg (1984), who studied managers in Fortune 500 firms, found that they combine both rational and intuitive methods in decision making. Parikh (1994) studied more than 1,300 managers and found that intuition is cross-national. Catford's (1987) study of 57 business professionals demonstrated that intuition was used commonly as a business tool. These and many other researchers have demonstrated that intuition is used regularly in the conduct of business (Fields, 2000).

Interestingly, more than half of today's intuition books are authored by females. Psychologists debate whether the intuition gap is truly intrinsic to gender. Whatever the reason, Western tradition has historically viewed rational thinking as masculine and intuition as feminine. Women's way of thinking gives greater latitude to subjective knowledge. Some personality tests show that nearly 6 in 10 men score as "thinkers" (claiming to make decisions objectively, using logic) while 3 in 4 women score as "feelers" (claiming to make decisions subjectively, based on what they feel is right; Meyers, 2002).

In recent years instinct appears ascendant. Decision makers have good reasons to prefer instinct. In a study, executives said they use their intuition as much as their analytical skills, but credited 80% of their success to instinct (Buchanan & O'Connell, 2006). Mintzberg and Westley (2001) explain that strategic thinking calls for creativity and synthesis, and this is better served by intuition than analysis. Buchanan and O'Connell cited some famous statements related to intuition:

"Pragmatists act on evidence. Heroes act on guts."

"Intuition is one of the X-factors separating the men from the boys."

One feature common to all the authors cited above is an inability to articulate a coherent, consistent, and verifiable theory of what underlies the intuitive phenomenon. These researchers unanimously declare that something really exists, but they cannot agree on just what exists or why it works as it does (Fields, 2000). Recent advances in cognitive science and artificial intelligence suggest that there is nothing mystical or magical about intuitive processes, and that they are not paranormal or irrational. Rather, intuitive processes evolve from long experience and learning and consist of the mass of facts, patterns, concepts, abstractions, and generally what we call formal knowledge or beliefs, which are impressed in our minds (Isenberg, 1984; Simon, 1987). Intuition is not the opposite of rationality, nor is it a random process of guessing, as we very often think. It is a sophisticated form of reasoning based on chunking that an expert hones over years of job-specific experience. Consequently, intuition does not come easily; it requires years of experience in problem solving and is founded upon a solid and complete grasp of the details of the business. However, in some cases, it compresses experience and learning into seconds, as it was shown in some cases during my interviews.

RATIONAL/INTUITIVE ORIENTATION

The lack of field studies in strategic decision-making processes called for a research study to examine concrete real-life cases and to analyze the following:

- How top-level managers really make strategic decisions.
- How entrepreneurs and executives differ, if at all, in their approach to strategic decision-making processes when they combine rational thinking with their intuition
- Similarities and differences, if any, in management skills between entrepreneurs and executives

Figure 1. The research model

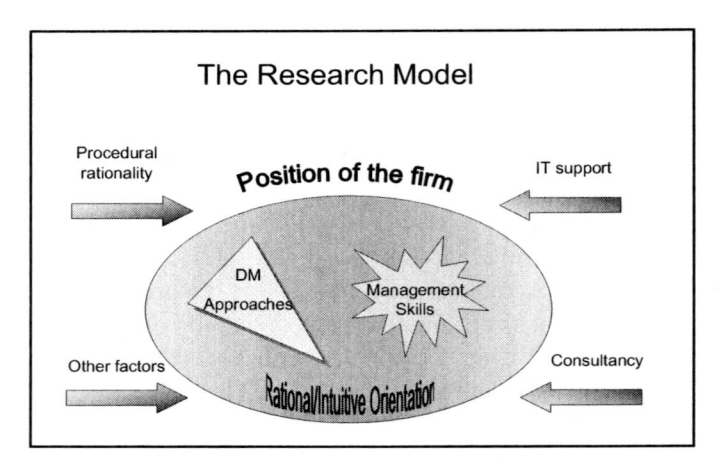

The logic of the research model can be described as seen in Figure 1.

Rational/intuitive orientation is a concept that has yet to make a significant impact on mainstream decision-making research. Consequently, no well-established indicators of rational/intuitive orientation exist. Based on understanding the concept, however, two optional indicators (decision-making approaches and management skills) were identified in this study.

In the literature of decision theory, several models of organisational decision making can be found. These differ from each other in the sense that they use other prerequisites of decision makers and also refer to the organisational connections of decision makers. On the basis of the above dimensions, four different models and decision-making mechanisms were identified (analytical, political, bounded rationality, and intuitive). Eleven management skills were investigated and rated as to whether they support analytical or intuitive thinking. In this article, we will focus on the core of the above-mentioned research model, namely on rational/intuitive orientation.

The main hypotheses of the research can be summarized as follows:

H1: Intuition plays a key role in strategic decision making since strategic problems are ill structured and hence cannot be programmed. Decision makers at the top level combine analytical and intuitive approaches, but more heavily rely on their intuition.

H2: Intuitive decision making is more favoured by independent decision makers (entrepreneurs) who have extended control over their firms and are more often in the final decision maker's position. When they put the dot on the i, they are almost always intuitive.

H3: The level of management skills is high. The creative/intuitive skills are even more developed in the sample.

Herbert Simon (1982) was the first to distinguish between the two extreme types of decisions. He called recurring, routine-like, or ready-made ones programmed decisions, while those being unique and unstructured with long-term impacts were called nonprogrammed decisions. Programmed and nonprogrammed decisions naturally set the two extreme poles of one continuum, and the appearance of interim cases is much more probable. In the course of company operations, it happens very rarely that a decision situation clearly corresponds to the terminology of the programmed or nonprogrammed decisions. On the other hand, most managers develop some kind of practice for the handling of nonprogrammed decision situations that can be successfully applied if a ready-made solution can be fitted to an actual situation. Certain nonprogrammed decisions may become programmed in the course of time in a company's practice. It is rather meaningful that programmed and nonprogrammed decisions are sometimes referred to as well structured and ill structured as well.

A central part of this survey consisted of the examination of 20 plus 60 real strategic decisions. At the beginning of the interview, every respondent could mention a big case that was mainly ill structured. When I asked the respondents to quote three more decision cases, they mainly mentioned semistructured problems that could be positioned somewhere between the well-structured and ill-structured extremes. These cases were not as big as the previous 20 decision situations, but they still had long-term consequences and strategic importance. Practically, each participant could mention four cases, one big case and three semistructured cases. This is how the database of the survey was built up based on the cases of the 20 contributors.

In the interest of comparability, the semistructured decision cases were classified into categories that are borrowed from the "Bradford Studies" (Hichson, Butler, Cray, Mallory, & Wilson, 1986). According to this, I distinguished the following types of decisions:

- Investment
- Reorganisation
- Acquisition
- Fundraising
- Marketing
- Service or product development
- Production
- Finding a site for investment
- Human resource management
- Quality management
- Other decisions

Decisions related to service or product development (10), investment (9), reorganisation (9), marketing (8), and finding a site for investment (7) were the most frequently mentioned cases. However, I also found at least a single case for each other category.

The respondents mixed the analytical and intuitive problem-solving approaches when they made these decisions. As they argued, they found it very difficult to use only the rational approach for these semiprogrammed decisions, therefore intuitive decision making was very often valuable and also applied. However, it was also typical that decision makers made their decisions and later developed rational-sounding reasons for the decision after the fact. It seemed that for some reason they like to be seen as rational. However, some of them were very proud of relying on their instinct in solving particular cases. Demonstrating the concept of bounded rationality, the respondents recognized that at least in part their decisions were based on intuition or a gut feeling. This was most typical in marketing cases, where the respondents needed more experience and judgment than sequential logic or explicit reasons to make those decisions. As they explained it, they made these decisions based upon what they believed to be right rather than upon what they could document with hard data. In the other categories, especially in cases of service or product development, investment, acquisition, and finding a site, they did not find it appropriate to apply this kind of logic.

When the respondents were given an extra opportunity to rethink their earlier answers concerning the analytical and intuitive approaches in their cases, they changed their minds only slightly. If they could repeat the same decisions, which will of course never happen, they would rely more on analysis in marketing decisions too, but in service and product development interestingly would give more room for intuition.

Clearly, there were major perceived differences between entrepreneurs' and executives' answers in terms of how their decisions were made. One of the main differences is that executives tend to exhibit more characteristics of analytical decision making than entrepreneurs do. Executives more heavily rely on the analytical approach. However, it is interesting to note that entrepreneurs are more careful in cases of investment decisions, where they insist on preliminary analytical investigation. A logical explanation could be that they risk their own money when investing and are therefore more careful about it.

The quality of the decision-making activity and the company's success is considerably influenced by the fact of who makes the decisions, what skills and capabilities they have, what their managerial style is, and also what techniques and methods they use in the course of decision making. Consequently, it is not only the applied decision-making approach and the managerial style that leave their mark on decision making, but equally important is the level of professional abilities, education, and experience the managers have.

What characteristics or individual skills must management have to be successful? The survey embraced the general abilities of management. What is more, in the in-depth interviews I encouraged respondents to make some self-evaluations. I asked them to define their strengths and weaknesses according to the investigated characteristics and skills by evaluating themselves on

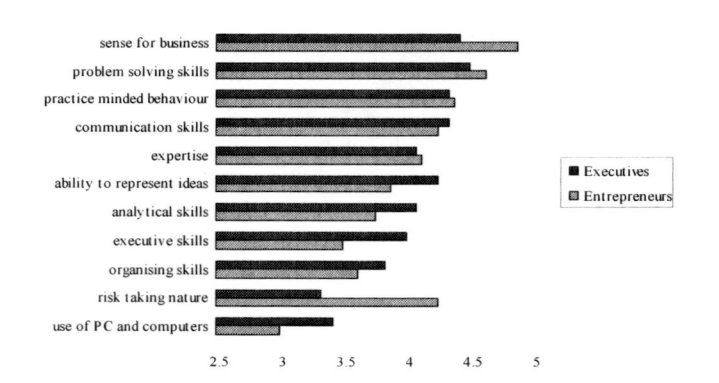

Figure 2. Differences in management skills of executives and entrepreneurs

a five-point Likert scale. However, the first task was to rank the skills according to their importance. Considering the opinions of all respondents (*N*=20), the "image of the ideal manager" fulfilling all expectations of management appeared in decreasing order:

- Excellent communication skills
- Sense for business
- Problem-solving skills
- Practice-minded behaviour
- Ability to represent ideas
- Risk-taking nature
- Expertise
- Organising skills
- Executive skills
- Analytical skills
- Use of PC and computers

Some interesting features are revealed from this ranking. Naturally, the top and the bottom of the list are worth attention, since the skills there outline a manager image frequently mentioned during the interviews. The major task of a manager is to communicate inside and outside of the company (as they stated they do most of the marketing) while the use of computers at top level is not a must since they can get all necessary IT support whenever they need. The other skills could be divided into two subgroups. As one of the respondents stated, the skills that are more important, which you cannot buy, happen to be in the upper part of the list, while those that are available through different channels, for example, consultancy, like organising skills, analytical skills, or IT knowledge, are in the second half of the list.

If we compare these results to the actual self-assessments, we can see interesting evidence of cognitive dissonance. The respondents ranked less important their weaknesses and more important their strengths. They were far beyond the average performers (if we define this category on a five-point scale with the middle position indicated by 3) on all criteria except one, the use of computers, but as we saw earlier, they did not feel that fact was a disadvantage. They are very good communicators, which I can confirm based on my personal experiences. They quite heavily rely on their accumulated knowledge, experiences, and expertise, and are equipped with the necessary problem-solving skills. They named as a real strength their sense for business. We cannot forget that two fifths of them are the founders and majority owners of their enterprises in the sample. Two of them started totally new businesses when they recognized new business opportunities. They left behind their emerging and safe careers and chose unknown and challenging new fields. Both of them are very successful in their new businesses.

We know that some skills and capabilities support more the intuitive way of problem solving than the others. My research method also involved interviewing a dozen university professors in an effort to link the management skills involved in this research with the analytical or intuitive way of problem solving. A quick survey was designed and the professors were asked to evaluate the above-mentioned skills by indicating whether these skills supported analytical or intuitive thinking strongly. They could mark only one answer for each skill. All of the respondents had strong management background since they were teaching either in the field of organisational behaviour or decision sciences.

The skills were split into two groups depending on their role supporting intuitive or analytical problem solving. According to the opinion of the university professors with management background, intuitive thinking and problem solving are best supported by the following skills: a willingness to take risks, a sense for business, the ability to represent ideas, practice-minded behaviour, and excellent communication skills. On the other hand, different skills take precedence when problems require analytical solutions. The skills that most support this approach were determined to be analytical skills, computer skills, organising skills, professional expertise, and problem-solving skills. Not surprisingly, executive skills are somewhere between these two groups of skills since effective leadership requires a combination of analytical and intuitive approaches.

Subsequently, I revised this distinction at two points. Most of the authors (Csikszentmihalyi, 1996; Klein, 2004; Sinclair & Ashkanasy, 2005) agree that intuition is nothing else than experience put into practice. This demystified definition of intuition shows how one can become expert in one's profession through one's cumulative experience or knowledge. Klein argues that intuition is a developed sense helping to put experience into recognizable patterns for future use. As it is well known, good communication skills often go with good analytical skills since both are the functions of the left hemisphere of the brain (Browning, 2005).

Putting this split into practice, the chart of the managers shows a rather balanced picture of their analytical and intuitive skills. Problem-solving skills lead the rank of the analytical skills while business sense is the most important strength among the intuitive skills. Among the 80 analyzed decision cases, I found much that confirms the importance of business sense as the path toward success. The weaknesses are compensated by the high level of strengths. Lack of computer knowledge or organising skills does not seem to be a big problem because top-level managers can easily find someone to do these jobs.

The largest gap could be recognized in the ability to represent ideas. Entrepreneurs do not have to sell their decisions because they are typically the final decision makers; consequently for them this skill is not a must. Their priorities are instead risk-taking nature, problem-solving skills, a sense for business, and communication skills. Executives consider the ability to represent ideas far more important than the entrepreneurs. Analytical and organising skills are ranked a little bit higher by them too.

Differences between groups that exceed 10% are considered to be very significant in survey research. There were relatively large differences in this research between the two responding groups according to the capabilities and skills based on their self-assessments (Figure 2). Entrepreneurs have better business sense and they are ready to take far more risks. They evaluated their problem-solving skills slightly higher than the executives. Executives' strengths are in the ability to represent ideas, analytical skills, and executive skills. The more balanced picture emerged when we compare practice-minded behaviour, communication skills, and expertise.

FUTURE TRENDS

When analyzing these findings, it must be remembered that these results were based on self-assessments. Rarely are self-assessments and independent (objective) assessments congruent. However, we do not have any techniques to measure the level of the different management skills and capabilities or decision-making approaches objectively yet. We feel that there might be a lack of agreement between the self-assessments and an imaginative objective assessment of these parameters. We call this gap "the coefficient of self–delusion." This coefficient can be positive (when the objective rating is higher than the self-assessment) or it can be negative (when the objective ratings are lower than the self-assessments). The positive coefficient of self-delusion occurs with people who either are genuinely humble or may be trying to avoid overinflating their self-ratings for a variety of reasons, for example, because of their cultural background. The negative coefficient of self-delusion usually occurs with people who are not conscious of the impact of their behaviours on others or they have an inflated sense of self. In either case, it is important to investigate why the assessment gap exists and reflect upon ways that it can be narrowed, perhaps even closed, which is a big research challenge.

There is a big debate at the present time whether the analytical or the intuitive way of thinking is more powerful in the business arena. Thomas Davenport (2006) argued that some companies have built their very businesses on their ability to collect, analyze, and act on data. Every company can learn from what these firms do. The popular "head vs. formula" controversy that is based mostly on laboratory studies in the past established the superiority of the rational-analytical approach over the soft judgmental or intuitive approach. The extension of this approach to strategic decision making is problematic, however. This is because strategic decisions are characterized by incomplete knowledge. Consequently, it may be impossible to identify quantitative equations among variables and find numeric values for parameters and initial states. That is why people still use their heads instead of formulas in strategic cases (Khatri & Alvin, 2000). As a conclusion of the very intensive debate, there is now an agreement that intuition is not an irrational process. It is based on a deep understanding of the situation. It is a complex phenomenon that draws from the store of knowledge in our subconscious and is rooted in past experience. It is quick, but not necessarily biased as presumed in previous research on rational decision making (Khatri & Alvin).

CONCLUSION

In everyday language, we tend to use the word intuitive with some connotation of irrational. This is probably due to Bergson (1911) who attached great importance to intuition but interpreted it as a mystic force that by definition could not be subject to rational means of inquiry (Wierzbicki, 1997). However, almost a hundred years of research in various fields of science now leads to a reversal of this interpretation. In the management literature of our days, we can read that intuition is not arbitrary or irrational because it is based on years of practice and hands-on experience, often stored in the subconscious. Managers started to accept that new interpretation and they believe that their intuition is part of their business knowledge. Decision support systems might help to strengthen this perception by providing user-friendly tools to obtain and sort the necessary knowledge for successful decisions. It will probably take time until this view is widely recognized.

This study showed that executives in a corporate setting tend to view decision making differently than entrepreneurs. Since they are typically given a fixed amount of budgeted resources to work with, they tend to define a problem in terms of what can be done with the resources on hand. Entrepreneurs, on the other hand, will likely pose the problem in terms of an objective. They usually state, "This is what I want to get done," and then start to worry about finding the resources to accomplish that objective. As a result, entrepreneurial decision makers feel less constrained by the lack of resources. They are famous for making "seat-of-the-pants" decisions, which means they make quick decisions based on a good feeling or intuition. This kind of challenge requires different skills from the entrepreneurs than from the executives.

There was another interesting finding when I compared the decision-making practices of the executives and the entrepreneurs. Both groups relied quite heavily on analysis in the preparation phase of the decision-making process, which gave room for decision support applications. However, executives were ready to follow the decision support systems' recommendations in the moment of choice while entrepreneurs preferred to follow their intuition. As a conclusion, we can state that entrepreneurs' support must focus mainly on the preparation phase, and decisions should be made by them vs. support systems.

REFERENCES

Agor, W. (1997). The measurement, use, and development of intellectual capital to increase public sector productivity. *Public Personnel Management*, 175-186.

Barnard, C. (1938). *Functions of the executive.* Cambridge, MA: Harvard University Press.

Bergson, H. (1911). *Introduction to metaphysics.* New York.

Browning, G. (2005). *Emergenetics: Tap into the new science of success.* Harper Collins.

Buchanan, L., & O'Connell, A. (2006). A brief history of decision making. *Harvard Business Review*, 32-42.

Catford, L. (1987). *Creative problem solving in business.* Doctoral dissertation, Stanford University, Stanford, CA. (UMI No.)

Csikszentmihalyi, M. (1996a). *Creativity: Flow and the psychology of discovery and invention.* Harper Collins Publishers.

Csikszentmihalyi, M. (1996b). *The work and lives of 91 eminent people.* Harper Collins.

Davenport, T. H. (2006). Competing on analytics. *Harvard Business Review*, 99-107.

Dean, J. W., & Sharfman, M. P. (1993). Procedural rationality in the strategic decision making process. *Journal of Management Studies*.

Eisenhardt, K. M. (1998). Strategy as strategic decision making. *Sloan Management Review*, 65.

Fields, A. F. (2000). *Intuition engineering*. Organizational Engineering Institute.

Frederickson, J. W. (1985). Effects of decision motive and organizational performance level on strategic decision processes. *Academy of Management Journal, 28*(4), 821-843.

Gladwell, M. (2005). *Ösztönösen: A döntésről másképp* [Blink: The power of thinking without thinking]. Budapest, Hungary: HVG Kiadó Rt.

Hichson, D., Butler, R., Cray, D., Mallory, G., & Wilson, D. (1986). *Top decisions: Strategic decision making in organizations*. Basil Blackwell.

Isenberg, D. (1984). How senior managers think. *Harvard Business Review*, 81-90.

Jung, C. G. (1934). *Modern man in search of a soul*. New York: Harcourt Brace.

Khatri, N., & Alvin, H. N. (2000). The role of intuition in strategic decision making. *Human Relations, 53*, 57-86.

Klein, G. (1998). *Sources of power: How people make decisions*. Cambridge, MA: MIT Press.

Klein, G. (2004). *The power of intuition: How to use your gut feelings to make better decisions at work*. Random House.

Leavitt, H. J. (1975). Beyond the analytic manager: Part II. *California Management Review, 17*(4), 11-21.

Maslow, A. (1954). *Motivation and personality*. New York: Harper & Row.

Meyers, D. G. (2002). The powers & perils of intuition. *Psychology Today*.

Mintzberg, H., & Westley, F. (2001). Decision making: It's not what you think. *MIT Sloan Management Review, 42*(3), 89-93.

Parikh, J. (1994). *Intuition: The new frontier of management*. Oxford, United Kingdom: Blackwell Business.

Restak, R. (2001). *Mozart's brain and the fighter pilot: Unleashing your brain's potential*. New York: Harmony Books.

Simon, H. A. (1982). *Korlátozott racionalitás: Válogatott tanulmányok*. Budapest, Hungary: KJK.

Simon, H. A. (1987). Making management decisions: The role of intuition and emotion. *Academy of Management Executive*, 57-64.

Sinclair, M., & Ashkanasy, N. M. (2005). Intuition. *Management Learning, 36*(3), 353-370.

Westcott, M. (1968). *Toward a contemporary psychology of intuition: A historical and empirical inquiry*. New York: Holt, Rinehart & Winston, Inc.

Whetton, D. A., & Cameron, K. S. (2005). *Developing management skills* (6th ed.). Prentice Hall.

Wierzbicki, A. J. (1997). On the role of intuition in decision making and some ways of multicriteria aid of intuition. *Journal of Multi-Criteria Decision Analysis, 6*, 65-76.

http://www.referenceforbusiness.com/management/De-Ele/Decision-Making.html

http://www.mlq.sagepub.com/cgi/content/abstract/36/3/353

http://www.oeinstutute.org/joe/Intuition_Engineering.html

http://breakthrough-business-school.com/ezines/ezine_5-10-05.html

http://www.findarticles.com/p/articles/mi_m1175/is_6_35/ai_92849363/print

http://sloanreview.mit.edu/smr/issuue/2001/spring/8/

http://referenceforbusiness.com/management/De-Ele/Decision-Making.html

http://www.au.af.mil/au/awc/awcgate/ndu/strat-ldr-dm/pt2ch9.html

http://www.jstor.org/jstor/gifcvdir/apr001004/00014273

http://www.aja4hr.co.uk/services/leadership/whole_brain.asp

http://www.people.uvawise.edu/pww8y/Reviews/OC/OCRev/OCrEV06DecMaking.html

KEY TERMS

Analytical Skills: The skills that most support the analytical approach in problem solving are determined as follows: analytical skills, computer skills, organising skills, professional expertise, problem-solving skills, and communication skills.

Intuition 1: Intuition is usually defined as knowing or sensing something without the use of rational processes.

Intuition 2: Intuition has been described as a perception of reality not known to consciousness, in which the intuition knows, but does not know how it knows.

Intuition 3: Intuition is a rational process in which an individual reaches a conclusion on the basis of less explicit information than is ordinarily required to reach that decision.

Intuition 4: Intuition is a nonsequential information processing mode, which comprises both cognitive and affective elements and results in direct knowing without any use of conscious reasoning.

Intuitive Skills: Intuitive thinking and problem solving are best supported by the following skills: the willingness to take risks, a sense for business, the ability to represent ideas, and practice-minded behaviour and expertise.

Nonprogrammed or Ill-Structured Decisions: Unique and unstructured decisions with long-term impacts are nonprogrammed decisions. Programmed and nonprogrammed decisions naturally set the two extreme poles of one continuum and the appearance of interim cases is much more probable. In the course of company operations, it happens very rarely that a decision situation clearly corresponds to the terminology of the programmed or nonprogrammed decisions. On the other hand, most managers develop some kind of practice for the handling of nonprogrammed-decision situations that can be successfully applied if a ready-made solution can be fitted to an actual situation. Certain nonprogrammed decisions may become programmed in the course of time in a company's practice. It is rather meaningful that programmed and nonprogrammed decisions are sometimes referred to as well-structured and ill-structured decisions as well.

Programmed or Well-Structured Decisions: Herbert Simon was the first to distinguish between the two extreme types of decisions. He called recurring, routine-like, or ready-made ones programmed decisions.

Strategic Decisions: Strategic decisions are those that affect the direction of the firm. These major decisions concern areas such as new products and markets, product or service developments, acquisitions and mergers, subsidiaries and affiliates, joint ventures, strategic alliances, finding a site for a new investment, reorganisation, and other important matters. Strategic decision making is usually conducted by the firm's top management, led by the CEO or president of the company.

The Analytic Hierarchy Process: Structuring, Measurement, and Synthesis

John Wang
Montclair State University, USA

Chandana Chakraborty
Montclair State University, USA

Huanyu Ouyang
The People's Hospital of Jiangxi Provence, China

INTRODUCTION

The challenges of evaluation and decision making are encountered in every sphere of life and on a regular basis. The nature of the required decisions, however, may vary between themselves. While some decisions may reflect individual solutions on simple problems, others may indicate collaborative solutions on complex issues. Regardless of their distinctive nature, all decisions are outcomes of a mental process. The process involves careful evaluation of merits of all the available options leading ultimately to the choice of a single solution. Numerous efforts have been made in the literature to develop decision models ideal for choosing the best solution for a given problem. The dilemma in using these decision models, however, can hardly be avoided. With differences in underlying methodology, each model serves a specific decision-making need of the decision maker. In the absence of a universal framework suitable for handling a variety of problems, decision makers are often required to identify the model best suited for their particular need. Furthermore, they need to take account of the advantages and disadvantages associated with the chosen model.

Recognizing the difficulty of model selection, Thomas L. Saaty, the mathematician, developed a decision-making approach known commonly as the analytic hierarchy process (AHP), which relies mainly on the innate human ability to make sound judgments about small problems (Saaty, 1994, 1996; Saaty & Alexander, 1981). The AHP is a popular method for assessing multiple criteria and deriving priorities for decision-making purposes. This model is different from all other models in that it is able to handle both tangible and intangible attributes of the decision maker. In addition, it has the ability to monitor the consistency with which a decision maker makes his or her judgments (Roper-Lowe & Sharp, 1990). Unlike other available models, AHP can be universally adapted to a wide range of problems and, hence, is an excellent choice for decision making in diverse problems in the fields of quality control, finance, balanced scorecard, and forecasting. It is for these reasons that AHP is now one of the most highly regarded and used models in a wide range of organizations including major corporations, government agencies, and academia (Liedtka, 2005).

BACKGROUND

Dr. Thomas L. Saaty worked for the U.S. Department of State in the 1960s. It was during this time that he realized that many of the available models were too general and abstract for application in a wide range of decision-making needs (Forman & Gass, 2001). In his attempt to create a universal framework as opposed to a specialized framework for modeling real-world problems, Saaty developed the AHP model in the 1970s while working as a professor at the Wharton School of Business (Saaty & Vargas, 1991). As narrated by Saaty, he utilized the methodology taught by his grandmother in developing the model. The methodology consisted of breaking down a complex problem and weighing the decision options against each other (Palmer, 1999).

AHP has three primary functions: structuring complexity, measurement, and synthesis. The first function, structuring, involves configuration of the problem into a hierarchy that describes the problem. With the overall goal placed at the top, the main attributes are placed at a level below the top one. These attributes can further be subdivided in consecutive lower levels thereby simplifying the decisions at hand. The second function, measurement, involves deriving weights for the lowest level of attributes. This is done by a series of pair-wise comparisons in which every attribute on each level is compared with its siblings in terms of its importance to the parent. Following this, the options available to the decision maker are scored with respect to the attributes. Finally, matrix algebra is used to calculate the final score for each available option (Roper-Lowe & Sharp, 1990).

MAIN FOCUS

Benefits of AHP

The AHP has the ability to elicit decision maker's responses on the relative importance of the problem in three different ways: numerically, verbally, and graphically. These elicited responses are inspired by a pair-wise comparison process. With an option to submit responses in alternative formats, decision makers using the AHP model provide meaningful responses and, thus, produce better results.

Structuring the problems into a hierarchy with the AHP allows the decision makers to deal with the associated complexity in a simple way. The methodology reflects Saaty's observation that human beings deal with complexity simply by structuring it into homogeneous clusters of factors (Forman & Gass, 2001). With problems broken up into clusters, individuals find it easier to evaluate the importance of each alternative available for solution. Other scientists have shared Saaty's views in this respect.

The effectiveness of structuring incorporated in the AHP model is backed up by evidence. Most of today's organizations use a hierarchy structure in order to ease the decision-making process.

Hierarchy building is a powerful instrument at the initial stages of setting up problems and considering alternatives. By allowing information to be organized, the structure allows the decision maker to better understand the interaction of the elements of a problem (Gass, 1985). Additionally, the structure minimizes the possibility of overlooking elements of the problem; issues and ideas ignored at previous levels can become apparent at advanced levels.

The ability to measure consistency is also a major strength of the AHP. AHP uses the eigenvalue technique that allows for computation of a consistency measure, an estimated arithmetical indicator of the inconsistencies or intransitivity in a set of pair-wise ratings (Warren, 2004). This measure is popularly referred as the consistency index. Pair-wise comparison ratings are considered consistent and acceptable as long as the consistency ratio (CR) is lower than 0.10. A ratio higher than 0.10 warrants additional review and evaluation of the results. The management team in charge of the evaluation process can take precautionary measures to avoid costly mistakes of repeated trials. In particular, the team should take precaution when dealing with a large number of alternatives capable of producing inconsistencies.

The AHP is also well known for its ability to compare intangible and tangible factors. This is easily accomplished through pair-wise comparisons with a nine-point scale. Even though it is feasible to do these comparisons, it has been suggested not to mix both factors in the same hierarchy. For cases that fail to satisfy this condition, an alternative approach of using a link attribute can prove useful. This link attribute helps to make a meaningful comparison of both tangible and intangible factors (Roper-Lowe & Sharp, 1990). The link attribute is weighed against the tangible and intangible factors in pair-wise comparisons. In the following stage, the intangible factors can be weighed against tangible ones by scaling the weight of the link attribute.

Finally, AHP is also useful in providing records about circumstances surrounding each decision. Records can be reviewed at a later point in time to determine how and why a particular decision was arrived at. This can become very useful when evaluating decisions that were previously made but need to be considered again for changes in circumstances. For example, additional information about the alternatives used in pair-wise comparisons can become available in the future. Decision makers can quickly process this new information in order to reevaluate original scores and measure the impact of new data on their initial decision. In cases where organizations are required to make similar decisions on an ongoing basis, the same hierarchy can be reused as a background for constructing a new hierarchy.

Shortcomings of AHP

Rank Reversal

One of the most highly commented about weaknesses of the AHP has been rank reversal. Rank reversal basically refers to a change in the rankings or the ordering of the alternatives if an additional alternative is added or an existing one is removed (Warren, 2004). It usually happens because of the implicit nature of the AHP. Under rank reversal, the linkage between alternatives is caused by normalization of the eigenvectors. Hence, the addition of an alternative or the removal of an alternative leads to a change in the weights of the other alternatives. This is opposed to the MAUT (multiattribute utility theory) model, which has an explicit nature and for which the addition of new alternatives does not affect the rank of the other alternatives.

Granted its existence, rank reversal is considered a secondary problem and its effects are seen only when the alternatives are closely related. There are additional questions of closed and open systems (Forman & Gass, 2001). A closed system is one in which there is a limited number of resources and, hence, one needs to allocate them evenly between the alternatives. Let us say that a company has limited construction supply and wants to allocate it efficiently between three different houses they are building. Given resource limitation, an additional housing project would require resources to be reallocated between the houses. Thus, in the real world where managers and CEOs are looking for increased efficiency with a given amount of resources, AHP appears to be a common choice. For cases representing open resources or unlimited resources, AHP can cause rank reversal.

Subjectivity and Time Consumption

An additional weakness of the AHP method is that it is subjective. In performing pair-wise comparisons, it often becomes apparent that different people have different ways of evaluating a particular component. Consequently quantifying components accurately can become extremely difficult. Recently, a solution for this problem was designed by integrating methods that deal with differences in evaluating techniques. An example of such a method is the fuzzy logic theory.

Another disadvantage of the AHP is the redundancy of entering rankings for different alternatives in pair-wise comparisons (Ishizaka, 2004). As the number of alternatives, criteria, and hierarchical levels increase, so does the number of comparisons needed to evaluate them. For example, a hierarchy with five criteria and nine alternatives would require the decision maker to perform 190 comparisons. With more alternatives, the total number of comparisons could increase infinitely. Clearly, therefore, AHP can become a time-consuming tool for evaluating solutions, especially in group settings, where some decisions can potentially turn into lengthy debates. Methods have been developed to address this issue by reducing the number of comparisons; however, making fewer comparisons can result in loss of accuracy. Many professionals suggest subdividing the alternatives into smaller clusters that reduce the number of comparisons needed. Many others have suggested that the time-consumption aspect of the AHP has very little relevance in today's technologically advanced societies; numerous software technologies are available to compute AHP models.

A Specific Example of Application of AHP

Let us now see an example of how AHP actually works and what kind of problems it can help solve in real-life business.

A hospital has a vacancy in its marketing department and is looking for a potential new employee to fill the position. The hospital is specifically looking for four different characteristics in its candidates: (a) experience, (b) salary requirement, (c) education, and (d) personality. The company has narrowed down its choices to three final candidates (John, Leon, and Leigh) and will use the AHP model to select the best candidate based on the identified criteria.

- Our Goal is: *Select the best candidate for the marketing position*
- Our Criteria are: *Experience, Salary Requirement, Education, and Personality*
- Our Alternatives are: *John, Leon, and Leigh*

There are two types of AHP models that we need to consider:

1. **Consistent:** In this model, the following conditions are true:
   a. Transitive property: If A is better than B and B is better than C, then A is better than C.
   b. Numerically consistent ratings: If A = 3B and A = 2C, then B = 2/3C
   c. The value of the CR is 0.
2. **Inconsistent:** This model pays no attention to transitive property or numerical consistency. However, to be in acceptable range, the value of CR should be less than 0.10.

Step 1: Create rankings for criteria and alternatives. The initial step is to compare the four criteria and decide which skills are more important for this marketing job. The comparisons are done via the use of a rating scale as proposed by Saaty himself.

So, if experience is more important than personality, we can give it a rating of anything from 2 to 9 based upon how much more important experience is than personality. A rating of 3 means that experience is moderately more important than personality. All of these decisions are made by the higher level personnel who have the ability to evaluate the importance of each skill in the context of their company's needs. Let us suppose the hospital develops the following pair-wise comparison matrix for the set of criteria referred to above.

Step 2: Normalize and figure out weights.
To normalize:

- Divide each column value by the total sum of the column and
- Take the average of each row

The sums of the columns are 2.25, 9, 3.375, and 6.75. After dividing each column value by their respective sums, we get the matrix in Table 3.

As can be seen from Table 3, since all the rows in a consistent AHP are multiples of each other, we really only need to normalize one column to get the weights. Hence, taking the average for each of the rows above, we get the following weights for the criteria:

Experience: 0.44; Salary Requirement: 0.11; Education: 0.298; Personality: 0.147

It is therefore apparent that the hospital is assigning major emphasis on the experience of the candidates; the weights are approximately 44% for experience, 29.8% for education, 14.7% for personality, and 11% for salary requirement.

Step 3: Do the same for each of the alternatives and figure out the weights. Following the same methodology used in Step 2, we need to figure out the weights for the other alternatives. So if Employee A has more

Table 1.

Intensity of Importance	Definition
1	Equal Importance
3	Moderate Importance
5	Strong Importance
7	Very Strong Importance
9	Extreme Importance
2, 4, 6, 8	For compromise between the above values

Table 2.

Criteria	Experience	Salary Req.	Education	Personality
Experience	1	4	1.5	3
Salary Req.	0.25	1	0.375	0.75
Education	0.67	2.67	1	2
Personality	0.33	1.33	0.5	1

CR = 0.0000
Since this is a consistent model, note that the value of CR as computed by the software is 0.0000.

Table 3.

Criteria	Experience	Salary Req.	Education	Personality
Experience	0.444	0.444	0.444	0.444
Salary Req.	0.111	0.111	0.111	0.111
Education	0.298	0.297	0.296	0.296
Personality	0.147	0.148	0.148	0.148

Table 4. Weights based on employee experience

Experience	John	Leon	Leigh
John	1	0.5	1.5
Leon	2	1	3
Leigh	0.67	0.33	1

CR = 0.0000
After normalization, the weights are the following.
John: 0.273; Leon: 0.545; Leigh: 0.182

Table 5. Weights based on employee salary requirement

Salary Req.	John	Leon	Leigh
John	1	5	3
Leon	0.2	1	0.6
Leigh	0.33	1.67	1

CR = 0.0000
After normalization, the weights are as follows.
John: 0.652; Leon: 0.130; Leigh: 0.218

Table 6. Weights based on employee education

Education	John	Leon	Leigh
John	1	0.75	0.25
Leon	1.33	1	0.33
Leigh	4	3	1

CR = 0.0000
After normalization, the weights are the following.
John: 0.158; Leon: 0.210; Leigh: 0.632

Table 7. Weights based on employee personality

Personality	John	Leon	Leigh
John	1	0.5	0.75
Leon	2	1	1.5
Leigh	1.33	0.67	1

CR = 0.0000
After normalization, the weights are as follows.
John: 0.231; Leon: 0.462; Leigh: 0.308

Table 8.

	Weights for Each Candidate Based on Alternatives				Weights for Criteria	
	Experience	Salary Req.	Education	Personality	Experience	0.44
John	0.273	0.652	0.158	0.231	Salary Requirement	0.11
Leon	0.545	0.13	0.21	0.462	Education	0.298
Leigh	0.182	0.218	0.632	0.308	Personality	0.147

experience than Employee B, we will give Employee A a higher rating for experience than Employee B. Using this strategy, the following weights have been calculated for each of the alternatives.

Step 4: Rank the candidates overall by priority. Synthesis of the previous steps yields the following weights:

To compute overall priority for each candidate, we will multiply the weight for each alternative by the weight for the corresponding criterion. So, the overall priority for the candidates would be the following:

John = (0.273 * 0.44) + (0.652 * 0.11) + (0.158 * 0.298) + (0.231 * 0.147) = 0.273

Leon = (0.545 * 0.44) + (0.130 * 0.11) + (0.210 * 0.298) + (0.462 * 0.147) = 0.385

Leigh = (0.182 * 0.44) + (0.218 * 0.11) + (0.632 * 0.298) + (0.308 * 0.147) = 0.338

To summarize, the overall weights for the employees are as follows:

John: 0.273; Leon: 0.385; Leigh: 0.338

Hospital executives have selected Leon to fill the position for their marketing vacancy because he has the highest ranking (0.385).

The above demonstration is based on a consistent model since an inconsistent model has a similar process.

Examples across Different Areas and Organizations

Over the years, AHP has been successfully applied to a broad range of difficult situations requiring more of a formal approach. Some of the examples include selection among competing alternatives, allocation of resources, and forecasting. Especially in multicriteria environments, AHP has widely been chosen to solve complex problems and forecast outcomes.

Much of its continued success can be attributed to Dr. Saaty's software company Expert Choice, which develops computer applications that utilize AHP and has been successful in helping countless organizations save millions of dollars. In addition, the software has made implementation of the AHP process less exhausting. The software keeps track of thousands of pair-wise comparisons while allowing the user to move and update variables. Also, calculations that would otherwise be too unwieldy and time consuming to do manually can now be done with relative ease.

Dr. Saaty has also developed a new version of his Expert Choice applications for businesses called Aliah. It is specifically being targeted for the Fortune 500 companies as a soup-to-nuts tool for business development. The aim is to make AHP the de facto standard of strategic planning (Palmer, 1999).

NASA: Optimal Project Selection

As a result of increased public awareness with regard to government spending on space exploration, Congressional mandates were put in place to hold the National Aeronautic and Space Administration (NASA) more accountable in the process of evaluating and selecting the best projects that maximize the return from the taxpayers' funds. NASA was forced to abandon its unstructured and intuitive process and replace it with a multicriteria group-decision model, known as CROSS (consensus-ranking organizational support system), which uses the AHP to help NASA scientists evaluate advanced technological projects (Tavana, 2003). With its successful implementation, NASA shortened the evaluation time, improved the quality of decisions, and reduced the number of costly decision reversals that were present under the old method. More importantly, it provided members of the decision-making group with a structured approach for systematic evaluation.

AHP in Health Care

The health care system consists of complex areas that are unique in their characteristics and that are a part of many dimensions fitted into singular unit; therefore, it is very difficult to approach the measurement of the performance of health care services. Most health care system delivery is evaluated through three categories of measurement—structure, process, and outcome—in order to improve the performance of multispecialty tertiary care. According to Hariharan, Dey, Moseley, Kumar, and Gora (2004), the AHP model was applied to two tertiary care teaching hospitals in Barbados and India. The results of application identified specific areas where neither hospital performed well; recommendations were provided for improvement in those areas. This study has established AHP as a useful tool for a process-based performance measurement of a tertiary care hospital. In addition, the study identified many advantages of the AHP in the performance measurement of a hospital: It is both objective and subjective in nature regarding the measurement of the performance, it allows for a group decision-making process and offers a sound mathematical basis, its application is user friendly, it identifies deficiencies in specific areas of the hospital, and it allows carrying out a sensitivity analysis that assists managers in understanding the effects of their decisions and prioritizing areas in need for improvement.

Other Industries: General Motors and Xerox Corporation

AHP has also been successfully implemented at some of the largest and well-known global corporations. For example, Xerox uses AHP for R&D (research and development) decisions, technology implementation, and design selection (Forman & Gass, 2001). In addition, the process is used to make marketing decisions, customer requirement structuring decisions, and market segment prioritization decisions. As a result of its successful implementation, Xerox successfully eliminated the selection of decisions that would normally be overturned under their old intuitive selection process.

In the automobile industry, General Motors (GM) has been very successful in using AHP. Advanced engineering staff use the AHP to assist them with automobile design evaluation and selection. The best and most cost-effective automobiles are selected with the model's assistance. The model's selection process is also credited for huge cost savings realized by GM. Moreover, the methodology enables GM to be efficient in its risk management functions.

Farm-Level Decisions

AHP has been successfully implemented in farm-level decisions with an objective to aid farmers in selecting one of the following farm systems: conventional, organic, or biological. Because of AHP's ability to deal with multiple criteria in agricultural economics, the methodology proved to be a valuable tool in helping farmers make their selections. These system selections are based on the following objectives, also known as subgoals in the AHP process: profit maximization, improvement of human health, and environmental protection through improved quality of land, water, and air (Mawapanga & Debertin, 1996).

FUTURE TRENDS

Dr. Saaty has created a foundation called Creative Decisions, which sponsors education, research, and software development in advanced methods of decision making involving the AHP. A software application called Super Decisions has been developed through this organization. This software implements a more advanced version of the AHP known as the analytic network process (ANP), which generalizes the pairwise comparisons into clusters that can influence one another's priorities (Saaty, 2005). The main concept of the ANP is that influence does not only flow downward as in the AHP, but can also flow upward and across factors causing nonlinear results of priorities of alternative choices (Super Decisions, 2005).

Another emerging development is the use of fuzzy logic with the AHP. In its traditional formulation, the AHP measurements are offered in exact numbers. In many practical situations, however, decision makers are often reluctant to assign an exact number on the basis of incomplete or uncertain information. Also, they are unable to provide an exact pair-wise comparison. To overcome this problem, scholars have integrated the AHP model with the fuzzy logic theory. The inclusion of fuzzy logic has helped with the accurate assessment of alternatives under incomplete or imprecise information sets (Wu, Chang, & Lin, 2006).

The future of the AHP looks exciting. The method continues to be a popular choice among governments, scholars, educators, and businesspeople all over the world. Further improvement in AHP is in progress and these expected improvements would only add to AHP's future popularity.

CONCLUSION

AHP is a dream come true for Saaty, whose main idea was to create a single unified model for all real-life decision-making problems. Organizations can easily implement AHP for their day-to-day decision-making processes. The use of AHP has been profitable. It has helped firms save millions by improving their overall operations and resource allocation techniques. With the development of Saaty's new foundation called Creative Decisions, we can expect a revision of the AHP model and the introduction of a more advanced model, the ANP. In the future, we can expect to see more and more industries starting to use the AHP model.

REFERENCES

Forman, E. H., & Gass, S. I. (2001). The analytic hierarchy process: An exposition. *Operations Research, 49*(4), 469-486.

Gass, S. I. (1985). *Decision making, models and algorithms: A first course.* New York: John Wiley & Sons, Inc.

Hariharan, S., Dey, P. K., Moseley, H. S. L., Kumar, A. Y., & Gora, J. (2004). A new tool of measurement of process based performance of multispecialty tertiary care hospitals. *International Journal of Health Care Quality Assurance, 17*(6), 302-312.

Ishizaka, A. (2004, September 22-24). *Advantages of clusters and pivots in AHP.* Paper presented at the 15th Mini-Euro Conference MUDSM (Managing Uncertainty in Decision Support Models).

Liedtka, S. L. (2005). Analytic hierarchy process and multi-criteria performance management systems. *Cost Management, 1*(6), 30-38.

Mawapanga, M. N., & Debertin, D. L. (1996). Choosing between alternative farming systems: An application of the analytic hierarchy process. *Review of Agricultural Economics, 18*(3), 385-401.

Palmer, B. (1999). Click here for decisions. *Fortune, 13*(9), 153-156.

Roper-Lowe, G. C., & Sharp, J. A. (1990). The analytic hierarchy process and its application to an information technology decision. *The Journal of the Operational Research Society, 41*(1), 49-59.

Saaty, T. L. (1994). How to make a decision: The analytic hierarchy process. *Interfaces, 24*(6), 19-43.

Saaty, T. L. (1996). *Decision making with dependence and feedback: The analytic network process.* Pittsburgh, PA: RWS Publications.

Saaty, T. L. (2005). *Theory and applications of the analytic network process.* Pittsburgh, PA: RWS Publications.

Saaty, T. L., & Alexander, J. M. (1981). *Thinking with models: Mathematical models in the physical, biological and social sciences.* New York: Pergamon Press.

Saaty, T. L., & Vargas, L. G. (1991). *Prediction, projection and forecasting.* Boston: Kluwer Academic Publishers.

Super Decisions. (2005). *The analytic network process for decision-making.* Retrieved July 29, 2007, from http://www.superdecisions.com/anp_intro.php3

Tavana, M. (2003). CROSS: A multicriteria group-decision-making model for evaluating and prioritizing advanced-technology projects at NASA. *Interfaces, Linthicum, 33*(3), 40-56.

Warren, L. (2004). Uncertainties in the analytic hierarchy process. *Australian Defense Science Magazine.* Retrieved July 29, 2007, from http://www.dsto.defence.gov.au/publications/3476/DSTO-TN-0597.pdf

Wu, C., Chang, C., & Lin, H. (2006). Evaluating the organizational performance of Taiwanese hospitals using the fuzzy analytic hierarchy process. *Journal of American Academy of Business, 9*(2), 201-210.

KEY TERMS

Alternatives: They are multiple choices from which you have to choose one based upon their weights on the different criteria. The alternative with the highest overall rating is selected as the most efficient choice in an AHP.

Consistency Measure (CM): Also known as consistency ratio or consistency index, it is an estimated arithmetical indicator of the inconsistencies or intransitivity in a set of pair-wise ratings.

Criteria: These are one of the three main parts of the AHP that need to be defined before solving a problem. A criterion is a standard on which your judgments are based.

Eigenvalue: An eigenvalue is a scalar associated with a given linear transformation of a vector space and having the property that there is some nonzero vector that when multiplied by the scalar is equal to the vector obtained by letting the transformation operate on the vector.

Eigenvector: An Eigenvector is a nonzero vector that is mapped by a given linear transformation of a vector space onto a vector that is the product of a scalar multiplied by the original vector.

Hierarchy: It is a system of ranking and organizing in which each component is a subordinate to another component directly above or below depending on the layout.

Rank Reversal: This is one of the secondary problems related to AHP that occurs when the rankings for the alternatives are changed with either the addition of or removal of an alternative.

Synthesis: Synthesis is the combining of separate elements to form a coherent whole.

An Attention-Based View on DSS

Sven A. Carlsson
Lund University, Sweden

INTRODUCTION

Commentators on decision support and decision support systems (DSS) have called for serious discussion of the discourses underpinning decision support and DSS (Huber, 1981; Stabell, 1987; Humphreys, 1998). Huber and Humphreys say that decision support and DSS discourses are critical to the advancement of the academic DSS field as well as to DSS practice, but the discourses are too seldom discussed. This article questions the influential "decision-making as choice" view. We suggest that the attention-based view of the firm (Ocasio, 1997) is a promising alternative view of organizational decision-making and that this view can be a basis for DSS design.

More than 50 years ago Herbert Simon suggested that to explain organizational behavior is to explain how organizations distribute and regulate the attention of their decision-makers (Simon, 1947). Simon was emphasizing the duality of structural processes and cognitive processes in structuring of organizational attention. More recent writings have either emphasized cognition and activity or structure. The attention-based view of the firm explicitly links structure, activity, and cognition and the view stresses that organizational decision-making is affected by both the limited attentional capacity of humans and the structural influences on a decision-maker's attention.

The purpose of the article is twofold. First, as an alternative to the decision-making as choice view, present the attention-based view of the firm. Although the concept of attention has a long tradition in the organization and decision-making literature, it has in the last years been used to develop what is called an attention-based view of the firm (Ocasio, 1997, 2001). Attention is also focused in current management literature: "Understanding and managing attention is now the single most important determinant of business success." (Davenport & Beck, 2001). Second, given the attention-based view of the firm, discuss what roles advanced information and communication technologies (ICTs) can play in supporting decision-making. DSS is not a particular ICT in a restricted sense, but primarily a vision and perspective on decision-making—in this article the attention-based view of the firm—and decision support, the role of ICTs as decision support and how to realize this vision in practice. Obviously, there is room for different perspectives on decision-making and decision support and also room for different perspectives on DSS. We will discuss implications of the attention-based view for the use of DSS and decision support portals (DS-Ps) to channel and distribute the attention of organizational decision-makers. A DS-P can be viewed as a personalized front end through which a user (decision-maker) can access "all" information, applications, and services needed to perform decision and knowledge related work and activities.

The remainder of the article is organized as follows: the next section discusses some limitations of the "decision-making as choice" view and argues that it can be fruitful to explore an attention-based view of the firm as a basis for decision support and DSS. It is followed by a section presenting the attention-based view of the firm. Given the attention-based view of the firm, the fourth section focuses on designing and managing DSS. Specifically, we discuss implications for the use of DS-Ps to channel and distribute the attention of decision-makers. The final section presents conclusions and discusses future research.

ON TRIAL: DSS BASED ON THE "DECISION-MAKING AS CHOICE" VIEW

A common view in the organizational decision-making literature is that the purpose of decision-making is to make rational choices (Brunsson, 1989, 2000; March, 1988, 1994). The "decision-making as choice" view has evolved into rational theories of choice: "Virtually all of modern economics and large parts of the rest of social science, as well as the applied fields that build upon them, embrace the idea that human action is the result of human choice. Standard theories of choice view decision making as intentional, consequential action based on knowledge of alternatives and their consequences evaluated in terms of a consistent preference ordering" (Cyert & March, 1992).

In part, contrary to the decision-making as choice view, March (1988) argues that one of the oldest ideas in the behavioral theories of organizational decision-making is that time and attention are scarce resources. In microeconomics, this has lead to the development of information and transaction cost theories where the cost of obtaining and processing information is an explicit part. Contrary to the microeconomic theories, behavioral theories of organizational decision-making have focused on developing behavioral theories of attention allocation: "That interest leads them [students of behavioral theories of organizational decision-making] to see the organization of attention as a central process out of which decisions arise, rather than simply one aspect of the cost structure" (March, 1988).

In some of the organizational decision-making literature, the attention problems are highlighted and brought into the center of theories and models. It is stressed that time and capabilities for attention are limited. Decision-makers receive too many signals and not every signal can be attended to at once or attended to at all. In many decision situations, many things are relevant to attend to and consider, but it is not possible for the decision-makers to attend to them. Because of these and other limitations, "… theories of decision making are often better described as theories of attention or search than as theories of choice. They are concerned with the way in which scarce attention is allocated" (March, 1994).

One of the insights of Simon's perspective on administrative behavior was that to explain firm behavior was to actually explain how firms and their structures channel and distribute the attention of the firms' decision-makers (Simon, 1947). Simon also noted that information and information systems (IS) might have a significant negative impact upon decision-makers' attention focus: "What information consumes is rather obvious: it consumes the attention of its recipients. Hence a wealth of information creates a poverty of attention" (Simon, 1997). If information and IS (incl. DSS) can have a negative impact on decision-makers' attention it is most likely that they can also have a significant negative impact upon organizational actions and moves and ultimately firm performance.

Attention plays also an important role in strategic renewal. Robert Simons, based on his study of how managers use IS to drive strategic renewal, states: "While it is difficult to specify the conditions under which the identification or creation of opportunities will occur, we can state that innovations and solutions cannot be created without organizational attention. … Organizational attention refers to the allocation of information processing capacity within the organization to a defined issue or agenda." (Simons, 1995).

To summarize: the DSS field has been heavily influenced by the "decision-making as choice" view. Given the critique of this view and that it has had a major impact on the DSS-field, it can be argued that alternative views should be explored as the basis for the design and management of DSS. The next section presents one such alternative view: an attention-based view of the firm.

AN ATTENTION-BASED VIEW OF THE FIRM

The main argument of the attention-based view of the firm is that firm behavior is the result of how firms channel and distribute the attention of their decision-makers. According to Ocasio (1997), the attention-based view of the firm is based on three interrelated theoretical principles: (1) *focus of attention*, (2) *situated attention*, and (3) *structural distribution of attention*. The *focus of attention principle* says that what a decision-maker is doing depends on what issues and answers the decision-maker focuses. The *situated attention principle* says that what issues and answers a decision-maker focuses, and what she does, depends on the specific context, setting, and situation she finds herself in. The *structural distribution of attention principle* says that what specific context, setting, and situation a decision-maker finds herself in, and how she attends to them, depends on how the firm's rules, resources, and social relationships regulate and control the distribution and allocation of issues, answers, and decision-makers into specific activities, communications, and procedurals.

Based on the three theoretical principles, Ocasio (1997) presents an attention-based view of the firm as a model of situated attention and firm behavior (Figure 1) The fundamental components of the model are: 1) *the environment of decisions and actions*, (2) *the repertoire of issues and answers*, (3) *procedural and communication channels*—the firm's situated activities, communications and procedures, (4) the firm's *attention*

Figure 1. Model of situated attention and firm behavior (Adapted from Ocasio, 1997). Note: The numbering of the mechanisms does not reflect a temporal order.

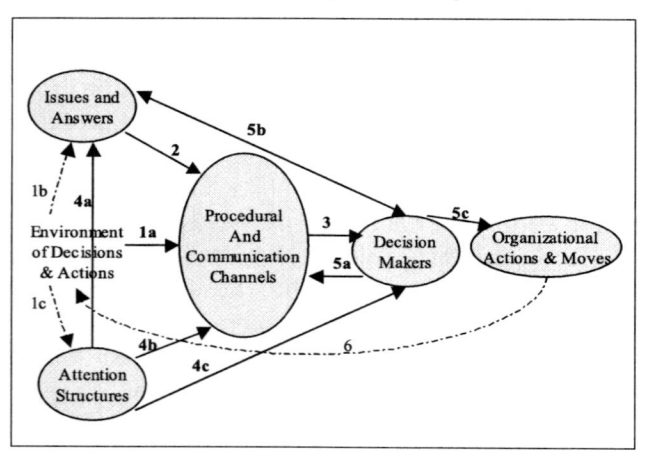

structures—its rules of the game, players, structural positions, and resources, (5) *decision-makers*, and (6) *organizational actions and moves* (Ocasio, 1997). A set of mechanisms links—the solid lines in Figure 1—the constructs of the model to the three principles of the attention-based view of the firm (the three principles are: focus of attention, situated attention, and structural distribution of attention). The dotted lines show additional mechanisms, not directly part of the model of firm behavior. The additional mechanisms show how the environment of decisions and actions is shaped by previous organizational actions and moves (arrow 6), and how a firm as a social and cultural system is shaped by the environment of decisions and actions (arrow 1b and 1c).

Environment of actions and decisions. External and internal social, material, and cultural elements and factors affect the decision activities of an organization's decision makers. The environment of decisions and actions forms the basis for the structuring of an organization's decision-making processes and practice. The complexity of the environment of decisions and actions and an organization's bounded capacity mean that an organization will be restricted in its attention. This means that decision-makers will be selective in the aspects of the environment of decisions and actions that they attend to, as different environmental stimuli are noticed, interpreted, and brought into conscious consideration (Weick, 1979). According to Ocasio (1997), three mechanisms are related to the environment of decisions and actions. The environmental stimuli mechanism (1a) says that a specific procedural or communication channel will be affected by external and internal physical, economic, and institutional factors and provide a set of stimuli for decision-making. The cultural and institutional mechanism (1b) says that the environment of decisions and actions provides decision-makers with a repertoire or "tool kit" of issues and answers from which the decision-makers construct actions and organizational moves. The environmental embeddedness mechanism (1c) says that an organization's economic, social, and institutional environment shape and embed the organization's rules, resources, and social relationships.

Issues and answers. The cultural and cognitive repertoire of schemas and scripts available to decision-makers are used to make sense of (*issues*) and to respond to (*answers*) environmental stimuli. The *embodiment of issues and answers mechanism* (2) implies that issues and answers, in part, are embodied in the cultural products and artifacts used to construct an organization's activities and communications (Ocasio, 1997), for example, different types of ICT-based IS.

Procedural and communication channels. Attention and action takes place in situational contexts. Procedural and communication channels are the informal and formal concrete activities, interactions, and communications set up by the organization to induce decision-makers to take action on a selected set of issues (Ocasio, 1997). Procedural and communication channels include, for example, meetings, administrative protocols, and key performance indicators reports in ERP systems. The specific form and characteristics of an organization's procedural and communication channels impact whether, when, and how decision-makers focus their attention, and how the attention of different decision-makers interacts within a channel. The procedural and communication channels also serve as conduits for processing of issues and answers in making organizational moves. The *availability and saliency of issues and answers mechanism* (3) says that the availability and saliency of issues and answers that decision-makers attend to are affected by the temporal, spatial, and procedural dimensions of an organization's communication and procedural channels (Ocasio, 1997).

Attention structures. The social, economic, and cultural structures governing the allocation of time, effort, and attentional focus of organizational decision-makers in their decision-making activities are the attention structures (March & Olsen, 1976). Four categories of attention regulators are at play: (1) *rules of the game*, (2) *players*, (3) *structural positions*, and (4) *resources* (Ocasio, 1997). *Players* in "organizational games" occupy *structural positions* and the players are constrained and enabled by organizational *rules of the game*. Players employ the organization's *resources* in their attention processes to direct what, how, and when the organization enacts and responds to the environment. An organization's attention structures govern the allocation and distribution of time, energy, effort, and attention through three separate mechanisms. The *valuation of issues and answers mechanism* (4a) says that an organization's valuation and legitimization of the repertoire of issues and answers available to decision-makers are governed by the organization's attention structures. The *channeling of decision-making mechanism* (4b) says that the decision-making activities of an organization are channeled and distributed into a set of procedural and communication channels through the organization's attention structure. The *structuring of interests and identities mechanism* (4c) says that decision-makers are motivated to act and their decision premises are structured by an organization's attention structures, which provide decision-makers with a structured system of interest and identities (Ocasio, 1997).

Decision-makers are the "concrete individuals who jointly participate, within any specific procedural and communication channel, in the enactment of the environment and the social construction of organizational moves." (Ocasio, 1997). The focusing of attention in organizations, or more specific in decision-making processes, is not given (Cyert & March, 1992; March & Olsen, 1976). It emerges from the social interactions among decision-makers who participate in any specific decision-oriented situation or activity. Hence, the focusing of attention is conditional on whether, when, how, and why decision-makers participate in an organization's procedural and communication channels. Further, decision-makers' time, effort, and energy affect their participation. A decision-maker's participation in a specific situation is also affected by other attentional demands. The *structuring of participation mechanism* (5a) says that an outcome of interactions among participants in an organization's procedural and communication channels is decision-making. Demands on decision-makers by alternative channels as well as time, interests, organizational identities, and so forth, affect the structuring of participation. The enactment of issues and answers is summarized in the following way: "Mechanism 5b: (enactment of issues and answers) Decision-makers will enact the environment of decisions by focusing their attention on a limited number of issues and answers. This attentional focus is shaped both by characteristics of the situation—the availability and saliency of issues and answers (3) and the interactions among participants within the channel (5a)—and by the structural determinants of attention—the values, legitimacy, and relevance accorded to the various issues and answers (4a) and the structured interests and identities of decision-makers." (Ocasio, 1997).

Organizational actions and moves. The output of attentional processing and decision-making—situated in procedural and communication channels—is organizational actions and moves, which "…are the myriad of actions undertaken by the firm and its decision-makers in response to or in anticipation of changes in its external and internal environment." (Ocasio, 1997). Organizational actions and moves include, for example:

- Implicit and explicit decisions
- Conscious (controlled) and unconscious (automatic) decisions
- Plans for actions and the actions themselves (the latter is implementation of the plans for actions).

The concept of moves stresses how the actions and moves are shaped by the rules of the games, its players, structural positions, and procedural and communication channels. The actions and moves are influenced and affected by the setting, context, order, and timing of other organizational actions and moves. These can be internal, inter-organizational, or external actions and moves. The *selection of organizational actions and moves mechanism* (5c) says that a decision-maker will select among alternative actions and moves depending on which issues and answers the decision-maker attend to. An organizational move becomes part of the organization's environment of decisions and actions and becomes an input into the construction of subsequent actions and moves. Consequently, the *effects on subsequent moves mechanism* (6) says that once enacted, organizational actions and moves become part of an organization's environment of decisions and actions and are inputs to the construction of subsequent organizational actions and moves.

DESIGNING AND MANAGING DSS BASED ON AN ATTENTION-BASED VIEW OF THE FIRM

The previous section presented the attention-based view of the firm. This section will first present our view on how computer-based decision support will be delivered in the Internet age. We then, from an attention-based view of the firm, discuss design and management of DSS.

Delivering Decision Support in the Internet Age

In the last years hardware and software companies, as well as service providers, have promoted a new approach to organizational information systems. The approach is based on the idea that organizations will increasingly buy or rent their information, applications, and services over the Internet rather than owning and maintaining their own hardware, software, and information. The approach has been launched under a number of different concepts: ".Net" (Microsoft), "Web services" (IBM), "network services" (Oracle), and "open network environment" (Sun). A result of the approach is that previous proprietary architecture—where companies built and maintained unique internal DSS—will to a growing extent be substituted by an open architecture where companies buy or rent data storage, processing power, specific applications, and other services from different types of external service providers. Hagel and Brown (2001) describe the approach as an architecture having three layers: 1) software standards and communication protocols, 2) service grid, and 3) application services. The first layer contains different communication protocols and software standards, for example, XML, WML, and SOAP (simple object access protocol). This layer allows data to be exchanged "easily" between different applications and it also allows data to be processed "easily" in different types of applications. The second layer builds upon the protocols and standards and provides a set of shared utilities. An example of a utility is data management containing data directories, data brokers, data repositories, and data transformation. This utility is critical for many DSS. The third layer contains different application services, for example, data mining tools, business intelligence tools, and statistical packages. The approach implies a number of changes regarding developing and maintaining DSS. First, DSS will increasingly be built and

Figure 2. Decision support portal components

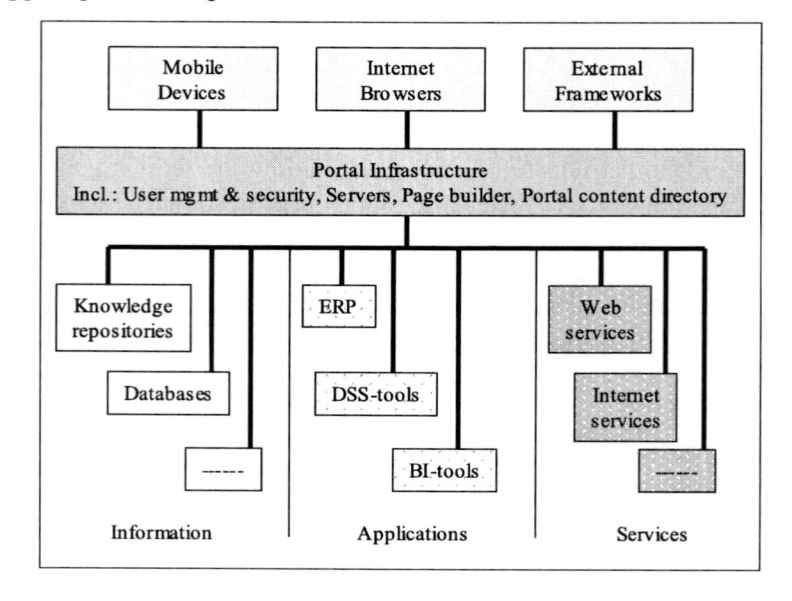

maintained using non-proprietary hardware, software, and information (Davenport & Harris, 2006). Second, using non-proprietary hardware, software, and information can make it easier to develop new DSS and change old DSS, which can lead to more flexible, adaptive, and dynamic DSS (Davenport & Harris, 2006).

Another trend is that access to different IS is increasingly through different types of gateways—called enterprise portals (Vering, Norris, Barth, Hurley, Mackay, & Duray, 2001; Mack, Ravin, & Byrd, 2001; Tsui, 2002; Carlsson & Hedman, 2004; Eckerson, 2006). A decision support portal (DS-P) is a single access point, often the Web and increasingly a mobile device, through which a decision-maker can access information, applications, and services needed to perform decision and knowledge related work and activities (Figure 2).

The information, applications, and services made available through a DS-P can be personalized and the DS-P keeps track of who in an organization is authorized to access different information, applications, and services.

The two trends are critical in designing DSS based on an attention-based view of the firm. They will make it more possible to design DSS that will be congruent with how a firm channels and distributes the attention of their decision-makers.

Designing DS-Ps Based on an Attention-Based View of the Firm

Designing DS-P based on the attention-based view of the firm will be based on the three theoretical principles (the third section). A DS-P affects a decision-maker's attention and the decision-maker's actions and moves by providing access to issues and answers (focus of attention principle). A DS-P is a part of a decision-maker's context, setting, and situation (the situated attention) and is also a part of the organization's rules, resources, and social relationships which regulate and control the distribution and allocation of issues, answers, and decision-makers into specific activities, communications, and procedurals (structural distribution of attention principle).

The attention-based view implies that DS-P designers' principal function is to design and manage DS-Ps that regulate and govern organizational attention. Whether a DS-P facilitates or inhibits organizational adaptation and performance is contingent on whether the DS-P focuses and distributes the attention of decision-makers in directions that are "congruent" with the organization's strengths, weaknesses, opportunities, and threats.

In designing a DS-P, designers and other stakeholders work iteratively through the model of situated attention and make specific design decisions. The design decisions are related to the model's six components and twelve mechanisms. For example, what features should a DS-P has to affect the specific mechanisms of the model. The attention-based view implies that DS-Ps will affect the temporal, spatial, and procedural dimensions of an organization's procedural and communication channels. Hence, it can be argued that DS-P differences, in some cases small differences, lead to changes in the procedural and communication channels and that these changes may have significant impact on organizational actions, moves, and performance.

CONCLUSION AND FURTHER RESEARCH

This article has presented Ocasio's (1997, 2001) attention-based view of the firm as an alternative to the decision-making as choice view. The former view highlights that both structural regularities and cognitive repertoires of issues and answers underlie attentional processes. Not only are they underlying the attentional processes, but they are so at the same time. This view is in line with the critical realist approach view on the relationship between agency and structure (Bhaskar, 1978; Layder, 1993).

The article argued that many DSS in the future will be decision support portals (DS-Ps), which are single access points through which decision-makers can access information, applications, and services needed to perform decision and knowledge related work and activities. We also proposed that DS-P design should be based on the attention-based view of the firm.

Future studies on the plausibility of designing and managing DS-P from an attention-based view of the firm are needed. More work is needed on how exactly the attention-based view can guide DSS and DS-P design. Also needed are studies focusing on individual and organizational impacts of DS-P use. Such impact studies can use the attention-based view of the firm as an evaluation framework.

REFERENCES

Bhaskar, R. (1978). *A realist theory of science*. Sussex: Harvester Press.

Brunsson, N. (1989). *The organization of hypocrisy: talk, decisions and actions in organizations*. New York: John Wiley & Sons.

Brunsson, N. (2000). *The irrational organization: irrationality as a basis for organizational action and change* (2nd ed.). Copenhagen: Copenhagen Business School Press.

Carlsson, S. A., & Hedman, J. (2004). From ERP systems to enterprise portals. In F. Adam & D. Sammon (Eds.), *The enterprise resource planning decade: Lessons learned and issues for the future* (pp. 263-287). Hershey, PA: Idea Publishing.

Cyert, R. M., & March, J. G. (1992). *A behavioral theory of the firm* (2nd ed.). Oxford: Blackwell.

Davenport, T. H., & Beck, J. C. (2001). *The attention economy*. Boston: Harvard Business School Press.

Davenport, T. H., & Harris, J. G. (2007). *Competing on analytics*. Boston: Harvard Business School Press.

Eckerson, W. W. (2006). *Performance dashboards: Measuring, monitoring, and managing your business*. Hoboken, NJ: Wiley.

Hagel, J., & Brown, J. S. (2001). Your next IT strategy. *Harvard Business Review, October*, 105-113.

Huber, G. P. (1981). The nature of organizational decision making and the design of decision support systems. *MIS Quarterly*, 5(2), 1-10.

Humphreys, P. C. (1998). Discourses underpinning decision support. In D. Berkeley, G. Widmeyer, P. Brezillon, & V. Rajkovic (Eds.), *Context sensitive decision support* (pp. 1-23). London: Chapman & Hall.

Layder, D. (1993). *New strategies in social research*. Cambridge, UK: Polity Press.

Mack, R., Ravin, Y., & Byrd, R. J. (2001). Knowledge portals and the emerging digital workplace. *IBM Systems Journal*, 40(4), 925-955.

March, J. G. (1988). Introduction: a chronicle of speculations about decision-making in organizations. In J. G. March (Ed.), *Decisions and organizations* (pp. 1-21). Oxford: Blackwell.

March, J. G. (1994). *A primer on decision making: how decisions happen*. New York: The Free Press.

March, J. G, & Olsen, J. P. (1976). *Ambiguity and choice in organizations*. Bergen, Norway: Universitetsforlaget.

Ocasio, W. (1997). Towards an attention-based view of the firm [Summer special issue]. *Strategic Management Journal*, 18, 187-206.

Ocasio, W. (2001). How do organizations think? In T. K Lant & Z. Shapira (Eds.), *Organizational cognition* (pp. 39-60). Mahway, NJ: Lawrence Erlbaum.

SAP. (2001). *Portal infrastructure: people-centric collaboration*. SAP White Paper.

Simon, H. A. (1947). *Administrative behaviour*. New York: Macmillan.

Simon, H. A. (1976). *Administrative behavior* (3rd ed.). New York: The Free Press.

Simon, H. A. (1977). *The new science of management decisions* (rev. edition), (pp. 187-202). Englewood Cliffs, NJ: Prentice-Hall.

Simon, H. A. (1988). Rationality as process and as product of thought. In D. E. Bell, H. Raiffa, & A. Tversky (Eds.), *Decision making: descriptive, normative, and prescriptive interactions* (pp. 58-77). Cambridge, UK: Cambridge University Press.

Simon, H. A. (1997). Designing organizations for an information-rich world. In D. M. Lamberton (Ed.), *The economics of communication and information* (p.187-202). Cheltenham, UK: Edward Elgar.

Simons, R. (1995). *Levers of control: how managers use innovative control systems to drive strategic renewal*. Boston: Harvard Business School Press.

Stabell, C. B. (1987). Decision support systems: alternative perspectives and schools. *Decision Support Systems*, 3, 243-251.

Tsui, E. (2003). Knowledge portal technologies. In C. W. Holsapple (Ed.), *Handbook on knowledge management*, vol.2: Knowledge activities, (pp. 5-27). Heidelberg, Germany: Springer-Verlag.

Vering, M., Norris, G., Barth, P., Hurley, J. R., Mackay, B., & Duray, D. J. (2001). *The e-business workplace*. New York: John Wiley & Sons.

Weick, K. E. (1979). *The social psychology of organizing* (2nd ed.). New York: Random House.

KEY TERMS

Attention-Based View: A view seeing the organization of attention as a central organizational process out of which decisions arise.

Decision-Making As Choice: A common view in the organizational decision-making and DSS literature which focuses the choice phase and assumes that the purpose of decision-making is to make rational choices

Decision Support Portals: A (single) access point through which a decision-maker can access information, applications, and services needed to make decisions and perform knowledge related work and activities.

Rational Decision Theories: Theories of decision making as intentional, consequential action based on knowledge of alternatives and their consequences evaluated in terms of a consistent preference ordering.

Balanced Scorecard Concepts, Technology, and Applications

Ricardo Colomo Palacios
Universidad Carlos III, Spain

Juan Miguel Gómez Berbís
Universidad Carlos III, Spain

Ángel García Crespo
Universidad Carlos III, Spain

INTRODUCTION

The balanced scorecard (BSC) harnesses the potential of checking and verifying the status of a company by evaluating and carefully assessing strategic aspects beyond the purely financial indicators. The significant impact of the BSC from a business standpoint has brought critical mass in use and the emergence of a number of technologies that will make a technology-supported BSC a reality. This article presents an overview of the concept and its history, evolution, major applications, and implications with a particular emphasis in decision making and decision support technologies.

BACKGROUND

The current business climate demands a high rate of change in which companies must adapt in a flexible and extremely agile manner. Hence, the need of relying on precise information, not necessarily narrowed to the financial, supporting the decision-based process in a business environment unveils itself as one of the key assets in modern organization management. The use of strictly financial criteria to establish the situation of a particular organization may lead to different management mistakes that must be avoided. Focusing on short-term results is probably the worst of these mistakes. Isolating both financial and nonfinancial components that enable organizational performance evaluation and, with that, setting up correcting criteria for deviations are not particularly groundbreaking and novel ideas. Earlier attempts in the BSC direction can be found from the 20th century in the dashboards that many followers of Scientific Management, established by Frederick W. Taylor (1911), adopted for business management and, more recently, the French Tableau de Bord of the 60s. The similarities of the French approach with BSC have been studied by a number of authors (e.g., Epstein & Manzoni, 1998; Lebas, 1994) and additionally, the Performance Measurement Pyramid has been identified as a first ancestor of the BSC (Lynch & Cross, 1995).

Apart from claims about its originality, the BSC is an overall control management tool that has deeply impacted organizations since its appearance in 1992. The BSC foundational work proposed by Kaplan and Norton (1992) has become the performance management model with more acceptance in its application to organizations despite the growing number of similar tools integrating intangible management, such as the del Intangible Asset Monitor developed by Karl Sveiby (1997) and the Skandia Navigator depicted by Edvinsson and Malone (1997). A more exhaustive report on tools for performance management can be found in Marr, Schiuma, and Neely (2004).

The ever-growing popularity of BSC has implied the appearance of a number of studies and surveys where it is analyzed and applied to various aspects of business, encompassing key areas such as human resources and IT management. As a proof of concept of the impact in academia, a particular report about business performance management (Marr & Schiuma, 2003) tools provides a survey of more than 301 papers with 4,464 citations. In the report, Kaplan and Norton are respectively the first and second most cited authors, and their book, *The Balance Scorecard* (1996), is the most referenced and cited book.

BALANCED SCORECARD

General Concepts

In 1992 Robert S. Kaplan of the Harvard School of Business and consultant David Norton developed BSC. The tool and its upcoming improved versions have become one of the key assets of day-to-day business management and can be defined as a multidimensional framework for describing, implementing, and managing strategy at all levels of an enterprise by linking, through a logical structure, objectives, initiatives, and measures to an organization's strategy (Kaplan & Norton, 1996). The result of its application in a particular company implies the creation of a framework depicting the different aspects that will determine the performance of an organization, encompassing the traditional financial signals with some others linked to customers, internal processes, and learning and growth. To summarize, the BSC is a conceptual framework for translating an organization's vision into a set of performance indicators distributed among four perspectives (see Figure 1): financial, customer, internal business processes, and learning and growth. These four perspectives provide answers to four basic questions.

- How do customers see us? (customer perspective)
- What must we excel at? (internal perspective)
- Can we continue to improve and create value? (learning and growth perspective)
- How do we look to shareholders? (financial perspective)

The four perspectives of the BSC are detailed in the following.

The financial perspective describes the tangible outcomes of the strategy in traditional financial terms, such as return on investment (ROI), shareholder value, return on capital, economic added value, profitability, revenue growth, and lower unit costs.

The customer perspective defines the drivers of revenue growth. It includes generic customer outcomes, such as satisfaction, acquisition, retention, and growth, as well as the differentiating value proposition the organization intends to offer to generate sales and loyalty from targeted customers.

The internal business process perspective focuses on the internal processes that will have the greatest impact on customer satisfaction, on achieving an organization's financial objectives, and on improving the quality and productivity of operating processes.

The learning and growth perspective identifies the infrastructure the organization has to build and manage to create long-term growth and improvement through people (human capital), IT systems (information capital), and organizational procedures and climate (organization capital).

Figure 1. BSC four visions

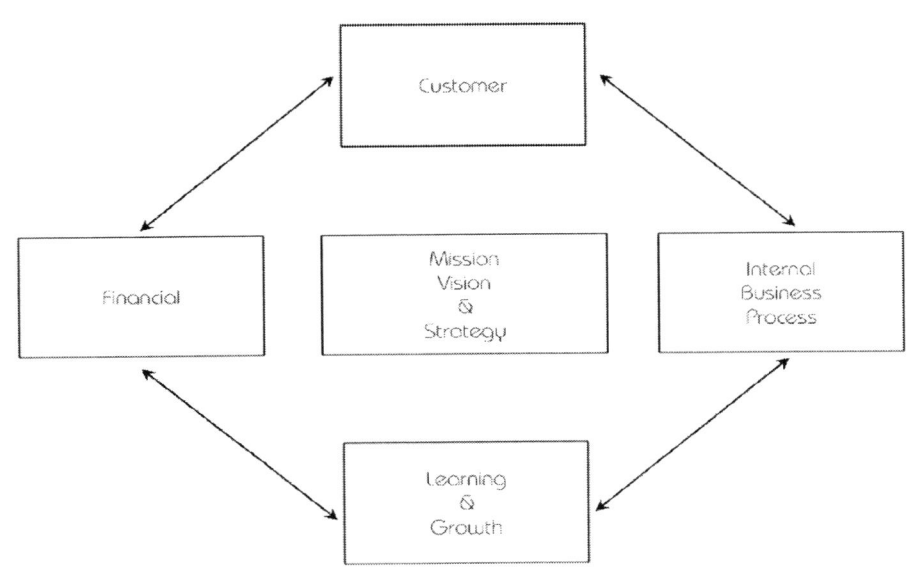

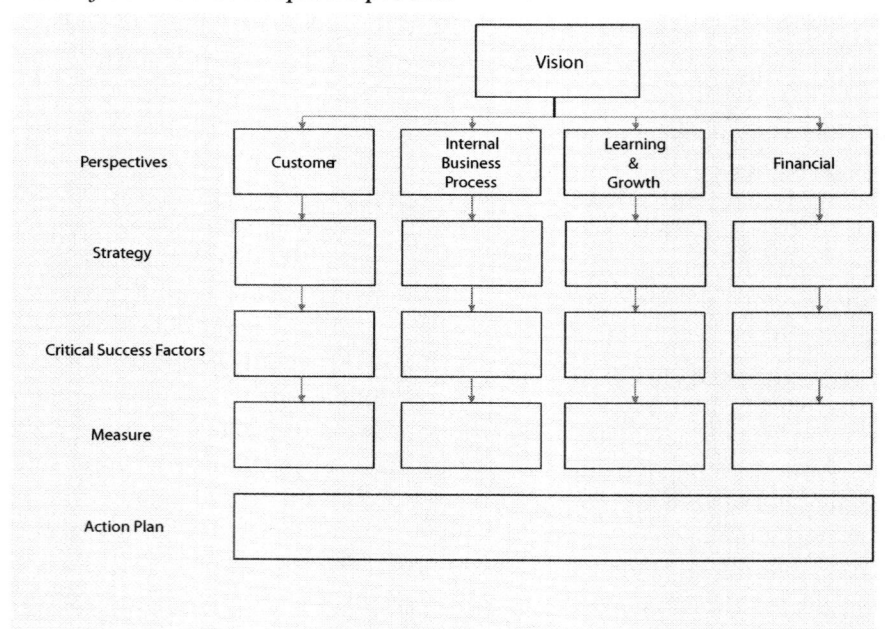

Figure 2. View of the BSC development process

Design and Transfer

A BSC kickoff is one of the fundamental elements for its suitable exploitation. Kaplan and Norton (1993) point out and stress, as it is shown in Figure 2, the BSC development process.

- **The vision:** It encompasses the goal of the organization for the future. This ensures that the performance measures developed in each perspective support accomplishment of the organization's strategic objectives.
- **Strategy:** Vision must be partitioned into decoupled real strategies, understandable and familiar with the company human resources with the aim of making them come true.
- **Critical success factors (CSFs):** CSFs are those key elements that must go right for the organization to achieve its aims in the development and implementation of a BSC.
- **Develop and identify measures and cause-effect relationships:** Measures must focus on the outcomes necessary to achieve the organizational vision by attaining objectives of the strategic plan. The most difficult task in this step is to find clear cause-and-effect relationships and to create a balance among the different measures in the selected objectives.
- **Action plan:** This describes the specifications and steps to be taken in order to achieve the above measurement levels. Goals must be set for every measure used, both for the short and long term.

BSC has been adopted by a huge number of organizations all over the world. Various studies on the adoption of the BSC show that one problem encountered by many organizations is their inability to develop a causal model of their strategy (Othman, 2006). This model is supposed to describe the cause-effect relationship of an organization's strategy. Substantial evidence of weaknesses from the organizations side to develop these models can be found in Finland (Malmi, 2001), Austria and Germany (Speckbacher, Bischof, & Pfeiffer, 2003), the USA (Davis & Albright, 2004), and Malaysia (Othman, 2006).

Nevertheless, and despite tremendous mistakes in the transfer of the BSC, a relevant number of checklists and key processes are ready to make it happen. In Table 1, recommendations made by Kaplan and Norton (1996) and Olve, Roy, and Wetter (1999) are gathered regarding how to kick off a BSC and have it up and running.

Both the steady need of the companies to quickly adapt to market changes and the inherent immediateness of business processes imply significant challenges for the correct application of tools such as the BSC.

Table 1. Recommendations for a BSC kick-off

Kaplan & Norton (1996)	Olve et al. (1999)
Clarify and update strategy	Communicate at all levels
Communicate strategy throughout the organization	Develop organizational goals
Align departmental and personal goals to the strategy	Offer training in improvement techniques
Identify and align strategic initiatives	Establish a reward and recognition system to foster performance improvements
Ling strategic objectives to long-term targets and annual budgets	Break down organizational barriers
Obtain feedback to learn about and improve strategy	Coordinate responsibilities
	Demonstrate a clear need for improvement
	Make a realistic initial attempt at implementation
	Integrate the scorecard into the organization
	Change the corporate culture
	Institutionalize the process

Nevertheless, technology as it is envisaged in the following stands as a suitable enabler for this kind of tools adoption, where best market practices are applied and are implemented in software solutions.

Technology

Complexity regarding the application and update of the BSC in today's organizations is highly tuned with the emergence of multiple software products available in the market. The maturity of the BSC had as an upshot the appearance of multiple initiatives for the automation of its exploitation and effective integration with available IT resources in organizations. During the last years, the aforementioned maturity has resulted in both BSC tools and BSC-oriented software providers. According to the Robert Frances Group (2001), BSC software vendors fall into four main categories:

- **Enterprise resource planning (ERP) vendors:** Vendors that supply ERP software but also offer BSC software as part of performance management suites.
- **Business intelligence (BI) vendors:** Vendors that provide software that has the capability to build a balanced scorecard; however, the software may not be specifically for this purpose.
- **BSC tool vendors:** Vendors that offer stand-alone BSC software as well as tools.
- **Specialist BSC software vendors:** Vendors that have well-integrated BSC stand-alone software as their main product.

A deeper analysis of tool capabilities supported by the BSC can be found in the book by Bernard Marr and Andy Neely (2003), where a lattice of 31 products belonging to all the four categories are surveyed and benchmarked. In this publication, stemming from a decision framework with a set of evaluation-enabled parameters (flexibility, customization, features and functions, technical specifications, analysis functionality, etc.), information about weaknesses and strengths are offered apart from the framework's positioning and the main features of the analyzed tools. This particular initiative represents the most rigorous, reliable, and precise source for BSC tools analysis despite the ever-growing number of Web sites devoted to knowledge management and independent IT consultancy firms, which publish on a regular basis useful reports related to management tools using as a basis their own tools and analysis methodologies.

Applications

In principle, BSC applications have outnumbered any forecast. The original and foundational perspective of its application to small and medium enterprises (SMEs) and brick-and-mortar organizations has been extended to small companies in any activity sector (technology, biotech, manufacturing, retail, education, etc.). In addition, within the organizations, the use of BSC has been tailored to a number of areas and business activities (customer relationship management [CRM], human resources management, etc.) with a specific emphasis on IT. The IT balanced scorecard has garnered headlines for its relevance and adaptability from its early inception by Gold (1992) and Willcocks (1995) and thereafter tested and tuned by multiple authors. Since then, it has ridden the crest of the IT management methodologies wave and emerged as the leading tool for gleaning knowledge about IT.

BSC in a Decision Support System

Business decisions must be coordinated and aligned with organizations' strategic goals. BSC is a powerful tool that allows depicting and defining strategy and organizing it from a business perspective, enabling one to design business activities on a sync-up basis from a business standpoint. Once defined, BSC provides a particular information structure that can be widely used with a decision support system (DSS) to present business information in a way such that decisions are made based on the value of the signals and markers of the BSC. Actually, DSSs offer information projection, trends, and "what-if" scenarios that, when applied to cause-effect relationships detailed in the BSC, complement and make more dynamic the capabilities of these systems.

However, BSC is not only useful in an automated DSS environment. According to Kaplan and Norton (1996), a typical balanced scorecard may employ 20 to 25 measures. Traditional research in decision making indicates that it is difficult for a person to process a large amount of information (Baddeley, 1994). Taking into account BSC decision support capabilities, Valiris, Chytas, and Glykas (2005) propose a methodology that will support BSC during the process of BSC design, implementation, and use in order to support the decision-making process.

FUTURE TRENDS

Future perspectives for BSC application span a vast number of fields. Despite some authors claiming the lack of applicability of the model for the so-called "innovation economy" (Voelpel, Leibold, & Eckhoff, 2006), the modifications, adaptations, additions, and forays of the BSC are shifting power away from the centralized old-fashioned management models and making of it a model with a future. Some of those future applications can be found in what follows:

- Interorganizational performance management framework development
- BSC integration with organizations' knowledge management and synergies with techniques and strategies related to knowledge management and knowledge discovery
- Nonexclusivity and complementary use with several other management tools, for example, the McKinsey 7-S model (Kaplan, 2005)
- Specific development model designed for business departments following the IT BSC guidelines

Thanks to the ERP tools designed from the application service provider (ASP) model and the new business models based on open-source software or low-cost software production, a proliferation of BSC-enabled systems in SMEs will take place.

CONCLUSION

The balanced scorecard is a powerful tool that, in addition to enhancing companies' performance management, is fundamental to streamline the decision-making process for current managers. Companies using the BSC can benefit through a number of signals and indicators, and create and attain a broad and reliable corporate vision based on its operational performance. This structural and efficient vision is vital for the decision-making process, which is currently lacking reliable, precise, and efficient information support.

From its very beginning, adaptations and improvements have made the BSC a powerful mechanism to hit the bull's eye. The set of signals and indicators of which it consists provides in its design a challenge and a chance for managers to benefits from its proper definition and exploitation. As it has been proven, the broad support of these tools has not unlocked the full potential of its strategic decision-making process. BSC adoption, as has also been proven in this work, has been stopped by the lack of strategic models in today's organizations. In the near future, the full adoption of technology will be an enabler to tackle this circumstance.

REFERENCES

Baddeley, A. (1994). The magical number seven: Still magic after all these years? *Psychological Review, 101*(2), 353-356.

Davis, S., & Albright, T. (2004). An investigation of the effect of balanced scorecard implementation on financial performance. *Management Accounting Research, 15*, 135-153.

Edvinsson, L., & Malone, T. (1997). *Intellectual capital: Realising your company's time value by finding its hidden brainpower.* New York: Harper Collins.

Epstein, M., & Manzoni, J. F. (1998). Implementing corporate strategy: From tableau de bord to balanced scorecard. *European Management Journal, 16*(2), 190-203.

Gold, C. (1992). *Total quality management in information services. IS measures: A balancing act.* Boston: Ernst & Young Center for Information Technology and Strategy.

Kaplan, R. S. (2005). How the balanced scorecard complements the McKinsey 7-S model. *Strategy and Leadership, 33*(3), 41-46.

Kaplan, R. S., & Norton, D. P. (1992). The balanced scorecard measures that drive performance. *Harvard Business Review, January-February 1992, 70*(1), pp. 171-179.

Kaplan, R. S., & Norton, D. P. (1993). *Putting the balanced scorecard to work.* Harvard Business School Press.

Kaplan, R. S., & Norton, D. P. (1996). *The balanced scorecard: Translating strategy into action.* Harvard Business School Press.

Lebas, M. (1994). Managerial accounting in France: Overview of past traditions and current practice. *European Accounting Review, 3*(3), 471-487.

Lynch, R. L., & Cross, K. F. (1995). *Measure up! How to measure corporate performance* (2nd ed.). Cambridge, MA: Blackwell Publishers.

Malmi, T. (2001). Balanced scorecards in Finnish companies: A research note. *Management Accounting Research, 12*, 207-220.

Marr, B., & Neely, A. (2003). *Automating your scorecard: The balanced scorecard software report.* Cranfield School of Management.

Marr, B., & Schiuma, G. (2003). Business performance measurement: Past, present, and future. *Management Decision, 41*(8), 680-687.

Marr, B., Schiuma, G., & Neely, A. (2004). Intellectual capital: Defining key performance indicators for organizational knowledge assets. *Business Process Management Journal, 10*(5), 551-569.

Olve, N., Roy, J., & Wetter, M. (1999). *Performance drivers: A practical guide to using the balanced scorecard.* Chichester, United Kingdom: John Wiley & Sons.

Othman, R. (2006). Balanced scorecard and causal model development: Preliminary findings. *Management Decision, 44*(5), 690-712.

Robert Frances Group (2001). *The Lowdown on Balanced Scorecard Software and Tools.* Retrieved from http://www.rfgonline.com/subsforum/archive/daily/043001/050201nt.html on 01/22/2008.

Speckbacher, G., Bischof, J., & Pfeiffer, T. (2003). A descriptive analysis of the implementation of balanced scorecard in German-speaking countries. *Management Accounting Research, 14*, 361-387.

Sveiby, K. E. (1997). *The new organisational wealth: Managing and measuring knowledge-based assets.* San Francisco: Berrett-Koelher.

Taylor, F. W. (1911). *The principles of scientific management.* New York: Harper Bros.

Valiris, G., Chytas, P., & Glykas, M. (2005). Making decisions using the balanced scorecard and the simple multi-attribute rating technique. *Performance Measurement and Metrics, 6*(3), 159-171.

Voelpel, S., Leibold, M., & Eckhoff, R. (2006). The tyranny of the balanced scorecard in the innovation economy. *Journal of Intellectual Capital, 7*(1), 43-60.

Willcocks, L. (1995). *Information management: The evaluation of information systems investments.* London: Chapman & Hall.

KEY TERMS

Balanced Scorecard: This is a framework that helps top management to select a set of measures that provide an integrated look at a company by dividing a list of measurable items into four perspectives: financial, customer, internal business processes, and learning and growth.

Balanced Scorecard Causal Model: This is a model that describes the cause-effect relationship of an organization's strategy.

Critical Success Factors: These are elements that are necessary for an organization or project to achieve its mission.

IT Balanced Scorecard: This is a framework that helps IT management to select a set of measures that provide an integrated look at an IT department by dividing a list of measurable items into four perspectives: user orientation, operational excellence, business contribution and future orientation.

Key Performance Indicators: These are financial and nonfinancial metrics used to quantify objectives to reflect the strategic performance of an organization.

Performance Management: It is a process by which an enterprise involves the whole of its resources in improving organizational effectiveness in the accomplishment of enterprise mission and goals.

A Bi-Criteria DSS Dedicated to Location Problems

Maria Eugénia Captivo
Universidade de Lisboa, Portugal

João Clímaco
Universidade de Coimbra and INESC – Coimbra, Portugal

Sérgio Fernandes
Instituto Politécnico de Setúbal, Portugal

INTRODUCTION

In *location problems* we want to determine the best way to serve a set of clients, or communities, whose location and demand are known.

This implies to decide the number and location of the facilities, the size or capacity of each facility, and the allocation of the demand points to the open facilities in order to optimize some objective function.

The type of optimality criterion depends on the nature of the activities or of the equipment to be installed.

Most location models deal with desirable facilities, such as warehouses, service and transportation centers, emergency services, and so forth, which interacts with the customers and where usually travel is involved. The typical criteria for such decisions include minimizing some function of the distances between facilities and/or clients.

However, during the last two or three decades, those responsible for the areas overall development, where the new equipment is going to be located (i.e., central government, local authorities) as well as those living there, are showing an increasing interest in preserving the area's quality of life.

The traditionally optimality criterion of "closeness" (to locate the facility as close as possible to the customers) is replaced by the opposite criterion (how far away from the customers can the facility be placed ensuring accessibility to the demand points).

The environmental issues on the approaches to undesirable facility location have generally been formulated as constraints or addressed by a surrogate criterion (distance) on a single objective structure.

Single objective models cannot be expected to accurately represent problems of this type (Erkut & Neuman, 1989). The modeling of environmental issues as objectives, as opposed to constraints, would generate more information regarding the cost and other implications of environmental considerations (Current, Min, & Schilling, 1990). It is an established fact that a number of different criteria are important in making locational decisions regarding public facilities (Ross & Soland, 1980).

Quite surprisingly the multi-objective decision tools have been scarcely used in undesirable facility location problems. Of the available literature in location models only a small percentage is on multi-objective optimization models in facility location.

Generally, the different criteria are formulated as constraints imposing some minimum or maximum value, or are addressed by a surrogate criterion (like distance) on a single objective structure.

To deal with this type of models we can choose one of the following approaches:

- Calculation of the whole efficient set of solutions (generating methods);
- A priori articulation of preferences of the decision-maker (utility function methods); or
- Progressive articulation of the decision-maker preferences (interactive methods) searching for a "compromise" efficient solution.

For this type of problem the number of efficient solutions can be very large. To present to the decision maker (DM) all the solutions and to expect him/her to be able to choose a good one is not realistic.

In general we do not believe that the DM has a process of defining an a priori utility function to be maximized.

We believe that interactive methods are the best choice, especially if they are thought of as learning procedures (improving the knowledge about the problem) and not as procedures seeking some "optimal" solution. They should also be designed so as to be useful in a group decision and negotiation environment.

The consideration of several criteria enables the stable part of the DM's preference structure to be fixed (Bouyssou, 1989). The use of a bi-criteria model will allow the DM to consider the model as the core of a learning-oriented decision support tool, enabling a reflection on the different non-dominated solutions and allowing negotiation with all the actors of the decision process while tolerating hesitations and ambiguities (dealing with the uncertainties associated with the aggregation of the preferences expressed by each criterion). The interactive process looks for a progressive and selective learning of the non-dominated solutions set, clarifying the criteria values aggregation meaning and consequences. Although in some situations it is possible to opt for one alternative, in many others the interactive process just enables the elimination of a greater part of the feasible solutions reducing the final choice to a small part of the non-dominated ones. In this case, if necessary, these alternatives can be scrutinized using another multi-criteria analysis tool dedicated to discrete problems, where the alternatives are known explicitly and in small number. Of course, this stage looks for a more detailed analysis of this subset of the non-dominated alternatives. However, it does not enable the combinatorial nature of feasible solutions to be explored. So, it just should be used for a deeper study of alternatives filtered by the phase one of the process.

In this article we propose the use of a bi-criteria decision support tool dedicated to the above referred to first phase of the process.

BACKGROUND

In Malczewski and Ogryczak (1990) the location of hospitals (a real application in Warsaw) is formulated as a multi-objective optimization problem and an interactive approach DINAS (Ogryczak, Studzinski, & Zorychta, 1989) based on the so-called reference point approach (Wierzbicki, 1982) is presented.

Erkut and Neuman (1992) propose a multi-objective mixed-integer program, assuming that the DM has selected a number of candidate sites for the location of several undesirable facilities, with different sizes, to meet regional demand for some service concentrated at population centers, in order to find a solution that has a low cost, is equitable, and results in acceptable levels of opposition.

Caruso, Colorni, and Paruccini (1993) present a model for planning an Urban Solid Waste Management System considering the last three phases of a well-known scheme structured into four phases: collection, transportation, processing, and disposal.

Wyman and Kuby (1993, 1995) present a Multi-objective Mixed Integer Programming Model for the location of hazardous material facilities (including the technology choice variables) with three objective functions (cost, risk, and equity).

Melachrinoudis, Min, and Wu (1995) propose a dynamic (multi-period) multi-objective capacitated mixed integer programming model for the location of sanitary landfills.

Fonseca and Captivo (1996, 2006) study the location of semi-obnoxious facilities as a discrete location problem on a network. Several bi-criteria models are presented considering two conflicting objectives, the minimization of the obnoxious effect, and the maximization of the accessibility of the communities to the closest open facility. Each of these objectives is considered in two different ways, trying to optimize its average value over all the communities or trying to optimize its worst value.

Ferreira, Santos, Captivo, Clímaco, & Silva (1996) present a bi-criteria mixed integer linear model for central facilities where the objectives are the minimization of total cost and the minimization of environmental pollution at facility sites. The interactive approach of Ferreira, Clímaco, and Paixão (1994) is used to obtain and analyze non-dominated solutions.

Ferreira (1997) also presents a bi-criteria mixed integer linear model for the location of semi-obnoxious facilities incorporating the routing phase, considering as objectives the minimization of total cost and the minimization of the obnoxious effect of the open facility and the risk associated with the transport phase.

Giannikos (1998) presents a multi-objective discrete model for the location of disposal or treatment facilities and transporting hazardous waste through a network linking the population centers that produce the waste and the candidate locations for the treatment facilities.

Cappanera, Gallo, and Maffioli (2004) present a model for the problem of locating semi-obnoxious facilities and simultaneously routing the undesirable materials between the communities and the facilities.

Dias, Captivo, and Clímaco (2003, 2006) propose the development of a DSS for dynamic location problems. Three types of facilities are considered: landfills, transshipment sites, and incinerators.

Rakas, Teodorovic, and Kim (2004) develop a model for the location of undesirable facilities such as landfills. To reduce the number of landfill candidate sites these authors use a multiple attribute decision making technique.

Haastrup et al. (1998) develop a DSS for waste management in the province of Sicily, allowing for the generation and evaluation of proper alternatives especially concerning environmental consequences.

Lahdelma, Salminen, and Hokkanen (2002) describe a real-life application of an ordinal multi-criteria method to choose the location for a waste treatment facility in a region in Finland.

THE MODEL

The bi-criteria location problem that was the object of this study can be formulated as following:

BSPLP (Bi-criteria Simple Plant Location Problem)

$$\text{Min} \quad Z_1(x,y) = \sum_{i \in I} \sum_{j \in J} l_{ij} x_{ij} + \sum_{i \in I} h_i y_i \quad (1)$$

$$\text{Min} \quad Z_2(x,y) = \sum_{i \in I} \sum_{j \in J} d_{ij} x_{ij} + \sum_{i \in I} g_i y_i \quad (2)$$

s.t.:
$$\sum_{i \in I} x_{ij} = 1 \quad j \in J \quad (3)$$

$$y_i \geq x_{ij} \quad i \in I, j \in J \quad (4)$$

$$y_i \in \{0,1\} \quad i \in I \quad (5)$$

$$x_{ij} \in \{0,1\} \quad i \in I, j \in J \quad (6)$$

where:

$J = \{1,\ldots,N\}$ is the set of clients or communities to be served,

$I = \{1,\ldots,M\}$ is the set of possible service locations,
h_i, g_i are fixed costs or values of opening service i,
l_{ij}, d_{ij} are transportation costs or values from assigning service i to client j,
and the variables can be defined as:

$$y_i = \begin{cases} 1 & \text{if service } i \text{ is opened} \\ 0 & \text{if service } i \text{ is closed} \end{cases} \quad i \in I$$

$$x_{ij} = \begin{cases} 1 & \text{if client } j \text{ is assigned to service } i \\ 0 & \text{if client } j \text{ is not assigned to service } i \end{cases} \quad i \in I, j \in J$$

Besides the cost it also considers the minimization of the obnoxious or disagreeable effect. It seems to be suitable and simple enough to be accepted as relevant by the DM and other actors, possibly associated with the decision process.

There are several examples in the literature (Hultz, Klingman, Ross, & Soland, 1981; Revelle & Laporte, 1996; Ross & Soland, 1980) where different meanings for the objective functions shown can be found. Considering the location of undesirable facilities, one of the objectives usually represents total costs and the other one total risk or noxiousness resulting from open services and transportation between clients and services. For instance, if h_{ij} represents the noxious or detrimental effect on location j of a facility located at i,

then $h_i = \sum_j h_{ij}$

can measure the total noxious effect of locating a facility at i. The noxious effect relating to the transportation of, for instance, undesirable materials between i and j can be represented by l_{ij}.

The two objective functions considered could be different from the ones shown as long as their weighted sum results in a linear objective function of the location variables y_i and the assignment variables x_{ij}.

Additional constraints can also be considered (constraints on the number or capacity of the open facilities, budget constraints, etc.).

THE INTERACTIVE APPROACH

Interactive decision-aid methods are widely accepted for dealing with multi-objective problems. In these methods, the DM is an active part in the process of discovering new non-dominated solutions. There is a calculation phase where non-dominated solutions are calculated, and a dialogue phase where the non-dominated solutions are presented to the DM giving the opportunity of expressing preferences, which will guide the next calculation phase and so forth. This process stops when the DM finds the preferred solution or feels satisfied with the knowledge gained about the problem.

In order to analyze the information provided by the bi-criteria model we use an interactive method based upon the progressive and selective learning of the non-dominated solutions set (see Clímaco, Antunes, & Alves, 2003; Ferreira et al., 1996).

According to Larichev and Nikiforov (1987), good interactive methods are those that use information relative to the objective function values in the dialogue with the DM, in order to create a system of preferences.

The interactive framework (see Figure 1) developed to this type of bi-criteria approach has several characteristics, namely:

- There are no irrevocable decisions along the process.

- The method is not too demanding with respect to the information required from the user in each interaction, that is, in the interaction phase the user is able to indicate a sub-region to carry on the search for non-dominated solutions in two (simple) different ways: (1) by choosing a pair of non-dominated solutions candidate to be adjacent (giving the solution indexes), and (2) by indicating upper bounds on Z_1 and Z_2.
- It enables the user to find any non-dominated solution of the problem namely: (1) supported non-dominated solutions (those located on the frontier of the convex hull) and (2) non-supported non-dominated solutions (in the duality 'gaps' between the points that define the convex hull).
- On the operational side, a single criterion mixed integer programming problem (whose structure remains almost unchanged, with computational advantages) has to be solved at each step.

This method (inspired by Ferreira et al., 1994) starts by calculating the two lexicographic minima and involves two main phases: a dialogue phase with the DM and a calculation phase.

Figure 1. General diagram of the interactive procedure inspired by Ferreira et al. (1994)

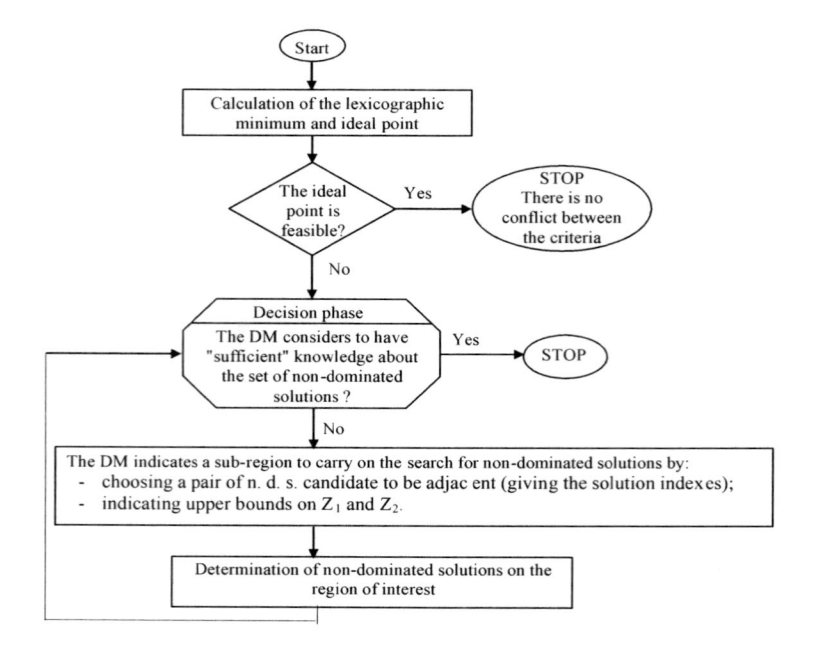

During the dialogue phase, the DM is asked to give indications about the sub-region to carry on the search for new non-dominated solutions. The information can be transmitted in two different ways: (1) by indicating upper bounds on the values of both objective functions or (2) by indicating two non-dominated solutions candidate to be adjacent.

In the calculation phase, the minimization of a weighted sum of the objective functions was used to determine non-dominated solutions on the region of interest.

In discrete problems, the optimization of weighted sums of the different objectives only allows for the computation of part of the non-dominated solutions set. As presented by Ross and Soland (1980), to obtain all non-dominated solutions of a bicriteria integer linear programming (BILP) model like, for example,

$$\min\ (Z_1\ x)$$
$$\min\ (Z_2\ x)$$
$$s.t.:\ x \in S$$

a parametric constrained problem of the type

$$\min\ (\lambda_1 Z_1\ x) + \lambda_2 Z_2(x)$$
$$s.\ t.:\ Z_1(x) \leq \varphi_1$$
$$(Z_2\ x) \leq \varphi_2$$
$$x \in S$$

can be solved for different values of (φ_1, φ_2) and considering (λ_1, λ_2) such that $\lambda_1 + \lambda_2 = 1$ and $\lambda_1 > 0, \lambda_2 > 0$. Obviously, some unsupported non-dominated solutions can be the most appropriate for the DM. So, this subset of non-dominated solutions must be considered.

In the calculation phase we optimize a single criterion problem representing the weighted sum of both objective functions, imposing limits on their values accordingly to the preferences expressed by the DM during the dialog phase. The weights are just operational parameters that can be fixed by the analyst or even by default using equal weights. In any case they are not elicited during the dialogue phase with the DM. The dialogue with the DMs regarding the elicitation of their preferences, concerns, by cognitive reasons, the objective function values, as pointed out by Larichev and Nikiforov (1987). This procedure seems to be easily understood by the DM.

A general solver for mixed integer linear programming (for instance CPLEX or MatLab) can be used to solve this single criterion problem. However, in many cases, there exist special algorithms dedicated to each problem taking advantage of its special structure. Of course, in terms of computational efficiency, they are much better than general solvers. So, different algorithms to solve the single criterion problem can be incorporated in the system.

An interactive decision support tool incorporating all these procedures was implemented in Visual C++

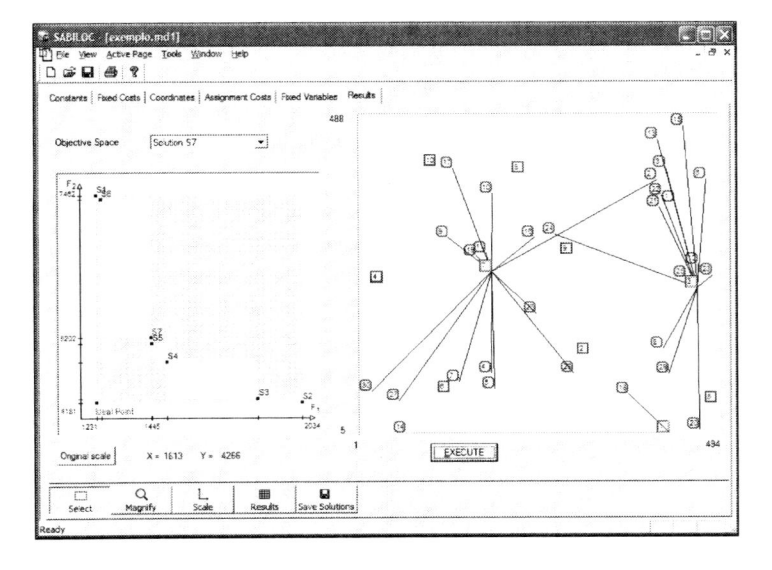

Figure 2. Software window

(Fernandes, Captivo, & Clímaco, 2005). It was developed in a modular way, allowing for the introduction of more models relevant in practical situations and/or procedures to solve them.

Two graphics are presented to the user (see Figure 2). In the left side, a graphic representation of the objective space is presented to the DM with the non-dominated solutions already known, indicating those that are adjacent and showing the regions where new non-dominated solutions may still exist. In the right side a graphical representation of the last non-dominated solution computed, showing the open facilities and their assignment to the communities.

If the DM wishes to continue the search for a new non-dominated solution in some of the white regions between two non-dominated solutions already known he/she just has to indicate which one. Then, in the calculation phase, the corresponding single criterion problem will be solved.

These two phases go on alternately, only ending when the DM considers having sufficient knowledge of the non-dominated solutions set. The DM has the option to calculate the entire non-dominated solutions set.

CONCLUSION AND FURTHER RESEARCH

The development of multi-criteria interactive decision support systems looking for a progressive and selective learning of the non-dominated solutions seems very adequate to location analysis. Particularly if we take into account the present environmental issues.

This is a new field of research dedicated to old problems involving new and more complex issues, such as:

- The existence of several actors/decision agents with (or without) hierarchical powers.
- The integration of negotiation support procedures, or specific Negotiation Support Systems (NSS), namely ε-NSS.
- Legal requirements (such as those imposed by the Environmental Impact Assessment[EIA]).

REFERENCES

Bouyssou, D. (1989). Modelling inaccurate determination, uncertainty, imprecision using multiple criteria. In A. G. Lockett & G. Islei (Eds.), *Improving decision making in organizations (pp. 78-87)*. Heidelberg, Germany: Springer Verlag.

Cappanera, P., Gallo, G., & Maffioli, F. (2004). Discrete facility location and routing of obnoxious facilities. *Discrete Applied Mathematics, 133,* 3-28.

Caruso, C., Colorni, A., & Paruccini, M. (1993). The regional urban solid waste management system: A modelling approach. *European Journal of Operational Research, 70,* 16-30.

Chalmet, L. G., Lemonidis, L., & Elzinga, D. J. (1986). An algorithm for the bi-criterion integer programming problem. *European Journal of Operational Research, 25,* 292-300.

Clímaco, J., Antunes, C. H., & Alves, M. J. (2003). *Programação Linear Multiobjectivo*. Portugal: Imprensa da Universidade de Coimbra.

Current, J., Min, H., & Schilling, D. (1990). Multiobjective analysis of facility location decisions. *European Journal of Operational Research, 49,* 295-307.

Dias, J., Captivo, M. E., & Clímaco, J. (2003). Desenvolvimento de um Sistema de Apoio à Decisão Dedicado ao Estudo de Problemas de Localização Dinâmica de Equipamentos para Transferência, Tratamento e Deposição de Resíduos Sólidos. *Anais do XXXV SBPO*, Natal, Brasil, 906-922.

Dias, J., Captivo, M. E., & Clímaco, J. (2006). Decision support system for location problems. In F. Adam, P. Brézillon, S. Carlsson, & P. Humphreys (Eds.), *Proceedings of CIDMDS 2006* (pp. 388-402). London.

Erkut, E., & Neuman, S. (1989). Analytical models for locating undesirable facilities. *European Journal of Operational Research, 40,* 275-291.

Erkut, E., & Neuman, S. (1992). A multiobjective model for locating undesirable facilities. *Annals of Operations Research, 40,* 209-227.

Ferreira, C. (1997). Problemas de Localização e Distribuição Multicritério - aproximações e estudo de alguns casos com implicações ambientais. PhD thesis, Universidade de Aveiro, Portugal.

Ferreira, C., Clímaco, J., & Paixão, J. (1994). The location-covering problem: A bicriterion interactive approach. *Investigación Operativa, 4,* 119-139.

Ferreira, C., Santos, B. S., Captivo, M. E., Clímaco, J., & Silva, C. C. (1996). Multiobjective location of unwelcome or central facilities involving environmental aspects—A prototype of a decision support system. *JORBEL, 36,* 159-172.

Fernandes, S., Captivo, M. E., & Clímaco, J. (2005). *Um Sistema de Apoio à Decisão para Análise de Problemas de Localização Bicritério.* Working paper 2/2005. Centro de Investigação Operacional, Universidade de Lisboa, Portugal.

Fonseca, M. C., & Captivo, M. E. (1996). Location of semiobnoxious facilities with capacity constraints. *Studies in Locational Analysis, 9,* 51-52.

Fonseca, M. C., & Captivo, M. E. (2006). Models for semiobnoxious facility location. In *Proceedings of the XIII CLAIO,* Montevideo, Uruguay.

Giannikos, I. (1998). A multiobjective programming model for locating treatment sites and routing hazardous wastes. *European Journal of Operational Research, 104,* 333-342.

Haastrup, P., Maniezzo, V., Mattarelli, M., Rinaldi, F., Mendes, I., & Paruccini, M. (1998). A decision support system for urban waste management. *European Journal of Operational Research, 109*(2), 330-341.

Hultz, J., Klingman, D., Ross, G. T., & Soland, R. (1981). An interactive computer system for multicriteria facility location. *Computers and Operations Research, 8*(4), 249-261.

Lahdelma, R., Salminen, P., & Hokkanen, J. (2002). Locating a waste treatment facility by using stochastic multicriteria acceptability analysis with ordinal criteria. *European Journal of Operational Research, 142*(2), 345-356.

Larichev, O., & Nikiforov, A. (1987). Analytical survey of procedures for solving multicriteria mathematical programming problems. In Y. Sawaragi, K. Inoue, & H. Nakayama (Eds.) *Towards interactive and intelligent decision support systems 1,* (pp. 95-104). Springer-Verlag.

Malczewski, J., & Ogryczak, W. (1990). An interactive approach to the central facility location problem: Locating pediatric hospitals in Warsaw. *Geographical Analysis, 22,* 244-258.

Melachrinoudis, E., Min, H., & Wu, X. (1995). A multiobjective model for the dynamic location of landfills. *Location Science, 3,* 143-166.

Ogryczak, W., Studzinski, K., & Zorychta, K. (1989). DINAS—Dynamic interactive network analysis system. In A. Lewandowski & A. P. Wierzbicki (Eds.), Aspiration based decision support systems. *Lecture Notes in Economics and Mathematical Systems, 331,* 385-387. Berlin, Germany: Springer-Verlag.

Rakas, J., Teodorovic, D., & Kim, T. (2004). Multi-objective modeling for determining location of undesirable facilities. *Transportation Research Part D, 9,* 125-138.

Revelle, C., & Laporte, G. (1996). The plant location problem: New models and research prospects. *Operations Research, 44*(6), 864-873.

Ross, G., & Soland, R. (1980). A multicriteria approach to the location of public facilities. *European Journal of Operational Research, 4,* 307-321.

Wierzbicki, A. P. (1982). A mathematical basis for satisficing decision making. *Mathematical Modelling 3,* (pp. 391-405).

Wyman, M., & Kuby, M. (1993). A multiobjective location-allocation model for assessing toxic waste processing technologies. *Studies in Locational Analysis, 4,* 193-196.

Wyman, M., & Kuby, M. (1995). Proactive optimization of toxic waste transportation, location and technology. *Location Science, 3*(3), 167-185.

KEY TERMS

Decision Support: Decision support consists of establishing, on recognized scientific bases, proposals to be submitted to the judgment of the decision maker.

Efficient (Non-Dominated) Solution: Efficient (non-dominated) solution is a feasible alternative not allowing to find another feasible solution improving some criteria without worsening another one.

Interactive Tools: Interactive tools are decision support tools incorporating, successively and alternatively, calculating and dialogue phases till some stopping condition is satisfied.

Location Analysis: Location analysis is the study and development of models, techniques, and tools to provide decision makers with good solutions to realistic locational decision problems.

Multi-Criteria Models: Multi-criteria models are models considering explicitly several conflicting dimensions of the problem.

Satisfactory Solution: Satisfactory solution is an efficient (or approximately efficient) solution acceptable by the decision maker.

Semi-Obnoxious Facilities: Semi-obnoxious facilities are useful but unwelcome facilities that produce environmental concerns.

Business Process Management Systems for Supporting Individual and Group Decision Making

Amit V. Deokar
Dakota State University, USA

Omar F. El-Gayar
Dakota State University, USA

INTRODUCTION

The complexities involved in managing intrafunctional as well as interfunctional activities have triggered many organizations to deploy large information technology (IT) systems such as ERP and CRM. While such systems have focused mainly on providing solutions to problems such as enterprise-wide application integration and customer driven revenue management, one of the prime issues of managing coordination among activities in organizational processes has not gained adequate attention and support. Business process management (BPM) systems have emerged as a key technology primarily in the past two decades with a goal of providing process support to organizations and supporting better decision making.

This article focuses on highlighting this role of BPM systems while discussing some of the recent advances and approaches from a decision making standpoint, both for supporting individual and collaborative decision making activities.

BACKGROUND

The original ideas upon which BPM systems are founded upon can be traced back to several different areas of computing and management. It is worthwhile to glance at the history to better understand the motivating factors for the advancement and role of BPM systems. One such area is that of office information systems. In the 1970s and 1980s, researchers like Holt (1985) focused on modeling routine office procedures with mathematical formalisms such as Petri Nets. These efforts did not gain much momentum due to the functional nature of organizations. Later, in the mid-1990s, management initiatives such as Business Process Re-engineering (BPR) (Hammer, 1990), and Total Quality Management (TQM) (Harrington, 1991) highlighted the importance of process oriented thinking in organizations, which helped in rejuvenating the interest in business process modeling and management.

During mid-1980s and early-1990s, another research stream of organizational decision support system (ODSS) emerged. It built upon Hackathorn and Keen's (1981) key ideas of decision support: individual, group, and organizational. From a decision standpoint, it laid out a foundation for focusing on organizational activities and further decomposing them into a sequence of subactivities performed by various organizational actors. Although process coordination was not the primary focus of ODSS, it supported the notion of coordinating and disseminating decision making across functional areas and hierarchical layers such that decisions are congruent with organization goals and management's shared interpretation of the competitive environment (Watson, 1990). The term ODSS was sometimes also referred to as "distributed decision support system" in the literature.

Also in the early 1990s, document imaging and management systems fostered the notion of automation of document-driven business processes by routing documents from person to person in an organization (Smith, 1993).

BPM AND RELATED TERMINOLOGY

The term BPM is often used by commercial vendors with different connotations. It is therefore essential to present operational definitions of related terms. Firstly, the term *process* itself is very broad. Medina-Mora,

Wong, and Flores's (1993) classification of organizational processes into material processes, information processes, and business processes is noteworthy here. Material processes relate human tasks to the physical world (e.g., assembly of machine parts). Information processes relate to automated tasks (i.e., performed by computer programs), and partially automated tasks (i.e., tasks performed by people with the assistance of computer programs). Business processes are a higher level abstraction of organizational activities that are operationalized through material processes and/or information processes (Georgakopoulos, Hornick, & Sheth, 1995). The term process in the BPM context relates to business processes implemented primarily as information processes, and is used in the discussion in this article.

Workflow is a related concept to automating business and information organizational processes. The Workflow Management Coalition (WfMC) defines *workflow* as: "The automation of a business process, in whole or part, during which documents, information, or tasks are passed from one participant to another for action, according to a set of procedural rules" (WfMC, 1999). Also, WfMC defines the term *Workflow Management System* (WFMS) as: "A system that defines, creates and manages the execution of workflows through the use of software, running on one or more workflow engines, which is able to interpret the process definition, interact with workflow participants and, where required, invoke the use of IT tools and applications" (WfMC, 1999). It can be seen that WfMC places strong emphasis on the execution aspect, which is limiting in many ways. While managing execution of workflows is essential, making use of information about workflows to analyze, diagnose, and redesign business processes at a conceptual level is critical to reap benefits from the technology, rather than focusing merely on process design, system configuration, and process enactment. With this realization, the term *BPM* has emerged, which involves "supporting business processes using methods, techniques, and software to design, enact, control, and analyze operational processes involving humans, organizations, applications, documents, and other sources of information" (Weske, van der Aalst, & Verbeek, 2004). Similarly, a *BPM system* can be defined as "a generic software system that is driven by explicit process designs to enact and manage operational business processes" (Weske et al., 2004).

The BPM life cycle can be viewed as the one involving process (re)design, system configuration, process enactment, and diagnosis. Thus, along with a strong workflow management component, BPM systems involve decision-making support for business managers through the diagnosis phase. The diagnosis phase mainly involves *business process analysis* (BPA) and *business activity monitoring* (BAM). In this context, a visionary characterization of workflow management infrastructure provided by Georgakopoulos et al. (1995) fits closely with the current BPM systems characterization. It indicates that workflow management involves a distributed computing infrastructure that is component-oriented (i.e., supports loose coupling between heterogeneous, autonomous, and/or distributed systems), supports workflow applications for accessing organizational information systems, ensures the correctness (in case of concurrency) and reliability (in case of failures and exceptions) of applications, and supports re-engineering business processes through modification of workflows.

WORKFLOW CHARACTERIZATION

Workflows can be classified in several different ways. The most widely accepted classification, one that has been used by the trade press and endorsed by the WfMC, divides workflow in four categories: *production, administrative, ad hoc,* and *collaborative* (Georgakopoulos et al., 1995; Stohr & Zhao, 2001). Different aspects of these workflows are shown in Figure 1.

Production workflows deal with highly structured and repetitive tasks, providing automation support for which can lead to great improvements in productivity. These workflows are characterized by minimal human intervention in process management (e.g., handling exceptions). From a system support perspective, production workflows are supported as either autonomous workflow engines or as embedded workflow components within enterprise systems such as ERP. Since various decisions in the process are made by the workflow system component, rather than humans, they involve high task complexity in addition to integration and interoperatibility of different enterprise applications. Also, with high transaction volumes, these workflows are mission critical and demand high accuracy, reliability, efficiency, security, and privacy. Typical examples

Figure 1. Characterization of workflows. Adapted from Georgakopoulos et al. (1995) and Stohr and Zhao (2001).

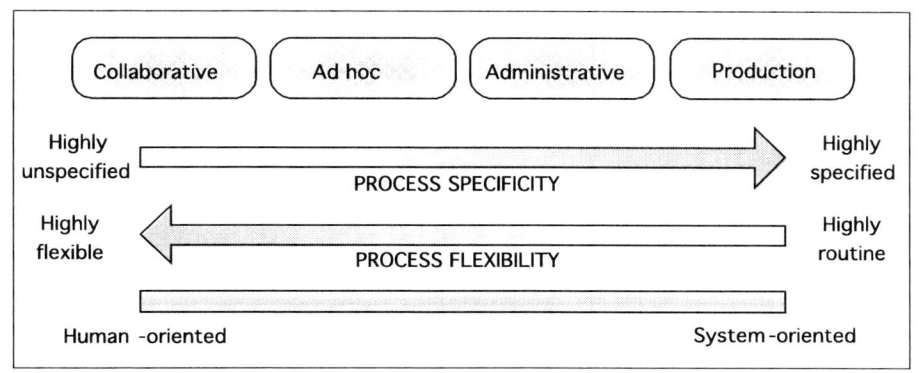

of production workflows are health claims processing and order entry and billing in manufacturing supply chains.

Administrative workflows are characterized by human decision-making and task execution (with the assistance of software applications). They involve simpler task coordination rules as compared to production workflows, thus having relatively less task complexity. Also, the emphasis is on routing and document approval functionalities such as in the case of travel expense reports. Most often, these workflows are nonmission critical from a business value standpoint. Coordination is achieved by prompting users to perform their tasks, most commonly by using electronic mail technology.

Ad hoc workflows are best suited where flexibility in processes is a key requirement. They are often used where spontaneous, user-controlled ordering, and coordination of tasks is needed. A typical example includes a small team of knowledge workers involved in a short term project involving a set of activities. These are most often nonmission critical and do not have high repeatability, thus ruling out the need for an automated task coordination and facilitation system, such as in the case of administrative or production workflows. Electronic mail, group calendaring, and conferencing systems (collectively termed as groupware tools) are commonly used for ad hoc workflows and thus advancements in computer supported cooperative work (CSCW) are relevant for enabling these workflows.

Collaborative workflows are activities which predominantly involve group decision making activities, which are mission critical. Quite differently from ad hoc workflows, collaborative workflows are knowledge intensive with collaborative intellectual problem solving involved, which requires expertise from multiple people. However, they may or may not be repeatable, depending on the process. For example, organizational processes such as strategic planning, engineering design, user requirements gathering, are not repeatable (as compared to production workflows), although they are critical to the business process. Traditionally, these processes have been supported by group decision support systems (GDSS) (Nunamaker, Dennis, Valacich, Vogel, & George, 1991), but deserve a place in the workflow spectrum.

Supporting Decision Making Through Coordination and Control

BPM systems can be used for coordinating and controlling interleaved individual and collaborative decision making tasks. With efficient coordination and control of the process, better decision making can be achieved. It is useful to look at a life cycle of a workflow schema to understand this mechanism.

Workflow Management for Coordination and Control of Tasks

The contemporary workflow management approach can be illustrated by considering the lifecycle of a workflow schema (process definition). Figure 2 illustrates the lifecycle of a workflow schema for a business process, through design and deployment, which forms the basis for coordination and control of tasks through workflow management in modern day BPM systems.

The lifecycle begins when business process analysts acquire and structure organizational processes into

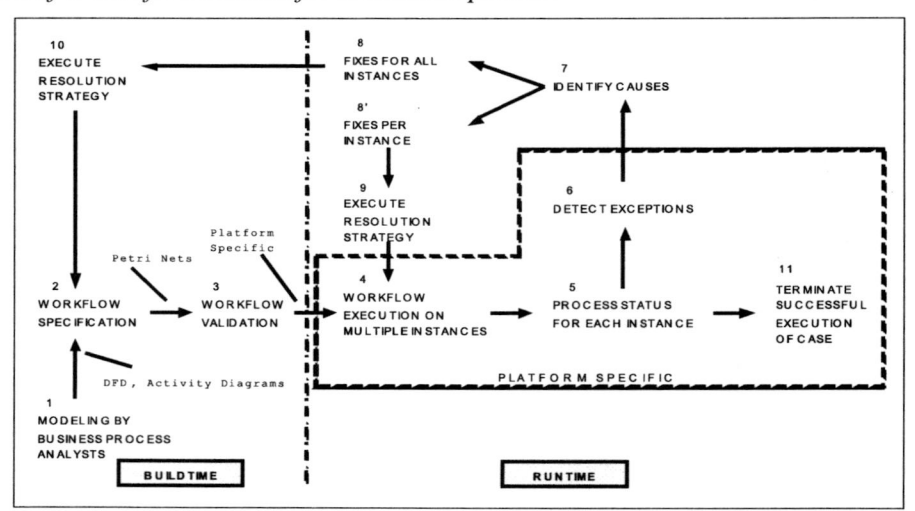

Figure 2. Lifecycle of a workflow schema for a business process

a workflow (Step 1). Defining a workflow schema involves identifying the different tasks that constitute a business process in an organization and then specifying the execution sequences along with the executing agents, control, and data dependencies for the various tasks. The workflow thus defined is verified, tested, and then executed (enacted) in a workflow engine (Steps 2, 3, and 4). A single workflow schema may cater to multiple workflow instances (or cases). Each executing case is monitored and tracked (Steps 5 and 6). Cases may execute normally without any errors or may lead to exceptions of various kinds. These exceptions may have a variety of causes and are handled by manual intervention (Step 7). The failures of the workflow cases are usually caused by underspecified or erroneously defined workflows during the modeling task, as it is usually difficult to acquire comprehensive knowledge to model all possible variations of a business process (which is one of the limitations of the procedural approaches used for workflow management). Further, the workflow implementation environment changes as the business evolves; organizational roles and task assignments change. Repairs may be applied to a single executing instance or organizationally it may be decided to update the initial workflow specification (Step 8, 8'). The process of updating single instances and generic definitions is a highly knowledge intensive task in organizations because of the complexity of the workflows (Steps 9 and 10). The workflow validation/verification step is usually done via simulation/animation.

The lifecycle in Figure 2 also indicates the different process representations that may be used during the various stages of the lifecycle. For example, data flow diagrams (DFDs) and unified modeling language (UML) activity diagrams may be used by business process analysts, which may be then encoded into a specification. Such a specification may be translated into a Petri Net based formalism for analysis. Note that the activities in the Figure 2 are classified into build time (design) and run time (execution) activities. Runtime models are highly dependent on the technology platform used to execute a workflow. Thus, the process of deploying a workflow model into production requires a consistent set of model transformations that need to occur through different stages of the lifecycle.

It can be noted that the contemporary approach presented is fundamentally programmatic or procedural, as the predefined rigid process structures (workflow schemas) rely on the process designer to search the design space (although implicitly) for seeking the right kind of process model to model the business process at hand and achieve the organizational goals. As a result, failure and change management approaches to support adaptive and dynamic processes are largely ad hoc. Once a workflow is deployed, maintenance of the workflow schema (or its instances) is manual and resource intensive. Manual intervention requires knowledge of the business processes as well as the underlying workflow technology. Also, simulation-based validation may not identify all the errors early because of the large number of test cases that need to be checked.

Alternatively, declarative, goal-driven workflow process design approaches have recently been explored for business process management in dynamic settings (Deokar, Madhusudan, Briggs, & Nunamaker, 2004). Instead on deriving generic schemas for business processes, these approaches use instance specific information to generate a customized process model for addressing the business process problem. Automated logic-based algorithms (such as artificial intelligence planning) may be used for these purposes (Myers & Berry, 1999). While these approaches are novel and useful, they involve a knowledge intensive process of encoding task descriptions based on domain knowledge in order for machine to be able to intelligently generate process models.

Individual Decision Making

Administrative workflows are typical examples where individual knowledge workers are involved in decision making in workflows. These decision making tasks are modeled and designed as any other task in a workflow process; however, the execution may be supported with the help of decision support systems (DSS) to aid the individual decision maker. For example, in a loan application process, the manager might have to make decisions based on the applicant's credit history and assets, among other factors. This decision may be facilitated using a DSS that is geared toward this task (Turban, Aronson, Liang, & Sharda, 2007).

Group Decision Making

Collaborative workflows involve group decision making tasks with high process complexity (due to high information unspecificity and flexibility). Systems supporting collaborative workflows are based on GDSS or group support systems (GSS) technology. Traditionally, such systems have been restricted to face-to-face and small group decision making through facilitator guided meeting sessions (e.g., GroupSystems) (Nunamaker et al., 1991). The process structure and support is also not explicated in such systems. To be embedded as a part of a BPM system, such systems need to contain an explicit embedded representation of the underlying group process (Deokar et al., 2004).

Over the past few years, researchers in the area of collaboration technology have been working on finding ways for teams to wield GSS successfully and manage their collaboration tasks for themselves with predictable results. Addressing this challenge is the domain of an emerging field of collaboration engineering. *Collaboration engineering* is an approach for designing, modeling, and deploying repeatable collaboration tasks for recurring high-value collaborative workflows that are executed by practitioners (knowledge workers) without the ongoing intervention of facilitators (de Vreede & Briggs, 2005). *Collaborative workflows* designed through this approach are processes that support a group effort towards a specific goal, mostly within a specific time frame. The workflow is built as a sequence of facilitation interventions that create patterns of collaboration; predictable group behavior with respect to a goal. As can be noted, the research efforts are moving towards making collaborative workflows "process-aware" in the true sense, thus expanding the horizons of typical GDSS systems from face-to-face to virtual collaboration.

The main thrust of the collaboration engineering research is thus on codifying and packaging key facilitation interventions in forms that can be readily and successfully reused by groups in collaborative workflows and that can produce predictable, repeatable interactions among people working toward their goal. These packaged facilitation interventions are termed as *thinkLets* (Briggs, de Vreede, & Nunamaker, 2003). These codified facilitation interventions are based on experiences of professional facilitators in conducting successful collaborative sessions (e.g., Lowry & Nunamaker, 2002). An example of thinkLet is a "LeafHopper" thinkLet, whose purpose is to have a group brainstorm ideas regarding a number of topics simultaneously. The detail description of this thinkLet can be found in Briggs et al. (2003). Each such thinkLet provides a concrete group dynamics intervention, complete with instructions for implementation as part of some group process. Researchers have formally documented approximately 70 such distinct thinkLets to date (Briggs et al., 2003). Field experiences suggest that these 70 thinkLets account for nearly 80% of a given collaboration process design. The other 20% of group interactions need to be designed with customized thinkLets for the group task at hand.

The underlying rationale behind the design of collaborative workflows using thinkLets is that each group task can be represented as a sequence of different collaboration patterns (thinkLets) with the goal of developing a process design (schema), which when executed (possibly repeatedly), can yield a predictable behavior from the group as a whole, while creating the different constituent patterns of collaboration among team members during the execution of a collaborative workflow.

Managerial Decision Support

As noted in earlier discussion, BPM systems involve BPA and BAM as key components for analysis and diagnosis of processes. These components can provide decision support for business managers who can track the performance of the business process from various standpoints such as productivity, and resource allocation. BPA primarily involves simulation of process models to improve the level of understanding of a business process and further assisting in limiting the amount of variation in the business process. BAM can benefit at multiple levels. At the activity level, it can provide the ability to track and monitor individual work requests, while at the process level, it can provide the ability to review resource productivity and work volume analysis.

BPA and BAM collectively can enable (re)engineering and optimization of business processes. Workflow audit history tracked by BAM tools may help in providing feedback on performance issues, which may be further analyzed to indicate bottlenecks in the process. Root causes for bottlenecks (such as ineffective process design and lack of resources) may be determined to reengineer the process.

FUTURE TRENDS

BPM systems are benefiting from advances in related areas of computing and information systems. Services science is one such emerging area where the focus is on provision and consumption of services. Each service is really a wrapper around a set of activities and would involve process-awareness for systems to fulfill and/or consume services.

In the same vein, work system framework, proposed by Alter, situates BPM systems in this broader context of services science. According to Alter, "a work system is a system in which human participants and/or machines perform work using information, technology, and other resources to produce products and services for internal or external customers" (Alter, 2006).

Also, Semantic Web is another area which has implications for BPM systems and decision making. Automated reasoning technologies and ontology-based frameworks founded primarily upon principles of RDF, OWL, and Description Logic, can be useful in improving decision making by associating semantics to process related information. Ongoing research in this area holds promise for the next generation of BPM systems for coordination, control, and decision making in organizations.

CONCLUSION

Recent advances in information technology are delivering decision support tools for enabling a variety of business activities. Hence, effective and efficient coordination and control between these activities is a key requirement of modern day organizations. In this article, we discussed the role of BPM systems in meeting this requirement. The discussion on the lifecycle of a workflow schema illustrates the contemporary workflow management approach. It is noted that facilitating integrated support for individual as well as group decision making involves many challenging issues and remains an open area for further research and development.

REFERENCES

Alter, S. (2006). *The work system method: Connecting people, processes, and IT for business results.* The Work System Press.

Briggs, R. O., de Vreede, G.-J., & Nunamaker, J. F., Jr. (2003). Collaboration engineering with thinkLets to pursue sustained sucess with group support systems. *Journal of Management Information Systems, 19*(4), 31-64.

Deokar, A. V., Madhusudan, T., Briggs, R. O., & Nunamaker, J. F., Jr. (2004). A structured approach to designing interleaved workflow and groupware tasks. In *Proceedings of the Tenth Americas Conference on Information Systems (AMCIS).* New York, NY.

de Vreede, G.-J., & Briggs, R. O. (2005). *Collaboration engineering: Designing repeatable processes for high-value collaborative tasks.* Paper presented at the

Proceedings of the 38th Annual Hawaii International Conference on System Sciences (HICSS-38), Big Island, HI.

Georgakopoulos, D., Hornick, M., & Sheth, A. (1995). An overview of workflow management: From process modeling to workflow automation infrastructure. *Distributed and Parallel Databases, 3*, 119-153.

Hackathorn, R. D., & Keen, P. G. W. (1981). Organizational strategies for personal computing in decision support systems. *MIS Quarterly, 5*(3).

Hammer, M. (1990). Reengineering work: Don't automate, obliterate. *Harvard Business Review, 68*, 104-112.

Harrington, H. J. (1991). *Business process improvement: The breakthrough strategy for total quality, productivity, and competitiveness*. New York.

Holt, A. W. (1985). Coordination technology and Petri nets. In G. Rozenberg (Ed.), *Advances in petri nets 1985* (pp. 278-296). Berlin, Germany: Springer-Verlag.

Lowry, P. B., & Nunamaker, J. F., Jr. (2002, January). *Using the thinkLet framework to improve distributed collaborative writing*. Paper presented at the Proceedings of the 35th Annual Hawaii International Conference on System Sciences (HICSS-35), Big Island, HI.

Medina-Mora, R., Wong, H., & Flores, R. (1993). Action workflow as the enterprise integration technology. *Bulletin of the Technical Committee on Data Engineering, IEEE Computer Society, 16*(2).

Myers, K. L., & Berry, P. M. (1999). *Workflow management systems: An AI perspective* (Technical Note). Menlo Park, CA: Artificial Intelligence Center, SRI International.

Nunamaker, J. F., Jr., Dennis, A. R., Valacich, J. S., Vogel, D. R., & George, J. F. (1991). Electronic meeting systems to support group work. *Communications of the ACM, 34*(7), 40-61.

Smith, T. (1993). The future of workflow software. *INFORM, 17*(4), 50-52.

Stohr, E. A., & Zhao, J. L. (2001). Workflow automation: Overview and research issues. *Information Systems Frontiers, 3*(3), 281-296.

Turban, E., Aronson, J. E., Liang, T.-P., & Sharda, R. (2007). *Decision support and business intelligence systems* (8th ed.). Pearson Prentice Hall.

Watson, R. T. (1990). A design for an infrastructure to organizational decision making. In *Proceedings of the Twenty-Third Hawaii International Conference on System Sciences (HICSS-23 '90)*. Kailua-Kona, HI: IEEE Computer Society Press.

Weske, M., van der Aalst, W. M. P., & Verbeek, H. M. W. (2004). Guest editorial: Advances in business process management. *Data and Knowledge Engineering, 50*, 1-8.

WfMC. (1999). *Terminology and glossary (3rd ed.)* (Document Number WFMC-TC-1011). Winchester, ID: Workflow Management Coalition.

KEY TERMS

Business Process Management (BPM): Supporting business processes using methods, techniques, and software to design, enact, control, and analyze operational processes involving humans, organizations, applications, documents, and other sources of information

Business Process Management Systems (BPMS): A generic software system that is driven by explicit process designs to enact and manage operational business processes.

Collaboration Engineering: An approach for designing, modeling, and deploying repeatable collaboration tasks for recurring high-value collaborative workflows that are executed by practitioners (knowledge workers) without the ongoing intervention of facilitators.

Group Support System (GSS): A software system used for improving team productivity in collaboration tasks.

Group Decision Support Systems (GDSS): A type of GSS geared towards collaborative decision making tasks.

Organizational Decision Support System (ODSS): A decision support system focused on coordinating and disseminating decision making across functional areas and hierarchical layers such that decisions are congruent with organization goals and management's shared interpretation of the competitive environment.

Workflow: The automation of a business process, in whole or part, during which documents, information, or tasks are passed from one participant to another for action, according to a set of procedural rules.

Workflow Management System (WFMS): A software system that defines, creates, and manages the execution of workflows through the use of software, running on one or more process engines, which is able to interpret the process definition, interact with workflow participants, and, where required, invoke the use of IT tools and applications.

Challenges for Decision Support in Urban Disaster Scenarios

Sergio F. Ochoa
Universidad de Chile, Chile

José A. Pino
Universidad de Chile, Chile

INTRODUCTION

An urgent challenge confronting society today is the vulnerability of urban areas to "eXtreme" Events (XEs) (Mileti, 1999; CWR, 2002; Godschalk, 2003). These hazardous situations include natural disasters such as earthquakes, hurricanes, and floods, as well as accidental and intentional disasters such as fires and terrorist attacks. At the global level, a total of 608 million people were affected by these disasters in 2002, out of which 24,500 died (IFRC, 2003). The economic damages to property and the environment were estimated at $27 billion dollars (IFRC, 2003). From January to October 2005, the number of people killed in disasters globally was estimated at 97,490 and the economical losses were approximately U.S. $159 billion (WHO, 2006). These significant human and economic costs emphasize the urgent need to reduce the vulnerability of urban areas to XEs (Mileti, 1999; CWR, 2002; Godschalk, 2003), improve the impact of relief team actions in these situations (NRC, 1999; NSTC, 2003), and the decision making process (Stewart, 2002; Mendonca, 2007).

When an XE affects an urban area, a variety of personnel and organizations with different expertise participate in the disaster relief process *(fire, police, health services, and government authorities)*. Typically, this process is composed of three phases: (a) the *preparedness* of first response plans for disasters, (b) the *response* process to reduce the impact of XEs, and (c) the *recovery* of the affected areas (Mileti, 1999; NSTC, 2003). Some countries have defined response plans specifying the role of each organization and the way the relief tasks have to be coordinated (FEMA, 1999). Additionally, these plans establish the superior authority in charge of coordinating the inter-organizational efforts.

Nevertheless, it is rare in practice to find a superior authority making macro-decisions and coordinating the inter-organization activities (Scalem, 2004). Typically, each organization has its own hierarchical structure and it establishes members' responsibilities, decision making levels, and protocols to coordinate its activities. The decision making process is local for each organization; thus, the decisions made by one of them can generate problems to other ones. The lack of cooperation and trust among these public and private agencies (Mileti, 1999; NCTA, 2004) and also the lack of coordination and information sharing (NRC, 1999; NCTA, 2004) often jeopardize the effectiveness of the mitigation process (Stewart, 2002).

Although this problem is complex, two important lessons have been learned from recent disasters: (a) the need to improve the collaboration among organizations in order to increase response effectiveness (NRC, 1999; Scalem, 2004) and (b) the use of IT solutions to support the coordination activities and the distributed decision-making processes (NRC, 2002; NSTC, 2003; Scalem, 2004). This article describes the challenges to face when carrying out distributed inter-organizational decision making and the technological requirements to be considered when supporting such process in urban disaster cases. The next section presents the key XE properties and the implications they have on the decision making process. The third section describes the decision making scenario in urban disasters. The fourth section describes the technological requirements for supporting this process. Finally, the fifth section presents the conclusions and further work.

CHARACTERIZING EXTREME EVENTS

Prior research has proposed six properties of extreme events that are important for decision making and decision support. These properties are: *rarity, uncertainty, high and broad consequences, complexity, time pressure,* and *multiple decision makers* (Stewart, 2002).

XEs are *rare*. Their low frequency of occurrence restricts the opportunities for preparation and learning from them. This rarity creates the need for diverse thinking, solutions, and skills. Furthermore, this rarity makes these events difficult of understand, model, and predict.

XEs are also *uncertain* because both its occurrence is unpredictable and its evolution is highly dynamic. The challenges to face and consequences of an XE are the joint product of an event, the affected community, and the organizations involved in preparation and response. Every disaster is different; therefore, disasters present varying challenges to decision making, for example, time availability and geographic scale.

When XEs affect urban areas they usually have *high and broad consequences*, leading to the need to manage interdependencies among a wide range of physical and social systems (Godschalk, 2003). The risks and the disaster evolution should be evaluated quickly and accurately. Thus, the decisions can be effective and on-time. Provided these processes involve several people and organizations, it may be appropriate to use tools to support interaction among these people and organizations.

Event *complexity* arises in part due to the severe consequences of XEs (CWR, 2002). It may also arise as a result of interdependencies among urban infrastructure systems (Godschalk, 2003). The complexity of the events requires the participation of experts in several areas (e.g., civil engineers, transportation/electrical engineers, and chemical experts) to support decision making.

Time pressure forces a convergence of planning and execution, so that opportunities for analysis are few (Stewart, 2002). It is therefore vital that accurate and timely information be gathered and delivered among the organizations participating in the disaster relief effort. Information supporting forecasting event impact and propagation is needed. This time pressure also creates a need for convergent thinking in order to generate a solution in a timely fashion.

Finally, we have to consider that *multiple decision makers* will be involved given the complexity and diversity of organizations participating in the relief activities. They may compete or negotiate while responding to the event. It may therefore be advisable to consider how decision support systems can support the management of shared resources and help people to converge soon to joint decisions.

All these XE properties add requirements and challenges to the decision making process. Communication, coordination, and information delivery become critical issues to make effective and on-time decisions in such scenario.

BACKGROUND

Typically, as soon as first responders are notified about the occurrence of an XE, they can start the response endeavor. The delay in the detection and notification of the XE, and the delay in starting the response process affect the consequences of the XE. For example, the physical infrastructure and lifelines systems that are affected by a fire could depend on the time spent by firefighters to detect the XE and initiate response actions. The number of survivors definitively depends on the elapsed time from the XE occurrence (Tadokoro, 2002). Therefore, the earlier the first response is, the higher is the probability to reduce the negative consequences of an XE. Early detection and fast alarm propagation play key roles as triggers for resistant activities and the decision making process. The inability to access information and the lack of standardization, coordination, and communication are all obstacles that need to be overcome in a disaster scenario in order to implement integral decision making accomplishment, and therefore effective relief actions (NRC, 1999).

Once the response process is triggered, the first actions are started by first responders, who are typically firefighters, police officers, and medical personnel. They make local decisions based on improvisations (Mendonca, 2007). While additional response groups are included to the relief endeavor, the most urgent need is having an ad-hoc inter-organizational structure able to establish responsibilities and decision making levels. Although proposals for this structure could be stated in some response plan, in practice it is the result of a self-organizing negotiation and even discussion process.

Typically, a critical response process should be carried out in this situation. This process involves multiple organizations and must be executed within the first 12 hours after the event occurrence. The time pressure also creates a need for convergent thinking in order to generate coordinated mitigation actions in a timely fashion. Therefore, the self-organization of this inter-organizational structure should be fast. The impact of the XE on human and economical losses depends on it. Once this structure is defined, holding control of the response activities can be attained.

On the other hand, there are several countries that have defined a strict National Response Plan that should be applied in case of major disasters. These plans establish the role of relief organizations and government agencies during response and recovery endeavors, and they provide basic recommendations on how to coordinate activities. The process to put these plans in action is difficult and slow, thus it is unsuitable to support response processes. For example, the period of time to implement the Federal Response Plan (USA) during a disaster is usually 24 hours (FEMA, 1999), while the probability of rescuing people under a collapse decreases 50% or more after 24 hours (Tadokoro, 2002). These plans are useful for recovery, but not for response.

Regardless of the way the structure is generated—by a self-organizing process or established by a national plan—two types of decision making processes are conducted during the response process: organizational decision making and improvisation. The next section briefly describes them.

Organizational Decision Making

Organizational decision making is the process to make decisions following the protocols, rules, and conventions defined by an organization. This process is usually done in a common command post or in the command post of each organization. The implementation of these decisions is carried out mainly using resources from the organization (e.g., equipment, human resources, and materials). These decisions have an effect on the relief effort and also on the activities of other first response organizations. Since the rules and protocols belonging to an organization are not usually designed to be used in inter-organizational activities, a decision made by an organization could imply negative effects on other ones. This lack of integration of procedures and decision making processes jeopardizes the trust and the possibility of collaboration among involved organizations. Several researchers have identified this situation (NCTA, 2004; Stewart, 2002).

On the other hand, some relief efforts tried to apply an integral response process facing an XE, but the results were unsuccessful (NCTA, 2004). The previously discussed lack of integration was a cause of problems; another cause was the absence of a jointly agreed authority. Typically, first responders belonging to an organization are unable to recognize as authority someone who does not belong to the same organization. Therefore, the decisions made by such persons do not have the required speed and effect. In fact, the consequences of a decision in this scenario have much uncertainty.

Local Decision Making (Improvisation)

Members of first response teams usually communicate among them using radio systems, because the fixed communication infrastructure is frequently collapsed, unreliable, or overloaded. They share few radio channels to carry out the communication process, which is insufficient and inappropriate for large relief efforts (Aldunate, 2006). The lack of control on the transmission channels and the poor capabilities to transmit information make several response teams become isolated or uninformed. In such situations, the only choice for such persons is the local decision making (or improvisation). Improvisation is typical of large relief efforts and it is mainly carried out in the work field (Mendonca, 2007). The decisions made during improvisation are based on the experience of the decision maker or the group. Little or no information supports such decisions and their implementation involves just local group resources.

Improvisations usually involve small scope activities; however, all these activities happening in parallel have important consequences on the global results of the relief effort. Some researchers propose to use mobile technological solutions to support improvisation (e.g., software applications running on mobile computing devices), in order to help first responders to make accurate decisions and reduce the gap among the organizational decisions and the local decisions (Aldunate, 2006; Ochoa, 2006). The use of technology has been identified as a way to solve several of the current problems in disaster management.

TECHNOLOGICAL REQUIREMENTS FOR DECISION SUPPORT

IT advances provide real opportunities to enhance the efficiency and effectiveness of response to an XE, mainly when it affects urban areas (NSTC, 2003). Digital communications, robotic, distributed real-time systems, GIS, collaborative systems, and mobile computing are some tools that could be used to face this challenge.

The adoption of IT solutions to support disaster response processes has been mainly focused on organizational decision making. These solutions perform risk management (CWR, 2002), disaster simulation (Tadokoro, 2002), and development of resilient critical infrastructure (DARPA, 2003). Some systems, such as DARPA-Encompass (DARPA, 2003), supports resources and victims information management. Other tools such as CATS (Swiatek, 1999) and OpenGIS (Farley, 1999) are intended to assist diagnosis tasks, based on graphical information.

On the other hand, some recent initiatives have developed prototype solutions that support the decision making done by first responders working on the field. It includes both the organizational and local decision making. Examples of these solutions are an ad-hoc distributed shared memory system providing consistent and reliable communication among first responders (Aldunate, 2006), the map based tools to represent and share information on response process evolution (Guerrero, 2006), and a tool to capture, represent and deliver contextual information to disaster managers and first responders (Ochoa, 2006). The next two sections describe the challenges, in terms of communication and information support, that must be faced to implement IT solutions able to support local and organizational decision making processes.

Communication Support

Communication support is a basic requirement for most disaster relief efforts. If this resource is not available, it is almost impossible to control the response process. If we assume the fixed communication infrastructure collapses or becomes overloaded immediately after a disaster, then the response process has to include provision of new communication infrastructure. Such infrastructure has traditionally been based on radio systems.

The limitations of radio systems to support interaction among first responders in such scenarios have been widely discussed by researchers of this area in recent years. Consequently, a set of technical requirements have been identified and they are listed.

Fast and easy to deploy. The communication system should be transported from the organizational store and put into production in the disaster area within a short time period. Thus, the first 12 hours are critical to rescue survivors. Moreover, the process to incorporate a new member to the rescue teams should be easy and fast. Digital communication systems based on Wireless (e.g., Wi-Fi and Wi-Fi mobile) appear as suitable candidates to replace traditional radio systems.

Mobile support. Since first responders must be on the move to do their activities, the communication support for them should be mobile wireless (e.g., Wi-Fi). In the case of decision makers located at the command post, the communication will also be wireless, but it is not required that it supports mobility (e.g., microwave).

High quality. Communication quality is in direct relationship with signal stability, communication range, and bandwidth provided by the system. The communication quality required in each disaster is different, depending on the number of people involved in the relief effort and the affected area evolution.

Support for routing. People with various hierarchies or technical skills can access a variety of data during relief tasks. The communication system must then provide support for routing information. Thus, information can be delivered to and accessed by the right persons.

Versatile. The system has to provide support for voice and data communication. In such case, digital systems have advantages over the analog ones.

Information Support

There are many cases when accurate and timely information was used to reduce disaster losses or make better decisions (NRC, 2002; NSTC, 2003). However, information has to satisfy several properties if it is going to be used to support decision making processes in urban relief scenarios. These properties are listed.

Available. The information has to be highly available. In an ideal situation, no matter if the communication system or computer servers are up or down, the information should be accessible to any person needing it and having applicable access rights. The use of computer-based distributed systems can help increase the information availability through replication techniques.

Standard. Several organizations collect, store, and represent common information as well as other data. They should represent such information in an understandable way for the organization members. Unfortunately, no standards for information representations are used; therefore, information understandable for one organization could be non-understandable for other ones. A possible solution involves decoupling the internal from the external information representation, by allowing multiples external (users') representations of the same data collection (Ochoa, 2006).

Easy to Understand. Since the time to analyze information is short, the information should be easy to understand. In such cases, graphical representations have advantages over text-based ones.

Accurate and Trustworthy. The information available to first responders and disaster managers should be accurate and trustworthy. Human and economical losses could depend on it. In order to deal with these properties, the gathering and updating process of basic information should be carefully implemented. Typical mechanisms of updating based on authority range, reputation, or technical roles can be used to deal with this challenge.

Easy to deliver and access. The information should be easy to deliver and access by the users, provided that several decision making processes occur during a relief effort. The information can be channeled from a source to one or more destinations, and also it can be accessed on demand by a user. The information has to be quickly available at a destination, because waiting is expensive (in losses) during relief activities.

FUTURE TRENDS

There are several research lines to explore in the future. Some interesting ones are distributed group decision making, coordination of distributed heterogeneous teams, IT adoption, organizational, social and cultural barriers, and real-time disaster modeling. Research on these areas may bring important improvements to the next generation of disaster relief efforts.

CONCLUSION

Given their size, complexity and rarity, XEs challenge the relief organization capabilities for responding; particularly when they affect urban areas. The collaboration among first response organizations and the decision making process have been identified as two key factors that produce a major impact on the results of the response process; therefore, research is being done to improve them.

Many pitfalls related to collaboration among first response organizations have been discussed and documented, such as lack of trust, information sharing, communication, and coordination (NRC, 1999; Stewart, 2002). Relief efforts are still "characterized by numerous shortcomings that inhibit optimal decision-making for disaster management" (NRC, 1999). In order to conduct integral responses and make effective decisions, "the inability to access information and the lack of standardization, coordination, and communication are all obstacles that need to be overcome" (NRC, 1999). Since all XEs are different and highly dynamic, the decision making process has to be dynamically adapted depending on the context of the mitigation effort, extreme event, and affected area (Ochoa, 2006).

Advances in IT provide opportunities to deal with these two key issues. Particularly, digital wireless communication and distributed collaborative systems have been considered as interesting tools to provide communication and information support. They are able to address most of the requirements involved in decision making and coordination activities. However, IT adoption by first responders and emergency managers represents an important challenge that is not discussed in this article. These technological solutions are not being used in real disaster relief efforts and thus it is not still possible to know the real advantages of IT adoption.

ACKNOWLEDGMENT

This work was partially supported by Fondecyt (Chile), grants N°: 11060467 and 1040952.

REFERENCES

Aldunate, R., Ochoa, S., Pena-Mora, F., & Nussbaum, M. (2006). Robust mobile ad-hoc space for collaboration to support disaster relief efforts involving critical physical infrastructure. *ASCE Journal of Computing in Civil Engineering, 20*(1), 13-27.

CWR: Columbia/Wharton Roundtable. (2002). *Risk management strategies in an uncertain world*. IBM Palisades Executive Conference Center.

DARPA: Defense Advanced Research Projects Agency. (2003). *Strategic plan*. www.darpa.mil/body/pdf/dsp_part1.pdf and ../dsp_part2.pdf

Farley, J., & Hecht, L. (1999). *Infrastructure for disaster management: building bridges between open geoprocessing technologies and the disaster management community*. Seamless Warehouse of Arkansas Geodata.

FEMA: Federal Emergency Management Agency. (1999). *Federal response plan*. (9230.1-PL).

Godschalk, D. (2003). Urban hazard mitigation: Creating resilient cities. *Natural Hazards Review, 4*(3), 136-143.

Guerrero, L., Ochoa, S., Pino, J., & Collazos, C. (2006). Selecting devices to support mobile collaboration. *Group Decision and Negotiation, 15*(3), 243-271.

IFRC: International Federation of Red Cross and Red Crescent Societies. (2003). *World disasters report 2003: Focus on ethics in aid*.

Mendonça, D. (2007). Decision support for improvisation in response to extreme events: Learning from the response to the 2001 world trade center attack. *Decision Support Systems, 43*(3), 952-967.

Mileti, D. (1999). *Disasters by design: A reassessment of natural hazards in United States*. Joseph Henry Press.

NCTA: National Commission on Terrorist Attacks Upon the United States. (2004). *The 9/11 commission report*. www.9-11commission.gov/report/index.htm

NRC: National Research Council. (1999). *Reducing disaster losses through better information*. Washington, D.C.: National Academic Press.

NRC: National Research Council. (2002). *Making the nation safer: The role of science and technology in countering terrorism*. Washington, D.C.: National Academic Press.

NSTC: National Science and Technology Council. (2003). *Reducing disaster vulnerability through science and technology*. Committee on the Environment and Natural Resources.

Ochoa, S., Neyem, A., Pino, J., & Borges, M. (2006). Using context to support group decision making in disaster affecting urban areas. In *Proceedings of the CIDMDS 2006*, London, England.

Scalem, M., Bandyopadhyay, S., & Sircar, A. (2004). An approach towards a decentralized disaster management information network. *Lecture Notes in Computer Science, 3285*.

Stewart, T., & Bostrom, A. (2002). *Extreme event decision making workshop report*. Center for Policy Research, Rockefeller College of Public Affairs and Policy. University of Albany, and Decision Risk and Management Science Program NSF. www.albany.edu/cpr/xedm

Swiatek, J. (1999). Crisis prediction disaster management. *SAIC Science and Technology Trends II*. www.saic.com/products/simulation/cats/VUPQPV4R.pdf

Tadokoro, S. (2002). *RoboCupRescue: A proposal of next-generation 'preparedness' as social infrastructure of urban cities*. Paper presented at the International Workshop and Project Presentation, Real-time Planning and Monitoring for Search and Rescue Operations, Foligno, Italy.

WHO: World Health Organization. (2006). Was 2005 the year of natural disasters? *Bulletin of the World Health Organization, 84*(1), 4-8.

KEY TERMS

Critical Response: This process involves multiple organizations and must be executed within the first 12 hours after the event occurrence.

Disaster Relief: The disaster relief process is composed of three phases: (a) the *preparedness* of first response plans for disasters, (b) the *response* process to reduce the impact of extreme events, and (c) the *recovery* of the affected areas.

Extreme Events: Hazardous situations including natural disasters such as earthquakes, hurricanes, and floods, as well as accidental and intentional disasters such as fires and terrorist attacks.

First Responders: First responders are typically firefighters, police officers, and medical personnel who initially work mitigating an extreme event.

Local Emergency Decision Making: The local decision making (or improvisation) is typical of large relief efforts and it is mainly carried out in the work field.

Classification and Ranking Belief Simplex

Malcolm J. Beynon
Cardiff University, UK

INTRODUCTION

The classification and ranking belief simplex (CaRBS), introduced in Beynon (2005a), is a nascent technique for the decision problems of object classification and ranking. With its rudiments based on the Dempster-Shafer theory of evidence—DST (Dempster, 1967; Shafer, 1976), the operation of CaRBS is closely associated with the notion of uncertain reasoning. This relates to the analysis of imperfect data, whether that is data quality or uncertainty of the relationship of the data to the study in question (Chen, 2001).

Previous applications which have employed the CaRBS technique include: the temporal identification of e-learning efficacy (Jones & Beynon, 2007) expositing osteoarthritic knee function (Jones, Beynon, Holt, & Roy, 2006), credit rating classification (Beynon, 2005b), and ranking regional long-term care systems (Beynon & Kitchener, 2005). These applications respectively demonstrate its use as a decision support system for academics, medical experts, credit companies, and governmental institutions.

Through its reliance on DST, the CaRBS technique allows the presence of ignorance in its analysis (Smets, 1991), in the case of the classification of objects this means that ambiguity is minimised but ignorance tolerated. Continuing the case of object classification, in the elucidation of CaRBS, two objective functions are considered here to quantify the level of classification achieved, which take into account differently the issues of classification ambiguity and classification ignorance. The use of the CaRBS technique allows the fullest visualisation of the decision support results, able through the depiction of the evidence from characteristics describing each object as a simplex coordinate in a simplex plot.

An associated issue is the ability of CaRBS to offer decision support based on incomplete data, without the need for any inhibiting external management of the missing values present (Beynon, 2005b). Within CaRBS, a missing value is considered an ignorant value and retained in the considered data, allowing the fullest real interpretation of results from the original data (Schafer & Graham, 2002). This article presents the rudiments of the CaRBS technique and an expository analysis using it on an example data set.

BACKGROUND

The classification and ranking belief simplex, introduced in Beynon (2005a, 2005b), is a novel object classification and ranking technique, where objects such as o_j are described by a series of characteristics $c_1, \ldots, c_n$. Considering the classification problem only here, these characteristics contribute evidence to whether the classification of an object is to a given hypothesis ($\{x\}$), its complement ($\{\neg x\}$), and a level of ignorance ($\{x, \neg x\}$). DST forms the basis for the operation of the CaRBS technique, as such it is termed around the formation of bodies of evidence (BOEs), made up of mass values representing the levels of exact belief in the focal elements of the hypothesis, not the hypothesis and concomitant ignorance.

More formally, the evidence from a characteristic c_i, for the object o_j, is defined a characteristic BOE, termed $m_{j,i}(\cdot)$, made up of a triplet of mass values; $m_{j,i}(\{x\})$, $m_{j,i}(\{x, \neg x\})$ and $m_{j,i}(\{\neg x\})$, where $\{x\}$, $\{\neg x\}$ and $\{x, \neg x\}$, are the focal elements discussed. The rudiments of the CaRBS technique can then be described by reference to Figure 1, where the construction of a characteristic BOE is shown.

In Figure 1, stage a) shows the transformation of a characteristic value v (j^{th} object, i^{th} characteristic) into a confidence value $cf_i(v)$, using a sigmoid function, with control variables k_i and θ_i. Stage b) transforms a $cf_i(v)$ value into a characteristic BOE $m_{j,i}(\cdot)$, made up of the three mass values, $m_{j,i}(\{x\})$, $m_{j,i}(\{\neg x\})$ and $m_{j,i}(\{x, \neg x\})$, defined by (Safranek et al., 1990):

$$m_{j,i}(\{x\}) = \max\left(0, \frac{B_i}{1-A_i} cf_i(v) - \frac{A_i B_i}{1-A_i}\right)$$

Classification and Ranking Belief Simplex

Figure 1. Stages within the CaRBS technique to construct a characteristic BOE from a characteristic value v

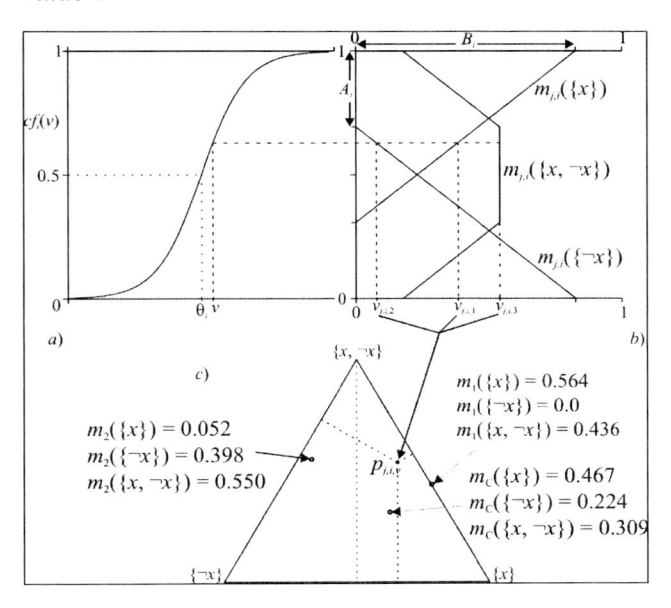

$$m_{j,i}(\{\neg x\}) = \max\left(0, \frac{-B_i}{1-A_i} cf_i(v) + B_i\right),$$

and $m_{j,i}(\{x, \neg x\}) = 1 - m_{j,i}(\{x\}) - m_{j,i}(\{\neg x\})$,

where A_i and B_i are two further control variables. Stage c) shows a BOE $m_{j,i}(\cdot)$; $m_{j,i}(\{x\}) = v_{j,i,1}$, $m_{j,i}(\{\neg x\}) = v_{j,i,2}$ and $m_{j,i}(\{x, \neg x\}) = v_{j,i,3}$, can be represented as a simplex coordinate ($p_{j,i,v}$) in a simplex plot (equilateral triangle). The point $p_{j,i,v}$ exists such that the least distance it is to each of the sides of the equilateral triangle are in the same proportion (ratio) to the values $v_{j,i,1}$, $v_{j,i,2}$ and $v_{j,i,3}$.

Within DST, Dempster's rule of combination is used to combine a series of characteristic BOEs, to produce an *object* BOE, associated with an object and their level of classification to $\{x\}$, $\{\neg x\}$, and $\{x, \neg x\}$. The combination of two BOEs, $m_i(\cdot)$ and $m_k(\cdot)$, defined $(m_i \oplus m_k)(\cdot)$, results in a combined BOE whose mass values are given by the equations in Box 1.

This process to combine two BOEs is demonstrated on $m_1(\cdot)$ and $m_2(\cdot)$, to produce $m_C(\cdot)$, see Figure 1c. The two BOEs, $m_1(\cdot)$ and $m_1(\cdot)$, have mass values in the vector form [$m_i(\{x\})$, $m_i(\{\neg x\})$, $m_i(\{x, \neg x\})$], as [0.564, 0.000, 0.436] and [0.052, 0.398, 0.550], respectively. The combination of $m_1(\cdot)$ and $m_2(\cdot)$, using the expressions, is evaluated to be [0.467, 0.224, 0.309] (= $m_C(\cdot)$). In Figure 1c, the simplex coordinates of the BOEs, $m_1(\cdot)$ and $m_2(\cdot)$, are shown along with that of the combined BOE $m_C(\cdot)$.

The described combination process can then be used iteratively to combine the characteristic BOEs describing each object into an *object* BOE. It is noted, the CaRBS system is appropriate for a problem where each related characteristic has a noticeable level of concomitant ignorance associated with it and its contribution to the problem (Gerig, Welti, Guttman, Colchester, & Szekely, 2000).

The effectiveness of the CaRBS system is governed by the values assigned to the incumbent control variables, k_i, θ_i, A_i and B_i ($i = 1, ..., n$). This necessary configuration is defined as a constrained optimisation problem, solved here using trigonometric differential evolution—TDE (Storn & Price, 1997; Fan & Lampinen, 2003). When the classification of a number of objects is known, the effectiveness of a configured CaRBS system can be measured by a defined objective function (OB). Two objective functions are considered

Box 1.

$$(m_i \oplus m_k)(\{x\}) = \frac{m_i(\{x\})m_k(\{x\}) + m_k(\{x\})m_i(\{x, \neg x\}) + m_i(\{x\})m_k(\{x, \neg x\})}{1 - (m_i(\{\neg x\})m_k(\{x\}) + m_i(\{x\})m_k(\{\neg x\}))}$$

$$(m_i \oplus m_k)(\{\neg x\}) = \frac{m_i(\{\neg x\})m_k(\{\neg x\}) + m_i(\{x, \neg x\})m_k(\{\neg x\}) + m_k(\{\neg x\})m_i(\{x, \neg x\})}{1 - (m_i(\{\neg x\})m_k(\{x\}) + m_i(\{x\})m_k(\{\neg x\}))}$$

$$(m_i \oplus m_k)(\{x, \neg x\}) = 1 - (m_i \oplus m_k)(\{x\}) - (m_i \oplus m_k)(\{\neg x\})$$

here, each based around the optimization of the final object BOEs, but take into account differently, the presence of ambiguity and ignorance.

Beynon (2005a) included an objective function which maximised the certainty in each object's final classification (minimising ambiguity and ignorance). This OB, defined OB1, uses the mean simplex coordinates of the final object BOEs of objects known to be classified to $\{x\}$ or $\{\neg x\}$, the sets of objects are termed equivalence classes ($E(\cdot)$), defined $E(x)$ and $E(\neg x)$. Then the mean simplex coordinate of an equivalence class $E(\cdot)$ is

$$\left(\frac{1}{|E(\cdot)|} \sum_{o_j \in E(\cdot)} x_j, \frac{1}{|E(\cdot)|} \sum_{o_j \in E(\cdot)} y_j \right),$$

where (x_j, y_j) is the simplex coordinate of the object BOE associated with the object o_j and $|E(\cdot)|$ is the number of objects in the respective equivalence class. It follows, the OB1 is given by:

$$OB1 = \frac{1}{2} \left(\sqrt{\left(x_H - \frac{1}{|E(x)|} \sum_{o_j \in E(x)} x_j \right)^2 + \left(y_H - \frac{1}{|E(x)|} \sum_{o_j \in E(x)} y_j \right)^2} + \sqrt{\left(x_N - \frac{1}{|E(\neg x)|} \sum_{o_j \in E(\neg x)} x_j \right)^2 + \left(y_N - \frac{1}{|E(\neg x)|} \sum_{o_j \in E(\neg x)} y_j \right)^2} \right)$$

where (x_H, y_H) and (x_N, y_N) are the simplex coordinates of the $\{x\}$ and $\{\neg x\}$ vertices in the domain of the simplex plot, respectively. The OB1 has range $0 \leq OB1 \leq \sqrt{(x_N - x_H)^2 + (y_N - y_H)^2}$. For a simplex plot with vertex coordinates $(1, 0)$, $(0, 0)$, and $(0.5, \sqrt{3}/2)$, it is an equilateral triangle with unit side, then $0 \leq OB1 \leq 1$.

The second objective function considered here was constructed in Beynon (2005b), which in contrast to OB1, considers optimisation through the minimisation of only the ambiguity in the classification of the set of objects. For objects in the equivalence classes, $E(x)$ and $E(\neg x)$, the optimum solution is to maximise the difference values $(m_j(\{x\}) - m_j(\{\neg x\}))$ and $(m_j(\{\neg x\}) - m_j(\{x\}))$, respectively. The OB2 is given by:

$$OB2 = \frac{1}{4} \left(\frac{1}{|E(x)|} \sum_{o_j \in E(x)} (1 - m_j(\{x\}) + m_j(\{\neg x\})) + \frac{1}{|E(\neg x)|} \sum_{o_j \in E(\neg x)} (1 + m_j(\{x\}) - m_j(\{\neg x\})) \right)$$

In the limit, each of the difference values, $(m_j(\{x\}) - m_j(\{\neg x\}))$ and $(m_j(\{\neg x\}) - m_j(\{x\}))$, has domain $[-1, 1]$, then $0 \leq OB2 \leq 1$. It is noted, maximising a difference value such as $(m_j(\{x\}) - m_j(\{\neg x\}))$ only indirectly affects the associated ignorance $(m_j(\{x, \neg x\}))$, rather than making it a direct issue, as with OB1.

There is one final feature of the CaRBS technique that separates it from the majority of other classification techniques, namely on how it models the presence of missing values. Moreover, if a characteristic value is missing its respective characteristic, BOE supports only ignorance, namely $m_{j,i}(\{x, \neg x\}) = 1$ (with $m_{j,i}(\{x\}) = 0$ and $m_{j,i}(\{\neg x\}) = 0$). That is, a missing value is considered an ignorant value and so offers no evidence in the subsequent classification of an object. This means that the missing values can be retained in the analysis rather than having to be imputed or managed in any way, which would change the data set considered (Huisman, 2000; Schafer & Graham, 2002).

CaRBS ANALYSES OF EXAMPLE DATA SET

The main thrust of this article elucidates the employment of the CaRBS technique on a small example data set. This data set is made up of 16 objects, $o_1, o_2, ..., o_{16}$, each described by five characteristics, $c_1, c_2, ..., c_5$, and known to be classified (d_1) to either a given hypothesis $\{x\}$ or its complement $\{\neg x\}$. The details of the 16 objects are reported in Table 1, for each characteristic, without loss of generality, the values are standardised, so they have zero mean and unit standard deviation.

When using the CaRBS technique, the descriptive characteristics are considered low level measurements. That is, no characteristic on its own offers certainty in the final classification of an object to either $\{x\}$ or

Classification and Ranking Belief Simplex

Table 1. Characteristic and classification details of 16 objects ($0 \equiv \{\neg x\}$, $1 \equiv \{x\}$)

	c_1	c_2	c_3	c_4	c_5	d_1		c_1	c_2	c_3	c_4	c_5	d_1
o_1	−1.348	0.275	0.722	−0.578	−0.791	0	o_9	−0.880	0.238	0.061	−0.365	−0.214	1
o_2	−0.641	0.340	−0.795	0.200	1.472	0	o_{10}	0.551	−3.853	3.289	−0.519	−0.117	1
o_3	0.981	0.264	−0.770	1.976	2.868	0	o_{11}	−0.247	0.227	−0.440	0.350	0.894	1
o_4	0.179	0.442	−0.091	−0.309	−0.743	0	o_{12}	−0.310	0.274	−0.298	−0.742	0.509	1
o_5	−0.075	0.411	−0.755	2.736	−0.743	0	o_{13}	1.180	0.232	−0.392	−0.225	−0.406	1
o_6	−0.416	0.279	0.451	−0.775	−0.695	0	o_{14}	0.623	0.106	−0.357	−0.409	−0.743	1
o_7	2.758	0.230	−0.723	−0.320	−1.032	0	o_{15}	−1.071	0.016	−0.250	−1.163	−0.647	1
o_8	−0.655	0.347	−0.676	0.696	0.172	0	o_{16}	−0.631	0.172	1.024	−0.553	0.220	1

Table 2. Control variable values associated with object characteristics, using OB1

Characteristic	c_1	c_2	c_3	c_4	c_5
k_i	−3.000	−3.000	3.000	−3.000	−3.000
θ_i	1.897	−1.335	−0.476	−0.009	1.227
A_i	0.104	0.928	0.303	0.030	0.269

$\{\neg x\}$. To assure this (see Beynon, 2005b), the control variables B_i, $i = 1, \ldots, 5$ are fixed as 0.5, signifying each characteristic will have an associated 'ignorance' mass value not less than 0.5 ($m_{j,i}(\{x, \neg x\}) \geq 0.5$ in a characteristic BOE). With the data standardised, consistent bounds on the other control variables present in CaRBS, k_i, θ_i and A_i, are set as; $-3 \leq k_i \leq 3$, $-2 \leq \theta_i \leq 2$, and $0 \leq A_i < 1$.

To configure a CaRBS system, a number of parameters are required for the employment of trigonometric differential evolution. Following Fan and Lampinen (2003), amplification control $F = 0.99$, crossover constant $CR = 0.85$, trigonometric mutation probability $M_t = 0.05$, and number of parameter vectors $NP = 10 \times$ number of control variables = 150. The TDE method was then employed with the different objective functions, the results are next described.

CaRBS Analysis With Objective Function OB1

The utilisation of the objective function OB1 in the configuration of a CaRBS system directly minimizes the levels of ambiguity and ignorance in the classification of objects. The TDE optimisation method was applied and found to converge to the optimum value OB1 = 0.370. The resultant control variables found from the TDE run are reported in Table 2.

An inspection of these results shows the uniformity in the k_i control variables taking the value −3.000 or 3.000, exhibiting the attempt to offer most discernment between $\{x\}$ and $\{\neg x\}$, see Figure 1. The role of these defined control variables is to allow the construction of characteristic BOEs, next demonstrated with the object o_{11} and the characteristic c_3. Starting with the evaluation of the confidence factor $cf_3(\cdot)$ (see Figure 1a), for the object o_{11}, from Table 1, and its characteristic value is $v = -0.440$, then:

$$cf_3(-0.440) = \frac{1}{1 + e^{-3.000(-0.440 + 0.476)}} = \frac{1}{1 + 0.896} = 0.527$$

using the control variables in Table 2. This confidence value is used in the expressions for the mass values in the characteristic BOE $m_{11,3}(\cdot)$, namely; $m_{11,3}(\{x\})$, $m_{11,3}(\{\neg x\})$ and $m_{11,3}(\{x, \neg x\})$, found to be:

$$m_{11,3}(\{x\}) = \max\left(0, \frac{0.5}{1-0.303} 0.527 - \frac{0.303 \times 0.5}{1-0.303}\right)$$
$$= \max(0, 0.378 - 0.217) = 0.161,$$

$$m_{11,3}(\{\neg x\}) = \max\left(0, \frac{-0.5}{1-0.303} 0.527 + 0.5\right)$$
$$= \max(0, -0.378 + 0.5) = 0.122,$$

$$m_{11,3}(\{x, \neg x\}) = 1 - 0.161 - 0.122 = 0.717.$$

For the object o_{11}, this characteristic BOE is representative of the characteristic BOEs $m_{11,i}(\cdot)$, presented in Table 3. These characteristic BOEs describe the evidential support from the characteristics to the o_{11} object's classification (known to be to $\{x\} \equiv 1$).

In Table 3, for the object o_{11}, to support correct classification, it would be expected the $m_{11,i}(\{x\})$ mass values to be larger than their respective $m_{11,i}(\{\neg x\})$ mass values, which is the case for the characteristics, c_1, c_3, and c_5. The large $m_{11,i}(\{x, \neg x\})$ mass values in all characteristic BOEs are a direct consequence of the imposed values on the B_i control variables. The majority of characteristic BOEs supporting correct classification is reflected in the final object BOE $m_{11}(\cdot)$ produced (through their combination), which suggests, with $m_{11}(\{x\}) = 0.486 > 0.370 = m_{11}(\{\neg x\})$, the correct classification. For further interpretation of the characteristic and object BOEs associated with the object o_{11} (and others), their representation as simplex coordinates in a simplex plot are reported in Figure 2.

Table 3. Characteristic and object BOEs for the object o_{11}, using OB1

BOE	c_1	c_2	c_3	c_4	c_5	Object BOE
$m_{11,i}(\{x\})$	0.499	0.000	0.161	0.115	0.316	0.486
$m_{11,i}(\{\neg x\})$	0.000	0.437	0.122	0.369	0.000	0.370
$m_{11,i}(\{x, \neg x\})$	0.501	0.563	0.717	0.516	0.684	0.144

Figure 2. Simplex coordinates of characteristic and object BOEs for o_{11} and other objects, using OB1

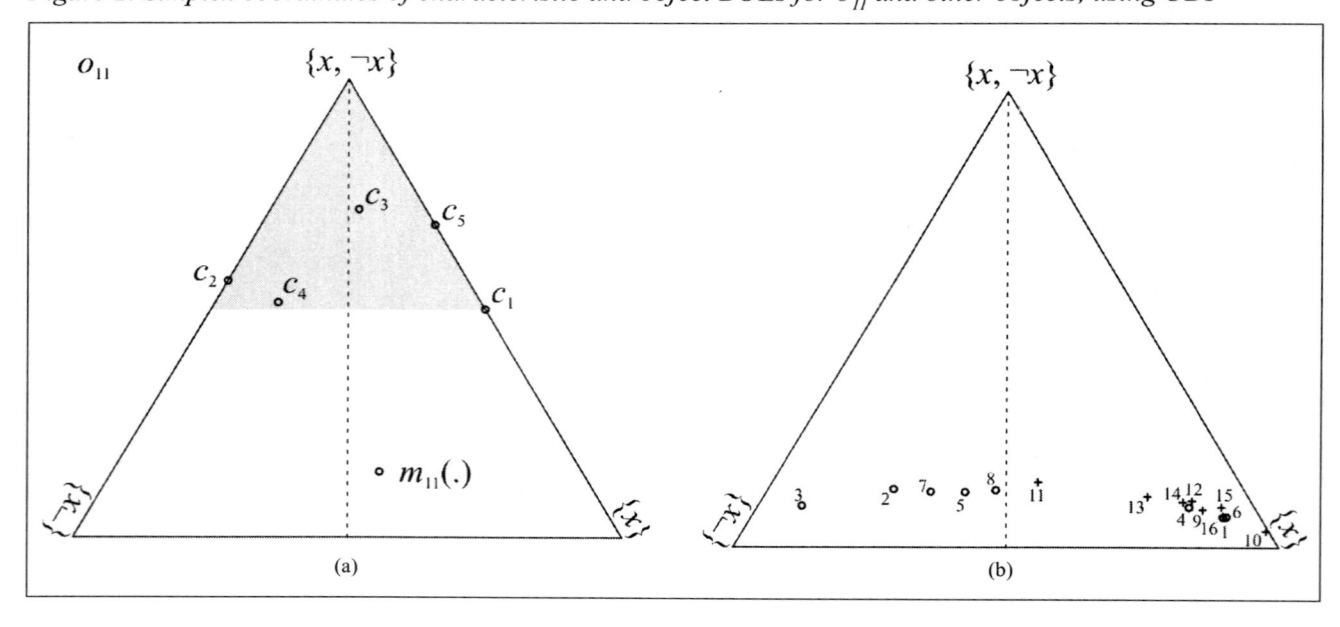

Figure 2a offers a visual representation of the supporting or non-supporting evidence from the five characteristics to the classification of the object o_{11}. The dashed vertical line partitions, in the simplex plot, where either of the mass values assigned to $\{\neg x\}$ (to the left) and $\{x\}$ (to the right) is the larger in a BOE. The characteristic BOEs $m_{11,i}(\cdot)$ are labelled with their respective c_i abbreviation (shown in a shaded area representing their known domain). The simplex coordinate of the object BOE $m_{11}(\cdot)$ is nearer the base line than those of the characteristic BOEs, due to the reduction of ignorance from the combination of evidence in the characteristic BOEs.

In Figure 2b the presentation of the objects' object BOEs between those associated with $\{x\}$ and $\{\neg x\}$ are labelled with a cross and circle, respectively, and labelled using their o_i index (see Table 1). The near consistent distances away from the base line of the simplex plot indicates similar levels of concomitant ignorance present in each object BOE, a consequence of the objective function used here (OB1), which directly attempts to minimise ignorance along with ambiguity in the final classification of the objects (within their object BOEs). Inspection of the simplex coordinates indicates 13 out of 16 objects were correctly classified. Importantly, a configured CaRBS system can be used to future predict the classification, including ignorance, of previously not considered objects, hence becomes a decision support system.

CaRBS Analysis with Objective Function OB2

This section briefly describes a CaRBS analysis of the example data set (see Table 1), using the other objective function OB2 previously defined. From its description, it is more tolerant of ignorance in the final classification of objects than in the case of OB1. The TDE method was again applied and found to converge to the optimum value OB2 = 0.324. The resultant control variables are reported in Table 4.

An inspection of these values, compared with those found when using OB1 (see Table 2), shows the generally larger values of A_i control variables here. From the description of the CaRBS system, this means there will be more ignorance associated with the evidence in the evaluated characteristic BOEs here. The resultant characteristic BOEs for the previously considered object o_{11} are reported in Table 5.

In Table 5, for the object o_{11}, only two characteristic BOEs offer non-ignorant evidence, namely c_2 and c_3, the others have $m_{11,i}(\{x, \neg x\}) = 1.000$ and offer no evidence to its final classification. The final object BOE $m_{11}(\cdot)$, produced through their combination, with $m_{11}(\{x\}) = 0.173 > 0.084 = m_{11}(\{\neg x\})$, offers correct classification. For further interpretation of the characteristic and object BOEs associated with the object o_{11} (and others), their representation as simplex coordinates in a simplex plot are reported in Figure 3.

Table 4. Control variable values associated with object characteristics, using OB2

Characteristic	c_1	c_2	c_3	c_4	c_5
k_i	−3.000	−3.000	3.000	−3.000	−3.000
θ_i	0.268	−0.664	−0.574	0.260	−0.268
A_i	0.941	0.925	0.366	0.567	0.970

Table 5. Characteristic and object BOEs for the object o_{11}, using OB2

BOE	c_1	c_2	c_3	c_4	c_5	Object BOE
$m_{11,i}(\{x\})$	0.000	0.000	0.184	0.000	0.000	0.173
$m_{11,i}(\{\neg x\})$	0.000	0.071	0.027	0.000	0.000	0.084
$m_{11,i}(\{x, \neg x\})$	1.000	0.929	0.789	1.000	1.000	0.743

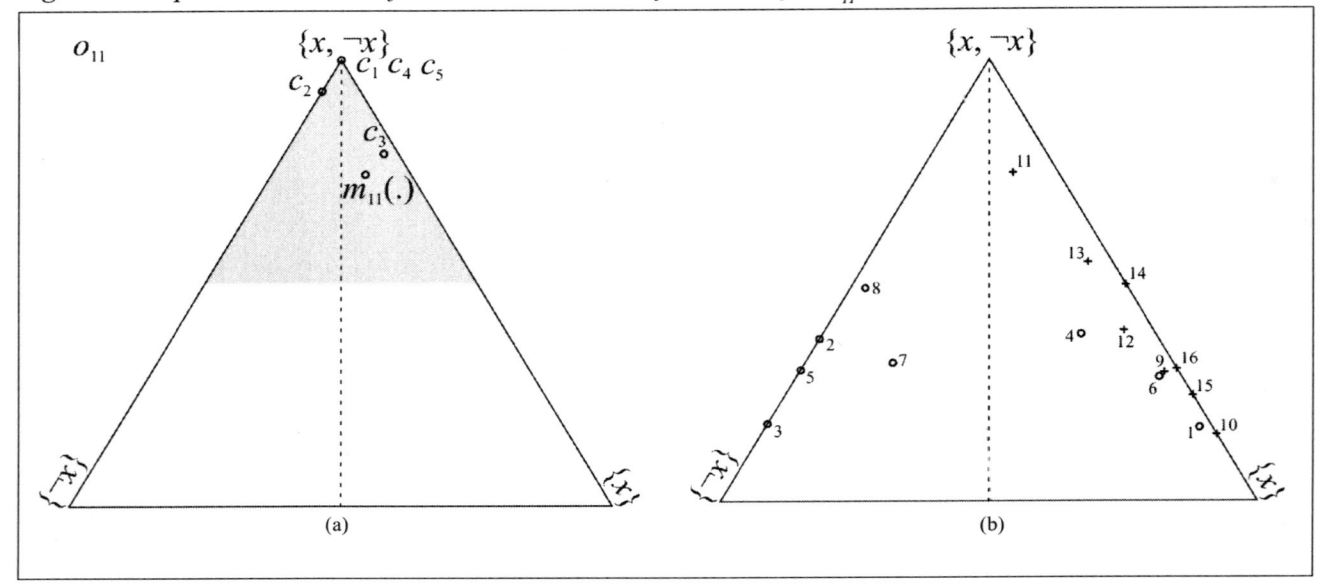

Figure 3. Simplex coordinates of characteristic and object BOEs for o_{11} and other objects, using OB2

In Figure 3a, the evidence from only the characteristics, c_2 and c_3 is clearly shown. As a consequence the final classification of the object, while correct, is heavily ignorant (high up in the simplex plot). Inspection of Figure 3b shows the simplex coordinates representing object BOEs are spread all over the simplex plot, indicating different levels of ignorance are associated with the classification of the objects. It can be seen, 13 out of the 16 objects are correctly classified, the same as when the objective function OB1 was employed.

Comparisons of the results from separately using the objective functions, OB1 and OB2, help discern the effects of differently minimising classification ambiguity and/or ignorance. Inspection of the final results in Figure 3b (for OB2) shows far less ambiguity in the classification of objects than that shown in Figure 2b (for OB1). This is especially noticeable for the objects associated with $\{\neg x\}$, in particular, o_2, o_5, o_7, and o_8.

FUTURE TRENDS

As a technique centred around uncertain reasoning, the future for CaRBS lies in the ability of decision makers to fully acknowledge its advantages over other, more traditional, techniques. In the case of object classification, the separate issues of classification ambiguity and ignorance are a good example of this.

The results from the two objective functions considered clearly demonstrate that there is something inherently different about the incumbent presences of ambiguity and ignorance in object classification. This has to be further elucidated so decision makers can make appropriate prior preparations that allow the CaRBS technique to perform the role it is intended for.

CONCLUSION

Object classification techniques form the cornerstone for many decision support systems, hence the range of techniques that exist. The CaRBS technique offers a novel perspective on the intended role played by such techniques.

The allowance for the perspective of ignorance in object classification is anecdotally a feature of computational intelligence that the CaRBS technique offers when employed. This is taken to the extreme by the allowance of missing values to be considered evidence of ignorance. However, this allowance means an incomplete data set can be analysed without inhibiting external management of the missing values present.

REFERENCES

Beynon, M. J. (2005a). A novel technique of object ranking and classification under ignorance: An application to the corporate failure risk problem. *European Journal of Operational Research, 167*, 493-517.

Beynon, M.J. (2005b). A novel approach to the credit rating problem: Object classification under ignorance. *International Journal of Intelligent Systems in Accounting, Finance and Management, 13*, 113-130.

Beynon, M. J., & Kitchener, M. (2005). Ranking the 'balance' of state long-term care systems: A comparative exposition of the SMARTER and CaRBS techniques. *Health Care Management Science, 8*, 157-166.

Chen, Z. (2001). *Data mining and uncertain reasoning: An integrated approach*. New York: John Wiley.

Dempster, A. P. (1967). Upper and lower probabilities induced by a multiple valued mapping. *Ann. Math. Statistics, 38*, 325-339.

Fan, H.-Y., & Lampinen, J. A. (2003). Trigonometric mutation operation to differential evolution. *Journal of Global Optimization, 27*, 105-129.

Gerig, G., Welti, D., Guttman C. R. G, Colchester, A.C.F., & Szekely, G. (2000). Exploring the discrimination power of the time domain for segmentation and characterisation of active lesions in serial MR data. *Medical Image Analysis, 4*, 31-42.

Huisman, M. (2000). Imputation of missing item responses: Some simple techniques. *Quality & Quantity, 34*, 331-351.

Jones, P., & Beynon, M. J. (2007). Temporal support in the identification of e-learning efficacy: An example of object classification in the presence of ignorance. *Expert Systems, 24*(1), 1-16.

Jones, A. L., Beynon, M. J., Holt, C. A., & Roy, S. (2006). A novel approach to the exposition of the temporal development of post-op osteoarthritic knee subjects. *Journal of Biomechanics, 39*(13), 2512-2520.

Safranek, R. J., Gottschlich, S., & Kak, A. C. (1990). Evidence accumulation using binary frames of discernment for verification vision. *IEEE Transactions on Robotics and Automation, 6*, 405-417.

Shafer, G. A. (1976). *Mathematical theory of evidence*. Princeton: Princeton University Press.

Schafer, J. L., & Graham, J. W. (2002). Missing data: Our view of the state of the art. *Psychological Methods, 7*(2), 147-177.

Smets, P. (1991). Varieties of ignorance and the need for well-founded theories. *Information Sciences, 57-58*, 135-144.

Storn, R., & Price, K. (1997). Differential evolution—a simple and efficient heuristic for global optimization over continuous spaces. *Journal of Global Optimisation, 11*, 341-59.

KEY TERMS

Confidence Value: A function to transform a value into a standard domain, such as between 0 and 1.

Equivalence Class: Set of objects considered the same subject to an equivalence relation (e.g., those objects classified to *x*).

Evolutionary Algorithm: An algorithm that incorporates aspects of natural selection or survival of the fittest.

Focal Element: A finite non-empty set of hypotheses.

Imputation: Replacement of a missing value by a surrogate.

Mass Values: A positive function of the level of exact belief in the associated proposition (focal element).

Objective Function: A positive function of the difference between predictions and data estimates that are chosen so as to optimize the function or criterion.

Simplex Plot: Equilateral triangle domain representation of triplets of non-negative values which sum to one.

Uncertain Reasoning: The attempt to represent uncertainty and reason about it when using uncertain knowledge, imprecise information, and so forth.

Computer Aided Facility Management (CAFM) as a New Branch of Decision Making Support Technologies in the Field of Facility Management

Thomas Madritsch
University for Applied Sciences, Kufstein Tirol, Austria
University for Health Sciences, Medical Informatics and Technology, Austria

Michael May
University of Applied Sciences, FHTW, Germany

Herwig Ostermann
University for Health Sciences, Medical Informatics and Technology, Austria

Roland Staudinger
University for Health Sciences, Medical Informatics and Technology, Austria

INTRODUCTION

Nowadays facility management (FM) and real estate activities contribute to about 5-10% of the gross domestic product (GDP) of advanced industrialized countries. For example the total value of FM activity including support services is about 8.2% UK GDP (Harris, 2002). Computer aided facility management (CAFM) software is a new class of information and communications technology (ICT) tools to support management in the preparation of relevant data in the decision making process especially in the area of illustration, evaluation, and control of relevant FM structures and processes. Recently, CAFM tools are developing from simple information systems to multifunctional decision support systems (DSSs) for private as well as public organizations. Until now however, little attention has been given to this relevant change in business and academic communities.

At the same time numerous software systems with various systematic approaches, functions, and varying success have been established on the market. Despite the multitude of suppliers and users in the different branches uncertainty concerning the procedures and achievable effects still prevails. This is closely related to the lack of well-documented, transparent, and successful case studies. In addition, little is known about how CAFM can be implemented successfully and the factors leading to its sustainable success. From an economic point of view it is very important to support this process in order to avoid wrong decisions and unnecessary investment. In particular, implementation strategies and formulae for success are of great interest (May, 2002).

The purpose of this chapter is to describe the relevance of CAFM as a decision support tool in the field of FM. The authors will illustrate the recent developments and market demands of FM and CAFM. The main part will provide an overview on the basic concept as well as building management, for example, CAFM and give detailed insight into the topic and how CAFM may serve as a DSS from an organizational perspective. The next part will introduce some examples of good practices. The chapter closes with an overview of future developments, trends, and research opportunities of CAFM as a decision support tool.

BACKGROUND

According to the survey by Berger (2001) we observe 70% of U.S. companies and 50% of European companies who consider their property and real estate as a strategic resource. The top management needs to regard this within their strategies and planning. The relevance of real estate is represented in the balance sheet. According to Cotts (1999) 25-50% of the assets are related to property or real estate. Life cycle costs are 5-7 times higher than the investment costs of buildings

Copyright © 2008, IGI Global, distributing in print or electronic forms without written permission of IGI Global is prohibited.

(Grabatin, 2001). This shows the need to optimize the operating costs.

A professional FM can help to raise the efficiency of the secondary processes of companies, for example, building facilities and services (Brown, Kevin, Lapides, & Rondeau, 1995). Therefore the management will need the relevant information of the building services engineer for their decision making. Companies are challenged by limited budgets and high customer expectations. Especially in the field of building services engineering there is a demand for integrated ICT to provide relevant data for the decision support process (May, 2005).

FACILITY MANAGEMENT

FM is developing in various European countries. Certain historical and cultural circumstances, organizations, and business areas have been the basis for different views and approaches. In general, all organizations, whether public or private, use buildings, assets, and services (facility services) to support their primary activities. By coordinating these assets and services, by using management skills, and by handling many changes in the organization's environment, FM influences its ability to act proactively and to meet all its requirements. This is done also in order to optimize the costs and performance of assets and services. "FM is an integrated process to support and improve the effectiveness of the primary activities of an organization by the management and delivery of agreed support services for the appropriate environment that is needed to achieve its changing objectives" (European Committee for Standardization, 2006).

The concept of FM was not new when the term "facility management" was formed in the U.S. in 1979, as the management of large facilities or properties for a profit had already been practiced before. The definition used by the International Facility Management Association (IFMA) is: "Facility management is a profession that encompasses multiple disciplines to ensure functionality of the built environment by integrating people, place, process and technology" (IFMA, 2007a).

Computer Aided Facility Management

CAFM means the support of FM activities by modern information technology during the life cycle of real estates. It is focussed on the supply of information related to the facilities. All relevant data in the life cycle of facilities are collected, processed and evaluated electronically (German Facility Management Association [GEFMA], 2002). Typical CAFM systems combine database technology with graphical systems, for example, CAD systems.

Without IT support the ambitious goals of FM cannot be reached efficiently. The appropriate use of IT has become a critical success factor for the implementation of FM. Thus IT is a fundamental "Enabling Technology" for FM (May, 2006, p.17).

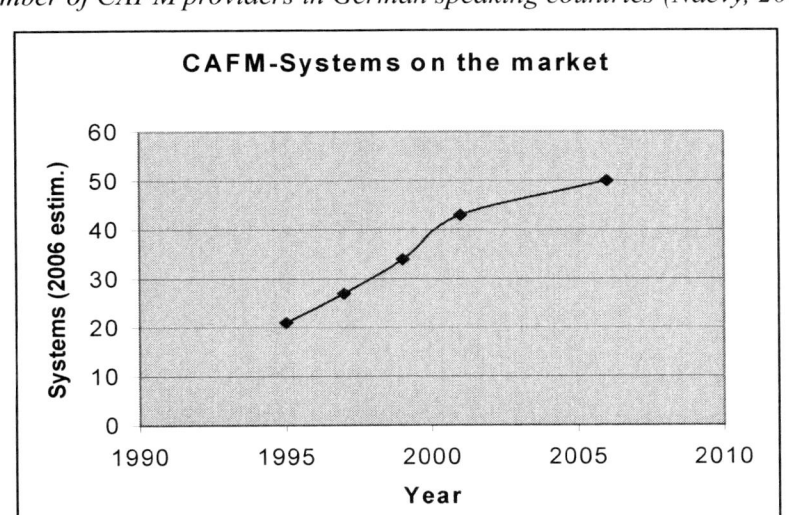

Figure 1. Growing number of CAFM providers in German speaking countries (Näevy, 2006)

Since the 1990s CAFM has been providing efficient IT tools for the illustration, evaluation, and control of FM structures and processes. During these years numerous software systems with various systematic approaches, functions, and varying success have been established on the market (May & Hohmann, 2004). Figure 1 (Naevy, 2006) shows the development of different CAFM systems/providers in German speaking countries.

The use of CAFM systems is very common. A Swiss FM study showed that approximately 30% of the enterprises are using CAFM systems. In the strategic range the support is considerably smaller. Only few companies are using data warehouses as management information systems for the decision support (FM-Monitor, 2004). The most common IT systems in FM are still office applications and commercial software such as enterprise resource planning (ERP) systems. In the future, companies expect more support in the business decision-making process.

CAFM as a Management Support System

The strategic value of real estate in companies makes it necessary that the management is supported by ICT. They are generally summarized under the generic term "management support system" (MMS) (König, Rommelfanger, & Ohse, 2003) as seen in Figures 2 and 3. CAFM systems are developed with the goal to generate relevant information from the existing real estate economical database and transfer it directly into planning and control processes. Primarily the decision relevant data and representations will be generated for the decision makers.

In a further development step CAFM systems will provide detailed and consolidated information for the decision makers via a partly automated report system. Most CAFM systems have limited interactivity for the users. In the sense of the previous categorization this first stage of development of CAFM systems can be called "management information system."

Concerning the amount of relevant data in real estate management the market demands effective support in the planning and decision making processes. Therefore CAFM systems must develop into real DSSs. With the use of interactive CAFM modules, the decision-making processes will be more effective in the simulation and evaluation of the decision relevant data. Contrary to the pure management information systems this will support managers in their planning and decision-making processes and improve the quality of decisions. In particular, these next generation CAFM systems can support the decision makers by generating and evaluating scenarios more effectively in the future.

Businesses rules management systems are modeling routine decisions, analyzing the criteria, and automating the decisions. If the basic conditions are changing, an enterprise can adapt the decisions with the help of the software within minutes. By the coupling of ICT with business processes, the management of the infrastructure is no longer a stand-alone process from the technical point of view, but is also integrated in the business context.

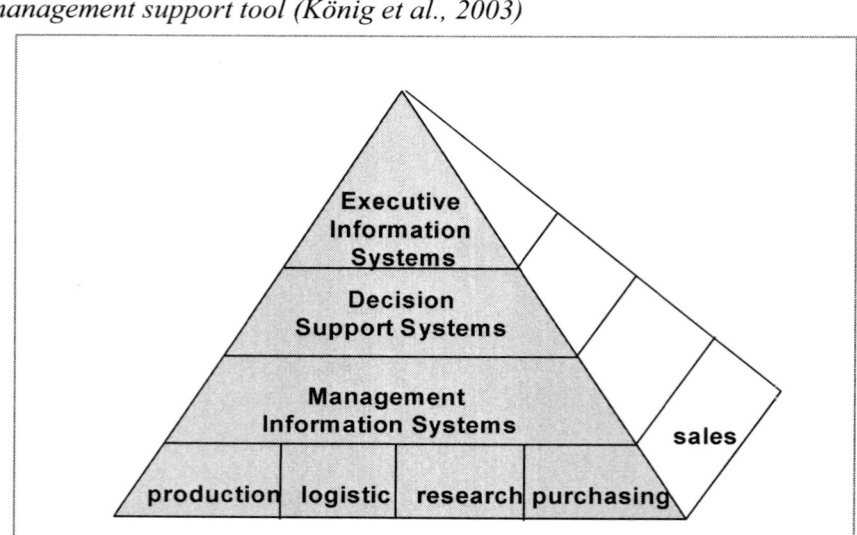

Figure 2. ICT as management support tool (König et al., 2003)

Figure 3. Management support systems (Stahlknecht, 2005)

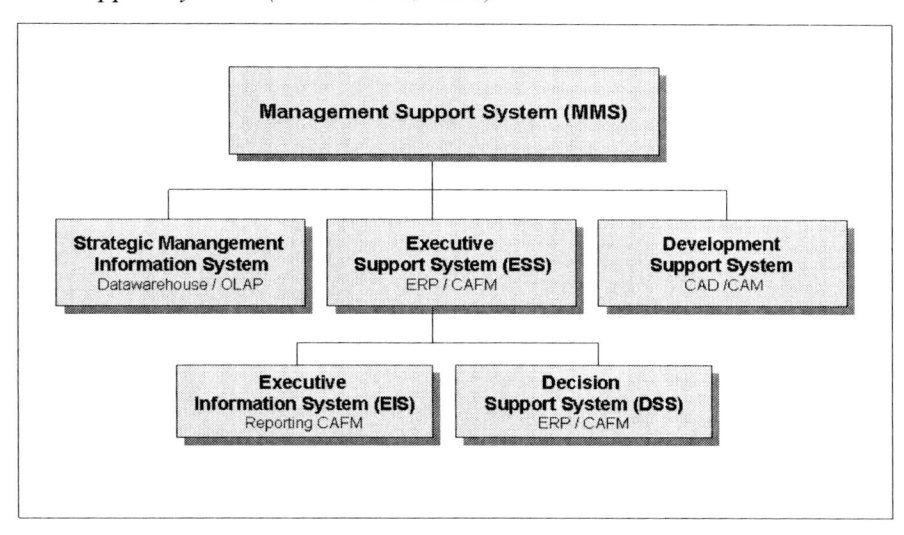

Figure 4. Benefits of CAFM implemenation (Naevy, 2006)

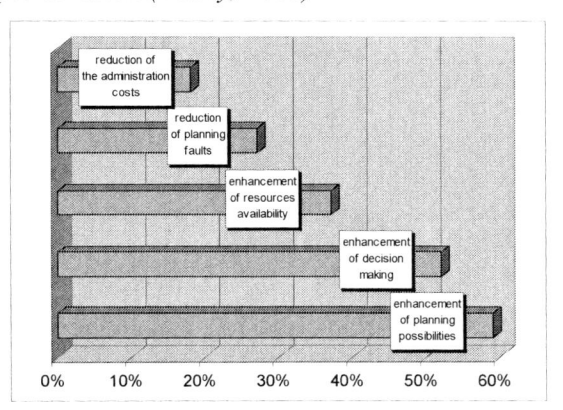

The Relevance of CAFM as a Decision Support System

FM contains the concepts of cost effectiveness, productivity improvement, efficiency, and the employee quality of life. Very often there are no set answers for fulfilling all expectations, but management decisions still have to be made (Cotts & Lee, 1992). Organizations cannot ignore the potential for cost saving within their real estate portfolios and increasingly they are using property-based information for corporate strategic decision making. The extent to which the information is fed back into strategic decision making varies depending on the implementation, experience in using the information produced, and the links made between departments within the organizations concerned (Fenwick, 1998).

After salary and wages, facility and real estate expenditure is the largest cost item for a company and any improvement of cost effectiveness results in a significant overall saving of costs (Finlay, 1998). CAFM systems are increasingly developing into a strategic planning tool in order to support decision making in facility and real estate management, for example, in the fields of space planning, cleaning, room conditions, and maintenance strategies.

CAFM as a Decision Support System

By using CAFM systems all decision relevant data are represented correctly, in time and transparently.

Economic data about real estate is the basis for the strategic management of the facilities. To optimize management processes in FM it is necessary to link real estate information with enterprise processes (Schach, 2005).

Decision makers demand more relevant data just in terms of quality and quantity. CAFM systems provide information on a whole range of FM functions enabling tactically pervasive decision-making performance for strategic long-term business success (Lunn & Stephenson, 2000).

The use and the saving potential of CAFM are evident in the chart (see Figure 4). In this investigation of the U.S. market (Naevy, 2006; Teicholz, 1995) the improvement potentials after the introduction of CAFM systems were examined. It becomes evident that enterprises regarded the improvement of decision making and improvement of the planning possibilities as the most important advantages of CAFM technology.

Design System Good Practice

In order to give an example on how CAFM tools can support very complex decision-making processes we consider assigning complex organizational structures of large organizations to existing spatial resources, that is, buildings, floors, offices, and work places. This problem usually occurs as part of relocation or reorganization processes. The underlying decision problem resembles the so-called quadratic assignment problem (QAP), which is known to be one of the most difficult (NP hard) combinatorial decision problems (Cela, 1998). Unfortunately, people can solve such optimization problems only for a very limited number of objects. When the number of n objects to be assigned is large it becomes impossible to enumerate all the possible assignments, even with the aid of very fast computers. For example, if n equals just 25 and a computer was able to evaluate 10 billion assignments per second, it would still take nearly *50 million year*s to evaluate all assignments. Thus, computer-based tools using heuristic mathematical algorithms are necessary. First results of integrating automated decision components into CAFM systems are provided (Rettinger, 2007). In this way we are able to solve this complex allocation problem almost in real time. Different solutions can be produced by modifying a number of parameters. These variants can be compared and quantified by applying a system of key performance indicators (KPIs) to the different scenarios. In this way we obtain a completely new quality of decision support based on data provided by CAFM systems.

The combination with a mobile CAFM solution allows a virtual workplace management for the users. It supports the following strategic guidance process in the real estate economy to support the management in the decision-making processes:

- Administration and management of real estate portfolios
- Analyzing and evaluating
- Controlling the complete life cycle of real estate
- Central reporting to the management
- Decision support for the real estate management.

Implementation

Despite the multitude of suppliers and users in different branches, there is still uncertainty concerning the procedures and achievable effects. This is closely related to the lack of well-documented, transparent, and successful case studies. In addition, little is known about how CAFM is implemented successfully and the factors leading to success. From the economic point of view it is very important to support this process in order to avoid wrong decisions and unnecessary investments. Especially implementation strategies and formulae for success are of great interest.

In 2006 the authors carried out a market survey about CAFM implementation (May, Madritsch, Koenig, Meier, & Scharer, 2007). This survey presents the first comparative analysis of CAFM projects in the German-speaking countries. Due to the geographical location of the project partners the entire German-speaking area is covered and thus the results of the analysis reflect the state of the art of CAFM implementation and use in the German-speaking area. The study of successful CAFM projects in companies and public institutions is intended to provide the know-how and practical experience to the public. It presents current trends and technologies and provides recommendations for the successful CAFM implementation. The authors recommend the steps as seen in Figure 5.

In addition further success factors are the participation of the management as well as the users of the CAFM

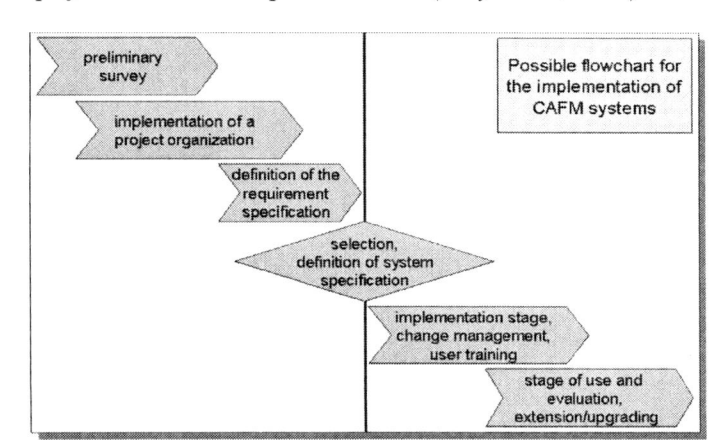

Figure 5. Recommended steps for the CAFM implementation (May et al., 2007)

tool in the project team as well as the data collection and the continuous data management.

Operation

The introduction of new work forms such as teleworking, desk sharing, and virtual enterprises leads to rapid changes of the use of real estate. FM develops into a know-how oriented technology. Modern information and communication systems will simulate different scenarios to find the optimum operating points in relation to the occupancy of buildings. In this context a bi-directional exchange of data between building automation and CAFM system will become necessary in the future (Schach, 2005).

A large potential is the use of information between CAFM systems and building automation. By simulating real estate processes important data can be created in order to support the management in the decision processes to find the potential efficient operation point. A further potential lies in the controlling of the efficiency of real estate management. When linking CAFM and building instrumentation, relevant building data can be generated, such as consumption data; malfunction and status messages; operation hours; and maintenance and inspection dates, as well as repair reports for the controlling process.

A further example for infrastructural building management concerns demand-related cleaning management (Schach, 2005). Instead of static cleaning cycles information about the actual degree of pollution determines the cleaning cycles. The degree of pollution is determined for example by the operational persons in the areas and the cleaning requirement. The user can be informed about this process and can make decisions for the cleaning process on the other hand.

FUTURE TECHNOLOGIES AND TRENDS

An increasing number of enterprises considers the further integration of FM with other supporting services. As a result we see the introduction of the integrated job management concept. This concept is based on the idea that it will be organized by a central department. That means that real estate management, FM, and IT management are concentrated in one organization.

The CAFM market is subject to a permanent development towards the needs of the customers. As mentioned before Web-based CAFM solutions are established in the market. In contrast to many standard CAFM systems with client/server architecture, Web-based CAFM solutions touch down on a multilevel (multi-tier) architecture. These applications are based frequently on three logical layers (3-tier architecture): presentation layer, business logic layer, and data layer. If an enterprise decides to outsource its CAFM solution additional extensive installations for remote access have to be accomplished for client/server systems. With a fully Web-based solution only inter-/intranet access is necessary.

The study by McAndrew, Anumba, and Hassan (2005) shows that a new wireless Web-based service for CAFM systems would be considered useful by facility managers and would improve current practice. Mobile CAFM solutions are usually not independent solutions; they are modules of CAFM solutions. The mobile devices update the data via an interface with the CAFM data. The operational areas of a mobile solution are various. It can be used, for example, for maintenance management and inventory management.

The development creates a further step to a management information system for FM. National and international enterprises need a holistic view of their real estate in order to optimize the real estate strategy in combination with the enterprise's strategy. This requirement can only be fulfilled if a high degree of transparency of the data and processes is available in the appropriate quality, in real time, and in the correct format at any time. Also the term "workplace management" comes up more often, which is a combination of FM, real estate management, project management, and other sections. Employee self-service systems guarantee a user-centerd approach; with helpdesks and self-service intranet it meets the needs of the customers.

CONCLUSION

By providing an overview about the major concepts and recent developments of CAFM, the authors have shown that FM essentially represents an integrated business function geared towards the improvement of the effectiveness of an organization's primary activities by delivering support services.

Based on such an understanding, CAFM is now recommended to form an integral building block of any management information system because besides salary and wages, facilities and real estate expenditure make up the largest cost item for the company.

The examples mentioned previously show which potentials a future CAFM software, as a DSS, can offer to the management. Moreover, key success factors as well as critical points have been identified for the implementation and operation of CAFM systems.

By taking a glimpse at emerging technologies, the authors conclude that further development of CAFM systems into decision support tools is meeting the requirements of a holistic integrated FM.

REFERENCES

Berger, R. (2001). *Trend Studie für Facility Management*. München, Germany: Roland Berger Strategy Consultants und GEFMA.

Brown, E., Kevin, R., Lapides, P., & Rondeau, P. (1995). *Facility management*. New York: John Wiley & Sons.

Cela, E. (1998). *The quadratic assignment problem. Theory and algorithms*. Kluwer Academic.

Cotts, D. G. (1999). *The facility management handbook*. New York: AMACOM.

European Committee for Standardization. (2006). *Facility management—Part 1: Terms and definition*, CEN/TC 348, (prEN 15221-1). Brussels, Belgium: Author.

Fenwick, J. (1998). Competitive advantage. *Premises & Facilities Management, 4*(1), 23-25.

Finlay, D. (1998). A commercial approach. *Premises & Facilities Management, 4*(1), 25.

FM-Monitor. (2004). *Swiss facility management monitor*. Zürich, Switzerland: pom+Consulting AG.

German Facility Management Association (GEFMA). (2002, April). *Computer aided facility management CAFM—Begriffsbestimmungen, Leistungsmerkmale: GEFMA Richtlinie 400*. Bonn, Germany: Author.

Grabatin, G. (2001). *Betriebswirtschaft für Facility Management*. Wuppertal, Germany: TAW-Verlag.

Harris, I. (2002). Bigger and better FM—To improve everyday life. In *European Facility Management Conference*. Madrid, Spain.

International Facility Management Association (IFMA). (2007a). *International Facility Management Association: What is FM?*. Retrieved January 30, 2007, from http://www.ifma.org/what_is_fm/index.cfm

International Facility Management Association (IFMA). (2007b). *International Facility Management Association: What is FM?*. Retrieved January 30, 2007, from http://www.ifma.org/what_is_fm/fm_definitions.cfm

König, W., Rommelfanger, H., & Ohse, D. (Eds.). (2003). *Taschenbuch der Wirtschaftsinformatik und Wirtschaftsmathematik.* Frankfurt am Main, Germany: Verlag Harri Deutsch.

Lunn, S. D., & Stephenson, P. (2000). The impact of tactical and strategic automation. *Facilities, 18*(7/8), 312-322.

May, M. (2002). How to implement CAFM successfully. In *Proceedings of the European Facility Management Conference* (pp. 41-52). Madrid, Spain.

May, M. (2005). CAFM-Einführung—(K)ein Buch mit sieben Siegeln—Tipps zur CAFM-Einführung. *Facility Management, 12*(6), 2-5.

May, M. (2006). *IT im Facility Management erfolgreich einsetzen: Das CAFM-Handbuch.* Berlin, Germany: Springer-Verlag Berlin Heidelberg New York.

May, M., Madritsch, T., Koenig, T., Meier, M., & Scharer, M. (2007). *Computer aided facility management im deutschsprachigen Raum—CAFM-Praxiserfahrungen aus Deutschland, Österreich und der Schweiz.* Norderstedt, Germany: BoD-Verlag.

May, M., & Hohmann, J. (2004). CAFM in Europe—Quo Vadis? In *Proceedings of the 4th European Facility Management Conference* (p. 8). Copenhagen, Denmark.

McAndrew, S. T., Anumba, C. J., & Hassan, T. M. (2005). Potential use of real-time data capture and job-tracking technology in the field. *Facilities, 23*(1), 31-46.

Naevy, J. (2006). *Facility management* (4th ed.). Berlin, Germany: Springer.

Oettl, R. (2005). *IT-Unterstützung von facility management prozessen durch den Einsatz von ERP- und CAFM-systemen* (cgmunich-report, 02). München, Germany: cgmunich GmbH.

Rettinger et al. (2007) Rettinger, C.; Marchionini, M.; May, M.: Computerbasiertes Generieren von Belegungsplänen bei Umzug oder Flächenverdichtung in großen Organisationen. In *Proceedings of the Facility Management 2007* (pp. 195-203). Frankfurt, Germany.

Schach, R. (2005). *Integriertes facility-management: Aus forschung und praxis* (Bd. 4). Renningen, Germany: expert-Verl.

Stahlknecht, P. (2005). *Einführung in die Wirtschaftsinformatik* (11th ed.). Heidelberg -New York: Springer-Verl.

Teicholz, E. (1995). Computer-aided facilities management and facility conditions assessment software. *Facilities, 13*(6), 16-19.

KEY TERMS

Benchmarking: Benchmarking is the continuous process of measuring products, services, and practices against the toughest competitors of those companies recognized as industry leaders (IFMA, 2007b).

Building Automation: Building automation calls the whole of monitoring, regulation, controlling, and optimization mechanisms in buildings in the context of the technical FM.

Building Management: Building management designates the administration from buildings and services to the support and improvement of the enterprise core processes. It is to ensure the task of the building management that everything is at the disposal for the co-workers, so that they can dedicate themselves fully and completely to their work. Building management extends from the lower level (e.g., caretaker at a school or a doorman) up to the complete support of all flow charts and holistic facility management.

Computer Aided Facility Management (CAFM): CAFM is an information technology system, which automates FM-specific tasks. CAFM is characterized usually by the fact that it unites drawing component (CAD) and alphanumeric data processing. The supply of decision relevant information about the facilities is the center of attention. CAFM provides decision makers with the ability to support the decision process.

Corporate Real Estate Management (CREM): CREM designates the success-oriented administration and marketing of corporate real estates.

Facility: Facility is something that is built, installed, or established to serve a purpose (IFMA, 2007b).

Facility Management (FM): FM is an integrated process to support and improve the effectiveness of the primary activities of an organization by the management and delivery of agreed support services for the appropriate environment that is needed to achieve its changing objectives.

Primary Activities: Primary activities are those that constitute the distinctive and indispensable competence of an organization in its value chain. The distinction between the primary activities and support services is decided by each organization individually; this distinction has to be continuously updated (European Committee for Standardization, 2006).

Service Level Agreement (SLA): SLA is an agreement between the client/customer and the service provider on performance and conditions of facility services delivery.

Context in Decision Support Systems Development

Alexandre Gachet
University of Hawaii at Manoa, USA

Ralph Sprague
University of Hawaii at Manoa, USA

INTRODUCTION

Finding appropriate decision support systems (DSS) development processes and methodologies is a topic that has kept researchers in the decision support community busy for the past three decades at least. Inspired by Gibson and Nolan's curve (Gibson & Nolan 1974; Nolan, 1979), it is fair to contend that the field of DSS development is reaching the end of its expansion (or contagion) stage, which is characterized by the proliferation of processes and methodologies in all areas of decision support. Studies on DSS development conducted during the last 15 years (e.g., Arinze, 1991; Saxena, 1992) have identified more than 30 different approaches to the design and construction of decision support methods and systems (Marakas, 2003). Interestingly enough, none of these approaches predominate and the various DSS development processes usually remain very distinct and project-specific. This situation can be interpreted as a sign that the field of DSS development should soon enter in its formalization (or control) stage. Therefore, we propose a unifying perspective of DSS development based on the notion of context.

In this article, we argue that the context of the target DSS (whether organizational, technological, or developmental) is not properly considered in the literature on DSS development. Researchers propose processes (e.g., Courbon, Drageof, & Tomasi, 1979; Stabell 1983), methodologies (e.g., Blanning, 1979; Martin, 1982; Saxena, 1991; Sprague & Carlson, 1982), cycles (e.g., Keen & Scott Morton, 1978; Sage, 1991), guidelines (e.g., for end-user computer), and frameworks, but often fail to explicitly describe the context in which the solution can be applied.

BACKGROUND

A DSS is broadly considered as "a computer-based system that aids the process of decision making" (Finlay, 1994). Sprague uses a definition that indicates key components of the DSS architecture. A DSS is a "computer-based system which helps decision makers confront ill-structured problems through direct interaction with data and analysis models" (Sprague, 1980). In a more detailed way, Turban (1995) defines it as "an interactive, flexible, and adaptable computer-based information system, especially developed for supporting the solution of a non-structured management problem for improved decision making. It utilizes data, provides an easy-to-use interface, and allows for the decision maker's own insights." This second definition gives a better idea of the underlying architecture of a DSS. Even though different authors identify different components in a DSS, academics and practitioners have come up with a generalized architecture made of six distinct parts: (a) the data management system, (b) the model management system, (c) the knowledge engine, (d) the user interface, (e) the DSS architecture and network, and (f) the user(s) (Marakas, 2003; Power, 2002).

One section this article, Key Terms, briefly defines nine DSS development methodologies popular in the DSS literature. A typical methodology is represented by the steps in Table 1.

Table 1. Phases of the DSS design and development life cycle (Sage, 1991)

1. Identify requirements specifications
2. Preliminary conceptual design
3. Logical design and architectural specifications
4. Detailed design and testing
5. Operational implementation
6. Evaluation and modification
7. Operational deployment

The exact number of steps can vary depending on the aggregation level of each phase. Moreover, steps are usually sequenced in an iterative manner, which means the process can iterate to an earlier phase if the results of the current phase are not satisfactory. Even though these processes are useful from a high-level perspective, we argue that they poorly support the DSS designers and builders to cope with contextual issues. The next paragraphs provide a couple of examples to illustrate this argument. The first example is related to the user interface. The DSS community widely recognizes that the user interface is a critical component of a DSS and that it should be designed and implemented with particular care. But how critical is this component? On the one hand, if we consider a DSS that is intended to be used by a wide range of nontechnical users (for example, a medical DSS for the triage of incoming patients in an emergency room that will be used by nurses and MDs working under pressure), then the user interface is indeed the single most critical component of the DSS, at least from a usability/acceptability point of view. In this context, the human-computer interaction (HCI) literature tells us that usability must definitely be considered before prototyping takes place, because the earlier critical design flaws are detected, the more likely they can be corrected (Holzinger, 2005). There are techniques (such as usability context analysis) intended to facilitate such early focus and commitment (Thomas & Bevan, 1996). On the other hand, if we consider a highly specific DSS that will be handled by a few power-users with a high level of computer literacy (sometimes the DSS builders themselves), then the user interface is less critical and usability considerations can be postponed until a later stage of the development process without threatening the acceptability of the system. This kind of decision has an impact on the entire development process but is rarely considered explicitly in the literature.

The second example deals with the expected lifetime of the DSS. On the one hand, some DSS are complex organizational systems connected to a dense network of transaction information systems. Their knowledge bases accumulate large quantities of models, rules, documents, and data over the years, sometimes over a few decades. They require important financial investments and are expected to have a long lifetime. For a computer-based system, a long lifetime inevitably implies maintenance and legacy issues. The legacy information systems (LIS) literature offers several approaches to deal with these issues, such as the big bang approach (Bateman & Murphy, 1994), the wrapping approach (Comella-Dorda, Wallnau, Seacord, & Roberts, 2000), the chicken little approach (Brodie & Stonebraker, 1995), the butterfly approach (Wu et al., 1997), and the iterative re-engineering approach (Bianchi, Caivano, Marengo, & Vissagio, 2003). Some authors also provide methods fostering the clear separation between the system part and the knowledge base part, in order to maximize reusability (Gachet & Haettenschwiler, 2005). On the other hand, some DSS are smaller systems used to deal with very specific—and sometimes unique—problems, that do not go past the prototyping stage, that require minimal finances, and use a time-limited knowledge base. Maintenance and legacy issues are less salient for these systems and their development follows a different process.

We describe in the coming sections of this article a unifying approach to DSS development allowing DSS designers to explicitly take these contextual aspects into considerations in order to guide the development process of a DSS. This new approach is based on the concept of value-based software engineering.

VALUE-BASED SOFTWARE ENGINEERING

Suggesting that the DSS community never considered the context of a DSS prior to its development would be unfair. Several authors acknowledge that a systems design process must be specifically related to the operational environment for which the final system is intended (Sage, 1991; Wallace et al., 1987). For example, Sprague and Carlson (1982) explicitly specified in their "DSS action plan" a phase consisting of steps to develop the DSS environment. The purpose of this phase is to "form the DSS group, articulate its mission, and define its relationships with other organizational units. Establish a minimal set of tools and data and operationalize them." (p. 68). Nevertheless, how these tasks should be carried out is not specified. In this section, we propose an approach allowing DSS designers to model contextual value propositions and perform feedback control of a DSS project. This approach is inspired by the concept of value-based software engineering (Boehm & Guo Huang, 2003).

Two frequently used techniques in value-based software engineering are the benefits realization approach

Context in Decision Support Systems Development

Figure 1. Benefits-realization approach results chain (adapted from Boehm & Guo Huang, 2003)

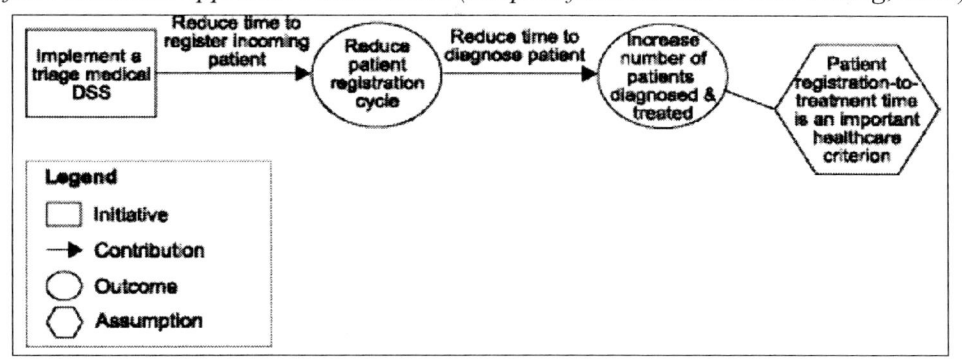

Figure 2. The realization feedback process (adapted from Boehm & Huo Huang, 2003)

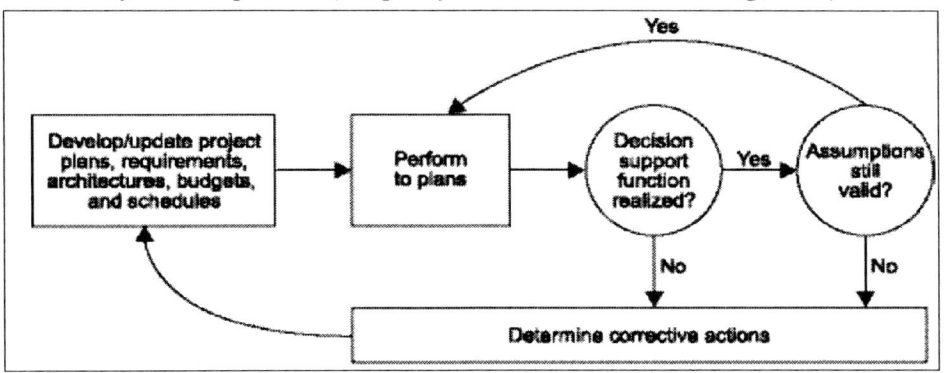

and the value-realization feedback process. The benefits realization approach (Thorp, 2003) allows developers to determine and reconcile the value propositions of the project's success-critical stakeholders. The centerpiece of this approach is the results chain (Figure 1). This chain establishes a framework linking initiatives that consume resources, such as implementing a new DSS, to contributions (describing the effects of the delivered system on existing operations) and outcomes (which can lead either to further contributions or to added value, such as increased profit). A results chain links to goal assumptions, which condition the realization of outcomes. Once the stakeholders agree on the initiatives of the final results chain, "they can elaborate them into project plans, requirements, architectures, budgets, and schedules." (Boehm & Guo Huang, 2003, p. 36)

Once the benefits-realization approach is completed, stakeholders can monitor the development of the project using the value-realization feedback process (Figure 2). As explained by Boehm and Guo Huang (2003):

The results chain, business case, and program plans set the baseline in terms of expected time-phased costs, benefit flows, returns on investment, and underlying assumptions. As the projects and program perform to plans, the actual or projected achievement of the cost and benefit flows and the assumptions' realism may become invalid, at which point the project team will need to determine and apply corrective actions by changing plans or initiatives, making associated changes in expected cost and benefit flows. (p. 37)

One obvious advantage of this feedback process is its ongoing consideration of the goal assumptions' validity. The development of an organizational DSS can take time and the project's plan can change several times during the whole process. It is therefore important to regularly monitor the process to be sure that the system still meets the local needs and helps answer the right questions (the popular "do the right thing" proposition). Otherwise, a DSS can be seen as very successful in terms of cost oriented earned value, but a complete disaster in terms of actual organizational value. The feedback process used in value-based software engineering focuses on value realization. Assessing the value of a transaction information system is a difficult task (Tillquist & Rodgers, 2005). However, assessing the value of a DSS is even more difficult, since its main function (supporting decision-makers) leads to effects that are very difficult to measure in isolation from the complementary processes and activities in which the DSS is embedded. Even worse, measuring the value of a DSS during its development is almost impossible. Therefore, the feedback process that we propose in Figure 2 focuses more of the realization of the decision support function of the DSS ("do the thing right") rather than on an objective measure of value realization. Another advantage of this process is that it clearly identifies the design and implementation feedback cycles of a DSS project. First, the upper loop where the two questions are answered positively represents the implementation cycle during which the DSS is gradually built by the DSS builder according to design plans. Second, the lower loop where either one of the two questions is answered negatively represents the design feedback cycle, during which the DSS design must be overhauled by the DSS designer to make sure that the DSS will "do the right thing right." This clear identification of both cycles is important because it overcomes a problem found in many DSS development processes that make an abundant use of feedback loops between their various phases, but fails to explain how the DSS designer and builder can go back to a previous stage in case of a goal failure at a later stage. Finally, another advantage of this feedback process is that it emphasizes the fact that context is not simply a state, but part of a process: "it is not sufficient for the system to behave correctly at a given instant: it must behave correctly during the process in which users are involved" (Coutaz, Crowley, Dobson, & Garlan, 2005, p. 50). Even though Coutaz et al. (2005) are mostly interested in the context of a system in use, we argue that the statement remains valid for the entire development process of a system.

Figure 3. Extended results chain for a triage medical DSS. Stakeholders and contextual information are explicitly considered

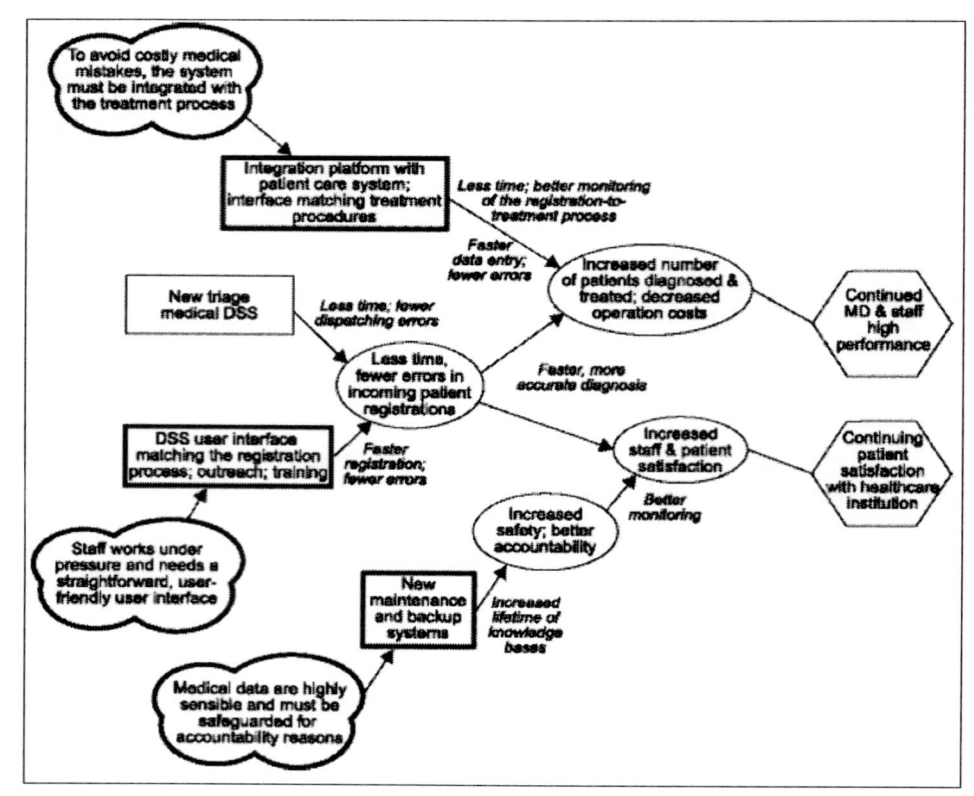

Modeling the context-based development of a DSS consists in defining the initiatives, contributions, outcomes, and goal assumptions of a results chain. For the purpose of this article, Figure 3 uses the example scenario of a medical DSS for the triage of patients in an emergency room and extends the results chain of Figure 1 by adding new initiatives explicitly dealing with the two issues we mentioned in Section 2, namely the user interface and the maintenance and legacy issues. A third issue, integration with the patient care system, is also considered. These additional initiatives are shown with bold borders. Needless to say, a realistic and complete results chain for a triage medical DSS would be much more complicated than Figure 3, with many more initiatives, outcomes, and goal assumptions related to other value propositions. For the sake of simplicity, however, we decided to limit the scope of the results chain in order to improve its readability. The ultimate purpose of the figure is to show how the benefits realization approach allows DSS designers to dynamically identify the project's success-critical stakeholders and to determine their propositions in terms of decision support.

Figure 3 also introduces a new kind of symbol, graphically represented as a cloud, which identifies contextual requirements. A contextual requirement is defined as a specification of a contextual imperative. The three contextual requirements of Figure 3 describe three imperatives related to the DSS integration with the rest of the patient care system, the DSS user interface, and the DSS maintenance, respectively.

Contextual requirements adequately supplement functional requirements. Traditional techniques to capture functional requirements (for example, UML use case diagrams in the object-oriented community at large) focus on describing how to achieve business goals or tasks. As such, they help define the inner environment of the target system. Defining the inner environment of the system, however, is only one part of the design phase. The DSS designer also needs to define the conditions for goal attainment, which are determined by the outer environment of the system. This is where contextual requirements come into play. The importance of contextual requirements to model the outer environment of the DSS can not be overemphasized. As Simon (1996) indicates, "in very many cases whether a particular system will achieve a particular goal of adaptation depends on only a few characteristics of the outer environment" (p. 11). For example, our example triage DSS is most likely to fail, independently from its intrinsic qualities (the inner environment), if it does not consider the working conditions of the medical staff, the sensitivity of medical data, and the tremendous risk associated with medical mistakes (three characteristics of the outer environment).

Obviously enough, functional requirements are driven by the contextual requirements. For example, the first contextual requirement in Figure 3 (in the top left corner) considers the legal environment of the system (medical mistakes can lead to costly malpractice lawsuits) and indicates how important it becomes to tightly integrate the triage DSS with the rest of the patient care system, to ensure patients are being given the drugs corresponding to the diagnosis. This integration also leads to an increased number of patients diagnosed and treated and keeps up the performance of the medical staff. Based on this contextual requirement, the DSS builder can derive a set of functional requirements to attain this integration goal.

The second contextual requirement in the results chain (in the middle left part of Figure 3) explicitly considers the work environment of the medical staff and shows that MDs, nurses, staff, and patients are considered as important stakeholders in the initiatives. Their satisfaction and acceptance of the new system are deemed critical for the DSS success and depend on a straightforward, user-friendly user interface. Expected outcomes such as the increased staff and patient satisfaction, or initiatives focusing on user and system interfaces acknowledge this fact.

Finally, the initiative to include maintenance and backup systems because medical data are highly sensible (last contextual requirement in Figure 3) illustrates the necessity to safeguard the data and knowledge bases of the entire infrastructure, for increased safety and better accountability.

With DSS more than with any other kind of IS, working on functional requirements that are not driven by contextual requirements is like shooting in the dark. You may end up with a great functionality from a technical point of view, but still be completely off target in the context of the target system. In short, contextual requirements are used by the DSS designer to define the outer environment of the system, which determines the conditions for goal attainment. Contextual requirements drive the functional requirements used by the

DSS builder to define an inner environment capable to achieve these goals.

Once the contextual requirements and the initiatives of the results chain are set, the DSS designer can turn them into plans, architectures, budgets, and schedules. At that stage, traditional DSS development processes and methodologies (see the section on Key Terms for examples) can be used with a context-based flavor. Instead of focusing on traditional performance issues, the context-aware DSS designer can focus on the most salient and relevant aspects of the target system. In our example DSS for medical triage, the requirements specification phase should focus on user interface requirements (to guarantee the system acceptability) and on data integration and workflow activities (to prepare a smooth integration with the global patient care system). Maintenance and backup considerations are traditionally postponed until the last step of the process (operational deployment). In our example, however, we clearly identified maintenance and backup as critical value propositions for the DSS. Therefore, it is wise to move the corresponding requirements to the first step of the process. Traditional methodologies defined in the Key Terms section, such as functional mapping (Blanning, 1979), decision graph (Martin, 1982), and descriptive and normative modeling (Stabell, 1983), can be used to identify functional requirements specifications.

CONCLUSION

In this article, we have described a unifying approach to formalizing the notion of context in the study of DSS development. The proposed solution relies on the concepts of value-based software engineering and contextual requirements. It provides DSS designers and builders with the appropriate techniques to explicitly consider the context of the target DSS during the entire development process.

The first technique is the benefits realization approach, which uses diagrams called results chains to determine and reconcile the value propositions of the project's success-critical stakeholders. The results chain establishes a framework linking contextual requirements to initiatives, contributions, and outcomes. The results chain also links to goal assumptions, which condition the realization of outcomes.

The second technique is the realization feedback process, which regularly monitors the realization of the expected decision support functionalities and the validity of the goal assumptions. If the decision support functionalities are not realized, or the assumptions' realism becomes invalid, the DSS designers need to determine and apply corrective actions by changing plans or initiatives.

Contextual requirements are used by the DSS designer to define the outer environment of the system, which determines the conditions for goal attainment. Contextual requirements then drive the functional requirements used by the DSS builder to define an inner environment capable of achieving these goals.

We provided an example to illustrate how a somewhat impractical, context-free DSS development life cycle can be turned into a context-based life cycle focusing on the most success-critical aspects of the target DSS, without overwhelming the DSS designers with long checklists that are not necessarily relevant in the context of the target system.

The inability of the DSS community to come up with unified and standardized methods to develop decision support systems is a recurring topic that has kept researchers and practitioners busy for the past three decades. We strongly believe that our approach finds a partial answer to the problem by explicitly acknowledging the fact that DSS can be widely different in their goals, scope, depth, lifetime, and costs. Rather than looking for an elusive context-free, one-size-fits-all solution, we propose a context-based set of tools able to formalize the DSS environment and context before choosing the appropriate development methodology. It is not our intention to define yet another solution in the existing proliferation of processes and methodologies for DSS development. Quite the opposite, we believe that our approach can help the field of DSS development enter in a formalization, or control, stage. Finally, it is our hope that the approach described in this article provides a vehicle for researchers and practitioners to develop better and more successful DSS.

REFERENCES

Arinze, B. (1991). A contigency model of DSS development methodology. *Journal of Management Information Systems, 8*(1), 149-166.

Bateman, A., & Murphy, J. (1994). *Migration of legacy systems*. Dublin City University, Dublin, Ireland: School of Computer Applications.

Bianchi, A., Caivano, D., Marengo, V., & Vissagio, G. (2003, March). Iterative reengineering of legacy systems. *IEEE Transactions on Software Engineering, 29*(3), 225-241.

Blanning, R. W. (1979, September). The functions of a decision support system. *Information and Management, 3,* 71-96.

Boehm, B., & Guo Huan, L. (2003). Value-based software engineering: A case study. *Computer, 36*(3), 33-41.

Brodie, M., & Stonebraker, M. (1995). *Migrating legacy systems: Gateways, interfaces and the incremental approach.* San Francisco: Morgan Kaufmann Publishers Inc.

Burback, R. L. (1997). *Software engineering methodology: The WaterSluice.* University of Stanford, Database Group. Retrieved December 16, 2007, http://wwwdb.stanford.edu/~burback/water_sluice/sluice6.25.97/ws/watersluice.html

Comella-Dorda, S., Wallnau, K., Seacord, R. C., & Roberts, J. (2000, April). *A survey of legacy modernisation approaches* (pp. 1-20). Carnegie Mellon University, Software Engineering Institute.

Courbon, J.-C., Drageof, J., & Tomasi, J. (1979). L'approche évolutive. Informatique et Gestion 103 (Janvier-Février).

Coutaz, J., Crowley, J. L., Dobson, S., & Garlan, D. (2005). Context is key. *Communications of the ACM, 48*(3), 49-53.

Finlay, P. N. (1994). *Introducing decision support systems.* Oxford, UK, Cambridge, MA: NCC Blackwell; Blackwell Publishers.

Gachet, A., & Haettenschwiler, P. (2005). Development processes of intelligent decision making support systems: Review and perspective. In J. Gupta, G. Forgionne & M. Mora (Eds.), *Intelligent decision-making support systems (I-DMSS): Foundations, applications and challenges.* London: Springer-Verlag.

Gibson, C., & Nolan, R. (1974). Managing the four stages of EDP growth. In P. Gray, W. King, E. McLean & H. Watson (Eds.), *MoIS: Management of information systems*. Forth Worth, TX: The Dryden Press.

Holzinger, A. (2005). Usability engineering methods for software developers. *Communications of the ACM, 48*(1), 71-74.

Keen, P. G. W., & Scott Morton, M. S. (1978). *Decision support systems: An organizational perspective.* Reading, MA: Addison-Wesley Publishing Company.

Marakas, G. M. (2003). *Decision support systems in the 21st century.* Upper Saddle River, NJ: Prentice Hall.

Martin, M. P. (1982, December). Determining information requirements for DSS. *Journal of Systems Management,* 14-21.

Nolan, R. (1979). Managing the crises in data processing. *Harvard Business Review, 57*(2), 115-126.

Paulk, M. C. (1998). The capability maturity model for software, Version 1.1. Software Engineering Institute, Carnegie Mellon University. Retrieved December 13, 2007, from ftp://ftp.sei.cmu.edu/pub/cmm/cmm-over.pdf

Power, D. J. (2002). *Decision support systems: Concepts and resources for managers.* Westport, CT: Quorum Books.

Sage, A. P. (1991). *Decision support systems engineering.* New York: Wiley.

Saxena, K. B. C. (1991). Decision support engineering: A DSS development methodology. In *24th Annual Hawaii International Conference on System Sciences (HICSS'91),* Los Alamitos, CA. IEEE Computer Society Press.

Saxena, K. B. C. (1992). DSS development methodologies: A comparative review. In *25th Annual Hawaii International Conference on System Sciences (HICSS'92),* Los Alamitos, CA. IEEE Computer Society Press.

Simon, H. A. (1996). *The sciences of the artificial.* Cambridge, MA: MIT Press.

Sprague, R. H., Jr., (1980, December). A framework for the development of decision support systems. *Management Information Systems Quarterly, 4*(4), 1-26.

Sprague, R. H., & Carlson, E. D. (1982). *Building effective decision support systems.* Englewood Cliffs, NJ: Prentice-Hall.

Stabell, C. B. (1983). A decision-oriented approach to building DSS. In J. L. Bennett (Ed.), *Building decision support systems* (pp. 221-260). Reading, MA: Addison-Wesley.

Thomas, C., & Bevan, N. (1996). *Usability context analysis: A practical guide*. Teddington, UK: National Physical Laboratory.

Thorp, J. (2003). *The information paradox: Realizing the business benefits of information technology*. Toronto, ON: McGraw-Hill Ryerson.

Tillquist, J., & Rodgers, W. (2005). Using asset specificity and asset scope to measure the value of IT. *Communications of the ACM, 48*(1), 75-80.

Turban, E. (1995). *Decision support and expert systems: Management support systems*. Englewood Cliffs, NJ: Prentice Hall.

Vaishnavi, V., & Kuechler, W. (2004). *Design research in information systems*. Retrieved December 13, 2007, from http://www.isworld.org/Researchdesign/drisISworld.htm

Wallace, R. H., Stockenberg, J. E., & Charette, R. N. (1987). *A unified methodology for developing systems*. New York, NY: Intertext Publications, McGraw-Hill.

Wu, B., Lawless, D., Bisbal, J., Richardson, R., Grimson, J., Wade, V. et al. (1997). The butterfly methodology: A gateway free approach for migrating legacy information systems. In *Proceedings of the ICECCS97*, Villa Olmo: Italy.

KEY TERMS

Design Cycle: DSS development methodology introduced by Keen and Scott Morton in 1978 (Keen & Scott Morton, 1978) which can be considered as the ancestor of most of the other DSS development processes and as an authoritative model. The global cycle is made of several steps focusing both on the decision support functionalities and their implementation in the actual system.

Decision Graph: DSS development methodology introduced by Martin in 1982 (Martin, 1982) as a modification of the descriptive system dynamics model. The methodology emphasizes graphic rather than computer simulation results, changes terminology from an engineering to a decision oriented context, and allows the use of a standard computer template. The methodology is purely graphical and uses symbols inspired by system dynamics structures. Decision graphs are used to create the decision model, with the purpose of identifying pertinent decisions.

Decision-Oriented DSS Development Process: DSS development process introduced by Stabell in 1983 (Stabell, 1983) in reaction to the technocentric, system oriented development methodologies proposed at the beginning of the 1980s. The development process relies on interrelated activities collectively labelled decision research. Emphasis in this decision-oriented, normative methodology is placed on changing the existing decision process to increase decision-making effectiveness.

Decision Support Engineering: DSS development methodology proposed by Saxena (1991) as a comprehensive methodology based on a life cycle model of DSS development, which encompasses an engineering approach to DSS analysis and design. Prototyping is also an important part of the methodology.

DSS Development Phases: DSS development methodology proposed by Sprague and Carlson in 1982 (Sprague & Carlson, 1982). The methodology can be broken down into two broad parts: an action plan and the ROMC methodology, a processing dependent model for organizing and conducting systems analysis in DSS.

DSS Prototyping (also known as evolutive approach): DSS development methodology defined by Courbon in 1979 (Courbon et al., 1979, 1980) as a methodology based on the progressive design of a DSS, going through multiple short-as-possible cycles in which successive versions of the system under construction are utilized by the end-user.

DSS Design and Development Life Cycle: DSS design and development methodology proposed by Sage in 1991 (Sage, 1991) as a phased life-cycle approach to DSS engineering. Its basic structure is very close to the software development life cycle (SDLC) methodology. However, it tries to avoid the drawbacks of the SDLC by embedding explicit feedback loops in the sequential life cycle and by promoting prototyping during system implementation in order to meet the iterative requirements of a DSS development process.

End-User DSS Development: Refers to people developing decision support applications for themselves or for others even though they are not trained IS professionals.

Functional Mapping (sometimes referred to as functional category analysis): DSS development methodology introduced by Blanning in 1979 (Blanning, 1979) as a DSS design approach mapping the functions of a DSS with the organizational units of the company. The methodology clearly identifies the responsibilities and/or benefits of the various organizational units vis-a-vis the DSS.

Contextualization in Decision Making and Decision Support

Patrick Brézillon
University Paris 6, France
Université Pierre et Marie Curie, France

Jean-Charles Pomerol
Université Pierre et Marie Curie, France

INTRODUCTION

Decision makers face a very large number of heterogeneous contextual cues; some of these pieces are always relevant (time period, unpredicted event, etc.), but others are only used in some cases (an accompanying person in the car, etc.). Actors then must deal with a set of heterogeneous and incomplete information on the problem-solving state to make their decisions. As a consequence, a variety of strategies are observed, including those involving an actor to another one, but also for the same actor according to the moment. It is not obvious how to get a comprehensive view of the mental representations at work in a person's brain during many human tasks, and the argumentation rather than the explicit decision proposal is crucial (Forslund, 1995): It is better to store advantages and disadvantages rather than the final decisions for representing decision making.

Procedures are diagnosis or action plans elaborated by the enterprise (Brézillon, Pomerol, & Pasquier, 2003; Pomerol, Brézillon, & Pasquier, 2002). Diagnosis and actions constitute a continuous interlocked process, not two distinct and successive phases. Actions introduce changes in the situation or in the knowledge about the situation, and imply a revision of the diagnosis, and thus of the decision-making process itself. As a consequence, actors prefer to adapt procedures to reality in order to deal with the richness of the situation. The actor establishes a practice that is based on procedures and a set of contextual cues depending on the actor's experience and situation characteristics. Practice results from a kind of contextualization of a procedure in which knowledge pieces and contextual cues are structured together in comprehensive knowledge about actions.

Modeling actors' reasoning through practices is a difficult task because a number of contextual elements are used. We propose in this article a formalism for an experience-based representation called contextual graphs for dealing with practices.

BACKGROUND

Context has played an important role for a long time in domains where reasoning must intervene, such as in decision making, understanding, interpretation, diagnosis, and so forth. This activity relies heavily on background or experience that is generally not made explicit but gives an enriched contextual dimension to the reasoning and the knowledge used. Context is always relative to the focus (the context of the reasoning, the context of an action, the context of an object, etc.) and gives meaning to items related to the focus. Thus, on the one hand, context guides the focus of attention, that is, the subset of common ground that is pertinent to the current task. On the other hand, the focus allows identifying the relevant elements to consider in the context. It specifies what must be contextual knowledge and external knowledge in the context at a given step of decision making. The focus evolves with the actions executed along the decision-making process, and its context also presents dynamics (some external events may also modify the context of the focus): Focus and its context are interlocked.

In reference to focus, Brézillon and Pomerol (1999) consider context as the sum of two types of knowledge. There is the part of the context that is relevant at this step of decision making, and the other part that is not relevant. The latter part is called external knowledge. External knowledge appears in different sources, such as the knowledge known by the decision maker but left implicit with respect to the current focus, the knowledge unknown to the decision maker (out of his competence), contextual knowledge of other actors in a team, and so forth. The former part is called contextual knowledge and obviously depends on the decision maker and on the decision at hand. Here, the focus acts as a discriminating factor between the external and contextual knowledge. However, the frontier between external and contextual knowledge is porous and moves with the progress of the focus and eventually with an unpredicted event.

A subset of the contextual knowledge is chosen and proceduralized for addressing specifically the current focus. We call it the proceduralized context. The proceduralized context is invoked, assembled, organized, structured, and situated according to the given focus and is common to the various people involved in decision making. A proceduralized context is quite similar, in the spirit, to the chunk of knowledge discussed in SOAR (Laird, Newell, & Rosenbloom, 1987). In a distinction reminiscent to cognitive ergonomics (Leplat & Hoc, 1983), we could say that the contextual knowledge is useful to identify the activity whereas the proceduralized context is relevant to characterize the task at hand (i.e., concerned by the activity).

An important point is the passage of elements from contextual knowledge to a proceduralized context. This is a proceduralization process that depends on the focus on a task and is task oriented just as the know-how and is often triggered by an event or primed by the recognition of a pattern. In its building view, the proceduralized context is similar to Clancey's view (1992) on diagnosis as the building of a situation-specific model. This proceduralization process provides a consistent explanatory framework to anticipate the results of a decision or an action. This consistency is obtained by reasoning about causes and consequences and particularly their relationships in a given situation. Thus, we can separate the reasoning between diagnosing the real context and anticipating the follow-up (Pomerol, 1997).

A second type of proceduralization is the instantiation of contextual elements (see also Grimshaw, Mott, & Roberts, 1997, for a similar observation). This means that the contextual knowledge or background knowledge needs some further specifications to perfectly fit the decision making at hand. For each instantiation of a contextual element, a particular action (e.g., a specific method for a task realization) will be executed. Once the corresponding action is executed, the instantiation does not matter anymore and the contextual element leaves the proceduralized context and goes back in the contextual knowledge. For example, arriving at a crossroad, a driver looks at the traffic light. If it is the green signal, then the driver will decide to cross. The instantiation of the contextual element *traffic light* (green signal) has guided the decision-making process and then the decision is made. The color of the traffic light does not matter after the decision is made (and this could be a problem if the light turns yellow immediately). We call this type of proceduralization by instantiation a contextualization process.

MAIN FOCUS OF THE ARTICLE

In this article, we present contextual graphs, a context-based formalism for representing reasoning. Contextual graphs are used in a large spectrum of domains such as decision support, medicine, ergonomics, psychology, army, information retrieval, computer security, road safety, and so forth.

A contextual graph proposes a representation of a problem-solving instance by a combination of diagnoses and actions as evoked in the introduction. Contextual nodes represent diagnoses. When a contextual node is encountered, an element of the situation is analyzed, and the value of the contextual element, its instantiation, is taken into account in the decision-making process. Thus, contextual graphs allow a wide category of diagnoses and action representations for a given problem-solving situation.

Contextual graphs are acyclic due to the time-directed representation and guarantees algorithm termination. Each contextual graph (and any subgraphs in it) has exactly one root and one end node because the decision-making process starts in a state of affairs and ends in another state of affairs (not necessarily with a unique solution for all the paths), and the branches express only different contextual-dependent ways to achieve this goal (i.e., different processes of contextualization). A path represents a practice developed by an actor, and there are as many paths as practices known by the system. Figure 1 gives the example of how to buy a subway ticket in Paris, on which we are working. This contextual graph represents the experience of persons living (and working) in Paris, a kind of expert for this problem solving. We develop also contextual graphs for tourists on the same problem solving (different types of novice) coming into Paris regularly or for the first time in order to compare the different graphs.

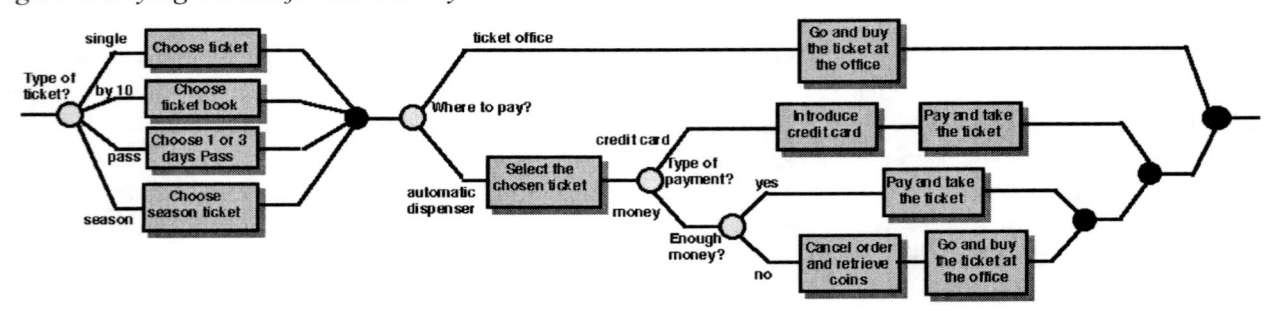

Figure 1. Buying a ticket for the subway in Paris

Elements of a contextual graph are actions, contextual elements, subgraphs, activities, and parallel action groupings (Brézillon, 2005). An action (rectangles in Figure 1) is the building block of contextual graphs. A contextual element is a pair of nodes, a contextual node (large circles in Figure 1), and a recombination node (small circles in Figure 1); a contextual node has one input and N outputs (branches) corresponding to the N instantiations of the contextual element. The recombination node is [N, 1] and represents the moment at which the instantiation of the contextual element does not matter anymore. Subgraphs are themselves contextual graphs. They are mainly used for obtaining different displays of the contextual graph by aggregation and expansion mechanisms like in Sowa's conceptual graphs (2000).

An activity is a particular subgraph that is identified by actors because it appears in different problem–solving instances. An activity is defined in terms of the actor, situation, task, and a set of actions. More precisely, an activity is a sequence of actions executed, in a given situation, for achieving a particular task that is to be accomplished by a given actor. In the decision-making area, an activity is identified by actors as a recurring structure in problem solving.

A parallel action grouping expresses the fact (and reduces the complexity of the representation) that a decision-making process must cross several subgraphs before continuing, but the order in which subgraphs are crossed is not important; they could even be crossed in parallel. The parallel action grouping could be considered like a kind of complex context. We discuss this point hereafter.

In a contextual graph, a proceduralized context is an ordered set of instantiated contextual elements that fit into each other like a nest of dolls (Russian dolls). As a consequence, the practice development leaves first the last contextual element entered. Thus, what is important is not so much the collection of contextual elements, but the way in which they are related and ordered in a practice to allow its execution. Note that this ordering of the contextual elements depends on the practice development by an actor and cannot be obtained from a domain ontology. Thus, representations in contextual graphs are experience based.

Once used, a proceduralized context is not lost but goes into the body of contextual knowledge from which its elements are coming. It is not only the chunk of contextual knowledge that is stored, but also all the ways in which this proceduralized context has been built, the reasons behind the choices (the contextual elements considered and their instantiations), the alternatives abandoned (the instantiations not retained for the decision making at hand in a practice and the corresponding abandoned actions or other practices), and so forth. The proceduralized context is integrated in the body of contextual knowledge. This is a kind of learning that results in an accommodation process. The proceduralized context could be recalled later either as a whole (like a part of a new proceduralized context) or explained in terms of the way in which it has been built and can be reused in the new proceduralized context. This is a type of learning by structuring the contextual knowledge, and the more a person experiments, the more the person possesses available structured knowledge (i.e., chunks of contextual knowledge).

FUTURE TRENDS

By the uniform representation of elements of reasoning and of contexts, contextual graphs allow us to learn the way in which all these elements (reasoning and contexts) are assembled in a practice. Based on such a context-based representation, an intelligent system will address more directly experience building than simple knowledge building. This is why we call such systems context-based intelligent assistant systems (CIASs) and this is now our concern in our current application: a design process in road safety (Brézillon, Brézillon, & Pomerol, 2006). The objective is to develop a CIAS for supporting the self-training of car drivers, especially like apprentices, but also later in the development of their experience by contextualization of the highway code learned at car school and on the road. For such CIASs, contextual graphs allow one to develop experience-oriented knowledge bases.

Anticipatory capability is enhanced in a representation by contextual graphs because a CIAS is able to develop a reasoning more directly related to the real situation, not in a mechanical way like with a procedure. Thus, the support to an actor concerns elements of reasoning and of contexts and how all these elements are assembled in practice. An anticipatory system uses knowledge about future states to decide what action to make at the moment and to know there is no better alternative. It should be able to predict what will probably happen and alert the driver for the occurrence of a crucial or time-critical event and its consequences. An anticipatory capability supposes a simulation component in the system.

Contextual graphs bring a solution to Henninger's claim (1992, p. 24) that "you won't know what is really needed until you're in the design process" because contextual graphs include a natural process for incrementally acquiring missing knowledge and jointly learning new practices. Incremental knowledge acquisition and practice learning intervene in contexts in which the system fails, that is, when the contextual graph does not include the right practice. Gathering and using knowledge in the context of use greatly simplifies knowledge acquisition because the knowledge provided by experts is always in a specific context and is essentially a justification of the expert's judgment in that context.

By its mechanism of incremental knowledge acquisition and practice learning, contextual graphs allow one to collect all the ways for problem solving. This is the policy followed in different real-world applications like the applications for incident solving in subways (Brézillon et al., 2003; Pomerol et al., 2002) or for information retrieval (Brézillon, 2005). In our current application for the training of car drivers, we explore a new use of contextual graphs by considering the good practices provided by the highway code (behaviors of good drivers) as well as the bad practices executed by novices, bad drivers, or drivers under drug influence (Brézillon et al., 2006). The interest of storing bad practices in contextual graphs is to allow a CIAS to identify online the current (good or bad) behavior of a driver, anticipate the consequences of the scenario chosen by the driver, and propose a scenario to allow drivers to evolve.

Other variants will be considered later. We study the representation of a given situation solved by all the drivers in a unique contextual graph to focus on all the practices developed by drivers independently of their individual experience. Another approach is to represent each driver's view (and all the practices imagined by the driver in a problem-solving situation) according to his or her experience, familiarity with driving, and so forth in a particular contextual graph. Then a contextual graph corresponds to the problem-solving occurrence and the actor. All these individual contextual graphs can be then classified from the totally novice to the deeply experienced driver. As shown in Figure 1, we are testing this approach in a simple decision-making scenario involving buying a subway ticket, solved by different persons more or less knowledgeable with the subway in Paris. The two approaches would lead to, on the one hand, a view of individual evolutions in the contextualization of theoretical knowledge, and, on the other hand, a collaborative view of the driver interacting with other drivers.

There are other problems yet open on a theoretical point of view as well as a practical one. First, we point out that contextual elements considered in a contextual graph constitute a heterogeneous population that is difficult to represent in a hierarchy or an ontology. A contextual element can concern the actor (e.g., I prefer a secure solution to a risky one) but does not belong directly to the domain of application. The understanding and representation of a set of such (heterogeneous) contextual elements is a challenge. Second, a contextual element may be itself a chunk of contextual knowledge where there are more underlying basic contextual elements. For example, a contextual element such as "Must I respect the yellow traffic light?" may cover contextual (or subcontextual) elements such as "I am in a hurry," "I can go ahead before the other car," and so forth. This aspect of contextual elements is related to the onion metaphor proposed in Brézillon, Cavalcanti,

Naveiro, and Pomerol (2000). The challenge here concerns the modeling of a contextual element at a finer granularity and, maybe, by extension, a modeling of parallel action groups.

Third, the introduction of the item *parallel action grouping* simplifies the representation of contextual graphs. A parallel action grouping generally represents (as a simplification) a complex entanglement of contextual elements corresponding to a low-level of description of the problem solving modeled in the contextual graph. In the popular example of the coffee preparation given in unified modelling language (UML) manuals, it is said that we must take the coffee and the filter in one order or the other (or in parallel). However, according to the type of coffee machine (e.g., we must pull the filter apart to fill the reservoir with water), the piece of the coffee machine where we must be put the filter can be independent of the coffee machine, mobile on the coffee machine, or fixed into the coffee machine. Each situation would be considered independently, but all situations will conclude in a unique action: Put the coffee in the filter. Thus, instead of making a complicated contextual graph for representing a natural complexity due to a low level of detail, we use parallel action groupings.

Fourth, an activity is a subgraph identified by actors as a recurring structure appearing in several contextual graphs. The introduction of activities relieves the representation by contextual graphs by introducing a subcontextual graph and leads to a network of contextual graphs, that is, of problem solving. However, the most interesting observation here is the fact that the notion of activity allows simplified interaction among actors: one actor giving the name of the activity and the other actor developing the activity. For example, turning right is an activity that a car driver translates into signaling a right turn, looking to see if the following car is not too close, braking to reduce speed, looking for pedestrians crossing the other road, and so forth. However, in a theoretical plan, we will then have to deal with a network of contextual graphs, not independent units of reasoning, if we consider a contextual graph (i.e., problem solving) as a unit of reasoning.

Finally, a proceduralized context is perceived as a chunk of contextual knowledge leading to the choice of an action to execute. However, the contextual elements intervening in this proceduralized context, their instantiations, and their relationships will stay available. This leads to the possibility of generating rich explanations, and even new types of explanations like the way in which a contextual graph grows from the initial procedure to the last practice introduced.

CONCLUSION

We propose contextual graphs for a uniform representation of elements of reasoning and contextual elements at the same level. This is different from the view of Campbell and Goodman (1988; and Hendrix, 1975, before for semantic networks), who consider context as a way to partition a graph. Moreover, context in our formalism intervenes more at the level of the links between elements of reasoning than elements themselves. Using contextual elements organized in contextual graphs in the spirit of a nest of dolls, we do not have a hierarchy of context because a given contextual element is itself contextualized and can appear encompassed in other contextual elements of various nature. Contextual elements are a factor of knowledge activation and intervene more in relationships between units of reasoning than the units themselves.

A contextual graph is a kind of micro corporate memory that provides a knowledge base that is more experience oriented than goal oriented. Contextual graphs are the experience-based representations of the knowledge and reasoning needs for intelligent systems. Relying on contextual knowledge and the possibility to acquire automatically most of the contextual information, an intelligent system is able to (a) identify a user's intention, (b) simulate (in accelerated time) the execution of the user's decision to anticipate consequences, (c) compare theoretical and user behaviors, and (d) alert the user either to a wrong decision (generally by lack of the right context) or to a discrepancy in planned and effective outcomes of the decision.

Context plays a role in many types of reasoning, and notably in decision making. Making explicit the context in the representation of a decision-making process allows us to integrate incremental knowledge acquisition and practice learning as part of the process of the decision making itself. Moreover, contextual graphs offering the possibility to represent good practices as well as bad practices become a tool for learning all the ways to solve a problem in a particular situation (good and bad practices), and a tool for identifying behaviors and proposing a rational way to improve our behavior. This seems to us a first step toward an attempt to rationalize the decision-making process.

ACKNOWLEDGMENT

The work presented in this article is part of the ACC project that is supported by PREDIT GO3 and the French Minister of Transportation.

REFERENCES

Brézillon, P. (2005). Task-realization models in contextual graphs. In A. Dey, B. Kokinov, D. Leake, & R. Turner (Eds.), *Modeling and using context (CONTEXT-05)* (LNCS 3554, pp. 55-68). Springer Verlag.

Brézillon, P., Brézillon, J., & Pomerol, J.-C. (2006). Decision making at a crossroad: A negotiation of contexts. In *Proceedings of the Joint International Conference on Computing and Decision Making in Civil and Building Engineering* (pp. 2574-2583).

Brézillon, P., Cavalcanti, M., Naveiro, R., & Pomerol, J.-C. (2000). SART: An intelligent assistant for subway control. *Pesquisa Operacional, 20*(2), 247-268.

Brézillon, P., & Pomerol, J.-C. (1999). Contextual knowledge sharing and cooperation in intelligent assistant systems. *Le Travail Humain, 62*(3), 223-246.

Brézillon, P., Pomerol, J.-C., & Pasquier, L. (2003). Learning and explanation in a context-based representation: Application to incident solving on subway lines. In R. Jain, A. Abraham, C. Faucher, & J. van der Zwaag (Eds.), *Innovations in knowledge engineering: International series on advanced intelligence* (chap. 6, pp. 129-149).

Campbell, B., & Goodman, J. (1988). HAM: A general purpose hypertext abstract machine. *Communications of the ACM, 31*(7), 856-861.

Clancey, W. J. (1992). Model construction operators. *Artificial Intelligence Journal, 53*, 1-115.

Forslund, G.: Toward Cooperative Advice-Giving Systems. IEEE Expert 10(4): 56-62 (1995)

Grimshaw, D. J., Mott, P. L., & Roberts, S. A. (1997). The role of context in decision making: Some implications for database design. *European Journal of Information Systems, 6*(2), 122-128.

Hendrix, G. (1975). Expanding the utility of semantic networks through partitioning. In *Proceedings of the Fourth IJCAI* (pp. 115-121).

Henninger, S. (1992). *The knowledge acquisition trap.* Paper presented at the IEEE Workshop on Applying Artificial Intelligence to Software Problems: Assessing Promises and Pitfalls (CAIA-92), (pp. 22-31). Monterey, Canada.

Laird, J. E., Newell, A., & Rosenbloom, P. S. (1987). SOAR: An architecture for general intelligence. *Artificial Intelligence, 33*, 1-64.

Leplat, J., & Hoc, J. M. (1983). Tâche et activité dans l'analyse psychologique des situations. *Cahiers de Psychologie Cognitive, 3*, 49-63.

Pomerol, J.-C. (1997). Artificial intelligence and human decision making. *European Journal of Operational Research, 99*, 3-25.

Pomerol, J.-C., Brézillon, P., & Pasquier, L. (2002). Operational knowledge representation for practical decision making. *Journal of Management Information Systems, 18*(4), 101-116.

Sowa, J. F. (2000). *Knowledge representation: Logical, philosophical, and computational foundations.* Pacific Grove, CA: Brooks Cole Publishing Co.

KEY TERMS

Context: Context is something that constrains a focus (e.g., decision making) without intervening in it explicitly. The context is defined relatively to the focus and evolves jointly with it. The focus allows us to discriminate in the context the contextual knowledge, directly related to the focus, and the external knowledge.

Contextual Element: This is the part of the context considered by an actor more or less related to the focus and from which the actor will extract elements for building the proceduralized context. Contextual elements constitute a heterogeneous population and have not necessarily the same granularity.

Contextual Graph: It is a directed acyclic graph with one input and one output that provides a uniform representation of elements of reasoning and of contexts in problem solving. A contextual graph represents problem solving, or at least a step of it. It is triggered when an unpredicted event occurs or there is a change in a contextual element belonging to it.

Contextualization: Contextualization is the process that transforms a procedure established by the organization in a practice that integrates the specificity of the situation and context.

Experience Base: It is a collection of practices that are expressed as chunks of knowledge, reasoning, and context. A contextual graph is an element of an experience base for a given problem-solving situation. This is the (future) knowledge base of intelligent systems, which are of higher granularity than previous knowledge bases in expert systems.

Practice: Practice is the application of a procedure (established by the head of the organization) by an actor that takes into account the situation and the context in which the procedure must be applied.

Proceduralized Context: This is the part of the contextual knowledge that is assembled, organized, and structured for exploitation at the current step of the decision-making process. In a contextual graph, a proceduralized context is an ordered sequence of instantiated contextual elements whose values (i.e., instantiations) matter for choosing among several methods at a given step of problem solving.

Cooperative Decision Support Systems

Pascale Zaraté
Université de Toulouse – INPT – IRIT, France

INTRODUCTION

The subject of our research aims to support in the most suitable way the collaborative decision-making process. Several scientific approaches deal with collaborative decision-making: decision analysis (Carlsson & Turban, 2002; Doyle & Thomason, 1999; Keeney & Raiffa, 1976) developing different analytical tools for optimal decision-making; in management sciences the observation of decision-making styles activity (Nuut, 2005; Fong, Wyer, & Robert 2003); decision-making as a group work (Esser, 1998; Matta & Corby, 1997); studies concerning different types of decisions focalised on number of actors: individual (Keeney & Raiffa, 1976), group (Shim, Warkentin, Courtney, Power, Sharda, & Carlsson, 2002), cooperative (Zaraté, 2005), and collaborative (Karacapilidis & Papadias, 2001). For the collaborative decision-making field, the situation is clear. In most of research studies, the concept of collaborative decision-making is used as a synonym for cooperative decision-making. Hence, the collaborative decision-making process is considered to be distributed and asynchronous (Chim, Anumba, & Carillo, 2004; Cil, Alpturk, & Yazgan, 2005). However, we can stand out several works, having different research approaches, considering collaborative decision-making process as multi-actor decision-making process, where actors have different goals. Considering (Panzarasa, Jennings, & Norman, 2002) the collaborative decision-making process is seen as "a group of logically decentralised agents that cooperate to achieve objectives that are typically beyond the capacities of an individual agent. In short, the collaborative decision-making has generally been viewed and modelled as a kind of distributed reasoning and search, whereby a collection of agents collaboratively go throughout the search space of the problem in order to find a solution." The main interrogation of this article is to study the best way to support collaborative decision-making process.

BACKGROUND

Many studies are based upon the work of Simon (Simon, 1977). Le Moigne (1990) develops the canonical model of decision-resolution process based upon the Simon's definition of the process. The working hypothesis adopted in this study is that "the decision can be represented as a work of symbolic computation," as Simon's model. The decision-making process, considered as a cognitive process of problem solving, is constituted of four main phases: intelligence, conception, selection, and review.

We notice that there have been changes influencing decision-making process (Teulier-Bourgine & Zaraté, 2001). Decision-making in organisation is becoming more and more multi-actor and complex. We could cite the work of Gorry and Scott Morton (1971) stating that the more one organisation is complex, the less are the chances that the decision will be taken by one single actor. Therefore, participants of one decision-making process have to integrate multiples points of view that are not necessarily in harmony. Due to the rapidly changing environment, every actor involved in a decision-making process has to augment his or her own vigilance and information research. Therefore, based upon the work of Simon, we propose a revisited decision-making process. The intelligence phase is becoming more complex and more active because of the environment to be taken into account. These changes have also influenced the decision-making progress. The actors have a prominent role of research of pertinence. Before these changes, the decision-makers have to search for efficient information in order to not forget important information; they must very rapidly sort out information that is very numerous. The conception step is also more frequent because every time the context is changing, every time the decision-maker must redesign a new solution.

Figure 1. The revisited decision-making process of Simon (1977)

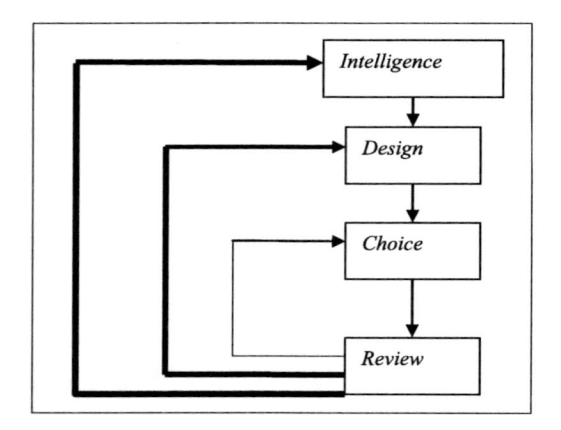

```
┌─────────────────────────┐
│  ┌──→ Intelligence      │
│  │       ↓              │
│  ├──→ Design            │
│  │       ↓              │
│  │   ┌→ Choice          │
│  │   │   ↓              │
│  └───┴─ Review          │
└─────────────────────────┘
```

The step of choice seems to stay the same because the very rapid sorting out process does not imply an alternatives generation and a systematic comparison among them and finally the choice of one of them.

The review process is then modified. As shown in Figure 1, the two first steps are visited more often than the third one. Several iterations are necessary for decision-makers before the choice by itself.

Summarising, the revisited cognitive decision making process is composed by four steps: intelligence, design, choice, and review and the two forts steps are visited very often, the decision makers must sort out the information in a very efficient may.

This process being modified, the need of new kind of decision support systems is obvious.

We present a study developing different situations of collaborative decision-making process and give an overview of different support adequate in each case. We develop a matrix of collective decision-making process taking into account two criteria: time and space.

Our purpose is to define what a collective decision making process is.

Authors consider collaborative decision-making process as a multi-agent socio-cognitive process. Thus, they incorporate beliefs, goals, desires, intentions, and preferences in what they call mental modeling. Panzarasa, Jennings et al. (2002) formalise a model giving the insight in: a) the agent's mental states and processes and b) a range of social behaviours that lead them to solicit and take part in decision-making process.

The authors also adopt a prescriptive approach in order to give a set of possible actions in every step of collaborative decision-making. The model is developed using social mental shaping, the process by which the mere social nature of agents may impact upon their mental states and motivate their behaviour. Their collaborative decision-making model consists of four phases:

1. The practical starting-point
2. Group ideas generation
3. Social practical reasoning
4. Negotiation.

This developed model, as the authors state, "aims at developing the theoretical foundation of collaborative decision-making by using a formal language." The authors do not propose a concrete help for decision makers in this process. Moreover, they consider the collaborative decision-making process in an idealised world and not to be iterative. The process is socially oriented and "captures underpinning motivations and social processes of each stage."

In order to clarify this collective decision making process, we intend to propose a typology of it according to the different situations. Decision makers could work:

- In one hand at different places or not, and
- In another hand at different times or not.

We then can find different types of collective decision making process (see Figure 2).

Collective decision making situations and the corresponding supports are defined as follows:

1. Face to face decision making: different decision makers are implied in the decisional process and meet them around a table. This is a very classical situation and it could be supported by every kind of group decision support systems (GDSSs) as well as GDSSs rooms.
2. Distributed synchronous decision making: different decision makers are implied in the decisional process and are not located in the same room but work together at the same time. This kind of situation is enough known and common in organizations and it could be supported by every

Figure 2. Collective decision making situations

	Same time	Different times
Same place	Face to face decision making	Asynchronous decision making
Different places	Distributed synchronous decision making	Distributed asynchronous decision making

kind of electronic meeting systems (EMS), videoconferences, telephone meetings, and so forth.

3. Asynchronous decision making: different decision makers are implied in the decisional process and they come in a specific room to make decisions but not at the same time. The specific room could play a role of memory for the whole process and also a virtual meeting point. This kind of situation is well known in the CSCW field and some real cases correspond to it, but for decision making it have no intrinsic meaning for a physical point of view, we cannot imagine decision made in organisation in this way: it is the reason why this case has a grey bottom in Figure 2.

4. Distributed asynchronous decision making: different decision makers are implied in the decisional process and they do not necessarily work together at the same time and in the same place; each of them give a contribution to the whole decisional process. This is a new kind of situation and decision-makers must cooperate. For this purpose cooperative decision support systems must be designed.

Summarising, for us a collective decision making process is defined as a decision making process in which several decision makers are involved that could happen in three kinds of situations: face to face, distributed synchronous, and distributed asynchronous situations.

COOPERATIVE DECISION SUPPORT SYSTEMS

Several systems have been designed for this purpose. One of them is designed by Karacapidilis and Papadias (2001) and is called the Hermes. Therefore, they develop the Hermes system as a "generic active system that efficiently captures users' rationale, stimulates knowledge elicitation, and argumentation on the issues under consideration, while it constantly (and automatically) checks for inconsistencies among users preferences and considers the whole set of argumentation items asserted to update the discourse status." In this argumentation process, Karacapilidis and Papadias (2001) present the argumentation basic elements: issues, alternatives, positions, and constraints representing preference relations.

The field of cooperative decision-making processes is mostly addressing distributed and asynchronous situation. When addressing likewise defined cooperative decision-making processes, we can state several research approaches, mostly support oriented:

- Multi-agent support systems and
- Cooperative decision support systems.

Multi-agent systems are systems constituted of different information processes that are realised at the time, that is, of different living agents, using the common resources and communicating between them.

In his work Bui and Lee (1999) defines a software agent as "a program that performs a specific task on behalf of a user, independently or with little guidance. An intelligent agent performs, reactively and/or proactively, interactive tasks tailored to a user's needs without humans or other agents telling it what to do." Researches in the field of multi-agent systems supporting decision-making processes can be illustrated by several studies:

- Bui and Lee (1999) propose a framework for building decision support systems using agent

technology. They propose taxonomy of agents' characteristics that can be used to help identify agent necessary to support different decision tasks. The authors propose a life-cycle for cooperative decision support building.
- Pinson, Louca, and Moraitis (1997) develop a general framework for building distributed decision support systems (DSDSS). The application is developed for strategic planning where "users intervene as human agents in the solution formation, and strategic knowledge and domain knowledge are distributed in different agents who communicate through various blackboards and message passing."
- Vahidov and Fazlollahi (2004) use agent technology for developing pluralistic multi-agent DSS. They develop a framework where agents are organised in groups according to the phases of the problem-solving.

As pointed out in the previous section and also by many other authors (Gachet & Haettenschwiler, 2001), the decision-making environment has changed. In order to support decision-making, the tools have to be able to support decisions in a dynamic environment that is rapidly changing and often distributed. Therefore, distributed decision support systems are defined by Gachet and Haettenschwiler (2001) as "a collection of services that are organised in a dynamic, self-managed, and self-healing federation of hard and software entities working cooperatively for supporting the solutions of semi-structured problems involving the contributions of several actors, for improved decision-making." This definition is based on several assertions:

1. A distributed DSS is not necessarily data intensive.
2. In a distributed DSS, two data units, which are not semantically related can always be physically stored in different storage devices.
3. A distributed DSS takes advantage of decentralized architectures.
4. A distributed DSS can survive on an unreliable network.
5. A distributed DSS enhances mobility.
6. A distributed DSS does not replace face-to-face meetings, it promotes and enhances them.

Other author defines collaborative decision support system (CDSS) as follows: "Collaborative decision support systems (CDSSs) are interactive computer-based systems, which facilitate the solution of ill-structured problems by a set of decision makers working together as a team." (Kreamer & King, 1998)

We find this definition very large and find it necessary to define the following architecture for these systems. Therefore, we propose a cooperative decision support framework. This framework is composed by several packages:

1. An interpersonal communication management system.
2. A task management system.
3. A knowledge management tool.
4. A dynamical man/machine interactions management tool.

This framework is described in Figure 3.

The interpersonal communication management tool is able, as in every kind of CSCW tool, to help users and decision-makers to very easily interact among themselves.

The dynamical man/machine interactions management tool guides the users in their processes of solving problems in order to solve the misunderstanding problems.

The knowledge management tool storages the previous decision made by the group or by other groups. The system proposes solutions or part of solutions to the group in very similar situations. In the case of a different situation, the system must be able to propose the solution the most appropriated and the users could accept it or not. This tool is based on a knowledge management tool and based reasoning tools.

Based on the DSSs' architecture defined by Sprague and Carlson (1982), the system includes also a data base management system, a model base management system. Nevertheless, this system is based on the development of knowledge based system and more particularly cooperative knowledge based system. Thus, the proposed system includes a knowledge base.

This tool is based on cooperative knowledge based system architecture. This cooperative knowledge based architecture is based on libraries of models: users' models, domain models (or problems models), and

Figure 3. Cooperative decision support framework architecture

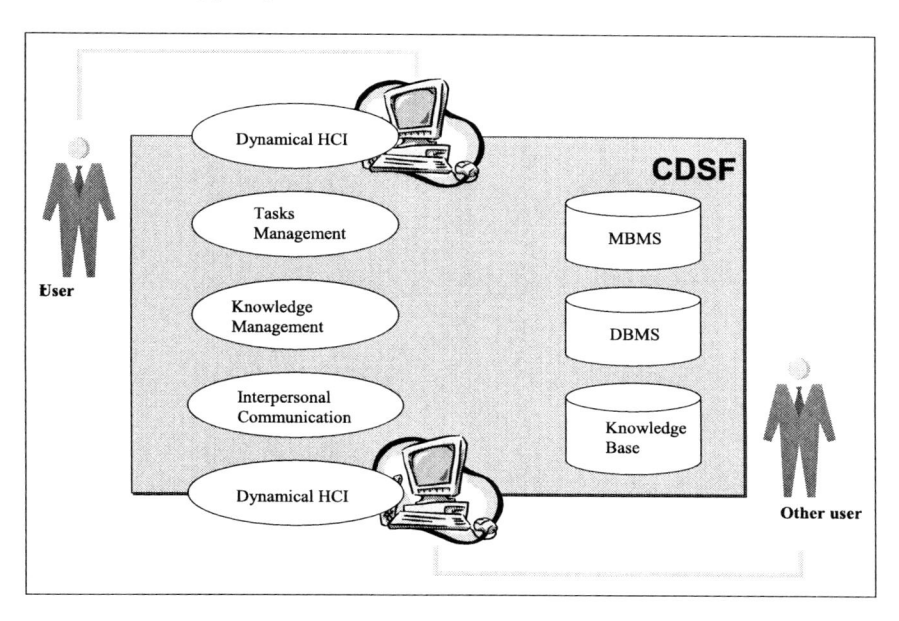

contextual models. The calculation of the proposed solutions is based on several techniques: planning tools (Camilleri, 2000), linear programming (Dargam, Gachet, Zaraté, & Barnhart, 2004). The main usage principle of this kind of tool is based on the interaction between the system and the users. The system proposes a solution to the group, the group takes in charge some tasks and then the system recalculates a new solution and proposes the new one to the group and so forth. The problem or the decision to make is solved step by step, each actor (system and users) solving parts of the problem.

The part of the system for which the development is deeper is the task management system. This tool has for objective to propose solutions or part of solutions to users. It calculates the scheduling of tasks and sub-tasks and each role that is assigned to each task. It also proposes an assignment of tasks to users or to the system itself.

FUTURE TRENDS

The cooperative decision support system is a proposal of architecture rather than a complete software package. The fundamental principle of this proposal is to support the users in an integrated approach. The main contribution of this kind of tool is the possibility given to the user to solve a part of the problem. The system must be able to dynamically react, that is, taking into account the users' answers, it must recalculate and propose a new assignment of the tasks to solve, to the different users. This is possible thanks to the interactive planning of decisions to make or tasks to realise. Nevertheless, the human confrontation stays essential for decision-making. This confrontation is possible through a solid argumentation among the decision-makers. Thus, we underline the fact that the use of this kind of tool will be efficient only if it is going with a methodology of the cooperative decision-making process management.

CONCLUSION

We have shown that the collaborative decision-making is a complex process. In order to support it, several kinds of tools are necessary depending of the king of collective situations. New kinds of systems are necessary: cooperative decision support systems. These systems are generally defined by several authors as frameworks integrating several tools. The main point of these frameworks is that the system must be able to support dynamically, decision-makers by proposing an "intelligent" assignment of tasks among the involved actors: decision-makers and software seen as agents.

REFERENCES

Bui, T., & Lee, J. (1999). An agent-based framework for building decision support systems. *Decision Support Systems, 25*(3), 225-237.

Camilleri, G. (2000). *Une approche, basée sur les plans, de la communication dans les systèmes à base de connaissances coopératifs*. Thèse de doctorat. Université Paul Sabatier, Toulouse, Décembre.

Carlsson, C., & Turban, E. (2002). DSS : directions for the next decade. *Decision Support Systems, 33*(2), 105-220.

Chim, M. Y., Anumba, C. J., & Carrillo, P. M. (2004). Internet-based collaborative decision-making system for construction. *Advances in Engineering Software, 35*(6), 357-371.

Cil, I., Alpturk, O., & Yazgan, H.R. (2005). A new collaborative system framework based on a multiple perspective approach: InteliTeam. *Decision Support Systems, 39*(4), 619-641.

Dargam, F., Gachet, A., Zaraté, P., & Barnhart, T. (2004). DSSs for planning distance education: A case study. In R. Meredith, G. Shanks, D. Arnott, & S. Carlsson (Eds), *Decision support in an uncertain and complex world* (pp. 169-179). Prato, Italie. ISBN 0 7326 2269 7.

Doyle, J., & Thomason, R. (1999). Background to qualitative decision theory. *AI Magazine, 20*(2), 55-68.

Esser, J. (1998). Alive and well after 25 years: a review of groupthink research. *Organizational Behavior and Human Decision Processes, 73*(2-3), 116-141.

Fong, C., Wyer, J., & Robert, S. (2003). Cultural, social, and emotional determinants of decisions under uncertainty. *Organizational Behavior and Human Decision Processes, 90*(2), 304-322.

Gachet, A., & Haettenschwiler, P. (2001). A decentralized approach to distributed decision support systems. *Journal of Decision Systems, 12*(2), 141-158.

Gorry, G., & Scott Morton, M. (1971). A framework for management information systems. *Sloan Management Review, 13*(1), 50-70.

Karacapidilis, N., & Papadias, D. (2001). Computer supported argumentation and collaborative decision making: the HERMES system. *Information System, 26*(4), 259-277.

Keeney, R., & Raiffa, H. (1976). *Decisions with multiple objectifs*. New York: Wiley.

Kreamer, K. L., & King, J. L. (1988). Computer based systems for cooperative work and group decision making. *ACM Computing Surveys, 20*(2), 115-146.

Le Moigne, J-L. (1990). *La modélisation des systèmes complexes*. Paris: Dunod.

Matta, N., & Corby, O. (1997). *Modèles génériques de gestion de conflits dans la conception concourante*. Paris: INRIA.

Nutt, P. (2005). Search during decision making. *European Journal of Operational Research, 160*(3), 851-876.

Panzarasa, P., Jennings, N. R., & Norman, T.J. (2002). Formalizing collaborative decision-making and practical reasoning in multi-agent systems. *Journal of Logic and Computation, 12*(1), 55-117.

Pinson, S., Louca, J., & Moraitis, P. (1997). A distributed decision support system for strategic planning. *Decision Support Systems, 20*(1), 35-51.

Shim, J. P., Warkentin, M., Courtney, J., Power, D., Sharda, R., & Carlsson, C. (2002). Past, present, and future of decision support technology. *Decision Support Systems, 33*(2), 111-126.

Simon, H. (1977). *The new science of management decision*. Englewood-Cliffs, NJ: Prentice Hall.

Sprague, R., & Carlson, E. (1982). *Building effective decision support systems*. Englewood-Cliffs, NJ: Prentice Hall.

Teulier-Bourgine, R., & Zaraté, P. (2001). Vers une problématique de l'aide à la décision utilisant les connaissances. In *Proceedings Conférence en Ingénierie des Connaissances IC'01, Grenoble*, France, (pp. 147-166).

Vahidov, R., & Fazlollahi, B. (2004). Pluralistic multi-agent decision support system: a framework and an empirical test. *Information & Management, 41*(7), 883-898.

Zaraté, P. (2005). *Des Systèmes Interactifs d'Aide à la Décision aux Systèmes Coopératifs d'Aide à la Décision: Contributions conceptuelles et fonctionnelles.* Habilitation à Diriger des Recherches. INPT.

Zaraté, P., & Soubie, J. L. (2004). An overview of supports for collective decision making. *Journal of Decision Systems, 13*(2), 211-221.

KEY TERMS

Collective Decision-Making Process: Collective decision making process is defined as a decision making process in which several decision makers are involved that could happen in three kinds of situations: face to face, distributed synchronous, and distributed asynchronous situations.

Cooperative Decision Support Systems: Is seen as a framework in which several packages are necessary for supporting in an efficient way, decision makers involved in cooperative decision making process. This framework is composed by: an interpersonal communication management system, a task management system, a knowledge management tool, and a dynamical man/machine interactions management tool.

Revisited Cognitive Decision-Making Process: Is composed by four steps: intelligence, design, choice, and review and the two forts steps are visited very often, the decision makers must sort out the information in a very efficient way.

Dashboards for Management

Werner Beuschel
Brandenburg University of Applied Sciences, Germany

INTRODUCTION

Dashboard system applications have been known in companies for several years. As the growing body of references shows, dashboards are now about to become more widespread, not only in numbers but also in terms of application areas (e.g., Eckerson, 2006; Few, 2006; Malik, 2005). The fact that almost every company is equipped with a great number of information systems, their infrastructure being largely dependent on software, supports the interest in high-level and condensed information representation. Originally, user interfaces and data representations of operational and administrative systems are not always designed for management-level use, so a need to bridge this gap develops.

Based on information technology infrastructure and forced to act in a complex and contingent environment, most organizations feel the need to create high-level overviews for managing tasks. The idea of dashboards is aimed at helping to visualize large amounts of data in a condensed representation, providing a quick overview of organizational processes and supporting managers in their decision-making tasks.

Dashboards started out to play a growing role not only in making data available in appropriate and concentrated formats, but also in representing these data in an easy-to-read display that makes reactions quick and easy. So, dashboards are increasingly used to act as mediating systems between the infrastructure technology and the need for information on decision-making levels. As an additional driver, the availability of vendor software and free software for graphical representations may contribute to growing dashboard diffusion. Finally, the ubiquity of complex systems on our own desks as day-to-day users may make us yearn for simpler representations. So, there is clearly a thrust to introduce more of these systems that deserves attention.

The article provides an introduction on dashboards and their position in the history of decision-making systems, not without pointing out the inherent problems the term as a metaphorical label for systems carries. Development issues and use factors are described and some examples are given to represent the multitude of practical solutions.

DASHBOARDS AS DECISION SUPPORT SYSTEMS FOR MANAGEMENT

Management information systems (MISs), executive information systems (EISs), and decision support systems (DSSs) were the academic fields that laid the foundations for dashboard functionalities in the 1970s (Laudon & Laudon, 2004; Marcus, 2006). The field of DSS introduced the idea that computer technology could help managers to make decisions. Increasing availability of data from all branches within an organization and use of enterprise-wide information systems provided the need as well as the base for easy-to-read information.

All functional areas in an enterprise, from manufacturing and production, finance and accounting to sales and marketing are now making use of decision support by computers. They all provide access to internal data sources that originate from the variety of systems in a company. MISs summarize and report on basic operations, while DSSs address decision problems where the solution-finding process may not be completely structured. DSSs may also incorporate external data sources, for example, from competitors or important institutions.

It is not quite clear when labeling decision support systems as dashboards started. It seems that about the mid-1990s, the term was applied to software systems (Few, 2006). It may also be a matter of definition if a decision support system is called a reporting system or a dashboard. Two examples may be quoted. The introduction of SAP/R3 in 1997 by the Nissan car manufacturing company in its Australian branch is quoted as an early success story of an EIS. Management had requests for profit analysis reports at that time. So the system was accompanied by a reporting facility that included "profit-and-loss reports, gross margin analysis, balance sheets, and wholesale and retail vehicles" (Laudon &

Laudon, 2004, p. 368). Another example of an early adopter (since 1998) and long-time user is General Electric, "where executives use dashboards to run their day-to-day operations, monitoring profits per product line and fill rates for orders" (Ante, 2006, p. 50).

Originally, a dashboard denoted a control panel of a vehicle, located below the windshield, where instruments and dials show basic functions of the engine to the driver (cf. "Digital Dashboard," n.d.). It is interesting to notice that from a current perspective, dashboards in cars and for management support are not so different as both now contain lots of software with a similar purpose: the quick overview of system-relevant data.

Characteristics of Dashboards

The literature on dashboards generally agrees on the following features:

- **Visualization:** Graphical representation of selected data
- **Selection of relevant data areas:** Information derived from and providing for key processing (or performance) indicators (KPI), their selection being dependent on specific contexts and objectives of an enterprise (or organizational unit)
- **Monitoring and interaction:** Interactive accessibility via the monitor of a computer system ("Digital Dashboards," n.d.; Eckerson, 2004; Few, 2006; Malik, 2005)

Stephen Few (2004, p. 1) provides a definition incorporating these characteristics:

A dashboard is a visual display of the most important information needed to achieve one or more objectives, consolidated and arranged on a single screen so the information can be monitored at a glance.

Visualization

All kinds of visual representations can be used as long as managers can interpret them from their task environment: alerts, summaries, bar charts, pie charts, gauges, and so forth (cf. "Digital Dashboards," n.d.). A frequently quoted example of visualization is the traffic light since it makes use of an easily understandable icon of day-to-day life that can be grasped with one glimpse. A red, yellow, or green light indicates the state of a certain area, like production numbers. This element of visualization could be compared to a minimalized version of an exception-reporting feature, known from controlling (Few, 2006). The main task is to signal positive or negative exceptions, caused by a deviance of data from given values. The goal of the visual signal is to indicate a potential need for action.

Selecting Relevant Data Areas (KPI)

Information systems for management support derive their value from representations of otherwise complex data that are permanently generated by a host of infrastructure systems in an enterprise. So a system must provide relevant data for the current state of an organization in its various units and situations. The selection of key indicators and their interpretation depends on the organizational context.

A dashboard basically follows the same intention by compressing informational complexity into simpler representations. The presentation of every detail is not important, but an appropriate condensation and visual representation so that structural properties and connections of organizational situations become visible.

From this perspective, dashboards are not systems in their own right but rather a front-end for all those complex systems an organization needs to store, process, and analyze data. On the other hand, it can be necessary for a user to reconstruct the data before interpreting a condensed representation. Thus, an important function in connection with KPIs is the drill-down capability, comparable to a looking glass allowing one to go back to a level of detail that is often buried deep in an enterprise.

Monitoring and Interaction

A dashboard can visualize large amounts of data, which were originally distributed among various software and even hardware systems, in a condensed representation. The granularity of the data and the visual form are dependent on managerial and business objectives and preferences. The reduction from mass data to comprehensive visual representation is executed by built-in algorithms. This requires quantifying and qualifying available data during the system development phases, a selection process that is highly sensitive and depending on the end user.

In case a company wants to monitor corporate performance, not all data and metrics might be in place. Models like the balanced scorecard methodology are applied in some cases to quantify data on qualitative areas (cf. Laudon & Laudon, 2004). Of course, it needs no explanation that even with a drill-down function it would not be possible to get ahead of the quantification step. This speaks for the importance of the underlying processes and models.

The time horizon a dashboard is focusing on for decision support can vary. Dashboards used in operations need a real-time database in order to deliver on real-time alerting. Dashboards for analytic purposes could also use real-time data in combination with snapshot data. They would need extensive drill-down capabilities and intelligent what-if functionality. Strategic dashboards do not require real-time access, but long-term data sets for comparison.

Application Categories

In their early years, dashboards were considered to be systems for top management. Over the past years, though, this has changed and dashboard applications can now be found throughout the firm. Dashboards are being deployed in almost all organizational areas and at all hierarchical levels. Malik (2005) provides a framework of categories for this comprehensive application view (Figure 1).

The area of classical top-level dashboards is contained in the column "Enterprise Performance." Here, the aforementioned KPIs are most difficult to identify as a high degree of data integration is needed for wide areas. Innovative areas of dashboard usage are represented in the columns of "Customer" and "Vendor." Vendor dashboards have especially found great acceptance with the supply industry as essential delivery requirements and production changes can be shown immediately (Malik, 2005).

System Development and Design Aspects

The goal of integrating a dashboard into an enterprise requires the decision to make or buy a system in the first place. Both ways are possible as there are many companies that develop their own systems as well as adapt and customize vendor solutions (Eckerson, 2006). Analyzing the literature, no clear preference for either way seems recognizable. Since a great number of dashboard vendors have established themselves over the past years, it seems reasonable to assume that customization of vendor solutions is on the rise.

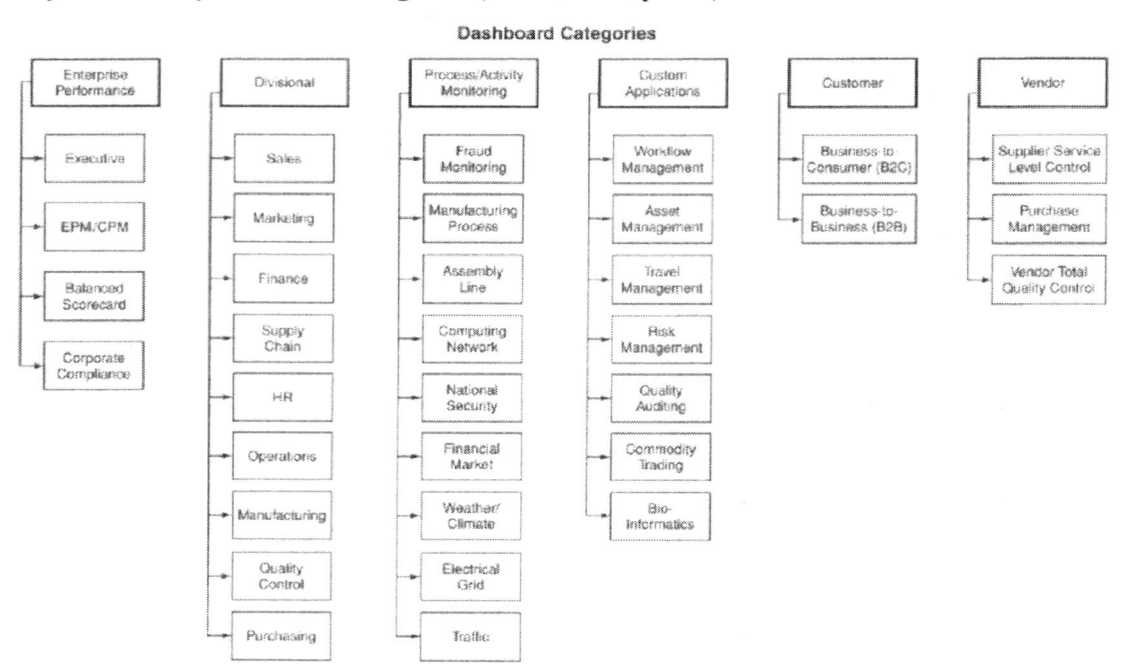

Figure 1. A framework of dashboard categories (Malik, 2005, p. 110)

The size of a company does not seem to be a critical factor for the deployment of a dashboard system. Vendor information claims that small, medium, and large companies use dashboards. According to Ante (2006), dashboard vendor NETSUIT reports to have sold 7,000 systems to small and medium companies. Forrester Research reports that 40% of large American companies use dashboards and Oracle claims to have their full sales force of 20,000 people using dashboards.

For in-house development of dashboards, experience and practice from software development methodology should apply. Participative, iterative methods of development, including prototyping, should prevail rather than the traditional waterfall model (König, 2006). In the case of dashboards, this is due to two factors.

Relevant data areas in an enterprise that need to be identified and condensed in a representation are not visible on first glimpse; the selection process requires us to go back and forth between development phases.

The selection regarding which business data are relevant should not be determined by software developers. Though developers have all the technical knowledge, it is the manager or the clerk in the office who knows best which data to use within which time frame and organizational situation.

The KPIs that lie behind the dashboard representations have to be selected carefully and with feedback after implementation. Areas where on occasion data field enlargements are required, via a looking-glass function or drill down, are dependent on the preselected data fields. If a certain data field is not available through the dashboard, there is no drill-down capability for it. According to many system development experiences, the best way to deal with such contingencies is to set up prototypes that can easily be reconfigured or redone when necessary. The usual division in must-have, should-have, and nice-to-have functions, known from interface development methodology, applies here. For the design of dashboard interfaces, advice from fields like human-computer interaction (e.g., Grudin, 2006), visual display, and graphics design (e.g., Tufte, 2001) should be utilized.

Finally, as all design usually goes back and forth between implementing features and redesigning according to the needs of system users, it helps to constantly remind those involved in the design process that the ultimate goal of a dashboard is not to build the most sophisticated device, but to support managers in their complex informational environment (Knemeyer, 2003).

Risks and Problems

As with every IT application development, risks and problems can occur from an organizational as well as a technical perspective. The high-level decision aspect with all its ramifications for a business as well as the interaction of managerial and technical factors, necessary to make dashboards work in an organizational setting, make it advisable to investigate risks and problems of dashboard use at some detail. While some aspects are general, mainly those pertaining to the specifics of dashboards shall be discussed.

Generalization based on data, as it is the main purpose of dashboards, always incorporates the danger of doing away with details that might turn out to be irrelevant under regular circumstances, but most critical and important in unexpected situations. While this sounds self-evident, it seems worthwhile to be repeated here. Relying on the data representations of a system might make a manager forget that the real value items in a company, a production system, or a customer relationship are something else than data. So, the advice to dashboard users is not to mistake the system for full reality and always to keep contact with the shop floor: "Management by walking around," as an article puts it in *Business Week* (Ante, 2006, p. 49).

A problem in the context of introducing a dashboard system might occur with workers and employees who feel alienated by real or perceived permanent control and surveillance. There is no general remedy as the individual and formal prerequisites of capturing and processing personal data differ in countries as well as in organizations. However, it should be in the best interest of a company to inform people about system features and objectives and assure alignment with company goals of educating and motivating its workforce.

It has already been emphasized that the selection of KPIs at the start of a system development is a crucial step. If the KPIs are not apt to represent important business processes, which possibly shows only in final test trials or even later during use, misguided decisions and mismanagement are likely to be the consequence. If false information is not owed to flawed algorithms in the system, only going back to the first phase and reselecting the KPI can help.

Time plays an important role in decision making. The time horizon of dashboard functionality was mentioned earlier. Marcus (2006) discusses short-term vs. long-term orientation in dashboards as a culture issue, among others; but there seems to be more to it. Another time-related problem is the time horizon of data validity. Data carry a time dependency with them that is not always immediately obvious. For example, a customer address has a different time horizon than a ticker value from a stock exchange. So, analyzing geographical changes in a customer database requires a different approach than following the stock value on a real-time basis. These aspects are usually implicitly incorporated in the algorithms, decisive for presenting an analysis or a summary on the dashboard. If the time frame chosen for the data to be processed is either too narrow or too wide, the consequence may be bad decision making (König, 2006).

Few (2005), in his basic critique on dashboard design promoted as cure-all by some vendors, warns of taking the metaphor of the dashboard too far. He cites examples where "visual noise" impedes the real objective of dashboards, namely, to quickly provide important information for further communication. Also, the extensive use of colors is scrutinized, as quite a large percentage of people are color blind.

Examples

Dashboard interfaces aimed at presenting business process results face endless opportunities. Without regarding their application context, it is almost impossible to provide further design hints. So the following illustrations serve mainly to provide examples of visual qualities of dashboards. The examples are also chosen to indicate that a great number of design elements and software packages are available from software companies as well as from open-source providers.

Figure 2 shows an example from the Web site Dashboardspy. The Weblog http://enterprise-dashboard.com, connected to the Web site, collects a great number of examples of business dashboards and covers a variety of up-to-date topics surrounding dashboards.

Further professional and extensive sources for design examples are the Laszlo company's Web site (http://www.laszlosystems.com/partners/support/demos/) and Componentart (http://www.componentart.com/). Apple has developed a number of "widgets" for the standardization of data representations on dashboards, so their use is confined to Mac operating systems (http://www.

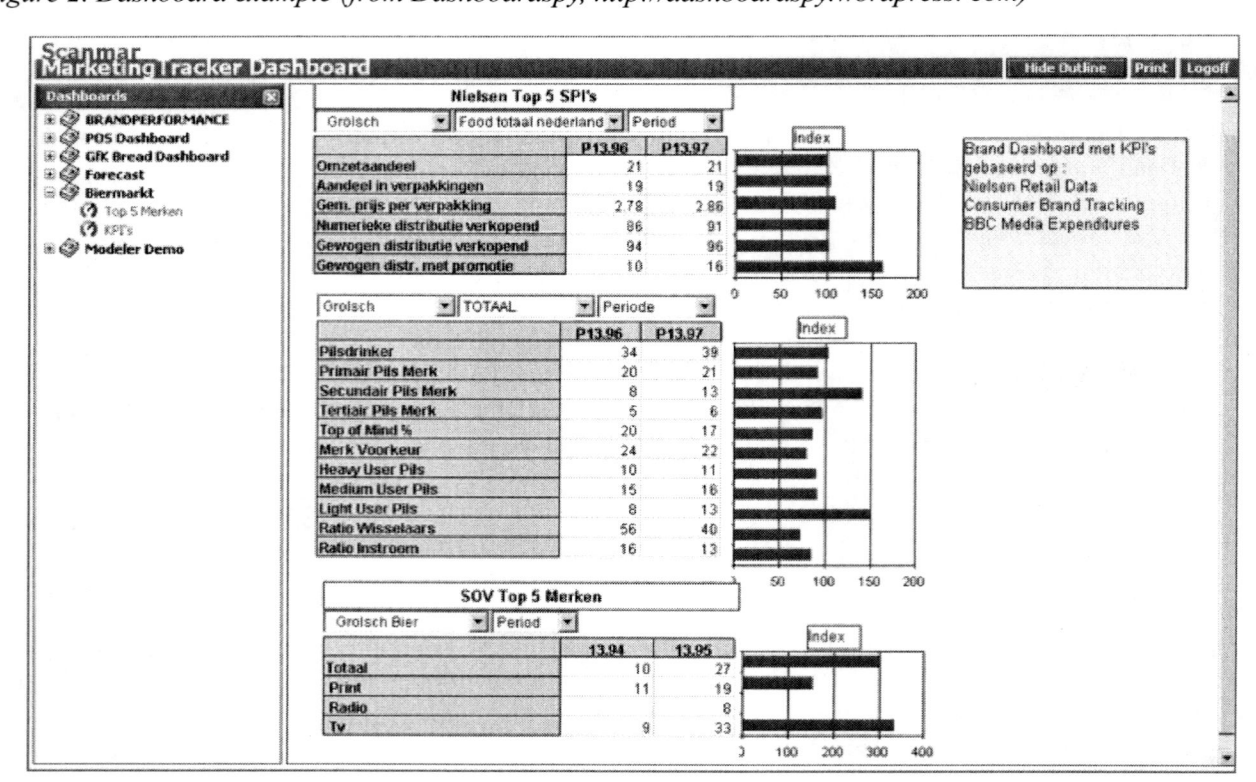

Figure 2. Dashboard example (from Dashboardspy, http://dashboardspy.wordpress. com)

Dashboards for Management

Figure 3. Dashboard widget (http://en.wikipedia.org/wiki/Image:Stocks_widget.png)

Figure 4. Dashboard of sustainability screenshot illustrating example dashboard layout (http://en.wikipedia.org/wiki/Executive_dashboard#Types_of_dashboards)

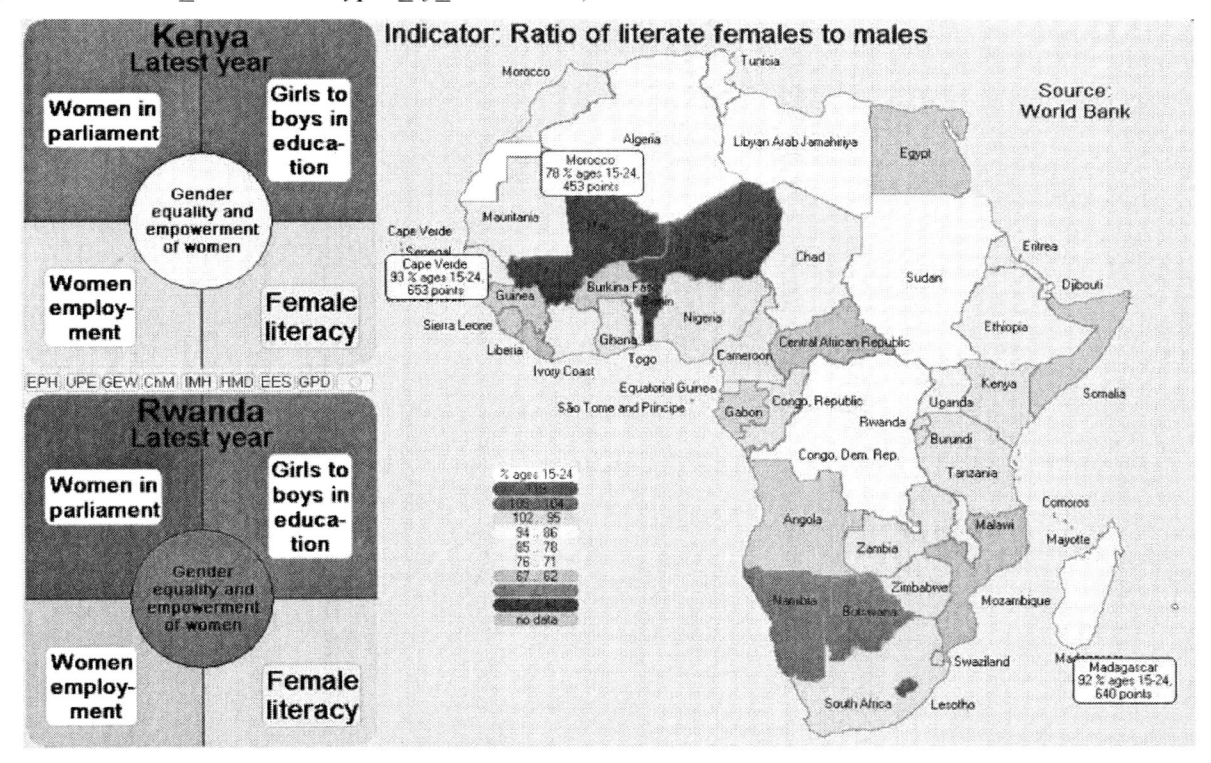

apple.com/downloads/dashboard/). Figure 3 shows a compact example of a widget for stocks.

The following example from Wikipedia (Figure 4) depicts an example of a dashboard layout. It combines various data collections and supports results by color. It was produced with a free and noncommercial software package (http://www.iisd.org/cgsdi/dashboard.asp).

FURTHER PERSPECTIVES

The current main drivers of IT in general, mobility, and networking issues can also be expected to influence dashboard developments. So the growing role of mobile devices suggests that we should devise dashboard displays adapted to small sizes (Marcus, 2006). Big companies are obviously striving to discard the current desktop metaphor as the leading design guide. It seems possible to create a mixture of one's own "versions of a favorite set of displays, gauges, latest results, latest news, etc." (Marcus, p. 49). Current industry experiments with customizable browser start pages point to the same direction. Their design is oriented on current TV screens, which more and more get filled not only by the transmitted picture, but also by icons for time, channel selection, and one or more news ticker lines. Marcus concludes, "The complexity of customization and possibly poor vendor and user-driven choices seem likely" (p. 49).

Another line of development could be characterized by increasing networking capabilities of devices and organizational processes, and an innovative form of delivery over the Internet: Web services. It is imaginable for the near future that dashboard functionality is delivered on demand over the Web (Ganesh & Anand, 2005). It remains to be seen to what degree this way of data sharing and remote service is able to meet managerial security demands and expectations on information validity. Unfortunately, there seems to be a lack of studies that observe and analyze dashboard use in its real business environment. In a similar reign, only anecdotal evidence of how dashboards are used in group decision situations is available. There seems to be a real need to investigate the development and use of dashboards with colocated as well as geographically distributed users, with an empirical focus on how decisions are reached.

SUMMARY

The subject of this article is an overview of and reflection on the role of dashboards in enterprises as decision support systems. As powerful business devices, they influence and include human, organizational, and technical aspects. From a technical viewpoint, dashboards are defined as software systems that process large amounts of carefully selected data areas and display them in condensed, at-a-glance, and easy-to-understand visual representations. By ways of interpreting the displays, managers can then communicate insights or demand for action deemed necessary to control an organizational unit or a whole business.

A critical look at dashboard functionality and examples across application areas provides reason to assume that the term is much more a metaphor geared toward the management function on all levels of an organization than a well-defined set of system functionalities.

The article reflects on aspects of terminology, history, and application areas of dashboards for business management. Examples of dashboard design and an outlook on future developments complete the picture. Special emphasis is put on development issues from a managerial aspect, taking a critical stance on potential problems inherent in dashboard development and use.

ACKNOWLEDGMENT

Reinhard C. König was very helpful on the basis of his thesis and practical work on dashboards for shaping the ideas expressed in this article.

REFERENCES

Ante, S. E. (2006, February 13). Giving the boss the big picture: A "dashboard" pulls up everything the CEO needs to run the show. *Business Week*, pp. 48-51.

Componentart. (n.d.). Retrieved August 15, 2006, from http://www.componentart.com/

Dashboardspy. (n.d.). Retrieved August 10, 2006, from http://dashboardspy.wordpress.com/

Digital dashboard. (n.d.). *Wikipedia.* Retrieved March 20, 2007, form http://en.wikipedia.org/wiki/Digital_dashboard

Eckerson, W. W. (2006). *Performance dashboards: Measuring, monitoring, and managing your business.* John Wiley & Sons, Inc.

Enterprise dashboards. (n.d.). Retrieved March 22, 2007, from http://enterprise-dashboard.com/

Few, S. (2005). Data visualization: Dashboard design. Taking a metaphor too far. *DM Review.* Retrieved from http://www.dmreview.com/article_sub.cfm?articleid=1021503

Few, S. (2006). *Information dashboard design: The effective visual communication of data.* O'Reilly Media.

Ganesh, J., & Anand, S. (2005). Web services, enterprise digital dashboards and shared data services: A proposed framework. In *Third European Conference on Web Service: ECOWS '05* (pp. 130-137). Retrieved from http.//doi.ieeecomputersociety.org/10.1109/ECOWS.2005.29

Grudin, J. (2006). Human factors, CHI, and MIS. In P. Zhang & D. Galletta (Eds.), *HCI in MIS* (Vol. 1). Foundations. M. E. Sharpe.

Knemeyer, D. (2003). *Executive dashboards: An information design approach*. Retrieved from http://www.experiencethread.com/articles/documents/article41.pdf

König, R. C. (2006). *Concept of a Web-based decision support system for upper-level management: Case study at a call center.* Unpublished master's thesis, Brandenburg University of Applied Sciences, Brandenburg, Germany.

Laudon, K. C., & Laudon, J. P. (2004). *Management information systems: Managing the digital firm* (8th ed.). Pearson Prentice Hall.

Laszlo Systems. (n.d.). Retrieved August 10, 2006, from http://www.laszlosystems.com/partners/support/demos/, accessed 08/10/2006

Malik, S. (2005). *Enterprise dashboards: Design and best practices for IT.* Wiley & Sons.

Marcus, A. (2006). Dashboards in your future. *Interactions*, pp. 48-49.

Tufte, E. R. (2001). *The visual display of quantitative information*.

Widgets. (n.d.). Retrieved March 20, 2007, from http://www.apple.com/downloads/dashboard/

KEY TERMS

Dashboard: In a horse-drawn wagon, the dashboard had to deflect mud and dirt. With the advent of the automobile, the term was used for the control panel under the windshield, containing all the important information for the driver to operate the vehicle.

Decision Support System (DSS): DSS is an academic field that laid the foundations for dashboard functionalities in the 1970s, introducing the idea that computer technology could help managers to make decisions.

Digital Dashboard: This is a business management tool used to provide a quick and concise visual overview of the status of a business enterprise through the elaboration of a more or less continuous stream of data from disparate in-house systems, interpreted as key business indicators. A dashboard can, for example, provide action information, alerts and warnings, next steps, and summaries of business conditions.

Executive Dashboard or Enterprise Dashboard: This is the same as a digital dashboard with emphasis on the decision-making and enterprise level.

Executive Information Systems (EIS): EIS is an academic field that emerged as part of the field of DSS, investigating the executive level of digital information system applications.

Key Processing Indicators or Key Performance Indicators (KPI): KPI is an undetermined variety of compressed data that are selected by the dashboard designers to represent the most relevant processes for the performance of a business unit or whole enterprise.

Drill Down: It is the functional ability in a dashboard system to present highly condensed data in more detail if necessary.

Visualization: Visualization is an important dimension in the human-machine interface of a dashboard system to show large amounts of complex data by a compact visual representation.

Widget: This term was coined by Apple Co. for a number of prefabricated tools that can be downloaded and used in the interface of a dashboard and other systems.

Data Warehousing for Decision Support

John Wang
Montclair State University, USA

James Yao
Montclair State University, USA

Qiyang Chen
Montclair State University, USA

INTRODUCTION

Today's business environment is dynamic and uncertain. Competition among business organizations is becoming more intensified and globalized. These business organizations' demand for both internal and external information is growing rapidly. This rapidly growing demand to analyze business information has quickly led to the emergence of data warehousing (Finnegan, Murphy, & O'Riordan, 1999). The strategic use of information from data warehousing assures the solution of the negative effects of many of the challenges facing organizations (Love, 1996). When the data warehousing technologies are well positioned and properly implemented, they can assist organizations in reducing business complexity, discovering ways to leverage information for new sources of competitive advantage, realizing business opportunities, and providing a high level of information readiness to respond quickly and decisively under conditions of uncertainty (Love; Park, 1997).

A data warehouse (or smaller scale data mart) is a specially prepared repository of data created to support decision making. Data are extracted from source systems, cleaned and scrubbed, transformed, and placed in data stores (Gorla, 2003). A data warehouse has data suppliers who are responsible for delivering data to the ultimate end users of the warehouse, such as analysts, operational personnel, and managers. The data suppliers make data available to end users either through structured query language (SQL) queries or custom-built decision support applications, including decision support systems (DSSs) and executive information systems (EISs).

During the mid to late 1990s, data warehousing became one of the most important developments in the information systems field. It has been estimated that about 95%t of the *Fortune 1000* companies either have a data warehouse in place or are planning to develop one (Wixon & Watson, 2001). Data warehousing is a product of business need and technological advances. Since the business environment has become more global, competitive, complex, and volatile, customer relationship management (CRM) and e-commerce initiatives are creating requirements for large, integrated data repositories and advanced analytical capabilities. More data are captured by organizational systems or can be purchased from a third party. Therefore, organizational desirability of implementing data warehousing technology has been on the rise.

Even though there are many success stories, a data warehousing project is an expensive, risky undertaking (Beitler & Leary, 1997). Organizations are spending millions each year on data warehouse development, but the majority of initial data warehousing efforts fail (Chenoweth, Corral, & Demirkan, 2006). The most common reasons for failure include weak sponsorship and management support, insufficient funding, inadequate user involvement, and organizational politics (Watson, Gerard, Gonzalez, Haywood, & Fenton, 1999).

Conventional wisdom holds that having a management champion with a tightly focused (data mart) design and restrictive tools will lead to success. However, Chenoweth et al. (2006) found out that the reverse situation can be just as successful. If the users see the potential of the data warehouse to deliver value to the organization, they can be the champions and convince management to adopt the technology. Furthermore, if users understand both the technology and the organization's business processes, a single data repository may actually be more satisfying for them.

This article is organized into several sections. In the background section, what a data warehouse is, five major elements of a data warehouse, and fundamental concepts of how a data warehouse works will be discussed. In the main-focus section, current issues that organizations are facing in implementing data warehouses, for example, the selection of data warehouse methodologies, management of data warehouse operational life cycles, and data warehouse security, will be discussed. Finally, the trends in data warehousing development, such as active data warehousing, integration of data warehousing, and CRM, will be discussed in the future-trends section.

BACKGROUND

Basic Concept of a Data Warehouse

In today's business environment, every business owner dreams of having the ability to know what is happening in all aspects of his or her operation and of being able to use that information to optimize the market and increase profit. In order for an organization to achieve competitive advantage, voluminous data need to be managed, analyzed, and fed into the decision-making process. The introduction of data warehouses, which provide decision support to organizations with the help of analytical databases and analytical applications like online analytical processing (OLAP), answers this need (Gorla, 2003). The technical definition of a data warehouse is a subject-oriented, integrated, time-variant, and nonvolatile collection of data that supports managerial decision making (Inmon, 2002). Typically, a data warehouse is housed on an enterprise's mainframe server, but it can reside with a storage service provider. Data in an OLAP data warehouse are extracted and loaded from various online transaction processing (OLTP) applications and other sources using extract, transfer, and load (ETL) tools. See Figure 1 for data warehouse architecture. Analytical applications such as OLAP tools, data mining, statistical modeling, geographical information systems (GISs), DSSs, and other user queries are then applied to the repository (Jones, 2001).

Data Warehouse Elements

There are five major elements of data warehousing, including data acquisition, data modeling and schema, metadata, data management, and data analysis (Inmon, 2002; Jones, 2001). Data acquisition involves identifying, capturing, and transforming data in operational systems so that the data can be loaded into a data warehouse or data mart. Data acquisition is a complex, time-consuming, and costly phase of building and managing a data warehouse, but if this phase is not correctly carried through, the data warehouse will not be effective. During data acquisition, data are extracted,

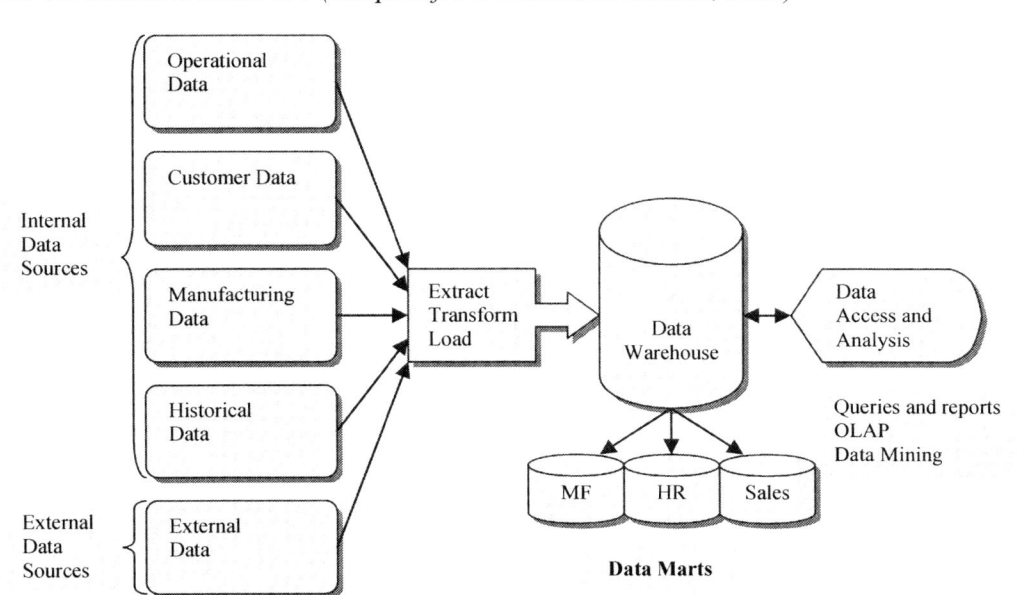

Figure 1. Data warehouse architecture (Adapted from Laudon & Laudon, 2007)

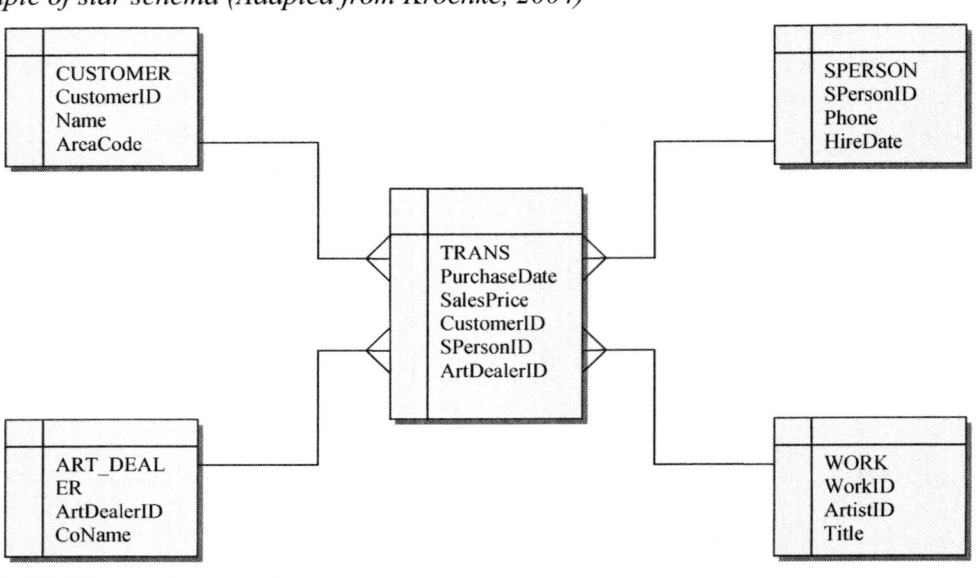

Figure 2. Example of star schema (Adapted from Kroenke, 2004)

transformed, transported, and loaded. Data modeling is the analysis of data objects used in a business or other context and the identification of the relationships among these data objects. A data model consists of objects (for example, a product, a product price, or a product sale) and expressions of the relationships between each of these objects. The activity of data modeling leads to a schema, which is the organization or structure for a database.

In terms of data modeling for data marts of a data warehouse, it is different from operational databases, for example, from OLTP and data modeling. This is because of the functional difference of the two systems. An operational system is a system that is used to run a business in real time based on current data. An information system, like a data warehouse, is designed to support decision making based on historical point-in-time and prediction data for complex queries or data-mining applications (Hoffer, Prescott, & McFadden, 2007). A data mart schema is viewed as a dimensional model that is composed of a central fact table and a set of surrounding dimension tables, each corresponding to one of the components or dimensions of the fact table (Levene & Loizou, 2003). There are a few types of data mart design schemas. One of the schemas is the star schema, which is the simplest database structure, containing a fact table in the center that is surrounded by the dimension tables (Ahmad, Azhar, & Lukauskis, 2004) as shown in Figure 2. As the figure illustrates, the fact table (TRANSACTION) is connected with the dimension tables using many-to-one relationships to ensure their hierarchy. The start schema can provide fast response time allowing database optimizers to work with simple database structures in order to yield better execution plans. Another one is called the snowflake schema, which is a variation of the star schema, in which all dimensional information is stored in the third normal form while keeping the fact-table structure the same. To take care of hierarchy, the dimension tables, as seen in Figure 3, are connected with subdimension tables using many-to-one relationships (Ahmad et al.). In general, the star schema requires greater storage, but it is faster to process than the snowflake schema (Kroenke, 2004).

Metadata is a definition or description of data, and it is the glue that holds together all components and views of a data warehouse. Data management includes the access and storage mechanisms that support the data warehouse. This is usually a relational, multidimensional, or other specialized database designed to facilitate complex queries. Data analysis applications enable end users to access and analyze data stored in data warehouses or data marts. There are many variants of data analysis software. The main types of data analy-

Figure 3. Example of snowflake scheme (Adapted from Kroenke, 2004)

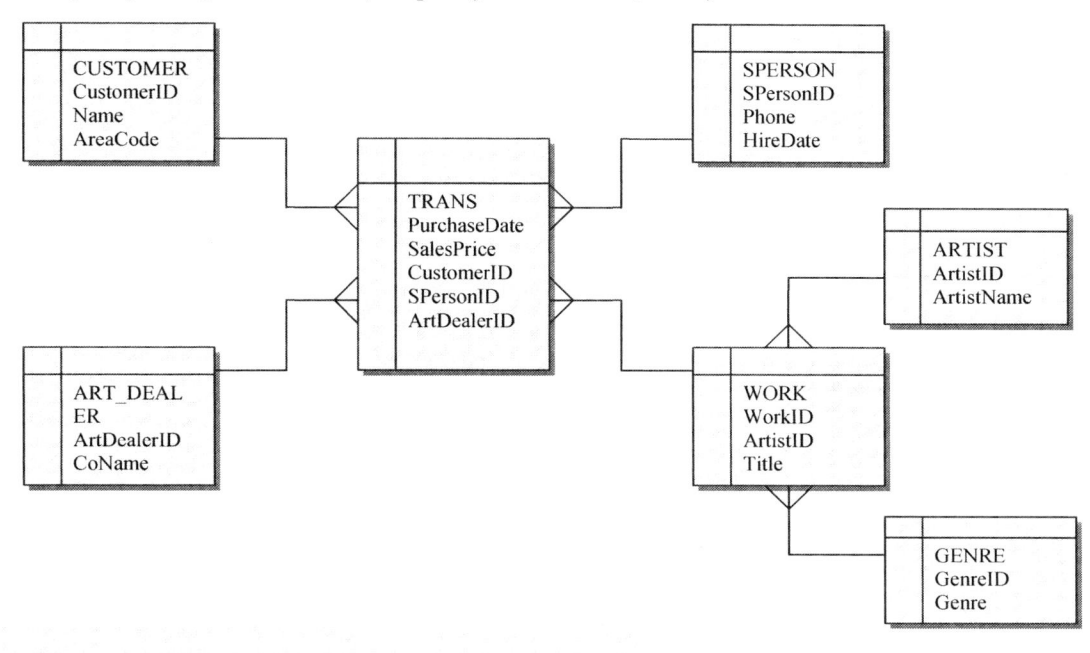

sis software include data mining tools, OLAP tools, enterprise business intelligence suites, and DSS.

Some Management Issues

There has been little empirical research on the implementation success of data warehousing projects. Wixon and Watson's (2001) empirical investigation suggests that management support and resources help to address organizational issues that arise during warehouse implementations. Furthermore, resources, user participation, and highly skilled project team members increase the likelihood that warehousing projects will finish on time, on budget, and with the right functionality. The implementation's success with organizational and project issues, in turn, influence the system quality of the data warehouse.

There are several issues of interest in the data warehousing literature. In this article, we focus on three issues. The first is data warehousing methodologies that organizations may choose, the second is the management of the data warehouse through its operational life cycle, and finally is the security of the data warehouse. The later issue is of importance because we believe that organizations must protect their valuable information assets.

MAIN FOCUS

When a small business decides to install a network for the first time, it must choose the operating systems, hardware, network, and software components. The same applies when an organization decides to build a data warehouse because there are several methodologies to choose from. Data integration technologies have experienced explosive growth, and a large number of data warehousing methodologies and tools are available to support market growth. As the business environment changes rapidly, the management of the data warehouse through its operational life and the security of the data become important because of the costs involved. Furthermore, nontechnical issues affecting the successful implementation of data warehouses have been identified. In this section, thoughts will be presented on the choice of data warehousing methodologies, managing the data warehousing through time, data warehouse security, business-driven data warehousing initiatives, senior-management sponsorship and commitment, and funding commitment.

Choosing Data Warehouse Methodology

With so many data warehousing methodologies to choose from, a major problem for many firms is which one the company should utilize for its situation. We believe that when a technology is in its growth stage, there is going to be a variety of methodologies and very little standardization. In such a case we expect that an organization would use different criteria to evaluate the different options and select the one that meets their need. To confirm our thoughts, we researched recent empirical studies on data warehousing methodologies (Sen & Sinha, 2005). In general, data warehousing methodologies can be classified into three broad categories as follows. (a) Core-technology vendors are those companies that sell database engines, such as NCR's Teradata-based methodology, Oracle's methodology, IBM's DB2-based methodology, Sybase's methodology, and Microsoft's SQL Server-based methodology. These vendors use data warehousing schemes that take advantage of the nuances of their database engines. (b) Infrastructure vendors are companies that sell database systems independent methodologies such as SAS's methodology, Informatica's methodology, Computer Associates' Platinum methodology, Visible Technologies' methodology, and Hyperion's methodology. These infrastructure tools are the mechanisms used to manage metadata using repositories; to help extract, transfer, and load data into the data warehouse; or to help create end-user solutions. (c) Information modeling vendors include ERP (enterprise resource planning) vendors (e.g., SAP and PeopleSoft), a general business consulting company (Cap Gemini Ernst Young), and two IT data warehouse consulting companies (Corporate Information Designs and Creative Data). These vendors focus on the techniques of capturing and modeling user requirements in a meaningful way.

Several attributes have been used to evaluate the various methodologies including core competence, modeling requirements, data modeling, support for OLAP queries, architecture design philosophy, ease of implementation, metadata management, scalability, and adaptability to changes (Sen & Sinha, 2005). Based on Sen and Sinha's qualitative evaluation of the various methodologies, it follows that none of the methodologies has achieved the status of a widely recognized standard, consistent with our hypothesis on technologies in the growth stage. The results from Sen and Sinha suggested that the core vendor-based methodologies are appropriate for those organizations that understand their business issues clearly and can create information models. Otherwise, the organizations should adopt the information-modeling-based methodologies. If the focus is on the infrastructure of the data warehouse such as using metadata or a cube design, it is best to use the infrastructure-based methodologies. We anticipate that as the field of data warehousing moves to the mature stage, there could be a convergence of the various methodologies.

Managing Data Warehouse Operational Cycle

Every business goes through changes in strategy as changes occur in the external and internal environment in which it operates. Organizations constantly assess their strengths, weaknesses, opportunities and threats in formulating and implementing new strategies. Because the business world is characterized by frequent changes, data warehouses must be adapted to these changes in order for them to continue to be relevant. The management of a data warehouse through these changes is a new area of research called data warehouse life cycle management (DWLM; Longman, 2004). This enables the organization to align information systems with the changing business operations they are designed to support.

Given the need to respond to internal and external changes, the design of the data warehouse must be flexible enough to adapt to changes in the business cycle. Without this flexibility, there will be additional high costs because any major change will require IT experts to hunt through large systems and identify what needs to be altered, and then make complex changes in the relevant places. One characteristic of an adaptive data warehouses is the use of generic storage rather than set a physical storage structure to meet predetermined business goals (Longman, 2004).

A second characteristic of an adaptable data warehouse is that it should allow the business users to manage the changes needed in the data warehouse, thus eliminating the need to have the IT function take charge of every little alteration needed. This is important because miscommunication between the business users who know what they need and the IT function who try to implement the change can lead to errors and costly translation processes. Thus, it makes sense for a financial manager to change the definition of net profit and add some new budget data to the data warehouse.

A third characteristic is consistency in the master data management. In a global corporation, for example, the same product can be referred to in different ways in different places, and this means that the transactional systems will not be sufficient to manage the master data to produce the desired analytical results for management. One recommendation is that adaptive warehouse design use a scheme that will give the business owners of the data the tools to improve, enrich, authorize, and publish master data in a form acceptable to the several systems used to run the business (Longman, 2004). Without well-managed master data, data warehouses will produce questionable results, which will significantly diminish their utility in running a business.

Finally, an adaptive data warehouse must be able to capture the history of an object of data in storage over time. This will allow the data warehouse to provide information about the behavior of these objects in the past, making it possible for the business to compare changes over time (Longman, 2004).

In our opinion, some of these characteristics are quite ideal, and in most cases a piecemeal implementation would be required to transform the data warehouse into an adaptive one. For example, it would not be 100% possible for business users to manage changes in the data warehouse themselves, meaning that there will always be a need for the IT function to be included in the transformations required. Furthermore, tracing historical changes in data objects, while ideal, should be done selectively within the master data structure.

Data Warehousing Security

In the IT world, the protection of IT systems against virus and spyware, and protecting customers' data are just a few of the security worries IT specialists face on a daily basis. Many of the basic requirements for security are well known and apply equally to a data warehouse like they would for any other system. We believe that these requirements are perhaps even more important in a data warehouse because a data warehouse contains data consolidated from multiple sources, and thus from the perspective of a malicious individual trying to steal information, a data warehouse can be one of the most lucrative targets in an enterprise. Therefore, the application must prevent unauthorized users from accessing or modifying data, the applications and underlying data must not be susceptible to data theft by hackers, the data must be available to the right users at the right time, and the system must keep a record of activities performed by its users.

There are further security provisions, in our opinion, that could be implemented in the data warehousing environment. First, an enterprise where there is a data warehouse that is widely used by many divisions and subsidiaries in a company needs a security infrastructure that ensures that the employees of each division only view the data that is relevant to their own division, while also allowing for employees in its corporate offices to view the overall picture. Second, when the data warehouse stores personal information, privacy laws that govern the use of such personal information must be strictly implemented. Furthermore, companies that sell data to their clients must ensure that those clients only view the data they are entitled to (Edwards & Lumpkin, 2005).

Recent research on data warehousing security and privacy suggest that organizations should ensure the security and confidentiality of customer data in a data warehouse by the establishment of a corporate security policy, logical security (such as the use of passwords and encryption technology), physical security, and periodic internal control reviews (Elson & LeClerc, 2005). Because in some cases the data warehouses were built with little consideration given to security during the development phase, a seven-phase process can be implemented (Warigon, 1997). These seven phases include identifying data, classifying data, quantifying the value of data, identifying data security vulnerabilities, identifying data protection measures and their costs, selecting cost-effective security measures, and evaluating the effectiveness of security measures (Warigon).

Business-Driven Data Warehousing Initiative

A research study on data warehouse implementation by Sammon and Finnegan ((2000) found that a common practice in data warehouse implementation in organizations is to implement an IT-driven initiative. It is not surprising to see such an initiative. As recent technology advancement, data warehousing is complicated, costly, and difficult to implement. It involves the process of extracting, transforming, and loading data from various transactional databases into a data warehouse. Then analytical tools are used to analyze the data to provide hidden patterns of business information to the business management team for wiser decision making. For that reason, most organizations view data warehousing implementation as an IT project initiative and hold the IT department solely responsible. Consequently, the initial stage of data warehousing implementation by those implementing organizations is not successful.

Implementing a data warehouse is a complex project that can cause difficulty for organizations. The chances of successful implementation are higher when the data warehousing project is planned, committed to, and managed as a business investment rather than a technology project initiative (Sammon & Finnegan, 2000). Sammon and Finnegan's study on data warehousing implementation reveals that when organizations start their data warehousing implementation projects initially as IT driven, commitment, funding, and management buy-in are consequently difficult to achieve and maintain. However, when the business takes over the initiatives and the initiatives become business driven, the warehouse design and scope is directly related to the business strategy. The business strategy is broken into a set of critical success factors that are in turn used to generate a set of key performance indicators. Thus, the problem of commitment is solved.

Senior-Management Sponsorship and Commitment

A senior-management champion is a key to the benefits of data warehouse implementation, especially when the project is enterprise-wide. The data warehouse is to be built on a number of subjects and across different business functional areas. It is difficult to balance, investigate, and solve the critical issues across these business areas. Without a senior-management champion, problems can occur at some stage in different areas and at different levels, and can be very difficult to solve and will eventually affect the implementation of data warehousing. To overcome similar problems, a data warehousing implementation project should have three areas of commitment: senior-management commitment, IT commitment, and business commitment (Sammon & Finnegan, 2000).

Funding Commitment

One of the problems of an IT-driven data warehousing initiative is the justification of funding. The traditional measurement of cost justification on a project of the scale of a data warehousing initiative is difficult to attain. The lack of a strong business case with measurable benefits will significantly reduce the chances of successful funding of a data warehousing project. If a data warehouse implementation initiative is IT driven, the only justifiable explanation the IT team can provide is that other organizations are using it because the benefits and expectations of a data warehouse are seldom quantifiable and difficult to track. In this case, an IT-driven data warehousing initiative is problematic in securing strong funding commitment (budgeted and unexpected) from senior management. When business units take over the initiative to propose benefits and expectations of a data warehousing initiative, they can justify the project funding from organization-level competitive advantages, organizational structure and business functional areas, and use of the information from a data warehouse such as for competitive threats and customer retention (Sammon & Finnegan, 2000).

FUTURE TRENDS

Organizations' business intelligence and data warehousing technology are rapidly expanding in the business industry globally, especially in the U.S. market. Data warehousing has several trends that are getting worldwide attention from organizations such as active data warehousing and the integration of CRM and data warehousing. These two trends are discussed briefly in this section.

One of the important trends in the data warehousing industry is that an active data warehouse provides an integrated information repository to drive strategic and tactical decision support within an organization (Brobst & Ballinger, 2003). Enterprises face competitive pressures to increase the speed of decision making so active data warehouses are designed to hold accurate, detailed, and integrated data from operational systems within an organization. Active data warehouses are becoming important for two key reasons. First, daily customer activities are supported by active data warehousing because all levels of decision makers can manage customers' information on a day-to-day basis. Businesses can manage customer relationships by real-time analysis such as responding to a customer's interactions, behaviors, and changing business conditions. Strong customer relationships are important to any information-driven business because direct interaction with customers will empower employees with information-based decision making. Employees will have the knowledge and experience to assist customers based on accurate information stored on their organization's data warehouse. Second, active data warehouses are the next-generation decision-support systems because they are one-to-one-relationship oriented. The next generation of data warehousing manages the customer relationship at any and all touch points and in understanding customers as individuals.

The next important data warehousing trend is the integration of data warehousing and CRM. In the business world today, many organizations are implementing a business strategy that supports their customers. Building and maintaining beneficial long-term customer relationships is critical for the implementation of CRM (Knight, 2001). The integration of data warehousing and CRM is essential because they both allow organizations to capture, analyze, and disseminate the proliferation of customer information to drive business decisions (Bull, 2002). A key success factor of any CRM strategy is the ability to make use of the available information on customers in order to understand the characteristics of the customer base and to influence the ways in which customers and the organization interact (Imhoff, Loftis, & Geiger, 2001). To achieve this integration, the organization should be able to use the data warehouse to recognize the different types of customers, their expectations, diverse requirements, and preferences. This will allow the organization to anticipate their customers' needs, by analyzing their buying habits. Effectively analyzing customer wants and needs through sales and marketing technologies will give customer-driven organizations a global competitive edge among rivals. Finally, understanding the value of each customer will positively affect a strong customer relationship because customers want to be recognized as loyal consumers. Therefore, the data warehouse must be accurate and up to date for this integration to be successful.

CONCLUSION

Every organization needs a view of its performance across all its operations. Many enterprises use data warehouses to store a copy of data drawn from operational systems so that they can be extracted for analysis. Such data warehouses present data on demand to business users and analysts via business intelligence, and reporting and analytical tools. By acting as a central source for management information, a data warehouse delivers a single version of the truth that spans multiple operations. This gives executives visibility of business performance, improving the organization's ability to react to competitive pressures.

Data integration technologies have experienced explosive growth and a large number of data warehousing methodologies and tools are available to support market growth. Because data warehousing is in its growth stage, there are several methodologies, and none of these methodologies have achieved the status of widely recognized standard. As the business environment changes, managers must think about adaptive data warehouses that could be easily aligned with the business or industry life cycles. Finally, the security and privacy of the information in the data warehouse must be protected because data warehouses are often very large systems, serving many user communities with varying security needs.

A common practice in data warehousing implementation in organizations is to implement an IT-driven initiative. As a result, it becomes problematic for the IT team to secure a senior-management commitment and strong funding commitment. To overcome and/or avoid these problems, a business-driven data warehousing implementation can offer a better solution by either in the planning stage having business units initiate the project or letting them take over the project. Thus, the benefits, as well as senior-management support and funding of implementing a data warehouse can be justified at the organizational level across different business functional areas.

REFERENCES

Ahmad, I., Azhar, S., & Lukauskis, P. (2004). Development of a decision support system using data warehousing to assist builders/developers in site selection. *Automation in Construction, 13*, 525-542.

Ariyachandra, T., & Watson, H. J. (2006). Which data warehouse architecture is most successful? *Business Intelligence Journal, 11*(1), 1-4.

Beitler, S. S., & Leary, R. (1997). Sears' EPIC transformation: Converting from mainframe legacy systems to on-line analytical processing (OLAP). *Journal of Data Warehousing, 2*(2), 5-16.

Brobst, S., & Ballinger, C. (2003). *Active warehousing: Why Teradata warehousing is the only proven platform.* Retrieved July 29, 2007, from http://www.teradata.com

Bull, A. (2002). *Integrating active data warehousing and CRM: The enterprise-wide imperative.* Retrieved July 29, 2007, from http://www.itweb.co.za/office/nds/020827052.html

Chenoweth, T., Corral, K., & Demirkan, H. (2006). Seven key interventions for data warehouse success. *Communications of the ACM, 49*(1), 115-119.

Cooper, B. L., Watson, H. J., Wixom, B. H., & Goodhue, D. L. (2000). Data warehousing supports corporate strategy at First American Corporation. *MIS Quarterly, 24*(4), 547-567.

Cope, J. (2000). New tools help Lockheed Martin prepare for takeoff. *Computerworld.* Retrieved July 29, 2007, from http://www.computerworld.com/databasetopics/data/software/story/ 0,10801,44221,00.html

Edwards, K. B., & Lumpkin, G. (2005). *Security and the data warehouse: An Oracle white paper.* Retrieved July 29, 2007, from http://www.oracle.com/technology/products/ bi/index.html

Elson, R. J., & LeClerc, R. (2005). Security and privacy concerns in the data warehouse environment. *Business Intelligence Journal, 10*(3), 51-59.

Finnegan, P., Murphy, C., & O'Riordan, J. (1999). Challenging the hierarchical perspective on information systems: Implications from external information analysis. *Journal of Information Technology, 14*(1), 23-37.

Gorla, N. (2003). Features to consider in a data warehousing system. *Communications of the ACM, 46*(11), 111-115.

Hoffer, J. A., Prescott, M. B., & McFadden, F. R. (2007). *Modern database management.* Saddle River, NJ: Person Education Inc.

Imhoff, C., Loftis, L., & Geiger, J. (2001). *Building the customer-centric enterprise: Data warehousing techniques for supporting customer relationship management.* John Wiley & Sons, Inc.

Inmon, W. H. (2002). *Building the data warehouse* (3rd ed.). New York: Wiley.

Jones, V. A. (2001). Data warehousing: Overview. *OfficeSolutions.* Retrieved March 26, 2007, from http://www.findarticles.com/p/articles/mi_m0FAU/is_7_18/ai_78357975

Knight, W. (2001). The CRM-ready data warehouse. *DM Review.* Retrieved July 29, 2007, from http://www.dmreview.com/article_sub.cfm?articleId=2924

Koutsoukis, N., Micra, G., & Lucas, C. (1999). Adapting on-line analytical processing to decision modeling: The interaction of information and decision technologies. *Decision Support Systems, 26*, 1-30.

Kroenke, D. M. (2004). *Database processing: Fundamentals, design and implementation* (9th ed.). Saddle River, NJ: Prentice Hall.

Laney, D. (2000). Data warehouse factors to address for success. *HP Professional, 14*(5), 21-22.

Laudon, K. C., & Laudon, J. P. (2007). *Essentials of business information systems* (7th ed.). Saddle River, NJ: Pearson Prentice Hall.

Levene, M., & Loizou, G. (2003). Why is the snowflake schema a good data warehouse design? *Information Systems, 28*(3), 225-240.

Longman, C. (2004). *Data warehouse lifecycle management: Concepts and principles.* Retrieved July 29, 2007, from http://www.kalido.com

Love, B. (1996). Strategic DSS/data warehouse: A case study in failure. *Journal of Data Warehousing, 1*(1), 36-40.

Park, Y. T. (1997). Strategic uses of data warehouses: An organization's suitability for data warehousing. *Journal of Data Warehousing, 2*(1), 13-22.

Sammon, D., & Finnegan, P. (2000). The ten commandments of data warehousing. *Database for Advances in Information Systems, 31*(4), 82-91.

Sen, A., & Sinha, A. P. (2005). Comparison of data warehousing methodologies. *Communications of the ACM, 48*(3), 79-84.

Warigon, S. (1997). Data warehouse control and security. *Ledger, 41*(2), 3-7.

Watson, H. J., Gerard, J. G., Gonzalez, L. E., Haywood, M. E., & Fenton, D. (1999). Data warehousing failures: Case studies and findings. *Journal of Data Warehousing, 4*(1), 44-55.

Wixon, B. H., & Watson, H. (2001). An empirical investigation of the factors affecting data warehousing success. *MIS Quarterly, 25*(1), 17-41.

KEY TERMS

Business Intelligence: Business intelligence is a corporation's ability to access and employ information usually contained in a data warehouse. With the information, the corporation can analyze and develop insights and understanding that lead to improved and informed business decision making.

Database Management System (DBMS): DBMS is computer system software that manages the physical data.

Data Mart: It is a subset of a data warehouse that focuses on one or more specific subject areas. The data usually are extracted from the data warehouse and further denormalized and indexed to support intense usage by targeted customers.

Data Warehouse: This is a database built to support information access. Typically, a data warehouse is fed from one or more transaction databases. The data need to be cleaned and restructured to support queries, summaries, and analyses.

Data Warehouse Life Cycle Management (DWLM): DWLM is the creation and ongoing management of a data warehouse throughout its operational life. DWLM delivers enterprise-scale data warehouses that adapt efficiently to change at lower cost than traditional software development methodologies.

Geographic Information System (GIS): A GIS is a computer system designed to allow users to collect, manage, and analyze large volumes of spatially referenced information and associated attribute data.

Metadata: Metadata are data about data. They include the attributes of and information about each piece of data that will be contained in the data warehouse.

Online Analytical Processing (OLAP): OLAP is a database designed to support analytical processing such as decision support.

Online Transaction Processing (OLTP): OLTP is a database designed to support transactional processing.

Debiasing Decision Makers Through Knowledge Management

Meliha Handzic
Sarajevo School of Science and Technology, Bosnia and Herzegovina

INTRODUCTION

The need to improve decision making is a longstanding concern in decision support research. As the accelerated technological development and fierce competition coming from global sources are becoming more apparent in the new 21st century, enhanced decision-making capabilities are required more than ever before to enable organisations to meet the new challenges.

Decision making can be viewed as a dynamic and iterative process comprising: (1) identification phase, which involves decision problem recognition and diagnosis activities; (2) development phase, which concerns search and design activities; and (3) selection phase, which comprises screening, evaluation, and authorisation activities (Mintzberg et al., 1976). The quality of the subsequent decisions will depend on the nature of the preceding diagnostic, design, and selection activities.

There is a considerable body of evidence indicating that people systematically deviate from the prescribed decision-making norms. Such deviations are termed *decision biases* and are described as cognitions or mental behaviours that prejudice decision quality (Arnott, 2002). The variety of biases documented in behavioural decision literature include: memory, statistical, confidence, adjustment, presentation, and situation-related biases. Most decision biases tend to cause poor decision outcomes. Therefore they are of concern to designers of decision support systems that aim to facilitate and improve decision makers' task performance.

Of particular interest to this study is to address biases that people experience in combining multiple cues into single judgmental responses. The problem of combination could be due to misperception and/or misaggregation (Lim & O'Connor, 1996). With respect of misperception, the literature shows that people are lacking the ability of correctly assigning the weights to the cues. Both tendencies to overestimate unimportant and underestimate important cues have been identified. With respect to misaggregation, the literature indicates that people have difficulties in performing mental calculations when combining multiple cues due to cognitive overload.

Knowledge management (KM) offers a promising new approach to reducing or eliminating biases from the cognitive strategies of a decision maker. Assuming that the decision maker is the primary source of the biased judgement (Fischhoff, 1982), our attention is focused on how to better manage the decision maker's knowledge. Two main trends are distinguishable in terms of this support. One is to focus on the use of information and communication technology (ICT) as tools to facilitate management of knowledge processes (e.g., Handzic, 2004). The other trend is the proposition of a set of prescribed social and structural mechanisms to create an enabling environment for knowledge development, transfer, and application (e.g., Holsapple, 2003).

While there is considerable theoretical support for suggesting efficiency and effectiveness benefits of different socio-technical KM initiatives for decision making, there is little empirical evidence regarding the actual impact of these initiatives on decision makers' working knowledge and performance (Alavi & Leidner, 2001). The main objective of this chapter is to fill the existing gap between theory and practice by providing some empirical evidence regarding the potential and limitations of specific technology-based KM initiatives for supporting individual decision makers in the context of judgemental time series forecasting.

Two knowledge management system (KMS) designs are considered that differ in how they attempt to "debias" decision makers' judgment strategies. One system focuses on automating knowledge integration in the attempt to reduce decision makers' cognitive overload and thus eliminate misaggregation bias. The other system focuses on organising and representing knowledge for human consumption in a way that would reduce misperception. It is implicitly assumed that the availability of such systems should lead to better decision performance. The study based on Handzic (2007) empirically tests this assumption.

BACKGROUND ON KNOWLEDGE MANAGEMENT AND DECISION SUPPORT

Various KMS implementations provide differing levels of support in locating, extracting, and utilising knowledge and impose differing burdens to their users. In this section, we discuss two approaches to KMS development (*automating* versus *informating*) that may help to overcome some of the negative influence of decision biases.

Automating

The artificial intelligence (AI) approach to KMSs focuses on "automating" knowledge processes. It involves the use of "smart" systems that apply knowledge to solve problems for and instead of humans. Typically, such systems can reason in a narrow domain and in relatively mechanistic way (Becerra-Fernandez, Gonzales, & Sabherwal, 2004). Examples of popular systems in this category include those that can facilitate activities of direction and routines. Other well known examples are knowledge-based systems (KBS) in the form of intelligent decision support and expert systems. These were devised as problem solving systems long before the term KM became popular (Hasan, 2003). Neural networks are another significant development by AI researchers. The most important feature of neural networks is their ability to learn from noisy, distorted, or incomplete data (Glorfeld & Hardgrave, 1996).

Of special interest to this study is an automated knowledge aggregation tool that mechanically combines multiple cues into a single judgemental response. It is argued that the provision of such a tool may help alleviate or even completely eliminate negative effects of misaggregation bias. In general, computers are considered to be better than people in making complex calculations and in making calculations rapidly and accurately (Stair & Reynolds, 2003). However, despite benefits offered by these systems they are not free from criticism. Some scholars warn that replacing people with machines may have important ethical implications. Most AI systems are of the "black-box" kind. This means that the tool produces conclusions without any explanation and justification of the reasons behind such conclusions. Consequently, it may have a detrimental effect on decision makers' working knowledge. Past empirical studies report general preference for heads over models in judgment (Dalrymple, 1987).

Informating

The previous discussion suggests that an alternative approach to KMS focusing on "informating" and guiding rather than "automating" knowledge work may be more useful to decision makers. Essentially, this approach involves organising and presenting knowledge to users in ways that would enhance their interpretation of the available knowledge and thus enable them to apply it more effectively in solving problems (O'Leary, 2003). Such approach can be considered as a "white box" kind of approach to managing knowledge. Resent empirical studies reported its beneficial effects in initiatives such as competency and procedural knowledge maps (Handzic, 2004).

EMPIRICAL STUDY

The focus of this study is on another white-box type of KMS, a knowledge weighting tool that provides users with a graphical image of task-relevant cues and their relative importance weights. It is argued that the provision of such a tool may help alleviate/eliminate negative effects of misperception bias. In addition, the white-box approach to KMS may help increase people's "trust" and reliance on helpful decision aids. Empirical evidence from recent knowledge tagging and content rating studies (Poston & Speirer, 2005; Shanks, 2001) also hint that such a tool may enhance users' working knowledge and performance.

Study Objectives

In view of the prior findings and concerns expressed, the main objective of the current study is to determine the nature of assistance, the extent of assistance, and the limitations of the aforementioned two approaches to KMS in supporting managerial decision making. In particular, the study examines whether and how KMSs of varying knowledge weighting and knowledge aggregation support may assist individual decision makers in enhancing their working knowledge and improving the quality of their subsequent decisions in a specific judgmental decision-making task.

Research Method

Experimental Task

The experimental task for the current study was a simple production planning activity in which subjects made decisions regarding daily production of fresh ice cream. The participants assumed the role of production manager for an imaginary dairy firm that sold ice cream from its outlet at the Bondi Beach in Sydney, Australia. The company incurred equally costly losses if production was set too low (due to loss of market to the competition) or too high (by spoilage of unsold product). The participants' goal was to minimise the costs incurred by incorrect production decisions. During the experiment, participants were asked at the end of each day to set production quotas for ice cream to be sold the following day. Subjects were required to make 10 production decisions over a period of 10 consecutive simulated days.

From pre-experiment discussions with actual store owners at Bondi Beach, three factors emerged as important in determining local demand for ice cream: the ambient air temperature, the amount of sunshine, and the number of visitors/tourists at the beach. All participants were provided with these contextual cues. Subjects were free to use the available knowledge as much or as little as they wished to. Contextual time series were artificially generated with cue weights set to 0.53, 0.30, and 0.17 to provide varying predictive power. Optimal decision was derived by using a weighted additive model with three contextual cues as independent and product demand as dependent variables in the equation.

The task differed with respect to the type of KMS received. One half of the subjects received a "black-box" system that automatically combined contextual cues into a single production decision without giving users any explicit analysis of the quality of the available contextual cues, or the rule applied to translate them into specific decisions. The other half received a "white-box" model with both the explicit analysis of the quality of the available contextual cues, and the rule applied to translate them into specific decisions. At the beginning of the experiment, task descriptions were provided to inform subjects about the task scenario and requirements. The given text differed with respect to the model provided.

Experimental Design and Variables

A laboratory experiment with random assignment to treatment groups was used for the study. This made it possible to draw stronger inferences about causal relationships between variables due to high controllability. The experimental design was a single factor design with the *KMS type* (black-box versus white-box) as the only independent variable.

The manipulation of different KMS types was achieved by changing the amount of explicit knowledge provided to the participants. The black-box version of KMS provided participants with a recommended decision only. The white-box version provided participants with additional explicit knowledge about the decision-relevant cues (in the form of relative importance weights) and the rule (in the form of weighted additive model) applied to integrate them into final decisions.

Subjects' performance was evaluated in terms of *decision accuracy* operationalised by absolute percentage error (APE) as suggested by Makridakis (1993). APE was calculated as the absolute difference between subject-estimated and actually demanded units of product per day, divided by actually demanded units and multiplied by 100%. In addition, the corresponding errors of their control and nominal optimal counterparts were calculated. These were actual subjects who produced their decisions without any KMS support and imaginary decision makers who made their decisions by using optimal decision strategies respectively. These scores were used to assess how much of the available KMS support was used by the experimental subjects in making their decisions.

Subjects and Procedure

Twenty-seven graduate students enrolled in the Master of Commerce course at the University of New South Wales, Sydney participated in the study on a voluntary basis. They had no prior knowledge of the task and received no monetary incentives for their performance. Generally, graduate students are considered to be appropriate subjects for this type of research (Ashton & Kramer, 1980; Remus, 1996; Whitecotton, 1996). The experiment was conducted as part of a guest lecture on KMSs and technology. Subjects were assigned randomly to one of the treatment or control groups by picking up an appropriate version of the research instrument to be used. Subjects were briefed about the purpose of the study, read the case descriptions, and performed the task. The session lasted about a half hour.

Results

The collected data were analysed statistically using a series of t-tests to examine the effect of two different types of KMSs on subjects' decision accuracy and to compare it with that of their nominal optimal and control (unsupported) counterparts. The results are presented in Table 1.

The results of the analysis shown in Table 1 indicate no significant change in decision accuracy due to the black-box type of KMS. The subjects provided with the black-box system made similarly high decision errors as those without any such support (10.759 versus 9.820, p=ns). Similar errors indicated low (if any) reliance and use of the available system support.

In contrast, Table 1 shows a significant difference in decision accuracy between the two KMS types. The mean error of the subjects supported with the white-box system was significantly smaller than that of the subjects with the black-box one (7.705 versus 10.759, p=0.018). Smaller errors indicated that the "opening" of the black box had a significant positive effect on decision makers' reliance and use of the system support provided.

Finally, the results in Table 1 show that subjects failed to reach optimal decision performance irrespective of the KMS type provided. The mean error of the subjects supported by the white-box system was significantly higher than that of their nominal optimal counterparts (7.705 versus 5.809, p=0.017). In real terms, these subjects managed to utilise only about one half (53%) of the system's maximum potential. This indicates a lot of room for further improvement.

Discussion

Main Findings

The main findings of the present study indicate that the opening of the black-box KMS was useful in improving decision making, however performance gains were less than theoretically possible. This was demonstrated by significantly smaller decision errors found among white-box subjects than their black-box counterparts, but greater decision errors compared to notional optimal counterparts.

The fact that the participants with the white-box system support performed better than those with the black-box one indicates that they were able to better understand and use the knowledge available from their system. The analysis found that these subjects tended to rely at least to some extent on explicit cues provided when making their decisions. As a result, they tended to achieve substantial improvement in their subsequent performance. In real terms, decision errors dropped by 28%. Such findings seem to contradict the overly pessimistic picture of human ability to utilise explicit knowledge painted by earlier laboratory research in judgment and decision making (e.g., Andreassen, 1991; Harvey, Bolger, & McClelland, 1994).

One potential explanation for the finding may be attributed to the "white-box" nature of the system support. Participants in the current study were given a small number of relevant contextual variables in a meaningful task context, graphical presentation of their relative importance weights to provide clues to causal relationships, and forecast values to suggest future behaviour. It is also possible that a graphical form of

Table 1. Summary results of T-tests for MAPE by KMS groups

	GROUP	N	Mean	t	df	Sig.(2-tail)
SCORE	Control	90	9.820	-.674	178	.501
	Black-box	90	10.759			
SCORE	Black-box	90	10.759	2.382	178	.018
	White-box	90	7.705			
SCORE	White-box	90	7.705	2.400	178	.017
	Optimal	90	5.809			

knowledge presentation facilitated interpretation and enabled the subjects to better judge the right size of future changes.

Despite this, the results indicate a lot of room for further improvement. The white-box subjects were found to make substantially greater decision errors than their nominal optimal counterparts. Greater than optimal errors indicate that the subjects tended to use much less of the available knowledge than they possibly could. Further analysis revealed that, on average, they tended to effectively internalise only 53% of the explicit knowledge provided to them. Such finding seems to agree with our earlier discovery of human ability to utilise between 40% and 60% of explicit knowledge (Handzic, 2004). The failure to achieve optimal performance resulted mainly from the participants' choice and application of inappropriate strategy placing too much reliance on their own judgment.

A potential explanation for the observed suboptimality may be the lack of vital knowledge regarding tool reliability. Subjects in the current research were not given any explicit analysis of the quality of their tool's past performance. As a result they tended to place less reliance than they should have on the seemingly helpful decision aid. Earlier studies on learning from feedback in multivariate tasks reported improved performance due to task and cognitive feedback (Remus, O'Connor, & Griggs, 1996). Another potential explanation for the observed suboptimality may be the lack of opportunity to learn from own experience through task repetition. Earlier studies on learning (for review see Klayman, 1988) indicate that people can learn multivariate tasks over a large number of trials reasonably well. However, it seems that the period of 10 trials was too short to induce effective learning.

Limitations

While the current study provides a number of interesting findings, some caution is necessary regarding their generalisability due to a number of limiting aspects. One of the limitations refers to the use of a laboratory experiment that may compromise external validity of research. Another limitation relates to artificial generation of time series data that may not reflect the true nature of real business. The subjects chosen for the study were students and not real-life decision makers. The fact that they were mature graduates may mitigate the potential differences. No incentives were offered to the subjects for their effort in the study. Consequently, they may have found the study tiring and unimportant and not tried as hard as possible. Most decisions in real business settings have significant consequences. Further research is necessary that would extend the study to other subjects and environmental conditions in order to ensure the generalisability of the present findings.

FUTURE TRENDS

Although limited, the findings of the current study may have some important implications for organisational decision support strategies. They suggest that decision makers could potentially benefit from additional KM initiatives that would enhance their understanding of the value of explicit knowledge captured in organisational systems. One possible solution is to provide systems with more meaningful analysis, task/performance feedback, and learning histories that might potentially help such workers better understand what works when and why (Kleiner & Roth, 1998). This, in turn, may result in better performance. Alternatively, organisations may employ trustworthy specialists trained in analytical and statistical reasoning who would perform a knowledge filtering process for professional and managerial knowledge workers (Godbout, 1999).

Initiatives aimed at creating working contexts that encourage communication and culture of knowledge sharing may also potentially have a beneficial effect on enhancing decision makers' working knowledge and performance. Organisations have come to realise that a large proportion of the knowledge needed by the business is not captured on hard drives or contained in filing cabinets, but kept in the heads of people; sources report that between 40% (Arthur Andersen Office of Training Education [AAOTE], 1998) and 90% (Hewson, 1999) of the needed knowledge is (in the lingo of the business) tacit. The spiral knowledge model postulates that the processes of sharing will result in the amplification and exponential growth of working knowledge (Nonaka, 1998; Nonaka & Takeuchi, 1995). Yet, little is known of the ways in which tacit knowledge is actually shared, conditions under which this sharing occurs, and the impact it has on performance.

Finally, by combining and integrating various KM initiatives organisations may potentially create synergy effects that would lead to even higher levels of knowledge and performance. According to Davenport and Prusak (1997) only by taking a holistic approach to management, may it be possible to realise the full power of knowledge ecology. Further research may look at some of these initiatives and approaches.

CONCLUSION

The main objective of this study was to investigate the effectiveness of two types of KMSs in supporting individual decision makers in a predictive judgment task context. The results indicate that only a white-box type of KMS was useful, although insufficient to maximally enhance individual decision performance. White-box participants were found to utilise more knowledge and make significantly smaller decision errors than their black-box counterparts. However, they tended to utilise less knowledge and make significantly larger decision errors compared to notional optimal counterparts. Although limited to the specific task and context, these findings may have important implications for decision support strategies, as they suggest that individuals could potentially benefit from additional KM initiatives to further enhance individual knowledge and performance. Therefore, more research is necessary to systematically address various KM initiatives in different tasks and contexts, and among different knowledge workers.

REFERENCES

Alavi, M., & Leidner, D. E. (2001). Knowledge management and knowledge management systems: Conceptual foundations and research issues. *MIS Quarterly, 25*(1), 107-136.

Andreassen, P. B. (1991). *Causal prediction versus extrapolation: Effects on information source on judgemental forecasting accuracy.* Working paper. Cambridge, MA: MIT.

Arnott, D. (2002). *Decision biases and decision support systems development* (Working Paper No. 2002/04). Melbourne, Australia: Monash University, Decision Support Systems Laboratory.

Arthur Andersen Office of Training and Education (AAOTE). (1998). *BC knowledge management.* Author.

Ashton, R. H., & Kramer, S. S. (1980). Students as surrogates in behavioural accounting research: Some evidence. *Journal of Accounting Research, 18*(1), 1-15.

Becerra-Fernandez, I., Gonzales, A., & Sabherwal, R. (2004). *Knowledge management: Challenges, solutions, and technologies.* Upper Saddle River, NJ: Pearson Education.

Dalrymple, D. J. (1987). Sales forecasting practices: Results from a United States survey. *International Journal of Forecasting, 3,* 379-391.

Davenport, T. H., & Prusak, L. (1997). *Information ecology.* Oxford, UK: Oxford University Press.

Fischhoff, B. (1982). Debiasing. In D. Kahneman, P. Slovic, & A. Tversky (Eds.), *Judgement under uncertainty: Heuristics and biases* (pp. 422-444). New York: Cambridge University Press.

Glorfeld, L. W., & Hardgrave, B. C. (1996). An improved method for developing neural networks: The case of evaluating commercial loan creditworthiness. *Computer Operation Research, 23*(10), 933-944.

Godbout, A. J. (1999). Filtering knowledge: Changing information into knowledge assets. *Journal of Systemic Knowledge Management, January,* 1-9.

Handzic, M. (2004). *Knowledge management: Through the technology glass.* Singapore: World Scientific Publishing.

Handzic, M. (2007). Supporting decision makers with knowledge management systems. In *Proceedings of the 11th Pacific-Asia Conference on Information Systems (PACIS 2007),* New Zealand.

Harvey, N., Bolger, F., & McClelland, A. (1994). On the nature of expectations. *British Journal of Psychology, 85,* 203-229.

Hasan, H. (2003). The role of computer-based KM systems. In H. Hasan & M. Handzic (Eds.), *Australian studies in knowledge management* (pp. 322-341). Wollongong, NSW, Australia: UOW Press.

Hewson, D. (1999). Start talking and get to work. *Business Life, November,* 72-76.

Holsapple, C. W. (Ed.). (2003). *Handbook on knowledge management.* Berlin, Germany: Springer.

Klayman, J. (1988). Learning from experience. In B. Brehmer & C. R. B. Joyce (Eds.), *Human judgement. The SJT view*. Amsterdam: North-Holland.

Kleiner, A., & Roth, G. (1998). How to make experience your company's best teacher. In *Harvard Business Review on Knowledge Management*. Boston: Harvard Business School Press.

Lim, J. S., & O'Connor, M. J. (1996). Judgemental forecasting with interactive forecasting support systems. *Decision Support Systems, 16*, 339-357.

Makridakis, S. (1993). Accuracy measures: Theoretical and practical concerns. *International Journal of Forecasting, 9*, 527-529.

Mintzberg, H., Raisinghani, D., & Theoret, A. (1976). The structure of unstructured decision process. *Administration Science Quarterly, 21*(2), 246-275.

Nonaka, I. (1998). The knowledge-creating company. In *Harvard Business Review on Knowledge Management*. Boston: Harvard Business School Press.

Nonaka, I., & Takeuchi, H. (1995). *The knowledge creating company: How Japanese companies create the dynamics of innovation*. New York: Oxford University Press.

O'Leary, D. E. (2003). Technologies for knowledge storage and assimilation. In C. W. Holsapple (Ed.), *Handbook on knowledge management* (Vol. 2, pp. 29-46). Berlin, Germany: Springer.

Poston, R. S., & Speirer, C. (2005). Effective use of knowledge management systems: A process model of content ratings and credibility indicators. *MIS Quarterly, 29*(2), 221-244.

Remus, W. (1996). Will behavioural research on managerial decision making generalise to managers? *Managerial and Decision Economics, 17*, 93-101.

Remus, W., O'Connor, M., & Griggs, K. (1996). *Does feedback improve the accuracy of recurrent judgemental forecasts*. Working paper. University of Hawaii.

Shanks, G. (2001, December). The impact of data quality tagging on decision outcomes. In *Proceedings of 12th Australasian Conference on Information Systems*, Coffs Harbour, Australia.

Stair, R. W., & Reynolds, G. W. (2003). *Principles of information systems* (6th ed.). Boston: Course Technology.

Whitecotton, S. M. (1996). The effects of experience and a decision aid on the slope, scatter, and bias of earnings forecasts. *Organisational Behaviour and Human Decision Processes, 66*(1), 111-121.

KEY TERMS

Absolute Percentage Error: Absolute percentage error is a popular measure of decision accuracy; calculated as the absolute difference between estimated and actual value, divided by the actual value and multiplied by 100%.

Black-Box System: Black-box system is a type of system that produces conclusions without any explanation and justification of the reasons behind such conclusions.

Debiasing: Debiasing consists of techniques and tools for reducing or eliminating biases from the cognitive strategies of a decision maker.

Decision Bias: Decision bias consists of cognitions or mental behaviours that prejudice decision quality; deviations from rational decision making.

Explicit Knowledge: Explicit knowledge is knowledge that has been or can be articulated, codified, and stored in certain media.

Knowledge Management (KM): KM is a range of practices and techniques used by an entity to consciously generate, transfer, and use its knowledge.

Knowledge Management System (KMS): KMS is a set of inter-related social/structural mechanisms and information/communication technologies that support the KM processes.

Decision Aiding Research Needs

Rex Brown
George Mason University, USA

INTRODUCTION

For more than 50 years, much research has been carried out on decision processes. Some has been descriptive, studying how decisions are being made. Some has been normative, studying how some ideally logical decider *would* make decisions. Prescriptive research, on how to help the decider advance from the descriptive to the normative has, however, been quite limited (Bell et al. 1993) and decision practice has not been much aided. There has, in fact, been little "useful" research, in the sense of leading toward decision technology that advances the interests of the decider, through decisions that are either more sound or more effectively communicated.

This article addresses, from the perspective of a professional decision aider, what hitherto-neglected decision research could improve decision aid usefulness, in the short or long run, and what can be done to make it happen.

The discussion will be developed mainly in the context of personal decision analysis (PDA), which quantifies judgment and processes it logically. That may be the most promising decision aiding approach available, and is the one with which I am most familiar. However, the argument should be broadly applicable to other decision tools.

BACKGROUND

An NAS panel of decision scientists, led by Herb Simon (1986) reported that decision tools of all kinds were used on only a tiny fraction of decisions that *could* benefit. That was 20 years ago, but progress since then has been modest, even in PDA. Institutions have been better served than individuals by decision tools. Because the stakes are higher, more effort can be justified and there may be more room for improvement, due to "organizational foolishness" (March & Simon, 1958). But even here the progress has been faltering.

General Motors, once a big corporate PDA user, appears to have all but given it up (Lieberman, 2000). Harvard Business School, the cradle of PDA, no longer makes it an MBA requirement (though it may be coming back). Numerous success stories have been reported, but often by support staff commissioning the work rather than deciders who have benefited from it. Moreover, advocacy, not decision-aiding, has commonly been the motivation. In any case, success stories must be a drop in a large bucket.

Respected authorities have disparaged PDA as practiced (including Nobel laureates Kahneman, Sen, and Simon, personal communications, 1995-2001) as have former PDA stars who became influential deciders themselves (Grayson, 1973; Watson, 1992) and top government policy advisors such as Edward Luttwak (Italy), Ivan Yablokov (Russia), Yezekiel Dror (Israel), and Herman Bondi (UK). Some of the original Harvard team (which I was a junior part of) became very successful deciders themselves.[1] Two of my students got to head a billion-dollar consulting corporation.

However, these all admitted that they do not now use PDA tools explicitly, though their informal decision-making has benefited from the training. I teach explicit PDA to deciders-in-training (Brown, 2005b), but with the main object of educating their informal reasoning, rather than having them use quantitative models (except with the support of specialized analysts).

MAIN FOCUS

Requirements of Successful Decision Aid

It takes more than logical soundness for a decision tool to improve on unaided judgment. In particular, it must:

- Use all the knowledge a decider normally uses.
- Call for inputs that people can readily and accurately provide.

- Produce output that the decider can use.
- Fit the institutional context.

Some of these essentials will be missing and the aid will fail[2] if:

1. Adequate decision aiding methods are lacking.
2. Such methods as exist are not learnt.[3]
3. Methods are misused (Brown, 2005b).

This article will only address the first issue, and, in particular, what research can enhance aiding methods and what it will take to get the research done.

Research to Enhance Decision Aid

After that discouraging NAS report, some decision aiders got together with Simon, Tversky, and other prominent researchers to review the practical impact and potential of decision research (Tolcott & Holt, 1988). They came away with the sobering finding that, though recent research had made important *scientific* advances, little had influenced decision aiding practice, and little current research was attacking the problems that were still holding back successful decision aiding.

Why has research not benefited decision-aiding more? And what can be done about it?

Nobel physicist Richard Feynman said, "Doing science is like making love. It may do some good,[4] but that's not why we do it." The "good" that decision research may do is to improve decisions, and it might do more good, if that *were* "why we do it." Instead, our priority is to pursue intellectual satisfaction and professional reward. Such personal and institutional priorities are perfectly legitimate and often do prove useful. But their dominance in decision research practice often diverts it from being useful.

Currently Prevailing Research Criteria

That dominance is largely the result of the institutional arrangements within which research talent is organized. Most research resources are housed in discipline-specific university departments, such as statistics, psychology, and economics. The researchers they employ are drawn, by their personal taste and professional incentives (such as career advancement, publication, and funding), to projects that are more scientific than useful.

Researchers tend to put highest priority on projects that promise well-specified, authoritative, universal knowledge within a single discipline. Researchers are discouraged from reporting tentative work, which could expose them to damaging criticism.

Science-driven research has certainly produced useful, even critical, findings. Some is normative (such as Savage on rationality axioms, Lindley on Bayesian statistics, Schlaifer on value of information and Raiffa on multi-attribute utility analysis). Some is descriptive (such as Edwards on probability assessment, Tversky and Kahneman on judgmental biases, Simon on bounded rationality, March on organizational processes, and Klein on naturalistic decision-making).

Much of it, including most research reported at professional conferences, however, grinds established research themes ever finer. It achieves welcome scientific closure on some decision aiding issues (such as Fishburn on utility and Schacter on influence diagrams[5]), but it often belabors them to the point of decreasing marginal usefulness.

Research for science sake is fine, and, in fact, the *prospect* of usefulness is often what prompted a scientific interest in the first place. However, the subsequent development of the research may owe nothing to that initial motivation.[6] Thomas Schelling's Nobel Prize work on "coordinated strategy" at the height of the Cold War is a case in point (Schelling, 1960), and may have spurred the U.S. foreign policy doctrine of "Mutual Assured Destruction." Although this work spawned much follow-up research, little of that was on his central "focal point" concept, because, some say (Sugden & Zamorron, 2006), it lacked theoretical tidiness.

It has been argued that institutional pressures to limit research funding and publication to monodisciplinary, closed-ended projects may not even serve scientific progress best. To encourage more divergent research, philosopher I.J. Good proposed a *Journal of Partly-Baked Ideas*, in which authors report a paper's degree of bakedness. Also, interdisciplinary research has been urged by funding agencies such as NSF, but this makes for less than fully baked findings, which may not best advance a researcher's academic career.

Distinctive Features of Practice-Driven Research

In order to advance, decision aiding practice needs more than science-driven research: it needs complementary practice-driven research, which is reactive, prompted by lessons learned in the field. It is typically untidy, open-ended, without predefined end product, and draws on whatever disciplines are called for.

Seeding research is the most critical and neglected type of practice-driven research. It identifies lessons learned during decision aiding, say, by developing a hunch into a testable hypothesis or by developing puzzlement into a lead for further research. However, it usually requires effort beyond what is needed to address whatever topical decision problem stimulated it. Seeding research may only produce partly-baked ideas for others to finish baking, but it is an essential ingredient of a useful overall research program (whether science- or practice-driven). Since it does not need to be constrained by the conventional standards of good research, practice-driven research is under-valued in the research community and little gets done.

Some argue that there is no need to fund partly-baked research, because the investment effort will be rewarded by conventional follow-up grants to complete the baking. However, in the case of practice-driven research—unlike science-driven research—the investors are not those who get the returns. Decision aiders do practice-driven research; academics do scientific research.

Nevertheless, decision aid practitioners have introduced much important decision aiding technique innovation, such as decision conferencing (Kraemer & Pinsonneault, 1989), without outside funding. They may justify the investment by the prospect of profitable new aiding resources. Occasionally, decision aiders do get funding to orchestrate the work of more conventional researchers. We had one evolving 10-year program that I believe developed plural evaluation methods by alternating a build-test-build-test sequence, engaging university-based psychologists and mathematicians, as needed (Brown, 2006).

ILLUSTRATIVE PROJECTS

Here are some illustrative practice-driven research topics that deserve development.

Topics Already Partly Explored

- How can learning formal decision aid educate informal decision-making (Baron & Brown, 1991)?
- How best to aid decision processes which involve incremental rather than once-and-for-all commitment (Brown, 2005d)?
- How to adapt decision aid to the institutional context? How does that context create an "incentive environment," which motivates deciders, decision aiders, and decision researchers (Brown, 2000)?
- What use is the construct of "ideal" judgment, that is, the perfect analysis of a person's psychological field (Brown, 1993)?
- How can plural PDA models be reconciled without ambitious metamodeling, for example, by judgmental adjustment.
- Many decision terms commonly used by technical specialists (such as "likelihood," "confidence interval," "expectation") are misleading or confusing to lay people. What alternative terms are cognitively and logically appropriate and likely to be widely adopted?

As Yet Undeveloped Topics

Decision Training

- If we wean people off counter-productive judgment heuristics (like "narrow framing") does it "help" to replace these with something else? Decision rules? PDA?
- Klein found that successful deciders use recognition-primed decision-making rather than "concurrent evaluation" of options, as in PDA (Brown, 2005c). How can others be trained to emulate them?
- How do we get people not just to think smart, but to act smart?

Decision Strategy

- How best to integrate informal analysis into informal reasoning without disrupting it?

General Decision Tool Design Principles

- How structure-intensive or judgment-intensive should decision models be, in given circumstances?
- How well can people make hypothetical value judgments (such as how they will enjoy some prospect not yet experienced) or hypothetical factual judgments (see next)?

Development of Specific Tools

- Some mathematical algorithms call for inputs that fit people's cognition better than others. Inference by Bayesian updating, for example, requires assessors to make hypothetical likelihood judgments. Are people better at making the resulting posterior assessments directly?
- What should be the form of utility elicitation? Holistic? Decomposed into additive pieces? Or further decomposed into factual and value judgments (as in Multiattribute Utility Analysis)?

Empirical Feedback on Aid Usefulness

- How have past decision-aiding efforts fared? Why? How could they have fared better?

Getting the Needed Research Done

It was once assumed that all aiders had to do was to tell researchers what research they needed and wait for it to get done. However, my and others' efforts to interest researchers (Brown, 1986; Brown & Vari, 1992) had no noticeable effect. Exhortation was clearly not enough. The research community has had the luxury of indulging priorities other than usefulness. Additional incentive is needed. Researchers and, more important, those that fund them will only pay real attention to usefulness if they are held accountable for it—or at least get credit for it.

To make a usefulness incentive work, two things are needed:

- A defensible method for rating how useful a research project promises to be, short- or long-term.
- A strategy for getting the research community to produce and use such ratings.

Rating Research Usefulness

The rating effort need not be very ambitious. It makes little sense to spend much of a modest research budget in planning how to spend the rest of it. Of course, the larger the stakes involved in research planning, the more careful and reviewable the rating has to be. For example, a funding agency might do well to develop a thorough repeatable procedure for rating *all* proposals.

The critical, and often sufficient, part of a rating methodology is to specify precisely what *form* rating should take. If usefulness is the sole object of research, nothing more than informal ranking may be needed, unless it is critical for the rating to be credible. If the usefulness rating is a letter grade or an undefined score, say from one to ten (as in the movie "Ten"), only qualitative issues need to be considered. However, if project usefulness is to be traded off against scientific or other criteria, interpretable numbers are needed.

A natural metric, like money, is attractive. A funding agent might say, "The most I could consider awarding for this proposal is $50k. They're asking $100k, so I'm declining it." However, no metric may fit the circumstances.

The best alternative may be a rating scale, say, from 0 to 100, with 0 the current decision quality and 100 a project that produces ideal decisions. Thus the 100-point range would be room for improvement in existing methods. For example a research evaluator might reason: "Medical research project A will improve the quality of surgical decisions 15 points on a scale where zero is current practice and 100 is some ideal medical practice. Although project B gets only a 10 for usefulness, it makes enough additional contribution to basic science to overcome the difference in usefulness."

Making the Evaluation

However the usefulness measure is defined, it can often be adequately rated holistically using direct judgment. The qualitative content of the rating, and the fact of quantifying it, may be more important than how well it is quantified. Whatever scale is used and however direct or formal the rating process, the same considerations in how a project influences human welfare must be taken into account.[7]

Considerations include:

- What decision tools will the project enhance and how? By improving decision tool quality or by its application?
- How much room for improvement is there, that is, how deficient are existing tools?
- Will the research affect the cost of the decision process or any institutional values (along with the quality of any action it results in)?
- What decisions and populations (applications, aid beneficiaries, decision roles) benefit from the research?

Which of these questions need to be considered in any given case depends on how different the projects compared are. You only need to consider issues that the comparison affects. The higher the level of research planning is, the more issues are affected by project choice.

If a PI is just choosing between research on different aspects of the same tool, only decision tool quality is relevant. If he is choosing among projects that address the same decision task, but with different aiding tools, he might also consider whether an indicated choice gets acted upon. (One project may study decision conferencing and the other expert systems, both of them for medical therapy purposes). If a funding agent is choosing among proposals involving different beneficiaries, decision tasks, and tools, a still richer range of questions needs to be addressed.

Getting Usefulness Rating Adopted

There is certainly much work to do on how to rate research, but the real problem is how to get people to do the rating. Deciders and aiders must somehow get the researchers and their funders to adopt usefulness rating as a standard practice.

The critical requirement is institutional. How do you get usefulness rating adopted as a general requirement, or at least acknowledged as standard practice, in research planning? In the case of private research funding, persuasion may do it. But with public funding, it may take political lobbying. Little support is likely to come from the research community itself and journal editors may be immovable.

A few years ago, NSF recruited a director from industry, Eric Bloch, whose mission was to make NSF research more useful (including the tiny decision research piece). He commissioned a study on how NSF should change proposal appraisals to foster more useful research. Program managers vigorously resisted the study and it was soon shelved.

There is, however, a precedent to funders requiring usefulness rating. NSF now has referees comment on the "broader impact" of proposed research in their appraisal (at least for psychology proposals). Since that criterion is neither defined nor quantified, referees still have much discretion in their final recommendations. Researchers have been heard to complain that, indeed, the NSF award process has become "biased" away from fundamental research, but how much toward long term usefulness is not clear.

NSF's Small Business Innovative Research program has its referees score proposals on a one-to-five scale of "anticipated technical and economic benefits," which corresponds to the commercial aspect of usefulness (which is a distinctive focus of the SBIR program). This score is added to four scientific and other criteria, as the basis for selecting proposals. This practice is encouraging, and should perhaps be extended to *all* competitive research procurement. The relative importance of usefulness could be fine-tuned by, for example, varying the maximum points that could be awarded for each criterion (rather than being fixed at five). Researchers are notorious for doing their own thing once they have secured a grant, but awarding an "exit" rating on *completion* of a project might combat that.

Getting the research community to make rating research usefulness standard practice is the big challenge. The deciders, and decision aiders who stand to benefit, may have to lobby funding agencies and the legislative sources of their funds. They may even have to take the campaign to the public, which is the ultimate beneficiary, via the press. It may be too much to hope that researchers themselves will take part in that lobbying.

The references below include further reading which expands on this discussion, in particular on aider motivation (Brown, 2005b), researcher motivation (Brown, 2006), research agenda (Brown & Vari, 1992), aiding technique (Brown, 2005a), and application to non-decision-research fields (Brown, 2005c).

CONCLUSION

Perhaps researchers (and even aiders) have avoided practice-driven research because two half-baked ideas do less for professional standing than one fully baked idea (even if it is less cost-effective). Even taking account of benefits other than usefulness, a community-wide research portfolio should surely include much more practice-driven research.

The thoughts in this article are themselves the fruits of "meta" seeding research. I am not arguing here that usefulness should be the pre-eminent consideration in planning research or evaluating proposals. That would depend on circumstances, such as whether an award is in the form of a grant or a contract. I am simply urging that usefulness be given greater saliency, possibly reinforced by some explicit rating and I suggest some promising avenues for practice-driven research.

REFERENCES

Bell, D.E., Raiffa, H., & Tversky, A. (1988). Descriptive, normative, and prescriptive interactions in decision making. In D. Bell, Raiffa, H. & A. Tversky (Eds.), *Decision making*. Cambridge University Press.

Brown, R.V. (1989). Toward a prescriptive science and technology of decision aiding. *Annals of Operations Research, Volume on Choice under Uncertainty, 19*, 467-483.

Brown, R.V. (1993). Impersonal probability as an ideal assessment based on accessible evidence: A viable construct? *Journal of Risk and Uncertainty, 7*, 215-235.

Brown, R.V. (2000). *Fitting decision aids to institutions: Organizational design issues.*

Brown, R.V. (2005a). *Rational choice and judgment: Decision analysis for the decider*. Wiley.

Brown, R.V. (2005b). The operation was a success but the patient died: Aider priorities influence decision aid usefulness. *Interfaces, 36*(1).

Brown, R.V. (2005c). Logic and motivation in risk research: A nuclear waste test case. *Risk Analysis, 25*, 125-140.

Brown, R.V. (2005d). *Managing incremental commitment.*

Brown, R.V. (2006, November). Making decision research useful—not just rewarding. *Journal of Decision Making, 1*(2).

Brown, R.V., & Vari, A. (1992). Towards an agenda for prescriptive decision research: The normative tempered by the descriptive. *Acta Psychologica, 80*, 33-47.

Grayson, C.J. (1973, July-August). Management science and business practice. *Harvard Business Review.*

Kraemer, K.L., & Pinsonneault, A. (1989). The impact of technological support on groups: An assessment of the empirical research. *Decision Support Systems.*

Lieberman, J. (2002). *Marketing of DA at GM: Rise and fall*. Paper presented at the Decision Analysis Affinity Group Conference, Las Vegas, NV.

Lindley, D.V., Tversky, A., & Brown, R.V. (1979). On the reconciliation of probability assessments. *Journal of the Royal Statistical Society, Series A, 142*(2), 146-180.

March, J.G., & Simon, H.A. (1958). *Organizations*. New York: Wiley.

Schelling, T.C. (1960). *The strategy of conflict*. Cambridge, MA: Harvard University Press.

Simon, H.A. (1986). Report of National Academy of Sciences Panel on research needs for decision making. In Impact and potential of decision research on decision aiding. NAS.

Sugden, R., & Zamarron, I.E. (2006, October). Finding the key: The riddle of focal points. *J. Econ. Psych., 27*, 5.

Tolcott, M.A., & Holt, V. (Eds.). (1988). *Impact and potential of decision research on decision aiding* (Report of a Department of Defense Research Roundtable Workshop sponsored by Decision Science Consortium, Inc. and the American Psychological Association.). APA.

Watson, S.R. (1992). The presumptions of prescription. *Acta Psych., 80*(1-3), 7-31.

KEY TERMS

Decision Research Usefulness: Fosters improved decision aid that serve decider's interests.

Prescriptive Effort: Intended to indicate a preferred choice.

Personal Decision Analysis (PDA): Prescriptive decision aid based on maximizing average personal utility ("subjective expected utility").

Practice-Driven Research: Designed to advance practical decision-aiding.

Science-Driven Research: Designed to advance pure science.

ENDNOTES

[1] Including: Andrew Kahr, business strategist; Bob Glauber, Assistant Secretary of the Treasury; and Ed Zschau, businessman and Member of Congress.

[2] Unaided judgment also has its flaws, of course.

[3] Surely reasoning belongs in a school curriculum alongside the three Rs!

[4] He may have had in mind nuclear power based on theoretical physics.

[5] See special issue of *Decision Analysis* on influence diagrams, 2005

[6] This covert usefulness motivation may be less prevalent in areas of science other than decision research. Einstein was surely not moved by the prospect that his efforts would help nuclear warfare or even power generation. However, his science-driven research may have proven more "useful" than all practice-driven research combined!

[7] Brown (2006) suggests a quantitative approach to modeling usefulness.

The Decision Hedgehog: Group Communication and Decision Support

Patrick Humphreys
London School of Economics and Political Science, UK

INTRODUCTION

The discourses established as the foundations of group decision support systems (GDSS) have been called into question not only in the interests of advancing the academic GDSS field (Bannon, 1997), but also out of the perceived need to plug gaps that sophisticated GDSS systems throw up in practice (Huber, 1981; Humphreys & Brezillon, 2002; Humphreys & Jones, 2006; Stabell, 1987). The limitations of rational perspectives of "decision-making as choice" have been raised (Carlsson, 2002; Cyert & March, 1992; Nappelbaum, 1997). The challenges relate to failures of implementation, the rise of unintended outcomes, the impact of cultures of fear and failure within organisations (Humphreys & Nappelbaum, 1997), and problems associated with externalisation of decision systems designers who "play God" by designing from outside the game for those who are inside (Humphreys, 1989).

Figure 1. The circular logic of choice

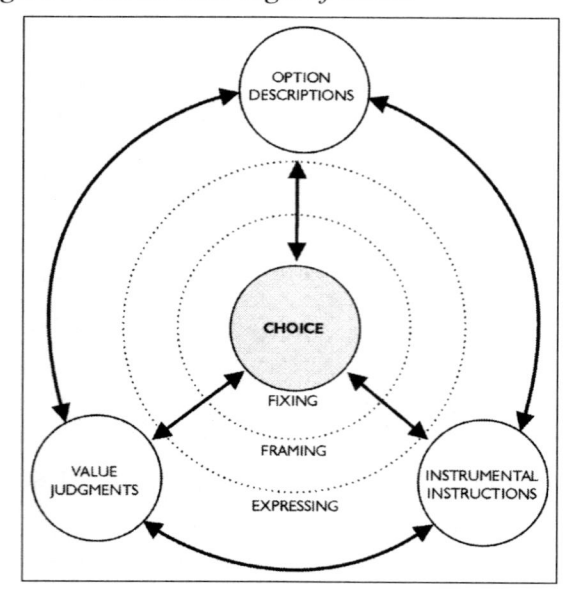

Alternative discourses have emerged. The attention-based view of the firm (Occasio, 1997) has its origins in the work of Herbert Simon (1960), who conceptualised decision making processes as linear, moving through three stages: intelligence, design, and choice. *Intelligence* involves a search for "the conditions that call for decisions." *Design* focuses on "inventing, developing, and analysing possible courses of action" through the construction of "a model of an existing or proposed real-world system." Decision-making is thus cast as problem solving, the model provides a representation of "the problem" which can be "solved by" implementing a prescribed course of action identified as "preferred" or "optimal" within this representation.

Yet, for the participants in the group decision-making process, the "representation of the problem" is cast within the plane of the symbolic/imaginary (Deleuze & Guattari, 1988), as are the prescriptions for action that emanate from its consideration within the group. So the "solution" to the decision problem is chosen on the basis of a collective fantasy by participants who do not always have sufficient resources for adequate "reality testing" before committing to a prescription for action (Humphreys, 1989).

The problem definition process is rooted in participants' issues of concern and spirals within what Nappelbaum (1997) called the *circular logic of choice* (Figure 1): the decision-making group progressively sharpens the description of the problem by cycling through option descriptions, value judgments, and instrumental instructions, reducing discretion in how these may be defined in spiralling towards the prescribed choice (Humphreys & Jones, 2007).

At the outset, all imaginable courses of action are candidates for implementation. The group process, aimed at developing a single, collectively agreed upon representation of "the problem" then progressively employs problem expressing, framing, and fixing processes to strengthen the constraints on how the problem is represented until only one course of action is prescribed: the one which "should be" actually embarked upon in

Figure 2. Decision-spine

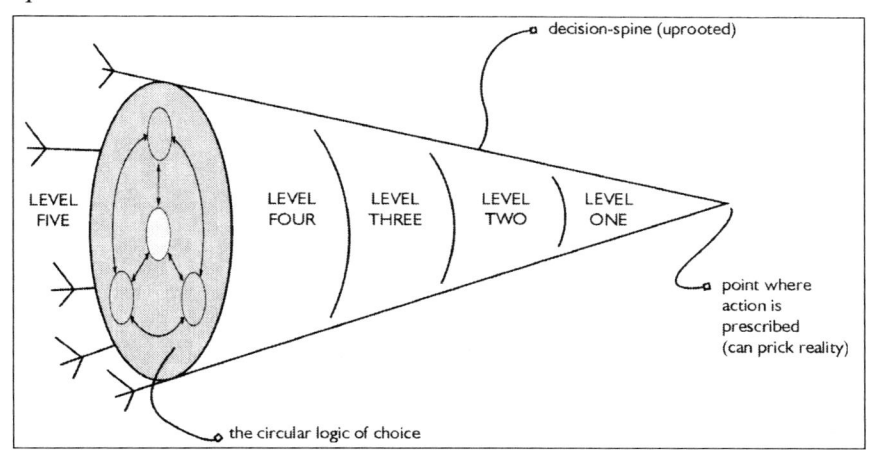

the *real*. Elsewhere (Humphreys, 2007; Humphreys & Jones, 2006), we have described how these constraints are negotiated and set at five qualitatively different levels of problem representation. These are *level 5,* exploring "what needs to be thought about"; *level 4,* expressing the problem and identifying frames in which it is to be represented; *level 3,* developing structure within a frame; *level 2,* exploring what-if questions within the frame;, and *level 1,* making best assessments. The way that participants in the group decision-making process agree to set the constraints at these five levels progressively establishes their view of the "truth about the decision situation."

According to Michel Foucault, "truth is a thing of this world: it is produced only by virtue of multiple forms of constraint" (Foucault, 1980, p. 131), and in this sense, all these discourses identified at the various levels, in the problem expressing, framing, and fixing processes, are involved in moving toward prescribing the *one and only best course of action* (the "true solution"), which can be considered as particularised and, sometimes, artificial *discourses of truth.* Conversely, the representation of the problem constructed through the use of this discourse does not reveal the "real" situation. Rather it is an artefact, which, as has been discussed elsewhere (Humphreys, 1998), is generally advanced, in organisational communications, through the other, more general, kinds of discourse of truth which may be coercive or rely upon cycles of seduction, challenge, and ruse between those people who are party to the decision.

Within these discourses of truth, naming identifies particular subjects and objects, thus giving them implicitly fixed identities extending through time and space (Lacan, 1977). Information about the relationships between them is provided entirely in the terms specified by the communicator (Eco, 1985). Such telling about what "is" or what "will be if these prescriptions are implemented" may be useful for establishing control or coordination in local decision making processes, but locks out consideration and exploration of potential resources and pathways that are not described explicitly and exhaustively in the structure of the problem representation (Humphreys & Brezillon, 2002).

In practice, decision-making processes founded in the circular logic of choice spiral within five levels of increasing constraint in problem representation, though a *decision-spine,* located in the symbolic-imaginary, capable of "pricking the *real*" at its point. The *decision-spine* is named by analogy with the structure and characteristics, in the real world, of an uprooted spine from a hedgehog, as illustrated in Figure 2.

THE DECISION HEDGEHOG

Located within the plane of the symbolic-imaginary, the decision spine is rooted in cognitive operations at level 5—exploring what needs to be thought about—(see Figure 2). Such explorations are *not* necessarily bounded within the spine, but can extend throughout the unbounded body of an imaginary and symbolic *decision-hedgehog*—a "body without organs" in the language of Deleuze and Guattari (1988, pp. 149-166). If we want to provide effective support for innovative and creative, rather than merely prescriptive, decision making, then we need to understand how cognitive operations beyond the spine provide the impetus for innovative and creative decision-making—understood as a rich and continuing process at the core of organisational and social life.

According to the conventional decision-theoretic logic, the act of choice within a single decision spine (i.e., gaining commitment of the participating group to implement the course of action prescribed within the spine as "preferred" or "optimal") "solves the problem" and therefore terminates the decision-making and the processes that support it (Kleindorfer, Kunreuther, & Schoemaker, 1993; Phillips, 1988). Narrative accounts of the decision making process that led to the chosen action tend to be justificatory (Humphreys, 1998). These justificatory stories trace back along paths framed within the decision spine, starting from the point of choice, ignoring (as "irrelevant" or "confusing") any narratives that traverse pathways that were not constrained within the spine. This is a major contributor to the failures of effort to support decision-making, predicated on this logic, which were identified by Humphreys and Nappelbaum (1997).

Conceptualising decision making as "learning" (Argyris & Schon, 1996; Senge, 2003) requires gaining feedback from the effects of embarking on "chosen" courses of action (pricking the *real* to gain information) that is not treated in isolation, like a diagnosis. Instead, this process, to allow learning through generating new knowledge relevant to decision making, must extend the rhizome that constitutes the body-without-organs of the *decision-hedgehog,* in which the roots of the decision spines are located, enriching the contextual knowledge for subsequent decision making along a plethora of other spines rooted in this rhizome (Figure 3).

The decision-hedgehog rhizome is not simply a reference structure or high-level frame informing the selection of decision spines. Deleuze and Guattari (1988. p. 12) point out:

The rhizome is altogether different. Make a map, not a tracing.... What distinguishes the map from the tracing is that it is entirely oriented toward an experimentation in contact with the real...It is itself part of the rhizome. The map is open and connectable in all of its dimensions; it is detachable, reversible, and susceptible to constant modifications. It can be torn, reversed, adapted to any kind of mounting, reworked by an individual, group or social formation

At the personal level in creative decision-making, the decision hedgehog rhizome is experienced as a map formed through exploring potential pathways to develop contextual knowledge, rather than as a tracing of "reality." Resources for conceptualisation of collaborative outcomes may be innovatively accessed and their transformation imagined through voyages along these pathways, doubled in imagination and in reality.

At the social level in creative decision making, the rhizome is activated, extended, and revised by the participants in the group, through making and exchanging stories about discovery and innovation in the conceptualisation, utilisation, and transformation of resources for living. When they are authored in multimedia, these stories involve *showing* as well as *telling* what is, and what *could* be, thus enriching context—rather than *being told* what *should* be, thus proceduralising particular aspects of context (Humphreys & Brezillon, 2002; Humphreys, Lorac, & Ramella, 2001).

Nurturing the Decision-Hedgehog Rhizome

In creative decision making, the fundamental dilemma about how to proceed, at least at the outset is: whether to aim for immediate decision taking (action) by spiralling down a decision spine, with the aim to "prick the real" or whether to nurture the decision hedgehog's body-without-organs by telling and exchanging stories which nurtures the decision hedgehog's rhizome and

Figure 3. Decision hedgehog: Open for exploration and nurturance in the plane of the symbolic/imaginary

Figure 4. Decision-hedgehog cross-section: decision-spines rooted in the rhizome

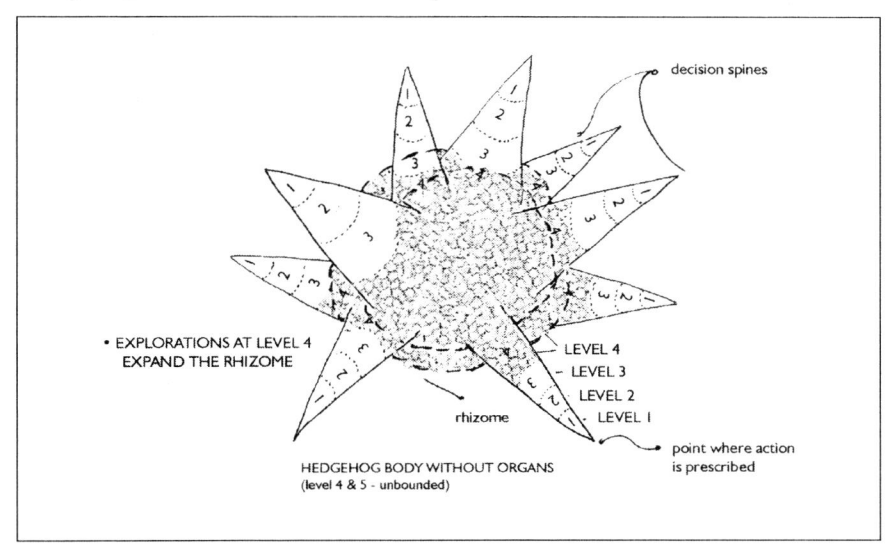

increasing its semantic diversity and intensity of connections. Thus two kinds of story telling are intertwined in creative decision-making:

- Telling and exchanging stories that support the process of spiralling down a spine to "prick the real," and the interpretation of the subsequent impact of the decision on local reality.
- Telling and exchanging stories that nurture the decision-hedgehog, as collaborating groups construct maps of potential possibilities and opportunities, thus enriching contextual knowledge.

Creative decision-making does not presume the hegemony of either type of outcome in directing the design of decision-making processes and support for these processes. Rather, it aims for a dynamic balance between them, through the manner in which the processes supporting their generation are designed.

Enabling Collaborative Authoring of Outcomes

The fundamental aim of storytelling that nurtures the decision hedgehog is to enrich contextual knowledge for decision making through authoring of narratives within the rhizome. This story telling activity can be linked with localised processes involved in proceduralising parts of this contextual knowledge, on a conditional basis, in constructing and exploring decision-spines. All these processes are doubled in the parallel planes of the *imaginary/symbolic* and the *real* (Deleuze & Guattari, 1988; Humphreys & Jones, 2006; Kaufman, 1998).

In reality, participants engage in story telling as associated creative activities involving improvisation and communication in rich media. They work with imaginary ideas and develop a variety of open symbolic representations (plateaus) within the rhizome. When we communicate these, we engage in real authoring activities using our imagination to create symbolic content and our production skills to communicate this content as mediated narrative.

GROUP DECISION AUTHORING AND COMMUNICATION SUPPORT (GDACS)

GDACS (Humphreys, 2007; Humphreys & Jones, 2006) supports creative authoring: enriching contextual knowledge that can both inform and improve the process of developing proceduralised context at levels 5 and 4 within a decision spine and also nurture the rhizome wherein decision-spines are rooted in the Decision-Hedgehog's body-without organs. GDACS provides comprehensive support for these processes through the convergence of the processes shown in Figure 5.

Facilitating environments for GDACS range from purpose built decision conferencing rooms and "pods" (Phillips, 1989), accelerated solutions environments (Jones & Lyden-Cowan, 2002), and flexible learning environments (Jones, 2005) to wireless hotspots and public infrastructure designed by architects to enable group work in the Internet-enabled laptop age. Such environments typically create knowledge-rich arenas, and involve interactive technology and feedback systems (visual and data). Event design and production support may be provided, together with spatial facilitation of group, private, and interpersonal work (Humphreys, 2007; Humphreys & Jones, 2006). In most cases, the idea of the *proscenium* exists: incorporating a back stage and a front stage, where participants are enabled, and the work mediated, by facilitators and support teams.

The use of participatory multimedia and authoring in rich language enables us to create a stage on which the players, actors, authors, stagehands, and audience are all present and where the proscenium shifts to the interface with the screen. The collaborative interactions that elicit conditions of "coming to know" within the framework of the proscenium, the interaction with the physical environment in constructing the rhizome that provides the pathways leading through the proscenium background (the "scene" of mise-en-scene), the actors and improvisation on the stage and the crafts associated with production of signifying artefacts in the proscenium foreground (or arena, theatre-in the-round), combine to enable sense-making and contingent encounters with the *real*.

The language of the design process has emerged as a means by which groups socially construct outcomes at every level of GDACS. Such language is used to enable the design of procedures for decision-making as well as providing frames within which the decisions may be manifest—supporting rapid iterative cycles of decision-making, anchored within artefacts leading in turn to rapid cycles of reflection and reaction. Use of rich, audiovisual language in authorship and production in multimedia within GDACS provides a rich set of constructs, better equipping us to co-author collaborative outcomes, showing as well as telling *what is* and *what could* be (Humphreys & Brezillon, 2002).

This convergence also raises new challenges for how we design, organise, and support creative decision making in groups, the physical environments we construct for ourselves to work in, the organisation of our knowledge systems, and how we organise ourselves to achieve desired outcomes.

REFERENCES

Argyris, C., & Schon, D. (1996). *Organizational learning II: Theory, method, and practice*. Reading, MA: Addison-Wesley Longman.

Bannon, L.J. (2007). CSCW – a challenge to certain (G)DSS perspectives on the role of decisions, information and technology in organizations? In P. Humphreys, S. Ayestaran, A. McCosh & B. Mayon-White (Eds.),

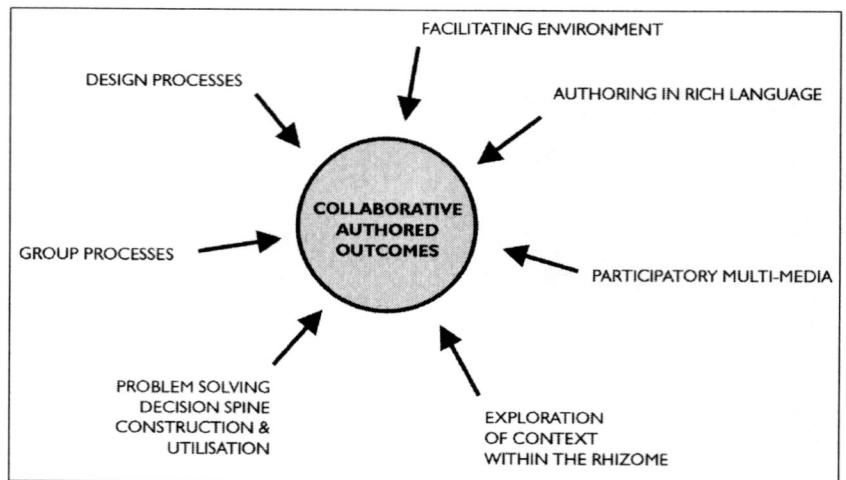

Figure 5. Converging processes in GDACS

Decision support in organisational transformation. London: Chapman and Hall.

Carlsson, S. (2002). Designing DSS based on an attention based view of the firm. In F. Adam, P. Brezillon, P. Humphreys & J.-C. Pomerol (Eds.), *Decision making and decision support in the Internet age.* Cork, Ireland: Oaktree Press.

Cyert, R.M., & March, J.G. (1992). *A behavioral theory of the firm* (2nd ed). Cambridge, MA: Blackwell Business.

Deleuze, G., & Guattari, F. (1988). *A thousand plateaus (capitalism and schizophrenia, Vol II).* London: The Athlone Press.

Eco, U. (1985). *Semiotics and the philosophy of language.* New York, Macmillan.

Foucault, M. (1980). *Power/knowledge: Selected interviews and other writings.* New York: Pantheon.

Huber, G. (1981). The nature of organizational decision making and the design of decision support systems. *MIS Quarterly, 5,* 1-10.

Humphreys, P.C. (1989). Intelligence in decision support: A process model. In G. Doukidis, F. Land & G. Miller (Eds.), *Knowledge based management support systems.* Chichester: Ellis Horwood.

Humphreys, P.C. (1998). Discourses underpinning decision support. In D. Berkeley, G. Widmeyer, P. Brezillon & V. Rajkovic (Eds.), *Context sensitive decision support systems.* London: Chapman & Hall.

Humphreys, P.C. (2007). *Decision support systems and representation levels in the decision spine.*

Humphreys, P.C., & Brezillon, P. (2002). Combining rich and restricted languages in multimedia: Enrichment of context for innovative decisions. In F. Adam, P. Brezillon, P. Humphreys & J.-C. Pomerol (Eds.), *Decision making and decision support in the Internet age.* Cork, Ireland: Oaktree Press.

Humphreys, P.C., & Jones, G.A. (2006). The evolution of group support systems to enable collaborative authoring of outcomes. *World Futures, 62,* 1-30.

Humphreys, P.C., Lorac, C., & Ramella, M. (2001). Creative support for innovative decision making. *Journal of Decision Systems, 10,* 241-264.

Humphreys, P.C., & Nappelbaum, E. (1997). Structure and communications in the process of organisational change. In P. Humphreys, S. Ayestaran, A. McCosh & B. Mayon-White (Eds.), *Decision support in organisational transformation.* London: Chapman and Hall.

Jones, G.A. (2005). *Learning environments for collaborative authored outcomes* (Research Report LML-LUDIC-RR-002). London: London Multimedia Lab for Audiovisual Composition and Communication.

Jones, G.A., & Lyden-Cowan, C. (2002). The bridge: Activating potent decision making in organizations. In F. Adam, P. Brezillon, P. Humphreys & J.-C. Pomerol (Eds.), *Decision making and decision support in the Internet age.* Cork, Ireland: Oaktree Press.

Kaufman, E. (1998). Madness and repetition: The absence of work in Deleuze, Foucault and Jacques Martin. In E. Kaufman & K. Heller (Eds.), *Deleuze and Guattari., new mappings in politics, philosophy and culture.* Minneapolis: University of Minnesota Free Press.

Kleindorfer, P.R., Kunreuther, H.C., & Shoemaker, P.H. (1993). *Decision sciences: An integrative perspective.* Cambridge: Cambridge University Press.

Lacan, J. (1977) The agency of the letter in the unconscious. In J. Lacan (Ed.) *Ecrits.* London: Tavistock

Nappelbaum, E.L. (1997). Systems logic for problem formulation and choice. In P. Humphreys, S. Ayestaran, A. McCosh & B. Mayon-White (Eds.), *Decision support in organizational transformation.* London: Chapman & Hall.

Occasio, W. (1997, Summer). Towards an attention-based view of the firm [Special issue]. *Strategic Management Journal, 18.*

Phillips, L.D. (1988). Conferencing to consensus. In J. Hawgood & P.C. Humphreys (Eds.), *Effective decision support systems.* Aldershot, UK: Gower.

Phillips, L.D. (1989). People-centred group decision support. In G. Doukidis, F. Land & G. Miller (Eds.), *Knowledge management support systems.* Chichester: Ellis Horwood.

Senge, P. (2003). *The fifth discipline fieldbook.* London: Nicholas Brealey Publishing.

Simon, H.A. (1960). *The new science of management decision.* New York: Harper & Row.

Stabell, C. (1987). Decision support systems: Alternative perspectives and schools. *Decision Support Systems, 3,* 243-251.

Decision Making and Support Tools for Design of Machining Systems

A. Dolgui
Ecole Nationale Supérieure des Mines de Saint-Etienne, France

O. Guschinskaya
Ecole Nationale Supérieure des Mines de Saint-Etienne, France

N. Guschinsky
United Institute of Informatics Problems, Belarus

G. Levin
United Institute of Informatics Problems, Belarus

INTRODUCTION

The *design of manufacturing systems* is a wide open area for development and application of decision making and decision support technologies. This domain is characterized by the necessity to combine the standard decision making methods, sophisticated operational research techniques, and some specific rules based on expert knowledge to take into account principal technological constraints and criteria.

A promising trend in this area deals with the development of integrated software tools (Brown, 2004; Grieves, 2005; Stark, 2005). Their main idea consists in integrating product and manufacturing data into a common database. This enables product designers to consider the manufacturing processes constraints at the early product design stage. At the same time, all data of product design should be used directly for optimizing the corresponding manufacturing system. That is why the core of these software tools is a powerful extendable database, supported by a user friendly software environment. This database normally contains digital models of product and processes. In order to find an optimal manufacturing system configuration, a set of advanced decision making and decision support methods are used for data processing.

In this work we present the main principles and ideas of decision making by the example of decision and support soluton for machining systems used for mass production. The used approach is based on several techniques:

- Powerful database of standard solutions and efficient mecanisms to search the existing elements
- Expert system to choose better solutions from database;
- Line balancing model based on shortest path approach;
- Set of problem oriented rules; and
- User friendly software environment.

These techniques are combined in the decision support software tool for optimal process planning, line balancing, and equipment selection for optimal design of a transfer machine with rotary or mobile table.

BACKGROUND

The studing of line design problems began by considering the simple *assembly line balancing problem* (SALBP) (Baybars, 1986; Scholl & Klein, 1998). The SALBP consists in assigning a set of operations to identical consecutive stations minimizing the number of stations required, subject to *precedence constraints* between operations and *cycle time* constraints. Many exact and heuristic approaches for SALBP were suggested in literature: lagrange relaxation techniques (Aghezzaf & Artiba, 1995), branch and bound algorithms (van Assche & Herroelen, 1998; Ugurdag, Papachristou, & Rachamadugu, 1997; Scholl & Klein, 1998), and heuristics and meta-heuristics (Arcus, 1966; Helgeson

& Birnie, 1961; Rekiek, De Lit, Pellichero, L'Eglise, Fouda, Falkenauer et al., 2001). This list is not exhaustive. A state-of-the-art can be found in (Baybars, 1986; Becker & Scholl, 2006; Erel & Sarin, 1998; Ghosh & Gagnon, 1989; Rekiek, Dolgui, Delchambre, & Bratcu, 2002).

The problem where line balancing is combined with equipment selection is often called *simple assembly line design problem* (SALDP) (Baybars, 1986; Becker & Scholl, 2006) or *single-product assembly system design problem* (SPASDP) (Gadidov & Wilhelm, 2000). SALDP considers the "high-level" logical layout design with equipment selection (one per station) from a set of alternatives. There are several equipment alternatives for each operation, and often a particular piece of equipment is efficient for some operations, but not for others (Bukchin & Tzur, 2000; Bukchin & Rubinovich, 2003). There is a given set of equipment types; each type is associated with a specific cost. The equipment cost is assumed to include the purchasing and operational cost. The duration of an operation depends on the equipment selected. An operation can be performed at any station, provided that the equipment selected for this station is appropriate and that precedence relations are satisfied. The total station time should not exceed the predetermined cycle time. The problem consists of selecting equipment and assigning operations to each station. The objective is to minimize the total equipment cost.

The *balancing of transfer lines and machines* (Dolgui, Guschinsky, & Levin, 2000) deals with grouping operations into a number of blocks (sets of operations performed by a spindle head) and assigning these blocks to stations. Each block requires a piece of equipment (a multi-spindle head), which incurs a purchase cost. Therefore, it is necessary to minimize both the number of stations and the number of blocks. To do it, all possible operations assignments to blocks and stations must be considered; otherwise the optimality of a solution cannot be guaranteed. The set of alternative blocks is not known in advance and the parameters of a block depend on the set of operations assigned to it. Therefore, the balancing of machining systems, as it was demonstrated in (Dolgui, Finel, Guschinsky, Levin, & Vernadat, 2006), is more complex than SALBP and SALDP.

MACHINE TOOL ENGINEERING

Transfer machines are dedicated to the mass production of a family of similar products and widely used in the automotive industry (Hitomi, 1996). Designing and balancing such machines is a very complex problem due to necessity to take into account the specific machining constraints. At the same time, to acquire a machine sell order, the manufacturers must provide their customers with the results of the preliminary design (general plans of the machine and an estimation of the price) as quickly as possible. Therefore, it is vitally important for manufacturers to have a decision making methodology and decision support system (Dolgui, Guschinskaya, Guschinsky, & Levin, 2005).

Thus, in order to help designers to find a high-quality (and if possible an optimal) architecture of transfer machine corresponding to the customer demand, we developed and implemented a methodology and a prototype of decision support system named "*machine tools engineering*" (MTE).

This decision support system deals with the optimization of the logical layout design of *transfer machines* and provides designers with an integrated design environment. We depicted the different design stages as well as the implemented in MTE software tool operational research and decision-aid methods.

A decision support system devoted to the design of transfer machines has to provide users with graphical tools to make the design process fast and easy. In addition, it must be capable to help designers to make decisions based on expert knowledge and technological requirements. To reach these objectives, MTE was developed in the design environment of popular commercial CAD system *AutoCad Mechanical Desktop 2006*. Its conceptual environment makes the creation, editing, and navigation of solids and surfaces simple and intuitive. The modules containing the developed optimization methods are plug-ins embedded to AutoCad Mechanical Desktop 2006. This system configuration enables designers to use the common data format at all preliminary design stages.

MTE is dedicated to the preliminary design of transfer unit head machines (machines composed from standard units) with the following configurations:

1. *Multi-positional machines with rotary table.*
   A part is sequentially machined on m working positions and is moved from one position to the

next one using a rotary table. The rotary table is divided into $m+1$ sectors: m of them correspond to the working positions and one sector is served for loading the billet and unloading the part. Therefore, at each moment m parts are machined—one per working position. Each working position may be accessible for one or two (one vertical and one horizontal) spindle heads. The spindle heads of each working position are activated simultaneously. Thus, all spindle heads perform operations on parts in parallel.

2. *Machines with mobile table*. These machines are used for the fabrication of parts that cannot be produced on multi-positional machines with rotary table because of their dimensions (this type of machine has a lower productivity than rotary table machines since only one part can be machined within the *cycle time*). Here, a part is machined on m ($m \leq 3$) working positions and is moved from one position to the next one using a mobile table. Each working position has one or two (one vertical and one horizontal, or two horizontal) spindle heads. The last working position may have three spindle heads (one vertical and two horizontal, or three horizontal). The spindle heads of each working position are activated simultaneously. At each moment only one position is active and the spindle heads of the active working position perform operations on the machined part. The first position is used also for unloading the part after machining and loading the billet.

DECISION MAKING METHODOLOGY

A design methodology for manufacturing systems can be defined as a set of procedures that analyzes and segregates a complex *manufacturing system design* task into simpler manageable sub-design tasks while still maintaining their links and interdependencies (Wilheim, Smith, & Bidanda, 1995). An illustration of *MTE decision support system* is given in Figure 1 and the corresponding decision making procedure is presented in Table 1 (Dolgui et al., 2005).

Product/Process Modeling

Part Modeling

The first step deals with the *modeling of a part* to be machined. The clients provide the machine tool manufacturer with the specifications of a part already designed,

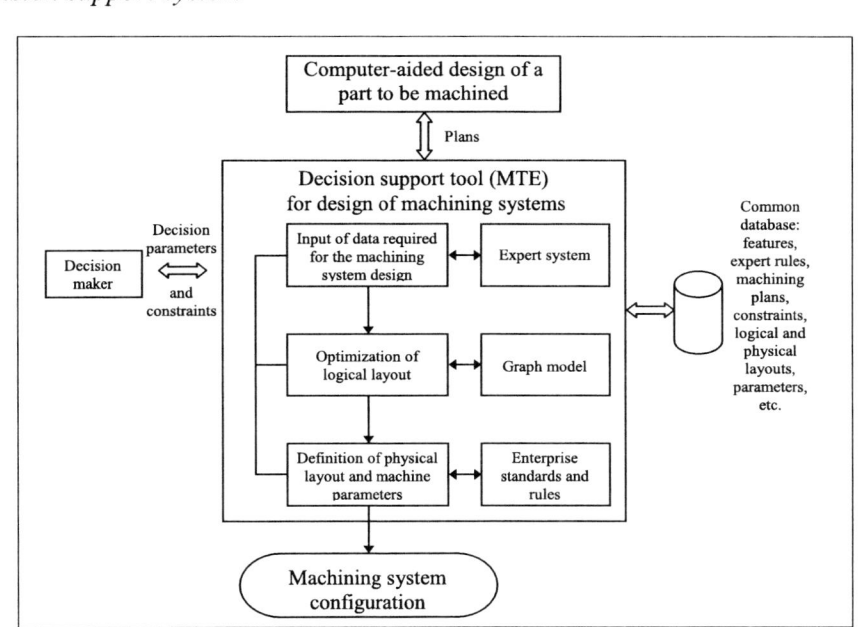

Figure 1. MTE decision support system

Table 1. General methodology of decision making for a machining system design

Stages and steps
Stage 1. Input of data required for the machining system design
Step 1.1. Part modeling with features
Step 1.2. Input of part and machine properties
Step 1.3. Process planning using an expert system
Step 1.4. Constraints generation based on machining data and user experience
Stage 2. Optimization of logical layout
Step 2.1. Finding all solutions minimizing the number of spindle heads and working positions while assigning operations to working positions and defining cutting modes for spindle heads
Step 2.2. Choice of a solution among the optimal ones (solution to be applied)
Stage 3. Definition of physical layout and machine parameters
Step 3.1 Working plan documentation
Step 3.2. Part positioning
Step 3.3. Equipment selection
Step 3.4. Preliminary 3D layout design
Step 3.5. Control equipment and additional devices selection
Step 3.6. Cost estimation

which they want to produce using a transfer machine. Usually, the manufacturing process includes milling, drilling, boring, and so forth, a set of part elements such as planes, facets, holes of different types (cylindrical, bevel, threaded, etc.). Each element concerns a certain side (or surface) of the part and is characterized by a set of technological parameters, like required tolerances and surface conditions. Figure 2 shows an example of a part that was modeled in the MTE system.

In order to use the same format for the geometric and technological data, the part is modeled with machining features. The concept of feature associates the technological characteristics of a machining element with its geometric parameters. Therefore, the part modeling step demands analyzing the part to be machined and identifying features, their geometric and topological relations.

To make the design of features easier and faster, we analyzed a certain number of standard elements. A graphic library of the most common parameterized features was developed and embedded to AutoCad Mechanical Desktop 2006. The corresponding technological characteristics are stored in the data fields associated with each feature.

When the part has been modeled, some additional characteristics of the part (for example, the material and its properties, the properties of the billet, etc.), and of the machine (for example, the desired productivity, the cooling method, the type of cooling liquid, etc.) must be defined as well as a desired type of machine (with rotary or mobile table) must be selected.

Process Planning

At this stage, the machining operations, required tools and their parameters for each part feature are determined. The *process plan* of a part feature, that is, a set of operations to be performed in order to provide the required geometric and technological characteristics, is chosen using the following parameters: the condition of surface before machining, the diameter of machining holes, and the required precision for each machining element. These parameters are stored in the data fields associated with the features. Analyzing their values and using the expert system, all possible process plans for each feature can be chosen from the process plans database. This database contains also dependences between the feature parameters and the set of all pos-

Figure 2. Part to be machined

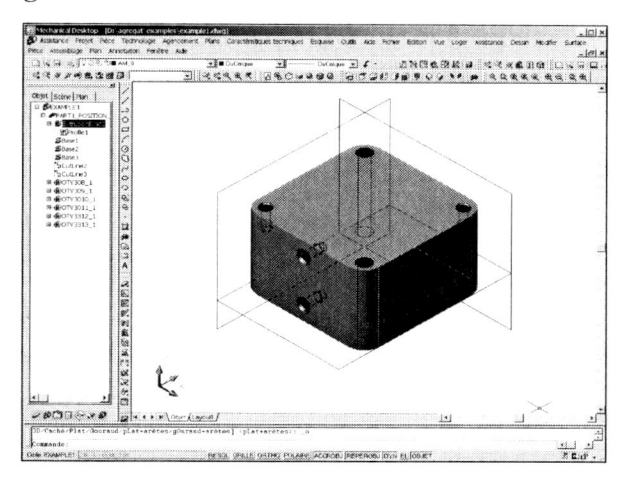

sible operations that a machine equipped by standard spindle heads can process. Then, for each feature and each possible process plan the corresponding tolerances are calculated. The obtained values of tolerances are compared with those required and the plan providing the values nearest to the required is chosen. For this chosen plan, the parameters of operations (like cutting depth, machining length, type and material of cutting tool, working stroke, and cutting mode) are determined automatically. Cutting mode is defined by minimal, maximum, and recommended values of the following parameters: cutting speed, feed rates per minute and per revolution. Then, the user, who can replace or modify automatically chosen plans, analyzes the plans suggested by the decision support tool. New process plans can be stored in the database.

In order to establish a total process plan, the individual machining plans selected for the features must be completed by introducing the existing relations between the operations of different features. These relations are introduced using different types of constraints.

Generation of Constraints

The decision support tool MTE considers the following types of relations between machining operations:

a. *Precedence constraints* which define possible sequences of operations and are determined by a number of known technological factors (fixed sequences of operations for machining features, the presence of roughing, semi-finishing and finishing operations, etc.).
b. *Inclusion constraints* reflect the necessity to perform some operations on the same working position or even by the same spindle head. They are implied by the required precision (tolerance) of mutual disposition of machined features as well as a number of additional factors.
c. *Exclusion constraints* are used in the cases when it is impossible to assign some pairs of operations to the same working position (or to the same spindle head). It can be caused by a number of constructional and technological constraints: mutual influence of these operations, a forbidden tool location, and so forth. This type of constraint must be fulfilled also for operations executed on the different sides of the part because they cannot be performed by the same spindle head.

Some constraints are automatically generated by the decision support tool MTE. For this, all operations can be divided into four groups according to the finish state:

1. Milling operations
2. Roughing operations (boring, drilling with the drill diameter more than 20 mm, countersinking with the countersink diameter more than 30 mm)
3. All other operations except threading operations
4. Threading operations.

Usually, no operation of a group can be started before the end of all previous group operations, therefore the corresponding precedence constraints are generated automatically. Generally, the same equipment cannot perform operations of two different groups. Thus, they cannot be assigned to the same spindle head. Since all spindle heads of a working position are activated simultaneously, operations from different groups can not be assigned to the same working position; therefore the corresponding *exclusion constraints* are also generated automatically. In accordance with their expert knowledge or preferences users can introduce complementary constraints of any type or remove the constraints generated automatically.

The overall equipment dimensions limit the total number of working positions and the number of blocks at each working position by the values of the parameters $\overline{m}$ and $\overline{n}$ respectively. The values of $\overline{m}$ and $\overline{n}$ are obtained taking into account the available machine configuration and economical constraints.

The objective production rate is obtained, if the machine *cycle time T(P)* does not exceed the maximum authorized value T_0.

Logical Layout Optimization

The manufacturing information as well as diverse constraints related to the design of spindle heads and working positions are used as input data for the second design stage, that is, *logical layout design* (Wilheim et al., 1995; Zhang, Zhang, & Xu, 2002). The quantity of equipment (spindle heads, working positions) required to produce a part with the given productivity rate defines the final cost of the *transfer machine*. Therefore, the goal of the logical layout optimization is to find a design variant that minimizes the number of working positions and the total number of spindle heads while satisfying all given technological and economical constraints (Dolgui, Guschinsky, Levin, & Proth, 2008).

Problem Statement

If the machining is organized on m working positions, then at the k-th working position $k=1, ..., m$, a subset N_k of the given set **N** of operations is performed. Each set N_k is uniquely partitioned into n_k subsets (N_{kl}, $l=1,...,n_k$), where the operations of each subset N_{kl} are performed by the same spindle head. Such a partition is unique due to the fact that each operation corresponds to one "side" of the part, and only the operations of the same side can be performed by one spindle head. Parameters of the kl-th spindle head and its execution time depend both on the set of operations N_{kl} and their cutting modes.

The logical layout optimization consist in determining simultaneously:

a. The number m of working positions;
b. The partitioning of the given set **N** of operations into subsets N_k, $k = 1,...,m$; and
c. The feed per minute X_{kl} for each N_{kl}, $l = 1,..., n_k$.

Let $P=<P_1,...,P_k,...,P_m>$ is a design solution with $P_k = (P_{k1}, ..., P_{kl},...,P_{kn_k})$ and $P_{kl} = (N_{kl}, X_{kl})$. Let C_1 and C_2 be the relative costs for one working position and one block, respectively. Then the objective function of the considered design problem can be formulated as follows:

$$Min\ Q(P) = C_1 m + C_2 \sum_{k=1}^{m} n_k \qquad (1)$$

Cycle Time Calculation

Let $\lambda(i)$ be the given length of the working stroke for operation $i \in \mathbf{N}$. The execution time $\tau^b(N_{kl}, X_{kl})$ of the set N_{kl} of operations performing by the kl-th spindle head working with the feed per minute X_{kl} is equal to:

$$\tau^b(N_{kl}, X_{kl}) = L(N_{kl})/X_{kl}, \qquad (2)$$

where $L(N_{kl}) = max\{\lambda(i) \mid i \in N_{kl}\}$.

The execution time for all operations of the k-th working position ($k=1,...,m$) is equal to:

$$\tau^p(P_k) = max\{\tau^b(N_{kl}, X_{kl}) \mid l=1,...,n_k\}. \qquad (3)$$

The *cycle time* for *machines with a rotary table* is defined by the maximum value among the execution times of the working positions:

$$T(P)=\tau'' + max\{\tau^p(P_k) \mid k=1, 2..., m\}, \qquad (4)$$

where τ'' is a given constant, an additional time for loading the billet and unloading the part after machining.

The cycle time for *machines with a mobile table* is defined by the sum of the machining times of the working positions:

$$T(P)=\tau'' + \sum_{k=1}^{m} \tau^p(P_k) \qquad (5)$$

Let $\mu(i)$ be a constant that characterizes the tool life rate, $[s_1(i), s_2(i)]$ and $[v_1(i), v_2(i)]$ the ranges of the feasible values of feed per revolution $s(i)$ and spindle speed (cutting speeds) $v(i)$, respectively, for each operation $i \in \mathbf{N}$; $s_0(i)$, $v_0(i)$ are their "recommended" values:

$$\begin{aligned} x_0(i) &= s_0(i)v_0(i), \\ x_1(i) &= s_1(i)v_1(i), \\ x_2(i) &= s_2(i)v_2(i). \end{aligned} \qquad (6)$$

The interval of possible values of the feed per minute for the spindle head which executes the set N of operations $\mathbf{X}(N) = [\underline{X}(N), \overline{X}(N)]$ is calculated as follows:

$$\underline{X}(N) = \max(\max\{x_1(i) | i \in N\}, L(N)/(T_0 - \tau')) \quad (7)$$
$$\overline{X}(N) = \min\{x_2(i) | i \in N\} \quad (8)$$

If the set $\mathbf{X}(N)$ is empty, then operations of the set N cannot be executed by one spindle head. Otherwise, a preliminary value $x \in \mathbf{X}(N)$ might be chosen in the following way:

$$x^*(N) = \min\{(L(N)/\lambda(i))^{\mu(i)} x_0(i) | i \in N\} \quad (9)$$
$$x^{**}(N) = \max\{\underline{X}(N), x^*\} \quad (10)$$
$$x(N) = \min\{x^{**}, \overline{X}(N)\} \quad (11)$$

In this case, the feed per revolution for operation i is equal to $s(i,x) = \min[s_2(i), x/v_1(i)]$, and the cutting speed is equal to $v(i,x) = x/s(i,x)$.

Modeling of Constraints

We assume that the given productivity is achieved, if the cycle time $T(P)$ (calculated) does not exceed the maximum value T_0.

$$T(P) \leq T_0 \quad (12)$$

The *precedence constraints* can be specified by an acyclic digraph $G^{OR} = (\mathbf{N}, D^{OR})$ where an arc $(i,j) \in D^{OR}$ if and only if the operation i has to be executed before the operation j. Thus, for each operation $j \in \mathbf{N}$, a set $Pred(j)$ of its immediate predecessors is determined.

The *inclusion constraints* can be given by undirected graphs $G^{SH} = (\mathbf{N}, E^{SH})$ and $G^{SP} = (\mathbf{N}, E^{SP})$ where the edge $(i,j) \in E^{SH}$ if and only if the operations i and j must be executed by the same spindle head, the edge $(i,j) \in E^{SP}$ if and only if the operations i and j must be executed on the same working position.

The *exclusion constraints* can also be defined by undirected graphs $G^{DH} = (\mathbf{N}, E^{DH})$ and $G^{DP} = (\mathbf{N}, E^{DP})$ where the edge $(i,j) \in E^{DH}$ if and only if the operations i and j cannot be executed by the same spindle head, the edge $(i,j) \in E^{DP}$ if and only if the operations i and j cannot be executed on the same working position.

Since for this type of machine the set N_k is partitioned into subsets for spindle heads uniquely, we can define a function $O(N_k)$ whose value is equal to the number of obtained spindle heads. We assume also that this function takes a sufficiently large value if the operations of the set N_k cannot be partitioned into subsets with regard to precedence, inclusion and exclusion constraints, that is, where one of the following conditions holds:

$$\{i,j\} \subseteq N_k, \ (i,j) \in (D^{OR} \cup E^{DP}) \quad (13)$$
$$|\{i,j\} \cap N_k| = 1, \ (i,j) \in E^{SP} \quad (14)$$
$$\{i,j\} \subseteq N_{kl}, \ (i,j) \in E^{DH}, \ l = 1, \ldots, n_k \quad (15)$$
$$|\{i,j\} \cap N_{kl}| = 1, \ l = 1, \ldots, n_k, \ (i,j) \in E^{SP} \quad (16)$$
$$\mathbf{X}(N_{kl}) = \varnothing, \ l = 1, \ldots, n_k \quad (17)$$

Optimization Model

The optimization model of the considered decision making problem for *logical layout design* can be formulated as follows:

$$\text{Minimize } Q(P) = C_1 m + C_2 \sum_{k=1}^{m} O(N_k), \quad (18)$$

subject to:

$$T(P) \leq T_0 \quad (19)$$

$$\bigcup_{k=1}^{m} N_k = \mathbf{N} \quad (20)$$

$$N_{k'} \cap N_{k''} = \varnothing, \ \forall \ k', k'' = 1, \ldots, m \text{ such that } k' \neq k'' \quad (21)$$

$$O(N_k) \leq \overline{n}, \text{ for all } k = 1, \ldots, m \quad (22)$$

$$X_{kl} \in \mathbf{X}(N_{kl}), \text{ for all } k = 1, \ldots, m; \ l = 1, \ldots, n_k \quad (23)$$

$$m = m(P) \leq \overline{m} \quad (24)$$

The objective function (18) is the estimation of the equipment cost; constraint (19) provides the required productivity rate; constraints (20-21) ensure the assignment of all the operations from $\mathbf{N}$, each operation to one and only one working position; (22) provides precedence constraints for operations, inclusion and *exclusion constraints* for spindle heads and working positions; (23) chooses feasible values of the feed per minute for each spindle head; and (24) is the constraint on the number of working positions.

The values $\bar{m}$ and $\bar{n}$ are defined by the type of the machine: for machines with rotary table $\bar{m} \leq 15$ and $\bar{n} = 2$, for machines with mobile table $\bar{m} \leq 3$ and $\bar{n} \leq 3$. For machines with mobile table the expression (22) is replaced by (22´):

$$O(N_k) \leq 2, \ k=1,\ldots,m\text{-}1; \ O(N_m) \leq 3 \qquad (22´)$$

Optimization algorithms are based on the shortest path approach (Dolgui et al., 2000; Dolgui et al., 2008). They find all optimal solutions corresponding to the different machine configurations with different operations' assignment or allocation of spindle heads to working positions. In order to choose a solution to be applied, these solutions can be evaluated by user with other criteria and user's preferences. If the results of the optimization do not satisfy user, it is possible to return to previous stages and make the necessary modifications of constraints and input data.

3D-MODEL AND COST ESTIMATION

The obtained logical layout defines the general configuration of a *transfer machine* and enables designers to complete this logical architecture by selecting the corresponding modular equipment from the library of standard units of *MTE*. At first, designers specify the overall dimensions of the movable table and place the part to be machined on it. The part position defines the angles and positions of the spindle heads.

Then, designers define the dimensions and the specifications of the required equipment that will automatically be designed using the graphical library of standard units. Finally, designers can obtain a preliminary 3D-model of the machine. Figure 3 illustrates a machine with rotary table which consists of six working positions and equipped by one vertical spindle head. Figure 4 shows a machine with mobile table, which consists of two working positions.

In order to estimate the total machine cost, additional devices are to be selected, like control, tool storage, and loading-unloading systems. This choice is guided by some automatically generated suggestions and accompanied by the verification of compatibility with all previous decisions. The costs of all selected devices are obtained from the database which contains market prices of standard units (spindle heads and other machine elements). The total cost estimation enables designers to formulate a commercial offer for customers. Therefore, using the decision support system MTE, machine tools manufacturers can provide their clients with technological plans and a commercial offer in really short times. If clients accept this offer then the detailed design of the machine with the chosen configuration is to be prepared in order to establish a manufacturing plan. At this stage more detailed analysis of machine properties is needed, the manufacturability of parts can be verified using, for example, the finite elements model and simulation (Daschenko, 2003).

Figure 3. 3D-model of a machine with rotary table

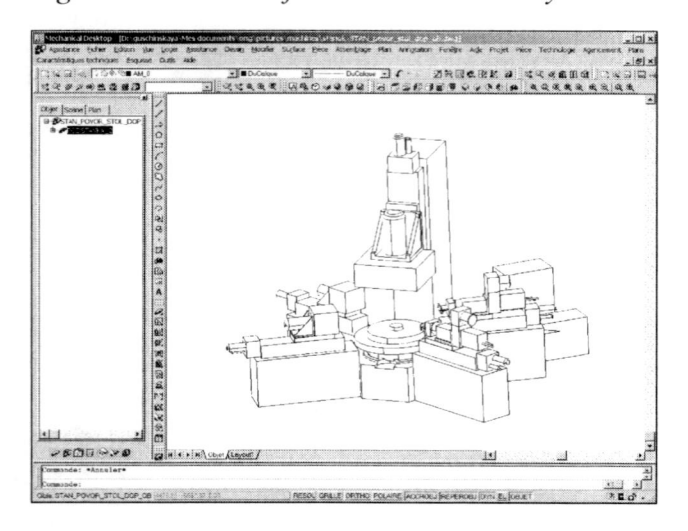

Figure 4. 3D-model of a machine with mobile table

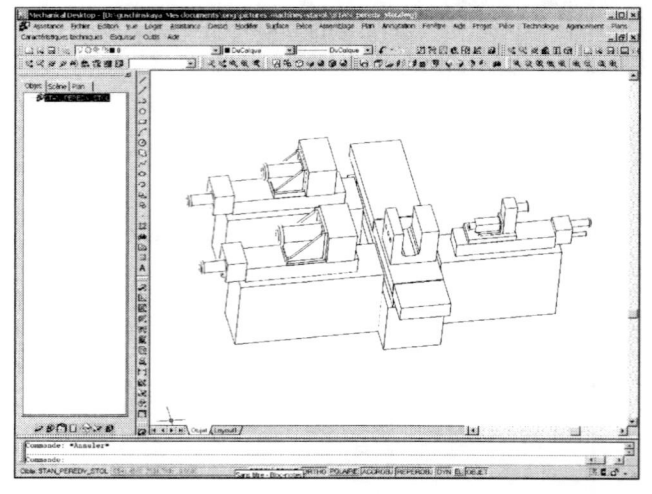

CONCLUSION AND FURTHER RESEARCH

A novel and promising applied area for decision making methods and decision support technologies is the development of decision-aid software tools for manufacturing system design. It is necessary to use conjointly advanced operational research methods, standard decision making approaches, decision support technologies and problem oriented specific rules. We have presented an example of such a decision support system for preliminary *design of machining systems* for mass production.

The integrated *decision support system* MTE was developed to help machine tool designers to obtain a high-quality (and if possible optimal) architecture of *transfer machines*. The system supports the different stages of the logical layout design of a transfer machine: modeling of a part to be machined, process planning, optimization of the machine configuration, its preliminary 3D layout, and cost estimation. The optimization problem of the logical layout is to find the number of working positions and the number of spindle heads, to assign the manufacturing operations to positions, and to choose the cutting modes for each spindle head while minimizing the total equipment cost.

The perspectives of this research consist in the improvement and extension of the suggested approach for a larger class of manufacturing systems: linear *transfer machines*, transfer lines with buffers, multi-flow transfer lines, assembly lines, and so forth. Another promising approach is the integration of the process planning and logical layout steps in a common optimization model using heuristics and meta-heuristics.

ACKNOWLEDGMENT

The authors thank Chris Yukna for the help in editing the English.

REFERENCES

Aghezzaf, E-H., & Artiba, A. (1995). Lagrangean relaxation technique for the general assembly line balancing problem. *Journal of Intelligent Manufacturing, 6*, 123-131.

Arcus, A.L. (1966). COMSOAL: A computer method of sequencing operations for assembly lines. *International Journal of Production Research, 4*, 259-277.

Askin R. G., & Standridge, C. R. (1993) *Modeling and analysis of manufacturing systems*. John Wiley & Sons, Inc.

Baybars, I. (1986). A survey of exact algorithms for the simple assembly line balancing. *Management Science, 32*, 909-932.

Becker, C., & Scholl, A. (2006). A survey on problems and methods in generalized assembly line balancing. *European Journal of Operational Research, 168*, 694-715.

Brown, J. (2004). *Digital manufacturing. The PLM approach to better manufacturing processes*. TechClarity.

Bukchin, J., & Rubinovich, J. (2003). A weighted approach for assembly line design with station paralleling and equipment selection. *IIE Transactions, 35*, 73-85.

Bukchin, J., & Tzur, M. (2000). Design of flexible assembly line to minimize equipment cost. *IIE Transactions, 32*, 585-598.

Dashchenko, A. I. (Ed). (2003). *Manufacturing technologies for machines of the future 21st century technologies*. Springer.

Dolgui, A., Finel, B., Guschinsky, N., Levin, G., & Vernadat, F. (2006). MIP approach to balancing transfer lines with blocks of parallel operations. *IIE Transactions, 38*, 869-882.

Dolgui, A., Guschinskaya, O., Guschinsky, N., & Levin, G. (2005). Conception de systèmes de fabrication: prototype d'un logiciel d'aide à la décision. *Journal of Decision Systems, 14*(4), 489-516.

Dolgui, A., Guschinsky, N., & Levin, G. (2000). *Approaches to balancing of transfer line with block of parallel operations*. Institute of Engineering Cybernetics, Minsk, Preprint No. 8, 42 pages.

Dolgui, A., Guschinsky, N., Levin, G., & Proth, J.-M. (2008). Optimisation of multi-position machines and transfer lines. *European Journal of Operational Research, 185*, 1375-1389.

Erel, E., & Sarin, S. C. (1998). A survey of the assembly line balancing procedures. *Production Planning and Control, 9*(5), 414-434.

Gadidov, R., & Wilhelm, W. (2000). A cutting plane approach for the single-product assembly system design problem. *International Journal of Production Research, 38*(8), 1731-1754.

Ghosh, S., & Gagnon, R. (1989). A comprehensive literature review and analysis of the design, balancing and scheduling of assembly lines. *International Journal Production Research, 27*(4), 637-670.

Grieves, M. (2005). *Product lifecycle management: Driving the next generation of lean thinking*. McGraw Hill.

Helgeson, W. B., & Birnie, D. P. (1961). Assembly line balancing using ranked positional weight technique. *Journal of Industrial Engineering, 12*, 394-398.

Hitomi, K. (1996). *Manufacturing systems engineering*. Taylor & Francis.

Rekiek, B., De Lit, P., Pellichero, F., L'Eglise, T., Fouda, P., Falkenauer, E. et al. (2001). A multiple objective grouping genetic algorithm for assembly line design. *Journal of Intelligent Manufacturing, 12,* 467-485.

Rekiek, B., Dolgui, A., Delchambre, A., & Bratcu, A. (2002). State of art of assembly lines design optimisation. *Annual Reviews in Control, 26*(2), 163-174.

Scholl, A., & Klein, R. (1998). Balancing assembly lines effectively: a computational comparison. *European Journal of Operational Research, 114*, 51-60.

Stark, J. (2005). *Product lifecycle management: 21st century paradigm for product realisation, series: decision engineering*. Springer.

Ugurdag, H. F., Papachristou, C. A., & Rachamadugu, R. (1997). Designing paced assembly lines with fixed number of stations. *European Journal of Operational Research, 102*, 488-501.

van Assche, F., & Herroelen, W. S. (1979). An optimal procedure for the single model deterministic assembly line balancing problems. *European Journal of Operational Research, 3*(2), 142-149.

Wilheim, M, Smith, A. E., & Bidanda, B. (1995). Integrating an expert system and a neural network for process planning. *Engineering Design and Automation, 1*(4), 259-269.

Zhang, G. W., Zhang, S. C., & Xu, Y.S. (2002). Research on flexible transfer line schematic design using hierarchical process planning. *Journal of Materials Processing Technology, 129*, 629-633.

KEY TERMS

Feature: A standard element characterized by both technological and geometrical parameters that have meaning in the definition and machining of a part.

Integrated Decision Support Tool for Design of Machining System: A software tool, which includes the functions of part modeling, process planning, logical and physical layouts optimization, and machining system cost estimation. It is used for the preliminary design of the machining systems.

Logical Layout: An assignment of all operations to be executed to pieces of equipment; usually an optimal logical layout is obtained by solving the corresponding line balancing problem.

Physical Layout: An arrangement of pieces of equipment in the production area.

Process Planning: The activity of taking the product design or specification, which is defined in terms of size, shape, tolerances, finish, material properties, and so forth, and transforming it into detailed list of manufacturing instructions such as specifications for materials, processes, sequences, and machining parameters.

Spindle Head (Spindle Box): A device where several tools are fixed to perform several operations in parallel; all tools of the same spindle head have the same parameters (working stroke, feed per minute) and are activated simultaneously.

Transfer Machine: A machine tool used in the mass production of a unique product or a family of similar products by processing the drilling, boring, milling, and other machining operations in a given order on each part machined.

Decision-Making and Support Tools for Design of Transmission Systems

A. Dolgui
Ecole Nationale Supérieure des Mines de Saint-Etienne, France

N. Guschinsky
United Institute of Informatics Problems, Belarus

G. Levin
United Institute of Informatics Problems, Belarus

INTRODUCTION

Transmission systems are crucial components of many machines and mechanisms. Ken Hurst (1998) highlights that whether you are designing power plants, cars, or washing machines, the power transmission system is an integral component responsible for product success or failure. The components that comprise a power transmission system include those that transfer power directly (coupling and shaft), speed and torque multiplication components (gears, belt drives, etc.), and the related mechanisms (clutches, brakes, etc.; see Freeman & Velinsky, 1995).

Transmission system design is a multistage iterative process of sequential generation and modification of design decisions. These decisions define in many respects the technical and economic characteristics of future products. Searching for suitable design decisions is a highly complex and time-consuming problem due to the necessity to consider and analyze many heterogeneous functional, technical, and economic factors. However, extensive computations, including solving very complex optimization tasks, are needed. As a rule, the design procedures are provided only by a very competent and experienced designer. With ever more complex and combinatorial decisions to be made, even the best designer will need competent design support, of which there is little. Therefore, the design of transmission systems is a wide open area for development and application of decision-making and decision support technologies.

The number of problems arising in the development of decision support systems (DSS) for the design of power transmissions is very large. In particular, the following apply:

- Development of computerized decision-making technology for each design stage with suitable partition of functions between designers and software tools
- Selection and analysis of main design tasks to be solved via software
- Formulation and study of a set of models for these problems providing different levels of model abstraction
- Development of methods and software for searching appropriate design decisions on the basis of these models, taking into account real requirements for accuracy and performances
- Creation of databases to support the decision-making process
- Embedding of optimization models into a user-friendly software environment

In this article, we present the main approaches and ideas of decision making for solving some above-mentioned problems of the initial stage of transmission design where the basic parameters of the transmission system are to be determined.

BACKGROUND

Transmission design is a very complex problem. In literature, the main publications concern the design of specific elements such as springs, gears, and shafts;

see, for example, Litvin (1994), Shigley, Mischke, and Budynas (2003), and Su and Qin (2003). Methods were suggested for the synthesis of structure and choice of parameters for some kinds of transmissions (Hsieh & Tsai, 1996; Nelson & Cipra, 2005; Yan & Hsieh, 1994).

For the design of complex power transmission systems, the functional decomposition approach is often used (Guillot, 1987). Here, a complex transmission system is decomposed to a set of basic elements, and each basic element is then separately optimized. To take into account external conditions for components, complementary constraints are added (Dadié, 1996). Expert systems are widely used in order to consider engineering experience and to integrate partial optimization models into the design process (Dixon, 1995; Su, 1998; Su & Chen, 2003; Su & Qin, 2003). Another method deals with hierarchical decomposition (Dolgui, Guschinsky, & Levin, 1999, 2000, 2007; Krishnamachari & Papalambros, 1997; Michelena & Papalambros, 1995). The optimization model is decomposed and solved as a set of smaller, coordinated subproblems. Such a process is often followed intuitively during the development of the model by adding together selected objectives of each subsystem to obtain an overall system objective. For subproblems, often metaheuristics are used. For example, in Kalyanmoy and Sachin (2003), multiobjective evolutionary algorithms are developed for a gearbox design. Some graph theory models are considered in Guschinsky, Levin, and Dolgui (2006), Liu and Chen (2001), Michelena and Papalambros (1997), and Talpasanu, Yih, and Simionescu (2006).

These and other problems in the development of decision support systems for the design of multiple-unit power transmission systems are also considered in Guschinsky and Levin (2000) and Guschinsky, Levin, and Dolgui (2006).

CONCEPTUAL PROBLEM STATEMENT

Modern industry uses a wide range of transmission systems. Each of them is defined by their functionality, their structure, as well as the characteristics and constructional features of each element and so forth. In this article, we consider mechanical power transmission

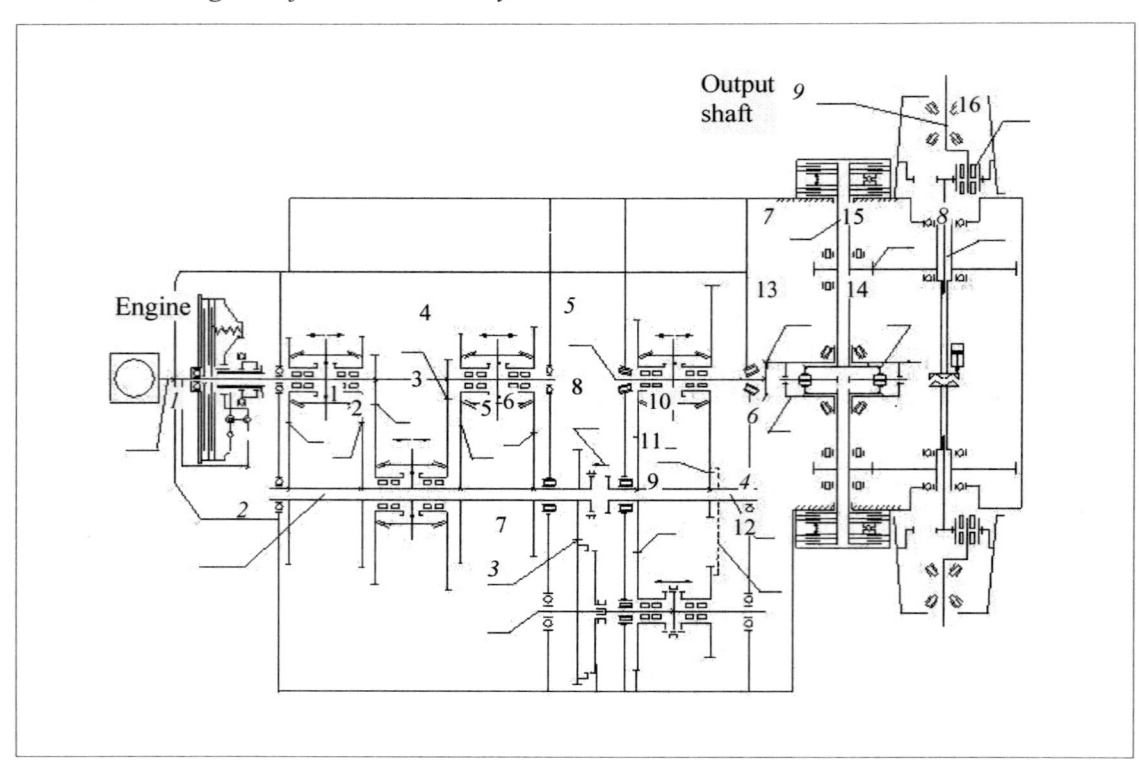

Figure 1. Kinematic diagram of a transmission system

systems that can involve a gearbox and gears of different types to transmit power and motion from the engine to the output shaft. An example of the kinematic scheme of such a transmission system is shown in Figure 1.

In the transmission system design, the following stages are traditionally present:

- Design of the transmission structure as a whole
- Determination of basic design parameters of the transmission system and its elements
- Physical layout design including 3-D modeling
- Refinement of design parameters of transmission elements taking into account the physical layout
- Analysis of the project and estimation of its basic technical and economic behaviors

We focus on the second stage, that is, the determination of the basic design parameters of the transmission system and its elements. This stage is the most complex from the combinatorial perspective. It is executed under the assumptions that the loading transmission conditions plus the strength characteristics of element materials are known, and the structure of a transmission system is already chosen. At this stage, we determine transmission ratios of all kinematic chains and the distribution of these transmission ratios to gears as well as the design parameters of gears (in particular, type, reference diameters and thickness, module and number of teeth, etc.) and shafts (outer diameter).

The following input data are considered:

- Nominal speed of an engine
- Desired set of nominal speeds for output shafts
- Loading transmission conditions for each kinematic chain
- Ranges of transmission ratios for gears and maximal speeds of shafts
- Strength characteristics of materials
- Required center distances

The main criteria for suitable design decisions are as follows:

- Deviation of output nominal speeds from the desired values (minimized)
- Transmission lifetime (maximized)
- Total mass of gears and shafts (minimized)

GENERAL SCHEME OF DECISION-MAKING AND DECISION-SUPPORT TOOL ARCHITECTURE

The following scheme can be used. It is based on simultaneous use of several methods of multicriteria optimization and decomposition techniques in combination with several methods of nonlinear optimization. This scheme takes into account the peculiarities of the design problem and supposes an active participation of an experienced designer in the decision making.

The main role of the designer in this scheme is to analyze solutions provided by the decision support system and to manage the general process of the design, including the choice of control parameters of the methods used. DSS solves complex mathematical problems in order to provide the designer with suitable decisions to be analyzed.

The scheme assumes sequential execution of the following procedures:

a. Specification of requirements for the considered design stage including input of necessary data for the whole problem
b. Kinematic computation of the transmission system, which consists of determining the transmission ratios of all kinematic chains. The result must provide minimal deviation of the nominal speeds of output shafts from the desired values while respecting the constraints on the admissible ranges of transmission ratios for gears and maximal speeds for shafts. The deviation is treated as a weighted sum of squares of the differences between the logarithms of the obtained speeds and that of the desired speeds. By changing the weights the designer can select a more suitable set of nominal speeds for output shafts.

The obtained nominal speeds for output shafts are used as input data at the next stages. In addition, the procedure determines transmission ratios for all gears that correspond to the nominal speeds for output shafts and constraints on gear ratio ranges and maximal speeds for shafts. These transmission ratios are preliminary and can be modified later.

c. Strength optimization for the transmission system consists of determining the transmission ratios for gears and the basic design parameters for gears and shafts (wheel diameters and thickness of gears, outer diameters of shafts, etc.) for a fixed value of the total transmission life. The obtained transmission ratios correspond to the nominal speeds of output shafts derived at the previous stage. The chosen design parameters provide a minimal estimation of the total mass for gears and shafts while satisfying constraints. By changing the required total transmission life, the designer can select design decisions with an appropriate combination of the two criteria.

d. Refined strength optimization coordinates basic design parameters with requirements on center distances and modules for groups of gears. Decisions are made on the basis of the results of the previous procedures. This process determines additional design parameters of gears: tooth number, module, profile correction factors, tooth angles, and so forth, as well as refines early obtained parameters and characteristics of the design decision.

e. Documenting step

After each step, the designer analyzes the recommended design decision. Then he or she can go to the next procedure or come back to a previous step and repeat it with modified data.

Procedures b and c are crucial in the proposed scheme. They were implemented on the basis of optimization approaches obtained from a general mathematical model of the considered design problem (see next section) and corresponding special optimization methods. The architecture of the DSS and the methods used are presented in Figure 2.

METHODS FOR DECISION MAKING

Optimization Model

We consider the case where the structure of the transmission system can be represented by a connected acyclic directed multigraph $G=(V,E)$. The set V of vertices and the set E of arcs are in one-to-one correspondence with shafts and gears of the transmission, respectively. An arc is oriented such that the direction is from drive- to driven shafts. It is supposed also that there is only one vertex v_0 with zero in-degree (the input shaft of the transmission) and one vertex v_s with zero out-degree (the output shaft of the transmission).

Let $v_1(e)$ and $v_2(e)$ be the initial and terminal vertices of the arc e, respectively. The graph G of the transmission system of Figure 1 is shown in Figure 3. In this

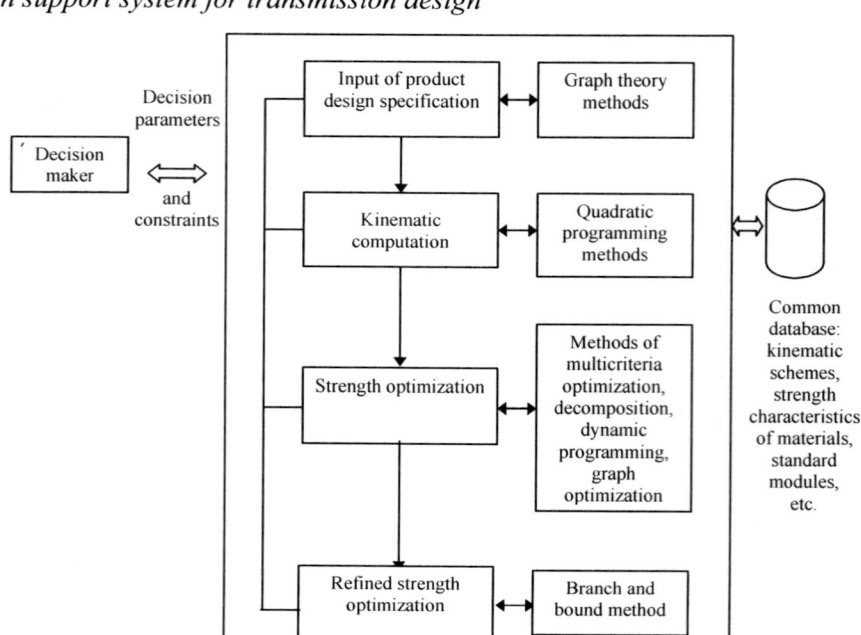

Figure 2. Decision support system for transmission design

Figure 3. Graph G of the transmission system

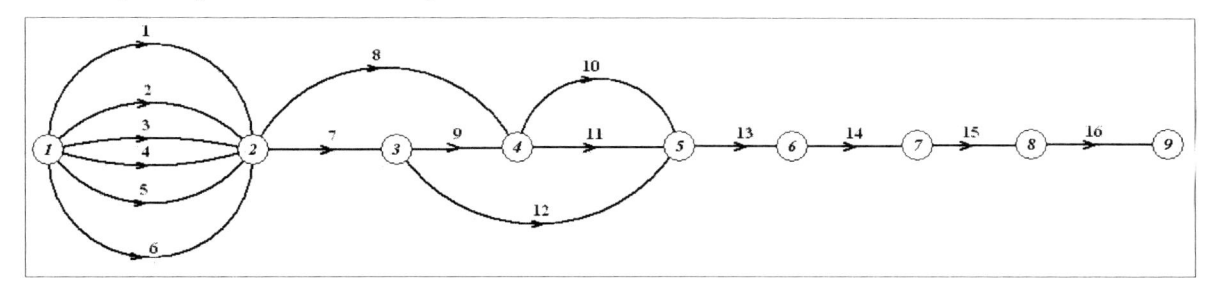

graph, arc 8 represents a clutch gear and couples shaft 2 and shaft 4; arc 4 represents a bevel differential gear and vertex 6 represents its body.

Each path in graph G from vertex v_0 to vertex $v \in V$ corresponds in one-to-one manner to a kinematic chain, connecting corresponding shafts. Later, we denote by $L(v) = \{L_k(v)| k = 1,...,r(v)\}$ a set of paths $L_k(v)$ in graph G from vertex v_0 to vertex $v \in V$.

Let us denote the following:

- given nominal speed of the engine (input shaft v_0) by n_0
- unknown transmission ratio of the gear $e \in E$ and its range by $x(e)$ and $[\underline{x}(e), \overline{x}(e)] \subset R$, respectively
- number of teeth of the gear $e \in E' \subseteq E$ by $z(e) = (z_1(e), z_2(e))$ and a set of its feasible values by $Z(e)$
- maximum allowable absolute speed of the shaft $v \in V$ by $\overline{n}(v)$
- collection of unknown design parameters of the gear $e \in E$ and a set of its feasible values by $u(e)$ and $U(e)$
- collection of unknown design parameters of the shaft $v \in V$ and a set of its feasible values by $w(v)$ and $W(v)$
- desired set of speeds of the output shaft by $c = (c_1,...,c_r)$, where $r = r(v_s)$
- coefficients of the relative importance for desired values c_k by $\alpha = (\alpha_1,...,\alpha_r)$

For fixed transmission ratios $x(e)$ of gears for the kinematic chain $L_k(v)$, $v \in V$, its transmission ratio is equal to $\prod_{e \in L_k(v)} x(e)$, and the speed $n_k(v,x)$ of the shaft $v \in V$ is equal to

$$n_k(v,x) = n_0 / \prod_{e \in L_k(v)} x(e) \quad (1)$$

Later, to simplify the presentation, we will use the following notations:

$V' = V \setminus \{v_0, v_s\}$
$x = (x(e)| e \in E)$
$X = \{x| x(e) \in [\underline{x}(e), \overline{x}(e)]\}$
$u = (u(e)| e \in E)$
$w = (w(v)| v \in V)$
$N(v,x) = (n_1(v,x),...,n_{r(v)}(v,x))$

For the given engine power and load conditions of the output shaft of the transmission system, the load conditions of the shaft $v \in V$ and of the gear $e \in E$ are defined by collections $N(v,x)$ and $(x(e), N(v_1(e),x))$, respectively. Based on well-known methods for calculating transmission elements (see, for example, Litvin, 1994; Shigley, Mischke, & Budynas, 2003; Su & Qin, 2003), the following functions can be constructed:

a. Function $T_e(x(e), N(v_1(e),x), u(e))$
   and $T_v(N(v,x), w(v))$,
   which determine the longevity for the gear $e \in E$ and the shaft $v \in V$ for fixed values of unknown parameters x, w, and u

b. Functions $M_v(w(v))$ and $M_e(u(e))$, which determine the mass of the shaft $v \in V$ and the mass of the gear $e \in E$ for fixed values of the unknown parameters w and u

Under these assumptions, the considered design can be reduced to the following multicriteria optimization problem:

$$\text{Min } g_1(x) = \sum_{k=1}^{r(v_s)} \alpha_k [\ln(n_0 / \prod_{e \in L_k(v_s)} x(e)) - \ln c_k]^2 \quad (2)$$

169

$$\text{Max } g_2(x,u,w) = \min[\min\{T_e(x(e), N(v_1(e),x), u(e)) | e \in E\}, \min\{T_v(N(v,x), w(v)) | v \in V\}] \quad (3)$$

$$\text{Min } g_3(u,w) = \sum_{e \in E} M_e(u(e)) + \sum_{v \in V} M_v(w(v)), \quad (4)$$

which is subject to V

$$x(e) \in [\underline{x}(e), \overline{x}(e)], \quad e \in E' \quad (5)$$

$$\prod_{e \in L_k(v)} x(e) \geq n_0 / \overline{n}(v), \quad k = 1, \ldots, r(v), \quad v \in V' \quad (6)$$

$$x(e) = z_2(e) / z_1(e), \quad z(e) \in Z(e), \quad e \in E' \quad (7)$$

$$u(e) \in U(e), \quad e \in E; \quad w(v) \in W(v), \quad v \in V \quad (8)$$

The first criterion $g_1(x)$ is to minimize the deviation of the obtained speeds from the desired speeds. The second $g_2(x,u,w)$ is to maximize the transmission life, and the third $g_3(u,w)$ is to minimize the total mass of the transmission. Equations 5 to 7 take into account ranges for transmission ratios of gears, their tooth numbers, and the maximum allowable nominal speeds of the intermediate shafts. Equation 8 provides the choice of design parameters for gears and shafts from their feasible sets.

Kinematic Computation

Kinematic computation (in terms of Equations 2 to 8) is to determine a set $(X_k = \prod_{e \in L_k(v_s)} x(e) | k = 1, \ldots, r)$ of transmission ratios for kinematic chains that minimizes the objective $g_1(x)$ under Equations 5 to 7.

The procedure is performed in two steps. First, the problem of minimizing the function $g_1(x)$ is solved under Equations 5 and 6 only. So, this step neglects the integrality of tooth numbers for gears of E' (problem B_{11}). Second, we then solve the whole problem for the choice of tooth numbers (problem B_{12}). For its solution, methods of quadratic programming and a branch-and-bound technique are used (Dolgui et al., 1999). Such an approach considers the importance of this subproblem to the overall solution procedure. It takes into account the uncertainty in parameters of kinematic constraints at the initial stages of design as well as the relatively small interval between adjacent discrete values of $x(e)$ determined by the integer number of gear teeth.

The kinematic computation includes the following:

- Input or modification of the data (the structure of the transmission, ranges of gear ratios, etc.)

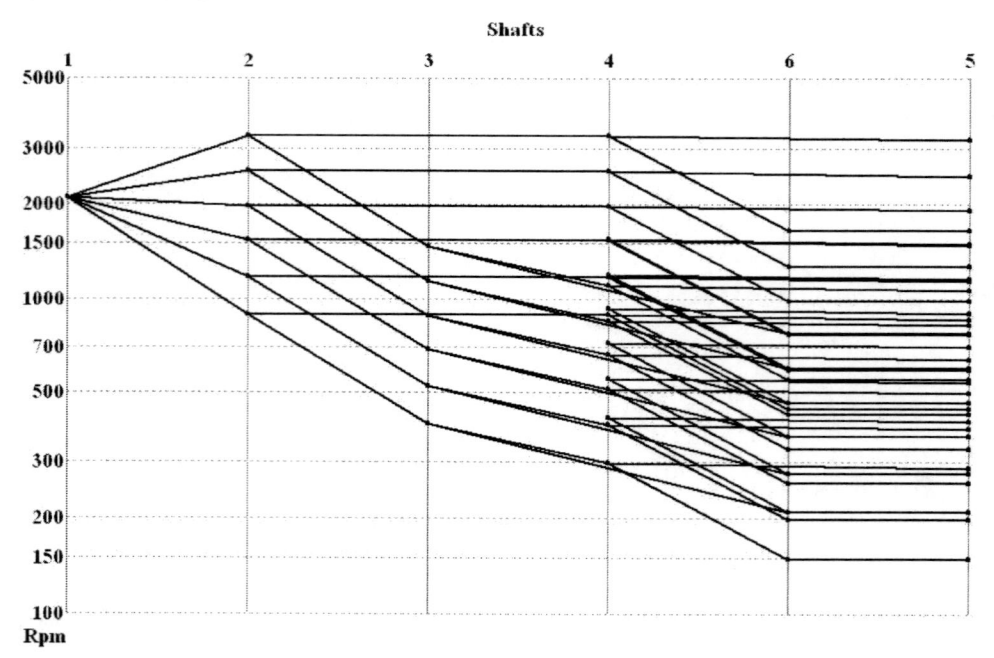

Figure 4. Diagram of shaft speeds

Decision-Making and Support Tools for Design of Transmission Systems

Figure 5. A fragment of the solution for the B_{21} problem

```
            RESULTS   OF   TRANSMISSION   CALCULATION
                          GEARS              PAGE  1

         GEAR NUMBER              1         2         3         4         5

         EQUIVALENT:
         POWER, KWT            C 77.26  C 77.17  C 77.27  C 77.20  C 77.13
                               B 77.26  B 77.17  B 77.27  B 77.20  B 77.13
         LIFE, HOURS           C    70  C   177  C   421  C   423  C   551
                               B    31  B   103  B   299  B   281  B   398
         OUTPUT SPEED, RPM      1026.6   1362.4   1774.5   2282.4   2929.7
         DESIGN PARAMETERS:

         TYPE                      SG       SG       SG       SG       SG
         TRANSMISSION RATIO       2.046    1.541    1.183    0.920    0.717
         REFERENCE DIAMETER OF GEAR 1, MM    96.0    115.1    134.0    152.3    170.4
         REFERENCE DIAMETER OF GEAR 2, MM   196.5    177.4    158.5    140.2    122.1
         THICKNESS OF GEAR, MM              21.1     25.3     29.5     30.8     26.9
         MASS OF GEAR, KG                  4.746    5.003    5.621    5.989    5.171
```

```
            RESULTS   OF   TRANSMISSION   CALCULATION
                          GEARS              PAGE  2

         GEAR NUMBER              6         7         8         9        10

         EQUIVALENT:
         POWER, KWT            C 77.36  C 74.94  C 60.00  C 58.20  C 57.06
```

and their analysis (checking the structure of the graph, compatibility of kinematic constraints)
- Solving of the problem B_{11}
- Analysis of the recommended design by the designer and selection of the next step (continue or return)
- Solving (if necessary) of the problem B_{12} with the choice of numbers of teeth for the gears according to Equation 7

For the obtained gear ratios, the procedure calculates basic kinematic characteristics of the design decision including nominal speeds of all intermediate shafts for all kinematic chains and maximum relative speeds of shafts and their analysis by the designer. An example of the shaft-speed diagram for the transmission system in Figure 1 is depicted in Figure 4.

Strength Optimization

Strength optimization is determining the design parameters (x,u,w) that minimize the function $g_3(u,w)$ under Equations 5 to 8 and the following additional constraints:

$$g_{2j}(x,u,w) \geq T_0 \qquad (9)$$

$$\prod_{e \in L_k(s)} x(e) = X_k^*, \quad k = 1,\ldots, r \qquad (10)$$

for fixed $T_0 \in \Delta$ and X^*.

Here:

T_0 is the required total transmission life,
Δ is a set of its acceptable values, and
$X^* = (X_k^* \mid k=1,\ldots, r)$ is a set of transmission ratios of kinematic chains obtained at the previous stage.

Figure 6. Data for the first (a) and the second (b) steps of the procedure

Grp	Gear	Mechanism type	Transmission ratio	Facewidth ratio	Center distance (mm) Obtained	Minimal	Required	Module Min	Max	Tooth numbers Driving Max	Min	Driven Max	Min
1	1	SG	2.046	0.22	146.25	63.24	146.25	1.75	5.5	55	17	100	34
	2	SG	1.541	0.22	146.25	61.56		1.50	6	76	19	100	29
	3	SG	1.183	0.22	146.25	62.27		1.50	7	89	19	100	22
	4	SG	0.92	0.202	146.25	60.18		1.50	8	100	18	93	17
	5	SG	0.717	0.158	146.25	66.42		1.25	7	100	23	97	17
	6	SG	0.551	0.121	146.25	72.29		1.20	6	100	30	86	17
2	8	SG	2.235	0.276	126.5	81.52	126.5	1.50	4.5	52	17	100	37
3	9	SG	1.331	0.22	126.5	71.36	126.5	2.00	6	54	18	72	23
4	10	SG	2.201	0.22	148.5	67.8	148.5	2.25	5.0	41	18	90	39
5	11	SG	1.198	0.22	146.25	74.31	146.25	1.75	8	76	16	91	19

a)

Grp	Gear	Mechanism type	Transmission ratio	Facewidth ratio	Center distance	Modules Min	Max	Required	Tooth numbers Driving Max	Min	Driven Max	Min
1	1	SG	2.046	0.22	146.25	1.75	5.5	4.5	55	17	100	34
	2	SG	1.541	0.22	146.25	1.50	6	4.5	76	19	100	29
	3	SG	1.183	0.22	146.25	1.50	7	4.5	89	19	100	22
	4	SG	0.92	0.202	146.25	1.50	8	4.5	100	18	93	17
	5	SG	0.717	0.158	146.25	1.25	7	4.5	100	23	97	17
	6	SG	0.551	0.121	146.25	1.20	6	4.5	100	30	86	17
2	8	SG	2.235	0.276	126.5	1.50	4.5	4.5	52	17	100	37
3	9	SG	1.331	0.22	126.5	2.00	6	4.5	54	18	72	23
4	10	SG	2.201	0.22	148.5	2.25	5.0	5	41	18	90	39
5	11	SG	1.198	0.22	146.25	1.75	8	5	76	16	91	19

b)

Figure 7. Results of the procedure for refined strength optimization

```
            R E Z U L T S  O F  G E A R S  C A L C U T A T I O N        PAGE   1

    GEAR NUMBER                                  1         2         3         4
    POWER EQUIVALENT, KWT              C      77.35     77.48     76.36     78.07
                                       B      77.35     77.48     76.36     78.07
    LIFE EQUIVALENT, HOURS             C         71       178       425       424
                                       B         31       103       307       284
    OUTPUT SPEED, RES/MIN                     1025.6    1365.0    1750.0    2303.2

    TYPE                                         SG        SG        SG        SG
    TRANSMISSION RATIO                        2.048     1.538     1.200     0.912
    REFERENCE DIAMETER OF GEAR 1, MM           94.5     117.0     135.0     153.0
    REFERENCE DIAMETER OF GEAR 2, MM          193.5     180.0     162.0     139.5
    THICKNESS OF GEAR, MM                      21.1      25.4      29.2      30.7
    MASS OF GEAR, KG                          4.746     5.006     5.564     5.952
    MODULE, MM                                 4.50      4.50      4.50      4.50
    DRIVING NUMBER OF TEETH                      21        26        30        34
    DRIVEN NUMBER OF TEETH                       43        40        36        31
    PROFILE CORRECTION FACTOR OF GEAR 1       0.278    -0.082    -0.112
    PROFILE CORRECTION FACTOR OF GEAR 2       0.250    -0.388    -0.358
    CENTER DISTANCE, MM                      146.25    146.25    146.25    146.25
    TEETH ANGLE DEG MIN SEC


            R E Z U L T S  O F  G E A R S  C A L C U T A T I O N        PAGE   2

    GEAR NUMBER                                  5         6         7         8
    POWER EQUIVALENT, KWT              C      77.97     78.01     75.03     60.56
```

The procedure is again performed in two steps. First, we determine preliminary values of design parameters without considering Equation 7 on the integrality of tooth numbers (problem B_{21}). Then, we can choose tooth numbers and refine the design parameters obtained in the first step (problem B_{22}).

The method of solving problem B_{21} is based on invariants (Dolgui et al., 1999) that reflect the interconnection between shaft speeds and transmission ratios for gears of the earlier determined set of nominal speeds of the output shaft. These invariants are calculated using Equation 10 before solving the problem B_{21}. The method applies the decomposition scheme proposed in Dolgui et al. (2000) with recursive procedures of series-parallel decomposition of the initial graph and its subgraphs.

The procedure of strength optimization involves the following:

- Input or modification of the data
- Computation of problem invariants and decomposition of graph G
- Solving problem B_{21} and the calculation of preliminary values of design parameters of gears and shafts
- Solving (if necessary) of problem B_{22} in order to choose numbers of teeth for the gears
- Analysis of the solution

As an illustration, in Figure 5 we give a fragment of B_{21} results for the transmission of Figure 1.

Refined Strength Optimization

Refining the strength optimization is done in dialog with the designer. At first, he or she specifies center distances and then modules for groups of gears taking into account a number of additional informal constructional, technological, and operational factors. The designer makes these decisions based both on the results of the previous procedures and on ranges of tooth numbers and modules provided by the DSS (see Figure 6). As a result, the sets $Z(e)$ are refined. Moreover, design parameters of gears and shafts are determined by solving the corresponding problem B_{22}. Results of this procedure are presented in Figure 7.

CONCLUSION AND FURTHER RESEARCH

The design of multiunit power transmissions is a very promising area for the development of specialized DSSs. The use of DSS results in a significant reduction of time and cost as well as an improvement of the quality and accuracy of design decisions. It concerns first of all those design stages where the overall layout and basic parameters of the future transmission system are defined.

Promising directions for DSS in transmission design are based on considering the following:

- More factors (e.g., overall dimensions)
- Uncertainty (possible real loading conditions, strength characteristics of materials, etc.)
- Mathematical models to represent the structure of a transmission system in more detail with specific features (e.g., gears have a common wheel)
- Elements when transmission ratios depend on loading conditions (e.g., hydraulic gears)
- Possibility of an end-to-end solution for problems in the structural and parametric synthesis of transmission systems including 3-D modeling as a whole

It will be interesting to develop and study other mathematical models truly dedicated to this subject. In addition, a wide area to exploit will be to apply various methods of decision making, including expert systems, methods of multiobjective optimization, different heuristics, and metaheuristics. Of equal importance will be taking into account engineering experience in solving similar problems, simulation and finite-element analysis, and so forth. This latter method is especially promising at the final design stage that is characterized a high level of detail and requirements.

ACKNOWLEDGMENT

The authors thank Chris Yukna for his help in English.

REFERENCES

Dadié, A. (1996). *Réalisation d'un logiciel de conception automatique appliquée à la détermination des engrenages cylindriques: Interfaçage avec un logiciel industriel de C.A.O.* Unpublished doctoral dissertation, INSA, Toulouse, France.

Dixon, J. R. (1995). Knowledge-based systems for design. *ASME Journal of Mechanical Design, 117*, 11-16.

Dolgui, A., Guschinsky, N., & Levin, G. (1999, August 31-September 3). *Models and methods of multicriteria optimization for computer aided design of multi-unit mechanical transmission systems.* Paper presented at the European Control Conference (ECC'99), Karlsruhe, Germany.

Dolgui, A., Guschinsky, N., & Levin, G. (2000). Optimization in design of multiunit mechanical transmission systems. In N. Mastorakis (Ed.), *Systems and control: Theory and applications (Electrical and computer engineering series)* (pp. 101-106). New York: WSES Press.

Dolgui, A., Guschinsky, N., & Levin, G. (2007). Optimization of power transmission systems using a multi-level decomposition approach. *RAIRO Operations Research, 41*, 213-229.

Freeman, J. S., & Velinsky, S. A. (1995). Design of vehicle power transmission systems. *ASME Journal of Mechanical Design, 117*, 113-120.

Guillot, J. (1987). *Méthodologie de définition des ensembles mécaniques en conception assistée par ordinateur, recherche des solutions optimales.* Unpublished doctoral dissertation, Université Paul Sabatier, Toulouse, France.

Guschinsky, N., & Levin, G. (2000). Mathematical models and methods for decision making in CAE of transmission systems. *Artificial Intelligence Kiev, 2*, 345-351.

Guschinsky, N., Levin, G., & Dolgui, A. (2006). *Decision-making support in transmission system design.* Minsk, Belarus: Belorusskaya Nauka.

Hsieh, H. I., & Tsai, L. W. (1996). Kinematic analysis of epicyclic-type transmission mechanisms using the concept of fundamental geared entities. *ASME Journal of Mechanical Design, 118*, 295-299.

Hurst, K. (1998). *Select and design optimal rotary power transmission systems.* McGraw-Hill.

Kahraman, A., Ligata, H., Kienzle, K., & Zini, D. M. (2004). A kinematics and flow analysis methodology for automatic transmission planetary gear trains. *ASME Journal of Mechanical Design, 126*, 1071-1081.

Kalyanmoy, D., & Sachin, J. (2003). Multi-speed gearbox design using multi-objective evolutionary algorithms. *ASME Journal of Mechanical Design, 125*, 609-619.

Krishnamachari, R. S., & Papalambros, P. Y. (1997). Hierarchical decomposition synthesis in optimal systems design. *ASME Journal of Mechanical Design, 119*, 448-457.

Litvin, F. L. (1994). *Gear geometry and applied theory.* Englewood Cliffs, NJ: Prentice Hall.

Liu, C.-P., & Chen, D.-Z. (2001). On the application of kinematic units to the topological analysis of geared mechanisms. *ASME Journal of Mechanical Design, 123*, 240-246.

Michelena, N. F., & Papalambros, P. Y. (1995). Optimal model-based decomposition of powertrain system design. *ASME Journal of Mechanical Design, 117*, 499-505.

Michelena, N. F., & Papalambros, P. Y. (1997). A hypergraph framework for optimal model-based decomposition of design problems. *Computational Optimization and Applications, 8*(2), 173-196.

Nelson, C. A., & Cipra, R. J. (2005). Simplified kinematic analysis of bevel epicyclic gear trains with application to power-flow and efficiency analyses. *ASME Journal of Mechanical Design, 127*, 278-286.

Shigley, J. E., Mischke, C. R., & Budynas, R. G. (2003). *Mechanical engineering design* (7th ed.). New York: McGraw Hill.

Su, D. (1998). Intelligent hybrid system for integration in design and manufacture. *Journal of Materials Processing Technology, 76*, 23-28.

Su, D., & Chen, X. (2003). Network support for integrated design. *Integrated Manufacturing Systems, 14*(6), 537-546.

Su, D., & Qin, D. (2003). Integration of numerical analysis, virtual simulation and finite element analysis for optimum design of worm gearing. *Journal of Processing Technology, 138*, 429-435.

Talpasanu, I., Yih, T. C., & Simionescu, P. A. (2006). Application of matroid method in kinematic analysis of parallel axes epicyclic gear trains. *ASME Journal of Mechanical Design, 128*(6), 1307-1314.

Yan, H. S., & Hsieh, L.-C. (1994). Conceptual design of gear differentials for automotive vehicles. *ASME Journal of Mechanical Design, 116*, 565-570.

KEY TERMS

Gear: A gear is a mechanism that transmits a rotary motion and power from a driving shaft to a driven shaft with possible changes in the speed, direction, and torque.

Gearbox: A gearbox is the system of gears with changeable connections that results in alternative kinematic chains from the input shaft of the gearbox to its output shaft with different transmission ratios.

Kinematic Chain: It is the sequence of gears such that the driven shaft of the previous gear is the driving shaft of the next gear.

Load Conditions for a Kinematic Chain: These are the speed and the torque of the output shaft of the chain as well as (if necessary) the operation time (total or relative) of the chain during the total life of the transmission.

Longevity of Transmission Element (Gear, Shaft): This is the duration of the element's ability to work.

Total Life of the Transmission System: This is the duration of operation for all elements.

Transmission Gear Ratio: This is the ratio of the speed of the driving shaft to the speed of the driven shaft.

Transmission Ratio of Kinematic Chain: It is the ratio of the speed of the driving shaft for the first gear and the speed of the driven shaft for the last gear.

Transmission System: The transmission system is an assembly of gears (not obligatorily sequentially interconnected) that transmits a rotary motion and power from the input shafts to the output shafts.

Decision Making by a Multiple-Rule Classifier: The Role of Rule Qualities

Ivan Bruha
McMaster University, Canada

INTRODUCTION

A rule-inducing learning algorithm yields a set of decision rules that depict knowledge discovered from a (usually large) dataset; therefore, this topic is often known as knowledge discovery from databases (KDD). Any classifier (or, expect system) then can utilize this decision set to derive a decision about given problems, observations, or diagnostics. The decision set (induced by a learning algorithm) may be either of the form of an ordered or unordered set of rules. The latter seems to be more understandable by humans and directly applicable in most expert systems, or generally, any decision-supporting one. However, classification utilizing the unordered-mode decision set may be accompanied by some conflict situations, particularly when several rules belonging to different classes match (are satisfied by, "fire" for) an input to-be-classified (unseen) object. One of the possible solutions to this conflict is to associate each decision rule induced by a learning algorithm with a numerical factor, which is commonly called the *rule quality* (An & Cercone, 2001; Bergadano et al., 1988; Bruha, 1997; Kononenko, 1992; Mingers, 1989; Tkadlec & Bruha, 2003).

This article first briefly introduces the underlying principles for defining rules qualities, including statistical tools such as contingency tables and then surveys empirical and statistical formulas of the rule quality and compares their characteristics. Afterwards, it presents an application of a machine learning algorithm utilizing various formulas of the rule qualities in medical area.

BACKGROUND

There are a few paradigms of extracting knowledge from databases. One commonly used paradigm is called *divide-and-conquer*. It is widely utilized by the family of top-down induction of decision trees (TDIDT) learning algorithms that induce decision trees. One of its first pioneers is the ID3 algorithm (Quinlan, 1986), but currently mostly used and well-known members are C4.5 and C5.0 algorithms (Quinlan, 1994).

Another widely used strategy in learning uses the *covering* paradigm that generates sets of decision rules; the AQx and CNx families as well as C4.5Rules or Ripper are the well-known algorithms generating knowledge bases as sets of decision rules. A decision rule has the following general form:

R: if *Cond* then class is C

Here R is the name of the rule, *Cond* represents the condition under which the rule is satisfied (fires), and C is the class of the rule, that is, an unseen object satisfying this condition is classified to the class C.

As we already stated a *decision set* of (decision) rules may be either ordered or unordered. To understand the situation better, here is an example of a very simple ordered decision set:

if outlook=overcast then class is +; quality=0.889
else if windy=false && humidity=normal then class is +; quality=0.867
else if humidity=high && outlook=sunny then class is -; quality=0.920
else if windy=true && outlook=rain then class is -; quality=0.880
else if true then class is +; quality=0.844

This case uses the well-known "weather" problem introduced by Quinlan (1986). Here windy, humidity, outlook, and temperature are attributes with two classes + and -. As we can see the order character of this decision set is arranged by if .. else if statement; notice that the last statement else if true then in fact represents else.

Corresponding unordered decision set induced by the same covering learning algorithm looks as follows:

if humidity=high && outlook=sunny
then class is -; quality=0.920
if outlook=overcast
then class is +; quality=0.889
if windy=false && humidity=normal
then class is +; quality=0.889
if windy=true && outlook=rain
then class is -; quality=0.880
if windy=false && outlook=rain
then class is +; quality=0.867
if humidity=normal && temperature=mild
then class is +; quality=0.844
if true
then class is +; quality=0.714

As we see the unordered decision set uses only the if statements. If the decision set is *ordered*, then classifying an input unseen (to-be-classified) object is quite straightforward: the classifier goes through the ordered list of rules from its beginning and looks for the first rule that matches (is satisfied by, "fires" for) the given input object; it is then categorized into the class attached to the rule.

However, the important and natural way seems to be the *unordered* mode that is utilized in various expert and decision-making systems. The classification utilizing an unordered set of decision rules exhibits a significant deficiency, not immediately apparent. When classifying an unseen object by a decision-making system consisting of an unordered set of decision rules, the system has to go through the entire decision set of rules; some rules will be satisfied (will fire), some not. Three cases are then possible:

1. If the unseen object satisfies one or more rules of the same class, then the object is categorized to the class assigned to the rule(s).
2. If the unseen object is not covered by any rule, then either the classifier informs the user about its inability to decide ("I do not know"), or the object is assigned by default to the majority class in the training set, or some similar techniques are invoked.
3. Difficulty arises if the object satisfies more rules assigned to different classes. Then some schemes have to be applied to assign the unseen input object to the most appropriate class.

One possibility to clarify the conflict situation (case 3) is to associate each rule in the decision scheme of the classifier with a numerical factor that can express its properties and characterize a measure of belief in the rule, its power, predictability, reliability, likelihood, and so forth. A collection of these properties is symbolized by a function commonly called the *rule quality*. This characteristic has been studied and applied in many research projects. One of the first studies was done by Bergadano et al. (1988). A similar approach can be found in Kononenko and Bratko (1992) and Kononenko (1992). A systematic survey of formulas of rule qualities is presented in Bruha (1997). A methodological and theoretical approach to this characteristic is delivered by Tkadlec and Bruha (2003).

Afterwards, when we choose a formula for the rule quality, we also have to select a *scheme for combining* these qualities. To solve the aforementioned conflict case, the qualities of fired rules of the same class have to be combined using a certain scheme (formula). Consequently, the rule-quality combination with the maximum value will determine the class of the unseen object. A survey of methods for the rule combination can be found, for example, in Kononenko (1992) and Bruha and Tkadlec (2003).

RULE QUALITY: CHARACTERISTICS, FORMULAS, AND COMBINATION SCHEMES

As we already stated, one eventuality in how to solve the multiple-rule decision-making problem is to associate each rule in the decision scheme (knowledge base) of a classifier with the *rule quality*. Formulas for the rule quality have been studied and tested in several aritcles (An & Cercone, 2001; Bergadano et al., 1992; Brazdil & Torgo, 1990; Bruha, 1997; Torgo, 1993). The previous conflict is then actually worked out by combining the qualities of rules that fire for (are satisfied, match) a given input object; the object is then assigned to the class for which the *quality combination* reaches the maximum.

We now discuss the general characteristics of any formula of the rule quality. The first feature required for the rule quality is its *monotony* (or, more precisely, *nondecreasibility*) towards its arguments. Its common arguments are the *consistency* and *completeness* factors of decision rules. Consistency of a decision rule exhibits its "purity" or reliability, that is, a rule with high consistency should cover the minimum of the objects that do not belong to the class of the given rule. A rule with high completeness factor, on the other hand, should cover the maximum of objects belonging to the rule's class. The reason for exploiting the aforementioned characteristics is obvious. Any machine learning/KDD algorithm dealing with real-world noisy data is to induce decision rules that cover larger numbers of training examples (objects) even with a few negative ones (not belonging to the class of the rule). In other words, the decision set induced must be not only reliable but also powerful. Its reliability is characterized by a consistency factor and its power by a completeness factor. A comprehensive analysis and empirical expertise of formulas of rule qualities and their combining schemes has been published in Bruha and Tkadlec (2003), its theoretical methodology in Tkadlec and Bruha (2003). The first one introduces quite a few statistical and empirical formulas of the rule quality, including the quality combinations and their comparison. The latter article introduces theoretical formalism and methodological tools for building multiple-rule systems. It focuses on four agents that cooperate with each other: Designer, Learner, Classifier, and Predictor. The article offers to a designer of a new multiple-rule system the minimum requirements for the aforementioned concepts and (mostly statistical) characteristics he/she can start with. It also exhibits a general flow chart for a decision-system builder.

Besides the rule quality discussed previously, there exist other rule measures such as its size (e.g., the size of its condition, usually the number of attribute pairs forming the condition), computational complexity, comprehensibility ("Is the rule telling humans something interesting about the application domain?"), understandability, redundancy (measured within the entire decision set of rules), and similar characteristics (Srivastava, 2005; Tan, Kumar, & Srivastava, 2002). However, some of these characteristics are subjective; on contrary, formulas of rule quality are supported by theoretical sources or profound empirical expertise.

Here we just briefly survey the most important characteristics and definitions used by the formulas of rule qualities follow. Let a given task to be classified be characterized by a set of training examples that belong to two classes, named C and $\overline{C}$ (or, not C). Let R be a decision rule of the class C (as definition previously).

	class C	not class C	
rule R covers	a_{11}	a_{12}	a_{1+}
R does not cover	a_{21}	a_{22}	a_{2+}
	a_{+1}	a_{+2}	a_{++}

Behavior of the aforementioned decision rule can be formally depicted by the 2×2 *contingency table* (Bishop, Fienberg, & Holland, 1991), which is commonly used in machine learning (Mingers, 1989; Quinlan, 1987) (see above):
where

a_{11} is the number of training examples that are covered by (satisfied by) the rule R and belong to the class C,

a_{12} is the number of examples covered by (satisfied by) the rule R but not belonging to the class C, etc.,

$a_{1+} = a_{11} + a_{12}$ is the number of examples covered by R,

$a_{+1} = a_{11} + a_{21}$ is the number of the training examples of the class C,

$a_{++} = a_{+1} + a_{+2} = a_{1+} + a_{2+}$ is the number of all training examples in the given task.

Using the elements of the contingency table, we may define the *consistency* of a rule R (also called *sensitivity*) by:

$$\mathrm{cons}(R) = \frac{a_{11}}{a_{1+}}$$

and its *completeness* (*coverage*, or *positive predictive value*) by

$$\mathrm{compl}(R) = \frac{a_{11}}{a_{+1}}$$

Note that other statistics can be easily defined by means of the elements of the previous contingency table; for example, the conditional probability $P(C|R)$ of the class C under the condition that the rule R matches an input object is, in fact, equal to $\mathrm{cons}(R)$; the prior probability of the class C is:

Decision Making by a Multiple-Rule Classifier: The Role of Rule Qualities

$$P(C) = \frac{a_{+1}}{a_{++}}$$

Similarly, the probability that the rule R fires under the condition the input object is from the class C is:

$$P(R|C) = \frac{a_{11}}{a_{+1}}$$

(which is identical to the rule's completeness).

Generally we may state that these formulas are functions of any previous characteristics, that is, all nine elements a_{11} to a_{++} of the contingency table, consistency, completeness, and various probabilities above classes and rules. There exist two groups of these formulas: empirical and statistical ones.

The *empirical* formulas for the rule qualities represent an ad hoc approach because they are based on intuitive logic and not necessarily backed by statistical or other theories. The common strategy is to use a weighted sum or multiplication of the consistency and completeness, which is more understandable to humans.

Here are two examples of empirical formulas. Rule quality as a *weighted sum* of the consistency and completeness has the form:

$$q^{weight}(R) = w_1 \, cons(R) + w_2 \, compl(R) \qquad (1)$$

where $w_1, w_2 \in (0,1)$ are user-defined weights, usually $w_1 + w_2 = 1$. This apprehensible formula is non-decreasing towards its arguments. It is used, for example, in Bergadano et al. (1988) as part of a more complex scenario.

However, this article does not state how to determine the above weights. Torgo (1993) specifies the aforementioned weights by a heuristic formula that emphasizes consistency:

$$w_1 = 0.5 + \tfrac{1}{4} \, cons(R) \qquad (2)$$
$$w_2 = 0.5 - \tfrac{1}{4} \, cons(R)$$

The second empirical formula defines rule quality as a *product* of consistency and completeness:

$$q^{product}(R) = cons(R) \cdot f(compl(R)) \qquad (3)$$

where f is an increasing function. The completeness works here as a factor that reflects a *confidence* to the consistency of the given rule. After a large number of experiments, Brazdil and Torgo (1990) selected an empiric form of the function f in the formula (3):

$$f(x) = \exp(x - 1) \qquad (4)$$

The *statistical* formulas for rule quality are supported by a few theoretical sources. The theory on contingency tables seems to be one of these sources, since the performance of any rule can be characterized by them. Information theory is another source of statistical measurements suitable for defining rule quality.

Again, just two examples of statistical formulas; the first one utilizes the theory of contingency tables. After theoretical analysis, Coleman (as cited in Bishop et al., 1991) came to the following formula that looks quite complex but it works:

$$q^{Coleman}(R) = \frac{a_{++} \, cons(R) - a_{+1}}{a_{++} - a_{+1}} \, \frac{1 + compl(R)}{2}$$

(5)

The second formula utilizes the information theory. Kononenko and Bratko (1991) define the *information score* for a rule R when classifying an unseen object as $-\log_2 P(C) + \log_2 P(C|R)$ where the logarithm is of base 2. This formula can be also applied to the rule quality:

$$q^{IS}(R) = -\log_2 \frac{a_{+1}}{a_{++}} + \log_2 cons(R)$$

(6)

As soon as a formula for rule quality is selected and an unordered set of decision rules is induced, we may utilize several different classification schemes for *combining the rule qualities*. The simplest way is to order an unordered set of decision rules by their qualities. Classification is then done in the same way as in the ordered mode, that is, the classifier goes through the list of rules starting with the best one (having the greatest quality) and looks for the first rule that matches ("fires" for) the given object; it is then categorized into the class attached to the rule. Another possibility is to calculate a weighted sum of qualities of "fired" rules for each class separately; the tested object is then categorized to the class for which this sum is the maximum. There

Table 1. Characteristics of three databases utilized in this small project

dataset	# classes	frequency of majority class	# examples	# attributes
Onco	3	50%	127	8
ThyroidGland	2	72%	269	10
BreastTumor	2	80%	288	10

Table 2. Classification accuracy for the five various formulas of rule qualities

dataset	q^{weight} $w_1=0.8, w_2=0.2$	q^{weight} with (2)	$q^{product}$	$q^{Coleman}$	q^{IS}
Onco	71	71.4	69.9	71.8	69.1
ThyroidGland	81.2	81.2	80	81.9	79.4
BreastTumor	75.5	75.6	76	77.5	74.4

exist also more sophisticated combination schemes that extend the scenario of the above weighted sum (Bruha & Tkadlec, 2003).

APPLICATION

As an application of the previous methodology, we present the results of inducing the decision sets by utilizing all previous formulas of rule qualities. As a covering paradigm algorithm we utilize our algorithm CN4 (Bruha & Kockova, 1993), a large extension of the well-known algorithm CN2 (Clark & Boswell, 1991). We have processed the following medical data(It should be noted that the actual research project involves 21 databases, Bruha & Tkadlec, 2003.):

- **Onco:** The oncological data were used for testing in the Czech Academy of Sciences, Prague, Czechland, and also in the project CN4 (Bruha & Kockova, 1993).
- **ThyroidGland:** This task of diagnosis of thyroid gland disease has been provided by the Institute of Nuclear Medicine of Inselspital, Bern, Switzerland. This database was used at the Deptartment of Advanced Mathematics, University of Bern, and also in the project CN4.
- **BreastTumor:** This dataset has been provided by the Jozef Stefan Institute, the research group of I. Bratko, Ljubljana.

Table 1 depicts the characteristics of the aforementioned databases. Table 2 comprises the classification accuracy (in %) for the formulas introduced previously. Table 3 compares the quality formulas by the paired t-test as the symmetrical matrix; therefore, only the right upper submatrix is presented. Here N/A means not applicable, + is to be interpreted as the quality formula in the row is significantly better than that in the column (measured on the classification accuracy, significance level 2.5%), the sign - means the opposite, and 0 exhibits that both formulas are statistically equivalent. From the viewpoint of the classification accuracy, the formulas q^{weight} for $w_1=0.8, w_2=0.2$, q^{weight} with the equation (2), and $q^{Coleman}$ exhibit the best performance. The second group is formed by $q^{product}$; the worst rule quality is portrayed by the formula q^{IS}.

The weighted-sum quality has quite an interesting characteristic. By selecting the weights w_1 and w_2 a user may select between inducing only reliable rules (when supporting consistency of rules) and only robust

Table 3. Comparison of the quality formulas by the paired t-test

	$q^{weight}_{w_1=0.8, w_2=0.2}$	q^{weight} with (2)	$q^{product}$	$q^{Coleman}$	q^{IS}
$q^{weight}_{w_1=0.8, w_2=0.2}$	N/A	0	+	0	+
q^{weight} with (2)		N/A	+	0	+
$q^{product}$			N/A	−	+
$q^{Coleman}$				N/A	+
q^{IS}					N/A

rules (when supporting completeness). However, our experiments undoubtedly revealed that a larger support of completeness deteriorates the classification accuracy.

By analyzing all the previous results of experiments we came to the following conclusions. Although the empirical formulas are not backed by any statistical theory, they work quite well. The statistical formulas work better but the difference in classification accuracy is almost negligible. To be more precise, even the statistical formulas used in machine learning are applied mostly in an ad hoc, empirical fashion, since most algorithms do not check the conditions or assumptions of their applicability. Unlike the genuine empirical formulas, however, we are aware of the error we have made when the conditions of applicability are not checked. If needed, the condition checking could in principle be embedded into the algorithm.

CONCLUSION AND FUTURE TRENDS

This article discusses one important characteristic of decision-making systems: the rule quality. It is utilized in the unordered decision sets of rules to overcome a conflict situation when an object to-be-classified satisfies more rules assigned to different classes. We have introduced elements of the theory above this topic, namely the contingency table, and defined several characteristics (such as consistency and completeness) that are exploited in formulas of rule quality. Afterwards, we introduced just a few such formulas; in fact, one can find in literature dozens of these formulas, although some of them are more or less identical.

As for the future trends in this research area, we introduce some directions.

In most decision-supporting systems, the rule qualities are static, constant, calculated a priori, before the actual classification or prediction. Their predictability can be improved by a dynamic change of their values during the classification process. One possible scheme implants a feedback loop from the classifier to the learner (Bruha, 2000); it refines (modifies) the rule qualities according to the correct/false predictions made by the classifier by changing the qualities of the rules that were involved in the current classification. This article indicates where the research of rule qualities can be directed.

Another direction of investigating the qualities is to define and analyze a quality above the entire decision set, that is, a decision set as a unit would be evaluated by a characteristic called *decision-set quality*. Some steps in this direction have already been done.

Let us introduce a metaphor before we sketch one possible future trend. One may imagine that any multiple-rule system can be represented by a "physician" who has to find a diagnosis of his/her patient. Thanks to the studies and experience in the field, he/she has in mind a set of decision rules about several diagnoses. He/she uses this set of decision rules for making his/her decision according to these rules. Therefore, we can observe a physician as a decision set. Now imagine that there is a "council" of physicians that has to make up the final verdict of the patient's diagnosis. This council then combines decision of single physicians according to their "qualities" (decision-set qualities). Such a scenario depicts a two-level decision system. This is, in fact, a promising direction in utilizing the concept of qualities in decision-making systems.

Another way of future research is in the following issue. Here we have focused on qualities from the classification viewpoint only. The learning phase has been considered as independent of the classification scheme. In other words, the evaluation heuristics invoked by an inductive (learning) algorithm are more or less expected to have no connection with the rule quality invoked by a classification scheme. We anticipate that it would be more natural that the heuristics of a learning algorithm and the rule quality of a classification scheme be selected *together* according to the demands of a client, an end user of a classifier. The most appropriate strategy would exploit any rule quality formula both within classification and within an inductive learning as evaluation heuristics.

REFERENCES

An, A., & Cercone, N. (2001). Rule quality measures for rule induction systems: Description and evaluation. *Computational Intelligence, 17*(3), 409-424.

Bergadano, F., et al. (1988). Measuring quality of concept descriptions. In *Proceedings of the Third European Working Session on Learning (EWSL-88)*, Glasgow (pp. 112-128).

Bergadano, F., et al. (1992). Learning two-tiered descriptions of flexible concepts: The Poseidon system. *Machine Learning, 8,* 5-43.

Bishop, Y. M. M., Fienberg, S. E., & Holland, P. W. (1991). *Discrete multivariate analysis: Theory and practice.* Cambridge, MA: MIT Press.

Brazdil, P., & Torgo, L. (1990). Knowledge acquisition via knowledge integration. In *Current trends in knowledge acquisition.* IOS Press.

Bruha, I. (1997). Quality of decision rules: Definitions and classification schemes for multiple rules. In G. Nakhaeizadeh & C. C. Taylor (Eds.), *Machine learning and statistics: The interface.* (pp. 107-131). New York: John Wiley.

Bruha, I. (2000). A feedback loop for refining rule qualities in a classifier: A reward-penalty strategy. *European Conference on Machine Learning (ECML-2000), Workshop Meta Learning*, Barcelona, Spain (pp. 15-27).

Bruha, I., & Kockova, S. (1993). A support for decision making: Cost-sensitive learning system. *Artificial Intelligence in Medicine, 6,* 67-82.

Bruha, I., & Tkadlec, J. (2003). Rule quality for multiple-rule classifier: Empirical expertise and theoretical methodology. *Intelligent Data Analysis, 7,* 99-124.

Clark, P., & Boswell, R. (1991). Rule induction with CN2: Some recent improvements. In *Proceedings of the European Working Session on Learning (EWSL-91)*, Porto, Portugal.

Kononenko, I. (1992). Combining decisions of multiple rules. In B. du Boulay & V. Sgurev (Eds.), *Artificial intelligence V: Methodology, systems, applications* (pp. 87-96). Elsevier Science.

Kononenko, I., & Bratko, I. (1991). Information-based evaluation criterion for classifier's performance. *Machine Learning, 6,* 67-80.

Mingers, J. (1989). An empirical comparison of selection measures for decision-tree induction. *Machine Learning, 3,* 319-342.

Quinlan, J. R. (1986). Induction of decision trees. *Machine Learning, 1,* 81-106.

Quinlan, J. R. (1987). Generating production rules from decision trees (Tech. Rep. No. 87.7). Sydney University.

Quinlan, J. R. (1994). *C4.5: Programs for machine learning.* Morgan Kaufmann.

Srivastava, M. S. (2005). Some tests concerning the covariance matrix in high dimensional data. *Journal of Japan Statistical Society, 35,* 251-272.

Tan, P. N., Kumar, V., & Srivastava, J. (2002). Selecting the right interestingness measure for association patterns. *Proceedings of the Eighth ACM SIGKDD International Conference on Knowledge Discovery and Data Mining (SIGKDD-2002)* (pp. 157-166).

Torgo, L. (1993). Controlled redundancy in incremental rule learning. In *Proceedings of the European Confer-*

ence on Machine Learning (ECML-93), Vienna (pp. 185-195).

Tkadlec, J., & Bruha, I. (2003). Formal aspects of a multiple-rule classifier. *International Journal of Pattern Recognition and Artificial Intelligence, 17*(4), 581-600.

KEY TERMS

Completeness: Completeness of a decision rule characterizes its power, that is, a rule with high completeness factor should cover the maximum of objects belonging to the rule's class.

Consistency: Consistency of a decision rule exhibits its reliability, that is, a rule with high consistency should cover the minimum of the objects that do not belong to the class of the given rule.

Contingency Table: A contingency table is a statistical tool, usually in the form of a matrix that exhibits the relation between two random variables; in case of decision rules, it portrays the relation between rule characteristics and the corresponding class.

Decision Rule: Decision rule is an element (piece) of knowledge, usually in the form of "if-then statement": if <Condition> then <Action>. If its Condition is satisfied (i.e., matches a fact in the corresponding database of a given problem), then its Action (e.g., classification or decision making) is performed.

Decision Set: Decision set is a set (list) of decision rules; a common knowledge representation tool (utilized, e.g., in most expert systems).

Decision-Set Quality: Decision-set quality is a numerical factor that characterizes a measure of belief in a given decision set; it is a conglomerate of the qualities of all its elements (decision rules).

Ordered or Unordered Set of Decision Rules: There are two modes of decision sets: either the order of its decision rules is substantial (ordered mode), or not (unordered mode). In the first mode, the system inspects the decision set from the beginning and stops at the first rule that is satisfied for a given object; in the latter, all rules must be inspected and decision is carried out according to a combination scheme.

Rule Quality: Rule quality is a numerical factor that characterizes a measure of belief in the given decision rule, its power, predictability, reliability, and likelihood.

Decision Making Support in Emergency Response

Viviane Barbosa Diniz
Federal University of Rio de Janeiro, Brazil

Marcos R. S. Borges
Federal University of Rio de Janeiro, Brazil

José Orlando Gomes
Federal University of Rio de Janeiro, Brazil

José H. Canós
Technical University of Valencia, Spain

INTRODUCTION

An emergency event can be chronologically divided into three phases: prevention, response, and investigation. Preventive actions attempt to anticipate all emergency situations and describe procedures intended to avoid undesirable outcomes. Unfortunately, not all circumstances can be predicted and some cannot be avoided. When undesirable situations occur, an emergency response action has to be set off. The response phase is very complex because decisions have to be made in a very short time and sometimes without the desirable information. An investigation usually follows any incident in order to find out the causes of the emergency, assess the effectiveness of the response, and generate recommendations for future preventive and response actions (Ochoa, Neyem, Pino, & Borges, 2006).

Concerning the emergency response phase, actions are usually carried out by several teams which should work in a manner as cooperative and articulated as possible to eliminate or reduce the impact of the disaster. These teams usually follow established procedures to deal with emergencies contained in emergency plans. In most events, actions are coordinated centrally but decisions are made at both central and local levels. Information plays an important role in these decisions. According to Dykstra (2003), when things go wrong in emergency management, the reasons are generally related to breakdowns in information, communication, and/or coordination.

During an emergency response, most decisions require knowledge from procedures, described in emergency plans, and from the previous experience of decision makers. A huge amount of contextual information has to be processed. This information comes from several sources, including the emergency field. The prompt capture and distribution of this information can play an important role in the decisions made by emergency teams. Most emergency response plans, however, are not designed to deal with this type of contextual information.

In some cases, contextual information is not available; in others the information exists but has not been disseminated. Conversely, team members have fresh information that could be useful to other teams, but they do not have the means to pass it on. A system processing information coming from the field and helping to propagate it to the right people at the right time would enable control rooms to better deal with emergencies (Brezillon & Naveiro, 2003).

The goal of this article is to describe a framework for understanding the interrelationship between the different types of knowledge. This framework should guide the design of systems able to store the captured contextual information and selectively disseminate it to decision makers and to emergency response teams. The system based on this framework should focus on the contextual information captured in the course of incident resolution, either by control room demand or incidentally by team members dealing with the emergency.

With such a system, people in control rooms should be able to make decisions assessing information derived from the event, in addition to, of course, from the procedures established by emergency plans. One of the main requirements of such a system is to provide decision makers with the right amount of information, avoiding both overloading and starvation. The system should help control personnel and manage the acquisition and dissemination of relevant contextual information among operation teams.

This article is divided as follows. We provide some background on the use of different types of knowledge during emergency response work, use the framework to review the information systems technology used to support decisions in emergency handling, and then conclude the article.

BACKGROUND

Emergencies are the concern of several organizations and researchers worldwide (Woods & Cook, 2002). Although the focus of each group is different, the groups usually recognize the need for better tools to promote interoperability among institutions that need to make decisions to resolve the emergency. An example of this shared thinking is the Seminar on Crisis Management and Information Technology (Seminar Report, 2002), which is a seminar aimed at finding better solutions for global crisis management, mainly peace support operations. In this seminar, it was stated that integrated Information and Communication Technology (ICT) systems, designed to support decision-making and communication in multilateral peace support operations, are an important tool.

Similarly, Smith (2003) argues that information sharing and interagency coordination are clearly needed to facilitate a successful emergency incident response. In that paper, a set of requirements is proposed for a consequence management solution, based on the principles of the Incident Command System (ICS), an all-hazard approach, established by the Federal Emergency Management Agency (FEMA) in the USA. Some examples of these requirements include: monitoring of multiple information sources for possible alerts to response participants and rapid risk communication/alert dissemination.

The examples above illustrated how researchers and practitioners are concerned with the cooperation aspects of emergency management. However, the issues are not only on helping the information reach people, but also on the quality of this information. Currion (2003) highlights a problem faced by humanitarian assistance teams: the growing gap between the supply of, and demand for, high quality information. There is a lack of information management, which makes people suffer either from data starvation or from information overload. They made several recommendations, such as investment in a framework for training and incentives for the staff to be more rigorous in collecting and using data, applying filter mechanisms (policy and structural).

Other works emphasize the need for decision support systems in emergency management. Gadomski, Balducelli, Bologna, and Costanzo (1998) propose an environment based on intelligent agents to guide decisions. An emergency response plan of an underground transportation company was turned into a multimedia system integrating text, audio, video, 3D models, and animations (Canós, Alonso, & Jaén, 2004). This solution has improved the usability of the emergency plan, though its lack of current contextual information was considered a serious limitation.

The emergency response phase starts when a dangerous situation needing immediate action occurs, and ends when such situation has been resolved. During this period, well-trained teams execute a set of actions under time pressure, aiming at saving lives or property. These teams usually belong to more than one organization; for instance, firefighters and policemen. Frequently, each organization has its own training and its own resources to coordinate its actions and to support communication among their team members. At the same time, these organizations must communicate with each other so that a large body of shared knowledge is built and used to make most decisions during the emergency response process.

The knowledge can be available in different forms, and be of different nature, as illustrated in Figure 1. First, the previous personal knowledge (PPK) is embedded in each emergency responder's mind. It has been acquired during past experiences, training, and simulations of real-life settings. This type of knowledge is fundamental in this domain because it reduces the time needed to make decisions. It is tacit, highly personal, and hard to formalize, as already pointed out by Nonaka and Takeuchi (1995).

Second, the previous formal knowledge (PFK) is usually explicit and does not change during the course of the emergency. One of its main sources is the emergency response plan, which describes the

Figure 1. Conceptual map of knowledge support during an emergency response phase (Diniz, Borges, Gomes, & Canós, 2005)

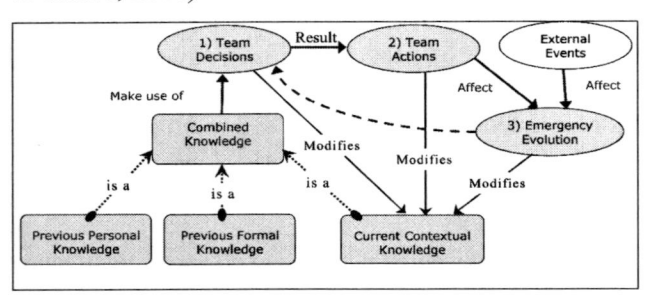

procedures that should be followed according to the type of incident. The emergency plan includes most information needed to perform the procedures, such as local maps, description of the infrastructures, and so forth. The PFK exists, it is essential to the emergency response work, and can be presented in many different ways. Recent work shows that rich user interfaces can be built using hypermedia technology (Canós, Borges, & Alonso, 2006).

The third key source of knowledge in emergencies is that originating from developments in the emergency settings, called current contextual knowledge (CCK). This knowledge about the event can be supplied either by human sources or automatic sources such as sensors. CCK is essential for the quality of decisions in the dynamic environments of emergency response. Examples of CCK are temperature measures captured by a sensor, aerial images about the incident sent by a helicopter or information from human sources expressed by sentences such as: "There are two people inside the building, one on the tenth floor and the other on the fifth," "the police have blocked all accesses to the premises," "this building will collapse soon," and "the police helicopter has seen a desperate person on the roof." Unlike the PFK, this type of information is made explicit as it is discovered. Human sources usually transmit this information by means of VHF radios or mobile phones. We can identify two types of CCK, one corresponding to the development of the emergency, and the other encompassing the actions performed by the emergency teams. In both cases, the information has to be perceived and processed in order to be considered contextual knowledge. Due to the dynamic nature of the current context, knowledge changes all the time.

During the event of an emergency, an initial plan is assigned to respond to the expected evolution of events. The plan includes any information needed to perform the procedures. It also takes into consideration the experience of emergency teams in dealing with the type of emergency. In other words, it is based on the personal knowledge (PPK) available. To generate the plan, the command also assesses the current context of the emergency situation, that is, the initial reports about the situation. Based on the initial plan, tasks are assigned to emergency teams, which start to perform them, and, at the same time, providing more accurate information about the context and the result of their actions.

In many emergency management systems, the CCK remains tacit. That is, there is no guarantee that the emergency teams will receive all information they need. In contrast, they might receive useless information that could dislodge their focus of attention. But how can situational awareness be improved? We argue that this can be achieved by increasing the quality of the information provided. How to measure the quality of knowledge is an interesting research issue, and can be addressed using the concepts of precision and recall (Baeza-Yates & Ribeiro-Neto, 1999). It is equally important to develop ways to present the combined knowledge to the decision makers effectively and efficiently. Canós and Zulueta (2004) developed an interesting example for the Metro Valencia. They used hypermedia to enhance the PFK and, hence, reduce the emergency response time. The emergency plan was enriched with multimedia objects; the expressive power of new media, along with the structure provided by hypertext helped to provide decision makers with richer information items in shorter time. The hyperlink structure came from the coordination rules established in the emergency plan.

Viewing the response to an emergency as the execution of a (flexible) process, the response teams must perform actions in the order defined by the process control flow. For each task in the flow, a set of information items must be brought to the user interface. Most of these elements belong to the PFK. Although CCK is equally relevant, in many emergency management systems (EMS) it remains tacit. The framework first described by Diniz et al. (2005) has been used in other works dealing with emergency response. Ochoa et al. (2006) use the framework to describe the work of different roles participating in disaster relief efforts. This work was further extended and the framework was used to explain the different contexts that should be dealt with when designing a supporting system (Ochoa, Neyem, Pino, & Borges, 2007).

MAIN FOCUS

In the following subsections, we use the framework presented in the previous section to describe some initiatives for using knowledge to support emergency response. In any case, in this work we are only dealing with explicit knowledge. As stated by French and Turoff (2007), "Many emergencies arise because of some unanticipated event or combination of events. In such circumstances, there is seldom sufficient explicit knowledge codified in databases and models to address the issues; one needs tacit knowledge" (p. 40). Although we recognize the importance of tacit knowledge in such situations, we believe that our proposed framework can help in providing more explicit knowledge to decision makers, reducing the uncertainties of many decisions.

Approaches Focused on Previous Personal Knowledge

One of the best-known computer approaches to stimulate cooperation among emergency response agents is training systems. Not only is cooperation treated in this kind of approach, an individual's ability to make quick decisions is, as well. The main idea included in these systems is that if people are well trained to make fast decisions and to cooperate among themselves, the probability of neglecting these issues is reduced. Although used during the prevention or preparation phases, training systems also feed previous formal knowledge, which is essential for making decisions in the response phase.

There are various reports in the literature about systems of this type, and some even have commercial versions. They share the ability to simulate real conditions to train agents' abilities to deal with emergencies. An example based on virtual reality and using some software agents that mimic human behaviour is ETOILE, defined by Dörner, Grimm, and Seiler (2001). This tool is divided into two principal parts: the execution platform, responsible for the training per se, and the emergency scenario creation tool, which permits training session planning. During training execution, individuals' actions are stored, allowing learning through later analysis.

An example of a commercial training system is MUSTER 2.0 – Multi-User System for Training Emergency Response (2001). This is an emergency simulation tool for doctors, nurses, and rescue teams, which seeks to provide training which takes into account the need for coordination among participants of various organizations (Andersen, 2001). Muster is based on a client/server architecture, as illustrated in Figure 2. The *server* is responsible for the progression of training. The supervisor begins and controls the session, and has a global vision of what is happening, as well as a local view of each individual's actions, which allows assessment of each participant. The scenarios are representations of real emergency situations, stored as scripts. The actors control the agents in the simulation and have facilities to communicate among themselves. Agents are rescue team members, such as doctor, nurse, and so forth. Each participant takes on an agent's role.

Approaches Focused on Previous Formal Knowledge

Another approach in the attempt to support decision-making is to make previous formal knowledge available

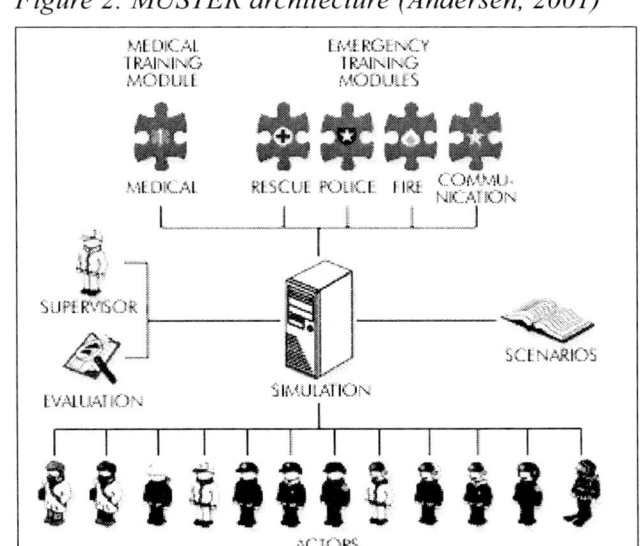

Figure 2. MUSTER architecture (Andersen, 2001)

more interactively and easier to access, thereby reducing the time taken by decision-makers searching for building plans, maps, emergency plans, and other documents. This was done by Canós et al. (2004), who transformed the Valencia subway company's emergency plan into a multimedia system, integrating text, audio, video, 3D models, and animation. "In a first stage, we replaced the printed, sequentially ordered plan by a hypermedia, multimedia document that allows context-sensitive and adaptive browsing of its contents. "In a second stage, we enriched the plan's multimedia content to facilitate interpretation and understanding under stressful situations." "Our goal was to reduce textual content and replace it with workflow-like graphical descriptions of the procedures" (p. 107). They also added maps and 3D animations to the workflows, making it easier to visualize infrastructure, safety equipment, and evacuation routes.

Systems that absorb previous formal knowledge frequently make use of the potential provided by workflow management systems (WfMS) to represent the action plans, for they have the ability to model, monitor, and control the execution of coordinated activities executed by different persons or groups (Dias & Carvalho, 2003). Some of these systems enrich the emergency plans with elements of current contextual knowledge, but as they are based on the plan, this article considers that they focus on previous formal knowledge.

Geographical information systems (GIS) are also used to represent previous formal knowledge. They substitute and improve upon maps and conventional blueprints, since besides representing these graphically, they allow the association of alphanumeric data to this representation and allow spatial queries and analyses. This is useful, for example, in hazard mapping and visualization as well as for improving situational awareness. Rauschert et al. (2002) developed a multimodal, multi-user GIS interface that puts geospatial data directly in the hands of decision makers. They highlight that in the emergency management domain it is fundamental to think of more user centred projects and interfaces. For them, geospatial information is critical to effective, collaborative decision-making during emergency management situations and the interfaces of current geographical information systems are not adequate for this.

Approaches Focused on Current Contextual Knowledge

As in the previous approach, this one seeks to help decision-making by making knowledge available, the difference being that the systems mentioned here attempt to incorporate current contextual knowledge as their main objective, and previous formal knowledge in a supporting role. Because of this, most systems for emergency response that target contextual information end up including elements of previous formal knowledge. The main reason it is difficult to treat current contextual information in isolation is that its relationship with previous formal knowledge must be made explicit. An example: the geographic location of the people involved is current contextual knowledge, but needs to be put in context on a map, which is previous formal knowledge.

The work described by Bui and Sankara (2001) is in the line that focuses current contextual knowledge and uses previous formal knowledge as a support. In this work, the issue of the large volume of information in humanitarian aid and disaster relief in large geographical scale operations, involving various organizations located in distant places. More than a technological solution, the system proposes a change in organizational structure. This change is the creation of a Virtual Information Centre (VIC), where there would be professionals specifically charged with monitoring information from sensors and a variety of crises related data bases, and processing them in decisions to save lives and assets. The authors envisioned that there will be several VICs each focusing on a specific type of disaster such as earthquake, floods, war/aggression.

As can be seen, this solution also proposes the use of computer technology. The two main requirements of the Virtual Information Centres were: "produce answers to requests for information (RFI) made by a participant/administrator of the emergency response, and research lower level data, make and send a request for attention (RFA), which was alert information to be examined by the deciders." To model the RFA request process, the authors adopted a workflow model. To implement an RFA, they suggested an event chain coupled with the use of intelligent software agents approach.

Another example of this approach is described by Gadomski et al. (1998), who propose an agent based environment with the objective of providing intelligent support for decision making during emergency response. The main idea is to reduce the probability of human error in management. This is done by not only providing data (selected according to situation assessment and intervention procedures from emergency plans) but providing an active decision support related to the choices of adequate actions.

FUTURE TRENDS

Many emergency management systems still rely on information stored on paper or other static forms of representation. However, emergency situations require a dynamic system environment with the most up-to-date information in order to anticipate the development of the incident and to deal with unexpected events. In this sense, a new generation of emergency response systems should support automatic acquisition of information coming from response and other supporting teams. This will provide a much better support for decision-making both in the control room and in the field.

Mobile communication is also a hot topic for the future of emergency response systems. The technology allows many new forms of operation, including those performed by automatic agents. These forms have been studied and some promising results have been published in a research seminar dedicated to the theme (Löffler & Klann, 2007).

The support for collaboration has been suggested by several authors (Canós et al., 2006; Diniz et al., 2005; Dugdale, Pavard, Pallamin, Jed, & Maugan, 2004; French & Turoff, 2007; Ochoa et al., 2006; Smith, 2003). Due to the complexity of emergency response operations, team members need support for collaboration to perform joint operations and synchronize efforts to achieve enhanced outcome. Moreover, collaboration is required among teams from different organizations. While there are group decision support systems that support collaboration, the deployment of their collaborative technologies within the context of emergency management is not common (French & Turoff, 2007). This is a topic that requires attention from researchers.

CONCLUSION

This article presented a general framework for understanding and supporting the use of knowledge in emergency response support systems. We have shown the three types of knowledge used and demonstrated the importance of Current Contextual Knowledge for the coordination of emergency response activities. We have also described a conceptual model to guide the design of knowledge management collaborative emergency response systems.

The definition of the conceptual model based on patterns is an important characteristic of the proposed model. It would enable interoperability and extensibility, two important requirements for dealing with several teams. Another important requirement, which has not yet been properly discussed, is the customization of the system to specific domains, both at emergency type level and at organization level (firefighters, police force, medical services, etc.).

Most of the requirements are obtained by analyzing reports from disasters (Dwyer, Flynn, & Fesseden, 2002; Gadomski et al., 1998; Seminar Report, 2002; The 9/11 Commission Report, 2005). However, a great amount of knowledge has also been obtained from visits and talks with experienced emergency workers. The latter will be particularly valuable when evaluating the system prior to implementation.

ACKNOWLEDGMENT

Marcos R. S. Borges and Jose Orlando Gomes were partially supported by grants from Conselho Nacional de Desenvolvimento Científico e Tecnológico – CNPq (Brazil), 305900/2005-6 and 484981/2006-4, respectively. José H. Canós has been funded by the Spanish "Comisión Interministerial de Ciencia y Tecnología" under grants DYNAMICA and META.

REFERENCES

Andersen, V. (2001). Training of medical teams on-site for individual and coordinated response in emergency management. *International Journal of Emergency Management, 1*(1), 3-12.

Baeza-Yates, R., & Ribeiro-Neto B. (1999). *Modern information retrieval*. New York: Addison-Wesley.

Brezillon, P., & Naveiro, R. (2003). Knowledge and context in design for a collaborative decision making. *Journal of Decision Systems, 12*(3-4), 253-270.

Bui, T., & Sankaran, S. (2001). Design considerations for a virtual information center for humanitarian assistance/disaster relief using workflow modeling. *Decision Support Systems, 31,* 165-179, 2001.

Canós, J.H., Alonso, G., & Jaén, J. (2004). A multimedia approach to the efficient implementation and use of emergency plans. *IEEE Multimedia, 11*(3), 106-110.

Canós, J.H., Borges, M.R.S., & Alonso, G. (2005). An IT view of emergency management. *IEEE Computer, 38*(12), 27.

Canós, J.H., & Zulueta, F. (2004). Using hypermedia to improve safety in underground metropolitan transportation. *Multimedia Tools and Applications, 22*(1), 75-87.

Currion P. (2003). Surviving droughts and floods: Stretching the metaphor for humanitarian information management. In *Proceedings of Toward an International System Model in Emergency Management,* Public Entity Risk Institute (pp. 1-7).

Diniz, V.B., Borges, M.R.S., Gomes, J.O., & Canós, J. H. (2005). Knowledge management support for collaborative emergency response. In *Proceedings of the 9th International Conference on Computer Supported Cooperative Work in Design* (Vol. 2, pp. 1188-1193). IEEE.

Dugdale, J., Pavard, B., Pallamin, N., Jed, M., & Maugan, L. (2004). Emergency fire incident training in a virtual world. In *Proceedings of the Conference of the International Community on Information Systems for Crisis Response and Management (ISCRAM)* (pp. 167-172).

Dwyer, J., Flynn K., & Fessenden, F. (2002, July 7). 9/11 exposed deadly flaws in rescue plan. *The New York Times*.

Dykstra, E. (2003). Concept paper: Toward an international system model in emergency management. In *Proceedings of Toward an International System Model in Emergency Management,* Public Entity Risk Institute.

French, S., & Turoff, M. (2007). Decision support systems. *Communications of the ACM, 50*(3), 39-40.

Gadomski, A.M., Balducelli, C. Bologna, S., & Costanzo, G. (1998). Integrated parallel bottom-up and top-down approach to the development of agent-based intelligent DSSs for emergency management. In *Proceedings of International Emergency Management Society Conference,* Washington (pp. 421-434).

Löffler, J., & Klann, M. (Eds.). (2007). Mobile response 2007 (LNCS 4458). Berlin, Germany: Springer-Verlag.

Nonaka, I., & Takeuchi, H. (1995). *The knowledge-creating company: How Japanese companies create the dynamics of innovation*. Oxford: Oxford University Press.

Ochoa, S., Neyem, A., Pino, J.A., & Borges, M.R.S. (2006). Using context to support group decision making in disaster affecting urban areas. In *IFIP International Conference on Decision Support System* (pp. 546-561). Ludic Publishing Ltd.

Ochoa, S., Neyem, A., Pino, J.A., & Borges, M.R.S. (2007). Supporting group decision making and coordination in urban disasters relief efforts. *Journal of Decision Systems*.

Rauschert, I. et al. (2002). Designing a human-centered, multimodal GIS interface to support emergency management. In *Proceedings of the GIS'02* (pp. 119-124). New York: ACM Press.

Seminar on Crisis Management and Information Technology. (2002). *Crisis management initiative* (Seminar report). Retrieved December 11, 2007, from http://www.ahtisaari.fi/files/ITCM_seminar_report.pdf. Access: Jun.2005

Smith, S. (2003). Inter-agency collaboration and consequence management: An all-hazard approach to emergency incident response. In *Proceedings of Toward an International System Model in Emergency Management,* Public Entity Risk Institute.

The 9/11 Commission Report. *Final report of the National Commission on terrorist attacks upon the United States*. Official Government Edition. Retrieved December 11, 2007, from http://www.9-11commission.gov/report/index.htm

Woods, D.D., & Cook, R.I. (2002). Nine steps to move forward from error. *Cognition, Technology & Work, 4*(2), 137-144.

KEY TERMS

Contextual Knowledge: Knowledge captured during an incident that provides information about the development of the event.

Decision Making Framework: A knowledge framework developed to understand how personal, formal, and contextual knowledge combine to provide information for decision-maker actions.

Emergency Response: A set of coordinated actions to handle unexpected and undesirable events during an emergency.

Formal Knowledge: Information made explicit and associated with a semantic meaning.

Personal Knowledge: The knowledge possessed by an individual as a result of previous experience and learning.

Decision Support and Problem Formulation Activity

David Paradice
Florida State University, USA

INTRODUCTION

While decision choices are certainly important and warrant appropriate attention, early stages of the decision-making process may be even more critical in terms of needing adequate support. The alternatives from which a decision maker may be able to choose are integrally tied to the assumptions made about the problem situation. Consequently, decision support systems (DSSs) may be more effective in helping decision makers to make good choices when support for problem formulation is provided. Research validates the notion that support for problem formulation and structuring leads to better decisions. This article explores this concept and looks at opportunities in emerging software trends to continue development of problem formulation support in DSS-type settings.

BACKGROUND

From its inception, the domain of DSS has focused on providing technological support for decision-making processes in ill-structured environments. Simon's (1977) model of decision-making processes has been a cornerstone of DSS design since the inception of the decision support movement. Simon outlined four processes that he believed account for most of what executives do:

The first phase of the decision-making process—searching the environment for conditions calling for decision—I shall call *intelligence* activity (borrowing the military meaning of intelligence). The second phase—inventing, developing, and analyzing possible courses of action—I shall call *design* activity. The third phase—selecting a particular course of action from those available—I shall call *choice* activity. The fourth phase, assessing past choices, I shall call *review* activity. (Simon 1977, p. 40)

Human nature being what it is, the success or failure of choices made in particular decision-making situations often gets the most attention. The early days of the DSS movement implicitly focused most heavily on the choice phase of Simon's model. At the beginning of the DSS movement, DSSs were still constructed from programming languages such as FORTRAN (formula translator) or PL/1 (programming language 1), although DSS environments containing interactive modeling languages were soon developed. In these environments, construction of the model that would form the basis of the decision process often fell on technical experts with little or no direct stake in the decision outcome. These experts simply translated a model specification into the appropriate programming code and returned a "system" to the ultimate decision makers. The actions of the decision makers involved executing the model, typically with varying combinations of input values, so that various scenarios could be examined to determine which set of input values led to the most desirable outcome. In other words, the function of the user was to choose one of several alternatives. In some cases, claims were made that the users had designed a solution and consequently that the DSS had supported the design stage of Simon's model. Closer examination, however, shows that the design stage of Simon's model was executed in the specification of the model to be programmed.

The power of the model was well documented in the work by Pounds (1969). Pounds learned that problem finding is essentially the recognition of a difference between reality and what a decision maker expected, where expectations were typically based upon some preexisting model. The model may be the decision maker's own mental model, based on historical events or personal experience, or it may be a model constructed by someone else. Regardless of their origin, the models used by decision makers were critical in their efforts to recognize and address problems. Pounds found that even though business models were quite naïve compared to decision-making models in scientific domains, model-building techniques were making significant contributions to management effectiveness.

Models are comforting because they provide a means of removing uncertainty. Humphreys and Berkeley (1985) note seven types of uncertainty in the process of conceptualizing decision problems. Decision theory can adequately account for only four of the uncertainty types. These uncertainties are primarily related to the likelihood of outcomes and events. Procedural uncertainty, such as specifying the relevant issues, what information to seek, and how to structure it, is not addressed by decision theory. When a decision model is constructed, much of the procedure for attacking the problem is then specified. One collects the appropriate data, executes the model, and assesses the results. These activities are much less cognitively straining than the construction of the model.

Of importance here is that these models, once specified and constructed, rarely have been examined at later times to determine whether they remain accurate models of reality. Decision makers (typically managers) specify a model to be constructed based on their experiences and perceptions, and programming professionals translate this specification into a functioning DSS. Once a model is producing acceptable results, rarely has anyone asked later, "Is this model still correct?" The assumptions underlying the model specification have been assumed to be accurate still. This is a critical aspect of DSS, for the alternatives from which a decision maker may be able to choose are integrally tied to the assumptions made about the problem situation.

Because decision makers "satisfice" (Simon, 1976), they will naturally be driven to consider ranges of feasible alternatives rather than choosing maximizing or optimizing behavior. Simon identified premises (i.e., assumptions) as the most fundamental unit of analysis in decision making. According to Simon, the premises that one recognizes are the most relevant to a decision situation. These control the alternatives considered. Consequently, premises dictate behavior. Schein (1985) has concluded that understanding a culture and a group's values and overt behavior requires understanding the underlying assumptions. These are typically unconscious but actually determine how group members perceive, think, and feel.

Churchman's (1971) examination of inquiring systems most clearly illustrates the fundamental dependence that models have on assumptions. Churchman developed the notion of inquiring systems—systems that create knowledge—by examining the design of such systems based on the philosophies of five Western philosophers. Beginning with Liebnitz and working through the philosophies of Locke, Kant, Hegel, and Singer, Churchman showed that the basic assumptions regarding how knowledge is created drive all other aspects of the system.

In the Liebnitzian system, formal logic is the guarantor of knowledge. Consequently, inputs to the system must be well formed and amenable to formal rules of logical conclusions. Lockean systems depend on consensus; therefore, agreement on labels and properties of objects becomes critical. Kantian systems allow for multiple realities, with the best fit of data to model determining how conclusions are drawn. Hegelian systems depend on the dialectic. It is in these systems that overt examination of the assumptions of different realities occurs. Singerian systems rely on continual measurement and a "sweeping in" of new model variables to refine models.

Churchman's students have certainly recognized the importance of assumptions. Mason (1969) and Mitroff, Emshoff, and Kilmann (1979) were early leaders in recognizing the need to identify assumptions in models. Mason recommended dialectic processes as a way to surface assumptions for review and reconsideration. He suggested this process could lead to the identification of new and relevant assumptions that strategic planners should consider. Mitroff and his colleagues demonstrated that Churchman's and Mason's ideas formed a good basis for formulating ill-structured problems.

Another of Churchman's students, Russell Ackoff (1981), has argued that examination of the models that are developed in decision-making situations leads to important and valuable knowledge. He argued that it is precisely due to making explicit that which is not normally made explicit (i.e., the assumptions of the model) that improvement of the decision-making system is possible. The assumptions should be made open for examination and criticism by decision makers and other researchers.

Later, Mitroff and Linstone (1993, p.15) built on Churchman's work to define a "new way of thinking." They argue for explicit consideration of multiple realities when dealing with complex problems. Their basic premise is that no one perspective of a complex situation will ever embody all of the assumptions of all of the stakeholders involved.

The importance of assumptions is not espoused solely by Churchman and his students. Huber (2004,

p. 72) also implicitly recognizes the importance of assumptions. He states that in the future, a firm's survival will depend on its ability to "rapidly and effectively sense and interpret environmental changes." Intuitively, decision-making models that are not revised to reflect environmental changes will be based on the wrong assumptions, with consequently poor support for the decision-making processes they are intended to support.

One can recognize that assumptions are most prevalent in the process of formulating the structure of a problem model. However, what empirical research exists to verify this preconception? In order to investigate support for problem formulation in DSS, a series of studies was executed under the direction of James Courtney (Courtney & Paradice, 1993). This research was grounded in the fields of cognitive psychology and systems engineering. From the work in cognitive psychology, problem formulation was determined to consist of three phases: problem identification, problem definition, and problem structuring.

Problem identification occurs when the need for a decision is perceived by the decision maker. When characterized as a problem situation, this need is typically perceived in the context of some perceived deviation from expectations. However, an opportunity could also create the need for a decision, so one should be careful to avoid the connotation that a problem situation is necessarily a bad situation. Problem definition involves determining the relevant properties of the situation. Problem structuring examines the problem situation to determine a strategy for addressing the situation.

HOW DSS CAN SUPPORT PROBLEM FORMULATION

Studies have shown that a critical part of problem solving is developing the problem structure (Abualsamh, Carlin, & McDaniel, 1990; Gettys, Pliske, Manning, & Casey, 1987; Mintzberg, Raisinghani, & Theoret, 1976; Mitroff & Featheringham, 1974). Consequently, some effort to support decision makers in this part of the decision process through appropriate DSS features should be valuable.

An initial DSS study that examined this argument was executed by Kasper (1985). Kasper had participants compete in a business-simulation gaming environment. The business simulation provided a complex decision-making environment, requiring participants to make up to 56 different decisions in each decision period. The game's outputs took into consideration the decisions made by all participants in determining how any one participant's decision inputs were processed. Participants had access to a database management system that provided access to their corporate data. It also provided access to competitors' data, but in such a way that mimicked the equivocal nature of acquiring information in real business environments.

Kasper (1985) divided his participants into three groups. The control group simply played the game using the database as they desired to make the best business decisions they could make. A second group was required to create a model of the decision environment. This group was required to specify the variables that they perceived as important to their decision-making process as well as the relationships between those variables. The third of Kasper's groups also created a model of the decision-making environment. However, unlike the second group, this group was required to actually use their model in their decision-making process.

Kasper's (1985) results indicated that the decision makers who built models outperformed the decision makers who did not build models. Furthermore, the decision makers who used the models they built outperformed the decision makers who only built the model but did not use it.

Pracht (1986) and Pracht and Courtney (1988) used Kasper's (1985) results as a starting point for their investigation. Additionally, they built upon work that showed that diagrams and images were useful in the problem formulation process. They hypothesized that participants with high spatial ability (i.e., a high degree of comfort with spatial orientation) would benefit from graphics-oriented problem structuring tools. They designed a 2x2 factorial design experiment where participants were categorized as having high or low spatial ability. The second factor isolated access to the graphics-oriented problem structuring tool. All participants were required to draw a structural model of the business simulation environment. The participants without access to the graphics-oriented tool drew their models by hand.

The results indicated that participants with high spatial ability who had access to the graphics-oriented problem structuring tool more closely formulated the correct structure of the business simulation environment than any other group. Participants with low spatial ability performed about the same regardless of having access to the tool. Notably, the participants with high spatial ability who did not have access to the tool performed the worst.

Loy (1986) extended these results to small-group environments. He used the same tool in two group-process environments. Some groups used the nominal group technique to structure their decision-making processes. The other groups were given no specific process to follow. To investigate whether spatial ability was again a factor, Loy computed a group spatial-ability score. Loy's results confirmed those obtained in the previous study. Groups with access to the graphics-oriented problem structuring tool outperformed groups without access to the tool. Groups with high spatial-ability scores who had access to the tool outperformed all other groups. Groups with high spatial ability without access to the tool performed the worst. The process factor was not significant. There were no significant results for any factor when groups using the nominal group technique were compared to those using no specific process.

Ata Mohammed, Courtney, and Paradice (1988) returned to the tool developed by Pracht and Courtney (1988) and focused their work there. They modified the tool to create causation trees, which are hierarchical diagrams similar to structural models. In this causation tree, the root node is a problem for which potential causes are sought. The branches of the tree represent paths from the problem to variables contributing to the base causes of the problem. The goal was to create an environment of semiautomated problem-structuring decision support.

Ata Mohammed et al. (1988) tested the new tool by taking models developed by Pracht and Courtney's (1988) participants as inputs to their DSS and checking the veracity of the base causes identified by the causation trees. The testing of the new tool inadvertently provided additional evidence for the importance of examining the assumptions upon which models are built. The tool was very sensitive to the accuracy of the model, and in an absolute sense the models developed by some of Pracht and Courtney's participants were not very good. Many of these models suffered from cognitive biases held by the participants. For example, the participants often believed that increasing a salesperson's commission would lead to increased sales. In the simulation, however, there is a point at which salespeople become comfortable with their annual salary and no amount of increased commission leads to more sales. In fact, increasing the commission can lead to fewer sales because fewer sales are required for the salespeople to achieve their desired level of income. Thus, even though the tool helped users formulate more accurate models, these models were not accurate enough to provide the basis for semiautomated problem-structuring support.

Such support was investigated by Paradice and Courtney (1987). They developed a new version of the DSS software developed by Ata Mohammed et al. (1988). This version attempted to control for the cognitive biases introduced into the models by the users through the use of linear and higher order statistical models. Rather than take the models at face value, Paradice and Courtney's system automatically examined the database created by the business simulation environment and statistically tested the relationships specified in the model.

Early testing of Paradice and Courtney's (1987) system exposed the need for an extended taxonomy of business-variable relationships. The system did not improve upon Ata Mohammed et al.'s (1988) approach when working with the simple notion of causality. However, incorporation of the extended taxonomy, in which variables could be described as redefining other variables—acting as upper and lower bounds on other variables, correlated with other variables, and participating in other relationships—began to lead to improved results. The addition of more sophisticated statistical analyses, such as the ability to conduct path analysis, further improved system performance. Finally, Paradice and Courtney constructed a manner for the system to report its confidence in its outputs.

This system was trained using Pracht and Courtney's (1988) participants' models. Models that passed statistical tests were stored in a knowledge base for use by an advisory module later. Paradice and Courtney's (1987) system was the first to provide explicit support for changing business environments through the use of its "rejection base." The rejection base was a knowledge base of proposed relationships that did not pass statistical analysis. Recognizing that relationships may be invalid now but valid later (or vice versa) due to changing business conditions, the system allowed the user to store the hypothesized relationships in the rejection base even when statistical support did not exist. The final validation of the system demonstrated that the system performed as well as the participants when the participants' models used to train the system were accurate. Notably, the system also outperformed the participants in other areas, particularly those where the participants' cognitive biases were evident.

Paradice and Courtney's (1987) system was a precursor to what would today be called a knowledge management system. It also contained rudimentary data mining capabilities, capabilities that would be extended in the next study conducted by Billman (1988). Billman extended Paradice and Courtney's system's advisory module and statistical capabilities by developing capabilities to discover relationships. Billman implemented three algorithms for assessing the strength of relationships between variables. She tested her system by allowing it to discover the relationships in the business simulation environment that was the basis for the studies that came before hers. When allowed to function without human intervention, Billman's system found 75% of the relationships implemented in the underlying business simulation game related to a target variable (cost of goods sold), but it also discovered six spurious relationships. Billman also tested her system using a composite model built from four of the best human-participant models constructed by players in the simulation game. Using this approach, her system discovered only 60% of the relationships involving the target variable, but it found no spurious relationships.

As these studies were under way, the field of group DSS (GDSS) was also beginning to see much activity. Over time, the GDSS field work merged into the domain of computer-supported collaborative work (CSCW). However, much of the research in CSCW can be interpreted as efforts to focus DSS effort on problem formulation activities.

Many of the GDSS and CSCW system characteristics support problem formulation and structuring. Anonymous brainstorming capabilities allowed GDSS users to suggest factors believed to be relevant to problem situations. Ranking and rating capabilities allowed the group to work collaboratively to define problem structures. Process techniques provided rules to assist meeting participants in attacking a particular problem well.

GDSS and CSCW studies focused on a wide range of dependent variables, but many of them are central to problem formulation and structuring activities. For example, Hartwick, Sheppard, and Davis (1982), Shaw (1981), and Stasser (1992) examined ways that individuals shared information that was held individually but not necessarily known to the group. Dennis, Valacich, and Nunamaker (1991) showed that shared information could be used synergistically by the group in ways that exceeded how the individuals would use privately held information. Shaw, and Laughlin, Vander Stoep, and Hollingshead (1991) showed that collective evaluation was more objective than individual judgment, leading to reduced bias in the problem formulations.

As the collaborative nature of work has become more widely recognized and supported, DSS researchers have begun to investigate more sophisticated means of supporting problem formulation. In the process, they have also indirectly shed some light on the least investigated phase of Simon's model: the review phase. Hall and Davis (2007) have revisited the work of Mason, Mitroff, and others. They recently report on the testing of a system designed to encourage decision makers to consider others' perspectives. Whereas Mason and his colleagues focused on Hegel's philosophy and dialectic processes, Hall and Davis have focused on Singer's philosophical concept of sweeping in new perspectives of a problem situation. Hall and Davis discovered that when participants consider perspectives that differ from their own innate system of values, they change their behavior as relates to weakly held value positions. Hosack (2007), building on Hall and Davis's work, has found that feedback in different forms can effect similar behavioral changes. Both of these studies force the users of these systems to review their prior decisions. These results suggest that in the absence of active support, decision makers will follow their own heuristics that may lead to biased problem formulations. When DSSs provide means for actively considering problem structures, reviewing one's prior decisions, and considering how others may see a problem differently, decision-making behavior changes. There can be little doubt that effort spent on defining a problem's structure helps in the process of solving that problem.

FUTURE TRENDS

Fortunately, today's systems are creating environments that naturally support collaborative problem structuring activities if DSS designers will only take advantage of them. Instant-messaging software, discussion boards, and chat rooms all provide environments conducive to soliciting multiple perspectives on problems, thus naturally creating the Singerian system of sweeping in new views of a problem situation. DSS designers must investigate ways of leveraging these environments in new DSS designs.

The electronic nature of these environments makes them amenable to incorporation into new DSS designs. For example, online archives of discussion boards could provide a new type of knowledge base to be accessed by a computer-based problem-structuring decision support environment. These archives often contain information on how to solve specific problems. In fact, frequently there are multiple approaches described.

Chat rooms and discussion boards may one day also provide immediate test environments for decision makers. In the same sense that spreadsheet technology led to scenario analysis in the early days of the DSS movement, chat rooms could provide decision makers with immediate responses to proposed alternative courses of action. This would be a type of scenario analysis that could exceed the benefits of even the best simulation because the audience would consist of the actual stakeholders in the problem situation.

CONCLUSION

As long as decision makers struggle with defining the problem they are trying to solve, problem formulation support in DSS will be valuable. When decision makers solve problems without giving adequate attention to the structure of the problem being faced, they run the risk of developing ineffective solutions. In the worst case, they solve the wrong problem completely. Research demonstrates that DSS support for problem formulation activities provides benefits, yet little continues to be done to exploit this finding in the development of new DSSs or new decision support environments. DSS designers should strive to always look for new opportunities to improve this aspect of decision support.

REFERENCES

Abualsamh, R. A., Carlin, B., & McDaniel, R. R., Jr. (1990). Problem structuring heuristics in strategic decision making. *Organizational Behavior and Human Decision Processes, 45*, 159-174.

Ackoff, R. L. (1981). *Creating the corporate future.* New York: John Wiley & Sons.

Ata Mohammed, N., Courtney, J. F., Jr., & Paradice, D. B. (1988). A prototype DSS for structuring and diagnosing managerial problems. *IEEE Transactions on Systems, Man, and Cybernetics, 18*(6), 899-907.

Billman, B. (1988). *Automated discovery of causal relationships in managerial problem domains.* Unpublished doctoral dissertation, Department of Business Analysis & Research, Texas A&M University, College Station, TX.

Churchman, C. W. (1971). *The design of inquiring systems.* New York: Basic Books, Inc.

Courtney, Jr., J.F. and Paradice, D.B. (1993). Studies in Managerial Problem Formulation Systems. *Decision Support Systems, 9*(4), 413-423.

Dennis, A. R, Valacich, J. S., & Nunamaker, J. F. (1991). A comparison of laboratory and field research in the study of electronic meeting systems. *Journal of Management Information Systems, 7*(3), 107-135.

Gettys, C. F., Pliske, R. M., Manning, C., & Casey, J. T. (1987). An evaluation of human act generation performance. *Organizational Behavior and Human Decision Processes, 39*, 23-51.

Hall, D., & Davis, R. A. (2007). Engaging multiple perspectives: A value-based decision making model. *Decision Support Systems, 43*(4), 1588-1604.

Hartwick, J., Sheppard, B. H., & Davis, J. H. (1982). Group remembering: Research and implications. In R. A. Guzzo (Ed.), *Improving group decision making in organizations: Approaches from theory and research* (pp. 41-72). New York: Academic Press.

Hosack, B. (2007). The effect of system feedback and decision context on value-based decision-making behavior. *Decision Support Systems, 43*(4), 1605-1614.

Huber, G. P. (2004). *The necessary nature of future firms.* Thousand Oaks, CA: Sage Publications.

Humphreys, P., & Berkeley, D. (1985). Handling uncertainty: Levels of analysis of decision problems. In G. Wright (Ed.), *Behavioral decision making* (pp. 257-282). New York: Plenum Press.

Kasper, G. M. (1985). The effect of user-developed DSS applications on forecasting decision-making performance. *Journal of Management Information Systems, 2*(2), 26-39.

Laughlin, P. R., Vander Stoep, S. W., & Hollingshead, A. B. (1991). Collective versus individual induction: Recognition of truth, rejection of error, and collective information processing. *Journal of Personality and Social Psychology, 61*(1), 50-67.

Loy, S. L. (1986). *An experimental investigation of a graphical problem-structuring aid and the nominal group technique for group decision support systems.* Unpublished doctoral dissertation, Department of Information Systems and Quantitative Sciences, Texas Tech University, Lubbock, TX.

Mason, R. O. (1969). A dialectical approach to strategic planning. *Management Science, 15*(8), B403-B414.

Mintzberg, H., Raisinghani, D., & Theoret, A. (1976). The structure of "unstructured" decisions. *Administrative Science Quarterly, 21*, 246-275.

Mitroff, I. I., Emshoff, J. R., & Kilmann, J. R. (1979). Assumptional analysis: A methodology for strategic problem solving. *Management Science, 25*(6), 583-593.

Mitroff, I. I., & Featheringham, T. R. (1974). On systemic problem solving and the error of the third kind. *Behavioral Science, 19*(6), 383-393.

Mitroff, I. I., & Linstone, H. A. (1993). *The unbounded mind: Breaking the chains of traditional business thinking.* New York: Oxford University Press.

Paradice, D. B., & Courtney, J. F., Jr. (1987). Causal and non-causal relationships and dynamic model construction in a managerial advisory system. *Journal of Management Information Systems, 3*(4), 39-53.

Pounds, W. F. (1969). The process of problem finding. *Industrial Management Review, 11*(1), 1-19.

Pracht, W. E. (1986). GISMO: A visual problem structuring and knowledge organization tool. *IEEE Transactions on Systems, Man, and Cybernetics, 16*, 265-270.

Pracht, W. E., & Courtney, J. F., Jr. (1988). The effects of an interactive, graphics-based DSS to support problem structuring. *Decision Sciences, 19*(3), 598-621.

Schein, E. (1985). *Organizational culture and leadership.* San Francisco: Jossey-Bass.

Shaw, M. (1981). *Group dynamics: The psychology of small group behavior* (3rd ed.). New York: McGraw Hill.

Simon, H. A. (1976). *Administrative behavior.* New York: Free Press.

Simon, H. A. (1977). *The new science of management decision* (Rev. ed.). Englewood Cliffs, NJ: Prentice Hall.

Stasser, G. (1992). Pooling of unshared information during group discussion. In S. Worchel, W. Wood, & J. Simpson (Eds.), *Group process and productivity* (pp. 48-67). Newbury Park, CA: Sage Publications.

KEY TERMS

Decision Model: It is a codified process for making a decision. An example of a decision model is Simon's intelligence-design-choice model, which specifies that one first determines the existence of a problem or an opportunity (intelligence in the military sense of the term), then designs alternative means to solve the problem (or exploit the opportunity), and then chooses the alternative deemed best.

Inquiring System: It is a system designed to systematically investigate a situation for the purpose of acquiring or creating knowledge.

Inquiry: Inquiry is a systematic process of investigation.

Intelligence-Design-Choice: This is an example of a decision model formulated by H. A. Simon. In this model, one first determines the existence of a problem or an opportunity (intelligence in the military sense of the term), then designs alternative means to solve the problem (or exploit the opportunity), and then chooses the alternative deemed best.

Messy Problem: A messy problem is a problem that is characterized by the absence of a correct solution. Messy problems are typically complex problems requiring significant judgment and involving multiple stakeholders who have conflicting goals.

Decision Support and Problem Formulation Activity

Problem Formulation: It is the process of determining the constituent parts of a problem: its important factors and variables, and the interrelationships between them.

Problem Structure: How the constituent parts of a problem (i.e., its important factors and variables) are believed to relate and interact with one another.

A Decision Support System for Evaluation of Investments in a Computer-Integrated Production System

Hannu Kivijärvi
Helsinki School of Economics, Finland

Markku Tuominen
Lappeenranta University of Technology, Finland

INTRODUCTION

Investments in new manufacturing systems are vital for the well-being of the company as they are means of achieving the objectives and goals the company is aiming at. Both long-term corporate success and short-term profitability are based on the company's investments. Managerial decision making is, however, becoming more difficult due to worldwide competition and the rapidly changing and increasingly complex environment.

A growing concern is that the selection of investment alternatives (manufacturing systems) that in the long run enhance the company's competitive position or other strategic goals cannot any longer be based on conventional financial analysis only. These financial analysis techniques do not provide the decision maker with sufficient support because they do not integrate the investments into the company's strategy sufficiently. Furthermore, the conventional investment planning based on these techniques does not fully respond to the way the investment decisions are actually made. The shortages of the conventional justification techniques include insufficient benefit analysis, a short-term focus, and misassessment of the appropriate discount rate. Therefore, conventional financial analysis techniques alone are not appropriate to justify more strategic investments, but a strategy-oriented investment justification is needed as well.

By an investment decision it is meant an irreversible commitment of resources in order to achieve uncertain future gains. The benefits of investments are not wholly exhausted in the short term and the investment decisions always, even if to a varying extent, involve a risk. Generally, investments can be classified to the following three groups:

- **Necessity investments:** These investments are different by nature. However, it is typical that negligence concerning the investments will cause considerable damage.
- **Investments for productivity improvement:** Investments belonging to this class include minor process improvements that are made in order to achieve cost savings or improve productivity.
- **Strategic investments:** These investments have a significant impact on the company as a whole, as well as on its long-term performance. They may be undesirable in the short term and difficult to justify economically. However, in the long run, the investments are necessary in order to maintain and enhance the company's position in the marketplace. Strategic investments are the special concern of this study.

In order to be successfully implemented and to enhance the company's strategic position, the investments ought to be evaluated consistently with the applied strategy and every phase of the investment process should be supported. The phases of the investment process we use here are based on Simon's (1976) general decision-making phases: intelligence, design, choice, implementation, and control. The investment process with its main inputs and outputs is described in Figure 1.

The organizational context cannot be ignored, and the information transmission and delegation of decision rights within the organization should be considered in the investment management process. A critical element in the investment management process is the decision support that transforms strategic plans into concrete investment decisions. Consistent and systematic decision support ensures that those investment alternatives that satisfy the strategic goals of the company best are

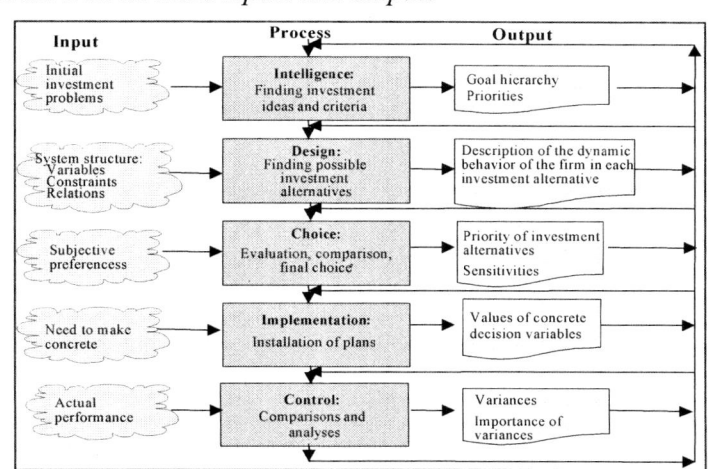

Figure 1. Investment process with its main inputs and outputs

identified, selected, and successfully implemented. This study presents how to support each phase of the investment process and provides appropriate techniques and tools for strategy-oriented investment justification and evaluation. According to the methodology, the emphasis is moved from technological aspects closer to substantive, managerial aspects. We believe that all phases of the development process can be supported by appropriate managerial decision models (Kivijärvi, 1997). The developed framework is versatile and can be applied to all strategic investments.

CONCEPTUAL BACKGROUND

Problem Structure and Intangible Investments

An essential characteristic of strategic decision making is its lack of structure, which might be due to a shortage of relevant information, high risk and uncertainty, novelty, and deficiencies in the decision-making process (Taylor, 1988). The degree of structure may vary situationally depending on the focus of the decision making, the personal capabilities of the decision makers, or on the strategy adopted. Porter (1980), for example, suggests three classes of competitive strategies—overall cost leadership, differentiation, and focusing—which may impose different kinds of information requirements, uncertainty, and so forth. Thus, it seems that the concept of problem structure is a key to the essence of strategic decision making and problem solving, and hence to the structure of a support system (Kivijärvi & Tuominen, 1993).

Smith (1988) classifies the existing conceptualizations of problem structure by four notions: goal state, problem space, knowledge, and process. The first conceptualization relates the degree of the problem structure to the clarity of the goal state of the problem. If the goal is adequately specified, the problem is structured. In the other extreme, if there are multiple goals or they are indefinite, then also, as a consequence, multiple solutions exist and justification and validation procedures are missing or they become more equivocal and demanding.

The second conceptualization relates the degree of the problem structure to its representability. If the characteristics of the problem can be easily measured, and the relationships between them can be formulated explicitly and quantitatively, then the problem is structured.

According to the third conceptualization, the problem structure is related to the solver's knowledge. How much is known of the relevant facts? How certain are they? Are they based on subjective evaluations or objective data? By this notion, the degree of the problem structure is regarded as person dependent rather than of a natural kind.

Finally, the degree of the problem structure can be seen in light of the solution process. If an effective solution procedure, no matter how complicated, is known and regularly used, then the problem is structured. On the other hand, if no solution strategy can be found, the problem is unstructured. Problems may also not be structured or unstructured in their entirety but only in terms of some stages in the solution procedure. Problems that are totally

Table 1. Problem structure and investment categories

Conceptualization of Problem Structure	Problem Structure		Investments	
	Structured ↔	Unstructured	Tangible ↔	Intangible
Goal State	• Definite • Single • Straightforward	• Indefinite • Multiple • Missing, equivocal or demanding	• Max the firm's present values • Financial justification	• Multiple goals • Hierarchical goal structure • Strategic justification
Problem Space	• Formal and quantitative	• Informal and qualitative	• All relevant variables can be expressed in terms of money	• Only a part can be formalized
Knowledge	• Known • Certain • Objective	• Unknown • Uncertain • Subjective	• Costs, revenues, interest rates, lifetime, etc. are known with certainty	• Subjective evaluations with high risk and uncertainty
Solution Process	• Exists and is regularly used • Repetitive	• Deficient procedure	• Traditional methods of investment analysis	• Multiple support methods

unstructured can be solved only with the help of human intuition, whereas the solution process of structured problems can be formalized or even automated.

The above four conceptualizations of the problem structure may overlap and correlate, but for our purposes they are distinguishable enough to characterize the dimensions and complexity of the concept of the problem structure. The four conceptualizations and their influence on structured and unstructured problems are summarized in the first three columns of Table 1.

Because the problem structure is rather a continuous than a dichotomous concept, there is always something between the two extremes, namely, semistructured problems. Semistructured problems may exist between the extremes according to any of the conceptualizations or they may be structured according to one conceptualization but unstructured according to another. In the solution process of semistructured problems, human judgment can be supported but not replaced by appropriate computer technology.

Strategic decision making typically deals with unstructured or semistructured problems. Strategic investment problems may, however, be structured, unstructured, or semistructured. Capital budgeting literature offers such an enormous amount of knowledge that conventional investment problems could be easily structured and solved by generally accepted routines. On the other hand, the semistructured investment problems, intangible investments, do not have such normative literature on their background, and other methods to solve them are needed.

In the fourth column of Table 1, the conventional (tangible) investments, as a class of structured problems, are conceptualized. The goal state of conventional investment problems is to maximize a firm's present value. Therefore, the investment alternative giving the greatest net present value is chosen. The justification and validation of the proposed solution is simply based upon the time-preference function. It is assumed that all the relevant factors can be expressed in terms of money, and that the data are available and certain. The solution process follows traditional investment analysis methods.

Intangible investments, as a class of semistructured problems, are characterized in the last column of Table 1. Within the intangible investments, the potential goal state the firm aims at is perhaps not best described by the firm's maximal present value, but several other descriptions of the goal state, in brief goals, can be used. Levy and Sarnat (1990), for example, list the following eight potential goals: maximization of profit, maximization of sales, survival of the firm, achievement of a satisfactory level of profits, achievement of a target market share, some minimum level of employee turnover, internal peace, and maximization of managerial salaries. In addition to these general goals, strategy- or problem-oriented lower level goals may be used. Among the goals there may exist hierarchical or other relationships that are determined by personal preferences. Thus, there may be several acceptable solutions to the intangible investment problems, and the alternative that is finally chosen depends on the personal preferences of the decision maker.

Within the intangible investments, only a part of the whole investment problem can be formally described.

There is only a limited number of facts available, and a significant part of the data is gathered by means of subjective evaluations. Data concerning revenues, costs, and other relevant factors may vary substantially across the alternatives, complicating the solution process. For the intangible investments, there is no well-defined solution procedure available, but different methods can be integrated to support the different phases of the process. The shortage of traditional methods and the need for a new, support-oriented methodology is discussed next. We will also illustrate with a concrete case how the solution process of intangible investments can be supported.

Shortages of Traditional Techniques and Some New Requirements

In general, the investment or the capital budgeting process can be divided into separate phases. According to Pike and Neale (1996), capital budgeting includes the following activities: determination of the budget; search for and development of projects; evaluation and authorization; and monitoring and control. McIntyre and Coulthurst (1987) use the following three-phase model: the creation phase, the decision phase, and the implementation phase. These classifications are general enough to cover conventional as well as intangible investments. The divergence of the phase models finally led us to use a more general process model of decision making.

In the literature of managerial economics (especially in capital budgeting literature), the main emphasis has been on the choice phase and the preceding appraisals and evaluations of the investment alternatives. Typically, the investment evaluation techniques involve the use of discounted cash flow, which is often given as a net present value formula. Other existing traditional evaluation techniques are the internal rate of return, profitability index, payback period, return on investment, present value of annuities, and benefit-cost ratio (see, e.g., Pike and Neale, 1996).

Investments can be made in the company's tangible assets like the plant and equipment, or intangible assets like information systems, logistics systems, know-how, patents, goodwill, brands, and so forth. As indicated in Table 1, intangible investments differ significantly from conventional investments. Indicatively, numerous studies have shown that there is a significant gap between theory and practice in investment processes. It has been found that simple techniques, such as the payback period, are more frequently used than discounted cash flow techniques (Pike and Neale, 1996).

Kaplan (1986) and Ordoobadi and Mulvaney (2001), for example, criticize the present state of investment analyses in computer-integrated production technologies. Kaplan (1986, p. 89) argues,

CIM technology provides many additional benefits—better quality, greater flexibility, reduced inventory and floor space, lower throughput times, experience with new technology—that a typical capital justification process does not quantify. Financial analyses that focus too narrowly on easily quantified savings in labor, material or energy will miss important benefits from CIM technology.

There is no doubt that the traditional techniques have significant deficiencies in the analysis of intangible investments. Most of the traditional investment criteria imply that the initial investment, the incremental cash flows, the cost of capital, and the economic time horizon of the investment alternative are known. It is assumed that all the effects of the investment can be traced, measured, and transformed into monetary units. Intangible costs and revenues are assumed to be zero, and subjective criteria are ignored.

According to the traditional investment techniques, the final choice is made on the basis of a single, cost-oriented criterion. The underlying assumption is that all investments aim at the cost-leadership strategy and that all firms in fact apply it only. However, firms may also have other strategies to meet their goals and objectives, for instance, product, service, technology, or distribution differentiation; focusing on a particular buyer group or a segment of the product line; and so forth (Porter, 1980). The traditional investment criteria are not strategy oriented; they are only cost oriented (Noble, 1989). This is a serious deficiency when the question is of strategic investments.

Whatever the corporate-wide strategy is, the traditional techniques are still needed. They should, however, be used in a more contributory fashion rather than dominantly. If a firm seeks to be a cost leader, even the tight cost-oriented measures are appropriate criteria for the investment justification. However, if the firm aims at its targets with other strategies, then the cost-oriented measures are only constraints that secure the minimum return on an investment alternative. The final choice is made on the basis of other criteria. The calculations will have multiple criteria and dimensions.

When the traditional criteria are used as constraints, lower present values and discount rates and longer planning horizons and payback periods can be used. However, the main difference is that other strategy-oriented measures are accepted as well. The strategy-oriented justification of investment projects is particularly appropriate, first, when the investment alternatives affect several areas of the firm, and second, when they have long-range effects—in other words, when it is a question of a strategic investment. The following investments are typical examples of intangible investments that have cross-functional, corporate-wide effects and where the investments should be strategically justified: logistics systems, information systems, corporate image, consumer service, and social overhead investments aimed at improving working conditions. Even the investments in new manufacturing facilities, flexible production systems, or automated factories have a strong impact on, for example, the flexibility, reliability, and quality of manufacturing, and can thus be considered as a class of intangible investments (Howell & Soucy, 1987).

As an illustrative case, we consider a class of strategic intangible investments in more detail: investments in manufacturing systems.

MULTIATTRIBUTE SUPPORT FOR THE SELECTION OF A COMPUTER-INTEGRATED PRODUCTION SYSTEM

Methodological Background

We have developed a decision support system for the analysis of intangible production investments where several tools are combined to support the different phases of the decision process. The design of the support system with its main inputs and outputs is described in Figure 2.

The key components of the system are a multiattribute evaluation tool and a dynamic simulation model. The evaluation tool can be used in the different tasks of the investment process, like problem decomposition, criteria selection, comparison of the alternatives, sensitivity and trade-off analyses, and in assessing the actual performance of the production system. The evaluation tool can be developed by a number of methodologies. In this case, however, the analytic hierarchy process (AHP; Saaty, 1999) is used. It is a procedure developed to tackle complex, multicriteria, political, and economic decision problems. As input, AHP uses the judgments of the decision makers about the alternatives, the evaluation criteria, the relationships between the criteria (importance), and the relationships between the alternatives (preference). In the evaluation process, subjective values, personal knowledge, and objective information can be linked together. As an output, a goal hierarchy and the priorities of alternatives and their sensitivities are reached.

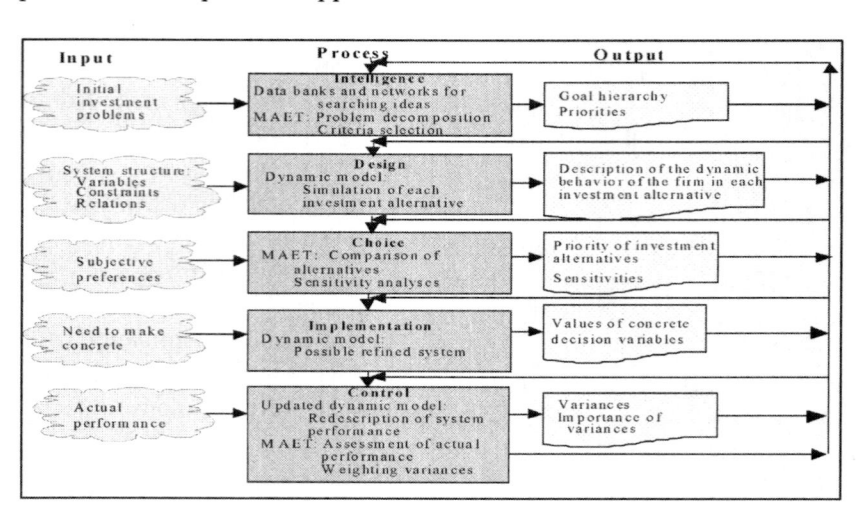

Figure 2. Investment process and respective support tools

Other potential evaluation procedures are, for example, Simple Multi-Attribute Rating Technique, SMART (Olson, 1996) and Analytic Network Process, ANP (Saaty, 2005). Simulation is a powerful tool for examining and comparing alternative designs for production systems, making it possible to both quantify and study their performance. The ability to support model construction and run models, and to generate animations with statistics is one of the main attractions of simulation. Today, there are many simulation packages available (Swain, 2007). In the planning of manufacturing systems, for example, the following simulation software are available: Flexsim, GoldSim, ShowFlow, SIGMA, SimCad Pro, SIMUL8, and SLIM. Software products like iThink, Stella, Vensim, and Powersim that are based on system thinking and system dynamics can be used to study larger systems with complicated feedback relations and to integrate managerial and technical elements. Simulation models can naturally be created with general programming systems or even with spreadsheets.

A number of people from different organizational units were involved in the system development process of this study. One of the leading ideas behind the development of the system was that human judgment has to be supported by an appropriate computer technology in every phase of the decision process (Sprague & Carlson, 1982; Turban, Aronson, & Liang, 2005). We cannot automate the phases but we can support the decision maker in performing them effectively. The second goal during the systems development was that subjective as well as objective data should be accepted flexibly. The best result is achieved through the integration of both types of input data.

In addition to the evaluation tool and the dynamic simulation model, networks, databases, and spreadsheets were integrated to the support context.

An Illustrative Case

The case company is a medium-sized metal-industry company. The management and representatives of manufacturing and the design office get together to set the manufacturing objectives for the company. Their background information includes marketing research and competitor analysis, as well as information about technological and economic trends in their own field and in the economy. Due to its relatively small size and distinct technical specialization, the company has chosen the differentiation strategy. This strategy has been made clear and delegated to the directors of the divisions. A large product range, tailored and high-quality products, and acceptable delivery times seem to bring competitive edge. However, the price is not allowed to rise too high. Therefore, quality and inventory costs have to be minimized. Consequently, varying the lot sizes and product mix require considerable flexibility. In spite of the future changes, the employees' positive attitude toward the company and its management has to be maintained.

In this case, due to the strategic point of view, the principles of system dynamics were applied (Sterman, 2000). A dynamic simulation model was developed using iThink software and in addition to the production process, it covers some company-wide elements from finance and marketing.[1]

The company-wide simulation model developed in this case is divided into two modules: production and finance. The production component includes some elements concerning marketing as well. The production module consists of the following items defined for both main product groups (A and B): production capacity, capacity utilization, inventories, shipments, raw-material inventories, raw-material purchasing, production levels, production costs, inventory costs, customer orders, pricing, market shares, and order backlog. Within the financial module some financial ratios are defined.

In the case company, AHP installed by the Expert Choice software package was selected as the evaluation tool because it can compare alternatives in regard to both subjective and objective criteria. It can also assess inconsistency in decision makers' judgments and give relative preference values for alternatives.

Decision Process

In the intelligence phase, new investment ideas were searched for on the Internet and in various databases. It soon became evident that there was a large number of different types of production solutions, the evaluation of which would not be a trivial task. AHP can be used to manage an extensive set of potential decision criteria and to evaluate the relative importance of these criteria. For this purpose, an evaluation hierarchy, as described in Figure 3, was constructed. The final criterion, the best manufacturing system, is at the top of the hierarchy. On the next two levels there are criteria and subcriteria. The elements at the lowest level are decision alternatives.

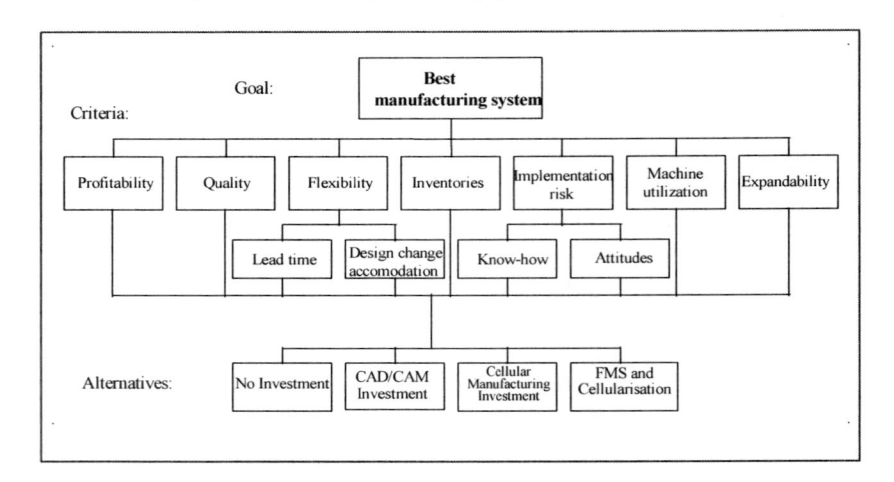

Figure 3. AHP for the selection of the best manufacturing system

AHP with its pair-wise comparisons was next used to set weights for the selected criteria (Figure 4). Priorities were produced by evaluating each set of elements in a pair-wise fashion with respect to each of the elements on a higher level. There is a verbal and a corresponding numerical scale in AHP to assess the dominance of each element over the others with respect to each element of the higher level of the hierarchy. Finally, the priorities are synthesized to determine the overall priorities. Based on these results, the following criteria and subcriteria were selected for the later phases of the decision process:

- **Profitability** (Net present value of investment in thousands of €)
- **Quality** (Defect rate; number of customer complaints per year)
- **Flexibility**
- **Lead time** (Average time from order receiving to delivery in days)
- **Design change accommodation** (Average number of design changes per week)
- **Inventories** (Production value per average inventory level)
- **Implementation risk**
- **Know-how**
- **Employees' attitude** (Number of absences per year)
- **Machine utilization** (Average working time/year (h))
- **Expandability**

After the evaluation criteria had been set for the new manufacturing system, a discussion about investment alternatives started in the design phase. In the group's opinion, waiting for better control systems alone would not bring the desired improvement in quality. Investments in new technology seemed to be essential. Therefore, a small team consisting of representatives of both the manufacturing department and the design office was formed. Their task was to generate investment proposals to fulfill the goals that were set earlier. Finally, the following proposals were generated by the team.

Alternative 1: No investment
Alternative 2: Computer aided design/computer-aided manufacturing (CAD/CAM) investment. Old manual and numerical control (NC) machines would be replaced with computerized numerical control (CNC) machines and their programming software would be compatible with the existing CAD software.
Alternative 3: Cellular manufacturing investment. Old machines would be replaced as in the previous CAD/CAM investment, and the functional layout would also be replaced with a group technology (GT) cellular layout.
Alternative 4: FMS and cellularisation. There would be GT cellular manufacturing for product group B and flexible manufacturing system (FMS) for product group A.

Figure 4. Weights of the criteria

Priorities with respect to Goal

Profitability	0.357
Quality	0.278
Flexibility	0.154
Inventories	0.005
Implementation	0.122
Utilization	0.047
Expandability	0.037

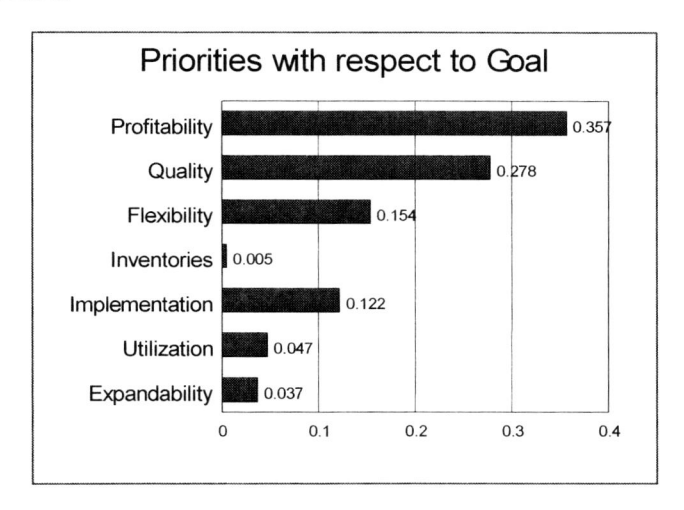

Figure 5. Alternative comparisons with respect to criterion X

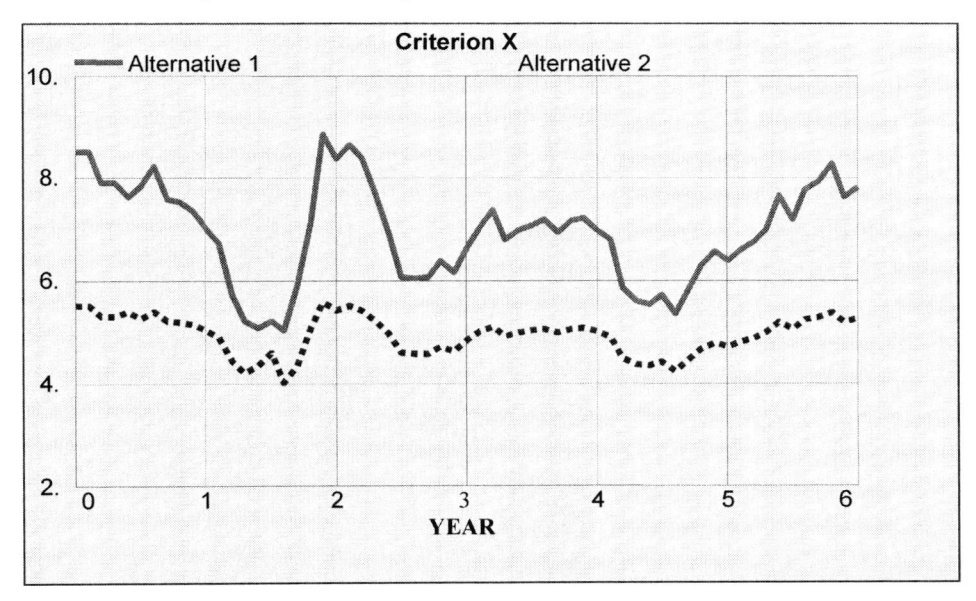

In the choice phase of the decision process, the simulated strategies are evaluated. When evaluating the investment alternatives according to the principles of the AHP, the alternatives are compared with respect to each criterion. In the evaluation process, for example, we judge which is more preferable: Alternative 1 or Alternative 2 with respect to criterion X and how preferable it is (Figure 5). Similarly, all other pairs of alternatives are compared under all criteria.

After the comparisons, the total priorities of the final ranking of the investment alternatives are synthesized. As presented in Figure 6, the cellular manufacturing investment is the best choice in the case illustrated. The next best alternative for the production system is based on FMS and cellularisation.

Analyzing strategic investments is a challenging task because all relevant inputs are subject to uncertainty and equivocality, and they are based on qualitative and quantitative data, subjective judgments, and conflicting goals. Values, preferences and goals, and strategic alternatives are not unambiguous, but they can be reevaluated, ordered differently, described in

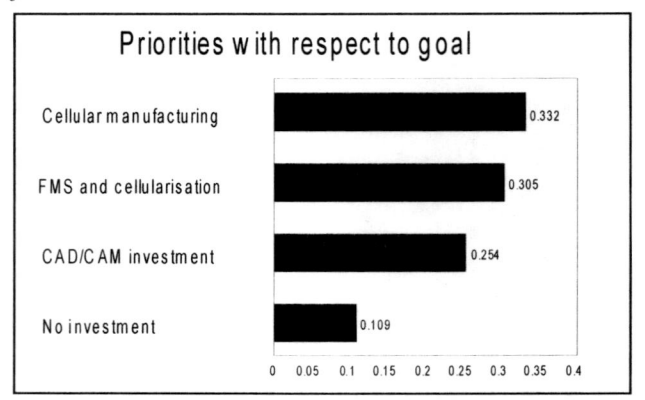

Figure 6. Overall priorities of the investment alternatives

Priorities with respect to goal

Alternative	Priority
Cellular manufacturing	0.332
FMS and cellularisation	0.305
CAD/CAM investment	0.254
No investment	0.109

more detail, and so forth. There is no single, exact way to solve intangible, strategic problems, nor a single solution to the problem. Sensitivity analysis forms an important part of strategic analysis, not least because it offers a means of examining the input uncertainty related to the output. Fortunately, the selected evaluation tool offers different types of sensitivity analyses (performance, dynamic, gradient, head to head, and two dimensional) that can be completed easily.

The success of an investment, however, does not only depend on finding an appropriate investment alternative, but also on the way the chosen alternative is implemented. The support system presented above has some characteristics that support even the implementation phase of the investment process. First, it is clear that intangible investments cannot be proposed, justified, or evaluated by a single person or a department only; joint efforts with diversified interests, goals, and objectives are needed. With the evaluation tool, different interests, goals, and objectives can be coordinated and harmonized in an efficient manner in the group context. The method proposed here is most suitable for participative group decision making and, as a consequence, people are accountable for the decisions they have participated in. Second, according to the presented method, the variables in the simulation model include disaggregated, operative, and well-documented pieces of information. This, of course, helps to concretize the strategic decisions to operative plans. Third, the implementation of the selected investment alternative can be effectively supported by a user interface with graphic and numeric outputs. The plans can also be easily distributed over the organization by means of network services. These characteristics make it easy to transform the plans into reality and to put theory into action.

When the investment is implemented, the actual results should be compared with the plans in the control phase. Generally, the comparison should be based on the same method of evaluation as was applied in the choice phase. A problem in controlling the investments is how to isolate the cash flow or other outputs of a particular investment from other cash flows. Thus, the control of an otherwise conventional investment may be an intangible task. Because the decisions are well documented in the system presented above, the outcome of the investment can subsequently be compared with the rationale and information used in arriving at the investment decision, and even better decisions can be made in the future. Also in the control phase, several decision makers may be involved. Therefore, it is necessary to use the same set of multiple criteria that was used in the design and choice phases.

CONCLUSION

In this article we have shown how the semistructured strategic decisions concerning intangible investments in manufacturing systems can be supported effectively by relating appropriate analysis methods to the different phases of the investment process. Intangible investments cannot be justified or evaluated by a single cost-oriented criterion alone, but several other criteria must be used as well. Intangible investments also have other characteristics that make special requirements for decision support. Within intangible investments, for example, only a part of the whole investment problem can be formally described, there is only a limited number of facts available, and a significant part of the data is gathered by subjective evaluations. Revenues, costs, and other relevant data may vary substantially across the alternatives, complicating the solution process. Therefore, for the intangible investments there is no well-defined solution procedure available, but different methods must be integrated to support the solution process.

Strategic planning is a managerial area where semistructured problems frequently exist. One of the key problems faced in strategic management is the issue of investment decisions. Investments in information systems, logistics systems, flexible production systems, corporate image, and so forth are examples of complex investment problems that are difficult to quantify and analyze with traditional techniques. Modern computer technology can enrich the analysis and improve the quality of strategic decision making.

Methodologically, our experiences emphasize some obvious advantages in integrating dynamic simulation and a multiattribute evaluation procedure like AHP. From the simulation point of view, AHP is a method that directs the development of the simulation model. During the development process, it is possible to determine by AHP the variables to be included in the model. The essential criteria and their relative weights can then be used as a starting point in formulating the simulation model as well. This way, problem restriction and variable selection are tied to the original problems and the goals and objectives of the firm. Perhaps the most important advantage is that AHP helps to find an efficient solution in the simulation context.

On the other hand, from the point of view of AHP, simulation provides long-felt dynamics to the static evaluation procedure. Typically, AHP evaluations are based only on subjective assessments. Simulation moves the evaluation toward a more factual basis. It is possible to utilize quantitative calculations behind the evaluations. Also, when describing and simulating the dynamic behavior of a network of complicated business processes, a more stable ground to evaluate the independence or dependence of the decision criteria is established.

REFERENCES

Dyer, R. F., & Forman, E. H. (1992). Group decision support with the analytic hierarchy process. *Decision Support Systems, 8*(2), 99-121.

Howell, R. A., & Soucy, S. E. (1987). Capital investment in the new manufacturing environment. *Management Accounting, 69*(5), 26-32.

Kaplan, R. S. (1986). Must CIM be justified by faith alone? *Harvard Business Review, 64*(5), 87-95.

Kivijärvi, H. (1997). A substance-theory-oriented approach to the implementation of organizational DSS. *Decision Support Systems, 20*(3), 215-241.

Kivijärvi, H., & Tuominen, M. (1993). A decision support system for evaluating intangible investments. *Computers and Industrial Engineering, 25*(1-4), 353-356.

Kivijärvi, H., Tuominen, M., & Ahola, J. (2001). Computer supported strategy analysis in a forest industry corporation: Implementation process of a corporate-wide decision support system. *Studies in Industrial Engineering and Management, 17*.

Levy, H., & Sarnat, M. (1990). *Capital investment and financial decisions.* Prentice Hall.

McIntyre, A., & Coulthurst, N. (1987). The planning and control of capital investments in medium-sized UK-companies. *Management Accounting, 65*(3), 39-40.

Noble, J. L. (1989). Techniques for cost justifying CIM. *The Journal of Business Strategy, 10*(1), 44-49.

Olson, D. L. (1996). *Decision aids for selection problems.* New York: Springer.

Ordoobadi, S. M., & Mulvaney, N. J. (2001). Development of a justification tool for advanced manufacturing technologies: System-wide benefits value analysis. *Journal of Engineering and Technology Management, 18*(2), 157-184.

Pike, R., & Neale, B. (1996). *Corporate finance & investments: Decisions and strategies.* London: Prentice Hall.

Porter, M. E. (1980). *Competitive strategy.* The Free Press.

Saaty, T. L. (1999). *Decision making for leaders.* Pittsburgh, PA: RSW Publications.

Saaty, T. L. (2005). *Theory and applications of the analytic network process: Decision making with benefits, opportunities, costs, and risks.* Pittsburgh, PA: RSW Publications.

Simon, H. (1976). *Administrative behavior.* New York: Free Press.

Smith, G. (1988). Towards a heuristic theory of problem structuring. *Management Science, 35*(12), 1489-1506.

Sprague, R. H., & Carlson, E. D. (1982). *Building effective decision support systems.* Prentice-Hall, Inc.

Sterman, J. D. (2000). *Business dynamics: Systems thinking and modeling for a complex world.* Irwin McGraw-Hill.

Swain, J.J. (2007), Simulation Software Survey - New Frontiers in Simulation, Biennial survey of discrete-event simulation software tools. *OR/MS Today, 34*(6), 32-43.

Taylor, L. A., III. (1988). Affective responses within a complex decision-making task: The influence of perceptually ill-structured problems. *Decision Sciences, 19*(1), 39-54.

Turban, E., Aronson, J. E., & Liang, T. P. (2005). *Decision support systems and intelligent systems.* Pearson Education.

KEY TERMS

Decision Making: Decision making is a cognitive process of choosing between alternative courses of action.

Manufacturing System: This is the arrangement and operation of production resources (machines, tools, material, people, and information) to produce planned products or services.

Multiattribute: It is a quality or characteristic of a system with a number of dimensions and subdimensions.

Simulation: Simulation is the imitation of certain key characteristics or behaviors of real systems.

ENDNOTE

[1] Due to some business secrets, the simulation model is not generally available. However, a very similar model from the forest industry is described in detail in Kivijärvi, Tuominen, and Ahola (2001).

A Decision Support System for Selecting Secure Web Services

Khaled M. Khan
Qatar University, Qatar

INTRODUCTION

Web service is becoming an important area of business processing and research for enterprise systems. Various Web service providers currently offer diverse computing services ranging from entertainment, finance, and health care to real-time application. With the widespread proliferation of Web Services, not only delivering secure services has become a critical challenge for the service providers, but users face constant challenges in selecting the appropriate Web services for their enterprise application systems. Security has become an important issue for information systems (IS) managers for a secure integration of Web services with their enterprise systems. Security is one of the determining factors in selecting appropriate Web services. The need for run-time composition of enterprise systems with third-party Web services requires a careful selection process of Web services with security assurances consistent with the enterprise business goal. Selection of appropriate Web services with required security assurances is essentially a problem of choice among several alternative services available in the market. The IS managers have little control of the actual security behavior of the third-party Web services, however, they can control the selection of right services which could likely comply their security requirements. Selecting third-party Web services arbitrarily over the Internet is critical as well as risky.

With increasing security challenges to the enterprise systems, there is a need for an automatic decision support system (DSS) for the selection of appropriate secure Web services. A DSS analyzes security profiles of candidate Web services and compares them with the security requirements of the enterprise system. The IS managers can make decisions from such systems more easily regarding which Web service is to be integrated with their applications. A DSS could make a comparative analysis of various security properties between a candidate Web service and the enclosing enterprise system including the consequences of different decision alternatives in selecting Web services. It could also project the likely additional security properties needed for the system if the candidate Web service lacked required properties. The complex nature of selecting secure Web services could not be easily managed without such a DSS support. With the rapidly evolving nature of security contexts in the field of enterprise systems, decision support systems for selecting secure Web services can play an increasingly important role.

This article proposes an architecture of an easy-to-use security decision support system (SDSS) for selecting Web services with security assurances consistent with the enterprise business goal. The SDSS stores security profiles of candidate Web services, compares properties with the security requirements of the enterprise system, and generates alternatives with consequences. Supporting the choice making process involves the evaluation and comparison of alternative Web services in terms of their security properties. To minimize the risks of selecting the wrong Web services for the enterprise systems, the SDSS can provide managers with consistent and concise guidance for the development of security criteria. Our proposed SDSS has been developed to provide IS managers with information necessary to make informed decisions regarding the selection of Web services. The basic components of the SDSS include a knowledge base of various security properties and an *inference mechanism* which uses a set of rules. The architecture consists of three components: (i) *Defining security criteria*; (ii) *Security profiling of Web services*; and (iii) *Generating alternatives*.

BACKGROUND

Making decisions concerning the selection of Web services with security compliances often strains the cognitive capabilities of the IS managers because many complex attributes are involved. Analyzing these complex attributes and predicting the security outcome of independent Web services is a daunting task. The human intuitive judgment and decision making capability is rather limited, and this ability deteriorates further with the complexity of assessing security issues manually. The final decision to select a particular Web service for an enterprise system is critical because such a decision is considerably influenced by many complex security attributes of the service. A computer-aided decision making process may manage this complexity in a more optimal way. One of many decision-making approaches in which decisions are made with the help of computer-aided process is generally called decision support system (DSS). A DSS can take many different forms. In general, a DSS is a computerized system for helping people make decisions (Alter, 1980; Power, 1997, 2007). According to Finlay (1994) and Turban (1995), a DSS is an interactive, flexible, and adaptable computer-based information system, especially developed for supporting the decision making. In our context in this article, we emphasize a knowledge-driven decision that helps managers to make a choice between alternative Web services based on their supporting security properties. It is an interactive computer-based system that aids IS managers in making judgments and choices regarding the selection of Web services which match their expectation. This article focuses primarily on the components that process various criteria against the provided data and generates best alternatives.

During the process of selecting appropriate Web services for the enterprises, IS managers often make decisions on which Web services should be integrated with their application. Considering the value of the information assets of the organizations, it is unlikely that managers only assess the business functionalities that Web services provide for their organizational need. They should also consider the security implications of using Web services with their applications. The decision making process of selecting security-aware Web services requires a systematic approach. A decision support system could aid managers with an automated system. In the current practice, IS managers use Web services without properly assessing the security compliances of the services (Khan, 2006, 2007). Managers could use decision support systems which could significantly improve the selection process of secure Web services.

Many decision making techniques already published in the literature can be used for the selection of an entity among various alternatives. Classical multi-attribute utility theory (MAUT) by Keeney and Raiffa (1976), analytical hierarchy process (AHP) by Saaty (1980), and a recent approach by Besharati, Azram, and Kannan (2005) for the selection of product design are among these approaches. MAUT has been used in many application domains for modeling decision maker's preferences for ranking a set of alternative decisions. AHP has been extensively used in marketing and management areas. However, using any of these models in security issues has not been reported yet. An agent-based DSS methodology reported in Choi, Kim, Park, and Whinston (2004) and a market-based allocation methodology (Parameswaran, Stallaert, & Whinston, 2001) are not also applicable in the security arena. Although these two DSS methodologies are used in product selection, their applicability in the selection of secure software product is limited.

Most research works in the area of Web services security often focus on how to make Web services secure. Some papers propose various security metrics models as reported in Berinato (2005) and Payne (2002). Khan (2006) proposes a scheme for assessing security properties of software components. The assessment scheme provides a numeric score to the candidate software component indicating a relative strength of the security properties of the component. Payne (2002) proposes a seven step methodology to guide the process of defining security metrics. Berinato (2005) argues for a constant measure of security incidents and it could be used to quantify the efficiency of the deployed security functions. The National Institute of Standards and Technology (Swanson, Bartol, Sabato, Hash, & Graffo, 2003) defines a security metrics guide for information technology systems. The document provides guidance on how an enterprise through the use of metrics identifies the security needs, security controls, policies, and procedures.

SECURITY DECISION SUPPORT SYSTEM (SDSS)

The environment of the proposed SDSS system consists of a preprocess and the architecture as illustrated in Figure 1. The preprocess has two related activities: (i) specification of the security requirements or security objectives of the identified functionality, and (ii) gathering security properties of the candidate Web services. These

A Decision Support System for Selecting Secure Web Services

two preprocess activities are required in the process of constructing the alternatives. Managers identify what security requirements their enterprise system needs from the Web services. This essentially sets the security requirements consistent with the enterprise-wide security requirements and assurances. For example, a financial enterprise system needs a service for *calculating tax offset*. Many third-party Web services may offer this functionality with various security functions such as confidentiality of data, integrity of the calculated data, and so forth. The managers must determine what type of security the identified functionality will have. Security requirements related to the functionality may be determined based on the threats, vulnerabilities, and risks associated with the functionality.

The selection of a list of candidate Web services is based on the identified functionality. At this stage the conformity of the defined security requirements is not checked. We select only those Web services which can provide the desired functionality such as calculating tax offset. This also involves gathering information regarding the security properties of the candidate Web services. We call it *security profiling*. In this activity, security properties of each candidate Web service are collected from the published security claim, available user's guide, and from enquiries (Khan, 2006). This profiling process enlists all security properties supporting the claimed security function of each Web service.

THE ARCHITECTURE

A DSS can consist of various types of components based on the domain of application and the type of system. Three fundamental components of DSS are identified by Sprague and Carlson (1982): the database management system, the model-based management system, and the user interface. Haag, Cummings, McCubbrey, Pinsonneault, and Donovan (2000) decompose these three components into more detail. Consistent with these, Figure 2 depicts three major components of the proposed SDSS. The identified security requirements and the security properties supported by each candidate Web service are the main input to the system. These data are structured and mapped into the same format by the system. The security profiles are stored in the knowledge base. The output of the system is a rating of the candidate Web services.

DEFINING SECURITY CRITERIA

This component of SDSS defines the criteria for the security requirements in a structured form based on the information provided by the IS managers. The elements of security criteria are defined according to the ISO/IEC Standard 15408, the Common Criteria (CC) for Information Technology Security Evaluation (Common Criteria, 1999). The CC provides evaluation measures of security by means of a common set of requirements of the security functions of a system, and a set of evaluation measures. The entire approach is quantitative and it describes the security behavior of functions expected of an information system. CC gives a comprehensive catalogue of high level security requirements and assurances for information systems products. CC consists of 11 classes for generic grouping of similar types of security requirements: security audit, communication, cryptographic support, user data protection, identification and authentication, security management, privacy, protection of system security functions, resource utilization, system access, and trusted path and channels.

The criteria are formulated in a tree structure. The idea is to decompose a complex decision making component into simpler subcomponents that are easily quantifiable and comparable in terms of values. In other words, security requirements are modeled into smaller subcomponents using a tree structure. The root of the tree (level 0) is the name of the functionality. Each node at level-1 represents a CC security class such as user data protection, authentication, security audit, and so forth. Level-2 and lower level nodes represent the decomposed security attributes of the requirements. The value associated with the each level-1 node signifies

Figure 1. The environment of security decision support system (SDSS)

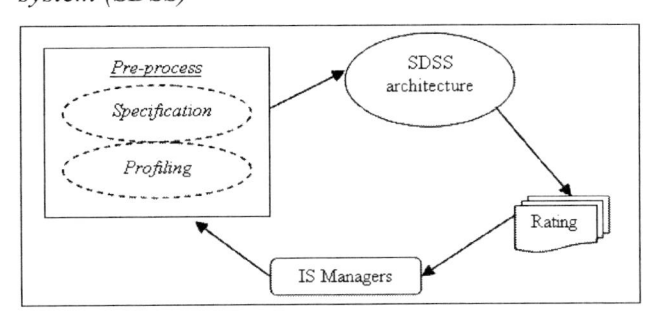

213

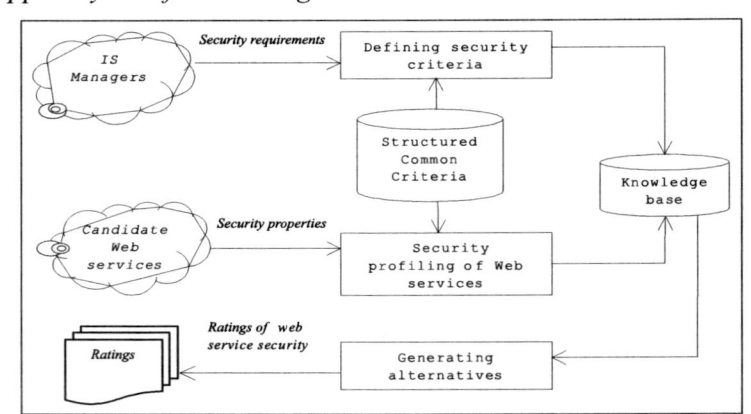

Figure 2. A decision support system for selecting secure Web services

Figure 3. An example of security criteria

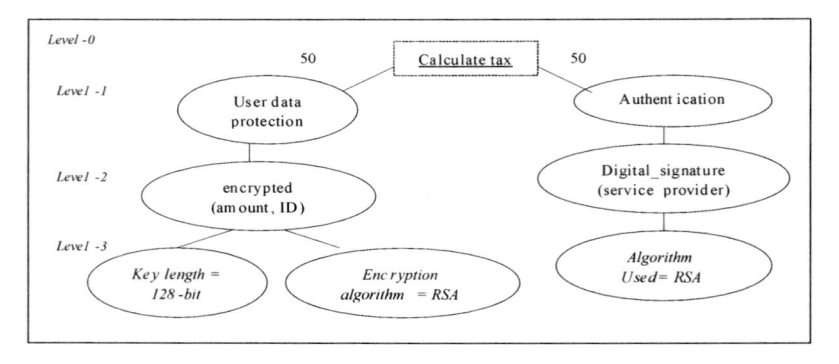

the relative importance of the node compared to other nodes at the same level. All values irrespective of the total number of nodes at level-1 must be summed up to 100. Figure 3 illustrates an example.

The example in Figure 3 illustrates the security requirements of the functionality *calculate tax*. The functionality has two security requirements: *user data protection* and *authentication*, as shown in level-2 nodes. Each of the two requirements has equal importance as shown with the value 50. The *user data protection* has one security property as shown at level-2 node: *encrypted(amount, ID)*. This property is further decomposed into two attributes: the *key length* should be 128-bit and *encryption algorithm* should be RSA. The requirement *authentication* has a security attribute: *digital_signature(service_provider)*. This property has one attribute: *algorithm used* which should be RSA. This information will be stored in the knowledge base.

In this example, several key issues are addressed in order to check the conformity of user data protection and authentication. For instance, if the user data protection is achieved by means of *encrypted data*, then next issues include what is the *length of the key* and which *algorithm* is used in the encryption. These are the specific criteria to check whether a Web service could provide the required functionality with the desired level of confidentiality of tax data.

STORING SECURITY PROFILE

The security information about each Web service gathered in the preprocess are entered into the system. The format of data is the same as shown in Figure 3. SDSS provides a template in order to capture the security requirements of the candidate services. Let us consider a scenario. Assume we have selected three candidate Web services called A, B, and C. All these services provide the same functionality, calculate tax, but with varying security properties. Web service A supports user data protection with encryption using a key length of 256-bit, but does not provide authentication. Service B provides authentication with digital signature using RSA algorithm, but does not support user data protection. All of the data are entered into the system.

Logic programming (Baral & Gelfond, 1993) can be used as a formal reasoning tool to characterize the security requirements and security profiles of the candidate Web services. The simple structure of the logic program allows us to represent a complicated form of security knowledge and its properties, and yet it is based on mathematical logic (Das, 1992). In logic programming, security properties can be expressed in symbolic notations such as *encrypted, digital_signature*. Some of the properties are identical with those defined in BAN logic (Burrows, Abadi, & Needham, 1989).

GENERATING ALTERNATIVES

This is the heart of the SDSS. This component produces a comparative rating of all candidate Web services based on the conformity of their security profiles with the enterprise-wide security criteria. Inference rules are used to calculate the deviation between the security criteria and the profiles. This component uses a rule-based approach in order to make a comparative rating of the candidate services. Security properties are reasoned about with the inference rules of logic programming. The inference rules are applied to check whether the security profile of a Web service is matched with the security requirements of the enterprise system. The rating of a candidate service is based on a value ranging from 0 to 100. The points are calculated on the basis of the presence or absence of certain security properties in the Web services. For example, if a node with a value 40 at level-1 has full compliance with the security criteria, the point will be 40 out of 100.

IS managers can evaluate the rating of the candidate services and make a decision regarding which Web service will be selected. They can also modify or adjust the security requirements differently and get a different rating of the same set of Web services. However, it is also possible to add newly identified security properties with the profile of a candidate Web service and process the properties for a new rating.

FUTURE TRENDS

We plan to implement the proposed approach as a prototype in order to test its applicability. We are currently evaluating some existing tools such as *smodels* and *lparse* (Syrjanen, 2000) which could be utilized as the supporting components of the SDSS in order to facilitate the inference mechanisms. The approach can be further expanded to select Web services with other nonfunctional properties such as usability, maintainability, reusability, and so forth. Further research includes the automatic verification of the security profile of Web services with their implementation. The more challenging research could be directed to automate the significant activities of the preprocess, such as automatic gathering of security profiles about the Web services.

CONCLUSION

The article has presented a framework for a security decision support system for selecting Web services with appropriate security assurances. The article argues that the selection process of appropriate Web services for the enterprise application needs an automatic tool support such as SDSS. The approach could be automated to aid enterprise decision support systems. This can be used in strategic planning of information systems as well. The main contribution of this article is a framework for the assessment of Web services security properties on which further work could be initiated. The evaluation method presented here is considered flexible enough, as security requirements can be altered by the IS managers as they see appropriate for their needs.

REFERENCES

Alter, S. L. (1980). *Decision support systems: Current practice and continuing challenges*. Reading, MA: Addison-Wesley Pub.

Baral, C., & Gelfond, M. (1993). Representing concurrent actions in extended logic programming. In *Proceedings of the 13th International Joint Conference on Artificial Intelligence,* Chambery, France (pp. 866-871).

Berinato, S. (2005, July). A few good metrics. *CIO-Asia Magazine*. Online version http://www.csoonline.com/read/070105/metrics.html

Besharati, B., Azram, S., & Kannan, P. K. (2005). A decision support system for product design selection: A generalized purchase modeling approach. *Decision Support Systems, 42*, 333-350.

Burrows, M., Abadi, M., & Needham, R. (1989, December). A logic of authentication. *ACM Operating Systems Review, 23*(5), 1-13. A fuller version was published as DEC System Research Centre Report Number 39, Palo Alto, California, February.

Choi, H.R., Kim, H. S., Park, Y.J., & Whinston, A.B. (2004, March). An agent for selecting optimal order set in EC marketplace. *Decision Support Systems, 36*(4), 371-383.

Common Criteria. (1999). Common criteria for information technology security evaluation (ISO/IEC 15408). NIST. Retrieved December 6, 2007, from http://csrc.nist.gov/cc/

Das, S. K. (1992). Deductive databases and logic programming. Addison-Wesley.

Finlay, P. N. (1994). *Introducing decision support systems*. Oxford, UK, Cambridge, MA: NCC Blackwell; Blackwell Publishers.

Haag, S., Cummings, M., McCubbrey, D., Pinsonneault, A., & Donovan, R. (2000). *Management information systems: For the information age*, (pp. 136-140). McGraw-Hill Ryerson Limited.

Keeney, R.L., & Raiffa, H. (1976). *Decisions with multiple objectives*. New York: John Wiley and Sons.

Khan, K. (2007). Selecting Web services with security compliances: A managerial perspective. To appear in *Proceedings of the Pacific Asia Conference on Information Systems (PACIS)*.

Khan, K., & Han, J. (2006, April). Assessing security properties of software components: A software engineer's perspective. In *Proceedings of the Australian Software Engineering Conference*, IEEE Computer Society.

Parameswaran, M., Stallaert, J., & Whinston, A. B. (2001, August). A market-based allocation mechanism for the DiffServ framework. *Decision Support Systems, 31*(3), 351-356.

Payne, S. (2002). *A guide to security metrics*. SANS Institute.

Power, D. J. (1997). What is a DSS? *The Online Executive Jo971021.htmlurnal for Data-Intensive Decision Support, 1*(3). Online version http://www.taborcommunications.com/dsstar/97/1021/

Power, D. J. (2004, February). Specifying an expanded framework for classifying and describing decision support systems. *Communications of the Association for Information Systems, 13*(13), 158-166.

Power, D. J. (2007). *A brief history of decision support systems*. DSSResources.COM. Retrieved December 6, 2007, from http://DSSResources.COM/history/dsshistory.html

Saaty, T. L. (1980). *The analytical hierarchy process*. New York: McGraw-Hill.

Sprague, R. H., & Carlson, E. D. (1982). *Building effective decision support systems*. Englewood Cliffs, NJ: Prentice-Hall.

Swanson, M., Bartol, N., Sabato, J., Hash, J., & Graffo, L. (2003, July). Security metrics guide for information technology systems [Special Publication 800-55]. *National Institute of Standard and Technology (NIST)*, (p. 99).

Syrjanen, T. (2000). *Lparse 1.0 user's manual*. University of Helsinki.

Turban, E. (1995). *Decision support and expert systems: Management support systems*. Englewood Cliffs, NJ: Prentice Hall.

KEY TERMS

Security Class: A security class represents a generic grouping of similar types of security objectives that share a common focus while differing in coverage of security functions as well as security properties.

Security Criteria: A security criteria is a rule with a set of security properties that can be used to assess a security function or security objective. A security criteria tests whether a security function has desired security properties.

Security Function: A security function is the implementation of a security policy as well as a security objective. It enforces the security policy and provides required capabilities. Security functions are defined to withstand certain security threats, vulnerabilities, and risks. A security function usually consists of one or more principals, resources, security properties, and security operations.

Security Objective: A security objective is an abstract representation of a security goal. A security objective defines a desired security state of an entity or data of the system. It represents the main goal of a security policy.

Security Profiling: Security profiling is the security characterization of an entity, a service, or a component in terms of security objectives as well as security properties. It spells out the actual implemented security characteristics of an entity.

Security Property: A security property is an implementation element used in a security function. A set of security properties can form a security function. A security property is an element at the lowest level of the implementation.

Web Services: A Web service is a platform-independent and self-contained software with defined functionality that can be available over the Internet. It provides a standard way of integrating mechanisms with enterprise applications over the net. A Web service can perform one or more functionalities for the complex application system.

Decision Support Systems and Decision-Making Processes

Udo Richard Averweg
eThekwini Municipality and University of KwaZulu-Natal, South Africa

INTRODUCTION

Decision support systems (DSS) deal with semi-structured problems. Such problems arise when managers in organisations are faced with decisions where some but not all aspects of a task or procedure are known. To solve these problems and use the results for decision-making requires judgement of the manager using the system. Typically such systems include models, data manipulation tools, and the ability to handle uncertainty and risk. These systems involve information and decision technology (Forgionne, 2003). Many organisations are turning to DSS to improve decision-making (Turban, McLean, & Wetherbe, 2004). This is a result of the conventional information systems (IS) not being sufficient to support an organisation's critical response activities—especially those requiring fast and/or complex decision-making. In general, DSS are a broad category of IS (Power, 2003).

A DSS is defined as "an interactive, flexible, and adaptable computer-based information system, specially developed for supporting the solution of a non-structured management problem for improved decision-making. It utilises data, it provides easy user interface, and it allows for the decision maker's own insights" (Turban, 1995). There is a growing trend to provide managers with IS that can assist them in their most important task—making decisions. All levels of management can benefit from the use of DSS capabilities. The highest level of support is usually for middle and upper management (Sprague & Watson, 1996). The question of how a DSS supports decision-making processes will be described in this article. This article is organised as follows: The background to decision-making is introduced. The main focus (of this article) describes the development of the DSS field. Some future trends for the DSS field are then suggested. Thereafter a conclusion is given.

BACKGROUND TO DECISION-MAKING

H. A. Simon is considered a pioneer in the development of human decision-making models (Ahituv & Neumann, 1990). His individual work (Simon, 1960) and his joint research with A. Newell (Newell & Simon, 1972) established the foundation for human decision-making models. His basic model depicts human decision-making as a three-stage process. These stages are:

- **Intelligence:** The identification of a problem (or opportunity) that requires a decision and the collection of information relevant to the decision
- **Design:** Creating, developing, and analysing alternative courses of action
- **Choice:** Selecting a course of action from those available.

The decision-making process is generally considered to consist of a set of phases or steps which are carried out in the course of making a decision (Sprague & Watson, 1996). Decision-making can be categorised as:

- Independent
- Sequential interdependent
- Pooled interdependent (Keen & Scott Morton, 1978).

Independent decision-making involves one decision-maker using a DSS to reach a decision without the need or assistance from other managers. This form of DSS use is found occasionally. Sprague & Watson (1996) contend that it is the exception because of the common need for collaboration with other managers. Sequential interdependent decisions involve decision-making at a decision point and are followed by a subsequent decision at another point. In this case the

Decision Support Systems and Decision-Making Processes

decision at one point serves as input to the decision at another point. A practical example is corporate planning and budgeting where a department formulates a plan which then serves as input to the development of the budget. Sprague & Watson (1996) indicate that DSS are frequently used in support of sequential dependent decision-making but not as frequently as pooled interdependent decision-making.

Pooled interdependent decision-making is a joint, collaborative decision-making process whereby all managers work together on the task. A group of product marketing managers getting together to develop a marketing plan is an example of this type of decision. Specialised hardware, software, and processes have been developed to support pooled interdependent decision-making but for the purposes of this study, these are not explored.

PROBLEMS AND DECISION-MAKING PROCESSES

Ackoff (1981) cites three kinds of things that can be done about problems—they can be *resolved, solved,* or *dissolved*:

- **Resolving:** This is to select a course of action that yields an outcome that is good enough that satisfices (satisfies and suffices).
- **Solving:** This is to select a course of action that is believed to yield the best possible outcome that optimises. It aspires to complete objectivity and this approach is used mostly by technologically oriented managers whose organisational objective tends to be thrival than mere survival.
- **Dissolving:** This to change the nature and/or the environment of the entity in which it is embedded so as to remove the problem.

Sauter (1997) indicates that a DSS will not solve all the problems of any given organisation. The author adds, "however, it does *solve* some problems" (italics added by author).

In a structured problem, the procedures for obtaining the best (or worst) solution are known. Whether the problem involves finding an optimal inventory level or deciding on the appropriate marketing campaign, the objectives are clearly defined. Common business objectives are profit maximisation or cost minimisation. Whilst a manager can use the support

Figure 1. Decision support framework (Source: adapted from Turban, McLean, & Wetherbe, 1999)

Type of Decision	Type of Control			Support Needed
	Operational Control	Managerial Control	Strategic Planning	
Structured	① Accounts receivable, order entry	② Budget analysis, short-term forecasting, personnel reports, make-or-buy analysis	③ Financial management (investment), warehouse location, distribution systems	Management information system, operations research models, transaction processing
Semi-structured	④ Production scheduling, inventory control	⑤ Credit evaluation, budget preparation, plant layout, project scheduling, reward systems design	⑥ Building of new plant, mergers and acquisitions, new product planning, quality assurance planning	DSS
Unstructured	⑦ Selecting a cover for a magazine, buying software, approving loans	⑧ Negotiating, recruiting an executive, buying hardware	⑨ R&D planning, new technology development, social responsibility planning	DSS, ES, neural networks
Support needed	Management information system, management science	Management science, DSS, ES, EIS	EIS, ES, neural networks	

of clerical, data processing, or management science models, management support systems such as DSS and expert system (ES) can be useful at times. One DSS vendor suggests that facts now supplement intuition as analysts, managers, and executives use Oracle DSS® to make more informed and efficient decisions (Oracle Corporation, 1997).

In an unstructured problem, human intuition is often the basis for decision-making. Typical unstructured problems include the planning of a new service to be offered or choosing a set of research and development projects for the next year. The semi-structured problems fall between the structured and the unstructured which involves a combination of both standard solution procedures and individual judgment. Keen & Scott Morton (1978) give the following examples of semi-structured problems: (USA) trading bonds, setting marketing budgets for consumer products and performing capital acquisition analysis. Here a DSS can improve the quality of the information on which the decision is based (and consequently the quality of the decision) by providing not only a single solution but a range of alternatives. These capabilities allow managers to better understand the nature of the problems so that they can make better decisions.

Before defining the specific management support technology of DSS, it will be useful to present a classical framework for decision support. This framework will assist in discussing the relationship among the technologies and the evolution of computerised systems. The framework, see Figure 1, was proposed by Gorry & Scott Morton (1971) who combined the work of Simon (1960) and Anthony (1965).

The details of this framework are: The left-hand side of the table is based on Simon's notion that decision-making processes fall along a continuum that ranges from highly structured (sometimes referred to as programmed) to highly unstructured (non programmed) decisions. Structured processes refer to routine and repetitive problems for which standard solutions already exist. Unstructured processes are "fuzzy" for which no cut-and-dried solutions exist. Decisions where some (but not all) of the phases are structured are referred to as semi-structured, by Gorry and Scott Morton (1971).

The second half of this framework (upper half of Figure 1) is based on Anthony's (1965) taxonomy which defines three broad categories that encompass all managerial activities:

- **Strategic planning:** The long-range goals and the policies for resource allocation.
- **Management control:** The acquisition and efficient utilisation of resources in the accomplishment of organisational goals.
- **Operational control:** The efficient and effective execution of specific tasks.

Anthony and Simon's taxonomies are combined in a nine-cell decision support framework in Figure 1. The right-hand column and the bottom row indicate the technologies needed to support the various decisions. For example, Gorry and Scott Morton (1971) suggest that for semi-structured and unstructured decisions, conventional management science approaches are insufficient. They proposed the use of a supportive information system, which they labelled a decision support system (DSS). ES, which were only introduced several years later, are most suitable for tasks requiring expertise.

The more structured and operational control-oriented tasks (cells 1, 2, and 4) are performed by low-level managers. The tasks in cells 6, 8, and 9 are the responsibility of top executives. This means that DSS, executive information systems (EIS), neural computing, and ES are more often applicable for top executives and professionals tackling specialised, complex problems.

The true test of a DSS is its ability to support the design phase of decision-making as the real core of any DSS is the model base which has been built to analyse a problem or decision. In the design phase, the decision-maker develops a specific and precise model that can be used to systematically examine the discovered problem or opportunity (Forgionne, 2003). The primary value to a decision-maker of a DSS is the ability of the decision-maker and the DSS to explore the models interactively as a means of identifying and evaluating alternative courses of action. This is of tremendous value to the decision-maker and represents the DSS's capability to support the design phase (Sprague & Watson, 1996). For the DSS choice phase, the most prevalent support is through "what if" analysis and goal seeking.

In terms of support from DSS, the choice phase of decision-making is the most variable. Traditionally, as DSS were not designed to make a decision but rather to show the impact of a defined scenario, choice has been supported only occasionally by a DSS. A practical example is where a DSS uses models which identify a best choice (e.g., linear programming) but generally they are not the rule.

DEVELOPMENT OF THE DSS FIELD

According to Sprague and Watson (1996), DSS evolved as a "field" of study and practice during the 1980s. This section discusses the principles of a theory for SS. During the early development of DSS, several principles evolved. Eventually, these principles became a widely accepted "structural theory" or framework—see Sprague and Carlson (1982). The four most important of these principles are now summarised.

The DDM Paradigm

The technology for DSS must consist of three sets of capabilities in the areas of dialog, data, and modeling and what Sprague and Carlson call the DDM paradigm. The researchers make the point that a good DSS should have balance among the three capabilities. It should be easy to use to allow non-technical decision-makers to interact fully with the system. It should have access to a wide variety of data and it should provide analysis and modeling in a variety of ways. Sprague and Watson (1996) contend that many early systems adopted the name DSS when they were strong in only one area and weak in the other. Figure 2 shows the relationship between these components in more detail and it should be noted that the models in the model base are linked with the data in the database. Models can draw coefficients, parameters, and variables from the database and enter results of the model's computation in the database. These results can then be used by other models later in the decision-making process.

Figure 2 also shows the three components of the dialog function wherein the database management system (DBMS) and the model base management system (MBMS) contain the necessary functions to manage the database and model base respectively. The dialog generation and management system (DGMS) manages the interface between the user and the rest of the system.

Even though the DDM paradigm eventually evolved into the dominant architecture for DSS, for the purposes of this article, none of the technical aspects is explored any further.

Levels of Technology

Three levels of technology are useful in developing DSS and this concept illustrates the usefulness of configuring DSS tools into a DSS generator which can be used to develop a variety of specific DSS quickly and easily to aid decision-makers; see Figure 3. The system which actually accomplishes the work is known as the specific DSS, shown as the circles at the top of the diagram. It is the software/hardware that allows a specific decision-maker to deal with a set of related problems. The second level of technology is known as the DSS generator. This

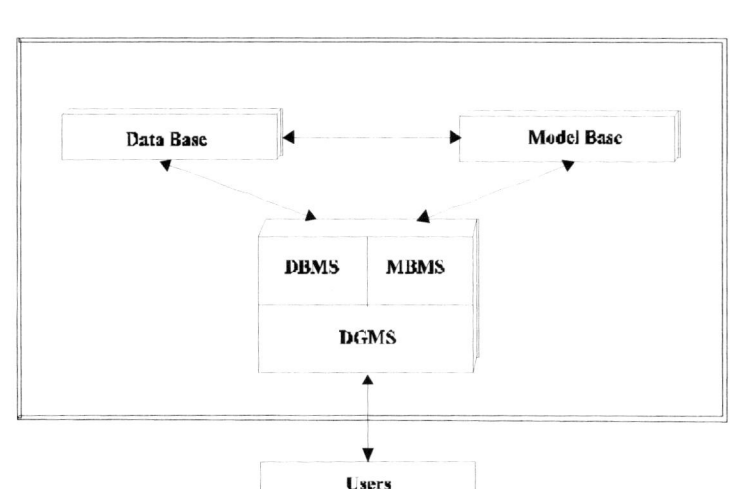

Figure 2. Components of DSS (Source: adapted from Sprague & Watson, 1996)

is a package of related hardware and software which provides a set of capabilities to quickly and easily build a specific DSS. The third level of technology is DSS tools which facilitate the development of either a DSS generator or a specific DSS.

DSS tools can be used to develop a specific DSS application strictly as indicated on the left-hand side of the diagram. This is the same approach used to develop most traditional applications with tools such as general purpose languages, subroutine packages, and data access software. The difficulty of the approach for developing DSS is the constant change and flexibility which characterises them. The development and use of DSS generators create a "platform" or staging area from which specific DSS can be constantly developed and modified with the co-operation of the user and with minimal time and effort.

Iterative Design

The nature of DSS requires a different design and development technique from traditional batch and online systems. Instead of the traditional development process, DSS require a form of iterative development which allows them to evolve and change as the problem or decision situation changes. They need to be built with short, rapid feedback from users thereby ensuring that development is proceeding correctly. In essence, they must be developed to permit change quickly and easily.

Organisational Environment

The effective development of DSS requires an organisational strategy to build an environment within which such systems can originate and evolve. The environment includes a group of people with interacting roles, a set of software and hardware technology, a set of data sources, and a set of analysis models.

DSS: PAST AND PRESENT

Van Schaik (1988) refers to the early 1970s as the era of the DSS concept because in this period the concept of DSS was introduced. DSS was a new philosophy of how computers could be used to support managerial decision-making. This philosophy embodied unique and exciting ideas for the design and implementation of such systems. There has been confusion and controversy over the interpretation of the notion decision support system and the origin of this notion is clear:

- Decision emphasises the primary focus on decision-making in a problem situation rather than the subordinate activities of simple information retrieval, processing, or reporting.

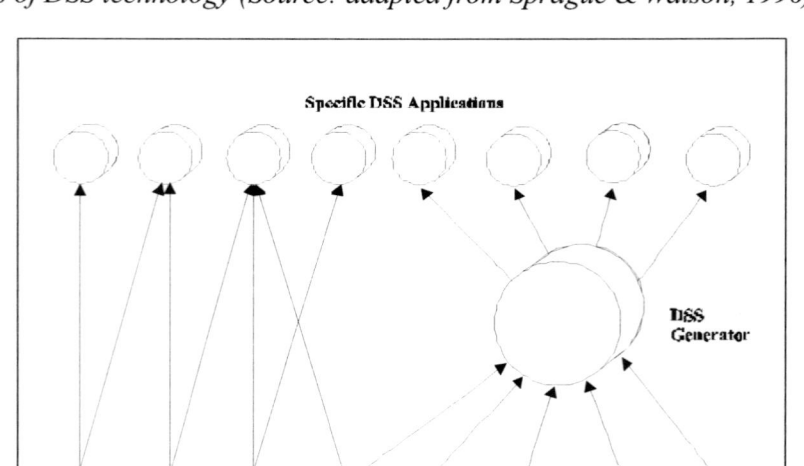

Figure 3. Three levels of DSS technology (Source: adapted from Sprague & Watson, 1996)

- Support clarifies the computer's role in aiding rather than replacing the decision-maker.
- System highlights the integrated nature of the overall approach, suggesting the wider context of machine, user and decision environment.

Sprague and Watson (1996) note that initially there were different conceptualisations about DSS. Some organisations and scholars began to develop and research DSS which became characterised as interactive computer based systems which help decision-makers utilise data and models to solve unstructured problems. According to Sprague and Watson (1974), the unique contribution of DSS resulted from these key words. They contend that the definition proved restrictive enough that few actual systems completely satisfied it. They believe that some authors have recently extended the definition of DSS to include any system that makes some contribution to decision-making; in this way the term can be applied to all but transaction processing. However, a serious definitional problem arises in that the words have certain "intuitive validity;" any system that supports a decision (in any way) is a "Decision Support System." As Sprague and Watson (1996) indicate, the term had such an instant intuitive appeal that it quickly became a "buzz word." Clearly, neither the restrictive nor the broad definition help much as they do not provide guidance for understanding the value, the technical requirements, or the approach for developing a DSS.

A further complicating factor is that people from different backgrounds and contexts view a DSS quite differently: a computer scientist and a manager seldom see things in the same way. Turban (1995) supports this stance as DSS is a content-free expression whereby it means different things to different people. He states that there is no universally accepted definition of DSS and that it is even sometimes used to describe any computerised system. It appears that the basis for defining DSS has been developed from the perceptions of what a DSS does (e.g., support decision-making in unstructured problems) and from ideas about how the DSS's objectives can be accomplished (e.g., the components required and the necessary development processes).

FUTURE TRENDS

New technology continues to affect the dialog, data, and models components. Differences in data, knowledge, and model structures may necessitate the development of new technologies for model retrieval tasks (Forgionne, 2003). Relational database technology and object-oriented databases and data warehousing are influencing how data is stored, updated, and retrieved. Drawing from artificial intelligence advances, there is the potential for representing and using models in new and different ways.

Decision support technology has also broadened to include monitoring, tracking, and communication tools to support the overall process of ill-structured problem solving. DSS implemented on a corporate intranet provides a means to deploy decision support applications in organisations with geographically distributed sites. Clearly these technologies and other emerging Web-based technologies will continue to expand the component parts of a DSS domain. An area of rapid growth is Web-based DSS. Even though Web-based technologies are the leading edge for building DSS, traditional programming languages or fourth generation languages are still used to build DSS (Power, 2003).

CONCLUSION

Moving from the early DSS concept era to almost 35 years later, DSS still comprise a class of IS intended to support the decision-making activities of managers in organisations. The concept has been buffeted by the hyperbole of marketing people and technologies have improved or changed (Power, 2003). While some major conceptual problems may be found with the current terms associated with computerised decision support (and which has been catalysed by marketing hype), the basic underlying concept of supporting decision-makers in their decision-making processes still remains important.

REFERENCES

Ackoff, R. L. (1981). The art and science of mess management. *Interfaces*, *11*(1), 20-26.

Ahituv, N., & Neumann, S. (1990). *Principles of information systems for management*. Dubuque: William C. Brown Publishers.

Anthony, R. N. (1965). *Planning and control systems: A framework for analysis*. Cambridge, MA: Harvard University Graduate School of Business.

Forgionne, G. (2003). An architecture for the integration of decision making support functionalities. In M. Mora, G. Forgionne, & J. N. D. Gupta (Eds.), *Decision making support systems* (pp. 1-19). Hershey, PA: Idea Group Publishing.

Gorry, G. M., & Scott Morton, M. S. (1971). A framework for management information systems. *Sloan Management Review*.

Keen, P. G. W., & Scott Morton, M. S. (1978). *Decision support systems: An organizational perspective*. Reading, MA: Addison-Wesley.

Newell, A., & Simon, H. A. (1972). *Human problem solving*. Englewood Cliffs, NJ: Prentice-Hall.

Oracle Corporation. (1997). *The oracle information catalogue*. Information Age Catalogue (part number Z23007-01).

Power, D. J. (2003). Categorizing decision support systems: A multidimensional approach. In M. Mora, G. Forgionne, & J. N. D. Gupta (Eds.), *Decision making support systems* (pp. 20-27). Hershey, PA: Idea Group Publishing.

Sauter, V. L. (1997). *Decision support systems: An applied managerial approach*. New York: John Wiley & Sons.

Simon, H. A. (1960). *The new science of management sciences*. New York: Harper and Row.

Sprague, R. H., & Carlson, E. D. (1982). *Building effective decision support systems*. Englewood Cliffs, NJ: Prentice-Hall.

Sprague, R. H., & Watson, H. J. (1974). Bit by bit: Toward decision support systems. *California Management Review, 22*(1), 60-67.

Sprague, R. H., & Watson, H. J. (1996). *Decision support for management*. Englewood Cliffs, NJ: Prentice-Hall.

Turban, E. (1995). *Decision support and expert systems*. Englewood Cliffs, NJ: Prentice-Hall.

Turban, E., McLean, E., & Wetherbe, J. (1999). *Information technology for management*. Chichester, NY: John Wiley & Sons.

Turban, E., McLean, E., & Wetherbe, J. (2004). *Information technology for management. Transforming organizations in the digital economy*. Hoboken, NJ: John Wiley & Sons.

Van Schaik, F. D. J. (1988). *Effectiveness of decision support systems*. PhD dissertation, Technische Universiteit, Delft, Holland.

KEY TERMS

Decision-Making: A three-stage process involving intelligence, design, and choice.

Decision Support System: An interactive, flexible, and adaptable computer-based information system, specially developed for supporting the solution of a non-structured management problem for improved decision-making.

Expert System: An IS which provides the stored knowledge of experts to non experts.

Management Science: An approach that takes the view the managers can follow a fairly systematic process for solving problems.

Pooled Interdependent Decision-Making: A joint, collaborative decision-making process whereby all managers work together on a task.

Semi-Structured Problem: Only some of the intelligence, design, and choice phases are structured and requiring a combination of standard solution procedures and individual judgement.

Structured Problem: The intelligence, design, and choice phases are all structured and the procedures for obtaining the best solution are known.

Unstructured Problem: None of the intelligence, design, and choice phases is structured and human intuition is frequently the basis for decision-making.

Decision Support Systems and Representation Levels in the Decision Spine

Patrick Humphreys
London School of Economics and Political Science, UK

INTRODUCTION: DECISION-MAKING AS PROBLEM SOLVING

Problem solving has been defined as the complex interplay of cognitive, affective, and behavioural processes with the aim to adapt to external or internal demands or challenges (Heppner & Krauskopf, 1987). In the realm of organizational decision-making, Herbert Simon (1977) describes the problem-solving process as moving through three stages: intelligence, design, and choice. In this context, design focuses on "inventing, developing and analysing possible courses of action," where the design artefact being constructed for this purpose constitutes the "representation of the problem."

While a wide range of representation means and calculi have been proposed for decision problem solving purposes, practical implementations generally involve applying one or more of these means to develop the structure of the problem within one or more frames. Typically, these are future-scenario frames, multi-attributed preference frames, and rule base-frames (Chatjoulis & Humphreys, 2007). Simon (1977) characterized decision problems according to the degree of problem-structure that was pre-established (or taken for granted as "received wisdom," or "the truth about the situation that calls for a decision") at the time participants embark on the decision problem solving process. He placed such problems on a continuum ranging from routine (programmed, structured) problems with well-specified solutions to novel, complex (unprogrammed, unstructured) with ambiguous solutions.

System thinking and soft systems methodologies (Checkland, 1999) have provided ways of looking at problem solving as an integrated whole throughout this continuum by modelling the process within a problem definition cycle, moving from the awareness that a problem exists to the moment of choice. Central to these models is the specification of a sequence of stages that the decision-making group has to follow in order to reduce uncertainty and increase structure, in transforming an ill-defined problem into a well defined one (Humphreys, 1989; Phillips, 1992). A great number of decision support systems (DSS) have been produced with the goal of providing mechanisms to help decision makers get through such sequences in processing uncertain and ambiguous decisions (Silver, 1991). The majority of these DSS are intended to support decision makers by increasing the structure of decision problem representations situated in already semi structured decision situations (Keen, 1980). However, as Meredith (2006, p. 31) points out:

At the extremely unstructured end of the continuum sits a class of decision problems for which a pre-existing solution either does not exist or is inadequate. Such problems require creative decision-making. DSS designed to support decision makers with such a task face a dilemma: too much structure may stifle the creative process, while too little structure provides inadequate support.

In such situations, participants embarking on the decision-making process can start out at the level of feeling, without being constrained (either explicitly or implicitly) by "received wisdom" about how the decision problem is already structured. Initially, participants have complete freedom and autonomy about how to think about translating this desire into action: all imaginable courses of action are candidates for implementation (Meredith, 2006). Conventional decision support methodologies, operating within the problem solving paradigm, intend to support a group process that aims at progressively strengthening the constraints on how the problem is represented at five qualitatively distinct levels, until only one course of action is prescribed: the one which should actually be embarked upon in the *real* (Humphreys & Jones, 2007).

LEVELS OF REPRESENTATION OF DECISION PROBLEMS

Each level of problem representation is associated with a different kind of discourse concerning how to structure the constraints at that level (Humphreys, 1998). The nature of the knowledge represented at each level and the cognitive operations involved in generating these knowledge representations has been discussed in detail elsewhere (Humphreys, 1984, 1989; Humphreys & Berkeley, 1986). These levels have been presented in a point-down triangle, or "decision spine" (Humphreys, 2007), as shown in Figure 1, indicating the progressive decrease in discretion in considering what knowledge can be included in the problem representation being developed as one moves downward from level 5 (exploring fantasy scenarios and dreams with conjecturality beyond formalization or structure) towards fixed structure (with all other knowledge now external to the representation of the problem), and zero discretion at level 1 (making "best assessments"). Three key formal properties of the 5-level scheme, taken as a whole, are as follows:

1. What is qualitatively different at each level are the cognitive operations carried out in thinking about the decision problem.
2. The results of the operations carried out on a particular level constrain the ways operations are carried out at all lower levels.
3. Any decision problem is represented at all levels, *doubled* in the symbolic/imaginary (where cognitive operations are carried out) and in the real (Deleuze & Guattari, 1988).

Therefore, we cannot treat levels like taxonomy, classifying decision problems as level 1, level 2, and so forth. We have to examine how each problem is handled at each level. In the actual decision making process, the sequence movement through the levels is not linear, but corresponds to a spiral through the circular logic of choice (Humphreys, 2007; Nappelbaum, 1997) to the point where a particular course of action is prescribed as the "true solution" to the decision problem. Decision conferencing methodologies essentially provide process designs to enable the decision making group to move efficiently and effectively through these levels within a general process which Phillips (1988, 1989) called "conferencing to consensus."

At Level 5

At the top level (level 5 in Figure 1), the roots of the decision problem are imagined through explorations carried out within a "small world" (Savage, 1955; Toda, 1976) whose bounds are defined by what each of the participants in the decision-making process is prepared to think about. However, small worlds complete with contents do not exist as complete entities pigeonholed away in a person's mind ready to be retrieved intact. From the outside, we infer the contents of the small world the person is using by looking at what he or she explores, and guessing its boundaries or possible holes within it by what he or she leaves out.

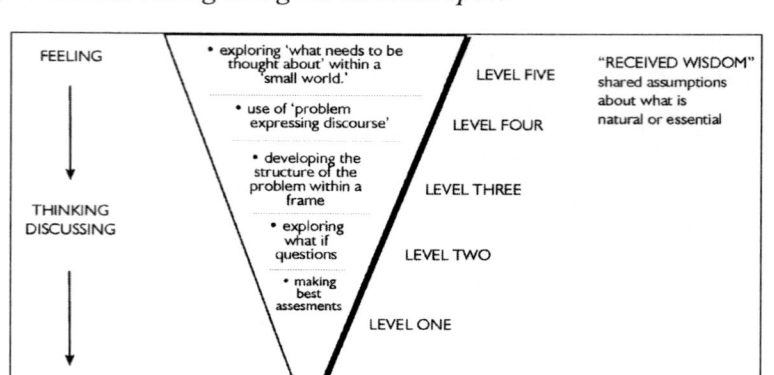

Figure 1. Five levels of constraint setting along the decision spine

We are left with uncertainty concerning the actual boundaries of this structure in the same way cartographers of the physical world in the middle ages experienced uncertainty about where to draw bounds when they had access only to explorers' reports and guesswork to fill in the gaps. As they made the maps, they were, at the same time, exploring and creating a rhizome (Deleuze & Guattari, 1988; Humphreys & Jones, 2006).

From the standpoint of this analogy, though, the person doing the thinking is not the cartographer, but an explorer within the rhizome. Exploring alternative futures in a territory for which there are no maps except those made during the explorations and where there may be considerable uncertainty: not only about where the boundary limiting the explorations could be set, but also about what unforeseen successes—or terrors—lie along the route.

In decision making under conditions of uncertainty, at level 5, it is generally necessary to explore worst case scenarios, which can be an extremely frightening process when the worst case is unbounded: offering the possibility that in exploring it a participant could stumble upon all kinds of terrors which he or she otherwise succeeded in keeping out of consciousness. Hence explorations within these bounds are generally made within what Sandler and Sandler (1978) called "the background of safety,"[1] and are themselves beyond language (Lacan, 1977), which can only be used to describe the results of what is found during such exploration. These results constitute the contextual knowledge that is available in forming the content elements of problem representations that are manipulated in problem structuring at lower levels.

Attempts to improve or enrich this contextual knowledge, by persuading participants to explore beyond their background of safety can be highly distressing to them, and are usually countered with what others (who consider such exploration to be "safe") experience as *paranoid discourse* as described by Colby (1975): discourse aimed at preventing other participants from exploring in areas that the speaker considers could be "unsafe" for them. Hence effective decision support techniques, at level 5, should aim to extend the background of safety for all participants, creating an arena where communication can be innovative and creative rather than paranoid. Techniques for doing this have been developed over many years in the field of drama. The role of the chorus in ancient Greek tragedies, providing ritualised, structured communication in unsafe areas where issues need to be resolved in coming to terms with tragedy, is one example; others involve improvisation techniques providing safe spaces for collectively acting out fantasies about alternative futures (Chatjoulis & Humphreys, 2007).

Humphreys and Jones (2006) describe how, within a flexible learning environment, a background of safety is created and maintained for participants through using dramatic techniques (construction and presentation of skits, enabling participants to explore future scenarios through the rhizome, enriching context, and allowing for more creative cognitive endeavours further down the decision spine).

At Level 4

At the next level down, (level 4 in Figure 1), problem-expressing discourse may be employed to make claims that particular elements of what was explored should (or should not) be included in the representation of the decision problem (Vari, Vecsenyi, & Paprika, 1986). This discourse determines the parts of the contextual knowledge, accessed by participants at level 5, which are expressed as "representatives in illocutionary acts" (Searle, 1979, following Austin, 1962) that will be proceduralised within the decision spine. This discourse is usually argumentative; *claims* about what aspects of context should be explicitly proceduralised. Claims are expressed by their advocates who support them with warrants and *backings* (Toulmin, 1958; van Eemeren, Grootendorst, Jackson, & Jacobs, 1997) in order to gain their acceptance by all participants in the decision making process.

The successful establishment of the claims of "what to include in the representation of the problem" is promoted and accepted through the use of *discourses of truth* (Foucault, 1981). These focus on establishing "unquestionable" or "natural" status for the backings for the claims made, in the minds of those participants in the decision making process who need to be persuaded to accept them. Thus problem-expressing discourse serves both to develop the proceduralised knowledge context within the decision spine and to define the constraints on what claims can be linked into frames so that their collective implications for potential prescriptions for action can be explored (Beach, 1990).

At Level 3

The claims thus established through problem expressing discourse need to be linked into frames so that their collective implications for the decision can be explored (Beach, 1990). Hence, at level 3, framing discourse is employed to develop the structure of the problem within a frame. Within "soft systems methodology" (Checkland, 1981; Checkland & Scholes, 1990; Humphreys, 1989), this process is described as "conceptual model building" and is located within proceduralised knowledge context established at level 4.

The problem structuring frames employed by participants developing problem structure within a decision spine usually fit into three principal categories (Chatjoulis & Humphreys, 2007). These are:

1. *Frames that structure future scenarios,* for example, through modelling act-event- sequences with decision trees. In this case, framing discourse serves to link imagined contingent acts and events in the future, forward through potential consequences of immediate acts, or backward from goals and imagined outcomes, with the aim of establishing course and action and investigating their potential consequences and side effects, usually under conditions of uncertainty.
2. *Frames that structure preferences between alternatives,* for example, through decomposition and recomposition within multi-attribute utility hierarchies. In this case, framing discourse seeks to identify value-laden attributes on alternative courses of action under consideration, (i.e., as explored within the other two categories of frames), and to make trade-offs (Keeney & Raiffa, 1976) or establish a dominance structure (Montgomery, 1983, 1989) between the alternatives to provide a rationale for "choice of the best alternative" (Berkeley, et al., 1991).
3. *Rule-based structures aimed at reducing the problem-solution search space.* In the extreme (bureaucratic) case, the framing discourse employed by participants tries to constrain possibilities for action by specifying a sufficient set of rules such that only one course of action is prescribed by the rule set, taken together.

Framing discourse is also employed to police the coherence of the material drawn from the proceduralised context into the frame until sufficient coherence is reached where it is possible to explore the structure so developed inside the frame.

Below Level 3

The result of the operations carried out at level 3 is a decision problem representation within one or more frames whose structure is conditionally fixed. Participants within the decision spine at this level no longer have any discretion over, say, which value-laden attributes may be considered within a preference structuring frame, but sensitivity analysis is possible within each frame, exploring what-if questions about the impact of changing values at nodes or reference points within structures developed at level 3. In this way it is possible to explore the decision problem within a frame. Hence at level 2, the content manipulated with the structured frames need not be represented as "facts" (where participants are expected to agree that there is a single "true" value), but as hypotheses (opinions, views, etc.). At this level, it is explicitly recognised, for example, that probabilities can vary according to individual participants' views on future states of the world and that utilities vary in reflecting the range of participants' interests and preferences.

Effective decision support systems, at this level, may employ "what-if" explorations to see the impact of changing the assessment of an element located at a particular node within the structure on the values of other nodes of interest within that structure. This kind of sensitivity analysis can discover points and areas within the frames where change of values across the range espoused by various participants makes very little impact on nodes of crucial interest, (e.g., those defining a choice between immediate courses of action) and so can be safely ignored. Conversely, where differences in espoused values are shown to have a crucial impact, a rationale is provided which could justify further effort in the *real* to refine participants' views on

At level 1, the only degree of discretion left for the participants in developing problem structure within the decision spine is to decide on how to make a "best assessment" of the of "the most likely value" at those points in the represented problem that have been represented as "uncertain" within the constructed decision-making frames, such that a particular course of action is prescribed.

If the resulting prescription is not acceptable to one or more stakeholders in the decision, this points to a re-examination of how the various higher-level constraints were set, to discover the level at which adjustment or negotiation is necessary, or for setting the constraints on how contextual knowledge is proceduralised in a new way, which will better reflect the interests of the parties to the decision.

DECISION SUPPORT WITHIN AND BEYOND THE DECISION SPINE:

From GDSS to GDACS

Figure 1 is not intended to indicate a prescriptive process model for decision-making (i.e., "start at level 5, establish constraints, then go down, one by one through the levels until action is prescribed at level 1"). All that can be established, *in general*, is that the employment, within the group decision-making process, of the discourses identified at each level in Figure 1 serves to constrain what can be explicitly considered, at the levels below it, in establishing the "truth about the decision situation" (Chatjoulis & Humphreys, 2007).

Group decision support systems (GDSS), following the approach instigated by the linear problem solving account of Herbert Simon, conventionally address the explicit modelling and support process at level 3 and below—working within one or more frames. What happens at levels 5 and 4, in identifying what these frames might be and in proceduralising the context which specifies the material to be structured within the frames, is seen as something a *priori* and external to the decision-making process. The participants in the decision making process are expected to have shared assumptions about this (as "received wisdom"). Generation of "sufficient" alternatives (as can only be known with hindsight) is considered, within this paradigm, as a problem of creativity prior to the decision process itself, rather than intrinsic to it (Kleindorfer, Kunreuther, & Shoemaker, 1993; Meredith, 2006).

Elsewhere, Humphreys and Jones (2006) have proposed a fundamental evolution of the group decision support model from one that provides support at levels 3 and below, presuming a single, pre-existing proceduralised context (Brezillon & Zarate, 2007) to comprehensive group communication and decision support (GDACS) at all levels. GDACS supports creative decision-making at levels 5 and 4 through construction of narratives with the fundamental aim of enriching contextual knowledge within the *rhizome* (Deleuze & Guattari, 1988) which constitutes the body-without-organs of a *decision-hedgehog* (Humphreys, 2007). Localised processes within a plethora of decision spines, developing problem structure through the five levels described above with the aim of "pricking the real" at the tip of the spine, are rooted in this rhizome.

REFERENCES

Austin, J. (1962). *How to do things with words.* Oxford: Oxford University Press.

Beach, L. R. (1990). *Image theory: Decision making in personal and organisational contexts.* Chichester: Wiley.

Berkeley, D., Humphreys, P., Larichev, O. & Moshkovich, H. (1991). Modeling and supporting the process of choice between alternatives: the focus of ASTRIDA. In H. G. Sol & J. Vecsenyi (Eds.), *Environments for supporting decision processes.* Amsterdam: Elsevier.

Brezillon, P., & Zarate, P. (2007). Group decision-making: A context-oriented view. *Journal of Decision Systems, 16*(2).

Chatjoulis, A., & Humphreys, P. (2007). A problem solving process model for personal decision support (PSPM-DS). *Journal of Decision Systems, 13.*

Checkland, P. (1999). *Systems thinking, systems practice (rev. ed.).* Chichester: Wiley.

Checkland, P., & Scholes, J. (1990). *Soft systems methodology in action.* Chichester: Wiley.

Colby, K. M. (1975). *Artificial paranoia.* Pergamon, Oxford.

Deleuze, G., & Guattari, F. (1988). *A thousand plateaus (capitalism and schizophrenia, Vol II).* London: The Athlone Press.

Foucault, M. (1980). *Power/knowledge: Selected interviews and other writings.* New York: Pantheon.

Hammond, J. S, Keeney, R. L., & Raiffa, H. (1998). *Smart choices: A practical guide to making better decisions.* Cambridge, MA: Harvard Business School Press.

Heppner, P. P., & Krauskopf, C. J. The integration of personal problem solving processes within counseling. *The Counseling Psychologist, 15,* 229-241.

Humphreys, P. C. (1984). Levels of representation of decision problems. *Journal of Applied Systems Analysis, 11,* 3-22.

Humphreys, P. C. (1989). Intelligence in decision support – a process model. In G. Doukidis, F. Land & G. Miller (Eds.), *Knowledge based management support systems.* Chichester: Ellis Horwood.

Humphreys, P. C. (1998). Discourses underpinning decision support. In D. Berkeley, G. Widmeyer, P. Brezillon & V. Rajkovic (Eds.), *Context sensitive decision support systems.* London: Chapman & Hall.

Humphreys, P. C. (2007). The decision hedgehog: Group communication and decision support. *$$ This volume $$*.

Humphreys, P. C., & Berkeley, D. (1986). Organizational knowledge for supporting decisions. In T. Jelassi & W. Mayon-White (Eds.), *Decision support systems: A decade in perspective.* Amsterdam: Elsevier.

Humphreys, P. C., & Brezillon, P. (2002). Combining rich and restricted languages in multimedia: Enrichment of context for innovative decisions. In F. Adam, P. Brezillon, P. Humphreys & J.-C. Pomerol (Eds.), *Decision making and decision support in the Internet age.* Cork, Ireland: Oaktree Press.

Humphreys, P. C., & Jones, G. A. (2006). The evolution of group support systems to enable collaborative authoring of outcomes. *World Futures, 62,* 1-30.

Humphreys, P. C., & Jones, G.A (2007). The decision hedgehog for creative decision making. In F. Burstein & C. Holsapple (Eds.), *Handbook on decision support systems.* Berlin: Springer.

Kaufman, E. (1998). Madness and repetition: The absence of work in Deleuze, Foucault and Jacques Martin. In E. Kaufman & K. Heller (Eds.), *Deleuze and Guattari, new mappings in politics, philosophy and culture.* Minneapolis, MN: University of Minnesota Free Press.

Keen, P. G. W. (1980) Adaptive design for decision support systems. *Data Base, 12,* 15-25.

Keeney, R.L. and Raiffa, H. (1976). *Decisions with multiple objectives: Preferences and value trade-offs.* New York: Wiley.

Kleindorfer, P. R., Kunreuther, H.C., & Shoemaker, P. H. (1993). *Decision sciences: An integrative perspective.* Cambridge: Cambridge University Press.

Lacan, J. (1977). *The agency of the letter in the unconscious.* In J. Lacan (Ed.), *Ecrits.* London: Tavistock.

Meredith, R. (2006). Creative freedom and decision support systems. In F. Adam, P. Brezillon, S. Carlsson & P. Humphreys (Eds.), *Innovation and creativity in decision making and decision support.* London: Decision Support Press.

Montgomery, H. (1983). Decision rules and the search for a dominance structure: Towards a process model of decision making,. In P. C. Humphreys, O. Svenson and A. Vari (Eds.), *Analysing and aiding decision processes.* North Holland, Amsterdam.

Montgomery, H. (1989). From cognition to action: The search for dominance in decision making. In H. Montgomery and O. Svenson (Eds.) *Process and structure in human decision making.* Chichester: Wiley.

Nappelbaum, E. L. (1997). Systems logic for problem formulation and choice. In P. Humphreys, S. Ayestaran, A. McCosh & B. Mayon-White (Eds.), *Decision support in organizational transformation.* London: Chapman & Hall.

Phillips, L. D. (1988). Conferencing to consensus. In J. Hawgood and P. C. Humphreys (Eds.) *Effective decision support systems,* (pp 176-183). Aldershot, UK: Gower.

Phillips, L. D. (1989). People-centred group decision support. In G. Doukidis, F. Land and G. Miller (Eds.), *Knowledge based management support systems.* Chichester: Wiley.

Phillips, L. D. (1992). Gaining corporate commitment to change. In C. Holtham (Ed.), *Executive information systems and decision support.* London: Chapman and Hall.

Sandler, A. M. (1987). *From safety to superego.* London: Karnac Books.

Sandler, J., & Sandler, A. M. (1978). On the development of object relations and affects. *International Journal of Psychoanalysis, 59,* 285-296.

Savage, L. (1955). *The foundations of statistics.* New York: Wiley.

Searle, J. (1969). *Speech acts.* Cambridge: Cambridge University Press.

Silver, M. S. (1991). *Systems that support decsion makers.* Chichester: Wiley.

Simon, H. A. (1977) *The new science of management decision (3rd rev. ed.).* Englewood Cliffs, NJ: Prentice Hall.

Toda, M. (1976). The decision process: A perspective. *International Journal of General Systems, 3,* 79-88.

Toulmin, S. (1958). *The uses of argument.* Cambridge: Cambridge University Press.

Van Eemeren, F. H., Grootendorst, R., Jackson, S., & Jacobs, S. (1997). Argumentation. In T. van Dijk (Ed.), *Discourse as structure and process.* London: Sage.

Vari, A., Vecsenyi, J., & Paprika, Z. (1986). Supporting problem structuring in high level decisions. In B. Brehmer, H. Jungermann, P. Lourens & G. Sevon (Eds.), *New directions in research in decision making.* Amsterdam: North Holland.

ENDNOTE

[1] The "background of safety" is built up over time through play; that is, structured and guided exploration of ways of setting bounds or having bounds provided initially by one's parents and subsequently by significant others, whose authority one accepts and trusts.

Decision Support Systems Concept

Daniel J. Power
University of Northern Iowa, USA

INTRODUCTION

Since the late 1960s, researchers have been developing and implementing computerized systems to support management decision makers. A number of decision support system (DSS) typologies were proposed in the early 1980s (Alter, 1980; Sprague & Carlson, 1982), but technology developments and new applications led to an expanded DSS framework (Power, 2000a, 2000b, 2001). The expanded DSS framework that is explained in detail in Power (2002b) helps decision makers and DSS developers understand and categorize decision support projects as well as existing decision support systems.

Many terms are used to describe decision support systems. For example, some vendors and managers use the terms business intelligence, collaborative systems, computationally oriented DSS, data warehousing, model-based DSS, and online analytical processing (OLAP) software to label decision support systems. Software vendors use these more specialized terms for both descriptive and marketing purposes. The terms used to describe decision support capabilities are important in making sense about what technologies have been deployed or are needed. Some DSSs are subsystems of other information systems and this integration adds to the complexity of categorizing and identifying DSSs. In general, decision support systems are a broad class of information systems used to assist people in decision-making activities (Power, 2004).

Decision support systems can "take on many different forms and can be used in many different ways" (Alter, 1980, p. 71). DSSs differ in terms of capabilities and targeted users of a specific system, and in terms of how the DSS is implemented and what it is called. Some DSSs focus on data, some on models, and some on facilitating communications and collaboration. DSSs also differ in scope: Some DSSs are intended for one primary user and are used as a stand-alone program on a personal computer for analysis, and other DSSs are intended for many users in an organization and are deployed as enterprise-wide Web-based systems.

BACKGROUND

Traditionally, academics and IS practitioners have discussed building decision support systems in terms of four major components: (a) the user interface, (b) the database, (c) the models and analytical tools, and (d) the DSS architecture and network (Sprague & Carlson, 1982). This traditional list of components identifies similarities and differences between categories or types of DSSs. The expanded DSS framework is primarily based on the differential emphasis placed on the DSS components when systems are actually constructed. The importance of each component in providing decision support functionality is the major differentiating factor among various categories of DSSs.

The expanded DSS framework focuses on one major dimension with five categories and three secondary dimensions. The major characteristic in the framework is the dominant technology component that drives or provides the decision support functionality. Five generic categories based on the dominant component are discussed in this section: communications-driven, data-driven, document-driven, knowledge-driven, and model-driven decision support systems. These categories can classify DSSs currently in use. Their explanations are based on Power (2001, 2002b, 2004).

Communications-driven DSSs include systems built using communication, collaboration, and decision support technologies. These systems were first developed in the late 1980s and were called groupware. Group DSSs (GDSSs) also involve communications, but many GDSSs derive their functionality by providing a group of users with access to quantitative decision models and hence are more appropriately classified as model-driven DSSs.

Data-driven DSSs include file-drawer and management reporting systems, data warehousing and analysis systems, executive information systems (EISs), and some spatial DSSs (SDSSs). Business intelligence (BI) systems are also examples of data-driven DSSs. Data-driven DSSs emphasize access to and manipulation of large databases of structured data and especially a

Decision Support Systems Concept

Table 1. Summary of Power's (2002b) expanded DSS framework

Dominant Component	User Group	Purpose	Enabling Technology
Communications Communications-Driven DSS	Intra- and interorganizational users	Conduct a meeting, post on a bulletin board	Web based or LAN (local area network)
Database Data-Driven DSS	Managers, staff, intra- and interorganizational users	Query a data warehouse, ad hoc analysis	Mainframe, LAN, Web based
Document Base Document-Driven DSS	Specialists, managers	Search Web pages, find documents	Web based
Knowledge Base Knowledge-Driven DSS	Internal users, customers	Management advice, choose products	LAN or Web based
Model Model-Driven DSS	Managers, staff, customers	Crew scheduling, decision analysis	Stand-alone PC, Web based

time series of internal company data and sometimes external data. Simple file systems accessed by query and retrieval tools provide the most elementary level of functionality. Data warehouse systems that allow the manipulation of data by computerized tools tailored to a specific task and setting or by more general tools and operators provide additional functionality. Data-driven DSSs with OLAP, drill down, and scorecards provide the highest level of functionality and decision support that is linked to the analysis of a large collection of historical data.

Document-driven DSSs integrate a variety of storage and processing technologies to provide complete document retrieval, summarization, and analysis. A search tool that creates text summaries and rates document relevance provides decision support functionality, but the dominant component is the document base. Examples of documents that might be included in a document database include policies and procedures, product specifications, catalogs, and corporate historical information, including minutes of meetings, corporate records, and important correspondence.

Knowledge-driven DSSs can suggest or recommend actions to managers. These DSSs contain specialized problem-solving expertise based upon artificial intelligence and statistics technologies. The expertise consists of knowledge about a particular domain, understanding of problems within that domain, and skill at solving some of these problems.

Model-driven DSSs include systems that use accounting and financial models, representational simulation models, and optimization models. Model-driven DSSs emphasize access to and manipulation of a model. A simple algebraic model with "what-if" analysis provides the most elementary level of model-driven DSS functionality.

Table 1 summarizes the five categories or types of decision support systems and the expanded DSS framework. Data-driven, document-driven, and knowledge-driven DSSs need very different and specialized database components to provide decision support. A data-driven DSS uses a relational or multidimensional database of structured data. A document-driven DSS has a specialized document repository and in some instances a relational database to assist in document searching. A knowledge-driven DSS stores knowledge using rules, frames, or likelihood data. A model-driven DSS derives functionality from the model component in the DSS architecture. Finally, the communications and networking component is the key driver for communications-driven DSSs.

FUTURE TRENDS

The number of DSSs in each generic category is expanding rapidly. In general, each general type of DSS can be targeted to the same user group. Also, a given decision process may benefit from implementation of multiple categories of DSS. Each DSS can have a narrow, specific purpose or a more general purpose. DSSs can serve multiple, overlapping purposes. For example, to provide business intelligence for managers, a company probably needs more than one DSS including both a data-driven and a document-driven DSS. Finally, each category of DSS can be deployed using various architectures and technologies. Today, Web technologies (Linux, Apache server, MySQL, PHP) provide a powerful DSS development environment. Decision support systems can, should, and will be categorized in terms of three secondary dimensions: targeted user groups, purpose of the system, and the enabling technology.

One can and should use all four dimensions in Table 1—dominant component, user group, purpose, and enabling technology—to describe a specific decision support system. Some specific questions for identifying the type of DSS include the following. What is the dominant component and driver of decision support? Who is the targeted user group? What is the purpose of the DSS? What is the enabling technology used for implementing the system? The answers to these questions should help classify the proposed DSS, the DSS product a vendor is trying to sell, or an existing system that was previously implemented in a company. For example, a manager may want to build a model-driven DSS for product design that is interorganizational and Web based; or a company might currently have a data-driven DSS for ad hoc query that is intraorganizational and client-server based. In the future, a checklist of questions will help DSS analysts and managers categorize and describe DSSs.

CONCLUSION

This article explained computerized decision support systems and summarized a broad conceptual framework that should be used for categorizing them. Discussion, debate, and efforts to use the framework can improve our understanding of decision support systems and make the framework more useful for both research and development of DSSs. The author hopes that the expanded framework improves our overall understanding of computerized systems intended to support decision making. The DSS concept has been reinterpreted and broadened over the past 30 years and technologies have changed and dramatically improved. There remain, however, conceptual overlap problems related to terms associated with computerized decision support and vendors still using too many marketing buzzwords for decision support development software. In general, the basic decision-support goal of supporting decision makers using computing technology remains crucial and important for any organization that is in a complex, rapidly changing environment.

REFERENCES

Alter, S. L. (1980). *Decision support systems: Current practice and continuing challenge.* Reading, MA: Addison-Wesley.

Power, D. J. (2000a). *Decision support systems hyperbook.* Retrieved from http://www.DSSResources.com

Power, D. J. (2000b, August 10-13). *Web-based and model-driven decision support systems: Concepts and issues.* Paper presented at the 2000 Americas Conference on Information Systems, Long Beach, CA.

Power, D. J. (2001, June 19-22). Supporting decision-makers: An expanded framework. In A. Harriger (Ed.), *E-Proceedings 2001 Informing Science Conference.*

Power, D. J. (2002a). Categorizing decision support systems: A multidimensional approach. In M. Mora, G. Forgionne, & J. N. D. Gupta (Eds.), *Decision making support systems: Achievements and challenges for the new decade* (pp. 20-27). Hershey, PA: Idea Group.

Power, D. J. (2002b). *Decision support systems: Concepts and resources for managers.* Westport, CT: Greenwood/Quorum Books.

Power, D. J. (2004). Specifying an expanded framework for classifying and describing decision support systems. *Communications of the Association for Information Systems, 13,* 158-166.

Power, D. J., & Kaparthi, S. (1998). The changing technological context of decision support systems. In

Decision Support Systems Concept

D. Berkeley, G. Widmeyer, P. Brezillion, & V. Rajkovic (Eds.), *Context-sensitive decision support systems* (pp. 42-54). London: Chapman & Hall.

Sprague, R. H., & Carlson, E. D. (1982). *Building effective decision support systems.* Englewood Cliffs, NJ: Prentice-Hall.

KEY TERMS

Business Intelligence (BI): Abbreviated BI, business intelligence "is a popularized, umbrella term introduced by Howard Dresner of the Gartner Group in 1989 to describe a set of concepts and methods to improve business decision making by using fact-based support systems. The term is sometimes used interchangeably with briefing books and executive information systems. A Business Intelligence System is a data-driven DSS." Decision support's purpose is to provide managers with information or business intelligence.

Data: Data are "binary (digital) representations of atomic facts," especially from financial transactions. Data may also be "text, graphics, bit-mapped images, sound, analog or digital live-video segments." Structured data are the "raw material" for analysis using a data-driven DSS. The data are "supplied by data producers and [are] used by managers and analysts to create information."

Decision Support Systems (DSSs): DSSs are a specific "class of computerized information system that support decision-making activities." "A DSS is an interactive computer-based system or subsystem intended to help decision makers use communications technologies, data, documents, knowledge and/or models to identify and solve problems…and make decisions….Five more specific Decision Support System types include: Communications-driven DSS, Data-driven DSS, Document-driven DSS, Knowledge-driven DSS, and Model-driven DSS."

Executive Information Systems (EISs): "An EIS is a computerized system intended to provide current and appropriate information to support decision making for [senior] managers using a networked workstation. The emphasis is on graphical displays and an easy to use interface..."

Online Analytical Processing (OLAP): "OLAP is software for manipulating multidimensional data from a variety of sources that has been stored in a data warehouse. The software can create various views and representations of the data. OLAP software provides fast, consistent, interactive access to shared, multidimensional data."

Web-Based DSS: This is "a computerized system that delivers decision support information or decision support tools to a manager or business analyst using a 'thin-client' Web browser like Netscape Navigator of Internet Explorer. The computer server that is hosting the DSS application is linked to the user's computer by a network with the TCP/IP protocol….Web-Based DSS can be communications-driven, data-driven, document-driven, knowledge-driven, model-driven or a hybrid."

What-If Analysis: This is "the capability of 'asking' the software package what the effect will be of changing some of the input data [decision variables] or independent variables." In a model-driven DSS, a decision variable is a changing factor in the model that is determined by a decision maker. The presence of this capability helps identify a model-driven DSS.

Development and Design Methodologies in DWM

James Yao
Montclair State University, USA

John Wang
Montclair State University, USA

Qiyang Chen
Montclair State University, USA

June Lu
University of Houston – Victoria, USA

INTRODUCTION

Information systems were developed in early 1960s to process orders, billings, inventory controls, payrolls, and accounts payables. Soon information systems research began. Harry Stern started the "Information Systems in Management Science" column in *Management Science* journal to provide a forum for discussion beyond just research papers (Banker & Kauffman, 2004). Ackoff (1967) led the earliest research on management information systems for decision-making purposes and published it in *Management Science*. Gorry and Scott Morton (1971) first used the term *decision support systems* (DSS) in a paper and constructed a framework for improving management information systems. The topics on information systems and DSS research diversifies. One of the major topics has been on how to get systems design right.

As an active component of DSS, data warehousing became one of the most important developments in the information systems field during the mid-to-late 1990s. It has been estimated that about 95% of the *Fortune 1000* companies either have a data warehouse in place or are planning to develop one (Wixon & Watson, 2001). Data warehousing is a product of business need and technological advances. Since business environment has become more global, competitive, complex, and volatile customer relationship management (CRM) and e-commerce initiatives are creating requirements for large, integrated data repositories and advanced analytical capabilities. By using a data warehouse, companies can make decisions about customer-specific strategies such as customer profiling, customer segmentation, and cross-selling analysis (Cunningham, Song, & Chen, 2006). To analyze these large quantities of data, data mining has been widely used to find hidden patterns in the data and even discover knowledge from the collected data. Thus how to design and develop a data warehouse and how to use data mining in the data warehouse development have become important issues for information systems designers and developers.

This article presents some of the currently discussed development and design methodologies in data warehousing and data mining, such as the multidimensional model vs. relational entity-relationship (ER) model, corporate information factory (CIF) vs. multidimensional methodologies, data-driven vs. metric-driven approaches, top-down vs. bottom-up design approaches, data partitioning and parallel processing, materialized view, data mining, and knowledge discovery in database (KDD).

BACKGROUND

Data warehouse design is a lengthy, time-consuming, and costly process. Any wrongly calculated step can lead to a failure. Therefore, researchers have placed important efforts to the study of design and development related issues and methodologies.

Data modeling for a data warehouse is different from operational database, for example, online transaction processing (OLTP), data modeling. An operational system is a system that is used to run a business in real time, based on current data. An OLTP system usually adopts ER modeling and application-oriented database design (Han & Kamber, 2006). An information system, like a data warehouse, is designed to support decision making based on historical point-in-time and prediction data for complex queries or data mining applications (Hoffer, Prescott, & McFadden, 2007). A data warehouse schema is viewed as a dimensional model (Ahmad, Azhar, & Lukauskis, 2004; Han & Kamber, 2006; Levene & Loizou, 2003). It typically adopts either a star or snowflake schema and a subject-oriented database design (Han & Kamber, 2006). The schema design is the most critical to the design of a data warehouse.

Many approaches and methodologies have been proposed in the design and development of data warehouses. Two major data warehouse design methodologies have been paid more attention. Inmon, Terdeman, and Imhoff (2000) proposed the CIF architecture. This architecture, in the design of the atomic-level data marts, uses denormalized entity-relationship diagram (ERD) schema. Kimball (1996, 1997) proposed multidimensional (MD) architecture. This architecture uses star schema at atomic-level data marts. Which architecture should an enterprise follow? Is one better than the other? Currently, the most popular data model for data warehouse design is the dimensional model (Bellatreche & Mohania, 2006; Han & Kamber, 2006). Some researchers call this model the data-driven design model. Artz (2006) advocates the metric-driven view, which, as another view of data warehouse design, begins by identifying key business processes that need to be measured and tracked over time in order for the organization to function more efficiently. There has always been the issue of top-down vs. bottom-up approaches in the design of information systems. The same is with a data warehouse design. These have been puzzling questions for business intelligent architects and data warehouse designers and developers. The next section will extend the discussion on issues related to data warehouse and mining design and development methodologies.

DESIGN AND DEVELOPMENT METHODOLOGIES

Data Warehouse Data Modeling

Database design is typically divided into a four-stage process (Raisinghani, 2000). After requirements are collected, conceptual design, logical design, and physical design follow. Of the four stages, logical design is the key focal point of the database design process and most critical to the design of a database. In terms of an OLTP system design, it usually adopts an ER data model and an application-oriented database design (Han & Kamber, 2006). The majority of modern enterprise information systems are built using the ER model (Raisinghani, 2000). The ER data model is commonly used in relational database design, where a database schema consists of a set of entities and the relationship between them. The ER model is used to demonstrate detailed relationships between the data elements. It focuses on removing redundancy of data elements in the database. The schema is a database design containing the logic and showing relationships between the data organized in different relations (Ahmad et al., 2004). Conversely, a data warehouse requires a concise, subject-oriented schema that facilitates online data analysis. A data warehouse schema is viewed as a dimensional model which is composed of a central fact table and a set of surrounding dimension tables, each corresponding to one of the components or dimensions of the fact table (Levene & Loizou, 2003). Dimensional models are oriented toward a specific business process or subject. This approach keeps the data elements associated with the business process only one join away. The most popular data model for a data warehouse is the multidimensional model. Such a model can exist in the form of a star schema, a snowflake schema, or a starflake schema.

The star schema (see Figure 1) is the simplest data base structure containing a fact table in the center, no redundancy, which is surrounded by a set of smaller dimension tables (Ahmad et al., 2004; Han & Kamber, 2006). The fact table is connected with the dimension tables using many-to-one relationships to ensure their hierarchy. The star schema can provide fast response

Figure 1. Example of a star schema (adapted from Kroenke, 2004)

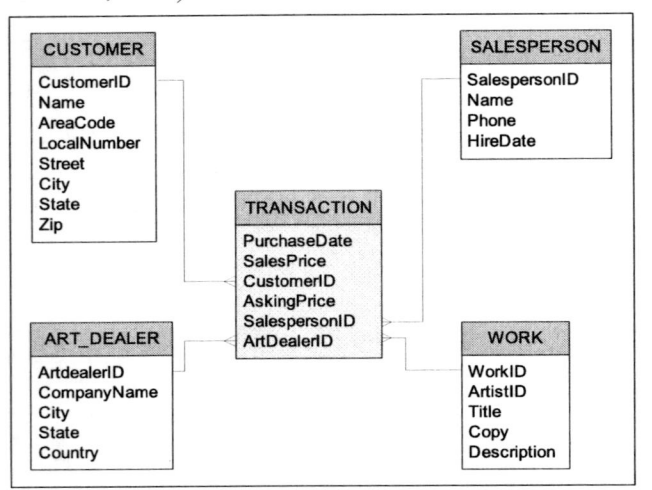

Figure 2. Example of a snowflake schema (adapted from Kroenke, 2004)

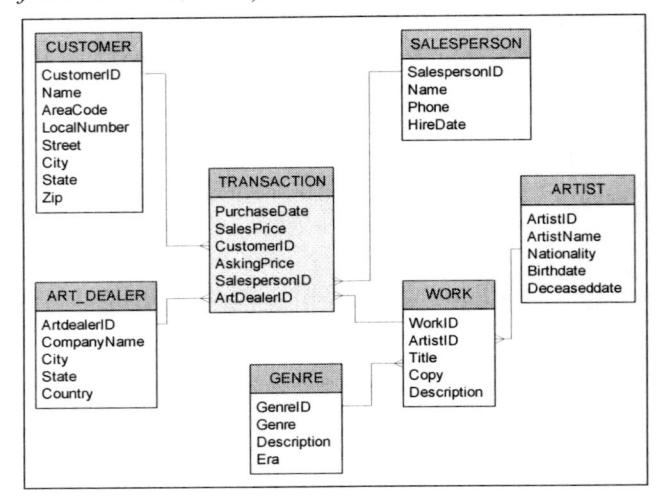

time allowing database optimizers to work with simple database structures in order to yield better execution plans.

The snowflake schema (see Figure 2) is a variation of the star schema model, in which all dimensional information is stored in the third normal form, thereby further splitting the data into additional tables, while keeping fact table structure the same. To take care of hierarchy, the dimension tables are connected with sub-dimension tables using many-to-one relationships. The resulting schema graph forms a shape similar to a snowflake (Ahmad et al., 2004; Han & Kamber, 2006). The snowflake schema can reduce redundancy and save storage space. However, it can also reduce the effectiveness of browsing and the system performance may be adversely impacted. Hence, the snowflake schema is not as popular as star schema in data warehouse design (Han & Kamber, 2006). In general, the star schema requires greater storage, but it is faster to process than the snowflake schema (Kroenke, 2004).

The starflake schema (Ahmad et al., 2004), also known as galaxy schema or fact constellation schema (Han & Kamber, 2006), is a combination of the denormalized star schema and the normalized snowflake schema (see Figure 3). The starflake schema is used in situations where it is difficult to restructure all entities into a set of distinct dimensions. It allows a degree of crossover between dimensions to answer distinct queries (Ahmad et al., 2004). Figure 3 illustrates the starflake schema.

What needs to be differentiated is that the three schemas are normally adopted according to the differences of design requirements. A data warehouse collects information about subjects that span the entire organization, such as customers, items, sales, and so forth. Its scope is enterprise-wide (Han & Kamber, 2006). Starflake (galaxy schema or fact constellation) schema can model multiple and interrelated subjects. Therefore, it is usually used to model an enterprise-wide data warehouse. A data mart, on the other hand, is similar to a data warehouse but limits its focus to a department subject of the data warehouse. Its scope is department-wide. The star schema and snowflake schema are geared towards modeling single subjects. Consequently, the star schema or snowflake schema is commonly used for a data mart modeling, although the star schema is more popular and efficient (Han & Kamber, 2006).

CIF vs. Multidimensional

Two major design methodologies have been paid more attention in the design and development of data warehouses. Kimball (1996, 1997) proposed MD architecture. Inmon et al. (2000) proposed the CIF architecture. Imhoff, Galemmco, and Geiger (2004) made a

Figure 3. Example of a starflake schema (galaxy schema or fact constellation) (adapted from Han & Kamber, 2006)

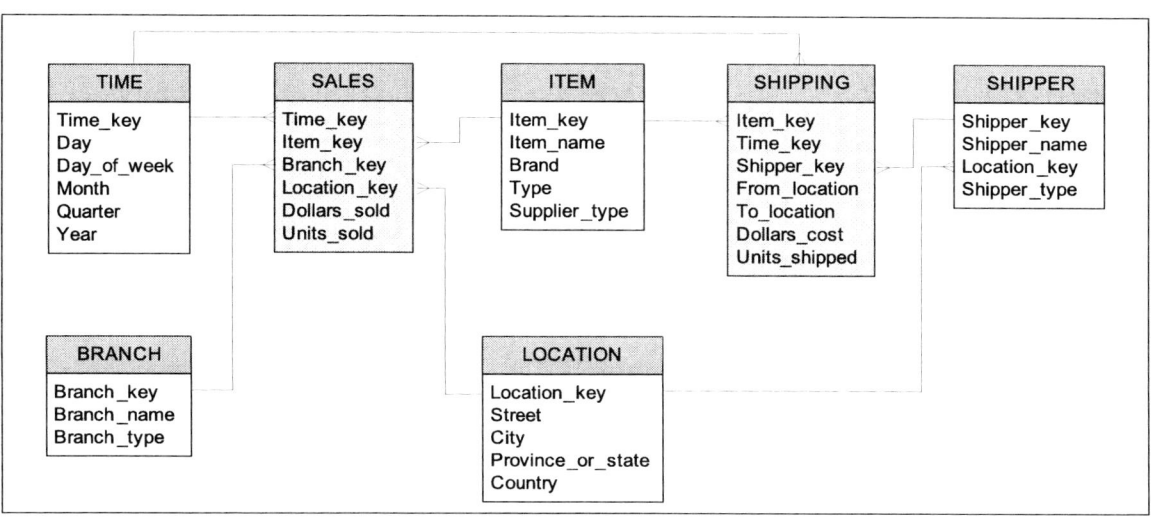

comparison between the two by using important criteria, such as scope, perspective, data flow, and so forth. One of the most significant differences between the CIF and MD architectures is the definition of the data mart. For MD architecture, the design of the atomic-level data marts is significantly different from the design of the CIF data warehouse, while its aggregated data mart schema is approximately the same as the data mart in the CIF architecture. MD architecture uses star schemas, whereas CIF architecture uses denormalized ERD schema. This data modeling difference constitutes the main design difference in the two architectures (Imhoff et al., 2004). A data warehouse may need both types of data marts in the data warehouse bus architecture depending on the business requirements. Unlike the CIF architecture, there is no physical repository equivalent to the data warehouse in the MD architecture.

The design of the two data marts is predominately multidimensional for both architecture, but the CIF architecture is not limited to just this design and can support a much broader set of data mart design techniques. In terms of scope, both architectures deal with enterprise scope and business unit scope, with CIF architecture putting a higher priority on enterprise scope and MD architecture placing a higher priority on business unit scope. With CIF architecture, the information technology (IT) side tackles the problem of supplying business intelligence source data from an enterprise point of view. With MD architecture, its proponents emphasize the perspective of consuming business unit data. For data flow, in general, the CIF approach is top-down, whereas the MD approach is bottom-up. The difference between the two in terms of implementation speed and cost involves long-term and short-term trade-offs. A CIF project, as it is at enterprise level, will most likely require more time and cost up front than the initial MD project, but the subsequent CIF projects tend to require less time and cost than subsequent MD projects. MD architecture claims that all its components must be multidimensional in design. Conversely, CIF architecture makes no such claim and is compatible with many different forms of business intelligence analyses and can support technologies that are not multidimensional in nature. For MD architecture, retrofitting is significantly harder to accomplish. Imhoff et al. (2004) encourage the application of a combination of the data modeling techniques in the two architectural approaches, namely, the ERD or normalization techniques for the data warehouse and the star schema data model for multidimensional data marts. A CIF architecture with only a data warehouse and no multidimensional marts is almost useless and a multidimensional data-mart-only environment risks the lack of an enterprise integration and support for other forms of business intelligence analyses.

Data-Driven vs. Metric-driven

Currently, the most popular data model for data warehouse design is the dimensional model (Bellatreche & Mohania, 2006; Han & Kamber, 2006). In this model, data from OLTP systems are collected to populated dimensional tables. Researchers term a data warehouse design based on this model as a data-driven design model since the information acquisition processes in the data warehouse are driven by the data made available in the underlying operational information systems. Another view of data warehouse design is called the metric-driven view (Artz, 2006), which begins by identifying key business processes that need to be measured and tracked over time in order for the organization to function more efficiently. Advantages of data-driven model include that it is more concrete, evolutionary, and uses derived summary data. Yet the information generated from the data warehouse may be meaningless to the user owing to the fact that the nature of the derived summary data from OLTP systems may not be clear. The metric-driven design approach, on the other hand, begins first by defining key business processes that need to be measured and tracked over time. After these key business processes are identified, then they are modeled in a dimensional data model. Further analysis follows to determine how the dimensional model will be populated (Artz, 2006).

According to Artz (2006), data-driven model to a data warehouse design has little future since information derived from a data-driven model is information about the data set. Metric-driven model, conversely, possibly has some key impacts and implications because information derived from a metric-driven model is information about the organization. Data-driven approach is dominating data warehouse design in organizations at present. Metric-driven, on the other hand, is at its research stage, needing practical application testimony of its speculated potentially dramatic implications.

Top-Down vs. Bottom-up

There are two approaches in general to building a data warehouse prior to the data warehouse construction commencement, including data marts: the top-down approach and bottom-up approach (Han & Kamber, 2006; Imhoff et al., 2004; Marakas, 2003). Top-down approach starts with a big picture of the overall, enterprise-wide design. The data warehouse to be built is large and integrated. However, this approach is risky (Ponniah, 2001). A top-down approach is to design the warehouse with an enterprise scope. The focus is on integrating the enterprise data for usage in any data mart from the very first project (Imhoff et al., 2004). It implies a strategic rather than an operational perspective of the data. It serves as the proper alignment of an organization's information systems with its business goals and objectives (Marakas, 2003). In contrast, a bottom-up approach is to design the warehouse with business-unit needs for operational systems. It starts with experiments and prototypes (Han & Kamber, 2006). With bottom-up, departmental data marts are built first one by one. It offers faster and easier implementation, favorable return on investment, and less risk of failure, but with a drawback of data fragmentation and redundancy. The focus of bottom-up approach is to meet unit-specific needs with minimum regards to the overall enterprise-wide data requirements (Imhoff et al., 2004).

An alternative to the previously discussed two approaches is to use a combined approach (Han & Kamber, 2006), with which "an organization can exploit the planned and strategic nature of the top-down approach while retaining the rapid implementation and opportunistic application of the bottom-up approach" (p. 129), when such an approach is necessitated in the undergoing organizational and business scenarios.

Materialized View

One of the advantages of data warehousing approach over traditional operational database approach to the integration of multiple sources is that the queries can be answered locally without accessing the original information sources (Theodoratos & Sellis, 1999). Queries to data warehouses often involve a huge number of complex aggregations over vast amount of data. As a result, data warehouses achieve high performances of query by building a large number of materialized views (Bellatreche & Mohania, 2006; Jixue, Millist, Vincent, & Mohania, 2003; Lee, Chang, & Lee, 2004; Theodoratos & Sellis, 1999). One of the common problems related to the materialized views is view selection. It seems infeasible to store all the materialized views as we are constrained by some resources such as data warehouse disk space and maintenance cost (Bellatreche & Mohania, 2006). Therefore, an appropriate set of views should be selected among the candidate views.

Studies have shown that materialized view selection problem is proven to be an NP-hard problem (Bellatreche & Mohania, 2006; Lee et al., 2004). Baralis, Paraboschi, and Teniente (1997); Mistry, Roy, Sudarshan, and Ramamritham (2001); and Theodoratos and Sellis (1997) researched on solving the materialized view selection problem, but they considered only the intermediate query results that appeared in the given workloads' execution plan as candidate materialized views (Lee et al., 2004). As a result, the views were excluded from the candidate view space if they joined the relations not referred to in the queries even though the views could have been used in the optimal query execution plan (Bellatreche & Mohania, 2006; Chang & Lee, 1999). Lee et al. (2004) developed a solution for identifying the candidate view space of materialization, which demonstrates that the candidate view space can be optimized by join-lossless property, partial-view and union-view. These methods can present better results when the database schema, especially the join relations, gets more complex.

Data Partitioning and Parallel Processing

Data partitioning is the process of decomposing large tables (fact tables, materialized views, indexes) into multiple small tables by applying the selection operators (Bellatreche & Mohania, 2006). A good partitioning scheme is an essential part of designing a database that will benefit from parallelism (Singh, 1998). With a well performed partitioning, significant improvements in availability, administration, and table scan performance can be achieved. Singh (1998) described five methods of partitioning: (1) hashing algorithm to distribute data uniformly across disks, (2) round-robin partitioning (assigning a row to partitions in sequence), (3) allocating rows to nodes based on ranges of values, (4) schema partitioning to tie a table to a particular partition, and (5) user-defined rules to allocate data in a particular partition. Bellatreche and Mohania (2006) and Bellatreche, Schneider, Mohania, and Bhargava (2002) on the other hand offer two types of partitioning: horizontal and vertical. In horizontal fragmentation, each partition consists of a set of rows of the original table. In the vertical fragmentation, each partition consists of a set of columns of the original table. Furthermore, horizontal fragmentation can be divided into two versions: primary horizontal partitioning and derived horizontal partition. The former one is performed using predicates that are defined on that table, the later one results from predicates defined on another relation.

Parallel processing is based on a parallel database, in which multiprocessors are in place. Parallel databases link multiple smaller machines to achieve the same throughput as a single, larger machine, often with greater scalability and reliability than single processor databases (Singh, 1998). In a context of relational online analytical processing (ROLAP), by partitioning data of ROLAP schema (star schema or snowflake schema) among a set of processors, OLAP queries can be executed in a parallel, potentially achieving a linear speedup and thus significantly improving query response time (Datta, Moon, & Thomas, 1998; Tan, 2006). Given the size of contemporary data warehousing repositories, multiprocessor solutions are crucial for the massive computational demands for current and future OLAP system (Dehne, Eavis, & Rau-Chaplin, 2006). The assumption of most of the fast computation algorithms is that their algorithms can be applied into the parallel processing system (Dehne et al., 2006; Tan, 2006). As a result, it is sometimes necessary to use parallel processing for data mining because large amounts of data and massive search efforts are involved in data mining (Turban, Aronson, & Liang, 2005). Therefore, data partitioning and parallel processing are two complementary techniques to achieve the reduction of query processing cost in data warehousing design and development (Bellatreche & Mohania, 2006).

Data Mining

As a process, data mining endeavors require certain steps necessary to achieve a successful outcome. A step common to data mining is infrastructure preparation. Without the infrastructure data mining activities simply will not occur. Minimum requirements for the infrastructure are: a hardware platform, database management system (DBMS) platform, and one or more tools for data mining (Marakas, 2003). The hardware platform, in most cases, is a separate platform than that which originally housed the data. The data mining environment is usually a client/server architecture or a Web-based architecture (Turban et al., 2005). To perform data mining, data must be removed from its host environment and prepared before it can be properly mined. This process is called extraction, transformation, and loading (ETL) process, in which the data is scrubbed/cleaned and transformed according to the requirements and then loaded to the hardware platform, usually a data warehouse or data mart (Han & Kamber, 2006; Marakas, 2003; Turban et al., 2005). A DBMS is the fundamental system for the database. Sophisticated tools and techniques for data mining are selected based on mining strategies and needs. A well-developed infrastructure is to be a pre-mining assurance for a successful data mining endeavor.

Data mining is the analysis of observational data sets to find unsuspected relationships and to summarize the data in novel ways that are both understandable and useful to the data owner (Hand, Mannila, & Smyth, 2001). Another term that is frequently used interchangeably with data mining is KDD. KDD was coined to describe all those methods that seek to find relations and regularity among the observed data and was gradually expanded to describe the whole process of extrapolating information from a database, from the identification of the initial business objectives to the application of the decision rules (Giudici, 2003). Although many people treat data mining as a synonym for KDD, there are differences between the two. Technically, KDD is the application of the scientific method to data mining (Roiger & Geatz, 2003). Apart from performing data mining, a typical KDD process model includes a methodology for extracting and preparing data as well as making decisions about actions to be taken once data mining has taken place. The KDD process involves selecting the target data, preprocessing the data, transforming them if necessary, performing data mining to extract patterns and relationships, and then interpreting and assessing the discovered structures (Hand et al., 2001). In contrast, data mining is the process of forming general concept definitions by observing specific examples of concepts to be learned. It is a process of business intelligence that can be used together with what is provided by IT to support company decisions (Giudici, 2003). A data warehouse has uses other than data mining. However, the fullest use of a data warehouse must include data mining (Marakas, 2003), which in turn, at an upper level, discovers knowledge for the user.

FUTURE TRENDS

Future information systems research will continue with the study of problems in information systems management, including systems analysis and design (Banker & Kauffman, 2004). According to Cunningham et al. (2006), there are no agreed upon standardized rules for how to design a data warehouse to support CRM and a taxonomy of CRM analyses needs to be developed to determine factors that affect design decisions for CRM data warehouse. Enterprises are moving towards building the operational data store, which derives data from enterprise resource planning (ERP) systems, solutions for real-time business analysis. There is a need for active integration of CRM with operational data store for real-time consulting and marketing (Bellatreche & Mohania, 2006).

In the data modeling area, to develop a more general solution for modeling data warehouse the current ER model and dimensional model need to be extended to the next level to combine the simplicity of the dimensional model and the efficiency of the ER model with the support of object oriented concepts (Raisinghani, 2000).

CONCLUSION

Several data warehousing and data mining development and design methodologies have been reviewed and discussed, followed by some trends in data warehousing design. There are more issues in relation to the topic but are limited due to the paper size. Some of the methodologies have been practiced in the real world and accepted by today's businesses. Yet new challenging methodologies, particularly in data modeling and models for physical data warehousing design, need to be further researched and developed.

REFERENCES

Ackoff, R. I. (1967). Management misinformation systems. *Management Science, 14*(4), 147-156.

Ahmad, I., Azhar, S., & Lukauskis, P. (2004). Development of a decision support system using data warehousing to assist builders/developers in site selection. *Automation in Construction, 13,* 525-542.

Artz, J. M. (2006). Data driven vs. metric driven data warehouse design. In J. Wang (Ed.), *Encyclopedia of data warehousing and mining* (pp. 223-227). Hershey, PA: Idea Group.

Banker, R. D., & Kauffman, R. J. (2004, March). The evolution of research on information systems: A fiftieth-year survey of the literature in *Management Science*. *Management Science, 50*(3), 281-298.

Baralis, E., Paraboschi, S., & Teniente, E. (1997). Materialized view selection in multidimensional database. In *Proceedings of the 23rd International Conference on Very Large Data Bases (VLDB '97)* (pp. 156-165).

Bellatreche, L., & Mohania, M. (2006). Physical data warehousing design. In J. Wang (Ed.), *Encyclopedia of data warehousing and mining* (pp. 906-911). Hershey, PA: Idea Group.

Bellatreche, L., Schneider, M., Mohania, M., & Bhargava, B. (2002). PartJoin: An efficient storage and query execution for data warehouses. In *Proceedings of the 4th International Conference on Data Warehousing and Knowledge Discovery (DAWAK '02)* (pp. 109-132).

Chang, J., & Lee, S. (1999). Extended conditions for answering an aggregate query using materialized views. *Information Processing Letters, 72*(5-6), 205-212.

Cunningham, C., Song, I., & Chen, P. P. (2006, April-June). Data warehouse design to support customer relationship management analyses. *Journal of Database Management, 17*(2), 62-84.

Datta, A., Moon, B., & Thomas, H. (1998). A case for parallelism in data warehousing and OLAP. *Proceedings of the 9th International Workshop on Database and Expert Systems Applications (DEXA '98)* (pp. 226-231).

Dehne, F., Eavis, T., & Rau-Chaplin, A. (2006). The cgmCUBE project: Optimizing parallel data cube generation for ROLAP. *Distributed and Parallel Databases, 19,* 29-62.

Giudici, P. (2003). *Applied data mining: Statistical methods for business and industry*. West Sussex, England.

Gorry, G. A., & Scott Morton, M. S. (1971). A framework for management information systems. *Sloan Management Review, 13*(1), 1-22.

Han, J., & Kamber, M. (2006). *Data mining: Concepts and techniques* (2nd ed.). San Francisco: Morgan Kaufmann.

Hand, D., Mannila, H., & Smyth, P. (2001). *Principles of data mining*. Cambridge, MA: MIT Press.

Hoffer, J. A., Prescott, M. B., & McFadden, F. R. (2007). *Modern database management* (8th ed.). Upper Saddle River, NJ: Pearson Prentice Hall.

Imhoff, C., Galemmco, M., & Geiger, J. G. (2004). Comparing two data warehouse methodologies. (Database and network intelligence). *Database and Network Journal, 34*(3), 3-9.

Inmon, W. H., Terdeman, R. H., & Imhoff, C. (2000). *Exploration warehousing: Turning business information into business opportunity*. New York: John Wiley & Sons, Inc.

Jixue, L., Millist, W., Vincent, M., & Mohania, K. (2003). Maintaining views in object-relational databases. *Knowledge and Information Systems, 5*(1), 50-82.

Kimball, R. (1996). *The data warehouse toolkit: Practical techniques for building dimensional data warehouses*. New York: John Wiley & Sons.

Kimball, R. (1997, August). A dimensional modeling manifesto. *DBMS, 10*(9), 58-70.

Kroenke, D. M. (2004). *Database processing: Fundamentals, design and implementation* (9th ed.). Saddle River, NJ: Prentice Hall.

Lee, T., Chang, J., & Lee, S. (2004). Using relational database constraints to design materialized views in data warehouses. *APWeb 2004,* 395-404.

Levene, M., & Loizou, G. (2003). Why is the snowflake schema a good data warehouse design? *Information Systems, 28*(3), 225-240.

Marakas, G. M. (2003). *Modern data warehousing, mining, and visualization: Core concepts*. Upper Saddle River, NJ: Pearson Education Inc.

Mistry, H., Roy, P., Sudarshan, S., & Ramamritham, K. (2001). Materialized view selection and maintenance using multi-query optimization. In *Proceedings of the ACM SIGMOD International Conference on Management of Data 2001* (pp. 310-318).

Ponniah, P. (2001). *Data warehousing fundamentals: A comprehensive guide for IT professionals*. New York: John Wiley & Sons, Inc.

Raisinghani, M. S. (2000). Adapting data modeling techniques for data warehouse design. *Journal of Computer Information Systems, 4*(3), 73-77.

Roiger, R. J., & Geatz, M. W. (2003). *Data mining: A tutorial-based primer*. New York: Addison-Wesley.

Singh, H. S. (1998). *Data warehousing: Concepts, technologies, implementations, and management*. Upper Saddle River, NJ: Prentice Hall PTR.

Tan, R. B. (2006). Online analytical processing systems. In J. Wang (Ed.), *Encyclopedia of data warehousing and mining* (pp. 876-884). Hershey, PA: Idea Group.

Theodoratos, D., & Sellis, T. (1997). Data warehouse configuration. In *Proceedings of the 23rd International Conference on Very Large Data Bases (VLDB '97)* (pp. 126-135).

Theodoratos, D., & Sellis, T. (1999). Designing data warehouses. *Data and Knowledge Engineering, 31*(3), 279-301.

Turban, E., Aronson, J. E., & Liang, T. (2005). *Decision support systems and intelligent systems* (7th ed.). Upper Saddle River, NJ: Pearson Education Inc.

Wixon, B. H., & Watson, H. (2001). An empirical investigation of the factors affecting data warehousing success. *MIS Quarterly, 25*(1), 17-41.

KEY TERMS

Dimensional Model: A dimensional model contains a central fact table and a set of surrounding dimension tables, each corresponding to one of the components or dimensions of the fact table.

Dimensions: Dimensions are the perspectives or entities with respect to which an organization wants to keep records (Han & Kamber, 2006, p. 110).

Entity-Relationship Data Model: An entity-relationship data model is a model that represents database schema as a set of entities and the relationships among them.

Fact Table: A fact table is the central table in a star schema, containing the names of the facts, or measures, as well as keys to each of the related dimension tables.

Knowledge Discovery in Databases (KDD): KDD is the process of extrapolating information from a database, from the identification of the initial business aims to the application of the decision rules (Giudici, 2003, p. 2).

Materialized View: Mmaterialized view are copies or replicas of data based on SQL queries created in the same manner as dynamic views (Hoffer et al., 2007, p. 298).

Metric-Drive Design: Metric-drive design is a data warehousing design approach which begins by defining key business processes that need to be measured and tracked over time. Then they are modeled in a dimensional model.

Parallel Processing: Parallel processing is the allocation of the operating system's processing load across several processors (Singh, 1998, p. 209).

Star Schema: Star schema is a modeling diagram that contains a large central table (fact table) and a set of smaller attendant tables (dimension tables) each represented by only one table with a set of attributes.

Diagrammatic Decision-Support Modeling Tools in the Context of Supply Chain Management

Dina Neiger
Monash University, Australia

Leonid Churilov
Monash University, Australia

INTRODUCTION

Recent research (Keller & Teufel, 1998; Klaus, Rosemann, & Gable, 2000; Powell, Schwaninger, & Trimble, 2001) has clearly demonstrated that years of increasing competition combined with the ongoing demand to improve the bottom line significantly reduced the business capacity to achieve greater efficiency (profitability) and effectiveness (market share) solely along organisational functional lines. To complement the functional paradigm of business development, a *business process paradigm* has evolved allowing a holistic view of the business as an entity focused on specific outcomes achieved through a sequence of tasks (Keller & Teufel; Klaus et al.). Existing common understanding of the concept of *business process* being "a continuous series of enterprise tasks, undertaken for the purpose of creating output" (Scheer, 1999) laid the foundation for several successful attempts by major *business process* modeling and ERP (enterprise resource planning) vendors, such as ARIS (Davis, 2001; Scheer, 1999, 2000) and SAP (Keller & Teufel), to link *business process* modeling and enterprise resource planning.

Diagrams used for process modeling are generally purely descriptive, reflecting their origins in information systems design and software engineering (Forrester, 1968; Hirschheim & Heinz, 1989; Howard & Matheson, 1989; Snowdown, 2001). While they provide a holistic view of *business processes*, they are not effective in modeling *decision* objectives, alternatives, and pathways. *Decision* modeling diagrams, on the other hand, originate from operational research and therefore are very effective in modeling *decision* components.

The objective of this article is to present a systematic and coherent view of business *decision* modeling diagrammatic tools. The discussion is structured around the process that can be regarded as the core of a business enterprise: the customer order management cycle (COM). Therefore, a simplified COM scenario as well as a generic *decision*-making model is introduced. A systematic and coherent view of *decision* modeling diagrammatic tools is presented.

BACKGROUND: A CUSTOMER ORDER MANAGEMENT SCENARIO MODELING AND DECISION-MAKING CONTEXT

Customer order management is one of the key components of *supply chain* management activities that, in turn, form an essential part of both modern management theory and practice (Ganeshan & Harrison, 1995/2001; Klaus et al., 2000; Scheer, 1999, 2000; Shapiro, 2001). A *supply chain* is commonly defined as a "network of facilities and distribution options that performs the functions of procurement of materials, transformation of these materials into intermediate and finished products, and the distribution of these finished products to customers" (Ganeshan & Harrison). *Supply chain*s exist in manufacturing and service industries, they can vary in complexity significantly, and they often provide the basis for various e-business industry solutions (Ganeshan & Harrison; Klaus et al.; Scheer, 1999, 2000; Shapiro).

Throughout this article, a simplified customer order management scenario based on Scheer's (1999) customer order processing example is used to illustrate key modeling concepts. The scenario is set within a generic manufacturing business enterprise; however, it could be easily modified for the settings of the service industry. Diagrammatic representation of this scenario can be found in Figure 1.

Figure 1. Customer order management scenario diagram

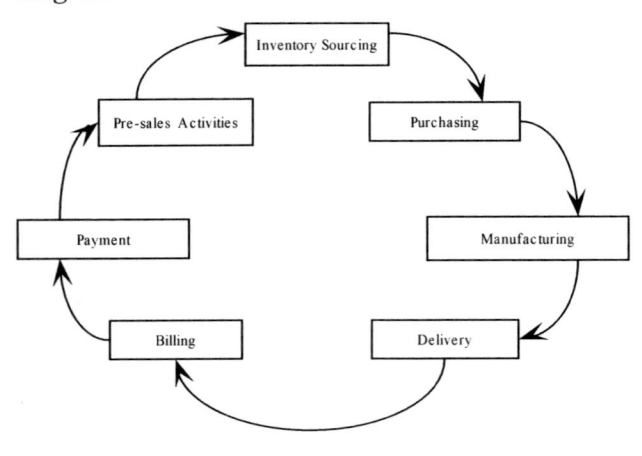

In other words, a simplified customer order management scenario can be described as follows. A manufacturing business enterprise has performed some presales and marketing activities and has identified a new product for sale. Before the product is produced, the materials required to manufacture the product are ordered from the supplier and stored in the business inventory. For illustration purposes, it is assumed that materials can be purchased in small, medium, or large quantity. Similarly, the demand for the final product can be small, medium, or large. The production process does not commence until a firm order from the customer is received. Then, the manufacturing process is planned, the identified goods are manufactured, and picking, packing, and shipping activities are performed. In this scenario, it is assumed that once the goods are produced they are immediately shipped to the customer (i.e., only materials inventory is kept). Once goods are issued, the customer accepts the product and makes a payment.

It is assumed that the business has one strategic objective: to maximize the profit from the sale of the product. The profit is determined as the sales revenue less production costs, which include fixed costs of the components inventory and variable costs of the materials purchased from the supplier, shipment costs, and goodwill or penalty costs resulting from delays in customer order or product shortages.

Note that the degree to which the stated strategic objective can be achieved depends very much on two basic components: solid and reliable *business processes* and rational business *decisions* made within the enterprise. The rest of this section is dedicated to the description of a generic rational *decision*-making model in the context of a customer order management scenario discussed above. This model is used extensively in the discussion throughout the article.

As far as the *decision*-making activities are concerned, there exists a general consensus (Clemen & Reilly, 2001; Winston, 1994) that a *decision* typically involves a choice from possible actions or alternatives to satisfy one or several given objectives. An example of a relatively simple *decision* in the context of a customer order management scenario is the choice between a small, medium, or large quantity of materials to be purchased to maximize the profit (excluding manufacturing and shipment costs) from the production of goods.

The small, medium, and large quantities define three possible actions or alternatives available to the *decision* maker. Generally speaking, a set of possible actions or choices defines the *decision* variable space. To construct a *decision* model, *decision* variables should be selected to adequately quantify a set of possible actions. The *decision* variables could be discrete or continuous, and could take on positive, negative, or integer values depending on a specific *decision* situation.

The *decision* variable space is usually defined using a set of functional constraints on the *decision* variables. In the above example, the constraints limit the set of choices to four possible quantities: no order, or small, medium, or large order. In other *decision* situations, constraint functions could be quite complex including linear, nonlinear, and probabilistic functions.

Depending on the *decision* situation, there may be one or more states of the world describing circumstances that affect the consequences of the *decision* and are completely outside of the *decision* maker's control. In the customer order management scenario, the states of the world describe possible levels of demand for the product. Each level of demand can have a known or unknown probability associated with it and can be either static or dynamic. Some *decision*-making situations, such as a blending problem, require the *decision* maker to choose an optimal blend of materials to achieve a prespecified quality and quantity of the final product; they are fully deterministic and therefore do not explicitly specify the state of the world. In a *decision* model, states of the world are usually described by a set of environment variables.

One of the essential elements of a *decision* situation is the consequence or outcome of the *decision*. In a *decision* made under uncertainty, the outcome would depend not only on the action chosen, but also on the states of the world. In some cases, uncertainty could be associated with outcomes as well as states of the world. In a *decision* model, utilities are used to quantitatively describe the outcome of the action via utility functions that model the objectives of the *decision*. In the customer order management scenario, the utility describing the outcome of the *decision* is the profit modeled by a function of revenue and costs.

Most *decision*-making situations and models include optimality criteria that specify utility preference such as maximum profit or minimum costs. However, there are some models, such as feasibility or constraint satisfaction models, that do not require optimality criteria to be specified.

Mathematical techniques and programming routines that are used to solve *decision* models constitute a subject of extensive operational research literature. For the purpose of this article, it is assumed that once the *decision* model is formulated, it can be solved using one of the existing mathematical and/or programming routines.

In the following sections, we review causal loop diagrams (CLDs), influence diagrams (IDs), and *decision trees* (DTs). These diagrammatic modeling tools are widely used for business *decision* support (Brans, Macharis, Kunsch, Chevalier, & Schwaninger, 1998; Clemen & Reilly, 2001; Davis, 2001; Forrester, 1968; Howard & Matheson, 1989; Keller & Teufel (1998), Kirkwood, 1998/2001; Klaus et al., 2000; Kros, 2001; Scheer, 1999, 2000; Snowdown, 2001; Spradlin, 1997/2001; Sterman, 2000; Winston 1994).

DIAGRAMS

Causal (Feedback) Loop Diagrams

CLD is part of the business dynamics tool kit aimed at translating the mental representation of the business into a structured system by describing the causal relationship between key business quantities and identifying feedback mechanisms within the business (Brans et al., 1998; Forrester, 1968; Kirkwood, 1998/2001; Sterman, 2000). In the customer order management scenario described in the previous section, the key quantities or variables are funds, costs, and revenue. These variables can be used to construct a performance indicator to evaluate the performance of the business with respect to the defined business objective, that is, maximization of the profit from the sale of the product.

CLD describes causal relationships between these key variables. For example, in the customer order management scenario, increases in costs will diminish business funds in the bank account (negative causal relationship), while increases in revenue will add to the business funds in the bank account (positive causal relationship). These causal relationships are pictured on the CLD (Figure 2) by linking the quantities with arrows and noting the sign of the relationship (as positive or negative). Arrows start at the quantity that causes changes and end at the quantity that changes in response.

One of the main advantages of the CLD compared to other modeling tools is that it is able to identify feedback loops created as a result of the information feedback within the system. For example, an increase in profit results in additional funds available for the production of goods. However, increase in production results in escalation of costs, thus diminishing the quantity of funds available to the business. This *funds → costs → funds* loop indicates that a negative feedback mechanism is operating between the costs and the funds.

The CLD depicted in Figure 2 is very limited as it does not reflect customer demand, supply of materials, shipment of goods, and other quantities influencing costs and revenues and the feedback mechanisms operating between them. A more complete CLD depicted

Figure 2. Causal loop diagram

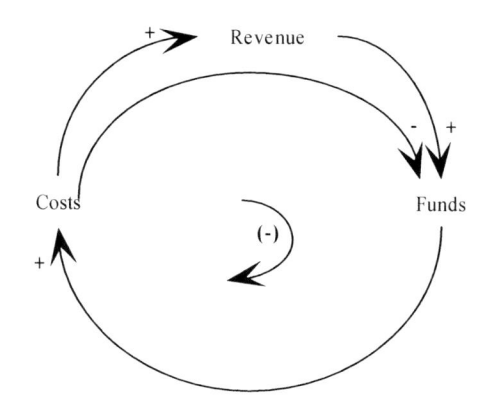

Figure 3. Extended causal loop diagram

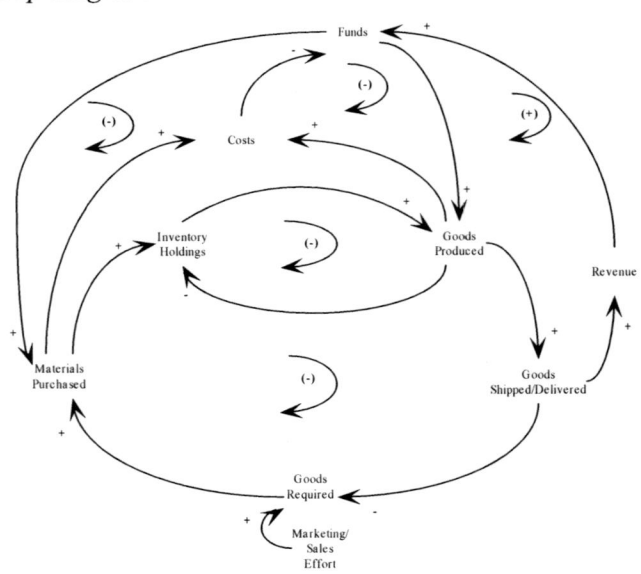

Figure 4. Organisational influence diagram

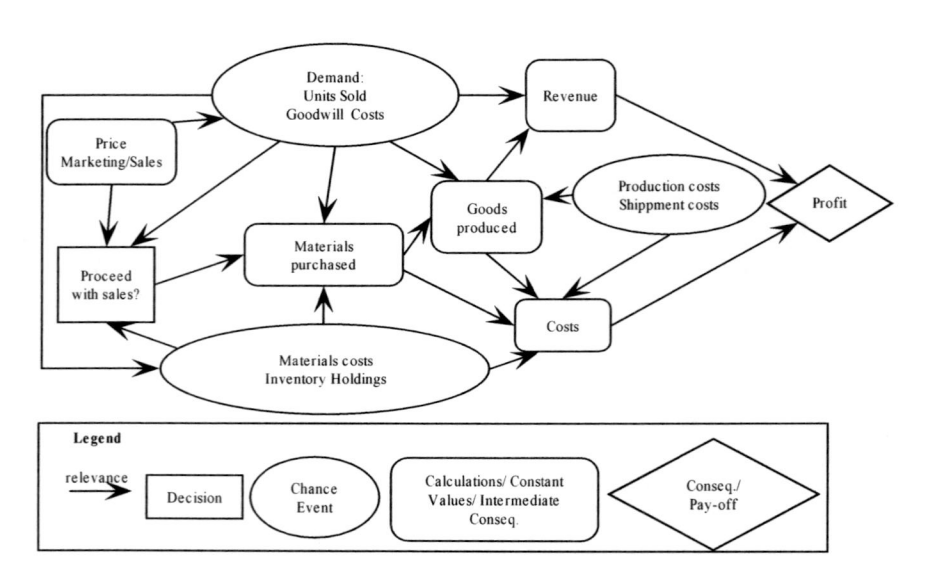

in Figure 3 illustrates other key causal relationship and feedback mechanisms apparent in the customer order management scenario.

While the CLD effectively represents causal relationships and feedback mechanisms, its capacity as a single tool to assist with the *decision* making is somewhat limited. In particular, the relationships between the variables are not quantified, alternatives available to the *decision* maker are not presented, and uncertain elements of the business situation are not identified.

Influence Diagrams

Some authors use the term *influence diagram* to describe an extended version of the CLD (Brans et al., 1998; Forrester, 1968). In this article, the term ID is used to describe a *decision* analysis tool focused on structuring complex *decision* problems by linking *decisions*, uncertain events, *decision* objectives, and calculation nodes (Clemen & Reilly, 2001; Howard & Matheson, 1989). In this representation, the ID takes the *decision*

Figure 5. Functional influence diagram

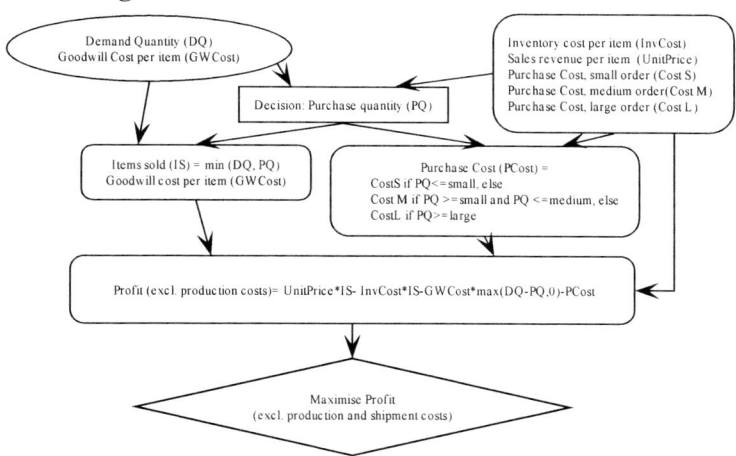

maker one step further than the causal loop toward solving the *decision* problem. It identifies key variables, *decision* objectives, objective functions, and sources of uncertainty influencing *decision* variables.

At the organisational level, the ID (Figure 4) can be used to identify the key factors and uncertainties influencing strategic organisational objectives. In the context of the customer order management scenario, the strategic objective is to maximize the profit. The price of goods and feedback from marketing and sales, the potential demand for the product, and the possible cost of materials will all influence the *decision* as to whether to proceed with the production and sale of goods. The demand and material costs are uncertain, while the quantity of materials purchased is an intermediate quantity calculated once demand, materials, and inventory costs are determined.

One of the most important modeling properties of an *ID* is that arrows, linking components of the ID, represent the direction of influence of the *decision* elements on each other rather than a sequence of events or a hierarchical structure of elements in the *decision* problem. For example, the arrow from the decision to the quantity purchased indicates that the quantity purchased is dependent on the outcome of the *decision*. Similarly, the quantity of materials purchased, materials and inventory costs, quantity of goods produced, and production and shipment costs need to be determined for the total cost calculations. The revenue is calculated based on the demand and quantity of goods produced. The goodwill or penalty costs are included in the revenue as these costs originate from the demand and can be considered as a cut in revenue.

While the ID does not explicitly describe the sequence of actions, the structural properties of ID can provide some useful information as far as corresponding *business processes* are concerned. For example, it is natural to expect that the elements at the start of the arrows (predecessors) be included in the process sequence before the elements at the end of the arrows (successors). Various process modeling tools, for example, event-driven process chains (Davis, 2001; Keller & Teufel, 1998; Klaus et al., 2000; Nuttgens et al., 1998; Scheer, 1999, 2000), can be used to model the sequence of actions required to achieve the objective specified in the strategic level ID.

At the functional or local level, the ID may be used to identify variables and relationships influencing the specific *decision* objectives, such as the objective to purchase quantity of materials so as to maximize the profit excluding production and shipment costs (Figure 5). At the functional level, the ID is easily translated into a *decision tree* diagram (DTD), which will enable the *decision* maker to choose an optimal action to satisfy the functional *decision* objective.

Decision Tree Diagrams

While the *decision tree* diagram and the ID can be considered as isomorphic (Clemen & Reilly, 2001), their origins and representations are sufficiently different to justify using them as separate business modeling tools.

DTD is a part of the *mathematical programming* family of tools used primarily to obtain solutions to

Figure 6. Decision tree diagram

Decision	Expected Profit	State of the World	Probability	Purchase Cost	Inventory Cost	Goodwill Cost	Sales Revenue	Profit (excl. manufacturing costs)
Order		Demand						
Small	2.65	Small	0.3	1	0	0	2	1
		Medium	0.5	1	0	0.5	2	0.5
		Large	0.3	1	0	1.5	2	-0.5
Medium =>	2.65	Small	0.2	5	3	0	2	-6
		Medium	0.5	5	2	0	12	5
		Large	0.3	5	2	0.5	12	4.5
Large	-3	Small	0.2	10	8	0	2	-16
		Medium	0.5	10	7	0	12	-5
		Large	0.3	10	6	0	25	9

specific structured and well-defined *decision*-making problems (Clemen & Reilly, 2001; Winston, 1994). *Mathematical programming* concerns itself with the "study of optimisation problems where we seek to minimize or maximize a real function of real or integer variables, subject to constraints on the variables" (Mathematical Programming Society, 2001). DTD is used to make an optimal choice between available alternatives when a *decision* has to be made under uncertainty. DTD provides the *decision* maker with a much more detailed view on the *decision* and the consequences of choosing a particular action—the characteristic that makes DTD better placed to represent the structure of complex *decision*-making situations (Clemen & Reilly; Winston).

A *decision tree* methodology is based on maximizing the value of the specified outcome for a given set of possible actions and corresponding utilities (Clemen & Reilly, 2001; Winston, 1994). Utility is defined as a reward associated with an outcome of the action for each of the possible states of the world influencing the outcome of the action. The utility is calculated so as to incorporate the *decision* maker's attitudes toward possible risk and reward values.

Figure 6 illustrates the *decision tree* methodology using the customer order management scenario. As shown by the corresponding ID, costs depend on the quantity of materials purchased and the revenue depends on the demand for goods. In the DTD, the costs and revenue are referred to as state variables. The utility, in this case the profit, is calculated as the difference between the costs and the revenue. A DTD is used to calculate the optimal path (the one with the maximum expected profit shown) for a given set of values for each of the quantities and a set of probabilities associated with each of the possible states of the world (levels of demand). To help interpretation of the DTD, the *decision tree* shown in Figure 6 is color coded, with the expected utility values shown in green, expected profit values in red, and the maximum expected profit in blue. The optimal path is marked with the arrow symbol (⇨).

DTD is one of a variety of modeling techniques used to assist the *decision* maker to make an optimal *decision* choice. Other commonly used *mathematical programming* techniques include, for example, linear and nonlinear programming, widely used to model and solve scheduling, short-term financial planning, product-mix, and production process problems; dynamic programming, which is used to model and solve inventory, equipment replacement, and resource allocation problems; and queuing theory used to model arrival and service processes and many other models (Winston, 1994).

Each of the above-mentioned models is highly effective in assisting the *decision* maker to make an optimal choice within a narrow, easily quantifiable, and well-defined context. Due to the very nature of the mathematical modeling tools, *mathematical programming* techniques can provide very powerful support to each function (e.g., scheduling, stock function, resource allocation, and transportation) of the *business process* separately. However, they do not offer simultaneous modeling capabilities of the interrelated and interdependent functions and do not describe well relationships of the *decision* variables within each function to the rest of the *business process* and *decision* variables within other functions. To summarize, the role of *mathematical programming* and other similar operational research techniques is to assist with sophisticated technical *decision* support effort at a given narrow segment of the business chain. Due to the highly numerical and abstract level of these tools, the effectiveness of their use rapidly diminishes as the scope of the *decision-making* situation becomes wider and includes more elements of an underlying *business process*.

CONCLUSION

This article provides the foundations for understanding how *decision* modeling tools can be used to translate the mental representation of the business into models that identify objectives, variables, influence, and feedback loops in the *business process*. The article on the integration of diagrammatic business modeling tools draws on the description of the *decision* modeling tools discussed in this article to present a classification framework that provides a systematic and coherent view of *business process* and *decision* modeling diagrammatic tools and to introduce a concept of a *decision*-enabled process modeling diagram that combines the modeling power of both process description and *decision* support tools.

REFERENCES

Brans, J. P., Macharis, C., Kunsch, P. L., Chevalier, A., & Schwaninger, M. (1998). Combining multicriteria decision aid and system dynamics for the control of socio-economic processes: An iterative real-time procedure. *European Journal of Operational Research, 109*, 428-441.

Clemen, R. T., & Reilly, T. (2001). *Making hard decisions with DecisionTools* (2nd ed.). Duxbury.

Davis, R. (2001). *Business process modelling with ARIS: A practical guide*. London: Springer-Verlag.

Forrester, J. W. (1968). *Principles of systems* (2nd ed.). Cambridge, MA: Wright-Allen Press.

Ganeshan, R., & Harrison, T. P. (1995, 2001). *An introduction to supply chain management*. Retrieved January 2007 from http://silmaril.smeal.psu.edu/misc/supply_chain_intro.html

Hirschheim, R., & Heinz, K. K. (1989). Four paradigms of information systems development. *Communications of the ACM, 32*(10), 1199-1216.

Howard, R. A., & Matheson, J. E. (1989). Influence diagrams. In R. Howard & J. Matheson (Eds.), *Readings on the principles and applications of decision analysis* (Vol. 2, pp. 719-762). Strategic Decisions Group.

Keller, G., & Teufel, T. (1998). *SAP R/3 process-oriented implementation: Iterative process prototyping*. Harlow, United Kingdom.

Kirkwood, C. W. (1998, 2001). *System dynamics methods: A quick introduction*. Retrieved January 2007 from http://www.public.asu.edu/~kirkwood/sysdyn/SDIntro/SDIntro.htm

Klaus, H., Rosemann, M., & Gable, G. G. (2000). What is ERP? *Information Systems Frontiers, 2*(2).

Kros, J. (2001). *The influence diagram: A tool for structuring relationships among variables*. Retrieved January 2007 from http://www.lapietra.edu/jkros/articles/infludia.htm

Mathematical Programming Society. (2001). *What's "mathematical programming?"* Retrieved January 2007 from http://www.mathprog.org

Nuttgens, M., Field, T., & Zimmerman, V. (2001). Business process modeling with EPC and UML: Transformation of integration? In M. Schader & A. Korthaus (Eds.), *The unified modelling language: Technical aspects and applications* (pp. 250-261). Heidelberg, Germany.

Powell, S. G., Schwaninger, M., & Trimble, C. (2001). Measurement and control of business processes. *Systems Dynamics Review, 17*(1), 63-91.

Scheer, A.-W. (1999). *ARIS: Business process frameworks* (3rd ed.). Berlin, Germany: Springer-Verlag.

Scheer, A.-W. (2000). *ARIS: Business process modeling* (3rd ed.). Berlin, Germany: Springer-Verlag.

Shapiro, J. (2001). Beyond supply chain optimization to enterprise optimization. *ASCET, 3*.

Snowdown, R. A. (2001). *Overview of process modelling*. Manchester, United Kingdom: Informatics Process Group, Manchester University. Retrieved January 2007 from http://www.cs.man.ac.uk/ipg/Docs/pmover.html

Spradlin, T. (1997, 2001). *A lexicon of decision making*. Retrieved January 2007 from http://faculty.fuqua.duke.edu/daweb/lexicon.htm

Sterman, J. D. (2000). *Business dynamics: Systems thinking and modelling for a complex world.* The McGraw-Hill Companies.

Winston, W. L. (1994). *Operations research: Applications and algorithms.* Wadsworth.

KEY TERMS

Business Process: It is a set of logically related tasks performed to achieve a defined business outcome (defined by Powell et al., 2001).

Business Process Paradigm: This is a holistic view of the business as an entity focused on specific outcomes achieved through a sequence of tasks.

Causal Loop Diagram (CLD): The CLD is a diagrammatic tool used to describe the causal relationship between key quantities and identify feedback mechanisms.

Decision: A decision typically involves a choice from possible actions or alternatives to satisfy one or several given objectives.

Decision Tree Diagram (DTD): DTD is a diagrammatic tool used to describe a decision and the consequences of choosing a particular action.

Influence Diagram (ID): ID is a diagrammatic tool used to describe a decision analysis tool focused on structuring complex decision problems by linking decisions, uncertain events, decision objectives, and calculation nodes.

Mathematical Programming: It is the study of optimisation problems where we seek to minimize or maximize a real function of real or integer variables, subject to constraints on the variables (defined by Mathematical Programming Society, 2001).

Supply Chain: It is a "network of facilities and distribution options that performs the functions of procurement of materials, transformation of these materials into intermediate and finished products, and the distribution of these finished products to customers" (Scheer, 1999).

The Disaster-Oriented Assessment of Urban Clusters for Locating Production Systems in China

Zhen Chen
Liverpool John Moores University, UK

Heng Li
The Hong Kong Polytechnic University, China

Qian Xu
Liverpool John Moores University, UK

Szu-Li Sun
The University of Reading, UK

INTRODUCTION

The choice of location is one of the most important decisions usually taken in the procedure of building any production system (Pavic & Babic, 1991). In order to solve the problem of location choice, Pavic and Babic indentified a group of location indicators, including basic location factors such as transportation costs, production costs, and duration of transport, and additional factors such as bottleneck time, building costs, infrastructure costs, labour costs, weather conditions, expansion possibility, and transportation possibilities. Based on these criteria, Pavic and Babic used the *preference ranking organisation method for enrichment evaluation* (PROMETHEE) method (Mattioli, 2005) to support decision making in location choice. However, there are two concerns about their study. The first concern is that whether those indicators are enough and appropriate in the location choice of production systems. In fact, they have lost some relevant important factors. For example, geographic and geological conditions; environmental pollution; climate change; industrial and technology policies; disaster containment; and emergency services are all necessary considerations before locating production systems. The second concern is that whether the PROMETHEE method is an appropriate approach to effectively and efficiently deal with problems in which structured hierarchies of indicators are used in modelling. In fact, researchers have begun to explore alternatives to overcome the weaknesses of the PROMETHEE method in multi-criteria decision making. For example, Macharis, Springael, De Brucker, and Verbeke (2004) discussed the strengths and weaknesses of the PROMETHEE method and recommended the integration of a number of useful features of the analytic hierarchy process (AHP) method (Saaty, 1980) into the PROMETHEE process; especially in regards to the design of the decision-making hierarchy (ordering of goals, sub-goals, dimensions, criteria, projects, etc.) and the determination of weights. Based on these two concerns, the authors think there are potentials in conducting operations research into the location choice problem by modelling the hierarchies or network of indicators.

There are many types of disasters such as natural disasters like earthquakes, tsunamis, volcanic eruptions, hurricanes, typhoons, tornadoes, floods, subsidence, rest fires, resource shortages, food and agriculture incidents, and so forth; technological disasters like chemical, biological, or radiological hazards, forest devastations, and cyber system disruptions, and so forth; and social disasters like infectious diseases, social chaos, economic crisis, terrorist attacks, and so forth (U.S. Department of Homeland Security [USDHS], 2004). All these natural and man-made disasters can bring widespread crucial destruction and distress to human beings natural or social environment (New Zealand Institute of Economic Research [NZIER], 2004; Redcross.org, 2005; United Nations Children's Fund [UNICEF], 2005). To protect human beings and the built environment from disaster strikes, the best way is to prepare ahead of time and to know what to do (Disaster Preparedness Office [DPO], 2005; Federal Emergency Management Agency [FEMA], 2005) by effective learning from post-disaster assessments (U.S. Agency for International Development [USAID], 1998). For example, the infrastructure risk management process highlights future strategies for managing risk to potable water, electric power, transportation, and other infrastructure systems threatened by earthquakes, tsunamis, landslides, severe storms, saboteurs, and various other hazards (Taylor & VanMarcke, 2005). In this regard, a major disaster-oriented assessment for the Great Lakes in the United States has been put forward (Changnon, 2004; H2ONotes, 2004), and the authors of this article believe it is also an effective approach to coping with any type of disaster due to tremendous natural and social variability. Regarding the location choice problem as mentioned previously, indicators used for major disaster-oriented assessment could actually provide a necessary complement in its modelling.

Based on all previous considerations, this article will focus on a multi-criteria decision-making model for the disaster-oriented assessment of urban clusters in order to facilitate the location choice of production systems in China. The decision-making model will be set up using analytic network process (ANP) method with regard to the disaster-oriented assessment of urban clusters. The significant contributions of this article include a set of criteria applied to the assessment of urban clusters in China, and an ANP model for the location selection of production systems in China. In order to improve the quality of decision making, the ANP model not only adopts commonly used indicators for location choice focusing on production management, but also adopts more indicators focusing on necessary multidisciplinary issues such as geographic and geological conditions; environmental pollution; industrial and technology policy; disaster containment and emergency services; and so forth. This article finally provides an experimental case study to demonstrate the usefulness of the ANP model. The evidence to be presented in this article includes the ANP model for selecting the most appropriate location for a production system; and an experimental case study to demonstrate the usefulness of the ANP model. It is concluded that the ANP is effective in decision-making support to find the most appropriate location for new production systems in China. As a pilot research, the ANP model described in this article needs further improvement based on collabrations from more experts as well as extrapolations from more historical data. It is the authors' expectation that practitioners can use the proposed ANP model to find ideal locations for their new production systems in China; moreover further improvement based on collabrations from more experts as well as extrapolations from historical data are also expected.

BACKGROUND

Currently, there have been about seven urban clusters in China, and these urban clusters are:

- Liaodong Peninsula, including Shenyang, Dalian, Anshan, Fushun, Benxi, Liaoyang, and so forth.
- Jing-Jin-Tang Region, including Beijing, Tianjin, Tangshan, Tanggu, and so forth;
- Shandong Peninsula, including Tsingtao, Jinan, Yantai, Weihai, Zibo, Weifang, and so forth;
- Yangtze River Delta, including Shanghai, Nanjing, Hangzhou, Suzhou, Wuxi, Changzhou, Ningbo, Nantong, and so forth;
- Minnan Region, including Fuzhou, Xiamen, Quanzhou, and so forth;
- South-West Region, including Chongqing, Chengdu, Mianyang, and so forth; and
- Pearl River Delta, including Hong Kong, Macao, Guangzhou, Shenzhen, Dongguan, Zhuhai, and so forth.

Among these urban clusters, Jing-Jin-Tang Region, Yangtze River Delta, and Pearl River Delta have been become the three most important urban clusters, which lead China to develop a more prosperous economy and to participate international economic competitions. Moreover, more and more wealth and economic activities will centripetally converge to urban clusters in China, especially to these three big urban clusters (Chinese Academy of Sciences [CAS], 2005). For example, the Pan-Bohai Bay Region is becaming a new urban cluster with the biggest territory in China (see Figure 1), which comprises Jing-Jin-Tang District, Liaodong Peninsula, and Shandong Peninsula.

Moreover, a new Yangtze River Economic Belt has become a confluence of two dominant cities (including

The Disaster-Oriented Assessment of Urban Clusters for Locating Production Systems in China

Shanghai and Chongqing) and seven provinces (including Jiangsu, Anhui, Jiangxi, Hubei, Hunan, Sichuan, and Yunnan) (see Figure 1). This Belt occupys 15% of the territory of China, owns 38% population of Chian, and contributes 46% gross domestic product (GDP) of China (CAS, 2005); and it is the biggest developable freshwater region in the world with large influence on Chinese economy.

Besides the concern about urban clusters in Chinese economic development, it has to concern some other relevant issues such as natural disasters too. In China, natural disasters usually happen and lead to huge damage and loss. According to the *2005 Report on Natural Disasters in China* (China MCA, 2006), there have been many natural disasters in 2005, including earthquakes, floods, snowstorm, typhoons, droughts, mud-rock flows, landslips, freezing injuries, and so forth. Among them, floods happened in the Pearl River valley, Huai River valley, Liao River valley, Min River valley, Yangtze River valley, and Yellow River valley. Moreover, there have been eight typhoons attacking the north and south coastal areas of China; and there have been 13 earthquakes above magnitude 5. In 2005, 2,475 people died and 2,264 buildings collapsed during these disasters in China; the direct economic loss is CNY204.21 billion (about USD25.3 billion). In order to deploy efficient response and to conduct effective management after natural disasters occur, the government of China has established a special department to make and to operate a series of national emergency response plans, including National Emergency Salvation Plan for Natural Disasters, and National Emergency Response Plan for Floods and Droughts (China GOV, 2006a, 2006b). Figures 2 and 3 provide general views into the risks of natural disasters such as earthquakes and floods in China. It is clear that the risks of natural disasters actually threaten urban clusters in China (see Table 1).

Based on the qualitative summary of the risks of potential natural disasters as provided in Table 1, there is not an urban cluster in China that has no or all low

Figure 1. The urban clusters outline map of China (CAS, 2005; Yeh & Xu, 1997)

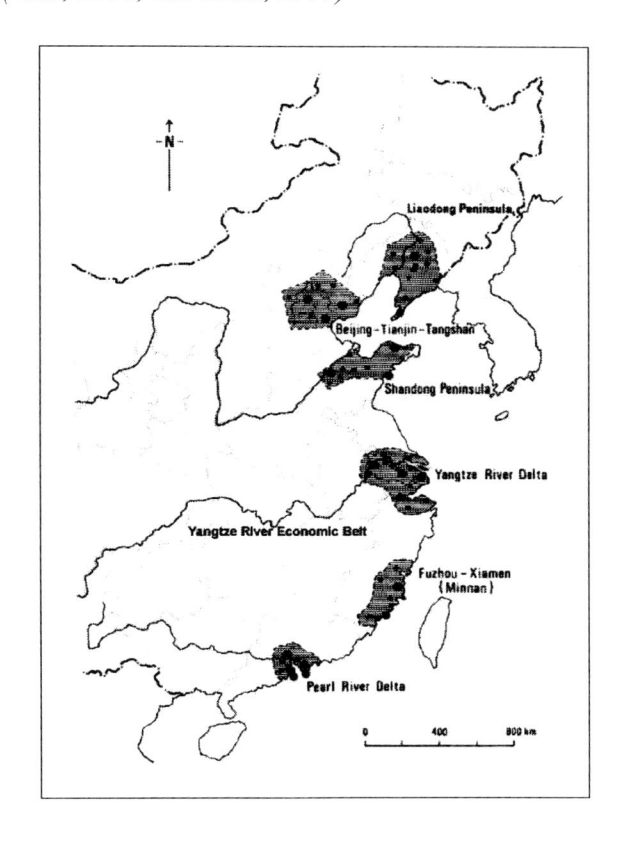

Figure 2. The seismic hazard map of East Asia

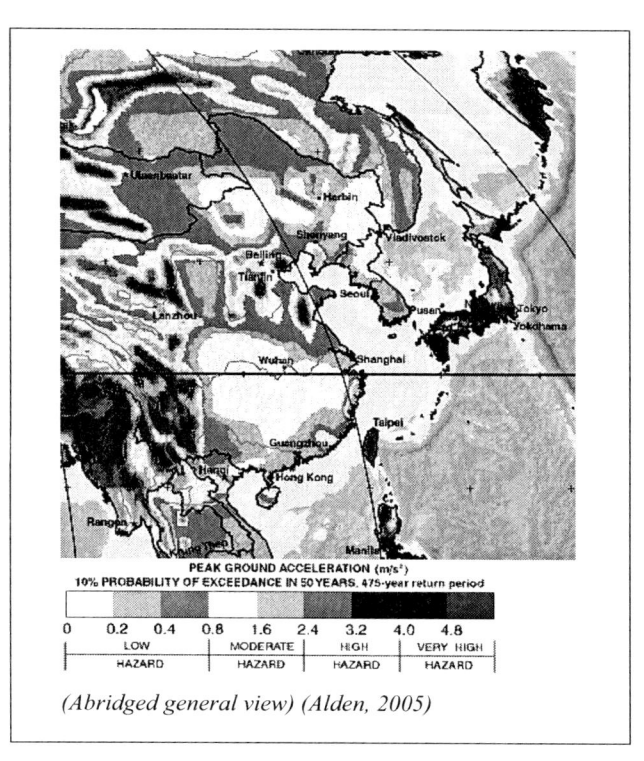

(Abridged general view) (Alden, 2005)

Table 1. The risks of natural disasters and urban clusters in China*

Urban clusters	The risks of potential natural disasters				
	Earthquake	Typhoon	Flood	Drought	Subsidence
Liaodong Peninsula	High	Low	Middle	Middle	Low
Jing-Jin-Tang Region	High	Low	High	High	Low
Shandong Peninsula	Middle	Middle	Middle	High	Low
Yangtze River Delta	Middle	High	High	Middle	High
Minnan Region	High	High	Low	Middle	Low
South-West Region	Low	Low	Low	Low	Low
Pearl River Delta	Low	High	Middle	Low	Low
Pan-Bohai Bay Region	High	Low	High	High	Low
Yangtze River Economic Belt	Middle	Low	High	Middle	Middle

*References: Alden, 2005; CAS, 2005; Wang & Plate, 2002; Yeh & Xu, 1997

Figure 3. Major rivers and areas of high flood risk in China

(Abridged general view) (Wang & Plate, 2002)

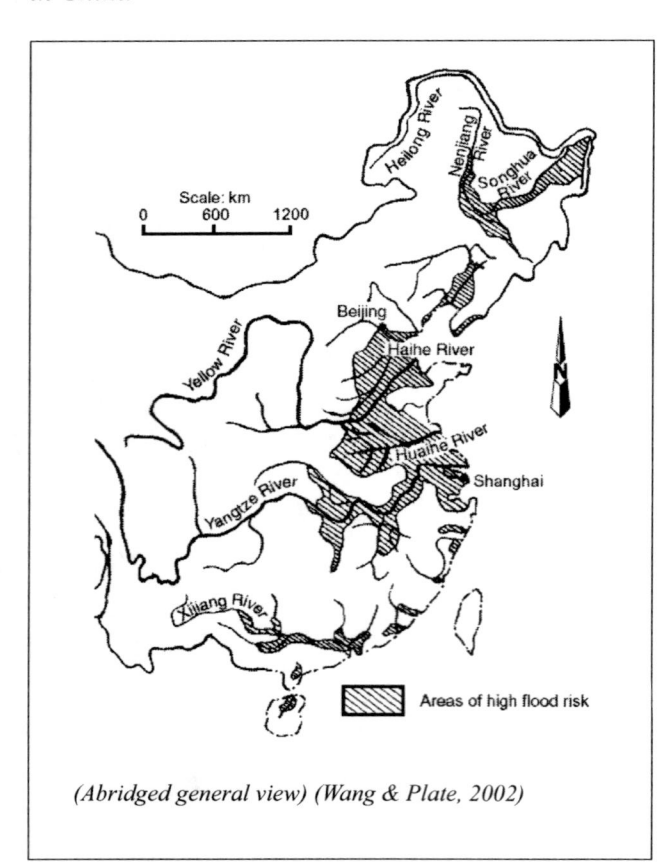

risks regarding potential natural disasters, including earthquake, typhoon, flood, drought, and subsidence. Although the authors have no intention to quantitatively describe these risks in this article, a quantitative measurement of the risks of natural disasters to the urban clusters in China is still constructive not only for urban development but also for locating production system. However, this section just provides background information about urban clusters and potential natural disasters in China, to pave the road to further descriptions and discussions of indicators and decision making for the location selection of production systems.

MAIN FOCUS

The Criteria for Assessment

To select the most appropriate location for a production system a set of reliable criteria is needed. Pavic and Babic (1991) gave two groups of criteria, including:

1. Basic criteria such as transportation costs, production costs, duration of transport, and so forth.
2. Additional criteria such as bottleneck time, building costs, infrastructure costs, labour costs, weather conditions, expansion possibility, transportation possibilities, and so forth.

Among these criteria, cost, time, and market are most important under general natural and social conditions; and many production systems have been located or relocated following these criteria in China. The Unilever N.V., a consumer goods producer, opened a new global production centre, that is, the Unilever Hefei Industrial Park, in Hefei (Asia Pulse, 2005), which is 600 km away from its original production centre in Shanghai. It is expected that the relocation of a production centre can reduce the total production cost by 30% (NF Editors, 2005). According to the annual *Survey Report on Investment Environment and Risks in Mainland China* conducted by Taiwan Electrical and Electronic Manufacturers' Association (TEEMA, 2005), investments to production systems in China have gradually flowed away from Shanghai and relocated in surrounding areas such as Xiaoshan, Kunshan, Jiangyin, Yangzhou, Nanchang, and so forth, or in north areas such as Shandong Peninsula and Jing-Jin-Tang Region. The direct reasons include the high cost of production and the shortage of energy supply, and so forth (Xie, 2006), which are leading to serious problems in sustainable development in some urban clusters such as Yangtze River Delta in China. However, as it is complex system engineering for decision makers to select the most appropriate locations for their production systems, these basic criteria and additional criteria as mention previously are not enough for making a good decision on location or relocation problems. Actually, concerns from other sectors such as insurance (Shen-Tu, Lai, & Guin, 2005) have suggested that risks of natural disasters such as typhoons, earthquakes and floods exist. In this regard, there are potential requirements to use a set of comprehensive criteria for assessing the conditions of any locating or relocating plans.

The Strategic Research Group of Sustainable Development from the CAS (2005) has developed an indicators system for evaluating the ability of urban development in China, which is the one of four urban

Table 2. The structure of the CAS urban development assessment system (CAS, 2005)

The 1st layer	The 2nd layer	The 3rd layer	No. of factors for the 4th layer
The ability of urban development	The index of urban strength	The amassment of resources	5
		The anount of economy	4
		The level of industrialisation	5
		The abilities of infrastructures	7
	The index of urban competition	The ability in creation and innovation	5
		The ability of learning	6
		The ability of intensivism	6
		The level of informationlisation	5
		The level of globalisation	7
	The index of urban society	The level of justice	5
		The level of insurance	6
		The level of advance	11
	The index of urban management	The level of efficiency	6
		The level of management	4
		The level of drive	4
	The index of urban sustainability	The level of ecological conditions	5
		The level of environmental quality	4
		The ability of harmony	5
		The ability of influence	3

Table 3. Indicators for assessing locations for production systems in China

The 1st layer (Clusters)	The 2nd layer (Indicators)	Criteria for the 3rd layer
Natural resources	Ecological diversity	Type, Area, Amount, Quality, etc.
	Minerals—Energy related	Type, Amount, Quality, Cost, etc.
	Minerals—Metallic	Type, Amount, Quality, Cost, etc.
	Minerals—Non-metallic	Type, Amount, Quality, Cost, etc.
Natural conditions	Climate conditions	Type, Curves, Probability, Forecast, etc.
	Geographic conditions	Location, Network, etc.
	Geological conditions	Stability, Probability, Forecast, etc.
	Environmental pollutions	Type, Degree, Sources, etc.
	Natural disasters	Type, Degree, Probability, Forecast, etc.
Social resources	Transportation	Type, Quality, Cost, etc.
	Water supply system	Type, Quality, Cost, etc.
	Energy supply	Type, Quality, Cost, etc.
	Real estates	Type, Quality, Amount, Cost, etc.
	Government services	Type, Amount, Quality, Cost, etc.
	Education services	Type, Quality, Location, etc.
	Human resources	Type, Quality, Amount, Cost, etc.
	Other business services	Type, Quality, Amount, Cost, etc.
Social conditions	Policy	Type, Coverage, Implementation, etc.
	Economy	Growth rate, Relevent industries, Consumers, etc.
	Shocks	Type, Degree, Probability, etc.

Note.
1. Energy-related minerals include oil, natural gas, coal, uranium, and so forth.
2. Metallic minerals include iron, manganese, copper, aluminum, lead, zinc, and so forth.
3. Non-metallic minerals include graphite, phosphorus, sulfur, sylvite, and so forth.
4. Social shocks include technological change; Change of economic agents' tastes; outbreaks of infectious diseases; war, terrorism, sabotage; technological risks such as chemical, biological, or radiological hazards, computer system disruptions; financial shocks (e.g., tightening of re-insurance markets); economic shocks (including shocks to world energy markets); and so forth.

development assessment systems and has advantages due to its integration of system theory and practical approach. There are four layers inside the CAS urban development assessment system, including general layer, system layer, condition layer, and factor layer. The assessment system has a structured hierarchy based on these layers and indicators; and the AHP approach (Saaty, 1980) is adopted to support final decision making. Table 2 gives the second and the third layers of the CAS urban development assessment system.

Further study on the CAS urban development assessment system reveals that, like the PROMETHEE model introduced by Pavic and Babic (1991), limitations exist in both indicators system and calculation method. For the indicators system, many essential factors, including geographic and geological conditions, the amount of environmental pollutions, industrial and technology policies, possibilities of various natural or social disasters, the ability of disasters containment, and so forth; however, these lost essential factors actually dominate the long-term development of urban clusters. On the other hand, there is no concern about interrelations between any two elements on the same layer. For example, users cannot define the relation between "The index of urban strength" and "The index of urban competition" on the second layer, or between "The amassment of resources" and "The ability of influence" on the third level. However, interrelationships actually exist there, and it will definitely decrease the possibility for decision makers to get more accurate results if they use this system. Therefore, it is necessary to further develop a new indicators system and to make an innovative calculation method for both location selection and urban clusters assessment problems.

Based on these analyses and the authors' understanding about relevant issues in China, Table 3 gives a group of indicators for the proposed ANP model, which is for selecting the most appropriate production system in China.

Experimental Case Study

Saaty (2005) introduced the ANP, which is a new generation of multi-criteria decision-making theory to replace the AHP. The ANP method is a general theory of relative measurement used to derive composite priority ratio scales from individual ratio scales that represent relative measurements of the influence of elements that interact with respect to control criteria. As mentioned by Saaty (2005), an ANP model consists of two main parts, including a network of interrelationships among each two nodes or clusters, and a control network of criteria or sub-criteria that controls interactions based on interdependencies and feedback. Here, nodes are indicators or criteria for model construction, while clusters are groups of indicators for classifying criteria. In order to conduct decision-making process, a control hierarchy is generally employed to build an ANP model. The control hierarchy is a hierarchy of criteria and sub-criteria for which priorities are derived in the usual way with respect to the goal of a system being considered. The criteria are used to compare the clusters of an ANP model, and the sub-criteria are used to compare the nodes inside a cluster. Regarding how to conduct location assessment by using ANP method, a four-step procedure is given:

- **Step A:** ANP model construction;
- **Step B:** Pairwise comparisons between each two clusters or nodes based on their interrelations;
- **Step C:** Supermatrix calculation based on results from paired comparisons; and
- **Step D:** Final assessment based on calculation result analysis.

The most significant advagtage of the ANP method than other multi-criteria decision-making methods such as the AHP method and the PROMETHEE model is that it makes it possible for decision makers to effectively measure interrelations among indicators. In this regard, this paper adopts the ANP mothod to make a multi-criteria decision-making model based on indicators for assessing locations for production systems in China.

ANP Model Construction

The objective of Step A is to build an ANP model for the location assessment of a production system. The ANP model is built based on determining the control hierarchies, as well as the corresponding criteria for comparing the clusters, including sub-clusters, of the model and sub-criteria for comparing the nodes inside each cluster and each sub-cluster, together with a determination of clusters and sub-clusters with their nodes for each control criteria or sub-criteria. Before finalising an ANP model, a set of indicators for the model construction has to be defined.

As the purpose of this article is to provide an alternative approach for evaluating locations for a proposed production system, the group of indicators summarised in Table 3 is directly used for the construction of ANP model. The goal of the ANP model is to select the most appropriate location from several alternative cities for a proposed production system in the process of evaluation. In accordance with the goal, Figure 4 gives an outline of the proposed ANP model.

It has to mention, Table 3 gives four groups of indicators at its first layer, including Natural resources, Natural conditions, Social resources, and Social conditions. In order to simplify the ANP model, Natural resources and Natural conditions are combined for one cluster, that is, the cluster of Natural indicators; and Social resources and Social conditions are combined for another cluster, that is, the cluster of Social indicators (see Figure 4). Therefore, there are two main clusters designed for the ANP model, including one Criteria cluster and one Alternative cluster (denoted as C_A). The Criteria cluster comprises two sub-network, that is, the cluster of Natural indicators (denoted as C_N) and the cluster of Social cluster (denoted as C_S). Inside these two sub-clusters, the cluster of Natural indicators consists of nine nodes (i.e., Indicator i (i=1,2,...,9)) in accordance with the nine indicators related to Natural resources and Natural conditions (see Table 3). In the mean while, the cluster of Social indicators consists of 11 nodes (i.e., Indicator j (j=1,2,...,11)) in accordance with the 11 indicators related to Social resources and

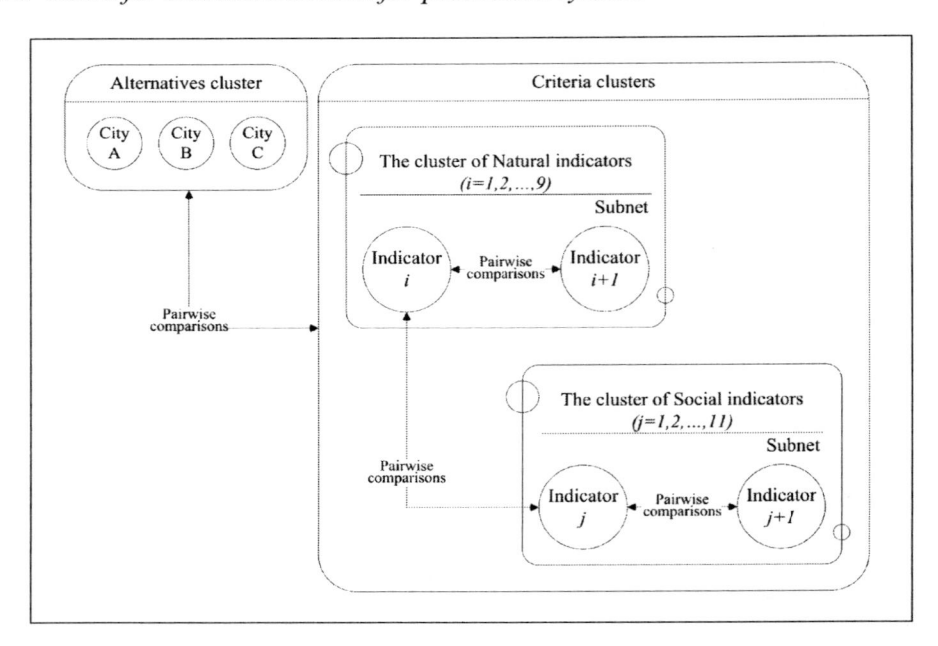

Figure 4. The ANP model for location selection for production systems

Social conditions (see Table 3). On the other hand, three anonymity urban clusters are selected from Table 1 for the cluster of Alternatives of the ANP model (see Figure 4), including City A, City B, and City C.

In accordance with these two main clusters and their total 23 nodes, the ANP model can thus be set up with interrelation connectivities between each two clusters and their nodes. Connections inside the two clusters finally generate a network with interrelations among clusters, subclusters, and nodes (refer to Table 6) including the Alternatives cluster (with three nodes), the Natural cluster (with nine nodes), and the Social cluster (with 11 nodes). The network connections are modelled by one-way or two-way and looped arrows to describe the interdependences existed between each two clusters or sub-clusters and each two nodes (see Figure 4).

Paired Comparisons

The objective of step B is to carry out pairwise comparisons among clusters and sub-clusters, as well as pairwise comparisons between each two nodes, because some indicators are actually interdependent on each other. The pairwise comparison is a quantitative description approach to interrelation connections illustrated in the ANP model (see Figure 4). In order to complete pairwise comparisons, the relative importance weight, denoted as a_{ij}, of interdependence is determined by using a scale of pairwise judgements, where the relative importance weight is valued from 1 to 9 (Saaty, 2005). Table 4 reproduces the fundamental scale of pairwise judgements generally applied in pairwise comparisons.

Pairwise comparisons have been modified in this research based on two considerations, including to maximise knowledge reuse for increasing benefits and to minimise knowledge retrieval for reducing time use. In this regards, the authors have paid further attentions to details in terms of how to reuse experts knowledge in ANP modelling. On the other hand, it is an effective way to ask experts to do pairwise comparisons for all pair indicators through in questionnaire survey; however, the pairwise comparison mechanism makes it very difficult to use on projects with large number of contractors and criteria (Kashiwagi, 2004). For example, there are 20 indicators selected by the authors to evaluate urban clusters in this research; and there will be hundreds of pairwise comparisons in setting up an ANP model. There should be no problem for research purpose, but it should be difficult to be accepted by practitioners.

Based on these considerations, a PairWiser tool is developed and it is presented in Table 4.

The PairWiser is a general tool to deal with problems with large amount pairwise comparison in ANP modelling. To use the tool, a specially designed questionnaire table, called the PairWiser Questionnaire Table is required to collect data from experts, which is regarded as knowledge retrieval; while the use a finalised ANP model for decision-making support is regarded as knowledge reuse. In this study, a two-page questionnaire table is adopted in a questionnaire survey, and it is presented in the Annex section. Delphi method (Turoff & Linstone, 2002) is recommended to collect experts' knowledge related to all indicators. To finally accumulate experts knowledge retrieved from the questionnaire survey, the PairWiser criteria (see the second column of Table 4) are used to input all data into the ANP model.

It has to be mentioned that the adoption of the PairWiser tool is to reduce burdens to experts in answering questionnaires, which allows them to pay attention to the importance rate of each indicator instead of boundless pairwise comparisons. On the other hand, there should be a person who deals with data input based on survey results. According to authors' experience, the use of PairWiser criteria has significantly accelerated the process of data input. In this regard, the PairWiser tool is adopted in this research.

Decision makers and a group of experts who are abreast with professional experience and relevant knowledge can use these scales for pairwise comparisons to determine the weight of interdependence. It is a process of knowledge acquisition. In this study, the authors determine this because the objective of this study is mainly to demonstrate the process and usefulness of the ANP model for location selection; in practice, the team of experts is required to make these comparisons. Table 5 gives some details for an experimental case study on location selection for a production center of consumer goods in China. Three anonymity urban clusters are selected from Table 1 as City candidate (see Figure 4), including City A, City B, and City C.

Table 6 gives a general form for pairwise judgement between each two nodes inside the ANP model. There are two types of pairwise judgements, one is the pairwise comparison between an indicator and a City candidate; and another is the pairwise comparison between two indicators. For example, for the node 1.9 Natural disasters (see Table 5), the pairwised judgements are given in Table 6. The results of pairwise judgements between 1.9 Natural disasters and each City candidate are for City C is 8, for City B is 6, and for City A is 4. Because an integrative review on the type, the degree, the probability, the forecast, and so forth about Natural disasters in these three cities re-

Table 4. Fundamental scale of pairwise judgment and PairWiser criteria

Scales of pair-wise judgment (Saaty, 2005)	Comparisons of pair indicator scores*
1= Equal	1:1
2= Equally to moderately dominant	2:1, 3:2, 4:3, 5:4, 6:5, 7:6, 8:7, 9:8
3= Moderately dominant	3:1, 4:2, 5:3, 6:4, 7:5, 8:6, 9:7
4= Moderately to strongly dominant	4:1, 5:2, 6:3, 7:4, 8:5, 9:6
5= Strongly dominant	5:1, 6:2, 7:3, 8:4, 9:5
6= Strongly to very strongly dominant	6:1, 7:2, 8:3, 9:4
7= Very strongly dominant	7:1, 8:2, 9:3
8= Very strongly to extremely dominant	8:1, 9:2
9= Extremely dominant	9:1

* Scores for indicators based on questionnaire survey; scales for scoring each indicator: 1=Not important, 2=Not to moderately important, 3=Moderately important, 4=Moderately to strongly important, 5=Strongly important, 6=Strongly to very strongly important, 7=Very strongly important, 8=Very strongly to extremely important, 9=Extremely important.

Table 5. A case details about indicators and their values for the ANP model

Clusters	Indicators	Scores of alternative locations*		
		City A	City B	City C
1 Natural cluster	1.1 Ecological diversity	60	65	70
	1.2 Minerals—Energy-related	35	50	50
	1.3 Minerals—Metallic	75	60	50
	1.4 Minerals—Non-metallic	80	30	50
	1.5 Climate conditions	65	70	75
	1.6 Geographic conditions	75	80	90
	1.7 Geological conditions	80	85	90
	1.8 Environmental pollutions	50	50	50
	1.9 Natural disasters	70	75	80
2 Social cluster	2.1 Transportation	85	90	90
	2.2 Water supply system	60	70	80
	2.3 Energy supply	70	70	85
	2.4 Real estate	80	85	80
	2.5 Government services	80	90	95
	2.6 Education services	80	85	95
	2.7 Human resources	75	85	90
	2.8 Other business services	70	80	95
	2.9 Policy	90	90	95
	2.10 Economy	70	75	90
	2.11 Shocks	80	85	90

* The criteria for scoring each indicator is a scale from 0 to 100, which means for each indicator, the score of City X is x ($x \in [0, 100]$). Each expert gives the score subjectively depending on facts and his/her knowledge.

Table 6. Pairwise judgements of indicator I_i (1.9 natural disasters) and I_j (2.11 shocks)

Pairwise judgements		1	2	3	4	5	6	7	8	9
Indicator I_i	City A	×	×	×	✓	×	×	×	×	×
	City B	×	×	×	×	×	✓	×	×	×
	City C	×	×	×	×	×	×	×	✓	×
Indicator I_i	Indicator I_j	×	×	×	×	×	×	✓	×	×

Note.
1. The fundamental scale of pairwise judgement is given in Table 4.
2. The symbol × denotes item under selection for pairwise judgement, and the symbol ✓ denotes selected pairwise judgement.

The Disaster-Oriented Assessment of Urban Clusters for Locating Production Systems in China

Table 7. Formulation of supermatrix and its sub-matrix for the ANP model

General format of supermatrix A	General format of submatrix
$W = \begin{bmatrix} W_{1,1} & W_{1,2} & W_{1,3} \\ W_{2,1} & W_{2,2} & W_{2,3} \\ W_{3,1} & W_{3,2} & W_{3,3} \end{bmatrix}$ $C_i = (C_A \quad C_N \quad C_S)$ $N_i = (N_A^2 \quad N_N^9 \quad N_S^{11})$	$W_{I,J} = \begin{bmatrix} w_1\|_{I,J} & \cdots & w_1\|_{I,J} \\ w_2\|_{I,J} & \cdots & w_2\|_{I,J} \\ \cdots & \cdots & \cdots \\ w_i\|_{I,J} & \cdots & w_i\|_{I,J} \\ \cdots & \cdots & \cdots \\ w_{N_{I_1}}\|_{I,J} & \cdots & w_{N_{I_n}}\|_{I,J} \end{bmatrix}$

Note. I is the index number of rows; and J is the index number of columns; both I and J correspond to the number of cluster and their nodes ($I, J \in (1, 2, \ldots, 23)$), N_I is the total number of nodes in cluster I, n is the total number of columns in cluster I. Thus a 23×23 supermatrix is formed.

veal that City A is in the inferior position, City B is in the middle, and City C is in the superior position (see Table 5 and Table 6). Therefore, quantitative pairwise judgements can be conducted to define priorities of each indicator for each City candidate, and the judgements are based on the quantitative attribute of each indicator from each City candidate (refer to Table 5). Besides the pairwise judgement between an indicator and a City candidate, the ANP model also contains all other pairwise judgements between any pair of indicators. For example, Indicator I_i (1.9 Natural disasters, as a representative) is *very strongly dominant* to Indicator I_j (2.11 Shocks, as a representative); therefore the judgement value equals 7 (as shown in Table 6). As a result, the essential initialisation for ANP modelling is set up based on the quantitative attribute (as described in Table 5) of indicators for each City candidate and inherent characteristics of each indicators.

Supermatrix Calculation

This step aims to form a synthesised supermatrix to allow for a resolution based on the effects of the interdependences that exist between the elements (including nodes, subclusters, and clusters) of the ANP model. The supermatrix is a two-dimensional partitioned matrix consisted of one nine submatrices (refer to Table 7).

Weights defined from pairwise judgements for all interdependences for each individual City candidate are then aggregated into a series of submatrices. For example, if the Alternatives cluster and its nodes are connected to nodes in the Natural cluster (denoted as C_N), pairwise judgements of the cluster thus result in relative weights of importance between each City candidate and each indicator inside the Natural cluster. The aggregation of the determined weights thus forms a 3×9 sub-matrix located at "W_{12}" and "W_{21}" in Table 7. It is necessary to note that pairwise comparisons are necessary to all connections among each node subcluster and cluster in the model, wherever interrelations exist, so as to identify the level of interdependences, which are fundamental in the ANP procedure. Upon the completion of pairwise judgements, a total of nine submatrices are then aggregated into a supermatrix, which is denoted to supermatrix A in this study (refer to Table 7). In addition, it is then used to derive the initial supermatrix in the later calculation in Step C, and the calculation of the ANP model can thus be conducted following Step C to D.

In order to obtain useful information for location assessment, the calculation of supermatrix is to be conducted following three sub-steps, which transform an initial supermatrix to a weighted supermatrix, and then to a synthesised supermatrix.

At first, an initial supermatrix of the ANP model is created. The initial supermatrix consists of local priority vectors obtained from the pairwise comparisons among clusters and nodes. A local priority vector is an array of weight priorities containing a single column (denoted as $w^T = (w_1, \ldots, w_i, \ldots, w_n)$), whose components (denoted as w_i) are derived from a judgment comparison matrix A and deduced by Equation 1 (Saaty, 2005).

$$w_i\big|_{I,J} = \sum_{i=1}^{I}\left(a_{ij}\bigg/\sum_{j=1}^{J}a_{ij}\right)\bigg/J \qquad (1)$$

where $w_i\big|_{I,J}$ is the weighted/derived priority of node i at row I and column J; a_{ij} is a matrix value assigned to the interdependence relationship of node i to node j. The initial supermatrix is constructed by substituting the submatrices into the supermatrix as indicated in Table 7. A detailed initial supermatrix, that is, unweighted supermatrix is given in Table 8.

After creating the initial supermatrix, a weighted supermatrix is therefore transformed (refer to Table 9). This process is to multiply all nodes in a cluster of the initial supermatrix by the weight of the cluster, which has been established by pairwise comparison among clusters using PairWiser tool. In the weighted supermatrix, each column is stochastic, that is, sum of the column amounts to 1 (Saaty, 2005).

The last substep of supermatrix calculation is to compose a limiting supermatrix, which is to raise the weighted supermatrix to powers until it converges or stabilises when all the columns in the supermatrix have the same values. Saaty (2005) indicated that as long as the weighted supermatrix is stochastic, a meaningful limiting result could then be obtained for prediction. The approach to getting a limiting supermatrix is to take repeatedly the power of the matrix, that is, the original weighted supermatrix, its square, its cube, and so forth, until the limit is attained, in which case the numbers in each row will all become identical. A calculus type algorithm is employed in the software environment of Super Decisions by Bill Adams and the Creative Decision Foundation to facilitate the formation of the limiting supermatrix and the calculation result is given in Table 10. As the limiting supermatrix is set up, the following step is to select a proper plan alternative using results from the limiting supermatrix.

Location Selection

This step aims to select the most appropriate location, that is, City candidate based on the computation results from the limiting supermatrix of the ANP model. The main results from ANP computations are the overall priorities of each City candidate, which can be obtained by synthesising the priorities of an individual City candidate against different indicators. The selection of the most appropriate City candidate, which should have the highest priority of locating a production system, is conducted by a limiting priority weight using Equation 2.

$$W_i = \frac{w_{C_{city},i}}{w_{C_{city}}} = \frac{w_{C_{city},i}}{\sum_i w_{C_{city},i}} \qquad (2)$$

where W_i is the synthesised priority weight of City candidate i ($i=1,\ldots, n$) (n is the total number of City candidates, $n=3$ in this paper), and $w_{C_{city},i}$ is the limited weight of City candidate i in the limiting supermatrix. Because the $w_{C_{city},i}$ is transformed from pairwise judgements conducted in Step B, it is reasonable to be treated as the priority of City candidate i and thus to be used in Equation 2. According to the computation results in the limiting supermatrix, $w_{C_{city},i}$ = (0.1495, 0.1145, 0.0432), so the W_i= (0.49, 0.37, 0.14), as a result, the most appropriate location is City A (refer to Table 11).

According to the attributes of each City candidate (see Table 5), the comparison results using W_i also implies that the most preferable location is the candidate that has better integrative natural and social conditions. This indicates that the ANP model provides a quite logical comparison result for the aim of a sense of emotional and physical well-being of people and lifespan energy efficiency of IBs and thus can be applied into practice.

The Disaster-Oriented Assessment of Urban Clusters for Locating Production Systems in China

Table 8. The unweighted super matrix of the ANP model

```
       1       2       3       1       2       3       4       5       6       7       8       9       1       2       3       4
       5       6       7       8       9      10      11
  1  0.00000 0.50000 0.50000 0.72222 0.72222 0.70588 0.60000 0.50000 0.71429 0.61538 0.75000 0.50000 0.78723 0.50000
     0.50000 0.50000 0.50000 0.50000 0.50000 0.50000 0.50000 0.50000 0.50000
  2  0.50000 0.00000 0.50000 0.27778 0.27778 0.29412 0.40000 0.50000 0.28571 0.38461 0.25000 0.50000 0.21277 0.50000
     0.50000 0.50000 0.50000 0.50000 0.50000 0.50000 0.50000 0.50000 0.50000
  3  0.50000 0.50000 0.00000 0.00000 0.00000 0.00000 0.00000 0.00000 0.00000 0.00000 0.00000 0.00000 0.00000 0.00000
     0.00000 0.00000 0.00000 0.00000 0.00000 0.00000 0.00000 0.00000 0.00000

  1  0.19962 0.21875 0.22398 0.00000 0.07736 0.21250 0.13679 0.10773 0.16331 0.12518 0.16342 0.22950 0.28289 0.11111
     0.11111 0.11111 0.11111 0.11111 0.11111 0.11111 0.11111 0.11111 0.11111
  2  0.12288 0.13441 0.12994 0.05852 0.00000 0.04452 0.03383 0.04592 0.05907 0.07632 0.03703 0.02414 0.09435 0.11111
     0.11111 0.11111 0.11111 0.11111 0.11111 0.11111 0.11111 0.11111 0.11111
  3  0.13349 0.11056 0.05612 0.16562 0.14251 0.00000 0.04972 0.09911 0.06321 0.14017 0.02679 0.02518 0.09435 0.11111
     0.11111 0.11111 0.11111 0.11111 0.11111 0.11111 0.11111 0.11111 0.11111
  4  0.09145 0.10523 0.06293 0.10163 0.07558 0.10694 0.00000 0.09420 0.18431 0.02553 0.07442 0.13755 0.09435 0.11111
     0.11111 0.11111 0.11111 0.11111 0.11111 0.11111 0.11111 0.11111 0.11111
  5  0.04348 0.04510 0.05361 0.01826 0.07761 0.03533 0.01541 0.00000 0.01317 0.18894 0.14258 0.15744 0.09435 0.11111
     0.11111 0.11111 0.11111 0.11111 0.11111 0.11111 0.11111 0.11111 0.11111
  6  0.03643 0.03515 0.03781 0.08458 0.02964 0.05285 0.28789 0.06572 0.00000 0.05423 0.10434 0.13705 0.05664 0.11111
     0.11111 0.11111 0.11111 0.11111 0.11111 0.11111 0.11111 0.11111 0.11111
  7  0.02407 0.02188 0.02176 0.08659 0.29212 0.33049 0.09000 0.22051 0.05404 0.00000 0.06551 0.02566 0.09435 0.11111
     0.11111 0.11111 0.11111 0.11111 0.11111 0.11111 0.11111 0.11111 0.11111
  8  0.01453 0.01341 0.01252 0.13220 0.02636 0.03172 0.05066 0.06104 0.13412 0.03376 0.00000 0.26350 0.09435 0.11111
     0.11111 0.11111 0.11111 0.11111 0.11111 0.11111 0.11111 0.11111 0.11111
  9  0.33406 0.31552 0.40133 0.35259 0.27884 0.18566 0.33571 0.30577 0.32877 0.35587 0.38592 0.00000 0.09435 0.11111
     0.11111 0.11111 0.11111 0.11111 0.11111 0.11111 0.11111 0.11111 0.11111

  1  0.30656 0.32464 0.31164 0.01771 0.14288 0.13363 0.15650 0.10954 0.12080 0.26345 0.23377 0.16116 0.00000 0.10000
     0.10000 0.10000 0.10000 0.10000 0.10000 0.10000 0.10000 0.10000 0.10000
  2  0.16852 0.20167 0.21604 0.15896 0.07672 0.09280 0.08143 0.12246 0.10293 0.16640 0.01114 0.11672 0.10000 0.00000
     0.10000 0.10000 0.10000 0.10000 0.10000 0.10000 0.10000 0.10000 0.10000
  3  0.16431 0.14318 0.16186 0.08110 0.11765 0.13527 0.04567 0.08399 0.10598 0.15891 0.15482 0.10261 0.10000 0.10000
     0.00000 0.10000 0.10000 0.10000 0.10000 0.10000 0.10000 0.10000 0.10000
  4  0.12528 0.11951 0.10002 0.06443 0.13858 0.09617 0.09023 0.18223 0.09241 0.10908 0.04251 0.17703 0.10000 0.10000
     0.10000 0.00000 0.10000 0.10000 0.10000 0.10000 0.10000 0.10000 0.10000
  5  0.07725 0.07269 0.07463 0.13854 0.04415 0.15207 0.10296 0.10513 0.09182 0.10209 0.08214 0.06321 0.10000 0.10000
     0.10000 0.10000 0.00000 0.10000 0.10000 0.10000 0.10000 0.10000 0.10000
  6  0.04929 0.04570 0.04976 0.03187 0.08994 0.11809 0.08688 0.06272 0.06524 0.06409 0.07446 0.06321 0.10000 0.10000
     0.10000 0.10000 0.10000 0.00000 0.10000 0.10000 0.10000 0.10000 0.10000
  7  0.03930 0.03489 0.03111 0.05663 0.10066 0.07605 0.12095 0.07171 0.09058 0.04873 0.10368 0.06321 0.10000 0.10000
     0.10000 0.10000 0.10000 0.10000 0.00000 0.10000 0.10000 0.10000 0.10000
  8  0.02558 0.02230 0.02282 0.05163 0.11296 0.06021 0.12996 0.08620 0.12367 0.03038 0.04301 0.06321 0.10000 0.10000
     0.10000 0.10000 0.10000 0.10000 0.10000 0.00000 0.10000 0.10000 0.10000
  9  0.02085 0.01663 0.01521 0.22296 0.05494 0.02167 0.05572 0.06854 0.05720 0.02746 0.16431 0.06321 0.10000 0.10000
     0.10000 0.10000 0.10000 0.10000 0.10000 0.10000 0.00000 0.10000 0.10000
 10  0.01357 0.01100 0.01014 0.14439 0.04932 0.03994 0.05117 0.05215 0.05929 0.01777 0.05181 0.06321 0.10000 0.10000
     0.10000 0.10000 0.10000 0.10000 0.10000 0.10000 0.10000 0.00000 0.10000
 11  0.00949 0.00781 0.00676 0.03178 0.07221 0.07411 0.07853 0.05531 0.09007 0.01162 0.03835 0.06321 0.10000 0.10000
     0.10000 0.10000 0.10000 0.10000 0.10000 0.10000 0.10000 0.10000 0.00000
```

Table 9. The weighted super matrix of the ANP model

	1	2	3	1	2	3	4	5	6	7	8	9	1	2	3	4	5	6	7	8	9	10	11
1	0.00000	0.16374	0.16374	0.20291	0.20291	0.19832	0.16858	0.14048	0.20068	0.17290	0.21072	0.14048	0.25780	0.16374	0.16374	0.16374	0.16374	0.16374	0.16374	0.16374	0.16374	0.16374	0.16374
2	0.16374	0.00000	0.16374	0.07804	0.07804	0.08264	0.11238	0.14048	0.08027	0.10806	0.07024	0.14048	0.06968	0.16374	0.16374	0.16374	0.16374	0.16374	0.16374	0.16374	0.16374	0.16374	0.16374
3	0.16374	0.16374	0.00000	0.00000	0.00000	0.00000	0.00000	0.00000	0.00000	0.00000	0.00000	0.00000	0.00000	0.00000	0.00000	0.00000	0.00000	0.00000	0.00000	0.00000	0.00000	0.00000	0.00000
1	0.08236	0.09026	0.09242	0.00000	0.03588	0.09856	0.06344	0.04997	0.07574	0.05806	0.07579	0.10644	0.11672	0.04584	0.04584	0.04584	0.04584	0.04584	0.04584	0.04584	0.04584	0.04584	0.04584
2	0.05070	0.05546	0.05361	0.02714	0.00000	0.02065	0.01569	0.02130	0.02740	0.03540	0.01717	0.01120	0.03893	0.04584	0.04584	0.04584	0.04584	0.04584	0.04584	0.04584	0.04584	0.04584	0.04584
3	0.05508	0.04562	0.02315	0.07682	0.06610	0.00000	0.02306	0.04597	0.02932	0.06501	0.01243	0.01168	0.03893	0.04584	0.04584	0.04584	0.04584	0.04584	0.04584	0.04584	0.04584	0.04584	0.04584
4	0.03773	0.04342	0.02597	0.04714	0.03505	0.04960	0.00000	0.04369	0.08548	0.01184	0.03452	0.06380	0.03893	0.04584	0.04584	0.04584	0.04584	0.04584	0.04584	0.04584	0.04584	0.04584	0.04584
5	0.01794	0.01861	0.02212	0.00847	0.03600	0.01639	0.00715	0.00000	0.00611	0.08763	0.06613	0.07302	0.03893	0.04584	0.04584	0.04584	0.04584	0.04584	0.04584	0.04584	0.04584	0.04584	0.04584
6	0.01503	0.01450	0.01560	0.03923	0.01375	0.02451	0.13353	0.03048	0.00000	0.02515	0.04839	0.06356	0.02337	0.04584	0.04584	0.04584	0.04584	0.04584	0.04584	0.04584	0.04584	0.04584	0.04584
7	0.00993	0.00903	0.00898	0.04016	0.13549	0.15328	0.04174	0.10227	0.02506	0.00000	0.03038	0.01190	0.03893	0.04584	0.04584	0.04584	0.04584	0.04584	0.04584	0.04584	0.04584	0.04584	0.04584
8	0.00599	0.00553	0.00517	0.06132	0.01222	0.01471	0.02349	0.02831	0.06221	0.01566	0.00000	0.12221	0.03893	0.04584	0.04584	0.04584	0.04584	0.04584	0.04584	0.04584	0.04584	0.04584	0.04584
9	0.13784	0.13019	0.16559	0.16353	0.12933	0.08611	0.15570	0.14182	0.15249	0.16505	0.17899	0.00000	0.03893	0.04584	0.04584	0.04584	0.04584	0.04584	0.04584	0.04584	0.04584	0.04584	0.04584
1	0.07968	0.08438	0.08100	0.00452	0.03647	0.03411	0.03994	0.02796	0.03083	0.06724	0.05967	0.04113	0.00000	0.02599	0.02599	0.02599	0.02599	0.02599	0.02599	0.02599	0.02599	0.02599	0.02599
2	0.04380	0.05242	0.05615	0.04057	0.01958	0.02369	0.02079	0.03126	0.02627	0.04247	0.00284	0.02979	0.02599	0.00000	0.02599	0.02599	0.02599	0.02599	0.02599	0.02599	0.02599	0.02599	0.02599
3	0.04271	0.03722	0.04207	0.02070	0.03003	0.03453	0.01166	0.02144	0.02705	0.04056	0.03952	0.02619	0.02599	0.02599	0.00000	0.02599	0.02599	0.02599	0.02599	0.02599	0.02599	0.02599	0.02599
4	0.03256	0.03106	0.02600	0.01645	0.03537	0.02455	0.02303	0.04651	0.02359	0.02784	0.01085	0.04519	0.02599	0.02599	0.02599	0.00000	0.02599	0.02599	0.02599	0.02599	0.02599	0.02599	0.02599
5	0.02008	0.01889	0.01940	0.03536	0.01127	0.03881	0.02628	0.02683	0.02344	0.02606	0.02096	0.01613	0.02599	0.02599	0.02599	0.02599	0.00000	0.02599	0.02599	0.02599	0.02599	0.02599	0.02599
6	0.01281	0.01188	0.01293	0.00813	0.02296	0.03014	0.02218	0.01601	0.01665	0.01636	0.01900	0.01613	0.02599	0.02599	0.02599	0.02599	0.02599	0.00000	0.02599	0.02599	0.02599	0.02599	0.02599
7	0.01022	0.00907	0.00809	0.01445	0.02569	0.01941	0.03087	0.01830	0.02312	0.01244	0.02646	0.01613	0.02599	0.02599	0.02599	0.02599	0.02599	0.02599	0.00000	0.02599	0.02599	0.02599	0.02599
8	0.00665	0.00580	0.00593	0.01318	0.02883	0.01537	0.03317	0.02200	0.03157	0.00775	0.01098	0.01613	0.02599	0.02599	0.02599	0.02599	0.02599	0.02599	0.02599	0.00000	0.02599	0.02599	0.02599
9	0.00542	0.00432	0.00396	0.05691	0.01402	0.00553	0.01422	0.01750	0.01460	0.00701	0.04194	0.01613	0.02599	0.02599	0.02599	0.02599	0.02599	0.02599	0.02599	0.02599	0.00000	0.02599	0.02599
10	0.00353	0.00286	0.00264	0.03685	0.01259	0.01019	0.01306	0.01331	0.01513	0.00454	0.01322	0.01613	0.02599	0.02599	0.02599	0.02599	0.02599	0.02599	0.02599	0.02599	0.02599	0.00000	0.02599
11	0.00247	0.00203	0.00176	0.00811	0.01843	0.01892	0.02005	0.01412	0.02299	0.00297	0.00979	0.01613	0.02599	0.02599	0.02599	0.02599	0.02599	0.02599	0.02599	0.02599	0.02599	0.02599	0.00000

Table 10. The limit matrix of the ANP model

	1	2	3	1	2	3	4	5	6	7	8	9	1	2	3	4	5	6	7	8	9	10	11
1	0.14955	0.14955	0.14955	0.14955	0.14955	0.14955	0.14955	0.14955	0.14955	0.14955	0.14955	0.14955	0.14955	0.14955	0.14955	0.14955	0.14955	0.14955	0.14955	0.14955	0.14955	0.14955	0.14955
2	0.11447	0.11447	0.11447	0.11447	0.11447	0.11447	0.11447	0.11447	0.11447	0.11447	0.11447	0.11447	0.11447	0.11447	0.11447	0.11447	0.11447	0.11447	0.11447	0.11447	0.11447	0.11447	0.11447
3	0.04323	0.04323	0.04323	0.04323	0.04323	0.04323	0.04323	0.04323	0.04323	0.04323	0.04323	0.04323	0.04323	0.04323	0.04323	0.04323	0.04323	0.04323	0.04323	0.04323	0.04323	0.04323	0.04323
1	0.07002	0.07002	0.07002	0.07002	0.07002	0.07002	0.07002	0.07002	0.07002	0.07002	0.07002	0.07002	0.07002	0.07002	0.07002	0.07002	0.07002	0.07002	0.07002	0.07002	0.07002	0.07002	0.07002
2	0.03594	0.03594	0.03594	0.03594	0.03594	0.03594	0.03594	0.03594	0.03594	0.03594	0.03594	0.03594	0.03594	0.03594	0.03594	0.03594	0.03594	0.03594	0.03594	0.03594	0.03594	0.03594	0.03594
3	0.04133	0.04133	0.04133	0.04133	0.04133	0.04133	0.04133	0.04133	0.04133	0.04133	0.04133	0.04133	0.04133	0.04133	0.04133	0.04133	0.04133	0.04133	0.04133	0.04133	0.04133	0.04133	0.04133
4	0.04261	0.04261	0.04261	0.04261	0.04261	0.04261	0.04261	0.04261	0.04261	0.04261	0.04261	0.04261	0.04261	0.04261	0.04261	0.04261	0.04261	0.04261	0.04261	0.04261	0.04261	0.04261	0.04261
5	0.03349	0.03349	0.03349	0.03349	0.03349	0.03349	0.03349	0.03349	0.03349	0.03349	0.03349	0.03349	0.03349	0.03349	0.03349	0.03349	0.03349	0.03349	0.03349	0.03349	0.03349	0.03349	0.03349
6	0.03555	0.03555	0.03555	0.03555	0.03555	0.03555	0.03555	0.03555	0.03555	0.03555	0.03555	0.03555	0.03555	0.03555	0.03555	0.03555	0.03555	0.03555	0.03555	0.03555	0.03555	0.03555	0.03555
7	0.03684	0.03684	0.03684	0.03684	0.03684	0.03684	0.03684	0.03684	0.03684	0.03684	0.03684	0.03684	0.03684	0.03684	0.03684	0.03684	0.03684	0.03684	0.03684	0.03684	0.03684	0.03684	0.03684
8	0.03594	0.03594	0.03594	0.03594	0.03594	0.03594	0.03594	0.03594	0.03594	0.03594	0.03594	0.03594	0.03594	0.03594	0.03594	0.03594	0.03594	0.03594	0.03594	0.03594	0.03594	0.03594	0.03594
9	0.10315	0.10315	0.10315	0.10315	0.10315	0.10315	0.10315	0.10315	0.10315	0.10315	0.10315	0.10315	0.10315	0.10315	0.10315	0.10315	0.10315	0.10315	0.10315	0.10315	0.10315	0.10315	0.10315
1	0.04621	0.04621	0.04621	0.04621	0.04621	0.04621	0.04621	0.04621	0.04621	0.04621	0.04621	0.04621	0.04621	0.04621	0.04621	0.04621	0.04621	0.04621	0.04621	0.04621	0.04621	0.04621	0.04621
2	0.03295	0.03295	0.03295	0.03295	0.03295	0.03295	0.03295	0.03295	0.03295	0.03295	0.03295	0.03295	0.03295	0.03295	0.03295	0.03295	0.03295	0.03295	0.03295	0.03295	0.03295	0.03295	0.03295
3	0.03013	0.03013	0.03013	0.03013	0.03013	0.03013	0.03013	0.03013	0.03013	0.03013	0.03013	0.03013	0.03013	0.03013	0.03013	0.03013	0.03013	0.03013	0.03013	0.03013	0.03013	0.03013	0.03013
4	0.02841	0.02841	0.02841	0.02841	0.02841	0.02841	0.02841	0.02841	0.02841	0.02841	0.02841	0.02841	0.02841	0.02841	0.02841	0.02841	0.02841	0.02841	0.02841	0.02841	0.02841	0.02841	0.02841
5	0.02283	0.02283	0.02283	0.02283	0.02283	0.02283	0.02283	0.02283	0.02283	0.02283	0.02283	0.02283	0.02283	0.02283	0.02283	0.02283	0.02283	0.02283	0.02283	0.02283	0.02283	0.02283	0.02283
6	0.01774	0.01774	0.01774	0.01774	0.01774	0.01774	0.01774	0.01774	0.01774	0.01774	0.01774	0.01774	0.01774	0.01774	0.01774	0.01774	0.01774	0.01774	0.01774	0.01774	0.01774	0.01774	0.01774
7	0.01772	0.01772	0.01772	0.01772	0.01772	0.01772	0.01772	0.01772	0.01772	0.01772	0.01772	0.01772	0.01772	0.01772	0.01772	0.01772	0.01772	0.01772	0.01772	0.01772	0.01772	0.01772	0.01772
8	0.01640	0.01640	0.01640	0.01640	0.01640	0.01640	0.01640	0.01640	0.01640	0.01640	0.01640	0.01640	0.01640	0.01640	0.01640	0.01640	0.01640	0.01640	0.01640	0.01640	0.01640	0.01640	0.01640
9	0.01758	0.01758	0.01758	0.01758	0.01758	0.01758	0.01758	0.01758	0.01758	0.01758	0.01758	0.01758	0.01758	0.01758	0.01758	0.01758	0.01758	0.01758	0.01758	0.01758	0.01758	0.01758	0.01758
10	0.01459	0.01459	0.01459	0.01459	0.01459	0.01459	0.01459	0.01459	0.01459	0.01459	0.01459	0.01459	0.01459	0.01459	0.01459	0.01459	0.01459	0.01459	0.01459	0.01459	0.01459	0.01459	0.01459
11	0.01332	0.01332	0.01332	0.01332	0.01332	0.01332	0.01332	0.01332	0.01332	0.01332	0.01332	0.01332	0.01332	0.01332	0.01332	0.01332	0.01332	0.01332	0.01332	0.01332	0.01332	0.01332	0.01332

Table 11. Selection of the most appropriate location

Model	No. of indivators	No. of alternatives	Synthesised priority weight W_i City A	City B	City C	Selection
ANP	20	3	0.49	0.37	0.14	City A

CONCLUSION

This article presents an ANP model for the disaster-oriented assessment of urban clusters in order to facilitate the location choice of production systems in China. A group of indicators focusing on natural and social conditions in China has been collected for the ANP model. Comparing with other relevant assessment systems such as the PROMETHEE model (Pavic & Babic, 1991) and CAS urban development assessment system (CAS, 2005), the proposed ANP model has a comprehensive group of criteria for location assessment. The experimental case study indicates that the ANP model is effective in assisting decision makers to find the most appropriate locations for their proposed production systems. As an exploiture of applying the ANP method to find the most appropriate location for new production systems in China, this article shows a practical procedure of how to adopt ANP to get final decision support. In order to apply the ANP model into practice, this article recommends the following steps:

1. Assess each City candidate on all indicators using Table 5.
2. Make pairwise comparisons among all indicators using Table 4 and Table 6.
3. Calculate supermatrix calculation to transform an initial supermatrix to a limiting supermatrix.
4. Calculate each limiting priority weight of City candidates using limiting supermatrix.
5. Select City candidate using Table 11.
6. If it is not satisfied, adjust the original plan and re-evaluate by repeating the previous procedure.

Finally, as a pilot research, the ANP model described in this article needs further improvement based on collabrations from more experts as well as extrapolations from more historical data. Moreover, real case studies are required to further test the ANP model.

REFERENCES

Alden, A. (2005). *Seismic hazard map, East Asia*. Retrieved May 30, 2007, from http://geology.about.com/library/bl/maps/blworldindex.htm

Asia Pulse. (2005, November 10). *Business in Asia today*. Asia Pulse Production Centre, Sydney, Australia. Retrieved May 30, 2007, from http://www.asiapulse.com/

Brans J. P., & Vincke, Ph. (1985). A preference ranking organisation method (The PROMETHEE method for multicriteria decision making). *Management Science, 31*(6), 647-656.

Brans, J. P., Vincke, Ph., & Mareschal, B. (1986). How to select and how to rank projects: The PROMETHEE method. *European Journal of Operational Research, 24*(2), 228-238.

Changnon, S. A. (2004). Temporal behavior of levels of the Great Lakes and climate variability. *Journal of Great Lakes Research, The International Association for Great Lakes Research (IAGLR), 30*(2), 184-200.

China GOV. (2006a). *National emergency salvation plan for natural disasters*. The Central Proples's Government of the People's Republic of China (China GOV). Retrieved May 30, 2007, from http://www.gov.cn/yjgl/index.htm

China GOV. (2006b). *National emergency response plan for floods and droughts*. The Central Proples's Government of the People's Republic of China (China GOV). Retrieved May 30, 2007, from http://www.gov.cn/yjgl/index.htm

China MCA. (2006, January 5). *News release: 2005 report on natural disasters in China*. Ministry of Civil Affairs (MCA). Retrieved May 30, 2007, from http://www.mca.gov.cn/news/content/recent/200615141759.html

Chinese Academy of Sciences (CAS). (2005). *2005 strategic report: China's suatainable development*. Sustainable Development Strategy Research Group (SDSRG). Retrieved May 30, 2007, from http://www.china.org.cn/chinese/zhuanti/2005cxfz/807367.htm

Disaster Preparedness Office (DPO). (2005). *Disaster preparedness*. U.S. Naval Support Activity, Naples, Italy. Retrieved May 30, 2007, from http://www.nsa.naples.navy.mil/disasterprep/home.htm

Department for Environment, Food and Rural Affairs (Defra). (2007). *Climate change and energy*. Retrieved May 30, 2007, from http://www.defra.gov.uk/environment/climatechange/index.htm

Federal Emergency Management Agency (FEMA). *(2005) Preparedness*. Retrieved May 30, 2007, from http://www.fema.gov/areyouready/basic_preparedness.shtm

H2ONotes. (2004). *A 141-year history of annual levels of the U.S. Great Lakes* (community weblog, 7/6/2004 - 17:57). Retrieved May 30, 2007, from http://h20notes.com/index2.asp?NGuid=1B8665D4D20A4C93BA1D8822F0CBDE51

Kashiwagi, D. T. (2004). *Best value procurement* (2nd ed.). Tempe: Arizona State University, Performance Based Studies Research Group (PBSRG).

Macharis, C., Springael, J., De Brucker, K., & Verbeke, A. (2004). PROMETHEE and AHP: The design of operational synergies in multicriteria analysis: Strengthening PROMETHEE with ideas of AHP. *European Journal of Operational Research, 153*(2), 307-317.

Mattioli, E. (2005). *The measurement of coherence in the evaluation of criteria and its effect on ranking problems illustrated using a mlticriteria decision method*. Performance Trading. Retrieved May 30, 2007, from http://www.performancetrading.it/Documents/EmMeasurement/EmM_Index.htm

NASA. (2007). *Natural disaster reference database*. Retrieved May 30, 2007, from http://ndrd.gsfc.nasa.gov/

New Zealand Institute of Economic Research (NZIER). (2004). *Sustainable infrastructure: A policy framework*. Retrieved May 30, 2007, from http://www.med.govt.nz/upload/18061/nzier.pdf

NF Editors. (2005). The rapid rise of business costs. *New Fortune, China, 4*, 56-59.

Organization for Economic Cooperation and Development (OECD). (2003). *Emerging systemic risks in the 21st century: An agenda for action*. Author.

Organization for Economic Cooperation and Development (OECD). (2005). *Large-scale disasters: Lessons learned*. Retrieved May 30, 2007, from http://www.oecdbookshop.org/oecd/display.asp?lang=EN&sf1=identifiers&st1=032004011p1

Pavic, I., & Babic, Z. (1991). The use of the PROMETHEE method in the location choice of a production system. *International Journal of Production Economics, 23*(1-3), 165-174.

Redcross.org (2005). *America's disasters 2004—Meeting the challenge*. Retrieved May 30, 2007, from http://www.redcross.org/pubs/dspubs/amdisasters2004.pdf

Shen-Tu, B., Lai, T., & Guin, J. (2005). *Modeling earthquake hazard and vulnerability in China*. (Originally published in the January 2005 issue of Reinsurance.) AIR Worldwide Corporation. Retrieved May 30, 2007, from http://www.air-worldwide.com/_public/html/air_innews_item.asp?ID=674

Saaty, T. L. (1980). *The analytic hierarchy process*. McGraw-Hill.

Saaty, T. L. (2005). Theory and applications of the analytic network process. Pittsburgh, PA: RWS Publications.

SPS. (2007). *Small urban area boundary determination before and after the 2000 U.S. census*. Retrieved May 30, 2007, from http://michigan.gov/documents/MDOT_smallurban_Attach3-Plan_Agencies_154588_7.pdf

Taiwan Electrical and Electronic Manufacturers' Association (TEEMA). (2005). *2005 survey report on investment environment and risks in Mainland China*. Taipei, Taiwan: Author.

Taylor, C., & VanMarcke, E. (2005). *Infrastructure risk management processes: Natural, accidental, and deliberate hazards*. ASCE Council on Disaster Risk Management No. 1, American Society of Civil Engineers (ASCE).

Turoff, M., & Linstone, H. A. (2002). *The Delphi method: Techniques and applications (Electronic Version)*. Newark, NJ: New Jersey Institute of Technology, Information Systems Department.

United Nations Children's Fund (UNICEF). (2005). *Emergency field handbook: A guide for UNICEF staff*. United Nations Publications.

U.S. Agency for International Development (USAID). (1998). *Field operations guide for disaster assessment and response* (Version 3.0). Washington, DC: Author.

U.S. Department of Homeland Security (USDHS). (2004). *National response plan*. Washington, DC: Author.

Wang, Z.-Y., & Plate, E. J. (2002). Recent flood disasters in China. *Water Management, Thomas Telford, 154*(3), 177-188.

Xie, J. (2006, January 6). The most anxious migration. *International Finance News*, (p. 18). Retrieved February 12, 2008, from http://www.people.com.cn/GB/paper66/16574/1460002.html

Yeh, A. G., & Xu, X. (1997). Globalization and the urban system in China. In F.-C. Lo & Y.-M. Yeung, (Eds.), *Emerging world cities in Pacific Asia*. Tokyo, New York, Paris: United Nations University Press. Retrieved May 30, 2007, from http://www.unu.edu/unupress/unupbooks/uu11ee/uu11ee00.htm#Contents

KEY TERMS

Analytic Network Process (ANP): According to Saaty (2005), the ANP is a general theory of relative measurement used to derive composite priority ratio scales from individual ratio scales that represent relative measurements of the influence of elements that interact with respect to control criteria. It is the most comprehensive framework for the analysis of societal, governmental, and corporate decisions that is available today to the decision maker.

Climate Change: According to Defra (2007), climate refers to the average weather experienced over a long period. This includes temperature, wind, and rainfall patterns. The climate of the Earth is not static and has changed many times in response to a variety of natural causes.

Natural Disaster: According to NASA (2007), there are a number of natural disasters, including wildfires, eruptions, avalanches, tsunamis, earthquakes, landslides, flooding, hurricanes, tornadoes, cyclones, storm surge, lahars, drought, typhoons, diseases, and so forth.

Production System: Production system is an industrial system that supports manufacturing and its logistics.

PROMETHEE: PROMETHEE is a multi-criteria decision-making method developed by Jean-Pierre Brans.

Urban Cluster: According to (SPS, 2007), urban cluster is a new statistical geographic entity designated by the Census Bureau for the 2000 Census, consisting of a central core and adjacent densely settled territory that together contains between 2,500 and 49,999 people. Typically, the overall population density is at least 1,000 people per square mile. Urban clusters are based on census block and block group density and do not coincide with official municipal boundaries.

ANNEX

PairWiser Questionnaire Table: the importance scores of indicators and their clusters

Clusters of Indicators			Indicators to evaluate contractor candidates		
No.	Name of Cluster	Score* of Cluster	No.	Name of Indicator	Score* of Indicator
1	Natural criteria		1.1	Ecological diversity	
			1.2	Minerals—Energy-related	
			1.3	Minerals—Metallic	
			1.4	Minerals—Non-metallic	
			1.5	Climate conditions	
			1.6	Geographic conditions	
			1.7	Geological conditions	
			1.8	Environmental pollutions	
			1.9	Natural disasters	
2	Social criteria		2.1	Transportation	
			2.2	Water supply system	
			2.3	Energy supply	
			2.4	Real estate	
			2.5	Government services	
			2.6	Education services	
			2.7	Human resources	
			2.8	Other business services	
			2.9	Policy	
			2.10	Economy	
			2.11	Shocks	

*Note. The scales for scoring with regard to sustainable (environmental, social and economic) issues relevant to construction projects:
1=Not important, 2=Not to moderately important, 3=Moderately important, 4=Moderately to strongly important, 5=Strongly important, 6=Strongly to very strongly important, 7=Very strongly important, 8=Very strongly to extremely important, 9=Extremely important.

Distributed Model Management: Current Status and Future Directions

Omar F. El-Gayar
Dakota State University, USA

Amit V. Deokar
Dakota State University, USA

INTRODUCTION

Modern organizations are faced with numerous information management challenges in an increasingly complex and dynamic environment. Vast amounts of data and myriads of models of reality are routinely used to predict key outcomes. *Decision support systems* (DSS) play a key role in facilitating decision making through management of quantitative models, data, and interactive interfaces (Power, 2000). The basic thrust of such applications is to enable decision-makers to focus on making decisions rather than being heavily involved in gathering data and conceiving and selecting analytical decision models. Accordingly, the number and complexity of decision models and of modeling platforms has dramatically increased, rendering such models a corporate (and national) resource (Muhanna & Pick, 1994).

Further, Internet technology has brought many new opportunities to conduct business electronically, leading to increased globalization. Managers and decision makers are increasingly collaborating in distributed environments in order to make efficient and effective use of organizational resources. Thus, the need for distributed decision support in general, and model sharing and reuse in particular, is greater today than ever before. This has attracted significant attention from researchers in information systems-related areas to develop a computing infrastructure to assist such distributed model management (Krishnan & Chari, 2000).

In this article, we focus on distributed model management advances, and the discussion is organized as follows. The next section provides a background on model management systems from a life-cycle perspective. This is followed by a critical review of current research status on distributed decision support systems from a model management viewpoint with a particular emphasis on Web services. Future trends in this area are then discussed, followed by concluding remarks.

BACKGROUND

The term model has been reviewed by many researchers and some common elements that characterize models have been noted. Krishnan and Chari (2000) depict a *model* (or a *model schema*) as a formal abstract representation of a decision problem. In other words, models can be conceived as specific formulations of decision situations amenable to certain problem solving techniques, such as simple linear regression, or a linear programming (LP) product mix formulation (Chang, Holsapple, & Whinston, 1993). Examples of models include a demand forecasting model for predicting customer calls in a call center and a production planning model to decide optimal product quantities to be produced. *Model instances* represent specific decision making situations created by instantiating model schemas with appropriate data, and are amenable to computational execution using *model solvers* to determine *model solutions*. Sometimes, models are generically considered as computational units (Orman, 1998) or objects (Lenard, 1993).

In general, models can be seen to conform to a *modeling lifecycle*, consisting of a complex, iterative process during which several modeling tasks need to be accomplished (Krishnan & Chari, 2000) (see Figure 1). Some of the modeling tasks are computationally intensive, while others are more subjective and need human judgment and domain expertise. Supporting the modeling life-cycle encompasses a variety of functionalities. For example, model creation may involve description, formulation, selection, integration, composition, and reuse of models. While model formulation focuses on the knowledge elicitation involved in the development of new models, model selection, composition, and integration aim at leveraging existing repositories of existing models. Model implementation is concerned with issues related to creating model representation amenable to execution by solvers. Issues of model-data, model-solver, and model-paradigm independence are of critical importance. Post-solution model interpretation deals with issues facilitating the interpretation of results by modelers and decision makers. Of particular importance is the analysis of the sensitivity of model results to parameter variations, as well as sensitivity of the model to structural changes in the model, thus enabling closer inspection of model structure. Supporting the modeling life cycle in particular, and the need for providing more expressive power to models in general is research on more explicit and expressive model representations such as the Structured Modeling (Geoffrion, 1987; Muhanna & Pick, 1994).

Model management as a term was coined back in the mid-1970s, noting the importance of managing models and the modeling life-cycle in DSS (Sprague & Watson, 1975). Model management advances have often followed the advances in database management, due to the analogy between managing models and data (Dolk, 1986). In this viewpoint, models are treated as "black boxes" with a set of named inputs and outputs, and the goal of model management is that of insulating the user from intricate details of storing and processing models (Dolk & Konsynski, 1984). In other words, models are considered as data that need to be closely managed for integrity, consistency, security, and currency (Dolk, 1986) using what are known as model management systems.

Model management systems (MMS) are computer based systems that aid in the creation, storage, retrieval, manipulation, and utilization of models for decision makers. The goal of MMS is to facilitate problem solving by relieving the decision maker of coding algorithms and specifying models in procedural syntax (Liang, 1988). In essence, MMS provides a way to access and manage various modeling resources and the modeling life cycle. These resources include specific solvers (special algorithms or processes for solving specific problems), modeling platforms (software for developing and analyzing agent-based models), modeling languages such as general algebraic modeling systems (GAMS) and a mathematical programming language (AMPL), test files representing model schemas as used in GAMS models and MATLAB (numerical computing environment and programming language) models, and executable models.

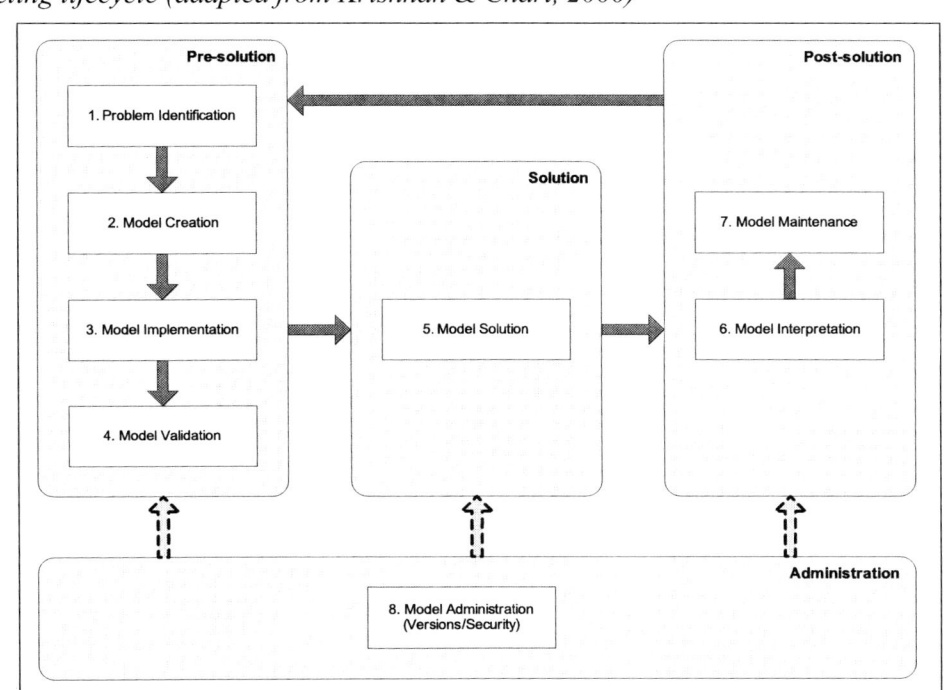

Figure 1. Modeling lifecycle (adapted from Krishnan & Chari, 2000)

DISTRIBUTED MODEL MANAGEMENT

With increased globalization, corporations are functioning in an increasingly distributed and collaborative manner. Further, mergers and acquisitions add to the diversity of models and data available to make appropriate decisions. In order to effectively provide decision support in such an environment, distributed decision support systems are becoming the focal point for both research and practice. Distributed model management plays an important role in these systems, either as stand-alone platforms or services or as embedded services.

DecisionNet, developed by Bhargava, Krishnan, and Mueller (1997), is a distributed decision support technology for the World Wide Web. The purpose of DecisionNet is to provide decision support technologies accessible electronically to consumers as a service over the World Wide Web instead of being purchased as stand-alone products. In this sense, DecisionNet performs the role of an "agent," mediating transactions between consumers and providers, in essence a "Yellow Pages" of services. Providers have the ability to register their products. DecisionNet's function involves data lookup and modification, as well as common fields of data for similar classes of entities. With this database interaction, queries with scripting languages can facilitate remote execution of decision support software. The DecisionNet prototype developed as a result of this research involves the use of relational databases that are directly accessed via common gateway interface (CGI) scripts. These CGI scripts are invoked by users with any Web browser.

Other examples include an integrated modeling environment that utilizes structured modeling for representing models, data warehouses for storing models, and a component-based architecture for plugging in software components based on user needs (Dolk, 2000). Structured models in the data warehouse are converted to the Unified Modeling Language (UML) which can be translated into executable code for model execution. In this architecture, model consumers and providers must be knowledgeable about the models to register and deploy them. Huh, Chung, and Kim (2000) propose a framework for collaborative model management systems in a distributed environment. The emphasis is on coordinating the changes made to a collection of shared models and propagating the effect of these changes throughout the organization.

In the context of optimization models, Ezechukwu and Maros (2003) propose an architecture supporting distributed optimization over the Internet. The architecture is comprised of Algebraic Modeling Language (AML) for representing models, an Optimization Reporting Markup Language (ORML) for representing model solutions, and a collection of Java programs referred to as Optimization Service Connectivity Protocol (OSCP) that are responsible for converting AML models to a target system for execution and converting model results to ORML.

Web Services and Distributed MM

The latest technological developments in Web services show great promise in distributed model management activities such as model creation and delivery, model composition, model execution, and model maintenance to fulfill dynamic decision-support and problem solving requests. These systems can be defined as a collection of logically related modeling resources distributed over an intra or inter computer network. In several ways, functions of Distributed Model Management Systems (DMMS) support the wide-spread sharing and usage of decision support models in a manner similar those of distributed database systems.

To facilitate the distribution process of model management, emerging Web services pose as a viable technology to accomplish the mediation task. The term Web services describes a standardized way of integrating Web-based applications using the extensible markup Language (XML), simple object access protocol (SOAP), Web services description language (WSDL) and universal description, discovery, and integration (UDDI) open standards over an Internet protocol backbone.

In that regard, Iyer, Shankaranarayanan, and Lenard (2005) propose a model management architecture emphasizing the use of structured modeling to represent models and an architecture supporting the sharing and reuse of models and data. The architecture focuses on sharing spreadsheet models and a prototype implementation features the use of Java Beans for implementing core engines, and Java Server Pages for client components.

At an abstract level, El-Gayar (2006) proposes a general framework based on service oriented architectures (SOA) design principles. The emphasis is on model sharing and reuse. The framework also accommodates distributed data as well as other decision support services such as discovery services, account management services, and user interface services.

Also, Madhusudan (2007) proposes an architecture for distributed model management based on Web services. The architecture adapts earlier work for Web services composition to model composition in a distributed setting. A "service platform" acts as a mediator by accepting service requests (e.g., from decision support clients), composing applicable models, and orchestrating the execution of the models.

Supporting model representation in a Web services environment, Kim (2001) and El-Gayar (2007) propose XML-based representations for analytical models. Both languages are based on the structured modeling paradigm (Geoffrion, 1987) for conceiving, manipulating, and representing models. The emphasis is on representing models at a higher level of abstraction to facilitate inferences about models. Such work will inevitably be the basis for further research on the use of ontologies in a model management context.

FUTURE TRENDS

It has been readily acknowledged that managing resources greatly enhances the ability for entities to utilize the full potential of these resources. This has become apparent with the research and development of data management systems. Model management is undoubtedly following a similar development process. The goal of distributed model management is to develop a generic infrastructure that offers productivity and efficiency improvements to builders of model-driven applications in a distributed environment. Earlier sections alluded to some of the recent developments in this area. However, to realize the vision for distributed model management there are a number of key research and development areas for consideration:

Models discovery and selection: Discovery and selection of models and services from a large collection of model/service libraries are critical functions supporting sharing and reuse of such entities. The proliferation of the Internet and intranets are key enablers providing access to an ever growing number of models. These models are heterogeneous, that is, pertaining to a variety of modeling paradigms, application domains, and modeling representations. Such scale and heterogeneity create unique challenges for model discovery and selection. Developing model ontologies and employing concepts from the semantic Web movement is a logical next step to facilitate and automate model discovery and selection in such environments.

Model composition: Further facilitating model reuse is the ability to compose existing models to develop new models. Automated composition of models is particularly critical in distributed environments as it reduces human time needed to manually compose such models, thereby improving efficiency. In a distributed setting, two main issues arise. First, how to ascertain model compatibility? Model inputs and outputs are not enough as they only capture the syntactic aspects. Capturing semantics will be necessary for successful model composition. Second, provided a set of models are identified, how do we handle interoperability among heterogeneous models that are distributed across diverse platforms?

Model representation: A variety of model representation paradigms and languages have been proposed in the literature. In a distributed setting, leveraging recent developments in Web technologies such as XML plays a key role in enabling model exchange and interpretation. Recent work by Kim (2001) and El-Gayar (2007) to leverage XML for model representation are steps along these lines. Further work is needed to operationalize these languages to a variety of domains and modeling concepts. Extending this work to include machine interpretable model semantics is critical rich model representation facilitating model selection, composition, and reuse.

Models as services: Conceptually, a model as a loosely coupled component delivering a specific functionality is a service in the context of a service oriented architecture. In effect, with the exception of model integration and model interpretation, a significant synergy exists between model management and service-oriented technologies and management.

Model data integration in a distributed setting: Similar to model composition where the emphasis is on coupling models, model-data integration emphasizes coupling models with data sets effectively creating model instances. In a distributed setting, a model can reside in one location while its data set resides in another. While the issue of model-data independence has been addressed in the literature, additional work is needed to extend these concepts to a distributed setting particularly as it related to leveraging XML, Web services, and ontologies to ensure that models are coupled with the "right" data sets and that data exchange occurs in a seemingly transparent manner.

CONCLUSION

Recent advances in information technology in general and distributed computing in particular are opening up new frontiers for model management. Models as a corporate and national resource can potentially be leveraged and reused within and across organizations. As noted in this article, the notion of "models as services" is particularly relevant as it provides a framework for capitalizing on the recent developments in Web services and supporting standards. Nevertheless, challenges remain and will have to be tackled if we are to further enact the inherent synergy between distributed model management and Web services. The issues and challenges noted in this article are but some of the critical ones at this point in time. Others will inevitably arise with further research and development.

REFERENCES

Bhargava, H. K., Krishnan, R., & Muller, R. (1997). Decision support on demand: Emerging electronic markets for decision technologies. *Decision Support Systems, 19*, 193-214.

Chang, A.-M., Holsapple, C. W., & Whinston, A. B. (1993). Model management issues and directions. *Decision Support Systems, 9*(1), 19-37.

Dolk, D. R. (1986). Data as models: An approach to implementing model management. *Decision Support Systems, 2*(1), 73-80.

Dolk, D. R. (2000). Integrated model management in the data warehouse era. *European Journal of Operational Research, 122*(2), 199-218.

Dolk, D. R., & Konsynski, B. R. (1984). Knowledge representation for model management systems. *IEEE Transactions on Software Engineering, SE-10*(6), 619-628.

El-Gayar, O. F. (2006). *A service-oriented architecture for distributed decision support systems.* Paper presented at the 37th Annual Meeting of the Decision Sciences Institute, San Antonio, TX, USA.

El-Gayar, O. F., & Tandekar, K. (2007). An XML-based schema definition for model sharing and reuse in a distributed environment. *Decision Support Systems, 43*, 791-808.

Ezechukwu, O. C., & Maros, I. (2003). *OOF: Open optimization framework* (Departmental Tech. Rep. No. 2003/7). London: Imperial College London, Department of Computing.

Geoffrion, A. M. (1987). An introduction to structural modeling. *Management Science, 33*(5), 547-588.

Huh, S. Y., Chung, Q. B., & Kim, H. M. (2000). Collaborative model management in departmental computing. *Infor, 38*(4), 373-389.

Iyer, B., Shankaranarayanan, G., & Lenard, M. L. (2005). Model management decision environment: A Web service prototype for spreadsheet models. *Decision Support Systems, 40*(2), 283-304.

Kim, H. (2001). An XML-based modeling language for the open interchange of decision models. *Decision Support Systems, 31*(4), 429-441.

Krishnan, R., & Chari, K. (2000). Model management: Survey, future research directions and a bibliography. *Interactive Transactions of OR/MS, 3*(1).

Lenard, M. L. (1993). An object-oriented approach to model management. *Decision Support Systems, 9*(1), 67-73.

Liang, T. P. (1988). Development of a knowledge-based model management system. *Operations Research, 36*(6), 849-863.

Madhusudan, T. (2007). A Web services framework for distributed model management. *Information Systems Frontiers, 9*(1), 9-27.

Muhanna, W. A., & Pick, R. A. (1994). Meta-modeling concepts and tools for model management: A systems approach. *Management Science, 40*(9), 1093-1123.

Orman, L. V. (1998). A model management approach to business process reengineering. *Journal of Management Information Systems, 15*(1), 187-212.

Power, D. J. (2000). *Web-based and model-driven decision support systems: Concepts and issues*. Paper presented at the Proceedings of the Americas Conference on Information Systems (AMCIS '00), Long Beach, CA.

Sprague, R. H., & Watson, H. J. (1975, November). *Model management in MIS*. Paper presented at the Proceedings of Seventeenth National AIDS, Cincinnati, OH.

KEY TERMS

Decision Support Systems (DSS): A decision support system is a computer-based system for supporting decision makers confront semistructured and ill-structured problems by leveraging data, knowledge, and models.

Distributed Model Management Systems (DMMS): DMMS are systems for managing models in a distributed environment where models, solvers, and client applications may be distributed over multiple heterogeneous platforms.

Model Management (MM): Analogous to data management, refers to the ability to create, retrieve, update, delete, and manipulate models. It also includes the need for managing models for integrity, consistency, security, and currency.

Model Management Systems (MMS): MMS are computer-based systems for supporting MM functions including but not limited to searching, selecting, retrieving, and composing models. MMS provide a way to access and manage various modeling resources and the modeling life cycle.

Service Oriented Architecture (SOA): The focus of SOA is to expose application logic as loosely coupled services. Design principles underlying SOA emphasize reuse, abstraction, autonomy, loose coupling, statelessness, composability, and discoverability.

Services: Services are independent building blocks that collaborate to deliver application functionality.

Web Services (WS): Web services are services that utilize XML and Web services technologies such as SOAP, WSDL, and UDDI to represent a Web-based implementation of an SOA.

DS/AHP

Malcolm J. Beynon
Cardiff University, UK

INTRODUCTION

DS/AHP was introduced in Beynon, Curry, and Morgan (2000) and Beynon (2002a), and is a nascent method of multi-criteria decision support. Following a hierarchical decision structure, similar to the analytic hierarchy process—AHP (Saaty, 1980), the identification of groups of alternatives (DAs) against the whole set of alternatives considered, over a number of different criteria, is operationalised using Dempster-Shafer theory—DST (Dempster, 1968; Shafer, 1976). As such, the utilisation of DS/AHP means the decision making is embedded with the realisation of the presence of ignorance and non-specificity in the decision judgements made (see Beynon, 2005).

Studies have acknowledged that the making of decisions is often difficult because of uncertainty and conflict in the judgement making process (Shafir, Simonson, & Tversky, 1993). Nutt (1998) references that a key incumbent in decision making is complexity, which prompts difficult decisions as well as manifesting how daunting a decision may appear. The notion of ignorance prevalent within DS/AHP, from DST, has been described as a general term for incompleteness, imprecision, and uncertainty (Smets, 1991), also relating to the subjective imperfection of a decision maker (Motro & Smets, 1997).

The judgement making made by a decision maker, when using DS/AHP, is through the comparisons of identified groups of DAs with respect to their increased belief in preference to that associated with all the DAs considered, over the different criteria. Pertinently, the decision maker does not have to discern between those DAs not preferred and those for which they are ignorant towards. This discernment is undertaken post analysis through the use of belief, plausibility, and pignistic probability measures, which view the presence of ignorance differently. A further measure of judgement making activity is the notion of non-specificity, which with DS/AHP, looks at the level of grouping of preferred DAs (Beynon, 2005b). The homogeneity of the combination process used in DS/AHP has allowed the approach to be effectively applied in a group decision 'consensus building' making environment (Beynon, 2006).

This article presents the rudiments of the DS/AHP technique, as well as a series of example results that exposit its operation in the presence of ignorance, and so forth.

BACKGROUND

For a full description of the fundamentals of the DS/AHP technique, see Beynon (2002a) and Beynon (2005). At various stages within a DS/AHP analysis, the construction of a body of evidence (BOE) is necessary, defined in DST (see Dempster, 1968; Shafer, 1976). A BOE is made up of mass values—$m(\cdot)$. Each $m(\cdot)$: $2^\Theta \to [0, 1]$ is a belief function, such that $m(\varnothing) = 0$ ($\varnothing$ - empty set), and

$$\sum_{x \in 2^\Theta} m(x) = 1,$$

where 2^Θ denotes the power set of Θ - the frame of discernment (finite set of hypotheses). Any subset x of the Θ for which $m(x)$ is non-zero is called a *focal element* and represents the exact belief in the proposition depicted by x, and $m(\Theta)$ is often interpreted as a level of ignorance, since this weight of evidence is not discernible amongst the hypotheses (Ducey, 2001).

With respect to a single criterion, the judgements made by a decision maker on the considered DAs, when using DS/AHP, are subject to:

a. The preference judgements on identified groups of DAs (focal elements) are with respect to a reference point, in this case all the DAs under consideration
b. Any preference judgements made on groups of DAs are towards the relative belief in the preference of that identified group against the underlying belief associated with the whole set of Das
c. Any DA identified in a group can only appear in one group of DAs

d. Each group of identified DAs should be assigned a unique preference scale value.

The evaluation of the evidence from the judgements made by a decision maker on a criterion, when using DS/AHP, was developed in Beynon (2002a), through the use of a comparison matrix of the form:

$$A_d = \begin{pmatrix} & s_1 & s_2 & \cdots & s_d & \Theta \\ s_1 & 1 & 0 & \cdots & 0 & pa_1 \\ s_2 & 0 & 1 & \ddots & 0 & pa_2 \\ \vdots & \vdots & \ddots & \ddots & 0 & \vdots \\ s_d & 0 & 0 & 0 & 1 & pa_d \\ \Theta & 1/(pa_1) & 1/(pa_2) & \cdots & 1/(pa_d) & 1 \end{pmatrix},$$

where p is the criteria importance value (CIV) for that criterion and, $a_1, a_2, \ldots, a_d$ are the preference scale values assigned to the d groups of DAs, $s_1, s_2, \ldots, s_d$, identified. The sparse matrix A_d shows comparisons are only made with identified groups of alternatives against all those considered, denoted by Θ. Following the process of identifying priority values from comparison matrices in AHP (see Saaty, 1980), the principle right eigenvector associated with the above matrix quantifies the evidence from the included judgements, in the form of a BOE. Moreover, for a criterion c_h, a *criterion* BOE is constructed, defined $m_h(\cdot)$, made up of the mass values:

$$m_h(s_i) = \frac{a_i p}{\sum_{j=1}^{d} a_j p + \sqrt{d}}, \quad i = 1, 2, \ldots, d$$

and $m_h(\Theta) = \dfrac{\sqrt{d}}{\sum_{j=1}^{d} a_j p + \sqrt{d}}$.

These expressions assign levels of exact belief to the DA groups, $s_1, s_2, \ldots, s_d$, as well as a level of local ignorance ($m_h(\Theta)$). The structure of these expressions indicates the utilised scale values, $a_1, a_2, \ldots, a_d$, need to be positive in nature to assure they form a BOE. These scale values quantify the verbal terms, ranging from moderately to extremely more preferred, used by the DM in their judgement making on groups of DAs compared to all those considered (Beynon et al., 2000).

Within DS/AHP, the setting of scale values began with an adherence to those employed in AHP (including the 1 to 9 scale). However, Beynon (2002a) considered the effect on the range of local ignorance allowed in the judgements made over a single criterion that the scale values available confer. This is a fundamental point within the DS/AHP (in particular DST) since without the presence of ignorance the combination process may exhibit an inhibiting level of conflict (see Murphy, 2000).

The criterion BOEs are independent pieces of evidence, all of which include information on the levels of exact belief in the preferences of groups of DAs. These criterion BOEs need to be combined to construct a final BOE, which includes all the evidence from the criteria on the preference of the DAs. To achieve this final BOE, Dempster's rule of combination is used which allows the combination of independent pieces of evidence. Moreover, considering two BOEs, $m_1(\cdot)$ and $m_2(\cdot)$, the combining function $[m_1 \oplus m_2]: 2^\Theta \to [0, 1]$, defined by:

$$[m_1 \oplus m_2](y) = \begin{cases} 0 & y = \varnothing \\ \dfrac{\sum_{s_1 \cap s_2 = y} m_1(s_1) m_2(s_2)}{1 - \sum_{s_1 \cap s_2 = \varnothing} m_1(s_1) m_2(s_2)} & y \neq \varnothing \end{cases}$$

is a mass value, where s_1 and s_2 are focal elements associated with the BOEs, $m_1(\cdot)$ and $m_2(\cdot)$, respectively. This combination rule can be used iteratively, to successively combine individual criterion BOE to the previously combined BOEs. The presence of the DAs in the focal elements in the final BOE, defined $m(\cdot)$, depends on their presence in the identified groups of DAs over the different criteria (in the respective criterion BOEs).

How this evidence is used depends on the decision maker, including whether the non-presence of individual DAs in identified groups of preferred DAs is due to their non-preferment or there is a more ignorance based reason. This is a novel viewpoint taken by DS/AHP, since it allows a decision maker to undertake their judgements, without the need to discern between non-preferred DAs and ignorance of DAs (over some or all the criteria). That is, without the allowance for both of these occurrences to exist, it means one may be sacrificed to allow for the other. To take account of the different reasons for the non-inclusion of DAs, a number of further measures are described (that take account of the presence of ignorance differently).

The belief function, defined

$$\text{Bel}(s_i) = \sum_{s_j \subseteq s_i} m(s_j)$$

for all $s_i \subseteq \Theta$, is the more ignorance averse of the measures considered, representing the confidence that a proposition y lies in s_i or any subset of s_i. With respect to DS/AHP, utilising the belief function means that no belief will come from the more ignorant focal elements (such as $m(\Theta)$), than that being considered (s_i).

The plausibility function, defined

$$\text{Pls}(s_i) = \sum_{s_j \cap s_i \neq \emptyset} m(s_j)$$

for all $s_i \subseteq \Theta$, is more inclusive of ignorance, representing the extent to which we fail to disbelieve a proposition y lies in s_i. With respect to DS/AHP, utilising the plausibility function means that preference belief will include evidence from the more ignorant focal elements (such as $m(\Theta)$).

Moving away from the use of the belief and plausibility measures, here the pignistic probability function, defined BetP(·), is also described (Denœux & Zouhal, 2001). The general expression for BetP(·) is given by:

$$\text{BetP}(s_i) = \sum_{s_j \subseteq \Theta, s_j \neq \emptyset} m(s_j) \frac{|s_i \cap s_j|}{|s_j|},$$

for a $s_i \subseteq \Theta$. With respect to DS/AHP, the BetP(·) function is a compromise option, between Bel(·) and Pls(·), since it is dependent on the level of presence of DAs in the focal elements making up a BOE.

The measures, Bel(·), Pls(·), and BetP(·) can be used to identify the most preferred DA(s). Since DS/AHP works with groups of DAs, the final results are also in terms of groups of DAs. That is, the notion of finding the best number of DAs is pertinent in DS/AHP, with the respective groups of DAs with the highest, Bel(·), Pls(·), or BetP(·), determining the required best DAs (see later).

Returning to the level of judgement making undertaken by a decision maker, the notion of non-specificity is next described. A non-specificity measure $N(\cdot)$ within DST was introduced by Dubois and Prade (1985), the formula for $N(\cdot)$ on a BOE $m(\cdot)$ is defined as:

$$N(m(\cdot)) = \sum_{s_i \in 2^\Theta} m(s_i) \log_2 |s_i|,$$

where $|s_i|$ is the number of elements in the focal element s_i. Hence, $N(m(\cdot))$ is considered the weighted average of the focal elements, with $m(\cdot)$ the degree of evidence focusing on s_i, while $\log_2|s_i|$ indicates the lack of specificity of this evidential claim. The general range of this measure is $[0, \log_2|\Theta|]$ (given in Klir & Wierman, 1998), where $|\Theta|$ is the number of DAs in the frame of discernment. Klir and Wierman (1998) suggest that measurements such as non-specificity are viewed as species of a higher uncertainty type, encapsulated by the term ambiguity, stating:

"... the latter (ambiguity) is associated with any situation in which it remains unclear which of several alternatives should be accepted as the genuine one."

In DS/AHP, the non-specificity measure $N(m(\cdot))$ for a criterion BOE can be written as:

$$N(m(\cdot)) = \sum_{i=1}^{d} \frac{a_i p}{\sum_{j=1}^{d} a_j p + \sqrt{d}} \log_2 |s_i|$$

$$+ \frac{\sqrt{d}}{\sum_{j=1}^{d} a_j p + \sqrt{d}} \log_2 |\Theta|$$

This expression takes into account the partition of the exact belief to the identified groups of DAs, $s_1, \ldots, s_d$, and the concomitant local ignorance. In the limit (considering DS/AHP), a value of $N(\cdot)$ near 0 implies very specific evidence on the DAs, namely individual DAs identified by the decision maker. While $N(\cdot)$ near $\log_2|\Theta|$ implies a lack of specificity, with evidence on large groups of DAs only.

DS/AHP ANALYSIS OF EXAMPLE DECISION PROBLEM

The main thrust of this article is an elucidation of the operations of DS/AHP through a small example. The example multi-criteria decision problem considered

DS/AHP

here concerns ten decision DAs, A, B, C, D, E, F, G, H, I, and J (making up the frame of discernment Θ), considered over three criteria, c_1, c_2 and c_3. Using DS/AHP, judgements are made on preferred identified groups of DAs over the different criteria, see Figure 1.

In Figure 1, two, three, and two groups of DAs have been identified for preference on the criteria, c_1, c_2 and c_3, respectively. Alongside each identified groups of DAs is their respective scale value assigned to them. Here, a '1 to 7' scale was adopted, with inference ranging from moderately preferred (1) to extremely preferred (7). Also shown in Figure 1 are the criterion importance values (CIVs) for the different criteria, c_1: $p_1 = 0.5$, c_2: $p_2 = 0.3$ and c_3: $p_3 = 0.2$. For the c_2 criterion, the respective comparison matrix is of the form:

$$\begin{array}{c} \\ \{E,H\} \\ \{F,I,J\} \\ \{A\} \\ \Theta \end{array} \begin{pmatrix} \{E,H\} & \{F,I,J\} & \{A\} & \Theta \\ 1 & 0 & 0 & 1p_2 \\ 0 & 1 & 0 & 2p_2 \\ 0 & 0 & 1 & 5p_2 \\ 1/(1p_2) & 1/(2p_2) & 1/(5p_2) & 1 \end{pmatrix},$$

which gives the respective mass values and focal elements (using general CIV p_2), which form the criterion BOE, defined $m_2(\cdot)$, given as:

$$m_2(\{E, H\}) = \frac{1p_2}{8p_2 + \sqrt{3}}, \ m_2(\{F, I, J\}) = \frac{2p_2}{8p_2 + \sqrt{3}},$$

$$m_2(\{A\}) = \frac{5p_2}{8p_2 + \sqrt{3}} \text{ and } m(\Theta) = \frac{\sqrt{3}}{8p_2 + \sqrt{3}}.$$

Figure 1. Judgements made on best DAs problem

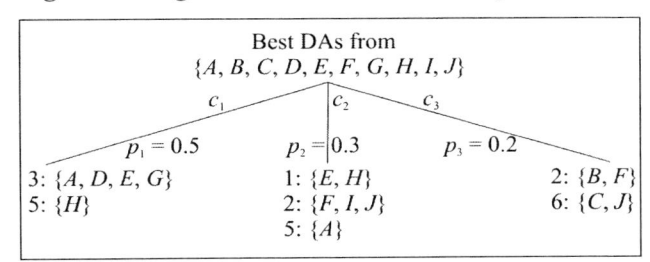

```
              Best DAs from
         {A, B, C, D, E, F, G, H, I, J}
          c₁         c₂         c₃
       p₁ = 0.5   p₂ = 0.3   p₃ = 0.2
    3: {A, D, E, G}  1: {E, H}      2: {B, F}
    5: {H}           2: {F, I, J}   6: {C, J}
                     5: {A}
```

These general expressions for the mass values in the criterion BOE $m_2(\cdot)$ and the other criterion BOEs, are further illustrated in Figure 2.

In Figure 2, the effect of a CIV (p_i value), on the formulisation of mass values in criterion BOEs is clearly exposited. As a CIV p_i tends to 0, the interpretation of little importance on the criterion means the majority of the exact belief is assigned to local ignorance. Similarly, as a CIV p_i tends to 1 (large importance) so more exact belief is assigned to the identified groups of DAs, with a subsequent reduction of the concomitant local ignorance. Also shown for each criterion are the specific mass values based on their respective CIVs of; $p_1 = 0.5$, $p_2 = 0.3$ and $p_3 = 0.2$. For the case of the c_1 criterion, the criterion BOE is (with $p_1 = 0.5$):

$m_1(\{A, D, E, G\}) = 0.277$, $m_1(\{H\}) = 0.462$ and $m_1(\Theta) = 0.261$.

For the other two criteria, the evidence in their respective criterion BOEs, $m_2(\cdot)$ and $m_3(\cdot)$, are:

For c_2 (with $p_2 = 0.3$): $m_2(\{E, H\}) = 0.073$, $m_2(\{F, I, J\}) = 0.145$, $m_2(\{A\}) = 0.363$ and $m_2(\Theta) = 0.419$.

For c_3 (with $p_3 = 0.2$): $m_3(\{B, F\}) = 0.133$, $m_3(\{C, J\}) = 0.398$ and $m_3(\Theta) = 0.469$.

Given these constructed criterion BOEs, the next consideration is on the level of judgement making by the decision maker over the different criteria, using the non-specificity $N(m(\cdot))$ expression given in the background section. To demonstrate the evaluation of the $N(m(\cdot))$ measure in DS/AHP, for the c_2 criterion, the $N(m_2(\cdot))$ value is given as:

$$N(m_2(\cdot)) = \frac{1p_2}{8p_2 + \sqrt{3}} \log_2|\{E, H\}|$$

$$+ \frac{2p_2}{8p_2 + \sqrt{3}} \log_2|\{F, I, J\}|$$

$$+ \frac{5p_2}{8p_2 + \sqrt{3}} \log_2|\{A\}| + \frac{\sqrt{3}}{8p_2 + \sqrt{3}} \log_2|\Theta|.$$

For the c_2 criterion, with CIV $p_2 = 0.3$, then $N(m_2(\cdot)) = 1.695$. Similar non-specificity values are found for the c_1 and c_3 criteria, in these cases they are $N(m_1(\cdot)) =$

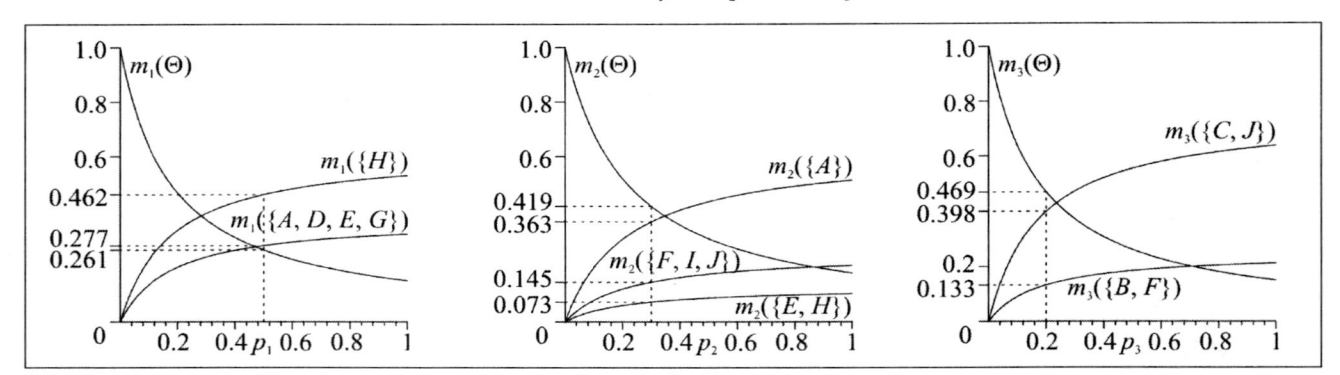

Figure 2. Mass value graphs of the criterion BOEs, $m_1(\cdot)$, $m_2(\cdot)$ and $m_3(\cdot)$

1.422 and $N(m_3(\cdot)) = 2.089$, respectively. The evaluated non-specificity values increase in value from c_1 to c_2 to c_3, a consequence of the size and number of the groups of DAs identified, as well as the decreasing level of CIV associated with them, respectively.

Dempster's combination rule can then be used to combine the evidence from the individual criterion BOEs. This is done iteratively, with the combination of the first two criterion BOEs, $m_1(\cdot)$ and $m_2(\cdot)$, first undertaken, the intermediate details of which are shown in Table 1.

The results in Table 1 come from the intersection and multiplication of focal elements and mass values from the two criterion BOEs, $m_1(\cdot)$ and $m_2(\cdot)$. On occasions the intersection of focal elements resulted in an empty set ($\emptyset$), the sum of the associated mass values is equal to

$$0.271 \left(= \sum_{s_1 \cap s_2 = \emptyset} m_1(s_1) m_2(s_2)\right),$$

it follows the denominator of the combination formula is:

$$1 - \sum_{s_1 \cap s_2 = \emptyset} m_1(s_1) m_2(s_2) = 1 - 0.271 = 0.729.$$

Bringing together the intermediate mass values of the same focal elements in Table 1 (e.g., the focal element $\{A\}$ appears twice), and dividing the sum by the 0.729 value in each case, allows the construction of the intermediate BOE. The intermediate BOE in this case, from the combination of the two criterion BOEs, $m_1(\cdot)$ and $m_2(\cdot)$, defined $m_{1-2}(\cdot)$, is found to be:

$m_{1-2}(\{A\}) = 0.269$, $m_{1-2}(\{E\}) = 0.028$, $m_{1-2}(\{H\}) = 0.313$, $m_{1-2}(\{E, H\}) = 0.026$, $m_{1-2}(\{F, I, J\}) = 0.052$, $m_{1-2}(\{A, D, E, G\}) = 0.160$, $m_{1-2}(\Theta) = 0.151$.

Further, using Dempster's combination rule to combine this intermediate BOE with the evidence contained in the third criterion BOE $m_3(\cdot)$, results in the final BOE, defined $m(\cdot)$, and is:

Table 1. Intermediate results from combining the criterion BOEs, $m_1(\cdot)$ and $m_2(\cdot)$

$m_2(\cdot) \setminus m_1(\cdot)$	$m_1(\{A, D, E, G\}) = 0.277$	$m_1(\{H\}) = 0.462$	$m_1(\Theta) = 0.261$
$m_2(\{E, H\}) = 0.073$	$\{E\}$, 0.020	$\{H\}$, 0.034	$\{E, H\}$, 0.191
$m_2(\{F, I, J\}) = 0.145$	$\emptyset$, 0.040	$\emptyset$, 0.006	$\{F, I, J\}$, 0.038
$m_2(\{A\}) = 0.363$	$\{A\}$, 0.101	$\emptyset$, 0.225	$\{A\}$, 0.095
$m_2(\Theta) = 0.419$	$\{A, D, E, G\}$, 0.116	$\{H\}$, 0.194	Θ, 0.109

Table 2. Groups of DAs of different sizes with largest belief, plausibility and pignistic probability values

Size	Belief - Bel(·)	Plausibility - Pls(·)	Pignistic - BetP(·)
1	{H}, 0.255	{A}, 0.472	{H}, 0.278
2	{A, H}, 0.474	{A, H}, 0.748	{A, H}, 0.541
3	{A, E, H}, 0.517	{A, H, J}, 0.931	{A, H, J}, 0.656
4	{A, C, H, J}, 0.614	{A, F, H, J}, 0.977	{A, E, H, J}, 0.734
5	{A, C, E, H, J}, 0.658	{A, E, F, H, J}, 1.000	{A, C, E, H, J}, 0.798

$m(\{A\}) = 0.219$, $m(\{E\}) = 0.023$, $m(\{F\}) = 0.012$, $m(\{H\}) = 0.255$, $m(\{J\}) = 0.036$, $m(\{B, F\}) = 0.035$, $m(\{C, J\}) = 0.104$, $m(\{E, H\}) = 0.021$, $m(\{F, I, J\}) = 0.043$, $m(\{A, D, E, G\}) = 0.130$, $m(\Theta) = 0.123$.

This final BOE contains all the evidence from the judgements made by the decision maker over the three criteria. How this evidence is used to identify the most preferred DA or groups of DAs is dependent on how the presence of ignorance is accommodated for. From this BOE, most preferred groups of DAs can be evaluated, see Table 2.

In Table 2, each row identifies the group of DAs, of a certain size, with the largest belief, plausibility, and pignistic probability values. To demonstrate, for a group of size one, the DAs, H, A, and H were identified as most preferred, based on the belief, plausibility, and pignistic probability values, respectively. The construction of their specific values is next shown:

$$\text{Bel}(\{H\}) = \sum_{s_j \subseteq \{H\}} m(s_j) = m(\{H\}) = 0.255,$$

$$\text{Pls}(\{A\}) = \sum_{s_j \cap \{A\} \neq \emptyset} m(s_j) = m(\{A\}) + m(\{A, D, E, G\}) + m(\Theta) = 0.472,$$

and

$$\text{BetP}(\{H\}) = \sum_{s_j \subseteq \Theta, s_j \neq \emptyset} m(s_j) \frac{|\{H\} \cap s_j|}{|s_j|},$$

$$= m(\{H\}) \frac{|\{H\} \cap \{H\}|}{|\{H\}|} + m(\{E, H\}) \frac{|\{H\} \cap \{E, H\}|}{|\{E, H\}|}$$

$$+ m(\Theta) \frac{|\{H\} \cap \Theta|}{|\Theta|},$$

$$= 0.278.$$

The same principle follows for identifying specific groups of DAs of other sizes. Inspection of the results in Table 2 shows similarities and variation. For example, when considering the most preferred groups of two DAs, all three measures identify the same group {A, H}. Whereas the best group of four DAs shows three different sets are identified, namely, {A, C, H, J}, {A, F, H, J}, and {A, E, H, J}.

FUTURE TRENDS

The future trends for DS/AHP lie in the general understanding of how it facilitates multi-criteria decision support to decision makers. Its operation is heavily centred in an uncertain environment, through the allowance for ignorance, is a novel direction for decision support, as such it does require a change of thinking by decision makers.

This change of thinking is demonstrated by considering further the allowance for ignorance and the optional use of the belief, plausibility, and pignistic probability values to measure DA preference. That is, these measures place different inference on the presence of ignorance, even taking consideration of the effect of ignorance after the judgments have been made. Moreover, their part in DS/AHP places the level of judgement effort in the control of the decision maker, rather than them being forced to make judgements beyond what they feel comfortable to do.

CONCLUSION

The aim of multi-criteria decision support techniques is to aid the decision maker in achieving their decision goals. This of course centres on the ability to have identified the most preferential DA or groups of DAs. However, the decision support should also be appropriate to the decision maker, including the allowance on them to have made as much effort in their judgement making as they felt happy to do so.

The DS/AHP technique, as described, through its allowance for ignorance, does allow the decision maker the control that a support system should. It follows, this technique would certainly be appropriate for problems where there are a large number of DAs to consider, since there may be more occurrence of ignorance due to the size of the problem. Moreover, DS/AHP could be used as a precursor to other techniques that operate effectively on problems with smaller number of DAs.

REFERENCES

Beynon, M. J. (2002a). DS/AHP method: A mathematical analysis, including an understanding of uncertainty. *European Journal of Operational Research, 140*(1), 149-165.

Beynon, M. J. (2002b). An investigation of the role of scale values in the DS/AHP method of multi-criteria decision making. *Journal of Multi-Criteria Decision Analysis, 11*(6), 327-343.

Beynon, M. J. (2005). Understanding local ignorance and non-specificity in the DS/AHP method of multi-criteria decision making. *European Journal of Operational Research, 163*, 403-417.

Beynon, M. J. (2006). The role of the DS/AHP in identifying inter-group alliances and majority rule within group decision making. *Group Decision and Negotiation, 15*(1), 21-42.

Beynon, M. J., Curry, B., & Morgan, P. H. (2000). The Dempster-Shafer theory of evidence: An alternative approach to multicriteria decision modelling. *OMEGA—International Journal of Management Science, 28*(1), 37-50.

Dempster, A. P. (1968). A generalization of Bayesian inference (with discussion). *Journal of Royal Statistical Society Series B, 30*, 205-247.

Denœux, T., & Zouhal, L. M. (2001). Handling possibilistic labels in pattern classification using evidential reasoning. *Fuzzy Sets and Systems, 122*, 409-424.

Dubois, D., & Prade, H. (1985). A note on measures of specificity for fuzzy sets. *International Journal of General Systems, 10*, 279-283.

Ducey, M. J. (2001). Representing uncertainty in silvicultural decisions: an application of the Dempster-Shafer theory of evidence. *Forest Ecology and Management, 150*, 199-211,

Klir, G. J., & Wierman, M. J. (1998). *Uncertainty-based information: Elements of generalized information theory*. Heidelberg: Physica-Verlag.

Motro, A., & Smets, P. (1997). Uncertainty management in information systems: From needs to solutions. Kluwer Academic Publishers, US.

Murphy, C. K. (2000). Combining belief functions when evidence conflicts. *Decision Support Systems, 29*, 1-9.

Nutt, P. C. (1998). How decision makers evaluate alternatives and the influence of complexity. *Management Science, 44*(8), 1148-1166.

Saaty, T. L. (1980). *The analytic hierarchy process*. New York: McGraw-Hill.

Shafer, G. A. (1976). *Mathematical theory of evidence*. Princeton: Princeton University Press.

Shafir, E., Simonson, I., & Tversky, A. (1993). Reason-based choice. *Cognition, 49*, 11-36.

Smets, P. (1991). Varieties of ignorance and the need for well-founded theories. *Information Sciences, 57-58*, 135-144.

KEY TERMS

AHP: The technique analytic hierarchy process to aid multi-criteria decision making.

Belief: In Dempster-Shafer theory, the level of representing the confidence that a proposition lies in a focal element or any subset of it.

Body of Evidence: In Dempster-Shafer theory, a series of focal elements and associated mass values.

Focal Element: In Dempster-Shafer theory, a set of hypothesis with positive mass value in a body of evidence.

Frame of Discernment: In Dempster-Shafer theory, the set of all hypotheses considered.

Dempster-Shafer Theory: General methodology, whose rudiments are closely associated with uncertain reasoning.

Ignorance: In Dempster-Shafer theory, the level of mass value not discernible among the hypotheses.

Mass Value: In Dempster-Shafer theory, the level of exact belief in a focal element.

Non-specificity: In Dempster-Shafer theory, the weighted average of the focal elements' mass values in a body of evidence, viewed as a species of a higher uncertainty type, encapsulated by the term ambiguity.

Pignistic Probability: In Dempster-Shafer theory, a measure to dissipate the mass values associated with focal elements to a specified focal element.

Plausibility: In Dempster-Shafer theory, the extent to which we fail to disbelieve a proposition lies in a focal element.

DSS and Multiple Perspectives of Complex Problems

David Paradice
Florida State University, USA

Robert A. Davis
Texas State University – San Marcos, USA

INTRODUCTION

Decision support systems have always had a goal of supporting decision-makers. Over time, DSS have taken many forms, or many forms of computer-based support have been considered in the context of DSS, depending on one's particular perspective. Regardless, there have been decision support systems (DSS), expert systems, executive information systems, group DSS (GDSS), group support systems (GSS), collaborative systems (or computer-supported collaborative work (CSCW) environments), knowledge-based systems, and inquiring systems, all of which are described elsewhere in this encyclopedia.

The progression of decision support system types that have emerged follows to some degree the increasing complexity of the problems being addressed. Some of the early DSS involved single decision-makers utilizing spreadsheet models to solve problems. Such an approach would be inadequate in addressing complex problems because one aspect of problem complexity is that multiple stakeholders typically exist.

Baldwin (1993) examined the need for supporting multiple views and provides the only attempt found in the information systems literature to operationalize the concept of a perspective. In his work, a view is defined as a set of beliefs that partially describe a general subject of discourse. He identified three major components of a view: the belief or notion to convey, a language to represent the notion, and a subject of discourse. He further described notions as comprising aspects and a vantage point. Aspects are the characteristics or attributes of a subject or situation that a particular notion emphasizes. A vantage point is described by the level of detail (i.e., overview or detailed analysis). Assuming the subject of discourse can be identified with the notion, Baldwin described how differences in views may occur via differences in the notion, the language, or both.

We agree with Baldwin's insights, but we take a different approach regarding the identification of DSS capabilities needed to accommodate different views. When multiple stakeholders confront a complex decision-making situation, each stakeholder may view the problem differently. We prefer to say the decision makers approach the problem from different perspectives. A decision maker's *perspective* is the cognitive sense-making structure the decision maker uses to construct an understanding of a problem. It is based on experiences, assumptions, and biases, among other things. What often makes resolution of complex problems so difficult is that difference stakeholders have different perspectives of complex problems. As such, the stakeholders bring to the problem different sets of experiences and different assumptions. They are guided by different biases and they often have different goals. These differences may not be distinct or mutually exclusive. Indeed, what makes resolution of complex problems possible is the overlap or commonality that exists in various perspectives. Simultaneously, the differences in the perspectives, when recognized as reasonable, contribute to better understanding of the problem situation by those that do not initially share those aspects of a perspective.

This article examines the nature of perspectives in greater detail and outlines issues that must be addressed for DSS to incorporate support for multiple perspectives into a decision maker's decision making process.

BACKGROUND

Janssen and Sage (2000) noted the existence of multiple perspectives and the need to support them in the area of policy making. They observe that complex decision-making environments are often attacked by drawing on the expertise of multiple experts. Often, the inputs of these experts are in summary form and without background information that would allow a policy-maker to assess the context in which the expert's perspective was developed. They developed a system that policy makers could use so that experts and decision makers with differing views could better understand each other's thought processes in complex situations. Their approach makes no effort to identify similarities or differences in individual perspectives.

Salipante and Bouwen (1995) see multiple perspectives as a way of understanding organizational conflict. They analyzed grievances filed in organizations and determined that grievances rarely fit into a single category (e.g., wages or discipline). Parties in a grievance form differing perspectives of the situation and hold to their perspective with great conviction for its veracity. Further, mediators tend to introduce their own perspectives when settling grievance disputes according to their preferred way for resolving disputes. Salipante and Bouwen's analysis points to the social construction of organizational reality, emphasizing that organizational reality is not a single objective thing but rather a negotiated reality based on the multiple perspectives of its stakeholders. While recognizing their existence, this work also does not attempt to explicitly model perspectives.

Why Perspectives Are Lost in GSS

Group support systems (GSS) emerged in recognition of the group-oriented decision making processes in organizations. GSS expanded DSS to include tools consistent with the role and function of groups in decision-making processes. These efforts were driven by acknowledgement that groups are often employed to solve problems, especially in situations exhibiting greater complexity. This research came to focus on group behaviors, and a shift of emphasis from group *decision* support to simply group support emerged. Often, the function of these group support systems is to synthesize whatever perspectives exist of a problem into a single perspective so that DSS approaches to problem solving can be used. For example, brainstorming capabilities are used to surface multiple perspectives of a problem, but group support system rating and voting functions effectively elevate the aspect(s) *most widely held* in the group to the status of being the aspect(s) *most important* in the decision-making behavior of the group. Typically, a voting process is employed to identify these aspects of a problem as the ones that will be adopted by the group to represent the problem at hand.

Users of group support systems often benefited from the surfacing of assumptions and beliefs that emerged during brainstorming sessions. However, these systems were not designed to maintain the integrity of the various perspectives of a problem being considered. We believe that a process that loses a perspective of a problem situation probably loses information valuable in constructing an approach to dealing with the problem in a sustainable, long-run fashion.

Philosophical Bases for Perspective Support in DSS

More recently, thought has been given to working with problem perspectives through the design of systems capable of inquiry (Courtney, 2001). These efforts trace their designs to Churchman's seminal book *The Design of Inquiring Systems* (1971) and the work of Mason and Mitroff (1973). Notably, the more sophisticated inquiring systems incorporate the notion of perspectives.

The first approach to inquiry described by Churchman that recognizes multiple perspectives is the Kantian inquirer. Though not expressed explicitly as "perspectives," the Kantian inquirer recognizes the value of multiple models of a situation, in that there is synergism in the multiple models (Linstone, 1999). Paradice and Courtney (1986, 1987) designed a system based on Churchman's description of the Kantian inquirer that performed as well as human subjects in identifying the underlying structure of a complex business simulation. In a few cases, it correctly identified relationships that human subjects had misidentified.

A different way of dealing with perspectives exists in Hegel's dialectic. Dialectic processes implicitly embody two perspectives, the thesis and the antithesis. Where the Kantian inquirer sees synergy in multiple perspectives, the Hegelian inquirer seeks to synthesize multiple perspectives into one. Hodges (1991) developed an information system based on dialectic analysis and demonstrated its effectiveness in supporting complex decision-making situations.

The final inquirer presented by Churchman is based on the philosophy of E.A. Singer. The essence of the

Singerian inquirer is that learning cannot take place where there is no disagreement (i.e., differing perspectives of a situation). Disagreements are addressed in a Singerian inquirer by "sweeping in" new variables to refine the knowledge in the system. These new variables originate in perspectives that are different from the original conception of the system. Thus, the Singerian inquirer implicitly recognizes the existence of multiple perspectives. Hall (2002) designed an information system based on Singerian philosophy and demonstrated how explicit consideration of multiple perspectives could influence decision-making behavior.

Vo, Paradice, and Courtney (2001) have also proposed a methodology for combining Linstone's technical, personal, and organizational perspectives (discussed in detail later) with Churchman's Singerian inquirer. The main argument in his work is that an organization learns when it consists of individuals who, through comparing their personal mental model with the organizational mental model, learn together by creating a shared vision. Vo's work does not maintain the integrity of individual perspectives, however.

Perspective Making & Perspective Taking

Boland and his colleagues (Boland & Tenkasi, 1995; Boland, Tenkasi, & Te'eni , 1994; Tenkasi & Boland, 1996) also draw on Churchman's Singerian inquirer. They begin with development of "distributed cognition," emphasizing the efforts of decision makers to interpret their situation and exchange that interpretation with others. In their distributed cognition environment, decision makers seek to act with an understanding of their own situation and that of others (Boland et al., 1994). Their emphasis is on coordinated outcomes that result from collaborative efforts as opposed to the traditional (group) DSS paradigm of constructing a pipeline of data believed to fit an ideal model to a decision maker who then selects an appropriate alternative. However, their focus is on an individual as a conversation maker, not a decision maker.

In their later work (Boland & Tenkasi, 1995) they explicitly speak of perspectives. They outline the design of communication systems to support "perspective making" and "perspective taking." Here they emphasize the growing numbers of "specialized and distinct knowledge communities" and the need for the integration of these communities to solve complex problems. They argue that working with perspectives is fundamental to solving problems in knowledge intensive firms because the complex problems dealt with by these firms are unsolvable by any one person. These problems require a variety of perspectives (Tenkasi & Boland, 1996).

One characteristic of Boland et al.'s work has been the identification of artifacts related to implementing systems that support "distributed cognition" and "perspective taking." Distributed cognition requires a "rich representation of understanding" and relies on the definition of actors, interpretations, and actions. They suggest increased use of forums to investigate and understand the perspectives held by others. Their systems to support perspective making and taking incorporate boundary objects such as cause maps, cognitive maps, and narrative maps. Cause maps, cognitive maps, and narrative maps are mental models held by decision makers. Their efficacy in modeling complex decision situations and the ease and effectiveness with which such maps are combined has been investigated by Vo, Poole, and Courtney (2002). Still, there is no explicit definition of what a perspective actually is.

Other System-Based Perspective Support Efforts

Among those attempts to improve task quality by adding a multiple perspective dimension into their tasks, Sugimoto, Hori, and Ohsuga (1998) developed a system that automatically generates different viewpoints from a large database.

Two techniques used to support the creation of multiple perspectives are (1) data organization and "virtualization of relationships" and (2) work group discussion and communication. First, data organization including data filtering, categorizing, structuring, and idea formation creates relationships among pieces of information. Then virtualization of those relationships helps generate multiple perspectives by enhancing a user's mental model through the use of a graphical interface. This technique reflects the belief that an individual's creativity comes partially from tacit knowledge. By explicating the knowledge, users will be able to notice what they have not noticed or what they have forgotten, draw relationships among pieces of information, and create a new, different mental model (Sugimoto et al., 1998). This approach implies that users already have the tacit knowledge, a required

DSS and Multiple Perspectives of Complex Problems

ingredient of new perspectives, but do not realize that the knowledge can be extended or that it reflects a new perspective. A benefit claimed by Sugimoto et al. is that their approach is a starting point for further communication among holders of different viewpoints.

A graphical user interface (GUI) is a primary feature supporting relationship virtualization as graphical representations are repeatedly found to be an effective tool for mental model construction (Loy, Pracht, & Courtney, 1987; Jarvenpaa & Dickson, 1988; Pracht & Courtney, 1988; Jarvenpaa, 1989; Roy & Lerch, 1996). Loy et al. (1987), Pracht and Courtney (1988), and Paradice and Courtney (1986, 1987) developed models like the ones shown in the figures included later in this article. Sugimoto et al. (1998) developed an example of a system supporting perspective creation based on the virtualization of relationship technique. This system automatically elicits different viewpoints by graphically providing lists of potentially related topics on the same screen based on the frequency of overlapping key terms. The lists then provide relationships among topics that help trigger users' different perspectives regarding the topic of interest. Information retrieval systems such as I^{3}R (Thompson & Croft, 1989), BEAD (Chalmers & Chitson, 1992), and InfoCrystal (Spoerri, 1993) form another genre of systems that emphasizes creating relationships among documents. However, these systems graphically present one pair of related information at a time. Therefore, they may be less effective in supporting the creation of multiple perspectives.

Work group discussion and communication is the second technique supporting creation of multiple perspectives. Examples of such systems include gIBIS (Conklin & Begeman, 1988), TeamWorkStation (Ishii, 1990), Cognoter (Tatar et al., 1991), and various GDSS applications. These systems provide tools for modeling arguments and thus facilitate discussions of different issue perspectives. They also provide tools for analyzing arguments and the positions taken by stakeholders. As such, these systems provide valuable decision-making aids and facilitate perspective generation activities through group discussion and communication.

While addressing the benefits of recognizing multiple perspectives, few researchers clearly define the term "perspective." The work by Goedicke, Enders, Meyer, and Taentzer (2000) regarding development of a framework supporting software development projects defines the term "viewpoint" as "a locally managed object or agent which encapsulates partial knowledge about the system and its domain... An entire system is described by a set of related, distributable viewpoints which are loosely coupled." However, this definition is relatively context-specific and difficult to generalize to other domains.

Goedicke et al. (2000) suggest the ViewPoints framework to build a support system integrating multiple perspectives in software development projects that normally involve members with different domain knowledge and development strategies. We believe the work in technical, personal, and organizational perspective analysis provides a solid foundation on which to build DSS support for decision situations involving multiple perspectives

DSS AND TECHNICAL, PERSONAL AND ORGANIZATIONAL PERSPECTIVES

A perspective indicates *how* one looks at a problem. Linstone (1999), working alone and with others (see, for example, Mitroff & Linstone, 1993), has developed the notion of three perspectives inherent in any complex problem situation: technical (T), personal (P), and organizational (O). This conception of perspectives provides one way to imagine DSS tools that support perspective integrity.

The T, P, and O perspectives yield quite distinct pictures of a situation. The P perspective provides an immediate grasp of the essential aspects of a situation, but it also reflects the bias of the analyst that constructed it. The T perspective may be a parsimonious model of a situation, but it can also be criticized, as it reflects an analyst's biases in the choice of assumptions, variables, and simplifications. An O perspective may give some indication of how an organization may be expected to move in a general sense. However, in the case of a strong organizational leader, one can argue that the O perspective is biased as well, since the leader's P perspective becomes adopted as the O perspective. These biases act as filters, blocking some aspects of a situation from view and allowing other aspects to be recognized.

Consider, for example, the rather complex situation that surrounds the plight of homeless persons in many metropolitan areas. (For our purpose here, we will not attempt to capture all of the complexity of this issue, but only parts of it to illustrate our points.) One person's P model of the homeless person's situation could be as depicted in Figure 1. This perspective reflects a belief that a lack of education leads to difficulty maintaining a job, which leads to job loss and thus little or no income. With no income, the uneducated person becomes homeless.

A second P-perspective model of the homelessness situation is given in Figure 2. It reflects a different root assumption: that the lack of healthcare is central to the problem.

On the other hand, a T-perspective model could approach the situation differently. It might focus on matching skills and job requirements to determine the best matches and resultant employment. Such a model may overlook education or health issues, or assume that users of the "system" already meet minimal education and health requirements to obtain and maintain employment. If asked to consider homelessness, the T-perspective modeler might simply add the result of income or no income onto the back end of the model. One such, a T-perspective model appears in Figure 3.

Finally, an O-perspective in this case may come from the city government, which must consider requests from various segments of the public to deal with the homeless issue. City administrators see the problem in terms of services that must be provided, which implies funds, facilities, and personnel. Funds must come from city revenues, that is, taxes, thus demanding public support for any proposal offered. Personnel to provide the services must be available and adequately trained. Facilities location itself becomes a difficult problem, as homeowners will fear a devaluing of their homes when shelters for homeless persons are located near by and shop owners will fear a reduction in customer traffic if shelters are too close to retail centers. The O-perspective is shown in Figure 4.

Perspectives are not independent. We can see some overlap among the models in the various figures. Each perspective gains from cues from the other perspectives. If one starts with a T perspective, one starts with, in some sense, an ideal representation. This perspective gains an aspect of reality from the O perspective in the form of organizational constraints. The P perspective provides motivations for pursuing a plan set forth by a T perspective. If one starts with an O perspective, the T perspective provides a plan of action and the P per-

Figure 1. One P-perspective model of homelessness

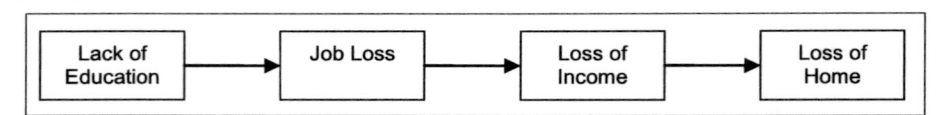

Lack of Education → Job Loss → Loss of Income → Loss of Home

Figure 2. A second P-perspective model of homelessness

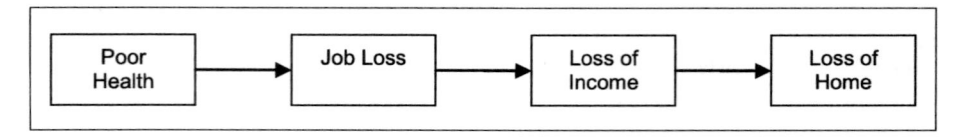

Poor Health → Job Loss → Loss of Income → Loss of Home

Figure 3. One T-perspective model of homelessness

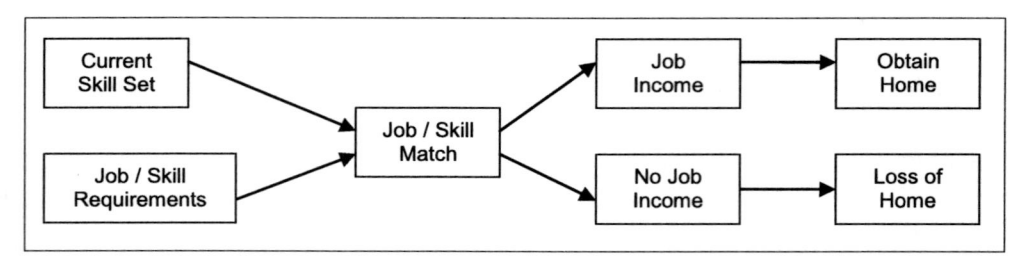

Current Skill Set, Job / Skill Requirements → Job / Skill Match → Job Income → Obtain Home; No Job Income → Loss of Home

DSS and Multiple Perspectives of Complex Problems

Figure 4. One O-perspective model of homelessness

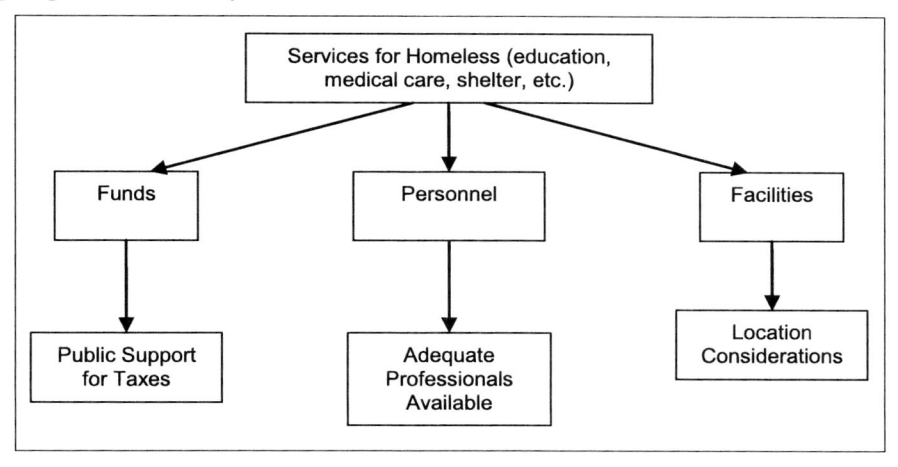

Figure 5. The beginnings of a combined-perspective model of homelessness

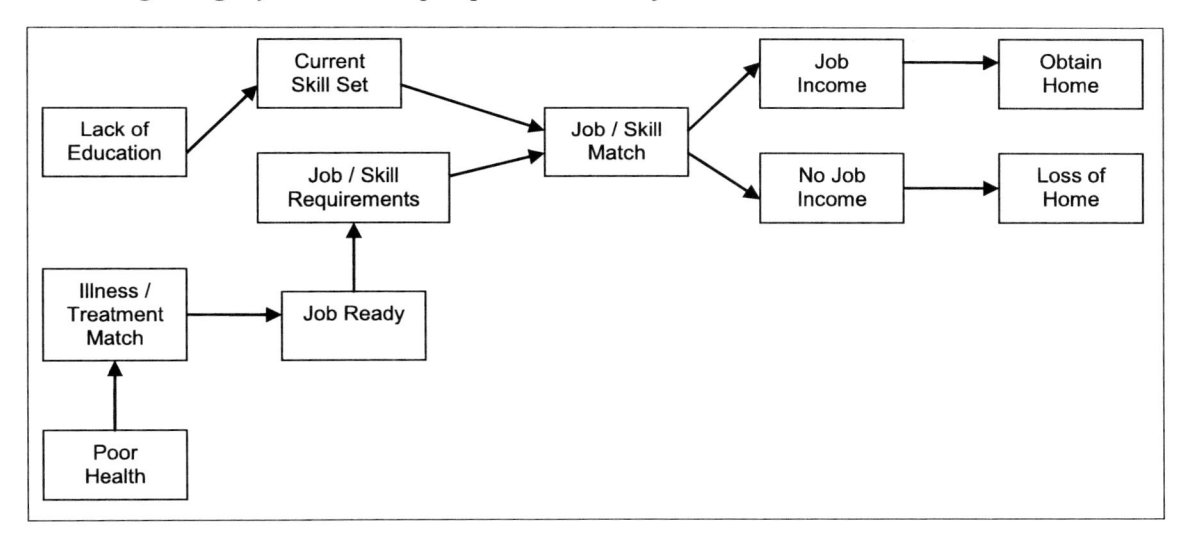

spective provides implementation for the plan. Starting from a P perspective, a T perspective can provide an initial starting point for formulating a strategy and an O perspective can provide information on the current context in which the strategy must be pursued.

We may imagine a single decision maker beginning with a DSS that supports the development of a model of that decision maker's perspective of a problem. This would be a classic P perspective. As this model is shared in a GSS environment, it may be merged with other individual models to create one or more T perspective models. Through various group processes of discussion and consensus, one would expect biases in P models to be refuted or validated, creating the "purer" T-type perspective model or models. There could be multiple models because some assumptions embedded in the P perspectives cannot be refuted or validated. We envision variations of combinations of the models illustrated in the figures. For example, the education-oriented P-perspective model and the healthcare-oriented P-perspective model could be combined and, in fact, a connection between education and healthcare might be established (a person needs to be healthy enough to attend training). The T-perspective model in Figure

3 could be introduced into the combined P-perspective models to help determine what kind of education is needed. A second T-perspective model that focuses on common illnesses in the homeless population could be produced to determine treatments needed. Figure 5 shows the progress of model development.

As the O-perspective model is folded into the combined model, we can envision where disagreement persists over assumptions. For example, the impact of a nearby homeless shelter on retail customer traffic might be contested. We envision multiple T-perspective models emerging to accommodate these differing assumptions, with one of these T perspective models being selected upon which to base the organization's decision making processes, at least until the assumptions in it are refuted. This selected model is embedded in the O-perspective model as the basis for decision making in our hypothetical DSS environment.

The DSS should maintain all of the models produced, not just the O perspective model that emerges. The different perspective models present different pictures of a situation because people have different ways of learning and different strategies for acquiring and processing information. They may also provide focused models for specific initiatives. For example, our education-oriented P-perspective model in the homeless issue analysis provides an excellent sub-model for assessing progress on that aspect of the problem. The importance of maintaining multiple perspectives of a situation is that more decision makers can be informed by doing so. Multiple perspectives provide pertinent information for each type of person from that person's accustomed point of view. More importantly, however, maintaining multiple perspectives allows a particular decision maker to see a situation from an alternate point of view.

The DSS should also help decision makers recognize that any particular perspective is unlikely to provide a "complete" view of a situation. Often, it is a partial view. The DSS could, for example, simply prompt the developer of the education-oriented P-perspective model in our homeless situation scenario whether there could be any other reasons a person is homeless. Such engagement by the DSS could force consideration of another perspective.

Participants in decision-making situations have partial views in two ways. First, they typically have one dominant perspective (T, P, or O) and thus information that would be represented in one of the other perspectives may not be incorporated. The norm is apparently a presence of all three perspective types in an unbalanced way (Linstone, 1999). The work by Hall and Davis (2007) reviewed in the article on problem formulation and DSS elsewhere in this volume speaks to the value of forcing decision makers to consider other perspectives.

Second, even the most ardent holder of any perspective often has incomplete information relevant to that perspective, whether through lack of accessibility to all relevant information, selective reduction that considers only subsets of relevant information, or personal bias that skews how relevant information is used to formulate the problem. "Groupthink" is a classic example of an O perspective that is, at best, a partial view of a situation. DSS must be designed to encourage decision makers to actively seek more relevant information (but avoid the information overload situation of seeking any information).

The T, P, and O perspectives have different perceptions of time and thus any DSS supporting these different perspectives must be able to accommodate different planning horizons. T perspectives have long-range planning horizons but often the decisions based on them are more immediate in nature. The assumptions underlying T perspectives are often believed to be valid for periods far longer than may be reasonable. (A good example is found in considering underlying assumptions in many business forecasting models.) P and O perspectives should have longer planning horizons because by their nature they should incorporate long-run consequences. However, both P and O dominant perspectives tend to give higher weight to short-run phenomena at the expense of long-run considerations. In our example, a P-perspective from a shop owner who believes a nearby shelter for homeless persons will negatively impact customer traffic will likely be focused on a short-term effect and not consider the long run impact of advertising, citizen education, and use of other distribution channels (e.g., mail order, Internet-based sales) in offsetting the reduced local traffic, if it actually occurs.

We believe that DSS supporting multiple perspectives may be most effective in addressing socio-technical problems and opportunities with short to moderate planning horizons. In these situations, the assumptions underlying T perspectives may be generally believed to hold, and by incorporating P and O perspectives with the T perspective, the DSS can help ensure that both social and technical considerations are examined.

The relative influence of each perspective can be driven by whether the problem or opportunity being addressed is novel or common. In novel situations, P perspectives may be more influential, as larger groups have not yet had time to assess the situation (i.e., the O perspective is thus under-developed) and little is known about the parameters of the situation (i.e., the T perspective is under-developed). A T perspective will likely carry more influence in a situation concerned with emerging technologies than in a situation concerning commonplace technologies since technical understanding may be prerequisite for any formulation of the problem at hand. The DSS interface could be programmed to ascertain these problem situation characteristics and then factor them into the manipulation of the models that reflect the various perspectives.

CONCLUSION AND FURTHER RESEARCH

We believe DSS will benefit from some working definition of perspective. The T, P, and O perspective taxonomy we have used here is one possible solution, but there are certainly others. Regardless of the starting point, the structural definition of a perspective will need to be developed so that issues such as individual biases, decision planning horizons, and competing assumptions among decision makers are handled effectively.

A critical aspect of our vision of future DSS is that they will be able to maintain the integrity of individual perspectives. Contrary to many approaches that have been implemented, the DSS should not synthesize models into a single problem representation. We believe that multiple models reflecting different assumptions may be more useful over different decision making horizons. Synthesis of multiple models reflects a reductionist approach in which rich details of a particular perspective of a problem may be lost to future decision makers. We encourage research into the design and development of DSS capable of maintaining and manipulating multiple model perspectives, especially a DSS that can proactively invoke a different model as the decision making characteristics change.

Graphical tools should be leveraged in new DSS to provide mental or causal maps of situations. Such maps may be a very effective first-approximation of a particular perspective. Some decision makers will more easily see where perspectives are similar and where they differ, leading to new avenues of discussion or investigation among decision makers confronting a complex problem situation.

In fact, a metric for determining similarities among perspectives needs to be developed. This could be based on a concept of distance, in which various components or factors that are important in the perspective definition are mapped into some type of "perspective space" in a multivariate sense. If such a metric could be developed, it would provide decision makers with a way of assessing when they moving closer together in the way they perceive a problem and when they are diverging. Both situations have positive and negative aspects. The DSS could help the decision makers cope with either situation.

Decision support systems are expected to support increasingly complex decision situations, and qualitative information typically associated with such situations is increasingly stored in electronic formats. The development of a rigorous concept of a perspective could provide a foundation for future efforts to automate environmental scanning (e.g., electronic news services) and policy analysis. Decision makers in complex situations would welcome such support.

REFERENCES

Baldwin, D. (1993). Applying multiple views to information systems: A preliminary framework. *Data Base*, 24(4), 15-30.

Boland, R., & Tenkasi, R. (1995). Perspective making and perspective taking in communities of knowing. *Organization Science*, 6(4), 350-372.

Boland, R., Tenkasi, R., & Te'eni, D. (1994). Designing information technology to support distributed cognition. *Organization Science*, 5(3), 456-475.

Chalmers, M., & Chitson, P. (1992). BEAD: Explorations in information visualization. In *Proceedings of the 15th Annual International ACM ISGIR Conference on Research and Development of Information Retrieval SIGIR '92* (pp. 160-169).

Churchman, C. W. (1971). *The design of inquiring systems*. Basic Books.

Conklin, J., & Begeman, M. (1988). gIBIS: A hypertext tool for exploratory policy discussion. *ACM Transactions on Office Information Systems, 6*(4), 303-331.

Courtney, J. (2001). Decision making and knowledge management in inquiring organizations: Toward a new decision-making paradigm for DSS. *Decision Support Systems, 31*(1), 17-38.

Goedicke, M., Enders, B., Meyer, T., & Taentzer, G. (2000). ViewPoint-oriented software development: Tool support for integrating multiple perspectives by distributed graph transformation. *Lecture Notes in Computer Science, 1779*, 369-377.

Hall, D. (2002). *Testing performance and perspective in an integrated knowledge management system*. Unpublished Ph.D. Dissertation, Texas A&M University.

Hall, D., and Davis, R. A. (2007). Engaging multiple perspectives: A value-based decision making model. *Decision Support Systems, 43*(4), 1588-1604.

Hodges, W. S. (1991). *DIALECTRON: A prototypical dialectic engine for the support of strategic planning and strategic decision making*. Unpublished Ph.D. Dissertation, Texas A&M University.

Ishii, H. (1990). TeamworkStation: Toward a seamless shared workspace. *Processing Computer-supported Cooperative Work*, 13-26.

Janssen, T., & Sage, A. P. (2000). A support system for multiple perspectives knowledge management and conflict resolution. *International Journal of Technology Management, 19*(3-5), 472-490.

Jarvenpaa, S. L. (1989). Effect of task demands and graphical format on information processing strategies. *Management Science, 35*(3), 285-303.

Jarvenpaa, S. L., & Dickson, G. W. (1988). Graphics and managerial decision making: Research based guidelines. *Communications of the ACM, 31*(6), 764-774.

Linstone, H. A. (1999). *Decision making for technology executives: Using multiple perspectives to improve performance*. Boston: Artech House.

Loy, S. L., Pracht, W. E., & Courtney, J. F. (1987). Effects of a graphical problem-structuring aid on small group decision making. In *Proceedings of the Twentieth Hawaii International Conference on Systems Sciences*, (pp. 566-574).

Mason, R. O., & Mitroff, I. I. (1973). A program for research on management information systems. *Management Science, 19*(5), 475-487.

Mitroff, I. I., & Linstone, H. A. (1993). *The unbounded mind*. Oxford: Oxford University Press.

Paradice, D. B., & Courtney, J. F. (1986). Controlling bias in user assertions in expert decision support systems for problem formulation. *Journal of Management Information Systems, 3*(1), 52-64.

Paradice, D. B., & Courtney, J. F. (1987). Causal and non-causal relationships and dynamic model construction in a managerial advisory system. *Journal of Management Information Systems, 3*(4), 39-53.

Pracht, W. E., & Courtney, J. F. (1988). The effects of an interactive, graphics-based DSS to support problem structuring. *Decision Sciences, 19*(3), 598-621.

Roy, M. C., & Lerch, F. J. (1996). Overcoming ineffective mental representations in base-rate problems. *Information Systems Research, 7*(2), 233-247.

Salipante, P., & Bouwen, R. (1995). The social construction of grievances: Organizational conflict as multiple perspectives. In D. Hosking, H. P. Dachler, and K. I. Gergen (Eds.), Management and organization: Relational alternatives to individualism (pp. 71-97).

Spoerri, (1993). InfoCrystal: A visual tool for information retrieval and management. In *Proceedings of the 2nd International Conference in Information and Knowledge Management* (pp. 11-20).

Sugimoto, M., Hori, K., & Ohsuga, S. (1998). A system for visualizing the viewpoints of information and its application to intelligent activity support. *IEEE Transactions on Systems, Man, and Cybernetics—Part C: Applications and Reviews, 28*(1), 124-136.

Tatar, D., Foster, G., & Bobrow, D. (1991). Design for conversation: Lessons from Cognoter. In S. Greenberg (Ed.), *Processing computer-supported cooperative work groupware* (pp. 55-79). New York: Academic.

Tenkasi, R., & Boland, R. (1996). Exploring knowledge diversity in knowledge intensive firms: a new role for information systems. *Journal of Organizational Change Management*, 9(1), 79-91.

Thompson, R., & Croft, W. (1989). Support for browsing in an intelligent text retrieval system. *International Journal of Man-Machine Study*, 30, 639-668.

Vo, H., Paradice, D. B., & Courtney, J. F. (2001). *Problem formulation in Singerian inquiring organizations: A multiple perspective approach*. Working paper.

Vo, H., Poole, M. S., & Courtney, J. F. (2002). Comparing methods of incorporating multiple perspectives into collective maps. In *Proceedings of the Eighth Americas Conference on Information Systems*, Dallas, (pp. 1783-1790).

KEY TERMS

Complex Problem: A problem characterized by relationships among the components of the problem whose inter-relationships are difficult to specify or whose behavior cannot be deduced simply from knowledge of the behaviors of the individual component parts.

Inquiry: A process followed in which the goal is to create or acquire knowledge.

Perspective: The way in which a subject or its component parts are mentally viewed.

Problem Formulation: (1) The process in which a problem situation is described or modeled, (2) problem structure.

Problem Structure: A description of a problem.

T, P, and O (Technical, Personal, and Organizational) Perspective: Three ways of describing perspectives of a problem.

DSS Using Visualization of Multi-Algorithms Voting

Ran M. Bittmann
Graduate School of Business Administration – Bar-Ilan University, Israel

Roy M. Gelbard
Graduate School of Business Administration – Bar-Ilan University, Israel

INTRODUCTION

The problem of analyzing datasets and classifying them into clusters based on known properties is a well known problem with implementations in fields such as finance (e.g., pricing), computer science (e.g., image processing), marketing (e.g., market segmentation), and medicine (e.g., diagnostics), among others (Cadez, Heckerman, Meek, Smyth, & White, 2003; Clifford & Stevenson, 2005; Erlich, Gelbard, & Spiegler, 2002; Jain & Dubes, 1988; Jain, Murty, & Flynn, 1999; Sharan & Shamir, 2002).

Currently, researchers and business analysts alike must try out and test out each diverse algorithm and parameter separately in order to set up and establish their preference concerning the individual decision problem they face. Moreover, there is no supportive model or tool available to help them compare different results-clusters yielded by these algorithm and parameter combinations. Commercial products neither show the resulting clusters of multiple methods, nor provide the researcher with effective tools with which to analyze and compare the outcomes of the different tools.

To overcome these challenges, a decision support system (DSS) has been developed. The DSS uses a matrix presentation of multiple cluster divisions based on the application of multiple algorithms. The presentation is independent of the actual algorithms used and it is up to the researcher to choose the most appropriate algorithms based on his or her personal expertise.

Within this context, the current study will demonstrate the following:

- How to evaluate different algorithms with respect to an existing clustering problem.
- Identify areas where the clustering is more effective and areas where the clustering is less effective.
- Identify problematic samples that may indicate difficult pricing and positioning of a product.

Visualization of the dataset and its classification is virtually impossible using legacy methods when more than three properties are used, as is the case in many problems, since displaying the dataset in such a case will require giving up some of the properties or using some other method to display the dataset's distribution over four or more dimensions. This makes it very difficult to relate to the dataset samples and understand which of these samples are difficult to classify, (even when they are classified correctly), and which samples and clusters stand out clearly (Boudjeloud & Poulet, 2005; De-Oliveira & Levkowitz, 2003; Grabmier & Rudolph, 2002; Shultz, Mareschal, & Schmidt, 1994).

Even when the researcher uses multiple algorithms in order to classify the dataset, there are no available tools that allow him/her to use the outcome of the algorithms' application. In addition, the researcher has no tools with which to analyze the difference in the results.

The current study demonstrates the usage of a developed decision support methodology based upon formal quantitative measures and a visual approach, enabling presentation, comparison, and evaluation of the multi-classification suggestions resulting from diverse algorithms. The suggested methodology and DSS support a cross-algorithm presentation; all resultant classifications are presented together in a "Tetris-like format" in which each column represents a specific classification algorithm and each line represents a specific sample case. Formal quantitative measures are then used to analyze these "Tetris blocks," arranging them according to their best structures, that is, the most agreed-upon classification, which is probably the most agreed-upon decision.

Copyright © 2008, IGI Global, distributing in print or electronic forms without written permission of IGI Global is prohibited.

Such a supportive model and DSS impact the ultimate business utility decision significantly. Not only can it save critical time, it also pinpoints all irregular sample cases, which may require specific examination. In this way, the decision process focuses on key issues instead of wasting time on technical aspects. The DSS is demonstrated using common clustering problems of wine categorizing, based on 13 measurable properties.

THEORETICAL BACKGROUND

Cluster Analysis

In order to classify a dataset of samples with a given set of properties, researchers use algorithms that associate each sample with a suggested group-cluster, based on its properties. The association is performed using likelihood measure that indicates the similarity between any two samples as well as between a sample, to be associated, and a certain group-cluster.

There are two main clustering-classification types:

- **Supervised** (also called categorization), in which a fixed number of clusters are predetermined, and the samples are divided-categorized into these groups.

- **Unsupervised** (called clustering), in which the preferred number of clusters, to classify the dataset into, is formed by the algorithm while processing the dataset.

There are unsupervised methods, such as hierarchical clustering methods, that provide visualization of entire "clustering space" (dendrogram), and in the same time enable predetermination of a fixed number of clusters.

A researcher therefore uses the following steps:

1. The researcher selects the best classification algorithm based on his/her experience and knowledge of the dataset.
2. The researcher tunes the chosen classification algorithm by determining parameters, such as the likelihood measure, and number of clusters.

Current study uses hierarchical clustering methods, which are briefly described in the following section.

Hierarchical Clustering Methods

Hierarchical clustering methods refer to a set of algorithms that work in a similar manner. These algorithms take the dataset properties that need to be clustered and start out by classifying the dataset in such a way that each sample represents a cluster. Next, it merges the clusters in steps. Each step merges two clusters into a single cluster until only one cluster (the dataset) remains. The algorithms differ in the way in which distance is measured between the clusters, mainly by using two parameters: the distance or likelihood measure, for example, Euclidean, Dice, and so forth, and the cluster method, for example, between group linkage, nearest neighbor, and so forth.

In the present study, we used the following well-known hierarchical methods to classify the datasets:

- **Average linkage (within groups):** This method calculates the distance between two clusters by applying the likelihood measure to all the samples in the two clusters. The clusters with the best average likelihood measure are then united.
- **Average linkage (between groups):** This method calculates the distance between two clusters by applying the likelihood measure to all the samples of one cluster and then comparing it with all the samples of the other cluster. Once again, the two clusters with the best likelihood measure are then united.
- **Single linkage (nearest neighbor):** This method, as in the average linkage (between groups) method, calculates the distance between two clusters by applying the likelihood measure to all the samples of one cluster and then comparing it with all the samples of the other cluster. The two clusters with the best likelihood measure, from a pair of samples, are united.
- **Median:** This method calculates the median of each cluster. The likelihood measure is applied to the medians of the clusters, after which the clusters with the best median likelihood are then united.
- **Ward:** This method calculates the centroid for each cluster and the square of the likelihood measure of each sample in both the cluster and

the centroid. The two clusters, which when united have the smallest (negative) affect on the sum of likelihood measures, are the clusters that need to be united.

Likelihood-Similarity Measure

In all the algorithms, we used the squared Euclidean distance measure as the likelihood-similarity measure. This measure calculates the distance between two samples as the square root of the sums of all the squared distances between the properties.

As seen previously, the algorithms and the likelihood measures differ in their definition of the task, that is, the clusters are different and the distance of a sample from a cluster is measured differently. This results in the fact that the dataset classification differs without obvious dependency between the applied algorithms. The analysis becomes even more complicated if the true classification is unknown and the researcher has no means of identifying the core of the correct classification and the samples that are difficult to classify.

Visualization: Dendrogram

Currently, the results can be displayed in numeric tables, in 2D and 3D graphs, and when hierarchical classification algorithms are applied, also in a dendrogram, which is a tree-like graph that presents entire "clustering space," that is, the merger of clusters from the initial case, where each sample is a different cluster to the total merger, where the whole dataset is one cluster. The vertical lines in a dendrogram represent clusters that are joined, while the horizontal lines represent the likelihood coefficient for the merger. The shorter the horizontal line, the higher the likelihood that the clusters will merge. Though the dendrogram provides the researcher with some sort of a visual representation, it is limited to a subset of the algorithms used. Furthermore, the information in the dendrogram relates to the used algorithm and does not compare or utilize additional algorithms. The information itself serves as a visual aid to joining clusters, but does not provide a clear indication of inconsistent samples in the sense that their position in the dataset spectrum, according to the chosen properties, is misleading, and likely to be wrongly classified. This is a common visual aid used by researchers but it is not applicable to all algorithms.

Among the tools that utilize the dendrogram visual aid is the Hierarchical Clustering Explorer. This tool tries to deal with the multidimensional presentation of datasets with multiple variables. It produces a dashboard of presentations around the dendrogram that shows the classification process of the hierarchical clustering and the scatter plot that is a human readable presentation of the dataset, but limited to two variables (Seo & Shneiderman, 2002, 2005).

Visualization: Additional Methods

Discriminant Analysis and Factor Analysis

The problem of clustering may be perceived as finding functions applied on the variables that discriminate between samples and decide to which cluster they belong. Since usually there are more than two or even three variables it is difficult to visualize the samples in such multidimensional spaces, some methods are using the discriminating functions, which are a transformation of the original variables and present them on two dimensional plots.

Discriminant function analysis is quit analogous to multiple regression. The two-group discriminant analysis is also called Fisher linear discriminant analysis after Fisher (1936). In general, in these approaches we fit a linear equation of the type:

$$\text{Group} = a + b_1 * x_1 + b_2 * x_2 + ... + b_m * x_m$$

Where a is a constant and b_1 through b_m are regression coefficients.

The variables (properties) with the significant regression coefficients are the ones that contribute most to the prediction of group membership. However, these coefficients do not tell us between which of the groups the respective functions discriminate. The means of the functions across groups identify the group's discrimination. It can be visualized by plotting the individual scores for the discriminant functions.

Factor analysis is another way to determine which variables (properties) define a particular discriminant function. The former correlations can be regarded as factor loadings of the variables on each discriminant function (Abdi, 2007).

It is also possible to visualize both correlations; between the variables in the model (using adjusted factor analysis) and discriminant functions, using a tool that combines these two methods (Raveh, 2000). Each ray represents one variable (property). The angle between any two rays presents correlation between these variables (possible factors).

Self-Organization Maps (SOM)

SOM also known as Kohonen network is a method that is based on neural network models, with the intention to simplify the presentation of multidimensional data into the simpler more intuitive two-dimensional map (Kohonen, 1995).

The process is an iterative process that tries to bring samples, in many cases a vector of properties, that are close, after applying on them the likelihood measure, next to each other in the two dimensional space. After a large number of iterations a map-like pattern is formed that groups similar data together, hence its use in clustering.

Visualization: Discussion

As described, these methodologies support visualization of a specific classification, based on a single set of parameters. Hence, current methodologies are usually incapable of making comparisons between different algorithms and leave the decision making, regarding which algorithm to choose, to the researcher. Furthermore, most of the visual aids, though giving a visual interpretation to the classification by the method of choice, lose some of the relevant information on the way, like in the case of discriminant analysis, where the actual relations between the dataset's variable is being lost when projected on the two-dimensional space.

This leaves the researcher with very limited visual assistance and prohibits the researcher from having a full view of the relations between the samples and a comparison between the dataset classifications based on the different available tools.

DSS USING VISUALIZATION OF MULTI-ALGORITHMS VOTING

This research presents the implementation of the multi-algorithm DSS. In particular, it demonstrates techniques to:

- Identify the strengths and weaknesses of each clustering algorithm
- Identify the profile of the dataset being researched
- Identify samples' characteristics

The model is implemented on known datasets to further demonstrate its usage in real-life research.

The Visual Analysis Model

The tool presented in the current study presents the classification model from a clear, two-dimensional perspective, together with tools used for the analysis of this perspective.

Vote Matrix

The "vote matrix" concept process recognizes that each algorithm represents a different view of the dataset and its clusters, based on how the algorithm defines a cluster and measures the distance of a sample from a cluster. Therefore, each algorithm is given a "vote" as to how it perceives the dataset should be classified.

The tool proposed in the current study presents the "vote matrix" generated by the "vote" of each algorithm used in the process. Each row represents a sample, while each column represents an algorithm and its vote for each sample about which cluster it should belong to, according to the algorithm's understanding of both clusters and distances.

Heterogeneity Meter

The challenge in this method is to associate the different classifications, since each algorithm divides the dataset into different clusters. Although the number of clusters in each case remains the same for each algorithm, the tool is necessary in order to associate the clusters of each algorithm; for example, cluster number 2 according to algorithm A1 is the same as cluster number 3 according to algorithm A2. To achieve this correlation, we will calculate a measure called the heterogeneity meter for each row, that is, the collection of votes for a particular sample, and sum it up for all the samples.

Multiple methods can be used to calculate the heterogeneity meter. These methods are described as follows:

Squared VE (Vote Error)

This heterogeneity meter is calculated as the square sum of all the votes that did not vote for the chosen classification. It is calculated as follows:

$$H = \sum_{i=1}^{n}(N - M_i)^2$$

Equation 1: Squared VE Heterogeneity Meter
Where:
H – is the heterogeneity meter
N – is the number of algorithms voting for the sample
M – is the maximum number of similar votes according to a specific association received for a single sample
i – is the sample number
n – is the total number of samples in the dataset

Distance From Second Best (DFSB)

This heterogeneity meter is calculated as the difference in the number of votes that the best vote, that is, the vote common to most algorithms, received and the number of votes the second-best vote received. The idea is to discover to what extent the best vote is distinguished from the rest. This meter is a reverse meter, as the higher it is, the less heterogenic the sample. It is calculated as follows:

$$H = \sum_{i=1}^{n}(B_i - SB_i)$$

Equation 2: DFSB Heterogeneity Meter
Where:
H – is the Heterogeneity Meter
B – is the best, that is, the cluster voted the most times as the cluster for a given sample
SB – is the second-best cluster for a given sample
i – is the sample number
n – is the total number of samples in the dataset

Heterogeneity Meter Implementation

In order to find the best association, the heterogeneity meter needs to be minimized, that is, identifying the association that makes the votes for each sample as homogeneous as possible.

The heterogeneity meter is then used to sort the voting matrix, giving the researcher a clear, two-dimensional perspective of the clusters and indicating how well each sample is associated with its designated cluster.

Visual Pattern Characteristics

In this section, we will demonstrate several typical patterns that can be recognized in the suggested DSS. In each pattern, we find the following columns:

S – Samples number
T – True clustering
A1, A2, A3, A4, A5, A6 – Three algorithms used to for clustering

For each example, there are five rows representing five different samples.

Well-Classified Samples

In Figure 1, we can see that sample 68 was classified correctly by all algorithms. This is an indication that the variables used to classify the dataset work well with the sample; if this is consistent with the cluster, it shows that these variables can be used to identify it.

Figure 1. Well-classified clusters

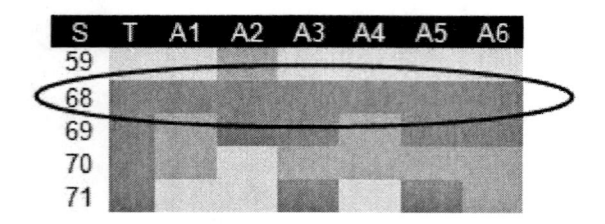

Figure 2. A hard-to-classify example

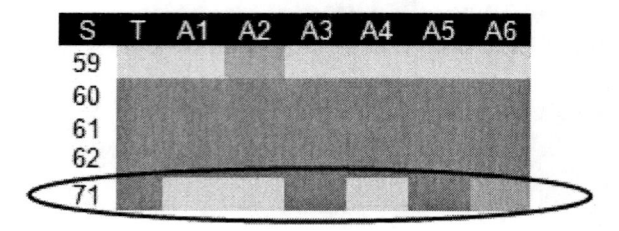

Figure 3. Algorithms that are effective for a certain cluster

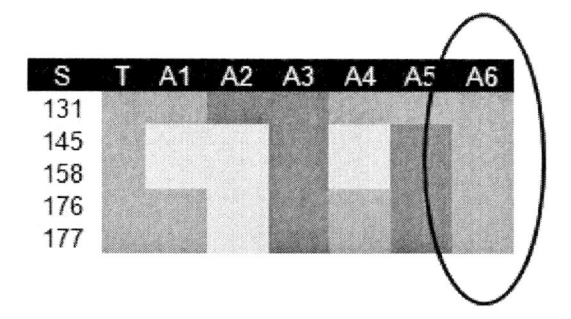

Figure 4. Wrongly classified samples

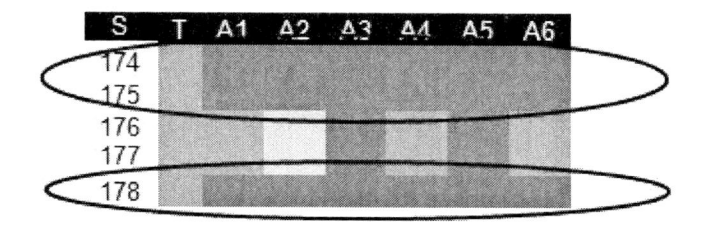

Samples that are Hard to Classify

In Figure 2, we see that while samples 59-62 are classified correctly and identically by nearly all the chosen methods, sample 71 is classified differently. This is an indication that this sample is hard to classify and that the parameters used for classification do not clearly designate it to any particular cluster.

Algorithms that are Effective for a Certain Cluster

In Figure 3, we see that algorithm A6 is more effective for classifying the medium grey cluster, as it is the only algorithm that succeeded in classifying it correctly. This does not mean that it is the best algorithm overall, but it does indicate that if the researcher wants to find candidates for that particular cluster algorithm, then A6 is a good choice.

Wrongly Classified Samples

In Figure 4, we see that some samples, mainly 174, 175, and 178 were classified incorrectly by all algorithms. It is evident since the cluster color of the classification by the algorithms, marked A1-A6, is different than the true classification, marked T. This is an indication that the parameters by which the dataset was classified are probably not ideal for some samples; if it is consistent with a certain cluster, we can then say that the set of variables used to classify the dataset is not effective for identifying this cluster.

IMPLEMENTATION: THE CASE OF WINE RECOGNITION

The Dataset

To demonstrate the implementation of the DSS, we chose the Wine Recognition Data (Forina, Leardi, Armanino, & Lanteri, 1988; Gelbard, Goldman, & Spiegler, 2007). This is a collection of wines classified using thirteen different variables. The variables are as follows:

1. Alcohol
2. Malic acid
3. Ash
4. Alcalinity of ash
5. Magnesium
6. Total phenols
7. Flavanoids
8. Non-flavanoid phenols
9. Proanthocyanins
10. Color intensity
11. Hue
12. OD280/OD315 of diluted wines
13. Proline

The target is to cluster the wines based on the given attributes into three different clusters, representing the three different cultivars from which the wines are derived.

Figure 5. Wine cases: Vote matrix part 1

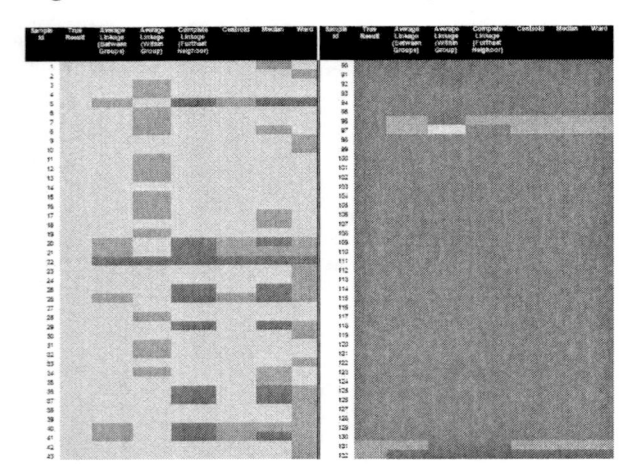

Figure 6. Wine cases: Vote matrix part 2

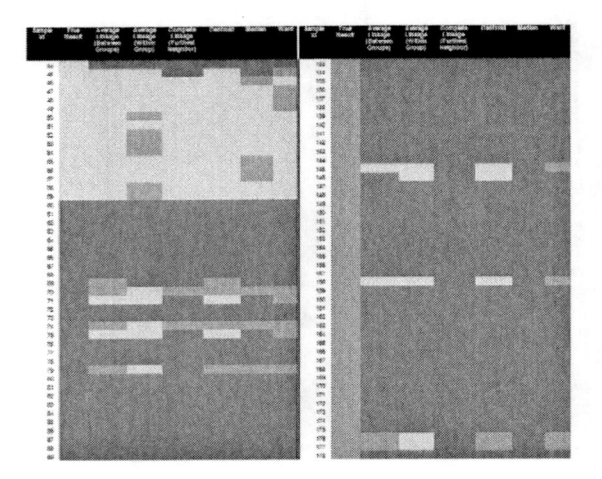

The Implementation

We used six hierarchical clustering methods:

1. Average linkage (between Groups)
2. Average linkage (within Group)
3. Complete linkage (Furthest Neighbor)
4. Centroid
5. Median
6. Ward

We performed the cluster association using the DFSB heterogeneity meter; the resulting vote matrix is depicted in Figures 5 6.

Figures 7 and Figure 8, in appendix A, rearrange the cases, that is, lines of Figures 5 and 6, in a way that agreed cases are placed close to each other, according to clusters order, creating a "Tetris-like" view. As aforesaid, each column represents a specific algorithm, each line represents a specific case, and each color represents a "vote", that is, decision suggestion.

Uni-color lines represent cases in which all algorithms vote for the same cluster (each cluster is represented by a different color). These agreed cases are "pushed down," while multi-color lines "float" above, in the same way it is used in a Tetris game.

DISCUSSION

The advantage of the visual representation of clustering the wine dataset is well depicted in Figures 5 and 6, as we get a graphical representation of the dataset and its classification. Examples of the immediate results from this presentation are as follows:

Looking at the vote matrix, it is easy to see that two of the three clusters are well detected using the hierarchical clustering algorithms.

It can also be seen that some samples, such as samples 70, 71, 74, and 75 are not easy to classify, while other samples, such as sample 44, are falsely associated.

Furthermore, it can be seen that the average linkage (within group) is probably not an algorithm that will work well with this dataset.

CONCLUSION AND FURTHER RESEARCH

The DSS presented in the current article uses different algorithm results to present the researcher with a clear picture of the data being researched.

The DSS is a tool that assists the researcher and allows the researcher to demonstrate his/her expertise in selecting the variables by which the data is classified and the algorithms used to classify it.

In some cases, the researcher knows the expected number of clusters to divide the dataset into, while in other cases, the researcher needs assistance. The discussed DSS works well in both cases, as it can present different pictures of the dataset as a result of the different classifications.

The result is a tool that can assist researchers in analyzing and presenting a dataset otherwise difficult to comprehend. The researcher can easily see, rather than calculate, both the trends and the classifications in the researched dataset and can clearly present it to his/her colleagues.

To activate the analysis, a tool was developed that performs the association of the different algorithms. This tool uses brute force and thus is still not scalable over a large number of clusters and algorithms. More efficient ways to perform the association require further research.

There are also multiple methods for calculating the heterogeneity meter. Two of them were presented in the current study, but there is still room for using/presenting other methods that allow us to associate the clusters based on different trends, such as prioritizing an association with a clear classifications in as many samples as possible vs. associations with minimum errors over all the vote matrix.

REFERENCES

Abdi, H. (2007). Discriminant correspondence analysis. In N. J. Salkind (Ed.), *Encyclopedia of Measurement and Statistics*. Sage.

Boudjeloud, L., & Poulet, F. (2005). *Visual interactive evolutionary algorithm for high dimensional data clustering and outlier detection*. (LNAI 3518, pp. 426-431).

Cadez, I., Heckerman, D., Meek, C., Smyth, P., & White, S. (2003). Model-based clustering and visualization of navigation patterns on a Web site. *Data Mining and Knowledge Discovery, 7,* 399-424.

Clifford, H. T., & Stevenson, W. (1975). *An introduction to numerical classification*. Academic Press.

De-Oliveira, M. C. F., & Levkowitz, H. (2003). From visual data exploration to visual data mining: A survey. *IEEE Transactions on Visualization and Computer Graphics, 9*(3), 378-394.

Erlich, Z., Gelbard, R., & Spiegler, I. (2002). Data mining by means of binary representation: A model for similarity and clustering. *Information Systems Frontiers, 4,* 187-197.

Forina, M., Leardi, R., Armanino, C., & Lanteri, S. (1988). *PARVUS—An extendible package for data exploration, classification and correlation*. Genova, Italy: Institute of Pharmaceutical and Food Analysis and Technologies.

Gelbard, R., Goldman, O., & Spiegler, I. (2007). *Investigating diversity of clustering methods: An empirical comparison*. Data & Knowledge Engineering, doi:10.1016/j.datak.2007.01.002.

Grabmier, J., & Rudolph, A. (2002). Techniques of cluster algorithms in data mining. *Data Mining and Knowledge Discovery, 6,* 303-360.

Jain, A. K., & Dubes, R. C. (1988). *Algorithms for clustering data*. Prentice Hall.

Jain, A. K., Murty, M. N., & Flynn, P. J. (1999). Data clustering: A review. *ACM Communication Surveys, 31,* 264-323.

Kohonen, T. (1995), Self-organizing maps. Series in *Information Sciences, 30.*

Raveh, A. (2000). Coplot: A graphic display method for geometrical representations of MCDM. *European Journal of Operational Research, 125,* 670-678.

Sharan, R., & Shamir, R. (2002). Algorithmic approaches to clustering gene expression data. In T. Jiang et al. (Eds.), *Current topics in computational molecular biology* (pp. 269-300). Cambridge, MA: MIT Press.

Shultz, T., Mareschal, D., & Schmidt, W. (1994). Modeling cognitive development on balance scale phenomena. *Machine Learning, 16,* 59-88.

Seo, J., & Shneiderman, B. (2002). Interactively exploring hierarchical clustering results. *IEEE Computer, 35*(7), 80-86.

Seo, J., & Shneiderman, B. (2005). A rank-by-feature framework for interactive exploration of multidimensional data. *Information Visualization, 4*(2), 99-113.

KEY TERMS

Decision Support System (DSS): DSS is a system used to help resolve certain problems or dilemmas.

Dendrogram: Dendrogram is a method of presenting the classification of a hierarchical clustering algorithm.

Distance From Second Best (DFSB): DFSB is a method of calculating the distribution of votes for a certain sample. This method is based on the difference between the highest number of similar associations and the second-highest number of similar associations.

Heterogeneity Meter: Heterogeneity meter is a meter of how heterogenic a certain association of clusters resulting from the implementation of an algorithm is.

Hierarchical Clustering Algorithms: Hierarchical clustering algorithms are clustering methods that classify datasets starting with all samples representing different clusters and gradually unite samples into clusters based on their likelihood measure.

Likelihood Measurement: Likelihood measurement is the measure that allows for the classification of a dataset using hierarchical clustering algorithms. It measures the extent to which a sample and a cluster are alike.

Vote Matrix: Vote matrix is a graphical tool used to present a dataset classification using multiple algorithms.

APPENDIX A: THE REARRANGED VOTE MATRIX

Figure 7. The rearranged vote matrix part 1

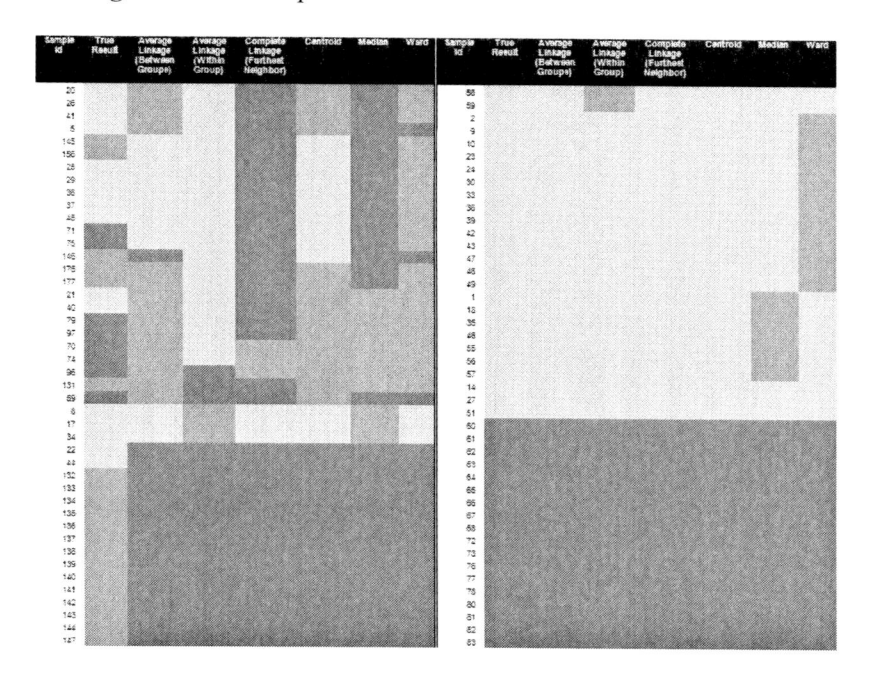

Figure 8. The rearranged vote matrix part 2

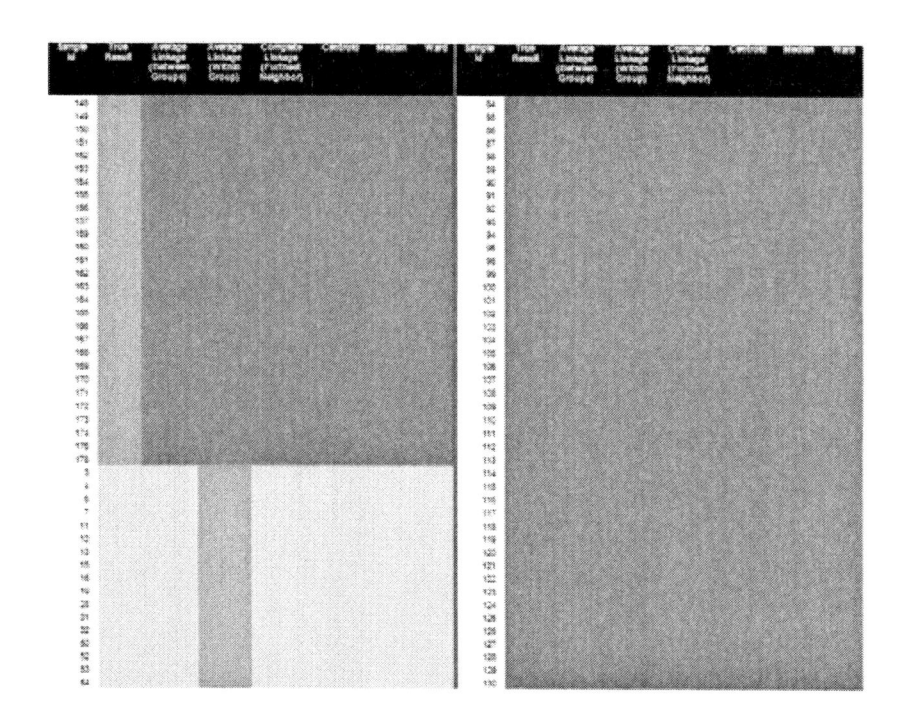

Dynamic System Simulation for Decision Support

Norman Pendegraft
University of Idaho, USA

Mark Rounds
University of Idaho, USA

Simulation is a powerful methodology for decision support because it allows managers to experiment with models prior to implementing a policy or decision. There are several approaches to computer simulation: continuous event simulation, discrete event simulation, and Monte Carlo simulation. Continuous event simulation can be used to model dynamic system which cannot otherwise be easily modeled.

INTRODUCTION

Simulation is a technique that uses models that imitate the behavior of the real system. There are several ways to describe simulation models (Winston, 1994).

- Static models describe the behavior of the system a specific point in time.
- Dynamic models describe the behavior of the system as it evolves over time.
- Deterministic models allow for no random behavior.
- Stochastic models use Monte Carlo techniques to model random behavior.
- Discrete event simulations model systems in which events change the state.
- Continuous simulations model systems in which the state variable changes continuously. Such systems can sometimes be described with systems of differential equations.

Simulation is valuable because it allows decision makers to experiment with models before they implement decisions or policies. They then may be able to better understand the impacts of their decisions before implementing them.

The remainder of the article is organized as follows. The second section discusses simulation as a mode of inquiry. The third section presents some background on Monte Carlo and discrete event simulation. The fourth section has the main discussion of continuous event simulation and systems dynamics. The fifth and sixth sections offer a discussion of current efforts and future trends. These are followed by definitions and references.

BACKGROUND

Simulation as a Mode of Inquiry

Scientific inquiry has traditionally had two components: theory and experimentation. Lax (1986) suggested that computer simulation constitutes a third form of inquiry. In particular, simulation provides the ability to study complex systems. Pagels (1988) suggested that this new mode of inquiry would have a great impact on decision making in a broad range of areas ranging from medicine to finance.

Since Lax made his prediction, an extensive literature on complex systems and nonlinear dynamics has arisen (see Sterman, 2000 for example). Complex systems are characterized by nonlinear behavior typically caused by feedback. Forrester (1961) notes that information feedback is present in every decision made by people. When the interaction between the components of a system dominates the aggregate behavior, the system can be described as complex. Further, such systems frequently display behavior that may vary radically depending on the values of the parameters.

Biological and social systems are inherently complex as are many physical systems. They typically do not achieve the "equilibrium" traditionally studied by economists. Even if they do, it is frequently their transient behavior that is interesting to decision makers. Some of these systems can be modeled with

Figure 1. Limits to growth (adapted from Senge)

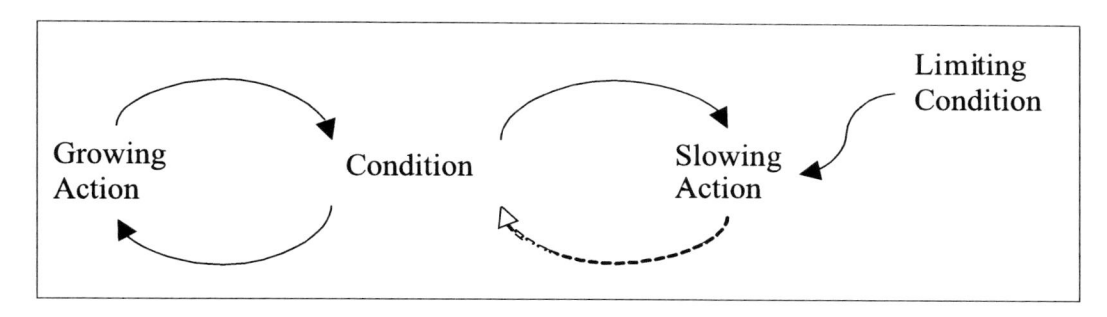

differential equations, but they are typically hard to solve analytically, simulation has become an attractive way to study their time evolution. Continuous event simulation (sometimes called "system dynamics" in this context) is well suited to studying such systems. These simulations use models consisting of systems of finite difference equations which are solved iteratively to model the dynamic behavior of the system. Until recently, numerical solution of such systems was expensive and required advanced programming skills. Recent advances in computer technology have made solutions of such systems much easier.

Senge (1990) presents an extensive discussion of dynamic models of social systems. He identifies several prototypes that describe common organizational problems. For example, his prototype I is "Limits to growth" (Figure 1). The management lesson that he extracts from the prototype is: "Don't push growth; remove the factors limiting growth." (Senge, 95ff.)

Discrete Event and Monte Carlo Simulation

In Monte Carlo simulation, some values are taken to be random variates. These are generated using some sort of pseudo random number generator. For example, a spread sheet calculating present value of an income stream might take the discount rate in each year to be random. In a queuing model, service and inter arrival times might be stochastic, and discrete event simulation is often useful. In such simulations the state of the system changes periodically due to the occurrence of events. In a queuing problem, the state could be the number of customers in the system and the busy/free states of the servers. Events would include: customer arrival, start of service, and completion of service. Each of these could cause the state to change. Typically, discrete event simulations use Monte Carlo methods to determine the times at which events occur and statistical means are used to evaluate the results (See Winston, 1994).

DYNAMIC SYSTEM SIMULATION

While Forrester (1961) did not invent simulation nor introduce it to management, his seminal *Industrial Dynamics*, may be the first comprehensive introduction to the use of computer simulation in support of management. He discusses key ideas like stock and flow models, information flows, and delays in flows. Stock and flow models are still a standard way of visualizing dynamic system models. Stocks represent the state of the system while the flows represent activities that result in changes to the state.

Forrester implemented his models in the computer language DYNAMO. More modern tools like IThink allow the user to write the code by manipulating graphical symbols on the computer screen. The program then translates those symbols into lines of code. The result in both cases is a set of finite difference equations which are solved iteratively using standard numerical algorithms.

Systems dynamics (SD) has been used to support decision making in a wide variety of fields. Strohhecker (2005) describes a project to support a bank planning for the euro conversion. Otto and Struben (2004) created a model to improve understanding of a fishery management problem. Stephens, Graham, and Lyneis (2005) describe the use of SD in a variety of legal disputes.

Figure 2a. Water tank model

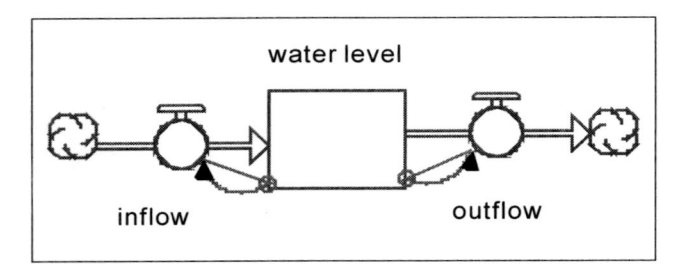

Figure 2b. Water tank equations

```
water_level(t) = water_level(t - dt) + (inflow - outflow) * dt
INIT water_level = 0

INFLOWS:
inflow = 1 + (4-water_level)/4
OUTFLOWS:
outflow = .25*water_level
```

Figure 2c. Water level vs. time

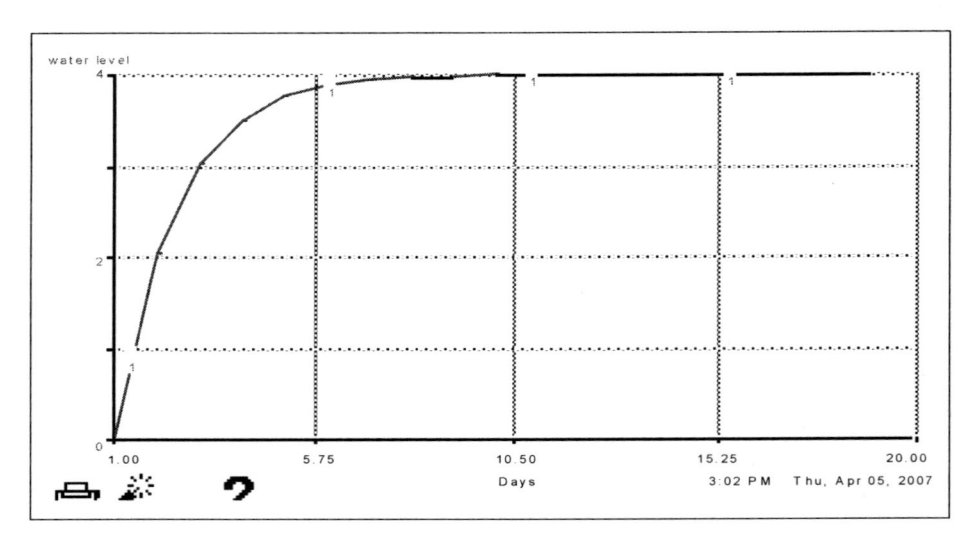

Homer, Hirsch, Minniti, and Pierson (2004) and Liddell and Powell (2004) describe projects assisting in health care planning. The use of systems dynamics in supply chain management is summarized by Akkermans and Dellaert (2005).

Continuous Event Simulation for a Simple Physical Process

Continuous event simulation is used to simulate physical systems that can be described with systems of differential equations. The differential equations are estimated with a series of difference equations, and these are solved numerically to obtain solutions of the system's behavior. The following example (from Clark, 1988) illustrates the use of CE simulation to solve a simple system. This system is so simple that it can be solved analytically, but it serves well to illustrate the general method.

Consider a water tank with an inflow and an outflow as follows.

T = time
$L(T)$ = water level in the tank at time T
$L(0)=0$
$I(T,L)$ = inflow rate $\qquad = 1 + (4-W(T))/4$
$O(T,L)$ = outflow rate $\qquad = .25\ W(T)$

Note that the rates are actually derivatives, so that this actually represents a differential equation.

$$dL/dT = 1 + (4-L(T))/4 - .2\ L(T)$$

Steady state conditions can be found by setting dL/dT = 0, leaving 2 - .45L=0 which gives L=4. Describing the transient state requires that the differential equation be solved which in this simple case is also easy:

L=a e^{bt} +c   with b= -.45, c=1/.45 and a=-1/.45.

While this particular system can be easily solved analytically, systems only slightly more complex are intractable, and can only be addressed numerically. Most social systems are much more complex.

This example also serves to illustrate the stock and flow model. In this simple case the stocks and flows are tangible: water. In social systems they may be less tangible. Figure 2a illustrates a solution to this problem using IThink. This model generated the code shown in Figure 2b, and Figure 2c illustrates the output showing the time trajectory of water level. Note the easy to understand graphic design of the program and the resultant code is illustrated. These are finite difference equations which can be solved numerically. In a finite difference equation, a first derivative is estimated with a finite difference:

dF/dt ~ {F(t) – F(t-δt)} / δt.

Similar estimates can be made for higher order terms (see for example Korn & Korn 737). The graph illustrates the water level over time.

Dynamic Systems Simulation for a More Complex System

One of the best known mathematical descriptions of a biological system is the Lotka Voltera equations (Jackson, 1987). This model consists of two differential equations that describe the interaction between a predator species and its prey. The first describes the population dynamics of the prey. The time rate of change of prey is proportional to the previous population times the birth rate less the death due to predation which is proportional to the population of predators. Similarly, the time rate of change of the predator population is proportional to the native death rate plus a prey interaction term. Here the interaction between the species is central to their behavior.

dY / dt = Y(b-aR)
dR / dt = -R(d-cY)

where   R is the number of some predator
Y is the number of its prey
t represents the time; and
b is the birthrate of the prey
d is the death rate of the predator
a and c describe the interaction of the two species.

This solution to this system can display varying behavior including extinction and oscillating popula-

Figure 3a. Predator prey model

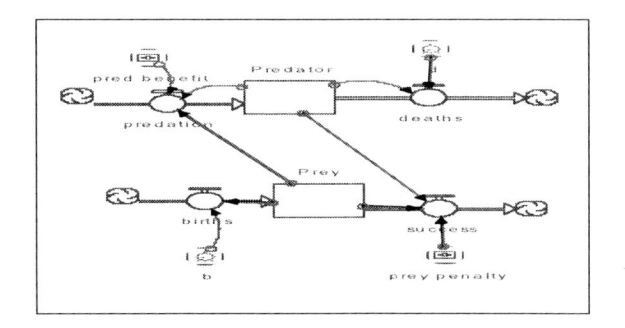

Figure 3b. Two population Trajectories

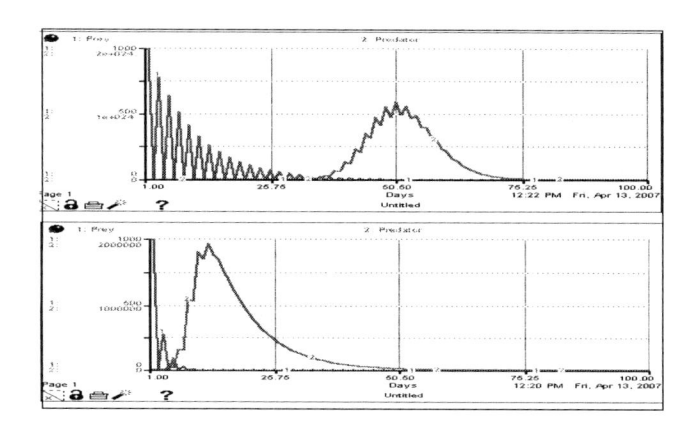

tions. Equilibrium conditions exist, but they are not stable. Hence, understanding the behavior of this system requires numerical solution. Figure 3a illustrates an IThink implementation of this model. The graphs (Figure 3b and 3c) illustrate possible population trajectories with different values of the parameters. As can be seen, the system displays radically different behavior depending on those values.

Systems Dynamics Example

The following example comes from the author's work with a student. A nursing home was concerned about the attrition rate of some of its certified nurses' assistants. A model based on Richmond and Peterson (1997) was built using IThink that calculates a simple quality of care metric and costs (Figure 4a). New hires are certified after several weeks of on the job training. This training cannot be suspended because it is a major attraction to new hires. Certified assistants get a substantial wage boost. One- hundred percent of certified help resulted in a cost of 100 / week (arbitrary units).

However, experimentation with the certified attrition rate showed that an attrition rate of 20% kept the same service level at a lower cost (Figure 4b). Thus the analysis gave the non intuitive insight that a low attrition rate can increase costs without significantly increasing service levels, and what was thought to be a severe problem, may instead be evidence of a healthy system.

Note the relatively high level of the model. Richmond and Person (1997) and Senge (1990) caution against too detailed a model, especially initially. The purpose of the model is to identify "point of leverage" and to evaluate aggregate behavior. In this case the insight was that a nonzero turnover rate was desirable.

FUTURE TRENDS

One expects that interest in simulation for decision support will increase. Akkermans and Dellaert (2005) point out the recent impact of system dynamics in supply chain management (SCM) and predict that use of systems dynamics will continue to improve SCM practice. Increased desktop computing power and improved software will make it easier for people to create and use simulation models. Efforts like Warren's and increasing numbers of success stories like those noted in the introduction will likely improve the visibility of simulation as a decision making tool.

CONCLUSION

Systems dynamics is, as noted, not without its detractors. Garner (2000) pointed out that simulation has not been widely used in education despite substantial effort and promise. Warren (2005) noted the relative lack of use of SD and has devoted efforts to making SD more

Figure 4a. Hiring / Promotion model

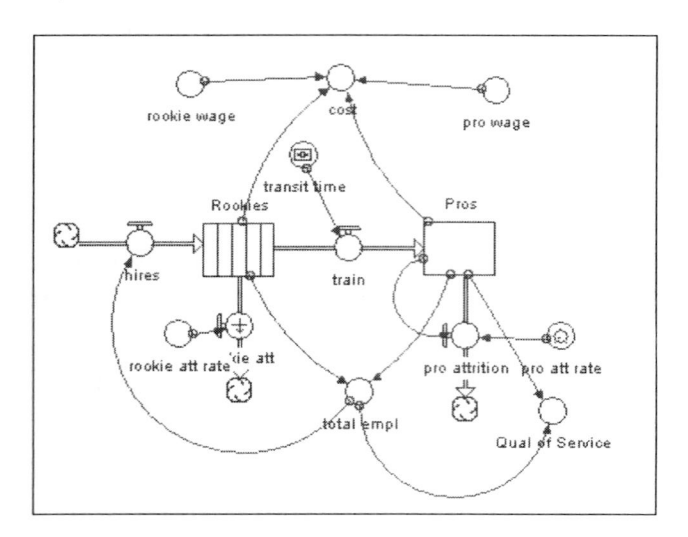

Figure 4b. A lower cost solution

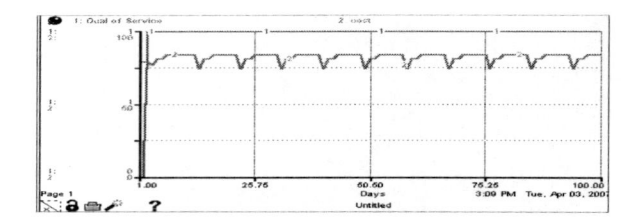

readily accessible to management. However, as noted in the introduction, there has been considerable use of system dynamics for decision support. There has also been considerable theoretical advancement in non linear dynamics and in the development of computer simulation languages. The great popular success of Senge's book suggests that there is an interest in systems thinking in the business community. As the tools become more powerful, that interest will likely increase.

REFERENCES

Akkermans, H., & Dellaert, N. (2005). The rediscovery of industrial dynamics: The contribution of system dynamics to supply chain management in a dynamic and fragmented world. *The System Dynamics Review, 21*(3),

Clark, R. (1988). *System dynamics and modeling.* Linthium MD: Institute for Operations Research and Management Science.

Forrester, J. (1961). *Industrial dynamics.* New York: John Wiley and Son.

Garson, D. G. (2000). The role of information technology in quality education in social dimensions of information technology. *Issues For The New Millennium,* 177-197.

Homer, H., Hirsch, G., Minniti, M., & Pierson, M. (2004). Models for collaboration: How systems dynamics help a community organize cost-effective care for chronic illness. *System Dynamics Review, 20*(3), 199-222.

Jackson, E. A. (1987). *Non linear dynamcs.* Cambridge: Cambridge University Press.

Korn, G. & Korn, T. (1968). *Mathematical handbook for scientists and engineers.* New York: McGraw-Hill.

Lax, P. D. (1986). Mathematics and computing. *Journal of Statistical Physics, 43*(5/6), 749-756.

Liddell, W. G., & Powell, J. H. (2004). Agreeing access policy in a general medial practice: A case study using QPID. *System Dynamics Review, 20*(1), 49-73.

Otto, P., & Struben, J. (2004). Gloucester fishery: Insight from a group modeling intervention. *System Dynamics Review, 20*(4), 287-312.

Pagels, H. (1988). *The dreams of reason.* New York: Simon and Shuster.

Richmond, B., & Peterson, S. (1997). *Introduction to systems thinking, high performance systems.* Hanover, NH.

Senge, P. (1990). *The fifth discipline.* New York: Currency Doubleday.

Stephens, C. A., Graham, A. K., & Lyneis, J. M. (2005). System dynamics modeling in the legal arena: meeting the challenges of expert witness admissibility. *System Dynamics Review, 21*(2), 95-122.

Sterman, J. D. (2000). *Business dynamics: Systems thinking and modeling for a complex world.* Boston: Irwin McGraw Hill.

Strohhecker, J. (2005). Scenarios and simulations for planning Dredner bank's e-day. *System Dynamics Review, 21*(1), 5-32.

Warren, K. (2005). Improving strategic management with fundamental principles of systems dynamics. *System Dynamics Review, 21*(4), 329-350.

Winston, W. (1994). *Operations research: Applications an algorithms* (3rd ed.). Belmont, CA: Duxbury.

KEY TERMS

Continuous Simulation: A simulation methodology in which uses the state of the system changes continuously in time.

Discrete Event Simulation: A simulation methodology in which events cause the state of the system to change at specific points in time.

Dynamic System: A system which has a state vector that changes over time.

Flow: An object in a dynamic systems simulation that represents changes in stocks.

Monte Carlo Simulation: A simulation in which random events are modeled using pseudo random number generators so that many replications of the random events may be evaluated statistically.

Simulation: Experimenting with a model (typically a computer model) of a system.

Stock: An object in a dynamic systems simulation that represents some aspect of the state of system which may change over time.

System Dynamics: A modeling approach developed by Forrester (1961) that models complex systems. An engineering discipline that deals with the mathematical analysis of dynamic systems.

Ethical Decision Making: A Critical Assessment and an Integrated Model

Norizah Mustamil
Curtin University of Technology, Australia

Mohammed Quaddus
Curtin University of Technology, Australia

INTRODUCTION

Studies have shown that organizations are putting more effort in enforcing the ethical practices in their decision making activities (Janet, Armen, & Ted, 2001). An increasing number of models have also been proposed that have attempted to explore and explain various philosophical approaches to ethical decision making behaviour. In addition, many empirical studies have been presented in various scholarly journals focusing on this subject with the aim of putting theory into practice (O'Fallon & Butterfield, 2005). Nevertheless, unethical practices including fraud, corruption, and bribery continue to be reported (Trevino & Victor, 1992). Bartlett (2003) claims that there is a large gap between theory and practice in ethical decision making research, as existing models are trapped either in undersocialized view (focus on individual factors only) or oversocialized view (focus on situational factor only).

Development of a theoretical framework in the ethical decision making area has proven to be very challenging due to the multitude of complex and varied factors that contribute to ethical behaviour. This article attempts to contribute in this challenging area by reviewing and examining the major existing models and presenting an integrated model of ethical decision making model.

This article is divided into three sections. The first section presents an analysis of the broad range of key determinants in major existing models of ethical decision making, namely, individual, organizational, moral intensity, and cultural factors. The second section proposes an integrated model of ethical decision making which is culturally based. In particular, the proposed model is developed based on Malaysian culture. Using culture as a basic determinant, the proposed model can be adapted for any specific culture or country. In the last section, suggestions on data collection to test the proposed model are provided.

BACKGROUND

The area of ethical decision making has been receiving increasing attention from ethical scholars. The main emphasis had been on individuals' behaviour in organizations and how they deal with ethical dilemma. Generally, four factors have been found to influence individual to engage in ethical decision making, namely: individual, organizational, moral intensity, and cultural dimensions. Table 1 provides a list of dimensions in each of the factors. In order to describe each of the dimensions, four major models in ethical decision making are reviewed including; (1) "A Person-Situation Interactionist Model" (Trevino, 1986); (2) "A General Theory of Marketing Ethics" (Hunt & Vitell, 1986); (3) "A Contingency Model of Ethical Decision Making in Marketing Organization" (Ferrel & Gresham, 1985); and (4) "An Issue Contingent Model" (Jones, 1991).

INDIVIDUAL FACTORS

Normative study emphasizes that, when dealing with ethical dilemma, individuals will develop their own beliefs and rules based on their own moral philosophy. Based on these beliefs, individuals will determine their ethical point of view in handling ethical dilemmas (Fritzsche, 1991). Thus, individual factors need to be considered to understand ethical behaviour. As shown in Table 1, a variety of dimensions have been proposed in the major models of ethical decision making to dem-

Table 1. Dimensions of key determinants in major ethical decision models

Individual Factor	Organizational Factor	Moral Intensity Factor	Cultural Factor
Trevino, 1986 Cognitive Moral Development Ego Strength Field Dependence Locus of Control **Ferrel & Gresham, 1985** Knowledge Values Attitudes Intentions **Hunt & Vitell, 1986** Deontological Norms Teleological Norms	**Trevino, 1986** Reinforcement Other Pressures Normative Structure Obedience to Authority Responsibility for Consequences Role Taking Resolution of Moral Conflict **Ferrel & Gresham, 1985** Professional Codes Corporate Policy Rewards/Punishment Differential Association Role Set Configuration **Hunt & Vitell, 1986** Organizational norms	**Jones, 1991** Magnitude of Consequences Social Consensus Probability of Effect Temporal Immediacy Proximity Concentration of Effect	**Hunt & Vitell, 1986** Cultural Environment **Ferrel & Gresham, 1985** Social and Cultural Environment

onstrate how individuals respond and reach different conclusions on morality issues. Hunt and Vitell (1986) proposed that deontological and teleological views effect the reaction of an individual's ethical behaviour. Those who hold the deontological view are concerned with the majority benefit. Therefore, the consequences of the action on majority benefit become their primary concern. On the other hand, those with a teleological view are concerned with the action rather than the consequences of the action.

Organizational Factor

An organization's environment reflects the individual's behaviour in ethical decision making. Individuals try to occupy their system of beliefs within the organizational setting, and any inconsistency will be modified based on the systems within the organization. Organizational culture provides behavioural cues and becomes a guideline for behavioral conduct (Karande, Rao, & Singhapakdi, 2002). Trevino's (1986) model has been known as the most accepted model to describe the influence of organizational culture. In this model, the author proposed that individual's ethical behavior is influenced by organizational components, which includes a number of dimensions (see Table 1). In addition, most of the major models of ethical decision making also propose the influence of organizational culture by proposing various dimensions of this construct.

Moral Intensity

Jones (1991) has addressed the importance of moral intensity in ethical decision making. He describes that the characteristics of the issue itself will determine whether the individual will be involved in ethical behaviour. The argument by Jones (1991) has been supported by Valentine and Fleischman (2003) who found the significant relationship between moral intensity and ethical behaviour. Jones (1991) proposed six dimensions to determine the moral intensity including: Magnitude of Consequences, Social Consensus, Probability of Effect, Temporal Immediacy, Proximity, and Concentration of Effect.

Cultural Dimension

Culture is recognised as a key determinant of how individuals behave, more or less ethically, in the organization (England, 1975). It is also increasingly understood that culture is an attribute to aid management to determine how individuals respond and perceive the ethical standards in the organization (Singhapakdi, Vitell, & Franke, 1999). Cultural background will help an individual to define what appropriate and inappropriate behaviour should be taken. This construct, however, received less attention in major models of ethical decision making compared to other factors (refer to Table 1). Hence, in the next section, this factor is discussed in detail to show how individual behaviour can be determined based on cultural background.

Culture and Ethical Decision Making

Individuals place their ethical standards based on their own perception; one person's unethical actions may not be unethical to others. Singhapakdi, Vitell et al. (1999) suggested that the reason for this discrepancy is due to varied cultural background. Culture has been found as an important determinant in ethical decision making. Christie, Kwon, Stoeberl, and Baumhart (2003) examined the effect of culture on ethical attitudes among business managers from India, Korea, and U.S. towards certain questionable practices. The results indicated that culture has a strong influence on business managers' attitude due to its effects on the development of personal integrity. In conclusion, individuals who were raised in different cultures have different value systems to interpret the ethical standard of certain practices (England, 1975).

Previous studies have acknowledged these differences. Hofstede (1984) has developed a quantitative classification scheme for measuring the characteristics of national culture on 67 countries based on 117,000 respondents. As a result, four dimensions have emerged, namely, Power Distance, Uncertainty Avoidance, Individualism/Collectivism, and Masculinity/Femininity. Hofstede (1984) concluded that there are systematic differences between different cultures, and these cultural values are the basis of the desirable characteristics of a particular person. Trompenaars (1993) reported a 10-year study examining the responses of over 15,000 managers from 23 countries and identified five relationship orientations that show how individuals in different cultures relate in the work place. These dimensions are: universalism vs. particularism, individualism vs. communitarianism, neutral vs. emotionalism, specific vs. diffuse, and achievement vs. ascription. In addition, the GLOBE project (House & Javidan, 2004) determined leadership behaviour and the role of national culture based on more than 18,000 middle managers in 62 countries. This project identified nine dimensions to distinguish the differences in culture. These include: performance orientation, future orientation, assertiveness, power distance, humane orientation, institutional collectivism, in-group collectivism, uncertainty avoidance, and gender egalitarianism. Regardless of the diversity of cultural dimensions, all of these research efforts reached a similar conclusion: an individual's behavioural characteristics reflect where the individual came from, that is, their cultural background.

Influence of Culture on Personal Values

Singhapakdi, Rawwas, Marta, and Ahmed (1999) proposed that the underlying foundation of a culture is individuals' values. Individuals learn and adapt their personal values based on their cultural backgrounds. These personal values then affect particular ethical norms and behaviours in dealing with ethical issues (Laczniak & Naor, 1985). In order to explain the personal values, we need to refer back to the moral philosophies in ethical behavior theory. Forsyth (1980) has developed a 20 item Ethics Position Questionnaire (EPQ) to determine the individual's personal values based on their moral ideology. He identified two broad categories, relativism (deontological) and idealism (teleological), to classify personal value systems.

Variations in idealism and relativism of individual behaviour could be explained on the basis of cultural differences. Differences in cultural background adopt a different view of ethical practices (Ferrell & Gresham, 1985; Hunt & Vitell, 1986). For example, one common practice in one culture might be unacceptable in another culture. In China, for instance, it is a common custom to give a variety of souvenirs including money to the business clients being dealt with. This practice is called "guangxi," which is accepted in the Eastern countries (Yeung & Tung, 1996). This is the way of showing kinship, close personal relationships, and respect to the manifestation of group orientation. However, it is often misinterpreted as bribery by the Western values.

To date, there are relatively few studies examining the relationship between culture and personal values (Armstrong, 1996). Hence, this article contributes by proposing a model incorporating the cultural influence in order to explain individuals' ethical decision making.

AN INTEGRATED MODEL OF ETHICAL DECISION MAKING: THE CASE OF MALAYSIA

In this section, "An Integrated Model of Ethical Decision Making" is proposed. Based on Malaysian culture, the model uses Hofstede's (1984) cultural dimensions as key determinants on Forsyth's (1980) typology of personal values in explaining individual's ethical decision making. Even though there are other factors that also influence this behaviour including individual, organizational, and moral intensity, the explanation in this section only focuses on the significance of cultural dimensions on personal values in ethical behavior. Malaysia is a country with cultures of collectivism, high power distance, low uncertainty avoidance, and lower masculinity (Hofstede, 1980).

Power distance: Hofstede (1984) ranked Malaysia very high with high Power Distance. This concept refers to the acceptance of power inequality in organizations. As described by Hofstede (1984), individuals in high power distance cultures behave in accordance to their position in organizations. They are expected to show loyalty, obey their superiors blindly, tend to use formal standard for ethical conduct, and support the status quo.

Collectivism: As a collectivism country, Malaysian societies think of themselves as benefiting from the group and accept that they need to sacrifice their personal interests to protect the group interest. Collectivism perceives that the nature of individual relationship is based on obligation of moral duties for group security and conformity. Group members collaborate to save face for group reputation and to try to avoid any disagreement among them to show their respect and loyalty (Hofstede, 1984).

Masculinity: Masculinity is defined in terms of being aggressive, ambitious, competitive, and materialistic (Hofstede, 1984). Malaysian is found to be low in masculinity culture. Hence, Malaysian societies are expected to be more interpersonally oriented and benevolent and define achievement in terms of close human relationship rather than material success.

Uncertainty avoidance: Uncertainty avoidance is related to the degree where members of a society feel uncomfortable with uncertainty and ambiguity. With the low uncertainty avoidance culture, Malaysians are expected to be less concerned with security, rely less on written rules and procedures, and be more tolerant of uncertainty.

With the culture of high power distance, collectivism, less masculinity, and lower uncertainty avoidance, Malaysian personal values in dealing with ethical decision making can be predicted (see Figure 1). The particular dimensions of culture drive Malaysian societies to place a "face" value among group member as an important obligation and consider social consensus in order to avoid any harm that affect a groups' benefits. Hence, Malaysians try to reach an agreement with any practices even if it might be questionable, especially if someone who has higher position has adopted this practice. Moreover, Malaysians believe

Figure 1. An integrated model of ethical decision making for Malaysia

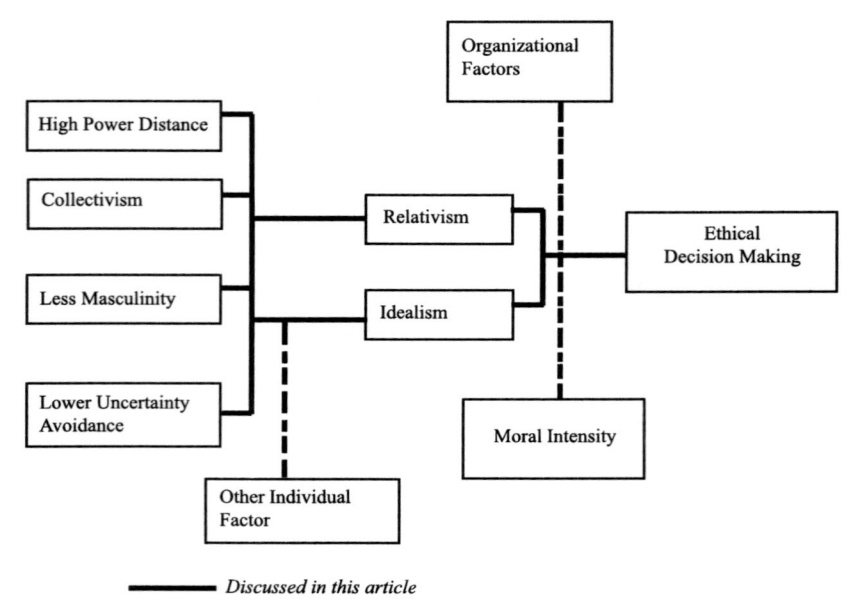

that the inequality of power is a common custom that societies must accept. This justification shows that Malaysians tend to be consistent with higher on relativism and lower on idealism. According to Sparks and Hunt (1998), relativism was negatively related with ethical sensitivity. People in this culture accepted the unethical practices as a normal practice in the business context. This conclusion is support by previous research, which shows that Malaysians are higher on relativism and lower on idealism (Singhapakdi, Rawwas et al., 1999). In a study to examine the perceived unethical practices in Malaysian business, Zabid and Alsagoff (1993) concluded that Malaysian managers accept that some unethical practices will exist because of its general acceptance in the community. Hence, the proposed model could be a good foundation to understanding how cultural dimension affects the values in individual's ethical decision making. It is noted that based on cultural dimensions, the model in Figure 1 can be adapted for any country.

FUTURE DIRECTIONS OF RESEARCH

Besides developing specific ethical decision making research models, the directions of future research should concentrate on collecting appropriate data needed for empirical studies in ethical behaviour. The process of collecting data in ethical behaviour is very challenging. In this article, no formal data has been collected to examine the effect of cultural dimensions on personal values and the ethical decision making. However, we offer some suggestions to this effect.

In measuring ethical behavior, the usage of close-ended questions is generally accepted. However, this method has been found to increase the likelihood of researcher bias. Moreover, it does not give the necessary freedom to the respondents and limits the process of capturing rich and in-depth data by narrowing the possible responses. Thus, to avoid this bias, the researcher can design alternative and creative means to explore ethical behaviour (O'Fallon & Butterfield, 2005). The use of opened-ended questions, for example, can help overcome difficulties posed by closed questions.

An issue of social desirability bias is common in ethical research. Respondents tend to underreport their actual behavior because of the subject sensitivity. As a result, it is difficult to measure the actual individual ethical behavior. It is important to acquire adequate information from respondents. Hence, researchers could use other methods rather than survey for data collection. For example, other alternative ways of collecting data in ethics research may include the field-experiments, in-basket exercises, and simulation techniques (O'Fallon & Butterfield, 2005). Researchers might also use qualitative method (e.g., interviews) to capture rich data from individuals and groups. This approach can serve as a valuable tool in exploring ethical decision making behaviour.

CONCLUSION

Understanding why and how individuals in organizations deal with ethical decision making could enhance the understanding of why certain behaviors are selected. Even though it is difficult to recognize the main influence of ethical behavior, previous studies have shown that there are four main factors (individual factors, organizational factors, moral intensity, and cultural dimension) in ethical decision making. Based on the review of ethical literature, culture has been determined as the main factor in influencing individuals in ethical decision making. Thus, the proposed model in the context of Malaysia can aid the researchers with a foundation of individual behavior based on cultural background. This article concludes with some suggestions for collecting empirical data in ethical research. We argue that a multitude of methods should be used for appropriate data collection needed for empirical study in ethical research.

REFERENCES

Armstrong, R. W. (1996). The relationship between culture and perception of ethical problems in international marketing. *Journal of Business Ethics, 15*(11), 1191-1208.

Barnett, T., Bass, K., & Brown, G. (1994). Ethical ideology and ethical judgment regarding ethical issues in business. *Journal of Business Ethics, 13*(6), 469.

Bartlett, D. (2003). Management and business ethics: A critique and integration of ethical decision-making models. *British Journal of Management, 14*(3), 223-235.

Christie, P. M. J., Kwon, I. G., Stoeberl, P. A., & Baumhart R, (2003). A cross-cultural comparison of ethical attitudes of business managers: India, Korea, and United States. *Journal of Business Ethics, 43*(3), 263-287.

England, G. (1975). *The manager and his values. International perspective.* Cambridge: Ballinger Publishing Co.

Ferrell, O., & Gresham, L. (1985). A contingency framework for understanding ethical decision making in marketing. *Journal of Marketing, 49*(3), 87-96.

Forsyth, D. (1980). A taxonomy of ethical ideologies. *Journal of Personality and Social Psychology, 39,* 175.

Fritzsche, D. J. (1991). A model of decision-making incorporating ethical values. *Journal of Business Ethics, 10*(11), 841.

Hofstede, G. (1980). *Culture's consequences: International differences in work related values.* Beverly Hills: Sage.

Hofstede, G. (1984). Culture's consequences; International differences in work related values. Beverly Hills, CA: SAGE.

House, R. J., & Javidan, M. (2004). Overview of GLOBE. In R. J. House, P. J. Hanges, M. Javidan, P. W. Dorfman & V. Gupta (Eds.), *Culture, leadership, and organizations: The GLOBE study of 62 societies.* Thousand Oaks, CA: Sage.

Hunt, S. D., & Vitell, S. J. (1986). A general theory of marketing ethics. *Journal of Macromarketing, 8*(2), 5.

Janet, S. A., Armen, T., & Ted, H. S. (2001). Codes of ethics as signals for ethical behavior. *Journal of Business Ethics, 29*(3), 199.

Jones, T. M. (1991). Ethical decision making by individuals in organizations: An issue-contingent model. *Academy of Management Review, 16*(2), 366-395.

Karande, K., Rao, C. P., & Singhapakdi, A. (2002). Moral philosophies of marketing managers: A comparison of American, Australian, and Malaysian cultures. *European Journal of Marketing, 36*(7/8), 768.

Laczniak, G., & Naor, J. (1985). Global ethics: Wrestling with corporation conscience. *Business, 35,* 3.

O'Fallon, M. J., & Butterfield, K. D. (2005). A review of the empirical ethical decision-making literature 1996-2003. *Journal of Business Ethics, 59*(4), 375.

Singhapakdi, A., Rawwas, M. Y. A., Marta, J., K. , & Ahmed, M. I. (1999). A cross-cultural study of consumer perceptions about marketing ethics. *The Journal of Consumer Marketing, 16*(3), 257.

Singhapakdi, A., Vitell, S. J., & Franke, G. R. (1999). Antecedents, consequences, and mediating effects of perceived moral intensity and personal moral philosophies. *Academy of Marketing Science Journal, 27*(1), 19.

Sparks, J., & Hunt, S. (1998). Marketing researcher ethical sensitivity: Conceptualization, measurement and exploratory investigation. *Journal of Marketing, 62*(2), 92-109.

Trevino, L. K. (1986). Ethical decision making in organizations: A person-situation interactionist model. *Academy of Management Review, 11*(3), 601-617.

Trevino, L. K., & Victor, B. (1992). Peer reporting of unethical behaviour: A social context perspective. *Academy of Management Journal, 35*(1), 38-64.

Trompenaars, F. (1993). *Riding the waves of culture.* London: Brealey.

Valentine, S., & Fleischman, G. (2003). Ethical reasoning in an equitable relief innocent spouse context. *Journal of Business Ethics, 45*(4), 325-339.

Yeung, I., & Tung, R. (1996). *Achieving business success in Confucian societies: The importance of guanxi (connections).* Organization Dynamics.

Zabid, A. R. M., & Alsagoff, S. K. (1993). Perceived ethical values of Malaysian managers. *Journal of Business Ethics, 12*(4), 331.

Ethical Decision Making

KEY TERMS

Ethical Decision Making: The practice that could give the benefit for the majority groups, no harm to others, and meet the rules and guidelines as given by legal parties. In other words, the behaviour follows the legal conduct and rules in the company and provides the benefit to the societies.

Idealism: Idealistic individuals "insist that one must always avoid harming others" (Forsyth, 1980, p. 244). They are concerned for the welfare of others. Idealistic individuals claim that everybody has a single common end to reach ethical standards. This common end will bind society together to show their obligation to reach an ethical practice.

Moral Intensity: The construct that captures the extent of an issue related to moral imperative in a situation (Jones, 1991). This construct will determine whether the issue faced by individuals in an organization includes the moral dilemma.

National Culture: The pattern of values, beliefs, and practices shared among members of an organization that influence thoughts and behaviour. Culture ca be viewed in terms of both what one does and how one thinks based on their beliefs, traditions, customs, norms, and even religion (Hofstede,1980).

Organizational Culture: Formal and informal systems in controlling behaviour of individuals in an organization. This system provides applicable and relevant information of behavioural conduct.

Relativism: This view holds the acceptance of the differences of ethical standard among cultures. They believe that individual have their own perceptions on ethical standard related to their culture values (Forsyth, 1980); therefore, we do not have any right to say whether others' standards are right or wrong. There is no universal standard to be applied to everyone at all times. As long as the individual believes that standard is accepted and right, it could be a standard for the individual.

Evaluation of Decision-Making Support Systems

Gloria E. Phillips-Wren
Loyola College in Maryland, USA

Manuel Mora
Autonomous University of Aguascalientes, Mexico

Guisseppi Forgionne
University of Maryland, Baltimore County, USA

INTRODUCTION

Decision support systems (DSSs) have been researched extensively over the years with the purpose of aiding the decision maker (DM) in an increasingly complex and rapidly changing environment (Sprague & Watson, 1996; Turban & Aronson, 1998). Newer intelligent systems, enabled by the advent of the Internet combined with artificial-intelligence (AI) techniques, have extended the reach of DSSs to assist with decisions in real time with multiple informaftion flows and dynamic data across geographical boundaries. All of these systems can be grouped under the broad classification of decision-making support systems (DMSS) and aim to improve human decision making. A DMSS in combination with the human DM can produce better decisions by, for example (Holsapple & Whinston, 1996), supplementing the DM's abilities; aiding one or more of Simon's (1997) phases of intelligence, design, and choice in decision making; facilitating problem solving; assisting with unstructured or semistructured problems (Keen & Scott Morton, 1978); providing expert guidance; and managing knowledge. Yet, the specific contribution of a DMSS toward improving decisions remains difficult to quantify.

Many researchers identify a single metric, or a series of single metrics, for evaluation of the DMSS in supporting decision making, if it is evaluated at all (Phillips-Wren, Mora, Forgionne, Garrido, & Gupta, 2006). The authors suggest outcome criteria such as decreased cost, or process criteria such as increased efficiency, to justify the DMSS. Yet no single integrated metric is proposed to determine the value of the DMSS to the decision maker.

The objective of this article is to review literature-based evaluation criteria and to provide a multicriteria evaluation model that determines the precise decision-making contributions of a DMSS. The model is implemented with the analytical hierarchy process (AHP), a formalized multicriteria method.

Building on other core studies (Forgionne, 1999; Forgionne & Kohli, 2000; Keen, 1981; Leidner & Elam, 1993; Money, Tromp, & Wegner, 1988; Phillips-Wren & Forgionne, 2002; Phillips-Wren, Hahn, & Forgionne, 2004; Phillips-Wren, Mora, Forgionne, Garrido, et al., 2006; Phillips-Wren, Mora, Forgionne, & Gupta, 2006; Pieptea & Anderson, 1987), this article focuses on the performance and evaluation of a planned or real DMSS in supporting decision making. Unlike previous DSS studies (Sanders & Courtney, 1985; Leidner, 1996; Wixom & Watson, 2001; Mora, Cervantes, Gelman, Forgionne, Mejia, & Weitzenfeld, 2002) or general information-system studies (DeLone & McLean, 1992, 2003), this study develops a DMSS evaluation model from a design research paradigm, that is, to be built and evaluated (Hevner & March, 2003).

BACKGROUND

Although developers of DMSSs generally report a single criterion for a DMSS, the use of multiple criteria to evaluate a DMSS has been reported in the literature. Chandler (1982) noted that information systems create a relationship between users and the system itself, so that its evaluation should consider both user and system constraints. He developed a multiple-goal programming approach to consider trade-offs between goals and performance. Adelman (1992) proposed a comprehensive evaluation for assessing specifically DSSs and expert systems using subjective, technical, and empirical methods to form a multifaceted approach. User and sponsor perspectives were included in the subjective methods. The analytical methods and correctness of the analysis were assessed in the technical evaluation. Finally, a comparison of performance with and without the system was evaluated in the empirical-methods section. The three approaches were combined to form an overall evaluation of the system. Turban and Aronson (1998) indicate that information systems, including DMSSs, should be evaluated with two major classes of performance measurement: effectiveness and efficiency. According to general systems principles (Checkland, 1999), effectiveness deals with how well the results or outputs contribute to the goals and achievements of the wider system, and efficiency measures how well the system processes inputs and resources to achieve outputs. A third measure, efficacy, deals with how well the system produces the expected outputs. This third measure complements the three general performance or value-based measures for any general system. For example, Maynard, Burstein, and Arnott (2001) proposed evaluating DMSSs by directly including the perspectives of different constituencies or stakeholders in a multicriteria evaluation.

DECISION VALUE OF DMSS

Multicriteria Model

Of the many studies of applied DMSSs published in the last 30 years, assessment usually consisted of characteristics associated with either the process or outcome of decision making using a DMSS (Forgionne, 1999; Phillips-Wren, Mora, Forgionne, Garrido, et al., 2006; Phillips-Wren, Mora, Forgionne, & Gupta, 2006). Process variables assess the improvement in the way that decisions are made and are often measured in qualitative terms. Process variables that have been used to judge a DMSS are increased efficiency, user satisfaction, time savings, more systematic processes, better understanding of the problem, and ability to generalize. Outcome variables assess the improvement in the decision quality when the DM uses the DMSS for a specific decision and are often measured in quantifiable terms. Outcome variables in the literature are, for example, increased profit, decreased cost, accuracy of predicting annual returns, and success in predicting failures.

These two categories of outcome and process are classical descriptions of decision making. Simon (1997) characterized decision making as consisting of the phases of intelligence, design, and choice. The intelligence phase concerns the identification of the problem and data collection, design includes the formulation of the model and search for alternatives, and choice includes the selection of the best alternative. Once the decision is made, the outcome of the decision can be evaluated. Since DMSSs affect both process and outcome, particularly in real-time systems, DMSSs should be evaluated on both criteria.

Previous research (Forgionne, 1999; Phillips-Wren & Forgionne, 2002; Phillips-Wren et al., 2004) has shown that a multicriteria model for the evaluation of DMSSs can be developed based on criteria in the literature. Although other authors have addressed multiple dimensions for information systems success in general (DeLone & McLean, 1992, 2003) and multiple factors for DSS evaluation in particular (Maynard et al., 2001; Sanders & Courtney, 1985), our proposed evaluation model focuses on how well the DMSS supports the specific decision for which it is intended. Our position is that the decision value of a DMSS should be evaluated based on its support for both the process and outcome of decision making. The decision value of the system can be determined quantitatively using a multiple-criteria model such as the AHP with the additional advantage that the precise contributions of the system to the subcomponents in the model can be determined. A stochastic enhancement of the AHP allows the determination of the statistical significance of the contributions (Phillips-Wren et al., 2004).

The AHP (Saaty, 1977) is a multicriteria model that provides a methodology for comparing alternatives by structuring criteria into a hierarchy, providing for pairwise comparisons of criteria at the lowest level of the hierarchy to be entered by the user, and synthesizing the results into a single numerical value. For example, the decision value of alternative DMSSs can be compared based on criteria and subcriteria. The AHP has been extensively used in decision making for applied problems (Saaty & Vargas, 1994). Once the hierarchy is established, the alternatives are evaluated by pairs with respect to the criteria on the next level. The criteria can be weighted, if desired, according to the priority of each criterion. An eigenvalue solution is utilized to reconcile the initial judgments, and a ranking of the alternatives on the specific criteria is produced using the judgments and the weighting of the criteria.

To evaluate a DMSS using the AHP, a hierarchy of criteria is needed. Although traditional DMSSs have been researched extensively, few, if any, studies have addressed a unifying architecture for the evaluation of DMSSs. A novel and first effort for such an architecture has been recently reported (Phillips-Wren, Mora, Forgionne, Garrido, et al., 2006; Phillips-Wren, Mora, Forgionne, & Gupta, 2006). The following description is a summarized analysis of the proposed evaluation architecture.

Unified Architecture for Evaluation and Design of DMSS

The authors recently reported a conceptualized framework to guide the design and evaluation of intelligent DMSSs for an integrated evaluation approach (Mora, Forgionne, Cervantes, Garrido, Gupta, & Gelman, 2005). It includes both management (i.e., process and outcome) and technical (i.e., services, architectural, and computer mechanisms) views. According to Mora et al. (2005), the primary research premise of intelligent DMSS research can be established as the following.

Decision-making phases and steps can be improved by the support of decisional services and tasks, which are provided by architectural capabilities that can or could in the future be computationally implemented by symbol- or program-based mechanisms.

These perspectives (Forgionne, 1999; Phillips-Wren & Forgionne, 2002; Phillips-Wren et al., 2004; Phillips-Wren, Mora, Forgionne, Garrido, et al., 2006; Phillips-Wren, Mora, Forgionne, & Gupta, 2006) propose that any improvement related to the phases and steps of the decision-making process will or should be related to impacts on outcomes to consider a DMSS as satisfactory. Consideration of both premises suggests that any DMSS evaluation must consider metrics associated with outcomes, phases, and steps of the decision-making process as well as with technical issues such as its decisional services, its architectural capabilities, and its internal computational mechanisms. Figure 1 (Mora et al., 2005) depicts the conceptual design and evaluation foundation framework with the four levels as follows:

- **Decision-making level:** To account for intelligence, design, choice, implementation, and learning in the decision-making phases and activities to be executed by a decision maker using a DMSS
- **Decisional service-task level:** To account for the decisional support services of the DMSS, for example, the Newell knowledge levels of task, method, and subtask

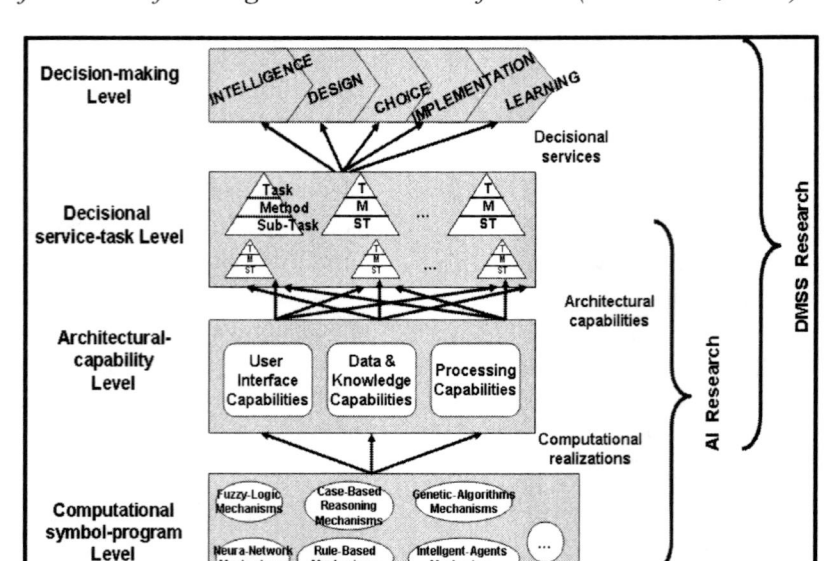

Figure 1. Conceptual framework for design and evaluation of DMSS (Mora et al., 2005)

Evaluation of Decision-Making Support Systems

Table 1. Classification of decisional services for DMSSs

Taxonomy of Decisional Services and Tasks			
TASK TYPE		**GENERIC SERVICES (inputs): outputs**	**GENERIC TASKS**
ANALYSIS		CLASSIFY(data): system state	CLASSIFICATION
		MONITOR(system): system variations	CLASSIFICATION
		INTERPRET(data): state assessment	IDENTIFICATION
		PREDICT(system): future system state	IDENTIFICATION
SYNTHESIS		CONFIGURE(parts, constraints, goals): system structure	DESIGN
		SCHEDULE(activities, constraints, goals): states sequence	DESIGN
		FORMULATE(elements, goals, constraints): system structure	COMPLEX DESIGN
		PLAN(activities, resources, constraints, goals): (states sequence, system structure)	COMPLEX DESIGN
HYBRID		EXPLAIN(data, system): system cause-effect links	COMPLEX
		RECOMMEND(system state): system recommendations	COMPLEX
		MODIFY(system, system changes): new system	COMPLEX
		CONTROL(system state, goals): input system actions	COMPLEX
		LEARN(system, knowledge on system): new knowledge	COMPLEX

Table 2. Requirements of decision-making phases and steps compared to analysis, synthesis, and hybrid services

DECISION PHASE	DECISION STEP	CLASSIFY	MONITOR	INTERPRET	PREDICT	CONFIGURE	SCHEDULE	FORMULATE	PLAN	EXPLAIN	RECOMMEND	MODIFY	CONTROL	LEARN
Intelligence	Problem Detection	√	√									√	√	
	Data Gathering		√										√	
	Problem Formulation			√				√		√	√			
Design	Model Classification	√								√				
	Model Building							√			√	√		
	Model Validation			√						√		√		
Choice	Evaluation	√		√						√				
	Sensitivity Analysis				√					√	√			
	Selection				√					√				
Implementation	Result Presentation					√				√				
	Task Planning						√		√					
	Task Monitoring		√										√	
Learning	Outcome-Process Analysis			√						√				√
	Outcome-Process Synthesis			√						√				√

323

- **Architectural capability level:** To account for the user interface capabilities, data and knowledge capabilities, and processing capabilities provided by the components of the architecture of the DMSS
- **Computational symbol-program level:** To account for specific AI computational mechanisms that implement the architectural components of the DMSS such as fuzzy logic, neural networks, case-based reasoning, genetic algorithms, and intelligent agents

In particular, the design and optimization of new mechanisms at the lowest level (i.e., Computational Symbol-Program Level) is an ongoing research area in AI and computer science to provide the design of new or improved algorithms. From the information-systems viewpoint, the lowest level contains mechanisms where input-output issues and computational efficiencies are the primary features of interest. In contrast, the next two levels (i.e., the Architectural Capability and Decisional Service-Task Levels) should be addressed jointly with the user in the design and evaluation tasks so that the DMSS designer or evaluator has a comprehensive and integrated view of the decision-making paradigm. The Architectural Capabilities Level has been discussed in previous work (Mora, Forgionne, Gupta, Cervantes, & Gelman, 2003) so it will not be repeated here.

In a study of the Decisional Service-Task Level, Mora et al. (2005) developed a synthesis of the relevant studies of intelligent DMSSs in the DSS and AI literature from 1980 to 2005. Table 1, borrowed from the authors, exhibits the analysis of the Decisional Service-Task Level. Decisional services are classified as services for analysis, synthesis, and hybrid tasks. Although the conceptual description is a high-level view, it also provides for core services that could be developed or implemented by component-based software engineering approaches in the near future as unit building blocks.

In turn, Table 2 reports a general analysis of the main decisional services (i.e., analysis, synthesis, or hybrid services) demanded by each step of the decision-making process.

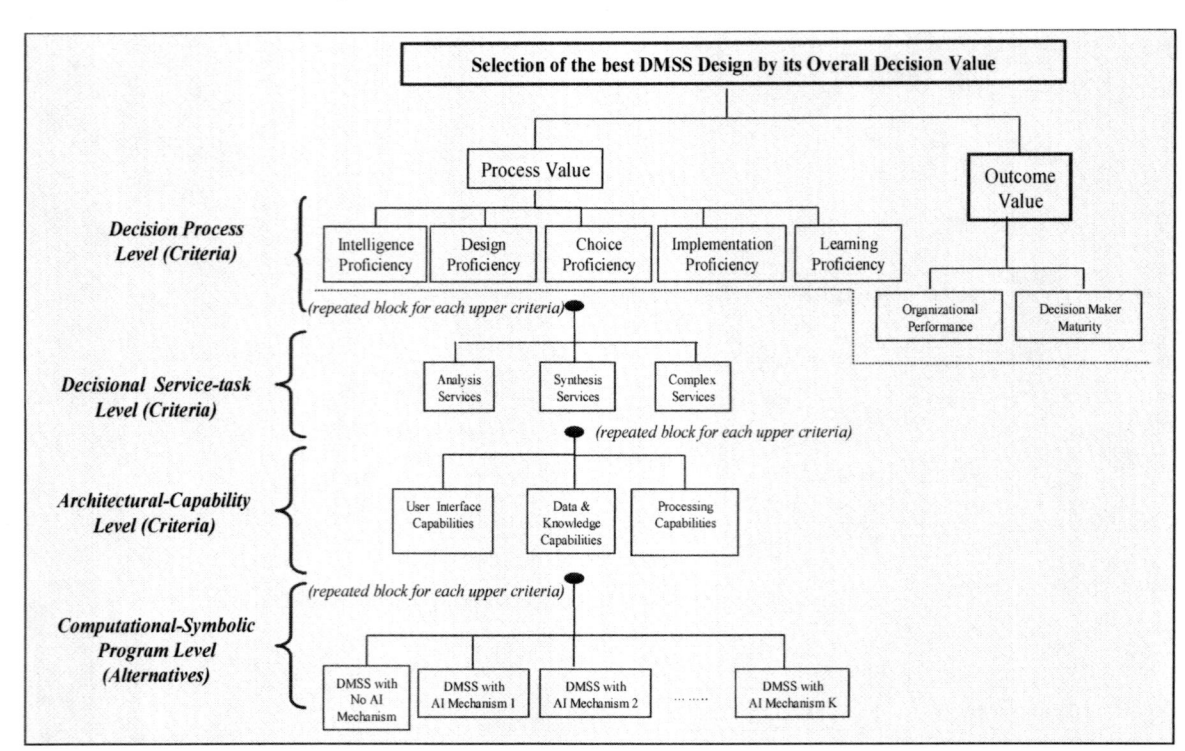

Figure 2. Multicriteria model implementation to evaluate DMSSs

Table 3. Illustration of decision value with user input alternatives

Alter-native	Column 1: Input Scores to UI, DK, and P Criteria	Column 2: Process Value (0.40)	Column 3: Outcome Value (0.60)	Column 4: Overall Decision Value
FL	0.1373, 0.0059, 0.1571	0.0853	0.0854	0.0854
NN	0.1346, 0.2867, 0.3176	0.2496	0.2510	0.2505
CBR	0.4090, 0.1709, 0.1971	0.2488	0.2471	0.2478
GA	0.1844, 0.3577, 0.0760	0.2311	0.2303	0.2306
IA	0.1347, 0.1789, 0.2522	0.1852	0.1862	0.1858

Example of Utilization of the Unified Architecture for Evaluation of DMSS

Given the architecture for a DMSS presented in Figure 1, the decision value of alternative DMSSs can be determined by evaluating their impact on the process and outcome of decision making. As suggested, the multicriteria model can be implemented with the AHP, and the structure is shown in Figure 2.

An advantage of the structure is that the precise contributions of each DMSS to each element of the architecture as well as to the process and outcome of decision making can be determined.

As an example, suppose that five alternative AI mechanisms are to be evaluated for incorporation into a DMSS: fuzzy logic (FL), neural network (NN), case-based reasoning (CBR), genetic algorithm (GA), and intelligent agent (IA). The alternatives are compared in pairs with regard to their contribution to the next level consisting of the user interface (UI), data and knowledge (DK), and processing (P) capabilities. An eigenvalue solution in the AHP reconciles the pair-wise comparisons to yield the input scores shown in Column 1 of Table 3. Each branch in Figure 2 can be weighted to indicate its importance to the next level. Each of our branches is weighted; for example, the outcome is weighted 0.6 compared to the process of 0.4 to indicate that the outcome is more important in our sample problem.

Column 1 shows the amount that each AI alternative contributes to three capabilities on the Architectural Capability Level in the opinion of the user. (Note that the sum of each subcolumn for the values under UI, DK, and P is equal to 1.0.) For instance, in Table 3 we see that the CBR contributes 0.4090 (Column 1) to the UI while GA at 0.3577 is most important to the DK capability (Column 1). The AHP then calculates that NN contributes most significantly to the process (Column 2) and outcome (Column 3). The overall decision value indicates that NN is preferred with the highest score, although NN and CBR are close. A stochastic enhancement of the AHP would permit one to determine if the differences are significant (Phillips-Wren et al., 2004). The analysis provides guidance to the decision maker in the selection of the AI method to be used. In a similar manner, we can trace the contribution of each alternative to each of the subcriteria in Figure 2.

FUTURE TRENDS

Previous AHP-based DMSS evaluations have offered hierarchies that define the nature of support to the outcome and process in decision making. In practice, outcome and process measures can vary across organizations and entities. The organizational and problem context, then, can serve as an additional layer in the AHP hierarchy between the system and the outcome and process levels. This expanded hierarchy would show how outcome and process results are determined by the organizational context and provide guidance for DMSS design, development, and implementation within the specific context.

There is another hierarchical expansion that can be instructive. In the original formulation, DMSS choices do not disclose the specific architectural elements within the compared systems. It is possible to add a level that would identify the specific decision-making tools delivered by the DMSS. This added hierarchy would link the tools to process and outcome, enabling the researcher or practitioner to identify the specific contributions of the tools to decision value.

Although the additional hierarchical levels can potentially provide useful information, it is not clear if the enhanced clarity would add to decision value. Research, then, is needed to determine if the added information is worth the added cost and complexity of the expanded hierarchy. Put another way, will the extra layers lead to a better (or even different) decision value than the original formulation?

Other unresolved issues involve the weighting and priority schemes used in the AHP methodology. Weights and priorities for the criteria and subcriteria are assigned by the decision maker or researcher and then are used to compute weighted averages from the evaluator's initial pair-wise comparisons. It would be useful to determine how sensitive the calculated decision value would be to alterations in the weights and priorities. Previous DMSS evaluations have not fully addressed this sensitivity analysis issue.

A final potentially fruitful area of further research deals with the data creation process for the AHP analysis. Since the AHP pair-wise comparisons are inherently subjective in nature, there has been a tendency to apply the concept through actual user studies. Such studies have typically involved small samples with dubiously representative participants. Simulation offers a potentially superior data creation approach. Each pair-wise comparison implicitly converts subjective user system alternative ratings to a 0-to-1 scale. Over a population of users, these 0-to-1 values can be expected to follow some probability distribution. It is possible, then, to use randomly generated values from theoretical probability distributions to generate the pair-wise comparisons in the AHP analysis. Analyses with various probability distributions can be used to determine the sensitivity of decision value to alterations in population characteristics

CONCLUSION

The proposed AHP-determined model of decision value provides a mechanism to integrate all previous measures of DMSS value. This formulation is comprehensive, intuitive, and complete. Moreover, the AHP analysis provides a single decision value that is linked to the outcomes and processes that generated the value. As such, the framework can serve as a guide to effective system design, development, and implementation.

REFERENCES

Adelman, L. (1992). *Evaluating decision support and expert systems*. New York: John Wiley & Sons, Inc.

Chandler, J. (1982). A multiple criteria approach to evaluation information systems. *Management Information Systems Quarterly, 6*(1), 61-74.

Checkland, P. (1999). *Systems thinking, systems practice*. Chichester, United Kingdom: John Wiley & Sons, Inc.

DeLone, W. H., & McLean, E. R. (1992). Information systems success: The quest for the dependent variable. *Information Systems Research, 3*(1), 60-95.

DeLone, W. H., & McLean, E. R. (2003). The DeLone and McLean model of information systems success: A ten-year update. *Journal of Management Information Systems, 19*(4), 9-30.

Forgionne, G. (1999). An AHP model of DSS effectiveness. *European Journal of Information Systems, 8*, 95-106.

Forgionne, G., & Kohli, R. (2000). Management support system effectiveness: Further empirical evidence. *Journal of the Association for Information Systems, 1*(3), 1-37.

Hevner, A. R., & March, S. T. (2003). The information systems research cycle. *Computer, 36*(11), 111-113.

Holsapple, C. W., & Whinston, A. B. (1996). *Decision support systems*. St. Paul, MN: West Publishing Company.

Keen, P. G. W. (1981). Value analysis: Justifying decision support systems. *Management Information Systems Quarterly, 5*(1), 1-15.

Keen, P. G. W., & Scott Morton, M. S. (1978). *Decision support systems: An organizational perspective*. Reading, MA: Addison-Wesley, Inc.

Leidner, D. (1996). The transition to open markets and modern management: The success of EIS in Mexico. In J. DeGross, S. Jarvenpaa, & A. Srinivasan (Eds.), *Proceedings of the Seventeenth International Conference on Information Systems*, Cleveland, Ohio (pp. 290-306).

Leidner, D., & Elam, J. (1993). Executive information systems: Their impact on executive decision making. *Journal of Management Information Systems, 10*(3), 139-155.

Maynard, S., Burstein, F., & Arnott, D. (2001). A multifaceted decision support system evaluation approach. *Journal of Decision Systems, 10*(3-4), 395-428.

Money, A., Tromp, D., & Wegner, T. (1988). The quantification of decision support benefits within the context of value analysis. *Management Information Systems Quarterly, 11*(4), 515-527.

Mora, M., Cervantes, F., Gelman, O., Forgionne, G., Mejia, M., & Weitzenfeld, A. (2002). DMSSs implementation research: A conceptual analysis of the contributions and limitations of the factor-based and stage-based streams. In M. Mora, G. Forgionne, & J. Gupta (Eds.), *Decision making support systems: Achievements, challenges and trends* (pp. 331-356). Hershey, PA: Idea Group.

Mora, M., Forgionne, G., Cervantes, F., Garrido, L., Gupta, J., & Gelman, O. (2005). Toward a comprehensive framework for the design and evaluation of intelligent decision-making support systems (i-DMSS). *Journal of Decision Systems, 14*(3), 321-344.

Mora, M., Forgionne, G., Gupta, J., Cervantes, F., & Gelman, O. (2003, September 4-7). A framework to assess intelligent decision-making support systems. In V. Palade, R. Howlett, & L. Jain (Eds.), *Proceedings of the 7th KES2003 Conference*, Oxford, United Kingdom (LNAI 2774, pp. 59-65). Heidelberg, Germany: Springer-Verlag.

Phillips-Wren, G., & Forgionne, G. (2002, July 4-7). Evaluating Web-based and real-time decision support systems. In F. Adam, P. Brézillon, P. Humphreys, & J. Pomerol (Eds.), *Decision making and decision support in the Internet age: Proceedings of the DSIage2002*, Cork, Ireland (pp. 166-175).

Phillips-Wren, G., Hahn, E., & Forgionne, G. (2004). A multiple criteria framework for the evaluation of decision support systems. *Omega, 32*(4), 323-332.

Phillips-Wren, G., Mora, M., Forgionne, G., Garrido, L., & Gupta, J. (2006). A multicriteria model for the evaluation of intelligent decision-making support systems. In J. Gupta, G. Forgionne, & M. Mora (Eds.), *Intelligent decision-making support systems (i-DMSS): Foundations, applications and challenges* (pp. 3-24). New York: Springer.

Phillips-Wren, G., Mora, M., Forgionne, G., & Gupta, J. (2006, June 28-July 1). Evaluation of decision-making support systems (DMSS): An integrated DMSS and AI approach. In F. Adam, P. Brezillon, S. Carlsson, & P. Humphreys (Eds.), *Creativity and innovation in decision making and decision support: CIDMDS 2006*, London (pp. 583-598).

Pieptea, D. R., & Anderson, E. (1987). Price and value of decision support systems. *Management Information Systems Quarterly, 11*(4), 515-527.

Saaty, T. L. (1977). A scaling method for priorities in hierarchical structures. *Journal of Mathematical Psychology, 15*, 234-281.

Saaty, T. L., & Vargas, L. (1994). *Decision making in economic, political, social and technological environments (The analytic hierarchy process series Vol. 7)*. Pittsburg, PA: RWS Publications.

Sanders, G. L., & Courtney, J. F. (1985). A field study of organizational factors influencing DSS success. *Management Information Systems Quarterly, 9*(1), 77-89.

Simon, H. (1997). *Administrative behavior* (4th ed.). New York: The Free Press.

Sprague, R. H., & Watson, H. J. (1996). *Decision support for management*. Englewood Cliffs, NJ: Prentice Hall.

Turban, E., & Aronson, J. (1998). *Decision support systems and intelligent systems*. Upper Saddle River, NJ: A. Simon & Schuster Company.

Wixom, B., & Watson, H. J. (2001). An empirical investigation of the factors affecting data warehousing success. *Management Information Systems Quarterly, 25*(1), 17-41.

KEY TERMS

Analytic Hierarchy Process (AHP): AHP is a multicriteria model that provides a methodology for comparing alternatives by structuring criteria into a hierarchy, providing for pair-wise comparisons of criteria at the lowest level of the hierarchy to be entered by the user, and synthesizing the results into a single numerical value.

Decision-Making Support System (DMSS): A DMSS is an information system whose purpose is to provide partial or full support for decision-making phases: intelligence, design, choice, implementation, and learning.

Decision Support System (DSS): A DSS is an information system that utilizes database or model-base resources to provide assistance to decision makers through analysis and output.

Decision Value: It is the metric provided by a multicriteria model of the DMSS that quantitatively combines both process and outcome criteria to form a single measure.

Evaluation Criteria: These are qualitative or quantitative metrics on which the DMSS is evaluated.

Multicriteria Method: This is the methodology that integrates two or more criteria to form a single value.

The Evaluation of Decision-Making Support Systems' Functionality

Giusseppi Forgionne
University of Maryland, Baltimore County, USA

Stephen Russell
University of Maryland, Baltimore County, USA

INTRODUCTION

Contemporary decision-making support systems (DMSSs) are large systems that vary in nature, combining functionality from two or more classically defined support systems, often blurring the lines of their definitions. For example, in practical implementations, it is rare to find a decision support system (DSS) without executive information system (EIS) capabilities or an expert system (ES) without a recommender system capability. *Decision-making support system* has become an umbrella term spanning a broad range of systems and functional support capabilities (Alter, 2004). Various information systems have been proposed to support the decision-making process. Among others, there are DSSs, ESs, and management support systems (MSSs). Studies have been conducted to evaluate the decision effectiveness of each proposed system (Brown, 2005; Jean-Charles & Frédéric, 2003; Kanungo, Sharma, & Jain, 2001; Rajiv & Sarv, 2004). Case studies, field studies, and laboratory experiments have been the evaluation vehicles of choice (Fjermestad & Hiltz, 2001; James, Ramakrishnan, & Kustim, 2002; Kaplan, 2000).

While for the most part each study has examined the decision effectiveness of an individual system, it has done so by examining the system as a whole using outcome- or user-related measures to quantify success and effectiveness (Etezadi-Amoli & Farhoomand, 1996; Holsapple & Sena, 2005; Jain, Ramamurthy, & Sundaram, 2006). When a study has included two or more systems, individual system effects typically have not been isolated. For example, Nemati, Steiger, Lyer, and Herschel (2002) presented an integrated system with both DSS and AI (artificial intelligence) functionality, but they did not explicitly test for the independent effects of the DSS and AI capabilities on the decision-making outcome and process. This article extends the previous work by examining the separate impacts of different DMSSs on decision effectiveness.

BACKGROUND

DMSSs are information systems that directly support the decision-making process for complex, high-level problems in an interactive manner (Alter, 2004; Mora, Forgionne, & Gupta, 2002). The specific DMSS can be a traditional DSS, EIS, ES, knowledge-based system (KBS), or a system that combines the functionalities of DSS, EIS, KBS/ES.

An architecture that incorporates the functionality of the various proposed systems is shown in Figure 1 (adapted from Forgionne, 2003).

In the typical DSS, the decision maker utilizes computer and information technology to (a) structure the problem by attaching the parameters to a model and (b) use the model to simulate (experiment with) alternatives and events and/or find the best solution to the problem (Borenstein, 1998; Raghunathan, 1999). Results are reported as parameter conditions (status reports), experimental outcome and parameter forecasts, and/or recommended actions. Feedback from user processing guides the decision maker to a problem solution, and created information is stored as an additional input for further processing. A DSS, then, would not include the knowledge base on the input side or offer explanations on the output side of Figure 1's conceptual architecture.

In a typical EIS, the decision maker utilizes computer and information technology to (a) access dispersed data, (b) organize the data into user-specified broad categories, (c) view the data from interesting perspectives, and (d) highlight important patterns by scanning current trends (Leidner & Elam, 1994; Seely & Targett,

Figure 1. General DMSS

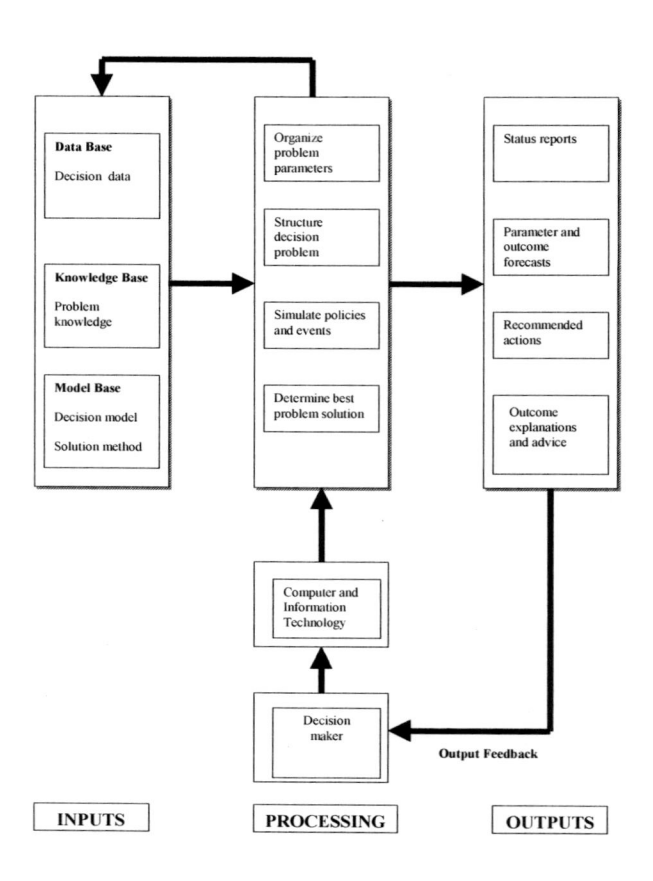

1999). Results are reported as categorical summaries and drill-down details (status reports) and/or suggested problem parameters (parameter forecasts). Feedback from the user processing guides the decision maker to a general problem understanding, and the created parameters are stored as additional inputs for further processing. An EIS, then, would have a limited model base and not include the knowledge base on the input side. Additionally, the system would not offer recommended actions or explanations on the output side of Figure 1's conceptual architecture.

A typical KBS/ES captures and stores as inputs problem-pertinent knowledge, either from experts, cases, or other sources, and the models (inference engine or reasoning mechanisms) needed to draw problem-solution advice from the knowledge (O'Leary, 1998; Preece, 1990; Ullman, 1988; Waterman, 1985). Results are reported as knowledge summaries (status reports), forecasted outcomes, and/or problem advice and explanations for the advice. Feedback from the user processing guides the decision maker to the advice, and the created events and advice pathways are stored as additional inputs for further processing. A KBS/ES, then, would have a limited model base and not include the database on the input side, and similar to an EIS, the system would not offer recommendations on the output side of Figure 1's conceptual architecture.

An MSS integrates the functions of a DSS, EIS, and KBS/ES into a single system (Turban, Aronson, & Liang, 2004). Similar to its component systems, an MSS will have a model base and a database. The database contains data relevant to the decision problem, including the values for the uncontrollable events, decision alternatives, and decision criteria. The knowledge base holds problem knowledge, such as guidance for selecting decision alternatives and uncontrollable inputs, problem relationships, or advice in interpreting possible outcomes. The model base is a repository for the formal models of the decision problem and the methodology for developing results (simulations and solutions) using these formal models. Processing will generate status reports on events and alternatives, simulated outcomes, decision recommendations, and explanations for the recommendations and further processing advice. Feedback provides additional data, knowledge, and models created from the processing.

As such, the MSS will enable the user to perform the operations and computations involved in all four processing tasks and generate all outputs shown in Figure 1.

EVALUATION OF DMSS COMPONENT SYSTEMS THROUGH SIMULATION

Issues, Controversies, and Problems

In theory, the support offered by DSS, EIS, and KBS/ES should improve the process of, and outcomes from, decision making (Forgionne, 1999; Kumar, 1999). Case studies (Lilien, Rangaswamy, Bruggen, & Starke, 2004; Sarter & Schroeder, 2001), field studies (Adelman, Gualtieri, & Riedel, 1994; Kanungo et al., 2001; Sojda, 2004), and experiments (Adleman, 1991; Maynard, Burstein, & Arnott, 2001; Parikh, Fazlollahi, & Verma, 2001; Pratyush & Abhijit, 2004) have all offered evidence that generally supports this theory. Conceptually, the synergistic effects from the integrated functionality of an MSS should further improve decision making when compared to individual DMSSs. There is also some experimental evidence to support this theory (Forgionne & Kohli, 2000). Yet, there are important gaps in this body of empirical testing. First, it is difficult to acquire and motivate case- and field-study participants, and the acquired participants may not be representative of the population. Second, few, if any, comparative studies measure the separate decision contributions of the individual DMSSs or functional components in the MSS.

These gaps are important for several reasons. Proper isolation of individual or functional contribution can contribute to a proper matching of system types with decision problems. Linking the effects of the isolated contribution to decision-making phases also will facilitate situational system design, development, and implementation. Such linkages can reduce the time and costs involved in the DMSS analysis and design process and provide direct measures of comparative system benefits. This approach combined with population studies will enable researchers and practitioners to generalize results and findings.

Solutions and Recommendations

Simulation can be used to gather pertinent data and conduct the comparative DMSS analyses. Since an extremely large number of trials can be performed in a very short period of time, simulation can generate the population information needed for generalization. While the approach is best suited to problems involving tangible variables, simulation also can incorporate intangible factors through the use of categorical and dummy variables (Coats, 1990; Wildberger, 1990). Once stated categorically, the intangible factors can be linked to the tangible factors through the simulation model equations.

The simulation study utilizes a complex semistructured problem, frequently used in management training and evaluation and typically requiring decision-making support (McLeod, 1986). This problem involves a market in which top management uses price, marketing, research and development, and plant investment to compete for a product's four-quarter total market potential. Demand for the organization's products will be influenced by (a) management actions, (b) competitors' behavior, and (c) the economic environment. The decision objective is to plan a four-quarter strategy that would generate as much total profit as possible.

Strategy making requires (a) setting the product price, marketing budget, research and development expenditures, and plant investment and (b) forecasting the competitors' price, competitors' marketing budget, a seasonal sales index, and an index of general economic conditions. Twelve additional variables, including plant capacity, raw-materials inventory, and administrative expenses, will be calculated from the strategy. Initial values for these twelve variables form the scenario for decision making. These 20 (controllable, uncontrollable, and calculated) variables jointly influence the profitability of the organization.

The problem is sequential in nature. Current decisions are affected by decisions and forecasts in previous and subsequent quarters. In this dynamic environment, poor strategies will have unrecoverable negative consequences over the planning horizon.

A precise and explicit model of the decision problem was programmed in the SAS System for Information Delivery. This software provided a robust programming environment where the decision support system simulation can be created and evaluated (Spector, 2001). Unlike other software approaches, SAS pro-

Figure 2. SAS program for normally distributed DSS inputs

```
Exhibit 1 SAS Program for Normally Distributed DSS Inputs

data simd;
do subject = 1 to 100;
   do year = 1 to 100;
      do quarter = 1 to 4;
/* controllable inputs           */
         P = 65 + (20 * RANNOR (0));
         M = 250000 + (70000 * RANNOR (0));
         RD = 0 + max(0,(1000000 * RANNOR (0)));
         PI = 10000000 + (333333 * RANNOR (0));
/* uncontrollable inputs         */
         CM = 350000 + (100000 * RANNOR (0));
         CP = 68 + (20 * RANNOR (0));
         E = 1.1 + (.3 * RANNOR (0));
         SI = .75 + (.25 * RANNOR (0));
         output;
      end;
   end;
end;
run;
```

Figure 3. SAS program for normally distributed EIS inputs

```
data simES;
   array pp[4] (64 64 63 63);
   array mp[4] (300000 300000 300000 300000);
   array pip[4] (1000000 1000000 1000000 1000000);
   array rdp[4] (0 1000000 0 0);
     do subject = 1 to 100;
      do year = 1 to 100;
       do quarter = 1 to 4;
/* Determine if the subject accepts the advice  */
         accept = RANNOR(0);
         if accept GT 0 then do;
         P = pp[quarter];
       M = mp[quarter];
       RD = rdp[quarter];
       PI = pip[quarter];
       CM = 350000 + (100000 * RANNOR (0));
       CP = 68 + (20 * RANNOR (0));
       E = 1.1 + (.3 * RANNOR (0));
       SI = .75 + (.25 * RANNOR (0));
       output;
       end;

/* Determine the values for nonaccepting subjects   */
         if accept LE 0 then do;
/* controllable inputs           */
         P = 65 + (20 * RANNOR (0));
         M = 250000 + (70000 * RANNOR (0));
         RD = 0 + max(0,(1000000 * RANNOR (0)));
         PI = 10000000 + (333333 * RANNOR (0));
/* uncontrollable inputs         */
         CM = 350000 + (100000 * RANNOR (0));
         CP = 68 + (20 * RANNOR (0));
         E = 1.1 + (.3 * RANNOR (0));
         SI = .75 + (.25 * RANNOR (0));
         output;
         end;
   end;
  end;
  end;
```

The Evaluation of Decision-Making Support Systems' Functionality

Figure 4. SAS program for normally distributed KBS/ES inputs

```
Exhibit 4 SAS Progam for Normally Distributed MSS Inputs

data simsub;
    array pp[4] (64 64 63 63);
    array mp[4] (300000 300000 300000 300000);
    array pip[4] (1000000 1000000 1000000 1000000);
    array rdp[4] (0 1000000 0 0);
    array ep[4] (1.15 1.18 1.18 1.20);
    array sip[4] (.8 1.1 1.3 .75);
    array cpp[4] (68 68 68 68);
    array cmp[4] (300000 325000 350000 350000);
    do subject = 1 to 100;
      do year = 1 to 100;
        do quarter = 1 to 4;
/* Determine if the subject accepts the advice */
          accept = RANNOR(0);
          if accept GT 0 then do;
            P = pp[quarter];
            M = mp[quarter];
            RD = rdp[quarter];
            PI = pip[quarter];
            E = ep[quarter];
            SI = sip[quarter];
            CM = cmp[quarter];
            CP = cpp[quarter];
            output;
          end;
/* Determine the values for nonaccepting subjects */
          if accept LE 0 then do;
/* controllable inputs */
            P = 65 + (20 * RANNOR (0));
            M = 250000 + (70000 * RANNOR (0));
            RD = 0 + max(0,(1000000 * RANNOR (0)));
            PI = 10000000 + (333333 * RANNOR (0));
/* uncontrollable inputs */
            CM = 350000 + (100000 * RANNOR (0));
            CP = 68 + (20 * RANNOR (0));
            E = 1.1 + (.3 * RANNOR (0));
            SI = .75 + (.25 * RANNOR (0));
            output;
          end;
        end;
      end;
    end;
run;
```

vides a series of linked modules that deliver, in an integrated and comprehensive manner, the wide range of mathematical and statistical tasks needed to perform the simulations.

In a typical DSS, the user would provide the controllable and uncontrollable variable values for the decision model. To incorporate the diversity of inputs from a population of users, each variable was assumed to follow a standard normal distribution with a mean of 0 and a standard deviation of 1. Using the scenario values, the permissible management game ranges, and SAS's random normal function, formulas were developed to ensure that input values would fall within the permissible ranges according to normal probability distributions. Figure 2 presents the corresponding SAS program.

The simulation study includes EIS capabilities within the management game. An EIS focuses on the intelligence (gaining a general problem understanding) phase of decision making. Insights about the decision environment, such as forecasted economic conditions and competitors' potential actions, are an essential form of intelligence. Within the management game, such intelligence can be expressed as guidance for selecting the values of the uncontrollable variables (economic index, seasonal index, competitor's price, and competitor's marketing). Guidance was provided for the selections through the documentation provided with the management game, and the guided values would generate good, although not likely optimal, profits for the organization.

In practice, users may not accept the intelligence guidance. To account for this possibility, guidance acceptance was assumed to follow a standard normal distribution with a mean of 0 and a standard deviation of 1. Simulated values greater than 0 from this distribution represented user acceptance of the guidance, while values of 0 or less constituted rejection of the advice. When users rejected guidance, uncontrollable-variable values were simulated with Figure 2's uncontrollable-inputs section. Figure 3 presents the relevant SAS program.

The simulation study also included KBS/ES capabilities. The focus in a KBS/ES is on the choice (selection of preferred alternatives) phase of decision making. Within the management game, this focus can be expressed as guidance for selecting the values of the controllable variables (price, marketing, research and development, and plant investment). The management-game documentation again provided the guidance for the selections. As with the EIS, guidance acceptance was assumed to follow a standard normal distribution with a mean of 0 and a standard deviation of 1, and simulated values greater than 0 represented user acceptance. When users rejected guidance, controllable-variable values were simulated with Figure 2's controllable-inputs section. Figure 4 presents the relevant SAS program.

Figure 5. SAS program for normally distributed MSS inputs

```
data simsub;
   array pp[4] (64 64 63 63);
   array mp[4] (300000 300000 300000 300000);
   array pip[4] (1000000 1000000 1000000 1000000);
   array rdp[4] (0 1000000 0 0);
   array ep[4] (1.15 1.18 1.18 1.20);
   array sip[4] (.8 1.1 1.3 .75);
   array cpp[4] (68 68 68 68);
   array cmp[4] (300000 325000 350000 350000);
   do subject = 1 to 100;
      do year = 1 to 100;
         do quarter = 1 to 4;
/* Determine if the subject accepts the advice */
            accept = RANNOR(0);
               if accept GT 0 then do;
               P = pp[quarter];
            M = mp[quarter];
            RD = rdp[quarter];
            PI = pip[quarter];
            E = ep[quarter];
            SI = sip[quarter];
            CM = cmp[quarter];
            CP = cpp[quarter];
               output;
         end;

/* Determine the values for nonaccepting subjects */
         if accept LE 0 then do;
/* controllable inputs */
            P = 65 + (20 * RANNOR (0));
            M = 250000 + (70000 * RANNOR (0));
            RD = 0 + max(0,(1000000 * RANNOR (0)));
            PI = 10000000 + (333333 * RANNOR (0));
/* uncontrollable inputs */
            CM = 350000 + (100000 * RANNOR (0));
            CP = 68 + (20 * RANNOR (0));
            E = 1.1 + (.3 * RANNOR (0));
            SI = .75 + (.25 * RANNOR (0));
            output;
         end;
      end;
   end;
end;
```

By combining the capabilities of DSS, EIS, and KBS/ES, the management game represents an MSS. Consequently, there would be guidance for both the controllable- and uncontrollable-variable values. As with the EIS and KBS/ES, (a) guidance acceptance was assumed to follow a standard normal distribution with a mean of 0 and a standard deviation of 1, (b) simulated values greater than 0 represented user acceptance, and (c) when users rejected guidance, variable values were simulated with Figure 2's program.

Figure 5 presents the relevant SAS program. The various simulations were run for 100 users across 100 years, with each year involving four quarters. This methodology generated 40,000 observations for the comparative analysis, including values for the controllable, uncontrollable, and calculated variables, including the organization's net profit after tax. These data were used in an ANOVA (analysis of variance) to test whether there were any significant differences in net profits from DSS, EIS, KBS/ES, and MSS use.

Figure 6 summarizes the ANOVA statistics, and this exhibit also presents means for net profit (the outcome variable in the study).

As Figure 6 demonstrates, there was a significant net-profit difference between the simulated DSS, EIS, KBS/ES, and MSS users. Furthermore, Scheffe's test indicates that EIS, KBS/ES, and MSS users all did better than DSS users. MSS and KBS/ES users also did better than EIS users, but there were no significant differences between the net profits of KBS/ES and MSS users. Although the analyses are not reported here, the same relative results occurred when only accepting-user data were utilized.

Since the differences can be traced to the guidance offered by each system, these results suggest that controllable-variable guidance is more important in this

Figure 6. ANOVA test for the organization's net profit

```
Dependent Variable: Net Profit
                                Sum of
        Source           DF     Squares        Mean Square      F Value    Pr > F

        Model             3     5.3123202E18   1.7707734E18     115076     <.0001

        Error        159996     2.4619876E18   1.5387807E13

        Corrected Total
                     159999     7.7743078E18

              R-Square    Coeff Var     Root MSE       NP Mean

              0.683317   -20.22143       3922730     -19398870

        Source           DF     ANOVA SS       Mean Square      F Value    Pr > F

        System Type       3     5.3123202E18   1.7707734E18     115076     <.0001

                          Scheffe's Test for NP
        NOTE: This test controls the Type I experiment-wise error rate.

                 Alpha                              0.1
                 Error Degrees of Freedom         159996
                 Error Mean Square              1.539E13
                 Critical Value of F             2.08383
                 Minimum Significant Difference    69353

        Means with the same letter are not significantly different.

                 Scheffe Grouping      Mean      N      System Type

                          A        -13614093   40000    KBS/ES
                          A
                          A        -13659634   40000    MSS

                          B        -25115608   40000    EIS

                          C        -25206144   40000    DSS
```

decision problem than uncontrollable-input advice. The negative profits across the system types suggest that the advice provided by the management-game documentation was flawed.

FUTURE TRENDS

As this simulation study illustrates, the type of advice can lead to different decision outcomes. This study examined the effects of static advice typically offered through EIS and KBS/ES. Other DMSSs may offer dynamic guidance, changing the advice depending on the evolving circumstances in the decision situation. Such dynamic advice can be derived from the decision model's mathematical relationships and rendered in real time through the system. The simulation approach can also be used to alter the mathematical relationships as the decision environment evolves.

Results from any simulation are only as good as the assumptions used in the analyses. This study assumed that the management game was a reasonable representation of many organizations' strategic decision-making problems. Different organizations, however, may utilize different management philosophies, accounting principles, and decision objectives. If so, the decision model should be changed to reflect the organization's practices, philosophies, objectives, and decision environments. In particular, the profit equation may be replaced with an alternative measure or measures of performance, some tangible and others intangible. Variables and relationships may be defined and measured differently. Additional environmental factors may be added to the equations. While such alterations would change the specific form of the simulation model, the general model and experimental methodology would still be applicable.

This study also assumed that acceptance rates and input values would follow normal distributions. A variety of other distributions is possible, including the binomial and Gamma distributions. Further studies, then, should examine the sensitivity of the results to changes in distributions.

Finally, this study examined only four types of DMSSs. There are others, including creativity-enhancing, decision technology, and machine learning systems. In addition, the functionality of the studied systems was operationalized in particular ways. Other operational possibilities exist, such as providing AI-based guidance to model formulations. The other DMSSs with different forms of guidance and assistance warrant further study.

CONCLUSION

The results of this study confirm that EIS, KBS, and MSS all improve decision making when compared to a basic DSS. In addition, these results suggest that guidance for controllable variables is relatively more important than guidance for uncontrollable variables in achieving decision objectives. Since the results are expressed in dollars of net profit, the findings provide an objective measure of determining the relative decision value of the various DMSS functions. Moreover, as large-scale simulation that approaches a census is studied, the evaluation results should be more generalizable in comparison to sample studies that use participants in laboratory, field, or case settings.

The study does not support the concept that higher synergistic value can be achieved through higher levels of functional integration. Instead, it may be sufficient in many circumstances to stop the integration at intelligent decision-making support, adding KBS/ES or other artificially intelligent capabilities to a basic DSS.

REFERENCES

Adleman, L. (1991). Experiments, quasi-experiments, and case studies: A review of empirical methods for evaluating decision support systems. *IEEE Transactions of Systems, Man and Cybernetics, 21*(2), 293-301.

Adelman, L., Gualtieri, J., & Riedel, S. L. (1994). A multifaceted approach to evaluating expert systems. *Artificial Intelligence for Engineering Design, Analysis and Manufacturing, 8*, 289-306.

Alter, S. (2004). A work system view of DSS in its fourth decade. *Decision Support Systems, 38*(3), 319-327.

Borenstein, D. (1998). Towards a practical method to validate decision support systems. *Decision Support Systems, 23*(3), 227-239.

Brown, A. (2005). Is evaluation in practice? *Electronic Journal of Information Systems Evaluation, 8*(3), 169-178.

Clerica, F. (2005). "Balancing" interest and reforming the common agricultural policy. *Farm Policy Journal, 2*(2), 33-39.

Coats, P. K. (1990). Combining an expert system with simulation to enhance planning for banking networks. *SIMULATION, 54*(6), 253-264.

Etezadi-Amoli, J., & Farhoomand, A. F. (1996). A structural model of end user computing satisfaction and user performance. *Information & Management, 30*, 65-73.

Fjermestad, J., & Hiltz, S. R. (2001). Group support systems: A descriptive evaluation of case and field studies. *Journal of Management Information Systems, 17*(3), 115-160.

Forgionne, G. A. (1999). An AHP model of DSS effectiveness. *European Journal of Information Systems, 8*, 95-106.

Forgionne, G. A., & Kohli, R. (2000). Management support system effectiveness: Further empirical evidence. *Journal of the AIS, 1*(1).

Holsapple, C. W., & Sena, M. P. (2005). ERP plans and decision-support benefits. *Decision Support Systems, 38*, 575-590.

Jain, H. K., Ramamurthy, K., & Sundaram, S. (2006). Effectiveness of visual interactive modeling in the context of multiple-criteria group decisions. *IEEE Transactions on Systems, Man and Cybernetics, 36*(2), 298-318.

James, R. M., Ramakrishnan, P., & Kustim, W. (2002). Decision making under time pressure with different information sources and performance-based financial incentives: Part 1. *Decision Support Systems, 34*(1), 75-97.

Jean-Charles, P., & Frédéric, A. (2003). From human decision making to DMSS architecture. In *Decision making support systems: Achievements, trends and challenges for* (pp. 40-70). Idea Group Publishing.

Kanungo, S., Sharma, S., & Jain, P. K. (2001). Evaluation of a decision support system for credit management decisions. *Decision Support Systems, 30*(4), 419-436.

Kaplan, B. (2000). Evaluating informatics applications: Clinical decision support systems literature review. *International Journal of Medical Informatics, 64*(1), 15-37.

Kumar, R. L. (1999). Understanding DSS value: An options perspective. *Omega, 27*(3), 295-304.

Leidner, D. E., & Elam, J. J. (1994). Executive information systems: Their impact on executive decision making. *Journal of Management Information Systems, 10*(3), 139-156.

Lilien, G. L., Rangaswamy, A., Bruggen, G. H. V., & Starke, K. (2004). DSS effectiveness in marketing resource allocation decisions: Reality vs. Perception. *Informs, 15*(3), 216-235.

Maynard, S., Burstein, F., & Arnott, D. (2001). A multifaceted decision support system evaluation approach. *Journal of Decision Systems, 10*(3-4), 395-428.

McLeod, R. J. (1986). *Software package 11*. College Station, TX: Academic Information Service (AIS).

Mora, M., Forgionne, G. A., & Gupta, J. N. D. (2002). *Decision making support systems: Achievements, trends and challenges for the new decade*. New York: Idea Group Publishing.

Nemati, H. R., Steiger, D. M., Lyer, L. S., & Herschel, R. T. (2002). Knowledge warehouse: An architectural integration of knowledge management, decision support, artificial intelligence and data warehousing. *Decision Support Systems, 33*(2), 143-161.

O'Leary, D. E. (1998, August 24-28). *Verification of multiple agent knowledge-based systems*. Paper presented at the Ninth International Workshop on Database and Expert Systems Applications (DEXA'98), Vienna.

Parikh, M., Fazlollahi, B., & Verma, S. (2001). The effectiveness of decisional guidance: An empirical evaluation. *Decision Sciences, 32*(2), 303-331.

Pratyush, B., & Abhijit, C. (2004). An empirical investigation of decision-making satisfaction in Web-based decision support systems. *Decision Support Systems, 37*(2), 187-197.

Preece, A. D. (1990). Towards a methodology for evaluating expert systems. *Expert Systems, 7*(4), 215-223.

Raghunathan, S. (1999). Impact of information quality and decision-maker quality on decision quality: A theoretical model and simulation analysis. *Decision Support Systems, 26*(4), 275-286.

Rajiv, K., & Sarv, D. (2004). Contribution of institutional DSS to organizational performance: Evidence from a longitudinal study. *Decision Support Systems, 37*(1), 103-118.

Sarter, N. B., & Schroeder, B. (2001). Supporting decision-making and action selection under time pressure and uncertainty: The case of in-flight icing. *Human Factors, 43*(4), 573-583.

Seely, M., & Targett, D. (1999). Patterns of senior executives' personal use of computers. *Information & Management, 35*(6), 315-330.

Sojda, R. S. (2004). *Empirical evaluation of decision support systems: Concepts and an example for trumpeter swan management*. Paper presented at the iEMSs 2004 International Congress: Complexity and Integrated Resources Management, Osnabrueck, Germany.

Spector, P. E. (2001). *SAS programming for researchers and social scientists* (2nd ed.). Thousand Oaks, CA: Sage Publications, Inc.

Turban, E., Aronson, J. E., & Liang, T.-P. (2004). *Decision support systems and intelligent systems* (7th ed.). Englewood, CA: Prentice Hall.

Ullman, J. D. (1988). *Principles of database and knowledge-base systems* (Vol. 1). Rockville, MD: Computer Science Press.

Waterman, D. A. (1985). *A guide to expert systems*. Boston: Addison-Wesley Longman Publishing Co., Inc.

Wildberger, A. M. (1990). AI & simulation. *Simulation, 55*.

KEY TERMS

Decision Making Process: This is the process of developing a general problem understanding, formulating the problem explicitly, evaluating alternatives systematically, and implementing the choice.

Decision Support System (DSS): A DSS is an information system that interactively supports the user's ability to evaluate decision alternatives and develop a recommended decision.

Executive Information System (EIS): An EIS is an information system that accesses, reports, and helps users interpret problem-pertinent information.

Knowledge-Based or Expert System (KBS or ES): This is an information system that captures and delivers problem-pertinent knowledge and advice for users.

Management Game: It is a model used by a participant to experiment with decision strategy plans in a simulated organization.

Management Support System (MSS): An MSS is an information system that integrates the functional capabilities of a decision support system, executive information system, and knowledge-based or expert system.

Simulation: A simulation is an approach to data creation and analysis that utilizes a model to represent reality.

Exploring the Risks That Affect Community College Decision Makers

Margaret W. Wood
George Mason University, USA

David C. Rine
George Mason University, USA

INTRODUCTION

For leaders, decision making is a charge that cannot be escaped. For those who prefer to avoid this responsibility, the startling truth is that not making a decision is a decision. Executives, including those who lead community colleges, have critical accountability to build a support network with easy access to pertinent information that carries out decisions as intended. Decision making's impending risks—particularly in this age of "I need it yesterday"—are amplified by the likelihood of misunderstanding and miscommunication. The man-hours of gathering, analyzing, and prioritizing information behind a good decision can be thwarted without a clear-cut strategy for how to make a decision with that information.

This chapter provides insights as to why a United States community college organization's leadership faltered as a result of decision making. For this domain, this long-neglected dynamic of identifying operational risks was explored using a tailored risk management methodology developed by the Software Engineering Institute (SEI). Community colleges, federal agencies, and small businesses have similar concerns about institutionalizing effective decision making; this chapter addresses those complexities specifically within community colleges and provides an understanding of managerial decision making at the executive level.

BACKGROUND

As a norm, lessons learned are not examined as a preventive measure in decision making. While elementary in nature, decision making does not necessarily get better with age or experience; rather, it is improved through the calculated assessment of potential outcomes.

Executive decision makers in all types of organizations are plagued with the tribulations of making effective decisions. Existing decision processes do not always result in informed communication. In addition to the misfortunes of a lack of communication, the decisions' contexts are not always well understood. Along with these factors, the rapid retirement of people who have capital knowledge creates an information exodus that has never been documented. Capital knowledge provides critical pieces of information necessary to make informed decisions.

It can be complicated, if it is even possible, to break free from the shackles of poor credibility once bad decisions have been made. The media has replayed too many sagas for this to be denied. In 1986, America was shocked by the destruction of the space shuttle *Challenger* and the death of its seven crew members due to the negligence of National Aeronautics and Space Administration (NASA) space shuttle decision makers (Presidential Commission, 1986), whose decision was shuttle efficiency over safety. Withholding information about faulty equipment demonstrated poor judgment when the worse possible consequence unfolded as millions of people watched this televised launch explode. The American calendar once again was tarnished by catastrophe on September 11th when, in 2001, one of the world's greatest defense tragedies unfurled on United States soil. Fingers continue to be pointed toward those who, it is rumored, did not heed warnings that might have prevented the hijacking of airplanes that subsequently were flown into the World Trade Center towers and the Pentagon (Borger, 2002). Decision making in this crisis was weak, at best, and the judgment lax. Imperative information was not disseminated throughout chains of authority, but instead rested where it ultimately served no purpose other than limited awareness. The unfortunate result of the decision to stifle a warning: nearly 3,600 people died.

Four years later, calamity smothered the United States again when Hurricane Katrina mounted into a Category 4 storm and slammed onto the Gulf Coast in 2005 (Davis, 2005). Water breached the levees, as predicted. Subsequently, Lake Pontchartrain and the Mississippi River submerged cities under 20 feet of water and left 1,300 dead, thousands homeless, and a damage tab of over $100 million. Yet, a few years earlier, the Federal Emergency Management Agency (FEMA) had predicted three American mega-catastrophes: a California earthquake, a Manhattan terrorist attack, and, oddly, the submergence of New Orleans.

In an abstract sense, these cases are lessons learned for all organizations. We must gain understanding by experience in order to develop new solutions. We must continuously analyze bad solutions that result in bad situations where the solution had great probability of being flawed from the start. In addition, we also must describe how to get out of bad situations and proceed from there to good solutions. We must thoroughly understand the contributing attributes that force conditions of harmony between today (what is) and the future (what is to be). The repercussions of not heeding these recommendations could yield yet more catastrophic occurrences that threaten to crumble every facet of our society.

According to Hammond, Keeney, and Raiffa (1999), a good decision-making method is a solid foundation to all occupations and the success of any organization. Organizations and the lives of those involved are enhanced when attention is paid to developing design methods for good decision making. Because everyone within an organization is impacted by the outcome of decisions regardless of their role, failure by leaders to exercise good judgment can prove detrimental to those in all ranks. In a community college setting, poorly designed decision methods have been widely exercised and have resulted in low staff morale and a decrease in staff retention.

Academic governance or management in the business sense—specifically within higher education institutions—has received much criticism over the past several decades. Fain (2004) reported that the Southern Association of Colleges and Schools revoked the accreditation of Morris Brown College in 2002 because of significant debt. In 2004, *The Chronicle of Higher Education* noted that numerous colleges were forced to downsize programs, merge, or close after a lack of advance budgetary planning: According to Lee (2004), legal battles surfaced when higher institutions lost their accreditation because, without that sanction, students were not able to matriculate. In cases such as these when conflict arises from executive decision makers' inappropriate planning, discord spreads beyond the executive level.

In a national study of faculty in governance in 1991, Dimond analyzed decision-making processes and found a large number of dissatisfied people (as cited in Kezar, 2004). Kezar wrote that of the faculty, staff, and administrators, 70% believed that decision-making processes worked ineffectively and noted that new approaches needed to be considered. He acknowledged the widespread governance problem of ineffective decision methods, and detailed that few solutions have been proposed; of those, none had improved decision making. He concluded that the common wisdom was that campus governance needed to radically alter its structure and formal processes. This was the same reason cited in a well-publicized 1998 study by Benjamin and Carroll of the RAND Corporation that campus management was perceived to be wholly ineffective (as cited in Kezar, 2004). All three authors found that campus governance structures and processes did not allow timely review or effective, expert decision making.

While governance examines structure, it remains an understudied area that has had only limited research (Kezar, 2004). Leslie stated in 1996 that what has been documented about governance in higher education rests on anecdote or, at best, a handful of teaching case studies (as cited in Kaplan, 2004). To obtain the maximum level of understanding that surrounds decision authority within governance structures, Kaplan (2004) suggested reviewing the various foundations and systems in place such that varying outcomes can be obtained.

This chapter centers on implementing a risk management program to identify potential problems for the community college to address in order to deliver knowledge that will develop risk management practitioners' abilities to handle continuing challenges such as the community college's increased societal demands and its decrease in funding from state and local levels. Implementing a risk management program increases an organization's success and ability to continue to handle our society's 21st century needs.

With such wide audiences, the academic sector has a responsibility to make and disseminate decisions with seamless transitions. Yet, this same community has made little effort to either explore or communicate their practical applications. Conversely, those who might seek the relevant research will find most of it inaccessible.

Where information is not complicated, sometimes it is merely antiquated. The old-fashioned quandary of who has power and authority is useless in a world that operates on too much information in too little time. The hindrance is that ways that were once ideal and rational required the impossible task of comprehensively understanding every facet of a problem. Today, decision makers are not afforded the luxury to perform comprehensive interpretations. Outdated decision-making models are failing, and their failure can be expected to accelerate (Dressel, 1981; Etzioni, 1989/2001).

With respect to the roles within academic governance, community college leaders are faced with numerous obstacles and frustrations (Vaughan, 1983). They must do more with less and still uphold the expectations to meet with governing boards, be models of ethical behavior, and provide vision for the entire community (Pierce, 1997). There is a need for decision-making systems that respond efficiently to change (Kaplan, 2004). Society's response to this need has been to apply decision-making technology to an already dysfunctional matter.

The community college's mission was instituted as a way to deliver quality education to all who would seek it, and as a way to convey social equality. The community college, after all, is the product of policy at all three levels of government—national, state, local—and provides a service to the community it serves (Dougherty, 2001). However, with greater demands and fewer resources, community college leaders run the potential risk of catastrophic failure in delivering upon a mission that is often unclear (Vaughan, 1983). Whether for these academic leaders or for corporate executives, the dilemma is the same: Daily organizational management leaves little time to actually lead (Addy, 1995). In short, executives are faced with multifaceted risks in decision making.

In answering the calls to reform governance, many administrators have invested in costly reengineering projects. Their responses have been based on the presumption that most processes do not work nearly as well as they should, and that a committed and urgent effort should be orchestrated to transform them (Keen & Knapp, 1996; Kezar, 2004). However, reengineering does not work when the problem's root cause has not been identified adequately. This disparity justifies the need for risk management to continuously evaluate proposed solutions in real-time. To identify good and bad contributing factors within their current solution space is simply good practice.

RISKS THAT AFFECT COMMUNITY COLLEGE DECISION MAKERS

In Spring 2004, a tailored software engineering methodology was implemented as a research strategy to address decision-making problems at a community college. The theoretical framework for the tailored methodology was derived from the software risk evaluation (SRE) method description defined by the SEI. The goal was to improve executive decision making by providing perspectives on the current problem through identifying and analyzing risks.

The units of analysis for this case study were centered on the first two activities of risk management: risk planning and risk assessments. Within the risk planning activity specific tailoring was performed on SRE method description tools. The taxonomy questionnaire specified by the SRE focused on identifying risks incurred in software development efforts (Williams, Pandelios, & Behrens, 1999). Thus, this taxonomy was tailored to identify operational risks.

Within the risk assessment activity the risk identification and risk analysis functions were used as specified by the SRE method description (Williams et al., 1999). The risk analysis function examined risks in detail to determine the risks' scope within the organization and quantifying the risks' consequences. During this analysis function, each risk was assessed for its likelihood of occurring and the potential adverse impacts to the organization if the risk occurred. Classifications and categorization were performed to create the taxonomy groups and review them for like themes.

Using the classifications, the scoring was reconciled by conducting validation on entries for impact and probability. After the validation procedure was completed the mean and standard deviation were calculated, sorting in descending order by standard deviation. This process concluded with the top 35% of the risks.

The research using the tailored SRE method description consisted of 11 interview sessions involving 56 participants, executives from a single urban northeastern United States community college. Executives within the community college participated by sharing their

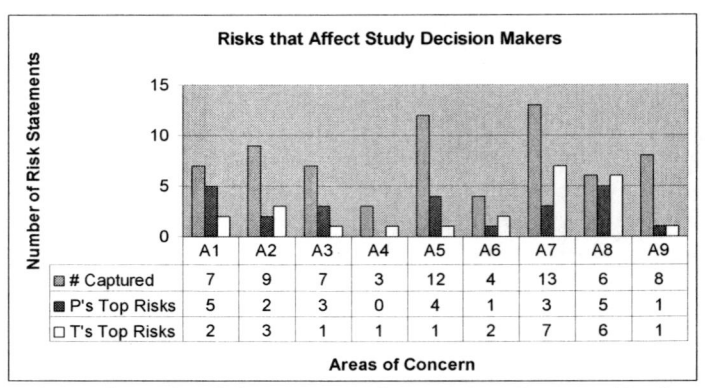

Figure 1. Risk areas of concern

Areas of Concern	A1	A2	A3	A4	A5	A6	A7	A8	A9
# Captured	7	9	7	3	12	4	13	6	8
P's Top Risks	5	2	3	0	4	1	3	5	1
T's Top Risks	2	3	1	1	1	2	7	6	1

Note. P = Participant, T = Team. A1 = Budget, A2 = Culture, A3 = Definition, A4 = Request, A5 = Resources, A6 = Scheduling, A7 = Suitability, A8 = Technology, A9 = Familiarity.

thoughts about what could happen if something went wrong. These interview sessions captured 69 risk statements with their risk impact, probability, and priority. The collection of risks formulated from the interviews formed this chapter's "risk list."

The 69 risk statements were captured, categorized, and ranked for perceived importance. Of the risk statements, the primary concern surrounded the suitability of the existing decision process and the lack of resources to effectively enact decisions.

Interview participants selected their top concerns according to the procedures specified in SRE method description. Table 1 illustrates the participants' top risks in ordinal sequence with the first risk statement being of most importance, the second most important risk statement listed as number 2. This sequence continues to the 24th risk statement.

In addition to classification and categorization the SRE method description discusses risk prioritization to analyze risk attributes to determine a risk category's relative priority or importance, yielding an *interrelationship digraph*. This digraph, illustrated in Figure 2, represents the relationships among the risk areas. If the conditions embodied in one risk area cause or influence conditions embodied in another risk area, a directional line was drawn between the two risk categories. The arrow shows the driving direction from one risk area to another. These relationships were qualitatively labeled as 1 for a weak relationship, 3 for a medium relationship, and 9 for a strong relationship.

The interrelationship digraph was transformed to a worksheet to show cause/driver and result/rider relationships. Any line that flowed from one risk area to another was a cause/driver. All risk areas that received drivers were result/riders. The total composite analysis resulted in Figure 3. This illustration represents the order of risk handling. The recommendation from this illustration is that by handling the resources concern, all other concerns can be addressed. Without handling resources, it would be impossible to gain maximum effectiveness.

Deficient resources cast the darkest cloud over the community college due to the fact that resources have the highest cause-and-effect relationship in this study. The resource issue must be handled first to improve unclear customer requests, nonexistent mission-suitable processes, and obsolete documentation. When the resource issue has been resolved, the community college must examine the decision-making process to capture requirements for change due to unsuitability. The risks discovered in this study become input in the "to be" process. With sufficient resources and a defined process, the community college can eliminate cultural biases imposed by its staff.

Issues that involve the staff can be monitored and controlled through effective leadership. However, it is impossible to ignore that no matter how great the leadership or how hard the people work, eventually the lack of budget will eradicate any efficiencies. Without adequate funding, the community college will need to creatively attract revenue. By proactively searching for risks, the community college can chart the course for a less turbulent future. With suitable resources assigned, existing processes can be improved and documented, and staff can be trained in the process. Addressing these issues will greatly improve the already defunct process.

Table 1. Participants' top risks

No.	Risk Statement and Possible Future Consequence(s)
1	Not all business processes are documented: presents a liability, loss of historic perspective, may lead to important information falling through the cracks, may be difficult for new hires to become familiar with the process
2	Poor communication: may lead to misinformation and frustration
3	Technology does not exist to facilitate process: may lead to manual processes, inefficient use of resources
4	"New" entire community unaware of where decisions are to be made: decisions likely to be made within the entire community
5	Potential for core knowledge to "walk" with retirees: single point of failure, reinvent the wheel, loss of effectiveness, disruption of strategic plan, degradation of service, lost data
6	Core Enterprise Resource Planning (ERP) lacks data and functionality: shadow database exists, pertinent information can be lost, sense of urgency to move toward being a "Learning Center" can be lost, complacency, lost college culture
7	Not all processes are institutionalized/documented: cannot provide assessments
8	Operation and capital funding does not keep up with the college and population demand: increase in tuition, cap on enrollment, affects hiring of quality people
9	Scarce resources: causes decision makers to be territorial
10	Process reliant on a few key people: disenfranchised
11	College as a whole does not adequately assess functions that cost money: service to stakeholders (students and faculty) can be affected
12	Adequate technological structure does not exist: deadlines can be missed, lack of ability to communicate and share
13	Decision processes may not be documented: decision authority may be unknown, inaction or no action is performed, wrong people can impact decisions
14	Proper analysis to identify root causes may not be performed: not solving the problem, misuse of resources likely
15	College mission/objectives may not be used to determine priorities: miss the mark, misuse of resources
16	Perception exists to be a collective entity of many institutions: dilutes focus, misuse of resources, set up for failure
17	Lack of unified approach to deal with institutional priorities: silo approach, goals not met
18	Lack of adequate funding: not enough resources, quantity overrides quality, lose "good" people
19	There can be a disconnect in communicating institution-wide decision making: some employees feel isolated from the process and that they had no input in the decision
20	There is a lack of tools to support/share decisions made at the cabinet and operational levels: inefficiencies, decisions can be based on incomplete data, processes are less efficient
21	Technology is not current: many procedures are time-consuming, reap inaccurate results
22	The budget is not adequate: some just do not do it, we do not evolve (design)
23	Not adequately staffed: lucrative options may not be exercised, dissatisfied customers
24	We have not been able to adequately secure budget for all needs: falling behind in information technology, not competitive in attracting and retaining faculty, higher tuition for students

The findings from the community college study confirmed that executives remain faced with challenges such as unclear customer requests, nonexistent mission-suitable processes, and obsolete or nonexistent documentation. Other issues of great discord related to various aspects of inadequate resources to perform the desired actions within the allotted time. Understaffing obstructs the goal of getting a job done well. Of the work that gets done, the process relies upon a few key people. Despite budget limitations, the community college process stays afloat, attributed mainly to the people who make it successful. A downside, though, is what occurs when—not if—these people experience burnout. Study participants stated that being overworked causes

Figure 2. Interrelationship digraph

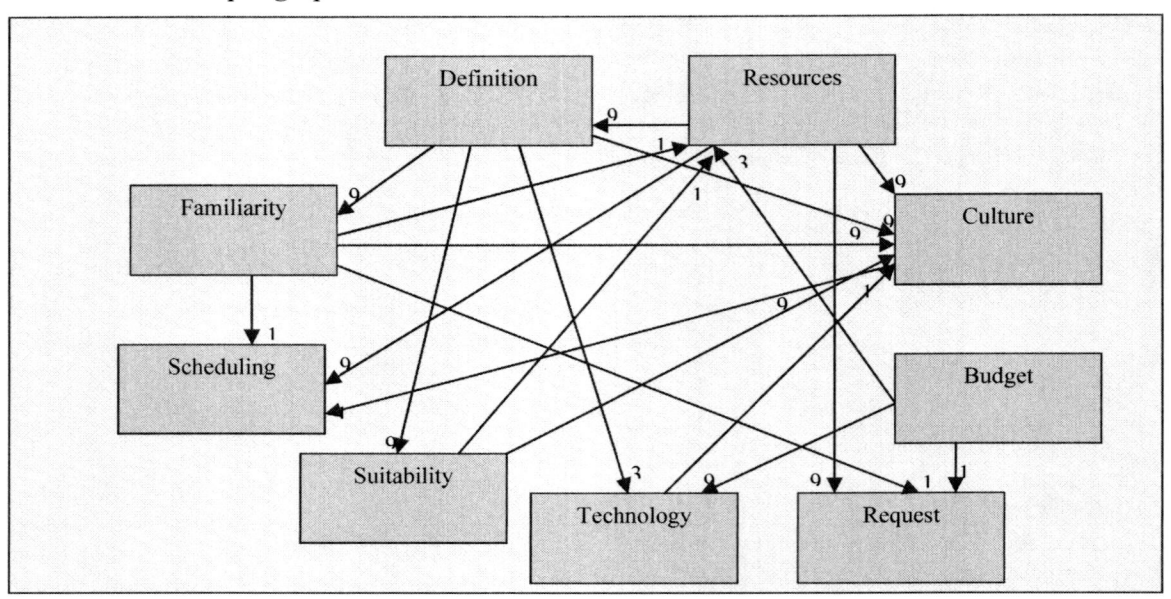

Figure 3. Interrelationship hierarchy digraph

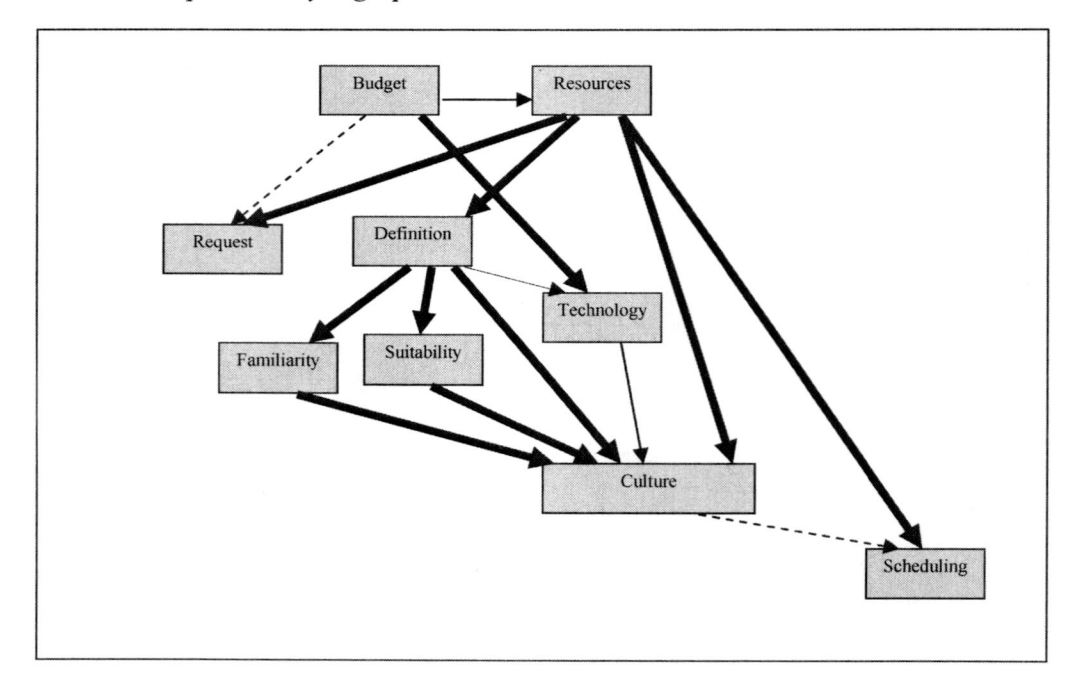

deterioration of staff morale and superficial decision making. They agreed that the perception is, "We do not have to be good; we just need to look good."

The best advice to avoid decision-making risks rests in information that has been presented in the current field. History suggests that bad decisions can be built from unclear alternatives, clamorous advice and no analysis (Hammond, Keeney, & Raiffa, 1998/2001).

Within an organization, the actual process often receives the blame for a bad decision. In such cases, the argument tends to be that the decision either was inept, not clearly defined, or the people involved were not sure who had the decision-making authority—or, worse, all of the above. Russo and Schoemaker

(2002) stated that the type of entity in which someone works—business, government, professional services, education, or non-profit sector—does not shield that person from the likelihood of being impacted by poorly made decisions. To improve the way business decisions are made, those involved in the process must become students of research—regardless of their domain—and continue to explore ways to chart new paths.

Welch (2002) linked having control of risks to being an effective decision maker, and acknowledged that studying and capturing risks are essential to improvements. Vaughan (1983) posed the question, "How can today's leaders utilize the experiences of the past to build a better future for the community college and thus the nation?" He challenges leaders to work tirelessly so that, in response, the community college can continue to contribute its best.

Vaughan and Weisman (1997) stated that leaders and executive management face the tough tests of balancing workloads, hidden agendas, and their personal lives. Exceptional leaders are necessary to a well-run organizational structure's success (Roueche, Baker, & Rose, 1989). Structures and processes need to be adapted to the culture of the institutions they serve (Kezar, 2004). If those institutions are dysfunctional, they must be analyzed to determine the best course of action. To be stagnant in this regard can be a cultural flaw. Furthermore, once new governance has been defined or dysfunctional governance has been corrected, periodic assessment of that governance must be implemented to determine its continued suitability (Addy, 1995).

FURTHER TRENDS AND CONCLUSION

To combat the problem of poor decision making, the recommendations resulting from this chapter are to continue exploring risks. In 2005, the SEI, a federal research center whose mission is to advance the practice of software engineering, came on board with the recognition that risks exist across all organizations, regardless of their mission, and produced a taxonomy of operational risks.

This chapter presented the results of a study that used an earlier SRE method description focusing on identifying risk in software development projects and tailored it to executive decision making. Researchers should continue this exploration and conduct additional studies within other community colleges. Reviewing and analyzing a thorough, combined set of risks will greatly enhance future definitions of governance structures, processes, roles, and chains of authority.

The concept of decision making is documented as long ago as Biblical times. Adam and Eve, believed in Christian theology to be the first couple created by God, were granted freedom with their sole directive being to not eat from the tree of knowledge of good and evil. When the pair found themselves tempted away from the other fruit-bearing trees toward the forbidden one, they had to make a choice: whether to disobey God. Their decision to sway from God's instructions is believed by some to have resulted in the irreversible affliction that generations to come would not avoid the clutches of suffering, evil, sickness, and death.

It is not always the decision that is difficult to make: It is more complicated to make a decision that reflects the best total judgment. Decision complexities are accurately addressed, and still relevant, in a commentary spoken by President John F. Kennedy more than 40 years ago (Sorensen, 2005):

The American Presidency is a formidable, exposed, and somewhat mysterious institution. It is formidable because it represents the point of ultimate decision in the American political system.... It is exposed because decisions cannot take place in a vacuum.... [President] Lincoln observed that we cannot escape history. It is equally true that we cannot escape choice; and, for an American President [sic], choice is charged with a peculiar and daunting responsibility for the safety and welfare of the nation. A President must choose among men, among measures, among methods.... 'The heart of the Presidency is therefore informed, prudent, and resolute choice—and the secret of the presidential enterprise is to be found in an examination of the way presidential choices are made. (p. xi)

Governmental systems, as they are operated in the United States, follow a framework set by the American presidency. Decisions made from the Oval Office create societal methods and rules for governing, including those of higher education. President Kennedy also addressed many other concerns that exist today regarding higher education governance and leadership.

Today's community college president is at the cusp of the ultimate decision making. He or she convenes a participating management team in a shared or bureaucratic governance structure. The governance process, its structures, and implementations are obscured and known only by those who have been involved long enough to have etched the process into their minds. Trends reveal that as people retire from community colleges, a shortage of executives with the requisite experience to immediately step into leadership positions and perform at maximum capacity will become prevalent. History's warnings have to be heeded.

Like the leaders before them, today's leaders are faced with the ultimate responsibilities to lead, influence, and motivate. This chapter challenges leaders to also become risk management practitioners within the community college environment. Practitioners can take knowledge gained from this case study and apply it as part of their overall management activities.

This chapter further challenges organizations—particularly community colleges—to implement a policy to perform risk management in accordance with a process standard applicable to the risk management paradigm that exists in the literature today. Implementing compliance with this process standard at the executive level will provide a cultural shift from firefighting and crisis management to proactive decision making that avoids problems before they arise. Anticipating what might go wrong will become a part of everyday business, and managing risks will be as integral to the organization as routine campus affairs.

REFERENCES

Addy, C. L. (1995). *The president's journey: Issues and ideals in the community college*. Bolton, MA: Anker.

Borger, J. (2002, May). Agent accuses FBI of "sabotage." *The Guardian*.

Butler, R. (1991). *Designing organizations: A decision-making perspective*. New York: Routledge.

Davis, M. (2005). *The predators of New Orleans*. Retrieved from http://mondediplo.com/2005/10/02katrina

Dougherty, K. J. (2001). *The contradictory college: The conflicting origins, impacts, and futures of the community college*. Albany: State University of New York Press.

Dressel, P. L. (1981). *Administrative leadership* (1st ed.). San Francisco: Jossey-Bass.

Etzioni, A. (2001). Humble decision making. In *Harvard Business Review on decision making* (pp. 45-57). Boston: Harvard Business School Press. (Reprinted from the *Harvard Business Review*, 1989, 67(4), 122-126)

Fain, P. (2004). Former Morris Brown president indicted. *The Chronicle of Higher Education, 51,* A35.

Hammond, J. S., Keeney, R. L., & Raiffa, H. (1999). *Smart choices: A practical guide to making better decisions*. Boston, MA: Harvard Business School Press.

Hammond, J. S., Keeney, R. L., & Raiffa, H. (2001). Even swaps. In *Harvard Business Review on decision making* (pp. 21-44). Boston: Harvard Business School Press. (Reprinted from the *Harvard Business Review*, 1998, 76(2), 137-149)

Kaplan, G. E. (2004). Do governance structures matter? *New Directions for Higher Education, 127,* 23-34.

Keen, P. G. W., & Knapp, E. M. (1996). *Every manager's guide to business processes: A glossary of key terms and concepts for today's business leader*. Boston: Harvard Business School Press.

Kezar, A. (2004). What is more important to effective governance: Relationships, trust, and leadership, or structures and formal processes? *New Directions for Higher Education, 127,* 35-46.

Lee, B. A. (2004). Colleges should plan now for a financial crunch. *The Chronicle of Higher Education, 50,* B8.

Moody, P. E. (1983). *Decision making: Proven methods for better decisions*. New York: McGraw-Hill.

Pierce, D. R. (1997). The community college presidency: Qualities for success. *New Directions for Community Colleges, 98,* 13-24.

Power, D. J. (2002). *Decision support systems: Concepts and resources for managers*. Westport, CT: Quorum Books.

Presidential Commission on the Space Shuttle *Challenger* Accident, The. (1986, June 6). *Report of the Presidential Commission on the Space Shuttle Challenger Accident*. Retrieved February 20, 2006, from http://history.nasa.gov/rogersrep/51lcover.htm

Roueche, J. E., Baker, G. A., & Rose, R. R. (1989). *Shared vision: Transformational leadership in Ameri-*

can community colleges. Washington, DC: Community College Press, National Center for Higher Education.

Russo, J. E., & Schoemaker, P. J. H. (2002). *Winning decisions: Getting it right the first time* (1st ed.). New York: Currency.

Secchi, P. (Ed.). (1999). *Proceedings of alerts and lessons learned: An effective way to prevent failures and problems* (Tech. Rep. No. WPP-167). Noordwijk, The Neitherlands: ESTEC.

Sorensen, T. C. (2005). *Decision-making in the White House: The olive branch or the arrows*. New York: Columbia University Press.

Vaughan, G. B. (1983). *Issues for community college leaders in a new era* (1st ed.). San Francisco: Jossey-Bass.

Vaughan, G. B., & Weisman, I. M. (1997). Selected characteristics of community college trustees and presidents. *New Directions for Community Colleges, 98*, 5-12.

Welch, D. A. (2002). *Decisions, decisions: The art of effective decision making*. Amherst, NY: Prometheus Books.

Williams, R. C., Pandelios, G. J., & Behrens, S. G. (1999). *Software risk evaluation (SRE) method description: Version 2.0*. Pittsburgh, PA: Carnegie Mellon University Software Engineering Institute.

KEY TERMS

Consequence: Consequence is part of a risk statement; a phrase that describes the key, possible negative outcomes of the current conditions that are creating uncertainties.

Context: Context is the circumstances, events, and interrelationships within the organization that provide background information for the risk.

Decision: Decision is an action that must be taken when there is no more time for gathering facts (Moody, 1983); the selection of a proposed course of action (Butler, 1991).

Decision Maker: Decision maker is each person who works in the business environment (Moody, 1983).

Decision Process: Decision process is the steps or analyses that lead to a decision. Decision processes are often part of a larger business processes (Power, 2002).

Lesson Learned: Lesson learned is knowledge or understanding gained by experience (Secchi, 1999).

Prioritization: Prioritization is a procedure to rank risks depending on their relationships.

Risk List: Risk list is a collection of risks affecting an organization. This list contains all the information necessary for a high-level review of the risks.

Risk Management: Risk management identifies, assesses, treats, and monitors risks during the entire life cycle, responding to each risk in terms of appropriate treatment and acceptance (ISO/IEC 15288, an industry standard).

Risk Probability: Risk probability is the likelihood that a risk will occur (Project Management Institute, 2000).

An Extended Model of Decision Making: A Devil's Advocate Workshop

David Sammon
University College Cork, Ireland

INTRODUCTION

Enterprise resource planning (ERP) packages can be described as the most sought after means of organisational transformation and IT innovation since the mid 1990s. Over the past decade, ERP packages have become a major part of the organisational landscape and form the cornerstone of IS architectures for an ever increasing percentage of organisations. Despite the strong push toward enterprise-wide ERP systems in the wider organisational community and the experience accumulated over 20 years of large scale integrated systems implementations, there is, in relation to ERP deployment, a lack of understanding of the specific project management required to counter the difficulties that can arise when organisations fail to ensure that all the required factors of success are present in their projects. Therefore, novel ideas to help managers and project managers to better prepare for enterprise-wide ERP projects are badly needed.

This entry presents a method of practical relevance for organisational decision-makers by introducing the concept of a devil's advocate workshop—reminiscent of Klein's premortem sessions (Klein, 1993, 2002), but tailor-made for large scale Information Systems projects—which leverages the concept of sense-making, in introducing a preplanning "intelligence" phase in any enterprise-wide ERP project life-cycle.

BACKGROUND

There seems to be a misguided perception in the managerial community that ERP packages are the modern day IT silver bullet and this has been revealed notably by Swanson and Ramiller (2004, p. 554) in their award winning MISQ research article titled "Innovating Mindfully with Information Technology," where they reported that

by the mid-1990s, ERP was a topic that was being banded about in boardrooms. It wasn't just an information technology (IT) project, but a strategic business imperative... the ERP genie was out of the bottle—every company needed to have an ERP implementation.

However, Swanson and Ramiller (2004, p. 554), borrowing Weick's concept of mindfulness, suggest that

adopting organisations entertain scant reasoning for their moves. Especially where the innovation achieves a high public profile, as with ERP, deliberative behaviour can be swamped by an acute urgency to join the stampeding herd, notwithstanding the high cost and apparent risk involved.

Indeed, this mindless behaviour in pursuit of "best practise" is the rule.

Paradoxically, the argument can also be made that investments in these ERP packages are amongst the most significant an organisation has engaged, or will ever, engage in; and this is not adequately matched by the low level of managerial understanding of the impacts of implementation of such systems on the organisation. This trend supports the contention that the level of managerial understanding of technological innovations is generally low, and that managers need to be empowered and made aware of what is critical for a successful project implementation of ERP applications. Therefore, specific tools and methods must be proposed to provide managers with a means of assessing their organisation's level of understanding before they embark on complex innovating pursuits (for example, enterprise-wide ERP projects) and, from this assessment, to offer the means to improve the starting point.

MAIN FOCUS

ERP projects are highly complex and challenging initiatives to undertake (regardless of organisational size) for reasons relating to: projects being difficult to scope, with issues becoming apparent only once the project is under way, the benefits being nebulous, and the scale of the project being greater than an organisation is prepared for, in implementation. In fact, success has not been easy to achieve and organisations that implement enterprise-wide ERP systems, based on a myopic mindset and only for an immediate return on investment, have been in for a "rude and expensive awakening" (Gargeya & Brady, 2005). Therefore, improving the likelihood of success prior to undertaking a project would prove hugely beneficial to most organisations. In fact, many organisations view their project implementations as failures. However, it has also been argued that the cause of these ERP implementation failures relates to a lack of appropriate culture and organisational (internal) readiness, which, if addressed, is also a feature of the most successful enterprise-wide ERP projects. This readiness is referred to as a "readiness to change" and it has been argued that not enough time and attention has been devoted to the "internal readiness" factor at the outset of an ERP project and the subsequent changes required during the implementation process (Davenport, 2000; Gargeya & Brady, 2005). As a result, an organisation's state of readiness is extremely important in order to undertake an enterprise-wide ERP implementation and, as a result, the awareness of managers should be reflected in the preparations made for the project initiative.

AWARENESS AND PREPAREDNESS

Very little academic research literature in the enterprise-wide ERP systems area focuses directly on the issue of organisational readiness for enterprise-wide ERP projects. However, numerous articles in the trade press highlight the importance of an organisation assessing its state of readiness to undertake an enterprise-wide ERP project. However, these readiness checks are promoted by ERP vendors and consultancy groups and are tightly integrated into a preferred implementation methodology, which ultimately positions these checks on readiness in the planning phase of the project. Indeed, it can be argued that the planning stage is too late for this self-assessment exercise, in that it should be a vendor/consultant-independent, methodology-independent and "preplanning" or "intelligence phase" thought process in relation to undertaking an enterprise-wide ERP project.

It seems that a critically important issue to consider with the introduction of any ERP package is the readiness of the organisation for such an initiative, prior to the project's initiation. This view is certainly supported by the available research literature and by the fact that a high number of enterprise-wide ERP projects fail in such a way that the cause of failure can be related to a lack of preparedness in the early stages of the project. Ideally, readiness is viewed as an organisational mindset and should be concerned with a straightforward and comprehensive assessment of the level of understanding that exists within an organisation, with regard to what is involved in undertaking an enterprise-wide ERP project, and the actual preparedness that is needed within the organisation for such a project undertaking. Therefore, organisational readiness is simply viewed as a "common sense" approach to an enterprise-wide ERP project. In fact, it can be argued that readiness leads to highlighting the criticality of certain factors a priori that may, if absent or unmanaged, lead to less than desirable project outcomes. As a result, organisational readiness should be concerned with providing focus and establishing the structures that should constitute an enterprise-wide ERP project.

While awareness is determined by the organisational decision makers' understanding of what an enterprise-wide ERP project entails, preparedness relates to the actions managers take to prepare themselves and the organisation for an enterprise-wide ERP project, thereby leveraging this awareness. As a result, a lack of preparedness can be as a result of a lack of awareness as to what is involved in such an undertaking and a lack of appreciation for the existing organisational configuration in the context of a managers own organisation. In accordance with Weick (1988, p. 306), if understanding is facilitated by action and "if action is a means to get feedback, learn, and build an understanding of unknown environments, then a reluctance to act could be associated with less understanding and more errors." Therefore, within implementing organisations a "delicate trade-off between dangerous action which produces understanding and safe inaction which produces confusion" exists (Weick, 1988, p. 306). This highlights the fact that low levels of awareness and preparedness is characteristic of safe inaction where organisational decision-makers display:

- Weak project management
- Myopic thinking

However, high levels of awareness and preparedness within an organisation is characteristic of dangerous action where organisational decision-makers display:

- Strong project management
- Hyperopic (strategic) thinking

Indeed, as Einhorn and Hogarth (1987, p. 69) argued "whether we like to acknowledge it or not, most of the time we do a poor job of thinking forward with any accuracy." Indeed, Mintzberg and Westley (2001, p. 90) also commented that "vision requires the courage to see what others do not," which equates to this notion of hyperopic thinking and dangerous action.

DESIGN OF THE DEVIL'S ADVOCATE WORKSHOP

The concept of devil's advocate[1] has been used by a number of researchers in the study of the strategic planning process (Boland, 1984; Mason, 1969) and psychological traps in decision making (Hammond, Keeney, & Raiffa, 2006). The devil's advocate workshop embraces the dialectical method and by its design suggests that theses and antitheses will be proposed by workshop participants. The dialectical approach (Mason & Mitroff, 1981) uses creative conflict to help identify and challenge assumptions to create new perceptions. Traditionally, the devil's advocate approach, while useful in exposing underlying assumptions, has a tendency to emphasise the negative, whereas dialectical inquiry has a more balanced approach.

As a result, the devil's advocate workshop avoids adversarial decision processes, where, for example, one workshop participant is deemed to win, while another workshop participant is deemed to lose with regard to deciding on the preferred course of action to take in preparing for a project. The nature of the workshop design is not intended to follow this adversarial process. However, the devil's advocate workshop does not simply want to satisfy all workshop participants through "soft" consensus through identifying and recording agreements that already exist, while they may not have been previously recognised. In fact, the merit of the devil's advocate workshop is that in embracing the dialectical processes, the focus of workshop participants is on disagreements which are turned into agreements, or indeed there is a transformation in the dialogue in that direction. Furthermore, workshop participants will raise their collective awareness and resolve disagreements through rational discussion around undertaking an ERP project implementation within their organisational context. As a result, from this dialectic between opposing views a greater understanding of the critical success factors (CSFs) for ERP implementation can emerge with a pooling of information in pursuit of better decision-making. Therefore, the devil's advocate workshop aims at being persuasive through dialogue, or at least results in a shared understanding (synthesis) amongst workshop participants who are the key organisational decision makers on the project.

The design of this devil's advocate workshop embraces the arguments of Mintzberg and Westley (2001, p. 89) who stated that "a *thinking first* model of decision making should be supplemented with two very different models—a *seeing first* and a *doing first* model." In fact, Mintzberg and Westley (2001) commented that when managers use all three models, the quality of their decisions can improve, and healthy organisations should have the capacity for all three. While the thinking first model is essentially the rational model of decision making, in practice it is uncommon in light of the mindless (Swanson & Ramiller, 2004) approach of managers to enterprise-wide ERP projects. However, inherent in the self-assessment method proposed here, managers are given the opportunity to think first, by analysing the outputs of the survey questions.

The seeing first model proposes that decisions or at least actions may be driven as much by "what is seen as by what is thought" (Mintzberg & Westley, 2001). Therefore, this proposes that understanding can be visual as well as conceptual. In the devil's advocate workshop,[2] a causal model of CSFs can be developed as a visual representation of the causal relationships between CSFs for ERP implementation. As a result, the outcomes of future decisions made around these CSFs can be visualised and with the increased understanding of these CSFs, the expected future actions may require further thought. Finally, the doing first model is described as being similar to that of sense-making (enactment, selection, retention) as proposed by Weick

An Extended Model of Decision Making

(1995). However, doing first requires action and the necessary thinking can happen after the action, based on trying something and then learning from it. In fact, Mintzberg and Westley (2001, p. 91) commented that doing first requires "doing various things, finding out which among them works, making sense of that and repeating the successful behaviours while discarding the rest." This illustrates the real value-added of the devil's advocate workshop, especially in relation to enterprise-wide ERP projects. Given how complex and resource intensive ERP projects are and given the prohibitive cost of incorrect action, or indeed safe inaction producing incorrect outcomes, implementing organisations cannot afford to get it wrong. Therefore, the positioning of the devil's advocate workshop in a preplanning environment, prior to project initiation, promotes a more inexpensive setting for the experimentation that doing first requires.

While action is important and produces learning, in the context of the devil's advocate workshop and the proposed method of organisational self-assessment, the action is being undertaken in an environment which may present managers with opportunities for improvisations, for example, identifying the skills required to execute the project, and, therefore, increasing their capacity for learning and understanding. However, managers may be able to use the benefit of foresight as opposed to hindsight, which has been a major defining characteristic of previous organisational approaches to selecting and implementing ERP packages because managers committed large expenditures in fees and licences early on in their projects.

THE BENEFITS OF A DEVIL'S ADVOCATE WORKSHOP

In this entry, it is argued that the devil's advocate workshop is extremely important to ensure that adequate planning and the associated level of understanding of potential consequences exist to govern decisions around an enterprise-wide ERP project. These devil's advocate workshops promote the importance of the intelligence phase of decision making (or the proper recognition of the problem in Klein's recognition-primed decision (RCP) model) for enterprise-wide ERP projects. Therefore, it is proposed that a workshop environment, promoting the enacted sense-making of project outcomes, in light of the level of managerial awareness of the CSFs (Critical Success Factors) for ERP implementation (before any decisions or actions are taken), will promote the establishment of a mindful (Swanson & Ramiller, 2004) approach to enterprise-wide ERP projects, as illustrated in Figure 1.

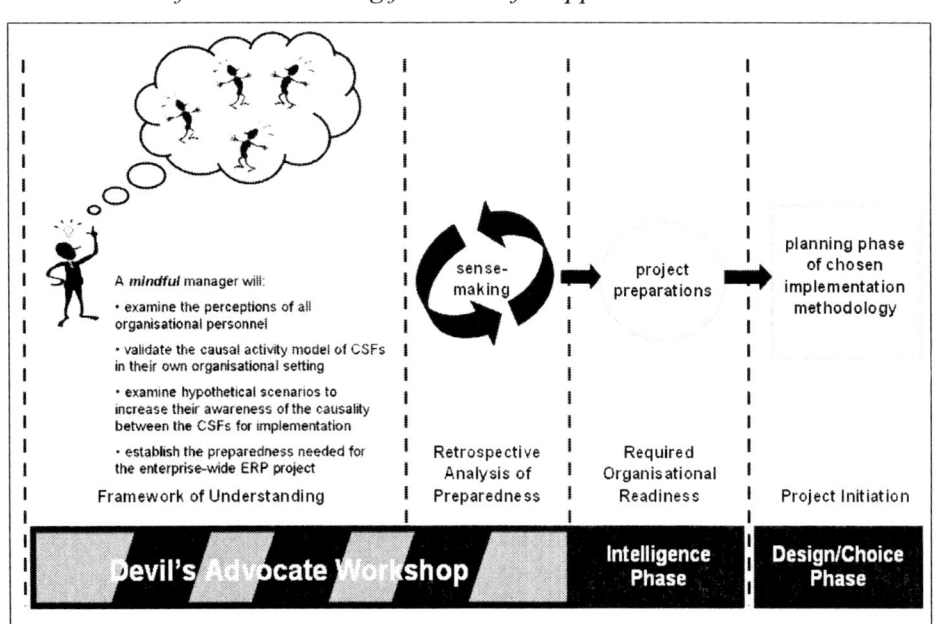

Figure 1. An extended model of decision making for a mindful approach to IT innovations

Table 1. The devil's advocate approach

Devil's Advocate Approach to Strategic Planning (Mason, 1969)	Devil's Advocate Workshop for Enterprise-Wide ERP Projects
• Normally used internally rather than with consultants	• Internal self-assessment of organisational readiness in a vendor-independent, methodology-independent and pre-implementation thought process
• Planner appears before the organisation's management and advocates a plan (in a manner similar to that of the expert[1] approach)	• All organisational personnel (impacted by the implementation of the ERP package) complete the survey with regard to their understanding of the CSFs for ERP implementation
• Management assumes the role of an adversary and often a critic of the plan. • Management attempts to determine all that is wrong with the plan and highlight the reasons why the plan should not be adopted	• The results are analysed and discussed by workshop participants (managers) as they become both advocates and critics of the findings • The causal nature of CSFs for ERP implementation is also analysed to assess the severity of the absence or presence of themes of understanding, which relate to the organisational personnels' perception of the CSFs in their organisational environment.

As illustrated in Figure 1, the devil's advocate workshop promotes a sense-making process (Weick, 1995). Therefore, preparedness for the project is a function of the level of awareness that managers have regarding the true nature of an enterprise-wide ERP project and developing it further requires going into the detail of how the system will fit their business processes (the devil is in the detail). Existing approaches to enterprise-wide ERP projects are characterised by their weakness in the activities included in the planning phase and the decisions made by organisational decision-makers within this phase. Therefore, a more mindful managerial decision making process to implementing ERP packages is missing in practice, which explains the inconsistency revealed in empirical studies of ERP between thought and action by decision makers. In essence, an organisation considering and preparing for an enterprise-wide ERP project should conduct such a sense-making exercise. In fact, this process can be viewed as an operationalisation of the concept of mindfulness discussed by Swanson and Ramiller (2004).

One main concern of this sense-making exercise centers on the need to understand the CSFs for ERP implementations, in a general sense initially, and then within one's organisation specifically. Thus, all managers whose business areas will be impacted by the introduction of the ERP package need to partake in the sense-making exercise so as to raise their perceptions of the absence or presence of certain CSFs within the organisation, for the project and to improve the quality of the organisation's overall preparedness. If awareness exists prior to project initiation, then adequate preparations can be made to address the CSFs and reduce the negative impact on the enterprise-wide ERP project outcomes. If awareness is not there, then it must be raised amongst participating personnel before the project can truly begin. Any shortcuts taken at this stage, for instance with greater reliance on external parties—consultants, vendors or implementers—will expose the organisation to the risk of abject failure as in the case of Foxmeyer, Mobil (Davenport, 1998) or the PPARS case (Sammon & Adam, 2006).

The value of the devil's advocate approach can be further demonstrated for this research study by referring back to the observations made by Mason (1969) with regard to the use of the devil's advocate approach for strategic planning. Mason (1969, p. 407) argued that "those who employ the devil's advocate approach assume that truly good plans will survive the most forceful opposition and that a sound judgment on a plan occurs when the plan is subjected to censure." In fact, Mason (1969) provided a description of how the devil's advocate approach worked in relation to planning, which is illustrated in Table 1. Table 1 has been extended to further illustrate the practicalities of using a devil's advocate workshop for the preplanning stage of an enterprise-wide ERP project.

To conclude, as argued throughout this section, the value-added the devil's advocate workshop is indeed compelling and promotes the establishment of a mindful (Swanson & Ramiller, 2004) approach to enterprise-wide ERP projects. However, this devil's advocate ideal type of organisational design (Mason, 1969) has not featured in organisations' approaches to adopting and implementing ERP projects.

FUTURE TRENDS

Hammond et al. (2006, p. 126) argued that the "best defence is always awareness" and stated that the best protection against all psychological traps—in isolation or in combination—is awareness. Forewarned is forearmed. Even if you cannot eradicate the distortions ingrained into the way your mind works, you can build tests and disciplines into your decision-making process that can uncover errors in thinking before they become errors in judgment. And taking action to understand and avoid psychological traps can have the added benefit of increasing your confidence in the choices you make.

It can be argued that the discussions presented by Hammond et al. (2006) are an effort to strengthen organisational decision-makers awareness, before committing to a course of action, with regard to the decision-making process they are about to follow. Indeed, this can be perceived as suggesting that foresight can be achieved to some degree by organisational decision-makers. In the context of this entry, foresight centres on an improved awareness of the causality between CSFs for ERP implementation and the impact of the presence or absence of CSFs on desired project outcomes. In fact, this suggestion of foresight would reduce the need to use hindsight with regard to decision-makers retrospectively making sense of the outcomes of their actions, which were informed by their decisions. Therefore, allowing a decision-maker the opportunity to retrospectively make sense of their proposed future decisions, using a devil's advocate workshop, would indeed embrace this concept of foresight and should ensure a more mindful (Swanson & Ramiller, 2004) approach to enterprise-wide ERP projects.

According to Brown (2000, p. 47) "there is a reasonable consensus that sense-making is accomplished through narratives," which makes the unexpected expectable (Robinson, 1981), allows us to comprehend causal relationships such that they can be predicted, understood, and possibly controlled (Sutton & Kahn, 1987), and which assist organisational participants to map their reality (Wilkins & Thompson, 1991). Therefore, a mindful manager (decision-maker) will have the opportunity to make sense of their state of internal readiness, through using the devil's advocate workshop; therefore, analysing the answers provided by organisational personnel to the survey questions and making sense of the causality between the CSFs for ERP implementation will result in an increased focus on preparedness, which will increase an organisation's ability to manage the actual enterprise-wide ERP project initiative. Therefore, sense-making is a thought process that uses retrospection to explain outcomes. In fact, these explanatory products of sense-making have been referred to as accounts and attributions in various strands of research, where statements are made to explain untoward behaviour and bridge the gap between actions and expectations, providing reasons for outcomes and discrepancies (Louis, 1980). As a result, a sense-making exercise as presented in Figure 1 may reduce an organisations tendency to accept the discourse of experts (ERP vendors and consultants), which has legitimised the actions and interests (sales discourse) of these dominant actors. Therefore, it is argued here that sense-making can promote and strengthen the needs discourse of an implementing organisation.

CONCLUSION

This proposed devil's advocate approach will work extremely well in any organisational setting. The key to its successful use is that managers need to approach its use with openness. It could be, however, that highly structured organisations where middle managers are not empowered to make any decisions and are not used to being asked to use their vision of reality, are a poor ground for running such initiatives. Participants need to be in a culture which is tolerant of contribution from managers closest to processes, rather than always relying on top managers of functional areas. Also, it is evidently a requirement that managers involved are allowed to follow through on correcting problems they have identified in the workshops rather than running the workshops for the sake of it.

REFERENCES

Adam, F., & Sammon, D. (2004). *The enterprise resource planning decade: Lessons learned and issues for the future.* Hershey, PA: Idea Publishing Group.

Boland, R. J. (1984). Sense-making of accounting data as a technique of organisational diagnosis. *Management Science, 30*(7), 868-882.

Brown, A.D. (2000). Making sense of inquiry sensemakin. *Journal of Management Studies, 37*(1), 45-75.

Davenport, T. (1998, July/August). Putting the enterprise into the enterprise system. *Harvard Business Review, 76*(4), 121-131.

Davenport, T. (2000). *Mission critical—realizing the promise of enterprise systems*. Boston, MA: Harvard Business School Publishing.

Einhorn, H. J., & Hogarth, R. M. (1987). Decision making: Going forward in reverse. *Harvard Business Review, 65*(1), 66-70.

Gargeya, V. B., & Brady, C. (2005). Success and failure factors of adopting SAP in ERP system implementation. *Business Process Management Journal, 11*(5), 501-516.

Hammond, J. S., Keeney, R. L., & Raiffa, H. (2006, January). The hidden traps in decision making. *Harvard Business Review*, 118-126.

Klein, G.A. (1993). A recognition-primed decision (RPD) model of rapid decision making. In G.A. Klein, J. Orasanu, R. Calderwood & C.E. Zsambok (Eds.), *Decision making in action, models and methods* (pp. 138-147). Nordwood, NJ: Ablex.

Klein, G.A. (2002). The fiction of optimization. In G. Gigerenzer & R. Selten (Eds.), *Bounded rationality: The adaptive toolbox* (pp. 103-121). MA: MIT Press.

Louis, M. R. (1980). Surprise and sensemaking: What newcomers experience in entering unfamiliar organisational settings. *Administrative Science Quarterly, 25*, 226-251.

Mason, R. O. (1969). A dialectical approach to strategic planning. *Management Science, 15*(8), 403-414.

Mason, R. O., & Mitroff, I. I. (1981). *Challenging strategic planning assumptions*. New York: Wiley.

Mintzberg, H., & Westley, F. (2001, Spring). Decision making: It's not what you think. *MIT Sloan Management Review*, 89-93.

Robinson, J. A. (1981). Personal narratives reconsidered. *Journal of American Folklore, 94*, 58-85.

Sammon, D., & Adam, F. (2006). Implementing radical changes with ERP—a case study in the Irish Health Service. In F. Adam, P. Brezillon, S. Carlsson & P. Humphreys (Eds.), *Creativity and innovation in decision making and decision support*. London, UK: Decision Support Press.

Sutton, R.I., & Kahn, R. L. (1987). Prediction, understanding, and control as antidotes to organizational stress. In J. W. Lorsch (Ed.), *Handbook of organizational behavior* (pp. 272-285). Englewood Cliffs, NJ: Prentice Hall.

Swanson, E.B., & Ramiller, N.C. (2004). Innovating mindfully with information technology. *MIS Quarterly, 28*(4), 553-583.

Weick, K.E. (1988). Enacted sensemaking in a crisis situation. *Journal of Management Studies, 25*, 305-317.

Weick, K.E. (1995). *Sensemaking in Organizations*. Thousand Oaks, CA: Sage.

Wilkins, A.L., & Thompson, M.P. (1991). On getting the story crooked (and straight). *Journal of Organizational Change Management, 4*(3), 18-26.

KEY TERMS

Critical Success Factors: CSFs have been applied to many aspects of organisational research and are defined as those critical areas where things must go right for the business or project to be successful.

Decision-Making: A decision-making process is a cognitive process which produces a final choice to take a course of action. Therefore, decision-making is a reasoning process which can appear to be rational or irrational and can be based on assumptions or preconceptions.

Devil's Advocate: To play devil's advocate is to argue against the decision that someone is contemplating. The concept of devil's advocate has a tendency to emphasise the negative aspect of dialectics. The devil's advocate approach is said to promote adversarial decision processes where one participant deems themselves to win, while another participant is deemed to lose with regard to deciding on the preferred course of action to take.

Dialectical Inquiry: The dialectical inquiry approach uses creative conflict to help identify and challenge assumptions to create new perceptions amongst decision makers. Usually, the dialectical process focuses on disagreements which are turned into agreements, or indeed there is a transformation in the dialogue in that direction.

Premortem: The opposite of postmortem, a premortem explores why a project might die in the future. A premortem would involve imagining that something has gone wrong with a project in the future and trying to establish what has caused this failure.

Sense-Making: The process of creating situational awareness and understanding in situations of high complexity or uncertainty in order to make decisions.

ENDNOTES

[1] The concept of devil's advocate has been used by a number of researchers in the study of the strategic planning process (Boland, 1984; Mason, 1969). Mason (1969) suggested that there were a variety of organisational designs used to cope with the problem of strategic planning, and suggested two "ideal types" as a means of achieving good organisational design for planning. One ideal type is referred to as the expert approach, where a planning department is established and serves as managements "alter ego." The other ideal type is the devil's advocate approach, where managers and planners of an organisational unit submit plans for extensive cross-examination by top management. Boland (1984) used retrospective analysis to get management groups to understand their actions during a period of time, why they had taken those actions, and how they felt about having taken those actions (this period was created through generating fictitious accounting reports to demonstrate plausible future scenarios for an organisation, in terms of alternative future directions an organisation could have taken) and to enhance the group process of inquiry during the initial stages of planning. "The impact of this exercise on the managers' cognitive and emotional experience and their commitment to use the method in other decisions suggest that sense-making can enhance the group process of inquiry during the initial stages of planning" (Boland, 1984, p. 868). Also, Hammond et al. (2006), when analysing the hidden psychological traps in decision making (workings of the confirming-evidence trap), suggested that to ensure a decision maker has made a smart choice, the decision maker can get some respected individual to play devil's advocate, to argue against the decision being contemplated.

[2] Mintzberg and Westley (2001) refer to having conducted "seeing first" workshops for managers as part of this distinction of the three models of decision making.

[3] The ideal type referred to as the expert approach, exists where a planning department is established and serves as managements "alter ego" (Mason, 1969).

Facilitation of Supply Chain Decision Processes in SMEs, Using Information Systems

Simon Woodworth
University College Cork, Ireland

Joe Cunningham
University College Cork, Ireland

INTRODUCTION

This article discusses how Small to Medium Enterprises (SMEs) apply information systems (IS) to facilitate decisions concerning their supply chains. In the collective decision—making environment of the Supply Chain, SMEs have to strike a balance between inventory reduction to minimise working capital costs and maintaining sufficient inventory to cater for demand fluctuation. These decisions take on an additional level of complexity for food SMEs, where the products have finite shelf lives and are subject to strict traceability requirements. Nevertheless, some of the smaller SMEs have proven successful in using IS to facilitate critical decisions to minimise inventory and therefore operating costs, while still retaining the ability to cope with demand fluctuation.

BACKGROUND

Traditionally, companies have been regarded as independent self-sufficient entities, which compete with each other to survive (Christopher, 1998). However, the rise since the 1950s of the "systems approach" has led to the idea that an organization (the subsystem) exists as part of a wider group (the supersystem) and its success or failure depends on other organisations or individuals in that group (Lowson, King, & Hunter, 1999). Such a group may be referred to as a *Supply Chain*.

A supply chain consists of several organisations working together to deliver a finished product to the end customer. These supply chains are not exclusive; a single organisation may be a member of two or more supply chains (Christopher, 1998; Lowson et al., 1999). The supply chain changes the way in which organisations compete. Competition between companies has been superseded by competition between supply chains (Christopher, 1998; Kalakota & Robinson, 2001), requiring collaboration and collective decision making processes among all organisations in the supply chain. The supply chain that can successfully deliver the right products at the right time for minimum cost and inventory is likely to gain competitive advantage over competing supply chains (Hendricks & Singhal, 2003). Therefore supply chain efficiency is regarded as a key factor for any firm seeking to gain an advantage over its competitors (Quayle, 2003). Large corporations have recognised this fact and have responded accordingly: annual investment in supply chain solutions has now reached $11.6 billion globally (Rossi, 2003).

The same cannot be said of small to medium enterprises (SMEs). In an Irish context, the Irish Business and Employers Confederation notes in its 2001 survey of supply chain management (SCM), that, while more than two thirds of large companies have an SCM strategy, less than a third of small companies do (IBEC, 2001). This imbalance is a threat to the overall success of supply chains; they can only be as strong as their weakest links (Lowson et al., 1999) and their success depends on the smaller as well as the larger participants (Smeltzer, 2001). SMEs face particular problems in supply chains because large-scale supply chain implementations are too expensive and are also unsuitable. In addition, SMEs may have little room for manoeuvre because they are strongly influenced by the larger companies in the supply chain (Bates & Slack, 1998; Webster, 1995) who are in a position to dictate standards and methods to the smaller participants. These problems expose the whole supply chain to the risk of becoming disconnected.

The benefits of supply chain management are well articulated, as is the need for collaboration and supply chain integration to facilitate collaborative decision making. IS as an integration enabler is also well documented. However, the literature falls short in several areas: supply chain management practices within SMEs receive very little attention (Quayle, 2003), the design and implementation of IS for SCM has not received enough attention (Gunasekaran & Ngai, 2004), and IS strategy use is under-researched and under-developed in SMEs (Levy & Powell, 2000; Levy, Powell, & Galliers, 1999). Consequently there is little understanding of how SMEs use IS to facilitate supply chain decisions they may need to take and the role of IS in collective supply-chain decision-making in SMEs has not been addressed.

SUPPLY CHAIN DECISION MAKING IN SMES

The Supply Chain and Supply Chain Management

Supply chains exist in almost every industry, particularly industries that involve manufacturing (Ashkenas, Ulrish, Jick, & Kerr, 1995; Strader, Lin, & Shaw, 1999). Definitions of supply chains tend to focus on a supply chain's structure or its function. These definitions can be synthesised into a unified definition of the supply chain as follows:

A supply chain is a network of distinct organisations, acting together in a coordinated fashion to transform inputs from original suppliers into finished products and services for end consumers.

A supply chain may simply be regarded as a group of organizations acting in concert to transform raw material (or services) into a finished product for the consumer. Those organisations are not all of the same size: While the major participants in any supply chain are frequently large corporations, as much as 80% of any given supply chain can be made up of SMEs (Smeltzer, 2001).

Supply chain models have evolved from the linear structural model described by Lowson et al. (1999) and Kalakota and Robinson (2001) to a more relationship-focused model as described by Poon (2000), Oliva (2003), and Tapscott, Ticoll, and Lowy (2000) and illustrated in Figure 1.

In the linear model, products and services move down the supply chain from the supplier, via manufacturer, distributor, and retailer, to the consumer. Payments move back up the supply chain from the consumer to the supplier. Information flows in both directions: Demand information (what the consumer wants) moves backward and supply information (what the supplier can provide) moves forward (Christiaanse & Kumar, 2000).

The relationship-focused model as illustrated in Figure 1, however, recognizes that the nature of a supply chain requires cooperation as distinct from competition as all parties in a supply chain are mutually interdependent (Horvath, 2001; Kalakota & Robinson, 2001; Romano, 2003). Competition then occurs between supply chains rather than individual organisations (Christopher, 1998; Kalakota & Robinson, 2001). Successful operation of the supply chain becomes critical to an organisation's competitive advantage or even survival (Humphreys, Lai, & Sculli, 2001; Quayle, 2003).

Most firms within a supply chain will have relationships with suppliers, customers, and possibly partners and competitors as well. The potential complexity of these supply chain structures implies that some form of oversight or management is required to maximise the supply chain's benefits and to optimize some or all of the relationships outlined above. These methods of coordinating and managing a supply chain are collectively referred to as supply chain management (SCM).

In 1996, Harland described the usage of the term supply chain management (SCM) as inconsistent and lacking in clarity (Harland, 1996). There is evidence

Figure 1. Key supply chain relationships

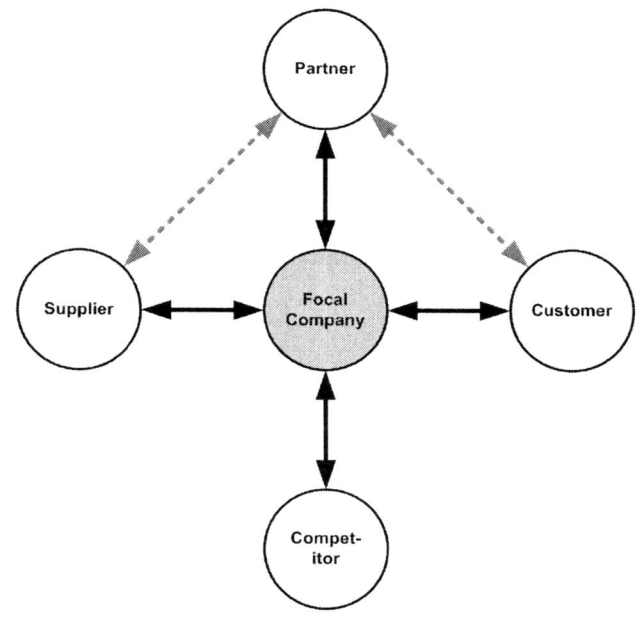

Adapted from Poon (2000), Oliva (2003), and Tapscott et al. (2000)

in the literature to suggest that this problem still persists: Quayle noted that SCM is an elusive term to define (Quayle, 2003) and that, "definitions of what it encompasses are at best vague" (Quayle, 2002).

This is reflected elsewhere in the literature where the concepts of SCM and the supply chain are confused and there is a profusion of related but misleading terms (Croom, Romano, & Giannakis, 2000; Kalakota & Robinson, 2001). However, the following definition of supply chain management may be synthesised from the literature:

The planning, organisation, coordination and control of all supply chain activities through the cooperation of all organisations in the supply chain, with the ultimate goal of maximising the competitive advantage of the supply chain.

The goal of SCM is to minimise the time and cost associated with each activity in the chain and to eliminate waste and maximise value to the consumer (Lowson et al., 1999). It is regarded as a significant strategy for improving organisational responsiveness, flexibility, and, ultimately, competitiveness (Gunasekaran, 2004). SCM extends in scope beyond one particular organisation to all organisations in the supply chain. The cooperative element of the supply chain is crucial as optimising one element of the supply chain may well be detrimental to others (Chen & Paulraj, 2004; Horvath, 2001). SCM is properly seen as an activity involving all participants in the chain—including the end consumer—and any SCM strategy is very dependent on a high degree of collaboration amongst organisations in the supply chain.

A collaborative approach to supply chain management is regarded as being more profitable than other alternatives (Themistocleous, Irani, & Love, 2003). Collaboration is seen as a fairly low-cost way to reduce waste and redundancy while improving service quality and relevancy (Stank, Keller, & Closs, 2001/2002). Collaboration cannot happen, however, without some means of exchanging information between supply chain partners.

An effectively managed and beneficial supply chain, therefore, needs to be integrated; it must support the forward and backward flow of information between all organisations in the supply chain. Interenterprise integration is a necessary goal of SCM (Kalakota & Robinson, 1999). Coordination of production and logistics activities requires supply chain integration which may be defined as "how closely, particularly at their interfaces, supply chain entities operate as a single unit" (Hill & Scudder, 2002, p. 376). Supply chain integration can be characterised as a synchronisation and coordination process that facilitates process alignment and information flow across all organisations in a supply chain, with the ultimate goal of reducing cost and improving customer service.

An integrated supply chain enables the flow of operational information—stock levels, purchasing information, delivery information, invoicing, orders, and so forth—that is essential for carrying out effective and efficient movement of raw materials and finished products (Stefansson, 2002). In addition, the flow of planning information, such as demand and inventory forecasts, is also enabled. Outsourcing and strategic alliances demand the use of an integrated supply chain to support information sharing.

Increasing competition and the need for much shorter order cycles requires that information be moved around the integrated supply chain as quickly and effectively as possible. Information Systems are the most obvious choice for this task as they can be particularly effective at moving information across organisational boundaries (Hill & Scudder, 2002). In fact, integration of the supply chain would not be economically possible without some electronic means of facilitating information exchange; this is due to the complexity of supply chain management (Gunasekaran & Ngai, 2004).

IS provides a multitude of integration mechanisms of varying sophistication and cost. For example, Talluri (2000) contends that IS plays a critical role in all the planning and execution phases of SCM and goes on to categorise these systems as covering Strategic, Tactical, and Operational—level planning and decision-making. While supply chain mechanisms using IS vary considerably in complexity and cost, much emphasis tends to be placed on large, expensive solutions (Friedman, 2002), though there is evidence that solutions vendors are now working to produce cheaper SCM applications more suited to smaller enterprises (Scannell & McCarthy, 2003). However, the focus of IS solutions on large expensive solutions presents serious problems for Small to Medium Enterprises: the available solutions are too large or complex to be economically implemented by smaller businesses.

The Small to Medium Enterprise in the Supply Chain

Definitions of SMEs vary from country to country (Forfás, 1998) and no single definition of SMEs is widely accepted (Ihlström & Nilsson, 2003). The European Commission defines Small to Medium Enterprises (SMEs) as follows: "Enterprises which employ fewer than 250 persons and which have an annual turnover not exceeding €50 million, and/or an annual balance sheet total not exceeding €43 million" (European Commission, 2003).

When SMEs are considered in an Irish context, then different criteria are applied: the National Competitiveness Council report on SME performance states that small enterprises are often defined as having 50 employees or fewer (Forfás, 1998). Since the research in this study was performed in an Irish context, the Forfás (1998) definition applies here.

SMEs contribute significantly to economic output and employment: in almost all industrialised countries, SMEs generate proportionally higher shares of employment than large companies (Conti, 2000). In Ireland, SMEs are recognised as a source of strength for the economy as a whole (Forfás, 1998). In the UK and other European countries, SMEs represent over half of total employment share and almost all European enterprises (Drew, 2003; Dutta & Evrard, 1999; Quayle, 2003). In an Irish context, businesses with fewer than 50 employees account for 98% of the country's business (Forfás, 1998).

In contrast to large organisations, SMEs tend to have centralised decision-making structures with a strong personal element and they often have simplified management structures (Vatne & Taylor, 2000). Cost advantages available to large firms through economies of scale and learning effects are not available to SMEs (O'Donnell, Gilmore, Carson, & Cummins, 2002; Vatne & Taylor, 2000). Also, SMEs have fewer resources than large firms (Manecke & Schoensleben, 2004; O'Donnell et al., 2002). Qian (2002) notes specifically that they have fewer resources for large-scale research and development. Such constraints are characterised by limited financial resources and also a lack of highly trained personnel (OECD, 2002). Consequently, SMEs approach human and technology resources differently from large organisations. They have a reactive approach to marketing (O'Donnell et al., 2002) and IS/IT investments (Hagmann & McCahon, 1993). Investment focus is likely to be on cost reduction.

Customer dominance is a major environmental factor influencing SMEs. SMEs that become a first-tier supplier to only a few large customers will always have a few customers (Levy, Powell, & Yetton, 2002). In addition, supplier dominance may become a factor if the supplier is in a monopoly position, or if the supplier is substantially bigger than the SME in question, or if the switching cost for the SME is very high (Bates & Slack, 1998). SMEs may lack market power because of their size and so suffer higher prices for supplies or finance (Forfás, 1998). Another environmental factor is that SMEs face greater uncertainty in market conditions (O'Donnel et al., 2002).

SMEs have adopted a number of behaviours and strategies to overcome some of the constraints outlined above. Such activities include networking, building inter-firm relationships, product differentiation, and targeting of niche segments in the market (Poon, 2000; Vatne & Taylor, 2000). Traditionally, SMEs have enjoyed the competitive advantage of being close to their customers (Huang, Soutar, & Brown, 2004) and are regarded as being adaptable and flexible (OECD, 2002). SMEs are also innovative: While R&D innovation is constrained by a lack of resources, SMEs innovate in other ways by creating or reengineering products to meet new market demands, by enhancing productivity, or by developing new techniques to expand sales (OECD, 2000).

SMEs are important in the context of the supply chain, as in many cases SMEs make up as much as 80% of any given supply chain (Smeltzer, 2001). Because of the large number and diversity of SMEs, large firms consequently have a greater choice of suppliers and customers (Forfás, 2000). This has consequences for supply chain integration: the prevalence of SMEs in any supply chain means that issues raised by using Information Systems for supply chain applications in SMEs must be addressed.

The particular situation of SMEs exposes a fundamental issue for supply chain integration. Given that supply chains are composed largely of SMEs (Smeltzer, 2001), the unsuitability of many solutions for SMEs poses potential problems for the integration of whole supply chain. Conversely, SMEs cannot ignore the developments in IS that are being driven by ongoing changes in their external supply chain environment (Dierckx & Stroeken, 1999).

The benefits of SCM are well articulated in the literature, as is the need for collaboration and supply chain integration. IS as an integration enabler is also well documented. However, SCM practices within SMEs receive very little attention (Quayle, 2003), the design and implementation of IS for SCM has not received enough attention, with a lack of empirical research and case studies (Gunasekaran & Ngai, 2004), and IS strategy use is under-researched and under-developed in SMEs (Levy & Powell, 2000; Levy et al., 1999).

Using IS to Facilitate Supply Chain Decisions in SMEs

The research objective was to explore the role of IS in facilitating supply chain related decisions and decision making processes in SMEs. Two research questions were formulated:

What is the role of IS in facilitating (1) Supply Chain decision making processes within SMEs? (2) Supply chain decisions taken by between SMEs, their suppliers, partners, customers, and competitors?

The unit of analysis was the Small to Medium Enterprise. A field study was selected as the research approach as it offered maximum realism. The research was performed using multiple cases to enhance generalisability (Galliers, 1991; Miles & Huberman, 1994).

A stratified purposeful sampling strategy, as described by Patton (1990), was used. The stratified nature of the sample can be seen by examining the sizes and supply chain positioning of eight cases in the study (see Table 1). Interviews, document analysis, and on-site inspections were used as data gathering techniques.

Supply Chain Decision Making Processes Within SMEs

The first research question refers specifically to issues with internal SME decision making processes that are related to supply chain activities such as purchasing, order fulfilment, stock control, and production.

The focus of the SMEs in the study was on improving internal processes to reduce costs rather than on utilising IS to provide tighter integration with their suppliers, customers, partners, or competitors. The respondents identified several supply chain processes where they felt IS played a role. These processes were stock control, traceability support, and production support. All are classified as supply chain processes on the grounds that how these processes are executed depend on external influences such as demand fluctuation and the regulatory environment and on internal influences such as the desire to track stock accurately and minimise inventory levels. The Information Systems used ranged from relatively simple systems such as Microsoft Excel and Sage Accounting packages to production support systems such as Caliach MRP.

Two of the medium-sized SMEs (see Table 1) had the turnover to support a large degree of stock retention and, indeed, did so to ensure they could meet sudden changes in demand. These SMEs decided to bear the cost of additional inventory to facilitate the needs of their customers. However, excess stock is a serious issue for the smaller SMEs as it consumes too much capital. Dingle Bay Seafood Soups illustrates the point: The respondent there was not so much concerned with demand fluctuation as with reducing inventory levels so as to minimise capital tied up in stock. The respondent stated, "I used to carry one hundred tons of frozen fish stock, which cost me a fortune. Now I carry just nine tons." Dingle Bay Seafood Soups decided to reduce its stock by careful management of its suppliers and also by pushing buffer stock to cope with demand fluctuation further down the supply chain to its distributors. Production planning with such a small inventory becomes a process critical to the success of the business. Dingle Bay Seafood Soups decides on production volumes by using weekly contact with its major customers to determine likely demand. In addition it uses the production records at its disposal (mainly on paper or Microsoft Excel) to predict demand and decide production output for the next two weeks. These decisions are based on production figures from 12 months previously.

An adjunct to stock control was traceability support. The Hazard Avoidance and Critical Control Point (HACCP) traceability standard requires full food traceability from finished product back to raw ingredients. All of the SMEs in the survey had implemented traceability systems, most based on paper production records but some based on Microsoft Excel. In general the SMEs that had IS for stock control and production support also used them for traceability. All batch numbers for raw stock were recorded and the batch numbers and best before dates of finished stock were also logged into the stock control system and associated with the relevant raw stock records. Batch number and best by date information was recorded on the product labelling so organisations further down the supply chain could trace products back to the producer.

In the event of contaminated product being sold to the consumer, the producer SMEs then need to decide which batches to recall. In ideal conditions, the relevant batch and best-by information is passed back up the supply chain to the producer. In reality, some precision is lost at the wholesaler stage of the supply chain, which necessitates recalling larger batches than is strictly necessary. In the case of Dingle Bay Seafoods Soups, a contaminated production batch led to the decision to lock down the manufacturing processes temporarily. The company decided to implement an extra production stage to reduce the risk of contamination in the future. This decision was facilitated by the data retained in stock and production records concerning both raw and finished stock.

Related to the stock control and traceability processes was the production process itself. While most of the producing SMEs used paper-based production support systems, there was some interest in using IS for production support but only under certain conditions. In particular, it was found that moving production support to an Information System would only be considered as an adjunct to stock control (J & L Grubb exemplified this view). Also, using an Information System to support traceability (as in the case of Dingle Bay Seafood Soups) would necessitate the support of production processes as well, as traceability standards require that those processes be tightly controlled. Production support was only implemented using an IS as an adjunct to stock control and traceability support.

The wholesaling SMEs had no production systems as such but both used IS for stock control and to manage the movement of stock into and out of the warehouse. Both carried substantial amounts of stock so inventory reduction was not seen as a motivator. However, both SMEs were keen to keep track of the large number of product lines they carried. One was seeking to introduce a stock control Information System to its warehouse floor. This would allow the existing stock control system to be kept up-to-date on a continuous basis by scanning all goods as they were received, warehoused, and dispatched. This sort of up-to-date information is vital as the wholesalers need to decide how to allocate stock to customer orders, especially since stock with

Table 1. SMEs in the field study

Company name	SME Size	Number of employees	Turnover	Nature of business	Supply chain position	Role of Information Systems in SME (all sites had e-mail and Office Applications)
Coolmore Foods	Medium	30	€3.5m	Bakery	Producer	Accounting, Manufacturing Resource Planning, Electronic Data Interchange
Dingle Bay Seafood Soups	Small	8	€500k §	Seafood products	Producer	Accounting, Production support, stock control, traceability
Gubbeen Farmhouse Products	Small	8	<€1m	Farmhouse Cheese	Producer	Quality control
J & L Grubb Ltd	Small	14	€1.4m	Farmhouse Cheese	Producer	Accounting
Munster Food Company	Micro	4	€ 1k (2001) §	Food Ingredients	Producer	Accounting, stock control, production support
Sheridans Cheesemongers	Medium	40	€2.9m	Cheesemonger	Wholesaler	Accounting, stock control
The Traditional Cheese Company	Medium	30	ST£2.5-ST£5m *	Cheesemonger	Wholesaler	Accounting, stock control, Electronic Data Interchange
Ummera Smoked Products	Micro	2	€210k	Smoked fish and meats	Producer	Accounting, stock control, CRM, goods shipment, online ordering by customers

* Turnover figures obtained from http://www.investni.com

§ Turnover figures obtained from http://www.bordbia.ie

a finite shelf life must also be allocated on a best-by date basis.

Supply Chain Decision Making Processes External to SMEs

For all of the SMEs in the study, telephone and fax were the preferred method for placing order with suppliers. This is explained by one respondent, who stated that, "We build up a relationship with our suppliers and customers over the telephone. Orders are placed by fax with delivery dates agreed in advance by telephone." Some of the respondents stated they experienced supplier issues such as late or lost orders. While such issues were rare, almost all of the SMEs in the survey considered it important to establish a relationship with their supplier first and then agree on a procedure for placing orders. Since a relationship between the SME and its supplier had already been established, any problems with missed or late orders could be dealt with effectively over the telephone.

No other supply chain activity was observed between SMEs and their suppliers. This lack of complexity in SME-supplier relationships removes the consequent need for extensive data sharing that might drive SMEs and their suppliers to employ Information Systems more extensively. Also, order volume from suppliers was low: Most of the SMEs in the study placed orders on a weekly basis or even less frequently than that. The only justification for daily orders was the perishability of the goods in question. Milk is one example; another is fresh fish, which was delivered daily to Ummera Smoked Products by local anglers.

However, there is a considerable degree of sophistication in the way the SMEs in the study used alliances and partnerships to compensate for their smaller size. A common theme in SCM literature is the outsourcing of non-core competencies to maximise competitive advantage (Carr & Pearson, 1999). A number of the SMEs in the study demonstrated this type of strategic behaviour. For instance, Coolmore Foods develops new products in conjunction with its customers. The respondent from Coolmore Foods stated, "We sit with our customers periodically to see what new products can be developed and introduced. Some new products are suggested by us, some are suggested by our customers."

While Coolmore Foods was the only SME in the study engaged in collaborative product development, other SMEs outsourced all or part of their production: Dingle Bay Seafood Soups had a reciprocal agreement with another food producer where one company manufactures products for the other. This collaboration was limited to a small subset of Dingle Bay Seafood Soup's products. The Munster Food Company outsourced all its production, warehousing, and distribution to two outside companies, leaving the company to focus on its core competencies such as marketing, supplier sourcing, product development, and sales.

Apart from the example of Munster Food Company, the coordination activities do not appear to need the sharing of large amounts of data which might have justified an Information System; in fact, they are probably more dependent on the sort of interpersonal relationships that are best facilitated by personal meetings or telephone conversations. In the case of all the SMEs in the study, relationships with other SMEs with whom they collaborated were maintained in this manner.

The role of IS in resolving supply chain issues between SMEs and their customers is mixed. Information Systems are used to a limited degree to assist with invoice and delivery note generation but the processing of orders from customers is handled mainly by telephone and fax. This is in line with the SME reliance on alliances and networks, leading to a preference for communication methods that enhance personal contact. The study revealed two examples, however, of the direct use of Information Systems to transmit orders from customers to he SMEs in the study. These two examples were Coolmore Foods and The Traditional Cheese Company.

Coolmore Foods, one of the medium sized SMEs in this study, provides cakes and muffins to the retail industry. It has several large retail customers, who prefer to use electronic data interchange (EDI) to place orders. The company, therefore, has put in place Information Systems to process these orders. The Traditional Cheese Company is a similarly-sized distributor SME which provides a wide range of products directly to the retail, catering, and hotel industries. Similarly, its large retail customers expect it to utilise EDI for reception of orders from its customers. In both cases these two medium-sized SMEs had invested in EDI simply because their customers—large retail multiples—expected them to do so.

While EDI makes sense for a large retail multiple because of its high volume of inventory turns and its wide product range, it is not a suitable order processing mechanism for the SMEs in this study, with their much smaller product ranges and a substantially lower rate of inventory turns. However, both of the SMEs have had to implement EDI to retain customer business. This illustrates a purely reactive form of IS expenditure where both SMEs implemented an Information System purely in response to external market forces.

The interaction between the SMEs, their suppliers, partners, and customers reveals a theme of collective decision making across the supply chain. While the use of IS was limited, there was much evidence of collective decision making at an operational level on production volumes and even at a more tactical or strategic level on production capacity allocation. This sort of collaborative decision-making behaviour is evidence of the tendency of SMEs to depend strongly on interpersonal relationships as a defence against external environmental influences.

Finally, the SMEs in the study demonstrated a range of coordinated activities with their competitors. The cheese makers coordinated joint marketing initiatives in an attempt to penetrate new markets abroad—this allowed them to market several farmhouse cheeses together rather than just one. The respondent from Dingle Bay Seafood Soups explained that seafood producers coordinate activities to defend their share of the seafood products market.

However, despite the sophistication of some of these coordination activities, Information Systems usage was extremely limited. While most of the alliances had Web sites, these were limited to providing directory information about the participating companies and their products. There were no communication or collaboration mechanisms such as bulletin boards or discussion groups, nor did any of the SMEs in the study use their own Information Systems to share data with their competitors. More traditional coordination mechanisms such as meetings, newsletters and telephone calls were used instead.

FUTURE TRENDS

The exploratory nature of this study suggests two directions for further research. The first is an explanatory study on a similar sample. An explanatory study could be used to explore the differentiating factors of SMEs and explain how each of those factors influences the role of Information Systems in resolving supply chain issues for those SMEs. One key differentiator is supply chain position: the decisions that need to be taken at producer level are different from those that need to be taken at wholesaler level. It is possible that such a study would have a predictive element, where the specific circumstances and characteristics if an individual SME could be used to determine the likely role of Information Systems in that organisation.

Second, an exploratory study aligned along the length of the food supply chain might yield some insight into inventory management practices with respect to best before dates. The supply chain from producer to wholesaler tends to be supply-driven, whereas it tends to be demand-driven from wholesaler to retailer. Inventory therefore tends to accumulate at the wholesaler and such a study might illustrate how the wholesaler decides how best to allocate stock to customers based on best by dates and demand. As these supply chains become more integrated, the effect of any emergent IS on collective decision making processes could also be observed.

CONCLUSION

The findings are summarised in Figure 2, which illustrates that most of the processes supported by IS and related to supply chain activities external to the SME sit within the SME itself. The role of IS in supporting supply chain decisions between the SME, its suppliers, and its competitors is limited. The role of Information Systems in supporting supply chain activities between the SME and its partners is less limited but is still constrained to very specific business processes, namely the need to share production and stock control data with outsourcing partners.

The role of IS in supporting supply chain activities between the SME and its customers is mainly focused on internal processes such as invoicing. However, demand data from customers is used collectively by the SMEs and their immediate customers in the supply chain to decide on appropriate production output. Information Systems play a significant role between the SME and its customers if those customers impose electronic ordering systems such as EDI—in this case the IS is not a consequence of collective decision making.

As SMEs are small and therefore more exposed to market pressures and external influences than larger organisations, they are more dependent on networks

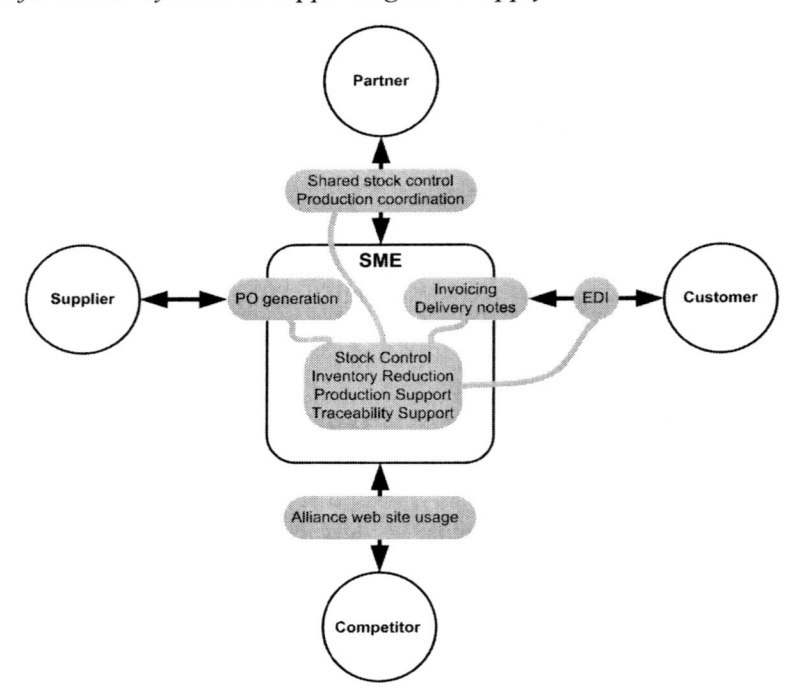

Figure 2. The role of information systems in supporting SME supply chain decisions

and alliances to counteract those influences. There was no desire among the respondents to replace the personal element of these relationships with Information Systems. Therefore any Information Systems deployed to address supply chain issues are focused on processes internal to the SME.

Finally, even though some of the stock control and production management Information Systems were rudimentary in nature, they provided a useful tool for some of the producer SMEs in deciding the appropriate inventory level and production output for the business and in anticipating fluctuations in demand as part of a collaborative decision making process with their customers.

REFERENCES

Ashkenas, R., Ulrish, D., Jick, T., & Kerr, S. (1995). *The boundaryless organization: Breaking the chains of organizational structure* (p. 192). Jossey—Bass Publishers.

Bates, H., & Slack, N. (1998). What happens when the supply chain manages you? A knowledge-based response. *European Journal of Purchasing and Supply Management, 4*, 63-72.

Carr, A.S., & Pearson, J.N. (1999). Strategically managed buyer-supplier relationships and performance outcomes. *Journal of Operations Management, 17*, 497-519.

Chen, I.J., & Paulraj, A. (2004). Understanding supply chain management: Critical research and a theoretical framework. *International Journal of Production Research, 42*(1), 131-163.

Christiaanse, E., & Kumar, K. (2000). ICT-enabled coordination of dynamic supply webs. *International Journal of Physical Distribution & Logistics Management, 30*(¾), 268-285.

Christopher, M. (1998). *Logistics and supply chain management* (2nd ed.). Financial Times/Prentice Hall.

Conti, S. (2000). *Small and medium enterprises in space: The plural economy in the networked firm in a global world: Small firms in new environments* (E. Vatne & M. Taylor, Eds.). Ashgate Publishing Ltd.

Croom, S. R., Romano, P., & Giannakis, M. (2000). Supply chain management: An analytical framework for critical literature review. *European Journal of Purchasing and Supply Management, 6*, 67-83.

Dierckx, M.A.F., & Stroeken, J.H.M. (1999). Information technology and innovation in small and medium-sized enterprises. *Technological Forecasting and Social Change, 60*, 149-166.

Drew, S. (2003). Strategic uses of e-commerce by SMEs in the east of England. *European Management Journal, 21*(1), 79-88.

Dutta, S., & Evrard, P. (1999). Information technology and organisation within European small enterprises. *European Management Journal, 17*(3), 239-251.

European Commission. (2003). *The new SME definition: User guide and model declaration*. Retrieved December 8, 2007, from http://ec.europa.eu/enterprise/enterprise_policy/sme_definition/sme_user_guide.pdf

Forfás. (1998, March). SME Performance, National Competitiveness Council. Retrieved January 21, 2008, from http://www.competitiveness.ie/reports/ncc/sme.htm

Friedman, M. (2002, November 29). Working out supply chain kinks. *Computing Canada, 28*(23), 22-23.

Galliers, R. (Ed.). (1991). *Information systems research* (pp. 28-60). Alfred Waller Ltd.

Gunasekaran, A. (2004): Editorial: Supply chain management: Theory and applications. *European Journal of Operational Research, 159*(2), 265-268.

Gunasekaran, A. and Ngai, E. W. T. (2004): Information systems in supply chain integration and management. *European Journal of Operational Research, 159*(2), 269-295.

Hagmann, C., & McCahon, C. (1993). Strategic IS and competitiveness. *Information and Management, 25*, 183-192.

Harland, C. M. (1996). Supply chain management: Relationships, chains and networks [Special issue]. *British Journal of Management, 7*, S63-S80.

Hendricks, K.B., & Singhal, V.R. (2003-2004). The effect of supply chain glitches on shareholder wealth. *Journal of Operations Management, 21*, 501-522.

Hill, C.A., & Scudder, G.D. (2002). The use of electronic data interchange for supply chain coordination in the food industry. *Journal of Operations Management, 20*(4), 375-387.

Horvath, L. (2001). Collaboration: The key to value creation in supply chain management. *Supply Chain Management: An International Journal, 6*(5), 205-207.

Huang, X., Soutar, G.N., & Brown, A. (2004). Measuring new product success: An empirical investigation of Australian SMEs. *Industrial Marketing Management, 33*, 117-123.

Humphreys, P.K., Lai, M.K., & Sculli, D. (2001). An inter-organizational information system for supply chain management. *International Journal of Production Economics, 70*, 245-255.

IBEC Transport and Logistics Council. (2001). *Survey of supply chain management, IBEC Research and Information Service*. Retrieved January 20, 2008, from http://www.ibec.ie

Ihlström, C., & Nilsson, M. (2003). E-business adoption by SMEs—prerequisites and attitude of SMEs in a Swedish network. *Journal of Organizational Computing and Electronic Commerce, 13*(3, 4), 211-223.

Kalakota, R., & Robinson, M. (2001). *E-business 2.0: Roadmap for success* (pp. 271-306). Addison Wesley.

Levy, M., & Powell, P. (2000). Information systems strategy for small and medium enterprises: An organisational perspective. *Journal of Strategic Information Systems, 9*, 63-84.

Levy, M., Powell, P., & Galliers, R. (1999). Assessing information systems strategy development frameworks in SMEs. *Information & Management, 36*, 247-261.

Levy, M., Powell, P., & Yetton, P. (2002). The dynamics of SME information systems. *Small Business Economics, 19*, 341-352.

Lowson, B., King, R., & Hunter, A. (1999). *Quick response: Managing the supply chain to meet consumer demand* (p. 33). John Wiley & Sons.

Manecke, N., & Schoensleben, P. (2004). Cost and benefit of Internet-based support of business processes. *International Journal of Production Economics, 87*, 213-229.

Miles, M.B., & Huberman, A.M. (1994). Qualitative data analysis: An expanded sourcebook (pp. 239-242). SAGE Publications, Inc.

O'Donnell, A., Gilmore, A., Carson, D., & Cummins, D. (2002). Competitive advantage in small to medium-sized enterprises. *Journal of Strategic Marketing, 10*, 205-223.

Oliva, R. (2003, November/December). Seeds of growth. *Marketing Management, 12*(6), 39-41.

Organisation for Economic Co-Operation and Development (OECD). (2000, June). Small and medium-sized enterprises: Local strength, global reach. OECD Observer Policy Brief. Retrieved January 20, 2008, from http://www.oecd.org/dataoecd/3/30/1918307.pdf

Organisation for Economic Co-Operation and Development (OECD). (2002, October 28-31). East West cluster conference panel I: Innovation and clusters, OECD Local Economic and Employment Development Programme. Retrieved January 20, 2008, from http://www.oecd.org/dataoecd/29/52/2398577.pdf

Patton, M.Q. (1990). Qualitative evaluation and research methods (2nd ed.). SAGE Publications, Inc.

Poon, S. (2000). Business environment and Internet commerce benefit—a small business perspective. *European Journal of Information Systems, 9*, 72-81.

Qian, G. (2002). Multinationality, product diversification and profitability of emerging US small- and medium-sized enterprises. *Journal of Business Venturing, 17*, 611-633.

Quayle, M. (2002). Supplier development and supply chain management in small and medium size enterprises. *International Journal of Technology Management, 23*(1/2/3), 172-188.

Quayle, M. (2003). A study of supply chain management practice in UK industrial SMEs. *Supply Chain Management: An International Journal, 8*(1), 79-86.

Romano, P. (2003). Co-ordination and integration mechanisms to manage logistics processes across supply networks. *Journal of Purchasing & Supply Management, 9*, 119-134.

Rossi, S. (2003). *Firms still disappointed by supply chain investments*. Retrieved December 8, 2007, from http://computerweekly.com

Scannell, E., & McCarthy, J. (2003). Think small (business). Retrieved December 8, 2007, from infoworld.com (pp. 53-56).

Smeltzer, L. (2001, September/October). Integration means everybody—big and small. *Supply Chain Management Review, 5*(5), 36-44.

Stank, T.P., Keller, S.B., & Closs, D.J. (2001, Winter/2002, Spring). Performance benefits of supply chain logistical integration. *Transportation Journal, 41*(2/3), 32-46.

Stefansson, G. (2002). Business-to-business data sharing: A source for integration of supply chains. *International Journal of Production Economics, 75*, 135-146.

Strader, T.J., Lin, F.-R., & Shaw, M.J. (1999). Business-to-business electronic commerce and convergent assembly supply chain management. *Journal of Information Technology, 14*, 361-373.

Talluri, S. (2000). An IT/IS acquisition and justification model for supply-chain management. *International Journal of Physical Distribution & Logistics, 30*(¾), 221-237.

Tapscott, D., Ticoll, D., & Lowy, A. (2000). Digital capital: Harnessing the power of business webs (p. 17). Harvard Business School Press.

Themistocleous, M., Irani, Z., & Love, P.E.D. (2004). Evaluating the integration of supply chain information systems: A case study. *European Journal of Operational Research, 159*(2), 393-405.

Vatne, E., & Taylor, M. (2000). *The networked firm in a global world: Small firms in new environments*. Ashgate Publishing Ltd.

Webster, J. (1995). Networks of collaboration or conflict? Electronic data interchange and power in the supply chain. *Journal of Strategic Information Systems, 4*(1), 31-42.

KEY TERMS

Small to Medium Enterprise (SME): In European terms, an enterprise which employs fewer than 250 persons and which has an annual turnover not exceeding €50 million, and/or an annual balance sheet total not exceeding €43 million.

Supply Chain: A network of distinct organisations acting together in a coordinated fashion to transform inputs from original suppliers into finished products and services for end consumers.

Supply Chain Integration: A synchronisation and coordination process that facilitates process alignment and information flow across all organisations in a supply chain, with the ultimate goal of reducing cost and improving customer service.

Supply Chain Management (SCM): The planning, organisation, coordination, and control of all supply chain activities through the cooperation of all organisations in the supply chain, with the ultimate goal of maximising the competitive advantage of the supply chain.

A Federative Approach of Decision-Making Aid in Urban Development

G. Kouamou
National High School of Engineering, Cameroon

C. Pettang
National High School of Engineering, Cameroon

INTRODUCTION

The interest in **urban planning and development** is a major preoccupation in the two last decades. In fact, the urban development is the act of improving living conditions, which are necessary for rest and for labour, for the health and education facilities, for the various exchanges and provisioning, for the moving of the population between their dwellings and their working place. However, the cities of the developing countries know serious problems of urbanization due not only with the non application of the urban guide (SDAU) when it exists, but also with the inadequacy of the policies of management of the city needed by the populations. That is why the proliferation of unstructured quarters around the cities, without the urban services necessary for their operation like drinking water network, electricity, and roadway system.

Facing these failures, the urban development is not any more the only fact of the municipal authorities. The populations through associations and the non governmental organisations are more implied, these activities are carried out under the impulse of the multilateral backers that support and finance the actions of the different actors.

In order to propose new approaches of the urban development, we started by defining a characterization of the city for better apprehending its morphology and its operation (Pettang, Kouamou, & Mbumbia, 1997). This characterization permits to deal with the land question, since the soil is the beginning of any installation (Pettang & Kouamou, 1999).

The purpose of this article recapitulates the steps recommended for a new approach of the decision making in **urban development**. It is based on:

- The identification of the characteristic parameters which describe a city.
- The determination of the criteria used to appreciate these parameters.
- The installation of an information systems which is able to store the urban data, to capitalize the actions and knowledge of the various urban actors since the democratization of the imagery survey allow the various municipalities to gradually build the numerical cartography of their space of action.

This study presents a new approach for solving the problem on urban development. This approach emerges on a decision support platform which consists of a set of specific applications for a collaborative work.

In the reminder of this article, we begin by discussing the passed solutions which were adopted by the municipalities. After that, we present the approach which allows a better analysis of the urban development problem. This approach could be explained with regard to the concept of observatory. Finally, we describe a kindly platform which could support such an approach by providing a collaborative decision support aid.

BACKGROUND

The **urban development** in the developing countries is focused mainly on the thorny question of the **spontaneous habitat**. This type of quarter are characterized by the poor quality of building materials that is used to make the dwellings and the lack of the infrastructures (roadway, water, and electricity supply …) necessary for a better quality of life in urban areas. The presence of this type of habitat in urban environments results from several combined factors: the demographic explosion, the poverty, and the failure of the policies of habitat. The traditional model of solution used by the authorities is based on the abandonment and the reorganization.

This solution consists in improving the accessibility of the dwellings by opening the roadway system. Consequently, the dwellings being on the road are destroyed. In spite of the multiple carried out actions, the effectiveness remains mitigated, initially because the interventions do not include coordination and do not take into account the correlation of the problems to be solved (Logone, 1992, Lebogo, 1994), then because they are interested in very few real problems of these districts (UNDP, 1993).

The decision in urban development must take into consideration the quality of life, the social cohesion, and the effectiveness of the urban services. In this process which is participative, we note the intervention of several actors divide up in the following categories: the authorities, the networks suppliers (electricity, water, telephone), NGO, populations through associations, researchers, and finally, the financial (bank, international organizations). These constraints induce a complexity on several levels:

- At the lower level, an intervention concerning an aspect can influence the others aspect.
- At the level of the actors, the efforts of the ones and others must be coordinated to avoid the interferences of the interventions.
- At the decision level, any actor can make strategic, tactical, or operational decisions.

Indeed, each actor is a decision maker on his level and each action of its own part constitutes a decision of urban development. It is necessary to especially avoid conflicts at the operational level where the actions are sectored. According to the United Nations, the decision must integrate the search for equilibrium between the various groups (UNO, 1991).

To harmonize the efforts made by all, each actor must intervene by taking account of the actions carried out by the others, thus the need for the capitalization of knowledge in a common space accessible to all.

Levine (1989) states that the main role of a DSS consists to store data and to present it to the decisions makers. That is, while a DSS software must include a data component capable of handling the databases and a component of dialog primitives that are used to manage interfaces (Luhandjula, 1996). But in the case of urban development and planning, this vision of DSS must be enhanced in order to facilitate the collaborative work between the users.

NEW APPROACHES OF THE URBAN DEVELOPMENT

Concept of Urban Observatory

The centralized management formerly monopolized by the authorities is obsolete today. The new orientation is based on the participative approach of urban management. It implies several categories of actors whose combined efforts are capitalized within the observatories.

An observatory is a unit made up of people and tools in charge of studying, supervising, and controlling a phenomenon or a set of phenomena that are social, economic, political, or environmental in order to facilitate their comprehension. An urban observatory is dissociated by its specificity in action (Assako, 1996). Indeed, an urban observatory is structured for research on the city and its development. Its purpose is to provide the relevant elements making it possible to include/understand the dynamics of the socio-economic and space phenomena of the city and its close periphery. The activities of an urban observatory deal with the acquisition, the treatment, and the analysis of the data, and the dissemination of knowledge on the city.

Components of a City

The city consists of a juxtaposition of identifiable entities generally called "quarter." These zones are characterised by a certain number of components which the most significant are: the site, the land, the habitat, the roadway system, networks, technical, and the equipments. The three first translate the morphology of the city whereas the others inform about the real operating condition of the city. The appreciation or the evaluation of these components is done using the criteria which make it possible to classify various urban areas. This characterization generates data from which one can evaluate the state and the level of degradation of a city.

Federation of the Tools for a Better Management of the Urban Development

The diversity of the data to be handled imposes the use of the varied systems of storage. The various forms of treatment and presentation of the results to the decision makers require adequate tools.

The Acquisition of the Data

The methods and the traditional tools used until now to collect the data and to analyze them include the surveys and the investigations since the financial, the human, and the technical effort do not make it possible to carry out collections through exhaustive censuses at satisfactory interval. Also, they are not enough alone any more to apprehend the contours of the problems arising. Today, these traditional techniques are rather complementary to modern techniques such as remote sensing (Weber, 1995). These new techniques are adapted to the follow-up of the dynamic phenomena whose temporality is very short like the migration. The data which result from it are heterogeneous including images, maps, and the qualitative and quantitative data. This diversity of the data requires the adequate tools of treatment and storage.

Data Processing and Storage

The functionalities are heterogeneous and they are varied in comparison with the diversity of the formats of data. The documents previously used to file the data are from now obsolete, because the volume of the data to be managed and their flexibility induced by dynamics of the urban phenomena are characteristics essential to take into account. Thus the need of computer tools in undeniable:

- Data bases able to store and integrate diverse sets of data in a common theme.
- Geographic information system (GIS) which provide the ability to computerise spatial query and analysis in an effective manner.
- The most modern algorithms in image processing to analyze and extract the relevant parameters from the satellite images.
- Mathematical models or statistical and models of simulation able to validate scenarios.

The maturity of the computerized information management systems, the evolution of the material, and the modernization of the techniques of data acquisition and processing make possible to note a progressive migration of the urban problems. At the core of the current concerns, we note the adequacy between data processing techniques and the activities of urban development undertaken in the observatories. The power of the data base management systems (DBMS) and the geographical information systems (GIS) lie in the storage and the management of the complex and huge data. Thus, they take part in the lightening of the function of storage and management of the data carried out in the urban observatories.

DISSEMINATION OF KNOWLEDGE

How to exploit the recent developments of the **communication and information technologies** to diffuse the urban data as well as the results of the research undertaken by the urban actors? The newspapers, the letters of observatory, and the reviews were often used for this purpose. But the frequency of the publication of these press releases does not always make possible to transmit new information available instantaneously.

However, we think that anyone shall be informed immediately when a project is done or when an action has been carried out in favor of an urban area. The adoption of the **IT** tools in this way let the authorities and the backers to have a large view of the projects carried out in favor of each urban area, thus to improve their policies of distributing funds by considering a significant part of the populations.

A Decision Support Platform for the Urban Activities

The city is currently structured in several components whose their knowledge informs about the urban phenomena. The identification of the descriptive elements of each of them allows:

- To collect a whole data which it is necessary to organize, store, and divide between various actors (Pettang et al., 1997);
- To develop simple or complex and interoperable models (Pettang & Kouamou, 1998); and

A Federative Approach of Decision-Making Aid in Urban Development

- To identify adequate technologies for their implementation.

The representation of these criteria raises several problems among which are: space localization, the temporal location, and the diversity of data types and data formats. The treatments which are applicable for them are varied and relate to mainly the statistical models, the cartography, the image processing, and the representation of knowledge. They call upon heterogeneous tools as well for their treatments as for their storage.

The heterogeneity of these tools must offer to the end users a global and coherent view of the whole environment, while avoiding a separation between the data and the processing tool (Gayte, Cheylan, Libourel, & Lardon, 1997). That is why the need for developing an integrated platform whose principal function is to assist the principal actors in the decision-making, which supposes the following functionalities:

- The data storage in various format.
- The unification of the user interface and the presentation of the data in adequate formats.
- The interaction among the various models implemented.

However, to duplicate the data at each actor is not indicated, this because of their volume which would require important hardware and significant software. Also, the replication of the tools for processing would complicate their updates. The first prototype was built exclusively for platforms MS Windows, only based on mechanism OLE, to define interoperability between the software which has been used. The database was implanted with Access and the maps were built under MapInfo. To unify the user interface to these software tools and to suitably manage the presentation of the various data types, we had chosen the language Visual BASIC.

However, this solution limits the portability of the developed platform; it does not take into account the exchanges of any nature (messages, documents) which are possible between the various actors. Meanwhile, the guiding principles that we initiated within the framework of the project SIMES (SIMES, 1997) was adopted, this is done in order to improve the existing platform and to provide specific applications for supporting collaboration. More precisely, the results of the project SIMES made it possible to offer a framework of collaborative work between the urban actors, to define mechanisms of interaction between the various tools for processing data, to develop a ubiquitous user interface.

Functional Architecture

Initially, the platform consists of two parts: a client machine and a server site. The server side is made up of an intranet with the following elements:

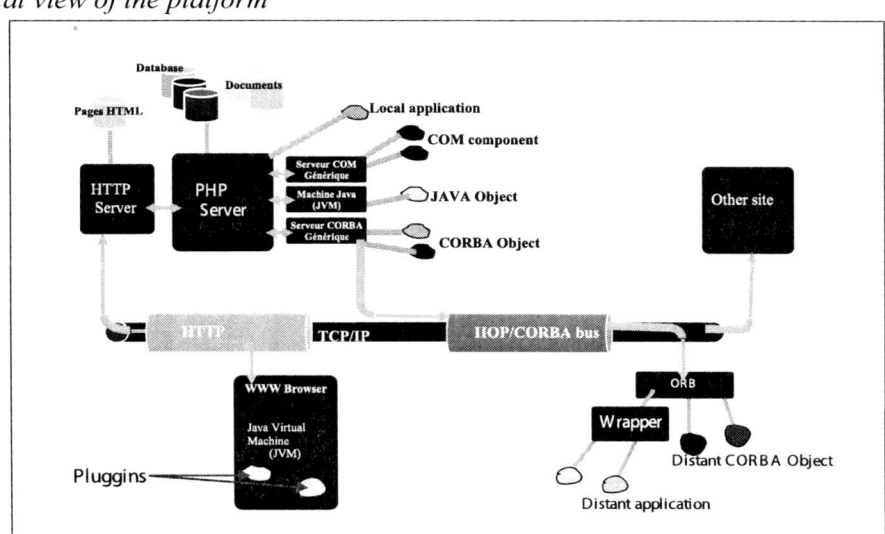

Figure 1. A logical view of the platform

- A main server on which are installed a HTTP server, the data storage system and the processing tools. It is connected directly to Internet and it is used as bridge between the intranet and the external world; and
- The secondary servers and the workstations which have other processing tools.

The client workstations do not have useful components for the platform, but they allow reaching the services offered by the platform. They have a HTTP navigator mainly.

The server share files and directory via NFS or SAMBA. This consideration is due quite simply to preserve the autonomy of the applications and the data.

An implementation of the platform is envisaged to be distributed on a network of the type Internet, and accessible from everywhere.

The tools are distributed on the server sites and must be invocable of everywhere. The user interface is simple and uniform as much as possible. To satisfy the generics, the opening and the extensibility of the platform, its architecture is based on emergent standards such as HTML for the description of the exchanges between the client stations and the server sites, SQL, and ODBC for the interfacing with the databases and the middlewares for distributing the applications.

The user interface is completely deployed at the end-user side. It is made up of specific applications and particularly of a tool for navigation in a document database.

The vertical tools relate to the administration of the server sites and the coordination of the processing tool.

The taking into account of the distribution is based mainly on CORBA (OMG, 1998) and related technology, a proposal of the OMG which is essential like a standard. It gives access to any object installed on a site equipped with an ORB (object request broker) (Vinoski, 1997).

CONCLUSION AND FURTHER TRENDS

We present in this article the complexity of the decisions in urban development. We propose an approach which consists of the separation of the main characteristics of a city. This methodology helps in organizing the data acquisition and their storage in database management system.

The methodology developed here allow considering the works done by all types of urban actors. Thus it is clearly demonstrated that there is a need to encourage collaborative decision-making to solve the problem of urban development. In this way we propose a platform that improves the public access to urban information and to share the knowledge between the main actors which participate in urban development.

We have showed how the current developments of the **information technologies** could be exploited to produce a platform able to enrich the municipal information system by supporting collaboration between the various urban actors. It is not possible to achieve this without the modernization of our urban administrations in order to use differently the IT tools. This recommendation is the next and very important step which could better externalize the results of this study.

REFERENCES

Gayte, O., Cheylan, J. P., Libourel, T., & Lardon, S. (1997). Conception des Systèmes d'Information sur l'Environnement. Hermes, 1997.

Lebogo, N. R. D. (1994). Douala : des titres fonciers à Nylon. *Cameroon Tribune. N°5755, December 1994*, SOPECAM editions, 4.

Levine, P., & Pomerol, J. C. (1989). *Systèmes interactifs d'aide à la décision et systèmes experts*. Hermès, Paris, 1989.

Logone, A. (1992). *Présentation du projet nylon à Douala*. Communication faite sur l'environnement et le développement urbain, Douala, 1992.

Luhandjula, M. K. (1996). On decision support systems. In *Proceedings of the 3rd CARI'96*, Libreville-Gabon, (pp. 447-456).

OMG. (1998, February). *The common object request broker: Architecture and specification*. Available on http://www.omg.org/corba/corbaiiop/htm

Pettang, C., & Kouamou, G. (1998). Construction indexes of low income housing policy in Cameroon. *African Journal of Building Materials, 2-20*, 8-22.

Pettang, C., & Kouamou, G. (1999). Un SIAD pour la régularisation foncière dans les tissus d'habitat spontané au. *Cameroun. Journal of Decision Systems*, Volume 8, N°3/1999, 307-323.

Pettang, C., Kouamou, G. E., & Mbumbia, L. (1997). Pour un système interactif d'aide à la décision pour la résorption de l'habitat spontané en milieu urbain. *Revue des systèmes de décision*, Vol. 6, n°2,1997, Hermès, Paris.

SIMES. (1997). *SIMES project proposal*. INCO-DC Programme (962820).

Tamo T. T. (1995). *Eléments pour une prise en compte de la participation des ménages aux développements des réseaux d'eau potable et d'électricité des villes des pays en développement: le cas du Cameroun*, thèse de Doctorat, INSA de Lyon, France.

UNDP. (1993, May). *Human development report*.

UNO. (1991). *World urbanisation prospects*. New York.

Vinoski.S. (1997). CORBA: Integrating diverse applications within distributed heterogeneous environments. *IEEE Communication Magazine*, 35(2).

Weber, C. (1995). *Images satellitaires et milieu urbain*. Hermès, Paris, Décembre 1995.

KEY TERMS

Characteristic Parameters: The set of elements which are necessary in the description of an urban area.

Database: Refers to computerized system used to store and query very huge data.

Federative Decision Support System (DSS): A type of information system which supports decision making activities among many groups of peoples.

GIS: Refers to a system for managing spatial data and associated attributes.

Information technology (IT): Refers to the techniques around computer science and telecommunication

Spontaneous Habitat: The unhealthy and not structured zones which are in urban environment.

Urban Development: The act of improving living conditions in a city.

Finite-Base Revision Supporting Knowledge Management and Decision Making

Fátima C.C. Dargam
SimTech Simulation Technology – Graz, Austria
ILTC, Instituto Doris Aragon – Rio de Janeiro, Brazil

INTRODUCTION

Generation and most of all sustainability of organizational success rely heavily on proper decision making and on the application of knowledge management (KM) concepts, where knowledge-based structures are fundamental components. KM can also be viewed as a means to support enhanced decision making through effective control of organizational knowledge. One of the main goals of KM is to capture, codify, organize, and store relevant knowledge into repositories, knowledge bases (KB), for later retrieval and use by organizations. However, there is always the danger of accumulating knowledge in an increasingly vast way, such that it becomes impossible to process it when necessary. Therefore, appropriate technologies have to be identified to protect us from irrelevant information. As the study in Handzic (2004) shows, decision-makers need to pursue primarily one KM strategy in order to use knowledge effectively. Moreover, the codification KM strategy using procedural knowledge maps was proven to be quite appropriate for solving decision problems of a complex nature. It is commonly agreed that KM can bridge the existing information and communication gaps within organizations, consequently improving decision making (Dargam & Rollett, 2007).

Interactions among the decision-makers may happen in many different ways. They may agree towards a common goal, or may have different arguments and points of view, which lead the process to contradictory objectives. They may know each other and work together, or they may work in different places and even in different times. Their influence on the decision-making process may also vary, according to their individual levels of responsibilities at work. Decision-making as well as KM require both information and knowledge. Information can be made explicit, while knowledge resides within its possessor and can only be made explicit via its articulation, that is, via the generation of "explicit knowledge." Following the studies of Carlsson and Kalling (2006), knowledge sharing is considered a fundamental aspect coming from KM to decision making (DM). Carlsson and Kalling (2006) say that knowledge sharing through the use of knowledge management systems (KMS) should be viewed as a means and not as an end, since it does not always lead to organizational overall improvement. Organizations face four particular representations of information or knowledge-based indeterminacy (Zack, 2004), namely: uncertainty, complexity, ambiguity, and equivocality, which are often present in many knowledge-based structured business applications. Compromise Finite-Base Revision can be applied as a specific KB revision approach. The "equivocality" problem is tackled, where multiple interpretations of information may occur, as well as contradictions and diversity of viewpoints, when updating a KB. Whenever an "equivocality" problem occurs, revision of finite-bases can be seen as a useful knowledge management approach for keeping consistency in the base, or for handling inconsistencies in a context-dependent way. We support the view of understanding the origin of the knowledge problem in hand in order to be able to apply the appropriate solutions, among the available ones.

BACKGROUND

As we rapidly move into a global knowledge society, proficiency in KM is increasingly important to the competitiveness of decision makers. When a decision is made, the decision-maker has to use his knowledge concerning the situation involved in order to deliver a solution by taking a decision. This aspect was also noticed and illustrated by Debilasic and Suknovic (2006). In Figure 1, the process of decision making is illustrated, explicating the use of knowledge for solving a problem.

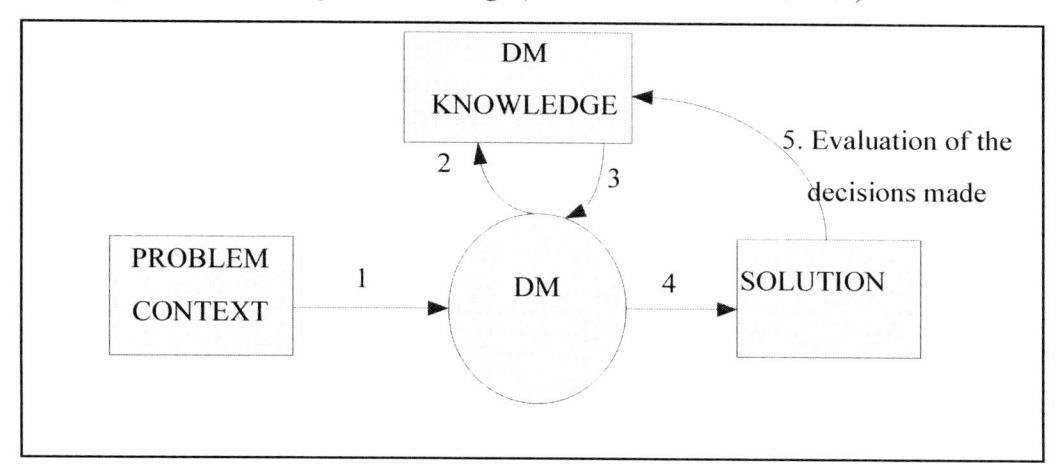

Figure 1. Interaction of decision-making and knowledge (Debilasic & Suknovic, 2006)

Knowledge is needed in almost all levels of decision-making, and therefore also for making business decisions. In KM, one of the main concerns is to use the available knowledge for supporting and evaluating the business decision process for efficiently improving decision-making.

As pointed out in Dargam (1996a, 1996b, 1999), inconsistency should be faced and formalized. Revision techniques should be applied, viewing inconsistency in a context-dependent way as a signal for external or internal actions. Dealing with inconsistencies is not necessarily a job for restoring consistency, but rather for supplying rules, which state how to act in the case of inconsistencies. In the AGM theory, Alchourrón and Makinson (1982, 1985), Alchourrón, Gärdenfors, and Makinson (1985), and Gärdenfors (1988) introduce their revising strategy by means of a set of postulates, which can be viewed as dynamic integrity constraints or transitions laws. Those postulates reflect the possible operations on belief sets, including three main types of belief change, namely:Expansion, Contraction, and Revision. In Belief Revision, the main concern is to solve the problem of revising derived beliefs whenever there is a change on the underlying set of beliefs. The approaches in this area adopt particular revising policies as strategies, which varies from temporal priority of facts to ordering definitions on the base, for instance, in order to restore consistency whenever the underlying set of base beliefs is modified. The revision operation reflects the following concept (Gärdenfors, 1988), that when we change our beliefs, we want to retain as much as possible of our old beliefs. Information is not in general gratuitous, and unnecessary losses of information are therefore to be avoided. Here we also follow this *informational economy* notion, by adopting a revision approach that allows more information to be kept in a base. A logical framework for reasoning about updates in the presence of contradictory data is used, where inconsistency is eliminated by managing safe-maximal sets within a reconciling strategy. Such strategy allows for consistent consequences of conflicting inputs to be kept in the resulting base.

FINITE-BASE REVISION AS A KM APPROACH

Compromise Reasoning

In Dargam (1999), the compromise reasoning model was presented as a revision mechanism for updates in KB. Basically, it proposes a method for reconciling logically conflicting inputs into knowledge bases, by imposing some restrictions on their consequences, among the many possible ways to invoke compromises in a disputing case. Hence, when a revision applies, as many as possible of the consistent consequences of the retracted sentences are kept in the base as a compromise. Compromise reasoning has been applied to decision making and negotiations in Dargam (1998, 2005), where decision support, negotiation, and argumentation systems were illustrated as suitable application areas. In cooperative as well as in negotiation decision support systems (DSS), the compromises considered by our revision approach can be well accepted, since the process of goal-achievement usually deals with arguments combined with factual pieces of information. From argumentation-based systems, in particular, we know that the goal of each argument is to maximize its gain, while the global goal of the system is to reach a settlement without undue inequity, possibly via some compromises. Within a cooperative/negotiating decision-making concept, the compromise approach can be considered as part of a broader decision support framework, which would provide different techniques and alternative approaches for reaching optimal decisions. To model a cooperative decision-making/negotiation scenario, we would have to capture some modes of common sense reasoning like supporting and attacking argumentation, as well as attacking the support of counter-argumentation. Three basic possibilities of support could be, for instance, taken into account: *support of only one party, support of all parties,* and *support of the mediator*. The compromise approach would mainly act as a support for the mediator, due to the fairness position of its compromise revision mechanism. The revision tries to consider as much as possible all the parties' positions (arguments), to reach a common settlement in the decision process.

Compromise Revision (CR)

The CR approach establishes some policies for dealing with the problem of inconsistency, by using a special process of reconciliation which considers restrictions of the effects of those inputs by compromising on their consequences. It allows for a maximal set of consistent consequences, which are generated from those conflicting updates with respect to the existing data, and to the integrity constraints which range over the base. By conflicting updates, we mean either simultaneous updates which interfere with each other, generating inconsistencies as part of their combined effects, or updates which are inconsistent to be performed because they conflict with the given database or scenario representation by violating some of their constraints. It is assumed that if an update satisfies its preconditions to be performed individually, it should also be allowed to be performed in parallel with other (perhaps conflicting) updates, as long as the performance process copes with inconsistency handling. By applying compromise revision (CR), a compromise solution, which presents some degree of impartiality, is derived. It is not always the case that there are established criteria, such as priority, preference, seniority, and so forth, to choose between conflicting updates. Also, by compromising on the performance of conflicting updates, we can keep track of the original update intention within the maximal set of consistent consequences, which is generated. We gain the property of building up, systematically, from the initial compromise solution, further in the direction of the original goal, via subsequent compromised results.

The formalization of the CR model was guided by the AGM model of belief revision. However, the theory representation of the compromise revision model is a set of sentences (base), which is not closed under logical consequence. This supports the fact that in real life, change operations are always applied to finite bases (Nebel, 1989). CR is presented for conventional bases and for bases driven by a protected subset of integrity constraints, accounting for theory changes in a more realistic way. One of the main aims of the CR model is to generate a consistent base, revised by the conflicting input, with a minimal loss of information from both the original base and the input. Hence, compromises apply with relation to what is being added to the knowledge base K and to what is being retracted from it.

Compromise Contraction and Compromise Revision Steps

In order to revise a base k with a sentence α, it is often necessary to retract some old sentences from k. Those sentences, which together with α generate inconsistency. In the CR approach, when contracting a sentence α from k, we are not only interested in removing from k a minimal subset whose removal prevents what remains from entailing α. We are also interested in keeping all the consistent consequences of α w.r.t. k, provided that they also do not interfere in the revision process. The contraction method supports the notion of minimal loss of information. That is, the retracted sentences are only removed from the base partially, in their informative sense, since some of their logical consequences remain available in the knowledge base. Basically, by CR we mean that an input sentence α, which is inconsistent with a knowledge base k, will either have its consistent consequences added to k, or will be itself added to k, provided that the final revised base is consistent. Alternatively, α can also be rejected, causing no revision k, in the case that it contradicts a tautology. So, a CR involving k and α, depends on how α is inconsistent with k. In the case that the base k contains a protected part of integrity constraints, if the input α which revises k, violates directly some of k's integrity constraints, then α is not present in (neither implied by) the revised base. And if α is indirectly inconsistent with k, then α is in the revised resulting base. In the case k that is a conventional base set, without integrity constraints α, is only rejected if it contradicts a tautology of the logical system considered.

Basic Definitions

A finite propositional language L is considered. The underlying logic includes classical propositional logic, so that L is closed under applications of the usual Boolean operators, namely, $\neg; \wedge; \vee$ and $\rightarrow$. The knowledge base k is initially defined as the set $K = \Delta k \cup Pk$, in which Δk and Pk are assumed to be finite sets of sentences of L, that are not necessarily closed under a logical consequence. Pk is a protected part of k. Therefore, its formulae cannot be modified by any update operation in k. Pk represents the integrity constraints ranging over Δk. It comprises two sets of well-formed formulae (wff) A. Those that must be in Δk, that is $A \in \Delta k$, and those that must remain out. The latter are conveniently written as $A \rightarrow \bot \in Pk$. $Cn(k)$ denotes the set of logical consequences of k, such that $Cn(k) = \{x \mid K \mapsto x\}$, $K \subseteq Cn(k)$, $Cn(k) = Cn(Cn(k))$, and $Cn(K_1) \subseteq Cn(K_2)$ whenever $K_1 \subseteq K_2$.

The consequence relation $\mapsto$ is assumed to be compact, and closed under the operators $\neg; \wedge; \vee$ and $\rightarrow$. Also $\mapsto$ is assumed to satisfy the deduction theorem, and if α is a classical tautology then $\mapsto \alpha$. $K \mapsto \alpha$ denotes that the knowledge base k logically entails α, where α is a sentence of L. $K \mapsto \alpha$ also expresses that $\alpha \in Cn(K)$. That is, either $\alpha \in K$ or `$\mapsto \alpha$; or there exists a β, such that $\beta \vee \alpha$ or $\beta \mapsto \alpha$ is in $Cn(K)$, and $\beta \in Cn(K)$. In the usual way, we assume that $k \mapsto \bot$ if $K \mapsto \alpha$ and $K \mapsto \neg \alpha$, or $K \mapsto \beta$ and $\beta \rightarrow \bot$ is in $Cn(K)$ ($\bot \in Cn(K)$). K is assumed to be initially consistent, that is, $K \mapsto \bot$. $K\bot$ denotes the inconsistent set, which contains the set of all sentences of L. The symbol $+$ is used to denote the AGM expansion operator, such that $K+\alpha$ denotes the expansion of K by α and its logical consequences. That is, $K+\alpha = Cn(K \cup \{\alpha\})$. The symbol "$-$" denotes the difference in the set-theoretical sense.

The Compromise Revision Postulates

The symbol "®" denotes the operator for CR. A revised base is denoted as , where $K = \Delta k \cup Pk$, and the sentence α is assumed to revise K in a compromised way. The postulates (®1)-(®10) below are defined as the basic requirements for achieving a revised base K® α. So, K® α is assumed to satisfy the postulates (®1)-(®10):

(®1) K® α is a base
(®2) If $\mapsto \neg \alpha$, then K® $\alpha = K$
(®3) If $Pk + \alpha \not\mapsto \bot$, then $\alpha \in K$® α
(®4) If $\alpha \in K$, then K® $\alpha = K$
(®5) If $K + \alpha \not\mapsto \bot$, then K® $\alpha = K \cup \{\alpha\}$
(®6) If $\not\mapsto \alpha$ and $Pk + \alpha \mapsto \bot$, the $K_{®}\alpha = \Delta_{K®\alpha} \cup P_{K_.}$, K® $\alpha \not\mapsto \alpha$ and $\Delta_{K®\alpha} = \Delta_k \cup max\ CI(\alpha)_®$

(®7) If $K + \alpha \mapsto \bot$ and $P_k + \alpha \not\mapsto \bot$, then $K_® \alpha = \Delta_{K®\alpha} = (\Delta_K - R_\alpha) \cup \{\alpha\} \cup maxCR\ (R_\alpha)_®$

(®8) $P_k \subseteq K$® α
(®9) For all bases K and sentences α, K® $\alpha \not\mapsto \bot$
(®10) If $\mapsto \alpha \leftrightarrow \beta$ then $Cn(K$® $\alpha) = Cn(K$® $\beta)$

Assumptions considered by the CR postulates:

- For the *input compromise case*, $CI(\alpha)$ is the chosen set of all the consequences of α w_w.r.t. ΔK, such that $CI(\alpha)$ is inclusion-maximal and the following conditions are satisfied: $CI(\alpha) \cup \Delta_k \not\mapsto \alpha$ and $CI(\alpha) \cup \Delta_k \not\mapsto \bot$.

- $MaxCI(\alpha)$ is the set of all inclusion-maximal consistent subsets of $CI(\alpha)$ w.r.t. K, such that for each $maxCI(\alpha)_i \in maxCI(\alpha)$, for $1 \leq i \leq r$, $maxCI(\alpha)_i \cup K \not\mapsto \bot$. These conditions involving $maxCI(\alpha)i$ and $CI(\alpha)$ guarantee that if a $maxCI(\alpha)$ is added to ΔK, the resulting base is consistent and does not imply the sentence α.

- $MaxCI(\alpha)_®$ is the final set of compromise consequences of α w_w.r.t. ΔK, which is obtained from the set $MaxCI(\alpha)$.

- When a sentence β has to be retracted from K to allow α to be admitted in K® α. β is said to be rejected w.r.t. α. R_α denotes the *chosen* set of sentences $\{\beta\} \subseteq K$, rejected w.r.t. α. R_α may not be necessarily unique, since when adding α to K, it may be possible to re-establish consistency in the new base in many different ways.

- For the *retracted sentences compromise case*, $CR(R\alpha)$ is the set of compromise consequences of the sentences in R_a w.r.t. K, such that $CR(R_a)$ satisfies the following conditions: $R_a \not\subseteq CR(R_a)$; $\forall y \in CR(R_a)$, $\Delta_k \mapsto y$ and $(\Delta_k - R_a) \not\mapsto y$; and $\forall \beta \in R_a$, $CR(R_a) \cup (\Delta_k - R_a) \not\mapsto \beta$. These conditions guarantee that the sentences in $CR(R_a)$ are consequences of K, which are justified by the sentences in R_a. And that if $CR(R_a)$ is added to $(\Delta_k - R_a)$, the resulting base does not imply any sentence in R_a. $CI(\alpha)$ and $CR(R_a)$ are defined using the notion of compromise consequence relation.

- $MaxCR(R_a)$ is the set of all inclusion-maximal consistent subsets of $CR(R_a)$ w.r.t. $(\Delta_k - R_a) + \alpha$, such that for each $maxCI(R_a)_i \in maxCI(\alpha)$, for $1 \leq i \leq m$, $maxCI(R_a)_i \cup (\Delta_k - R_a) \cup P_k \cup \{\alpha\} \not\mapsto \bot$.

- $MaxCR(R_a)_\circledR$ is the final set of compromise consequences of R_a w.r.t. K, which is obtained from the set $MaxCR(R_a)$. The set $MaxCR(R_a)_\circledR$ can be obtained in many different ways. In the compromise revision approach $maxCR(R_a)_\circledR$, is defined under the notion of *safe-maximality*.

Some Issues of Compromise Revision and their Adopted Solutions

CR faces two main problems: *the irrelevant consequences problem*, that is the problem of keeping in the revised knowledge base derivations which are not relevant to the changes that have been applied to the base, and *the non-uniqueness problem*, that is the problem of coping with nonuniqueness of maximal consistent sets. These problems also occur in standard revision approaches and some solutions are presented in the literature.

Concerning the *irrelevant-consequences problem*, Ryan (1992) proposed the notion of a "natural consequence relation." Such a relation is defined as a subrelation of ordinary consequence, which selects relevant consequences from unwanted ones by preventing the addition of irrelevant disjuncts as conclusions. It is shown to be substructural, but it satisfies reflexivity, weak monotonicity and weak cut. In the CR approach, Ryan's notion of *Natural Consequence* is adapted to provide a *Compromise Consequence Relation (CCR)*. This solution to the problem of irrelevant distinguishes the wanted and the unwanted consequences, among the retracted formulae's consequences, to be added to the base as a consequence of the compromise revision. In the formalization of the compromise revision model, the CCR is defined as a restricted version of the classical consequence relation, as it imposes some logical restrictions to its ordinary notion. It takes into account a set of sentences and a particular sentence, which is involved in the compromise, in order to capture the following requirements. (1) Deals with the compromise consequences of the nonallowed updating inputs. (2) Deals with the compromise consequences of the retracted sentences from the base, to accomplish a revision. By doing so, the CCR is able to express the notion of compromise reasoning, without allowing the introduction of irrelevant consequences to the base.

Concerning the *nonuniqueness problem*, many solutions were proposed in belief revision, based on the definition of special contraction functions to obtain the revision of a base. Those contraction functions usually make use of selection mechanisms to get a unique final resulting set. In CR, however, the solutions for such problems had to account for some compromise reasoning criteria in order to express the adopted compromise notion within the revision method. The notion of *"safe-maximality"* was adopted (Dargam, 1996a) to solve the problem of nonuniqueness of maximal consistent sets resultant from compromise revision. In general, the standard approach using maximal subsets does not consider preferences or restrictions. However, by adopting the skeptical view of taking the intersection of all the maximal subsets as a final result, one might not get an intuitive solution, not to mention that too much information can be lost. In order to express restrictions or preferences, we have to be able to consider a more credulous view of handling not all the maximal subsets, but a selection of them. Such a selection should express the essence of the restrictions that we want to make on the sets available. One method for selecting the sentences to be retracted is by using an *ordering* of the sentences in the base. This approach seems to be quite natural and intuitive, since we can import preferences from the world being modelled.

In CR, whenever we need to give up some sentences in order to get an inclusion-maximal subset of the base, which satisfies a particular condition, we adopt the notion of *safe-maximality*. This notion requires that an *ordering* be employed in the database. A partial order $\leq$ on the elements of Δ_k is adopted. This ordering is supposed to give an intuitive meaning of relevance to the elements of Δ_k, according to the requirements of the application area to which the system is applied. We assume that the ordering ≤ satisfies the properties of reflexivity, transitivity, and antisymmetry. The order ≤ propagates to newly inserted sentences in Δ_k, such that when the input sentence α is present in the revised base K® α, α gets the highest priority w.r.t. ≤ on Δ_k, due to its novelty status. In the case of a compromise (either input or retraction), we may add to a revised base K® α some compromise consequences. Hence, relevance is defined w.r.t. ≤ (the ordering propagation) that those consequences will have. For an arbitrary set Δ_k ordered by ≤, the notion of ordering propagation relates each consequence y of Δ_k to the premises, which were necessary to derive y. This way, we state that the logical consequence y of Δ_k has at least the same relevance of the sentences in Δ_k which contributed, in a minimal way, to its derivation. Intuitively, we want to be able to know which elements K of conflict with the updating sentence α, so that we can build up a set containing these elements, and then determine the set R_α (where R_α denotes the *chosen* set of sentences {β} ⊆ K, rejected w.r.t. α, when a sentence β has to be retracted from K to allow α to be admitted in K® α). In this way, an ordering on Δ_k helps to determine the elements of R_α, as well as to determine a general (not skeptical) notion for dealing with the problem of choosing among various maximal subsets of the base. A safe-maximal set is viewed as a cautious restriction of a maximal set. It does not choose arbitrarily the elements to retract from the original base. Instead, it discards a *convenient* subset of the minimal elements, which fail to accomplish the condition given. The selection of those minimal elements is performed in a unique way. The safe-maximality option can be seen as *"the impartial-choice for safe-minimal change."*

User-choice for minimal-change x impartial-choice for safe-minimal-change

An alternative to this option would be to allow the current application to define which elements to retract from Δ_k. This option is free from a nonjustifiable general choice mechanism. Instead, it can be viewed as a user-choice approach, since it allows the user to decide which minimal element to discard from each set of minimals of $\perp_\alpha$. Thus, only one minimal element from each set of $\perp_\alpha$ minimals of is retracted from Δ_k. Consequently, within this option, called *"the user-choice for minimal change,"* the conservativity principle can be fully satisfied. In the *retracted sentences compromise cas*e, the set R_α is defined by adopting a combined approach, with both *"the impartial-choice for safe-minimal change"* and *"the user-choice for minimal change"* options. R_α selects the minimal elements to be retracted from Δ_k, in order to accomplish K® α, by having *"the user-choice for minimal change"* as the main option, when it applies, and *"the impartial-choice for safe-minimal change"* as default. The CR model was designed based on a user-oriented choice for a minimal loss of information of the original base K, and on an impartial solution via the notion of safe-maximality. The motivation to allow the user to choose a minimal element from each set of minimal elements to be retracted from the set Δ_k, is based the following arguments: (1) In the case where the sentences on the base are not comparable by the partial ordering, according to the application's requirements, we lack the application background knowledge in order to design a selection function for choosing one of the minimal elements. (2) By allowing the user to make the choice, we are not imposing that the contraction function of the system is the only option to retract conflicting data. Instead, we are offering a combined choice between the function and the application-oriented option, hoping for a more adequate result. (3) The high persistence results that the user-option brings to the system meets our basic goals of contracting the former base minimally when revising it, without having to apply unjustified selection mechanisms with relation to the current application. The user-oriented alternative to the safe-maximality notion is also more appropriate for the application of the CR model to decision making and negotiations.

FUTURE TRENDS

The future trends for the CR approach lie in the need to adapt it to more realistic formalizations of knowledge bases, in which real case-studies can be exploited. Two knowledge management case-studies using the compromise reasoning concept are under development phases. CR is having its formalization adapted to attend needs of the case-studies, so that it can be used for handling conflicting updates of information, for generating new knowledge. The use of the safe-maximality notion of the CR method adapted for the studies, seems to be well-accepted when dealing with matches of knowledge coming from different sources within the organizations involved. Those organizations act on different activities. They are, namely, a software company and a cultural association, which both aim at improving collection, integration, organization, and transfer of internal and external knowledge for supporting better decision making. The case-studies scenarios were described in Dargam (2005). Knowledge bases were considered, containing the internal knowledge of the organizations' processes in order to control the documented knowledge available and to achieve the defined goals. Results are currently being worked for further publications.

CONCLUSION

A finite-base revision approach based on compromise reasoning was revisited as a mechanism to serve as knowledge management technology for helping the KM processes of knowledge creation and organization, also supporting decision making. This approach caters for the specific case where compromise solutions apply, when conflicts involving the inputs (updates/actions/beliefs) occur. This work has concentrated its interests on tackling the "equivocality" knowledge problem type that KM processes and technologies have to face, in order to cope with multiple interpretations of information, as well as contradictions and diversity of viewpoints. We have supported the premise that the *compromise revision* mechanism can be considered as a context-dependent module of a broader KM framework for decision support, which is able to handle different techniques and alternative approaches for reaching optimal decisions. Further reports about how the compromise revision approach can be adapted to effectively support KM and decision-making will follow, as the work progresses.

REFERENCES

Alchourrón, C., Gärdenfors, P., & Makinson, D. (1985). On the logic of theory change: Partial meet functions for contraction and revision. *Journal of Symbolic Logic, 50*.

Alchourrón, C., & Makinson, D. (1982). The logic of theory change: Contraction functions and their associated functions. *Theoria, 48*.

Alchourrón, C., & Makinson, D. (1985). On the logic of theory change: Safe contractions. *Studia Logica, 44*.

Carlsson, S.A, & Kalling, T. (2006). Decision support through knowledge management: What works and what breaks. In F. Adam, P. Brézillon, S. Carlsson & P. Humpreys (Eds.), *Creativity and innovation in decision making and decision support* (Vol. II, pp. 693-710). Decision Support Press/Ludic Publishing Ltd.

Dargam, F.C.C. (1996a). *On reconciling conflicting updates: A compromise revision approach*. Ph.D. thesis, Department of Computing, Imperial College, University of London, UK.

Dargam, F.C.C. (1996b). Compromise updates in labelled databases. In J. Calmet, J. Campbell & J. Pfalzgraf (Eds.), *Artificial intelligence and symbolic mathematical computations* (LNCS 1138, pp. 49-70). Springer-Verlag.

Dargam, F.C.C. (1998). On supporting decision making and negotiations via compromise revision. *Journal of Decision Systems, 7,* 157-178.

Dargam, F.C.C. (1999). A compromise model for reconciling updates. In R. Pareschi & B. Fronhoefer (Eds.), *Dynamic worlds - from the frame problem to knowledge management* (pp. 149-194). Kluwer Academic Publishers.

Dargam, F.C.C. (2005). On supporting finite-base revision as a knowledge management approach for decision making. In *Proceedings of the Joint-Workshop on Decision Support Systems, Experimental Economics & E-Participation,* Graz, Austria (pp.72-84)..

Dargam, F.C.C., & Rollett, H. (2007). Decision Making and Knowledge Management: A two-way road. In *Proceedings of the 22nd European Conference on Operational Research,* EURO XXII, (p. 61). Prague, Czech Republic.

Delibašić, B., & Suknović, M. (2006). A loan granting knowledge system. *Journal of Decision Systems, 15*(2-3), 309-329.

Gärdenfors, P. (1988). *Knowledge in flux: Modeling the dynamics of epistemic states.* Cambridge, MA: Bradford Books/The MIT Press.

Handzic, M. (2004). Decision support through knowledge management: An empirical examination of two strategies. In *Proceedings of DSS2004, the 2004 IFIP*

International Conference on Decision Support Systems: Decision Support in an Uncertain and Complex World, Prato, Italy (pp. 306-315).

Nebel, B. (1989). A knowledge level analysis of belief revision. In *First Conference on Principles of Knowledge Representation and Reasoning.*

Ryan, M. (1992). *Ordered presentations of theories - default reasoning and belief revision*. Ph.D. thesis, Department of Computing, Imperial College, London, UK.

Zack, M.H. (2004). The role of DSS technology in knowledge management. In *Proceedings of DSS2004, the 2004 IFIP International Conference on Decision Support Systems: Decision Support in an Uncertain and Complex World*, Prato, Italy (pp. 861-871).

KEY TERMS

Ambiguity: In the context of this work, the fact of not having a conceptual framework for interpreting information.

Belief Revision: This approach reflects the kind of information change in which an agent reasoning about his beliefs about the world is forced to adjust them in face of a new, and possibly contradictory, piece of information.

Belief Set: When the set of beliefs held by an agent is closed under the consequence relation of some formal language, it is usually called a belief set.

Complexity: In the context of this work, the case of having more information than one can easily process.

Compromise Revision: A finite base revision approach originally proposed in Dargam (1996). The compromises adopted are of two types: (1) If the input sentence cannot be added to the knowledge base K, we compromise by allowing its consistent consequences to be added to K. This case is referred to as *"the input compromise."* (2) The input can be added to the base, K is revised and we compromise by allowing the consistent consequences of the retracted sentences to be in the revised base. This case is referred to as *"the retracted sentences compromise."* By adopting these compromises, less loss of information from the requested update of the knowledge base is achieved.

Contraction: Belief change that happens when the agent is forced to retract some beliefs.

Equivocality: In the context of this work, the state of having several competing or contradictory conceptual frameworks.

Expansion: Belief change that occurs when new information is consistent with the belief set.

Finite Base Revision: When the focus of the revision approach is done on a finite set of beliefs, it is then usually called *Base Revision* or *Finite-Base Revision.*

Revision: Belief change that deals with the acceptance of new information contradicting the current belief set; therefore, a subsequent process of restoring the consistency of that belief set is needed, whenever the new information is not itself contradictory. The notion of revision was introduced with the AGM belief revision theory (Alchourrón & Makinson, 1982, 1985, 1986; Alchourrón et al., 1985).

Safe-Maximal Set: A set that is obtained either in the input compromise case and or in the retracted sentences compromise case, by using the safe-maximality notion. It is not necessarily inclusion-maximal.

Uncertainty: In the context of this work, the state of absence of information.

Fuzzy Decision Trees

Malcolm J. Beynon
Cardiff University, UK

INTRODUCTION

The first (crisp) decision tree techniques were introduced in the 1960s (Hunt, Marin, & Stone, 1966), their appeal to decision makers is due in no part to their comprehensibility in classifying objects based on their attribute values (Janikow, 1998). With early techniques such as the ID3 algorithm (Quinlan, 1979), the general approach involves the repetitive partitioning of the objects in a data set through the augmentation of attributes down a tree structure from the root node, until each subset of objects is associated with the same decision class or no attribute is available for further decomposition, ending in a number of leaf nodes.

This article considers the notion of decision trees in a fuzzy environment (Zadeh, 1965). The first fuzzy decision tree (FDT) reference is attributed to Chang and Pavlidis (1977), which defined a binary tree using a branch-bound-backtrack algorithm, but limited instruction on FDT construction. Later developments included fuzzy versions of crisp decision techniques, such as fuzzy ID3, and so forth (see Ichihashi, Shirai, Nagasaka, & Miyoshi, 1996; Pal & Chakraborty, 2001) and other versions (Olaru & Wehenkel, 2003). The expectations that come with the utilisation of FDTs are succinctly stated by Li, Zhao, and Chow (2006):

Decision trees based on fuzzy set theory combines the advantages of good comprehensibility of decision trees and the ability of fuzzy representation to deal with inexact and uncertain information.

A fuzzy environment is embodied through the utilisation of fuzzy membership functions (MFs), which enable levels of association to the linguistic variable representation of numerical attributes (Kecman, 2001). Indeed, it is the notion of MFs that is a relatively unique feature of fuzzy set theory techniques (Li, Deng, & Wei, 2002), namely they allow linguistic and numerical descriptions of the decision rules identified in the case of FDTs.

The FDT technique employed here was first presented in Yuan and Shaw (1995) and Wang, Chen, Qian, and Ye (2000), and attempts to include the cognitive uncertainties evident in data values. Chen, Sheu, and Liu (2007) suggest cognitive uncertainties and the fuzzy maintenance problem, in particular, may be well-represented by Yuan and Shaw's FDT methodology. A further application that utilised this technique was presented in Beynon, Peel, and Tang (2004), which investigated the capabilities of FDTs to predict the levels of audit fees for companies.

BACKGROUND

In classical set theory, an element (value) either belongs to a certain set or it does not. It follows, the definition of a set can be defined by a two-valued membership function (MF), which takes values 0 or 1, defining membership or non-membership to the set, respectively. In fuzzy set theory (Zadeh, 1965), a grade of membership exists to characterise the association of a value x to a set S. The concomitant MF, defined $\mu_S(x)$, has range [0, 1].

The domain of a numerical attribute can be described by a finite series of MFs that each offers a grade of membership to describe a value x, which form its concomitant fuzzy number (see Kecman, 2001). The finite set of MFs defining a numerical attribute's domain can be denoted a linguistic variable (Herrera, Herrera-Viedma, & Martinez, 2000). Different types of MFs have been proposed to describe fuzzy numbers, including triangular and trapezoidal functions, with Yu and Li (2001) highlighting that MFs may be (advantageously) constructed from mixed shapes, supporting the use of piecewise linear MFs. The functional forms of two piecewise linear MFs, including the type utilised here (in the context of the jth linguistic term T_j^k of a linguistic variable A_k), are given by:

Fuzzy Decision Trees

$$\mu_{T_j^k}(x) \begin{cases} 0 & \text{if } x \leq \alpha_{j,1} \\ \dfrac{x - \alpha_{j,1}}{\alpha_{j,2} - \alpha_{j,1}} & \text{if } \alpha_{j,1} < x \leq \alpha_{j,2} \\ 1 & \text{if } x = \alpha_{j,2} \\ 1 - \dfrac{x - \alpha_{j,2}}{\alpha_{j,3} - \alpha_{j,2}} & \text{if } \alpha_{j,2} < x \leq \alpha_{j,3} \\ 0 & \text{if } \alpha_{j,3} < x \end{cases}$$

and

$$\mu_{T_j^k}(x) \begin{cases} 0 & \text{if } x \leq \alpha_{j,1} \\ 0.5 \dfrac{x - \alpha_{j,1}}{\alpha_{j,2} - \alpha_{j,1}} & \text{if } \alpha_{j,1} < x \leq \alpha_{j,2} \\ 0.5 + 0.5 \dfrac{x - \alpha_{j,2}}{\alpha_{j,3} - \alpha_{j,2}} & \text{if } \alpha_{j,2} < x \leq \alpha_{j,3} \\ 1 & \text{if } x = \alpha_{j,3} \\ 1 - 0.5 \dfrac{x - \alpha_{j,3}}{\alpha_{j,4} - \alpha_{j,3}} & \text{if } \alpha_{j,3} < x \leq \alpha_{j,4} \\ 0.5 - 0.5 \dfrac{x - \alpha_{j,4}}{\alpha_{j,5} - \alpha_{j,4}} & \text{if } \alpha_{j,4} < x \leq \alpha_{j,5} \\ 0 & \text{if } \alpha_{j,5} < x \end{cases}$$

with the respective *defining values* in list form, [$\alpha_{j,1}$, $\alpha_{j,2}$, $\alpha_{j,3}$] and [$\alpha_{j,1}$, $\alpha_{j,2}$, $\alpha_{j,3}$, $\alpha_{j,4}$, $\alpha_{j,5}$]. Visual representations of these MF definitions are presented in Figure 1, which elucidate their general structure along with the role played by the sets of defining values.

The general forms of MFs presented in Figure 1 ($\mu_{T_j^k}(\cdot)$) shows how the value of a MF is constrained within 0 and 1. In Figure 1a, a regularly used triangular MF is shown, based on only three defining values, whereas a more piecewise form is shown in Figure 1b, which requires five defining values. The implication of the defining values is also illustrated, including the idea of associated support (the domains [$\alpha_{j,1}$, $\alpha_{j,3}$] in Figure 1a and [$\alpha_{j,1}$, $\alpha_{j,5}$] in Figure 1b). Further, the notion of dominant support can also be considered where a MF is most closely associated with an attribute value, the domain [$\alpha_{j,2}$, $\alpha_{j,4}$] in Figure 1b.

The FDT approach considered here was introduced in Yuan and Shaw (1995) and Wang et al. (2000), which focuses on the minimization of classification ambiguity in the presence of fuzzy evidence. Underlying knowledge related to a decision outcome can be represented as a set of fuzzy '*if .. then ..*' decision rules, each of the form:

If (A_1 is $T_{l_1}^1$) and (A_2 is $T_{l_2}^2$) ... and (A_k is $T_{l_k}^k$) then C is C_j,

where $A = \{A_1, A_2, .., A_k\}$ and C are linguistic variables in the multiple antecedents (A_is) and consequent (C) statements, respectively, and $T(A_k) = \{T_1^k, T_2^k, .. T_{S_l}^k\}$ and $\{C_1, C_2, ..., C_L\}$ are their linguistic terms. Each linguistic term T_j^k is defined by the MF $\mu_{T_j^k}(x)$, which transforms a value in its associated domain to a grade of membership value to between 0 and 1. The MFs, $\mu_{T_j^k}(x)$ and $\mu_{C_j}(y)$, represent the grade of membership of an object's antecedent A_j being T_j^k and consequent C being C_j, respectively.

A MF $\mu(x)$ from the set describing a fuzzy linguistic variable Y defined on X can be viewed as a possibility distribution of Y on X, that is $\pi(x) = \mu(x)$, for all $x \in X$ (also normalized so $\max_{x \in X} \pi(x) = 1$).

Figure 1. General definition of two types of MFs (including defining values)

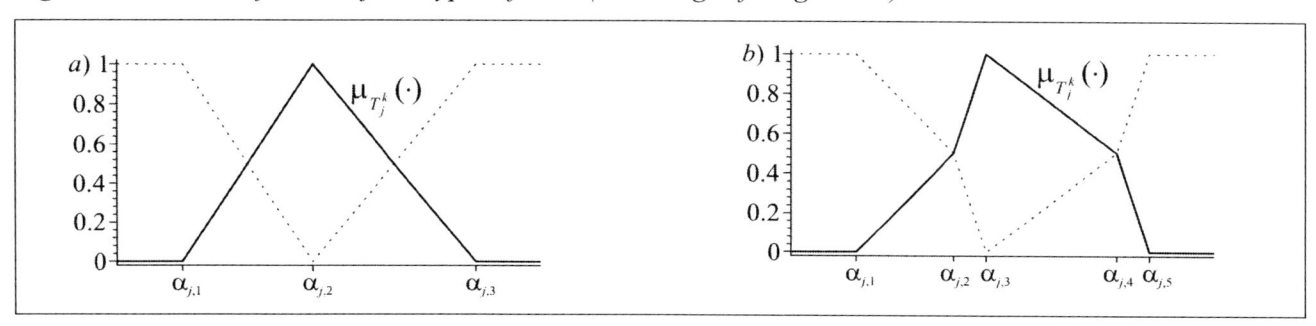

The possibility measure $E_\alpha(Y)$ of ambiguity is defined by

$$E_\alpha(Y) = g(\pi) = \sum_{i=1}^{n}(\pi_i^* - \pi_{i+1}^*)\ln[i],$$

where $\pi^* = \{\pi_1^*, \pi_2^*, ..., \pi_n^*\}$ is the permutation of the normalized possibility distribution $\pi = \{\pi(x_1), \pi(x_2), ..., \pi(x_n)\}$, sorted so that $\pi_i^* \geq \pi_{i+1}^*$ for $i = 1, .., n$, and $\pi_{n+1}^* = 0$ (see Zadeh, 1978). In the limit, if $\pi_n^* = 0$ then $E_\alpha(Y) = 0$ indicates no ambiguity, whereas if $\pi_n^* = 1$ then $E_\alpha(Y) = \ln[n]$, which indicates all values are fully possible for Y, representing the greatest ambiguity.

The ambiguity of attribute A (over the objects $u_1, .., u_m$, a universe of discourse U) is given as:

$$E_\alpha(A) = \frac{1}{m}\sum_{i=1}^{m} E_\alpha(A(u_i)),$$

where $E_\alpha(A(u_i)) = g(\mu_{T_s}(u_i)/\max_{1\leq j\leq s}(\mu_{T_j}(u_i)))$,

with $T_1, ..., T_s$ the linguistic terms of an attribute (antecedent) with m objects. When there is overlapping between linguistic terms (MFs) of an attribute or between consequents, then ambiguity exists. The fuzzy subsethood $S(A, B)$ measures the degree to which A is a subset of B, and is given by;

$$S(A, B) = \sum_{u\in U}\min(\mu_A(u), \mu_B(u)) \Big/ \sum_{u\in U}\mu_A(u).$$

Given fuzzy evidence E, the possibility of classifying an object to the consequent C_i can be defined as:

$$\pi(C_i|E) = S(E, C_i) / \max_j S(E, C_j),$$

where $S(E, C_i)$ represents the degree of truth for the classification rule, '*if E then* C_i.' With a single piece of evidence (a fuzzy number for an attribute value), then the classification ambiguity based on this fuzzy evidence is defined as: $G(E) = g(\pi(C|E))$, which is measured based on the possibility distribution $\pi(C|E) = (\pi(C_1|E), ..., \pi(C_L|E))$.

The classification ambiguity with fuzzy partitioning $P = \{E_1, ..., E_k\}$ on the evidence F, denoted as $G(P|F)$, is the weighted average of classification ambiguity with each subset of partition:

$$G(P|F) = \sum_{i=1}^{k} w(E_i|F)G(E_i \cap F),$$

where $G(E_i \cap F)$ is the classification ambiguity with fuzzy evidence $E_i \cap F$, and $w(E_i|F)$ is the weight which represents the relative size of subset $E_i \cap F$ in F; $w(E_i|F) =$

$$\sum_{u\in U}\min(\mu_{E_i}(u), \mu_F(u)) \Big/ \sum_{j=1}^{k}\left(\sum_{u\in U}\min(\mu_{E_j}(u), \mu_F(u))\right)$$

In summary, attributes are assigned to nodes based on the lowest level of classification ambiguity. A node becomes a leaf node if the level of subsethood is higher than some truth value β assigned to the whole of the FDT. The classification from the leaf node is to the decision class with the largest subsethood value. The truth level threshold β controls the growth of the tree; lower β may lead to a smaller tree (with lower classification accuracy), higher β may lead to a larger tree (with higher classification accuracy).

Fuzzy Decision Tree Analyses of Example Data Set

The main thrust of this article is the exposition of the construction processes involved with the FDT method described in the background section. Two analyses are described here that form different FDTs for a same small example data set, consisting of four objects described by three condition (T1, T2, and T3) and one decision (C) attribute, see Table 1.

Using the data set presented in Table 1, the two FDT analyses are next exposited, in each case starting with the fuzzification of the individual attribute values. The two analyses are different in the levels of fuzzification employed; the first analysis uses two MFs to describe each condition attribute, whereas in the second analysis three MFs are employed. For consistency, two MFs are used to fuzzify the single decision attribute C, see Figure 2.

Table 1. Example small data set

Object	T1	T2	T3	C
u_1	13	15	26	7
u_2	10	20	28	8
u_3	8	18	19	5
u_4	15	12	11	10

Fuzzy Decision Trees

Figure 2. Fuzzification of C using two MFs (labeled C_L and C_H)

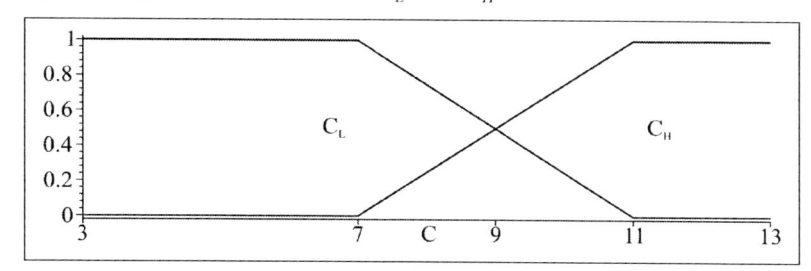

Figure 3. Fuzzification of condition attributes using two MFs

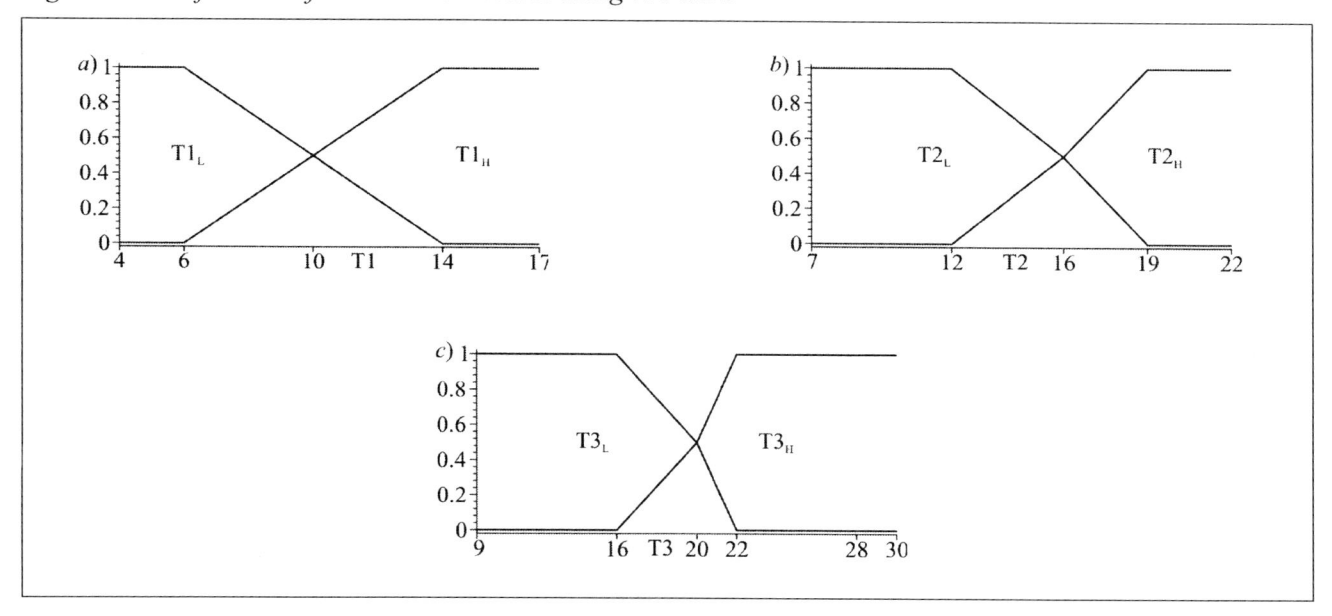

Table 2. Fuzzy data set using two MFs for each condition attribute

Object	T1 = [T1$_L$, T1$_H$]	T2 = [T2$_L$, T2$_H$]	T3 = [T3$_L$, T3$_H$]	C = [C$_L$, C$_H$]
u_1	[0.125, **0.875**]	[**0.625**, 0.375]	[0.000, **1.000**]	[**1.000**, 0.000]
u_2	[**0.500**, **0.500**]	[0.000, **1.000**]	[0.000, **1.000**]	[**0.750**, 0.250]
u_3	[**0.750**, 0.250]	[0.167, **0.833**]	[**0.625**, 0.375]	[**1.000**, 0.000]
u_4	[0.000, **1.000**]	[**1.000**, 0.000]	[**1.000**, 0.000]	[0.250, **0.750**]

In Figure 2, two MFs, $\mu_L(C)$ (labelled C_L) and $\mu_H(C)$ (C_H), are shown to cover the domain of the decision attribute C, the concomitant defining values are, for C_L: $[-\infty, -\infty, 7, 9, 11]$ and C_H: $[7, 9, 11, \infty, \infty]$. An interpretation could then simply be the association of a decision attribute value to being low (L) and/or high (H), with the two MFs showing the linguistic partition.

Analysis With Two MF Based Fuzzication of Condition Attributes

This section analyses the example data set using two MFs to fuzzify each condition attribute, see Figure 3.

The MFs described in Figure 3 are each found from a series of defining values, in this case for; T1 - $[[-\infty, -\infty, 6, 10, 11], [6, 10, 11, \infty, \infty]]$, T2 - $[[-\infty, -\infty, 12, 16, 19], [12, 16, 19, \infty, \infty]]$ and T2 - $[[-\infty, -\infty, 16, 20, 22], [16, 20, 22, \infty, \infty]]$. Applying these MFs on the example data set achieves a fuzzy data set, see Table 2.

In Table 2, each condition attribute, T1, T2, and T3 is described by two values associated with two fuzzy labels. For the construction of a FDT, the classification ambiguity of each condition attribute with respect to the decision attributes is first considered, namely the evaluation of the $G(E)$ values. Further, a threshold value of $\beta = 0.95$ was used throughout this construction process. The evaluation of a $G(E)$ value is shown for the attribute T1 ($= g(\pi(C|\ T1))$), where it is broken down to the fuzzy labels L and H, so for L:

$$\pi(C|\ T1_L) = S(T1_L, C_i) / \max_j S(T1_L, C_j),$$

considering C_L and C_H with the information in Table 1:

$$S(T1_L, C_L) = \sum_{u \in U} \min(\mu_{T1_L}(u), \mu_{C_L}(u)) \Big/ \sum_{u \in U} \mu_{T1_L}(u)$$

$= (\min(0.125, 1.000) + \min(0.500, 0.750)$
$+ \min(0.750, 1.000)$
$\quad + \min(0.000, 0.250))$
$\quad / (0.125 + 0.500 + 0.750 + 0.000)$

$= (0.125 + 0.500 + 0.750 + 0.000)/1.375 = 1.375/1.375$
$= 1.000,$

whereas $S(T1_L, C_H) = 0.182$. Hence $\pi = \{1.000, 0.182\}$, giving $\pi^* = \{1.000, 0.182\}$, with $\pi_3^* = 0$, then:

$$G(T1_L) = g(\pi(C|\ T1_L)) = \sum_{i=1}^{2} (\pi_i^* - \pi_{i+1}^*) \ln[i]$$

$= (1.000 - 0.182)\ln[1] + (0.182 - 0.000)\ln[2]$

$= 0.126,$

with $G(T1_H) = 0.370$, then $G(T1) = (0.126 + 0.370)/2 = 0.248$. Compared with $G(T2) = 0.294$ and $G(T3) = 0.338$, it follows the T1 attribute, with the least classification ambiguity, forms the root node in this case. The subsethood values in this case are; for T1: $S(T1_L, C_L) = \mathbf{1.000}$ and $S(T1_L, C_H) = 0.182$; $S(T1_H, C_L) = \mathbf{0.714}$ and $S(T1_H, C_H) = 0.381$. In each case the linguistic term with larger subsethood value (in bold), indicates the possible augmentation of the path. For $T1_L$, this is to C_L, with largest subsethood value above the desired truth value of 0.95. For $T1_H$, its largest subsethood value is 0.714 ($S(T1_H, C_L)$), hence is not able to be a leaf node and further possible augmentation needs to be considered.

With only three condition attributes considered, the possible augmentation of $T1_H$ is with T2 or T3, where with $G(T1_H) = 0.370$, the ambiguity with partition evaluated for T2 ($G(T1_H$ and T2$|\ C)$) or T3 ($G(T1_H$ and T3$|\ C)$) has to be less than this value. In the case of T2:

$$G(T1_H \text{ and } T2|\ C) = \sum_{i=1}^{k} w(T2_i |\ T1_H) G(T1_H \cap T2_i).$$

Starting with the weight values, in the case of $T1_H$ and $T2_L$, it follows:

$$w(T2_L |\ T1_H) = \frac{\sum_{u \in U} \min(\mu_{T2_L}(u), \mu_{T1_H}(u))}{\sum_{j=1}^{k} \left(\sum_{u \in U} \min(\mu_{T2_j}(u), \mu_{T1_H}(u)) \right)}$$

$= (\min(0.625, 0.875) + \min(0.000, 0.500)$
$+ \min(0.167, 0.250)$
$\quad + \min(1.000, 1.000)) /$
$\sum_{j=1}^{k} \left(\sum_{u \in U} \min(\mu_{T2_j}(u), \mu_{T1_H}(u)) \right)$

Fuzzy Decision Trees

where $\sum_{j=1}^{k}\left(\sum_{u\in U}\min(\mu_{T2_j}(u),\mu_{T1_H}(u))\right)=2.917$,

so $w(T2_L|T1_H) = 1.792/2.917 = 0.614$. Similarly, $w(T2_H|T1_H) = 0.386$, hence:

$G(T1_H$ and $T2|C) = 0.614 \times G(T1_H \cap T2_L) + 0.386 \times G(T1_H \cap T2_H)$
$= 0.614 \times 0.499 + 0.386 \times 0.154$
$= 0.366$,

Figure 4. FDT for example data set with two MFs describing each condition attribute

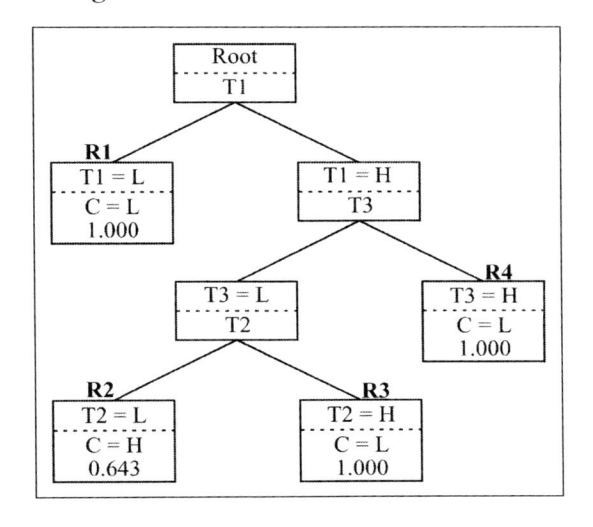

similarly, $G(T1_H$ and $T3|C) = 0.261$. With $G(T1_H$ and $T3|C) = 0.261$, the lowest of these two values, and lower than the concomitant $G(T1_H) = 0.370$ value, so less ambiguity would be found if the T3 attribute was augmented to the T1 = H path.

The subsequent subsethood values in this case for each new path are; $T3_L$; $S(T1_H \cap T3_L, C_L) = 0.400$ and $S(T1_H \cap T3_L, C_H) = \mathbf{0.600}$; $T1_H$: $S(T1_H \cap T3_H, C_L) = \mathbf{1.000}$ and $S(T1_H \cap T1_H, C_H) = 0.154$. These subsethood results show one path $T1_H \cap T3_H$ ends in a leaf node, the other $T1_H \cap T3_L$ would require the possible further augmentation of other condition attribute linguistic terms. This process continues until either all paths end at a leaf node or no further augmentation will reduce classification ambiguity, or there are no further condition attributes to augment. The resultant FDT in this case is presented in Figure 4.

The tree structure in Figure 4 clearly demonstrates the visual form of the results described previously. Only shown in each node box is the truth level associated with the highest subsethood value to a decision attribute class. There are three levels of the tree showing the use of all the considered condition attributes. There are four leaf nodes which each have a defined decision rule associated with them.

Analysis with Three MF Based Fuzzication Of Condition Attributes

This section analyses the example data set using three MFs to fuzzify each condition attribute, see Figure 5.

Figure 5. Fuzzification of condition attributes using three MFs

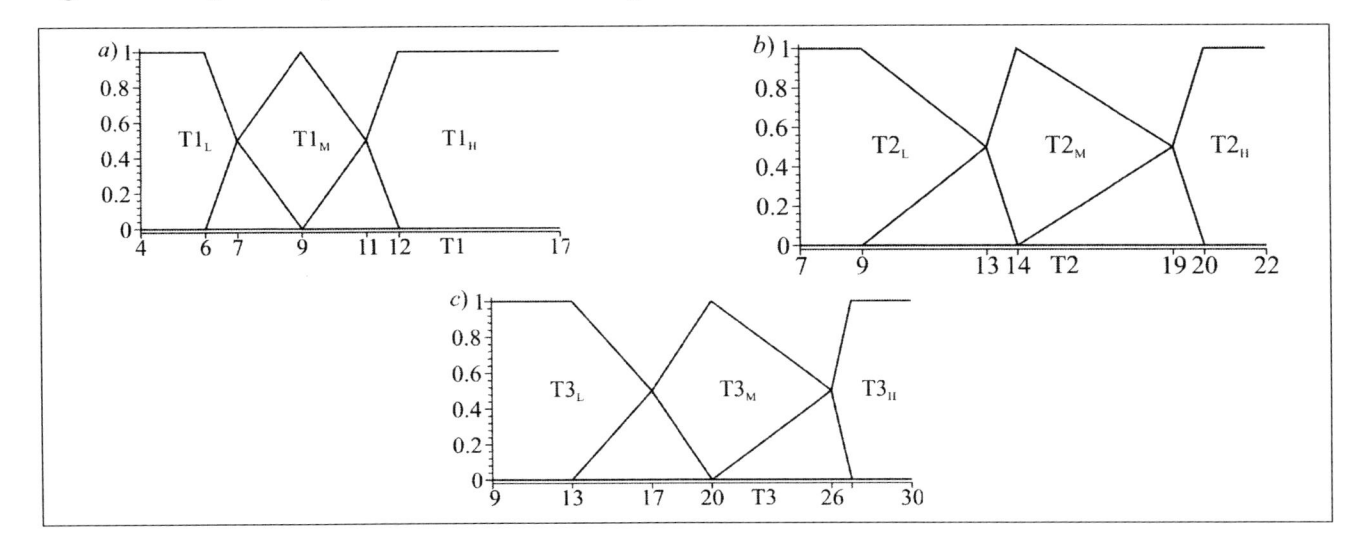

Table 3. Fuzzy data set using three MFs for each condition attribute

Object	T1 = [T1$_L$, T1$_M$, T1$_H$]	T2 = [T2$_L$, T2$_M$, T2$_H$]	T3 = [T3$_L$, T3$_M$, T3$_H$]	C = [C$_L$, C$_H$]
u_1	[0.000, 0.000, **1.000**]	[0.000, **0.900**, 0.100]	[0.000, **0.500**, **0.500**]	[**1.000**, 0.000]
u_2	[0.000, **0.750**, 0.250]	[0.000, 0.000, **1.000**]	[0.000, 0.000, **1.000**]	[**0.750**, 0.250]
u_3	[0.250, **0.750**, 0.000]	[0.000, **0.600**, 0.400]	[0.167, **0.833**, 0.000]	[**1.000**, 0.000]
u_4	[0.000, 0.000, **1.000**]	[**0.625**, 0.375, 0.000]	[**1.000**, 0.000, 0.000]	[0.250, **0.750**]

Figure 6. FDT for example data set with three MFs describing each condition attribute

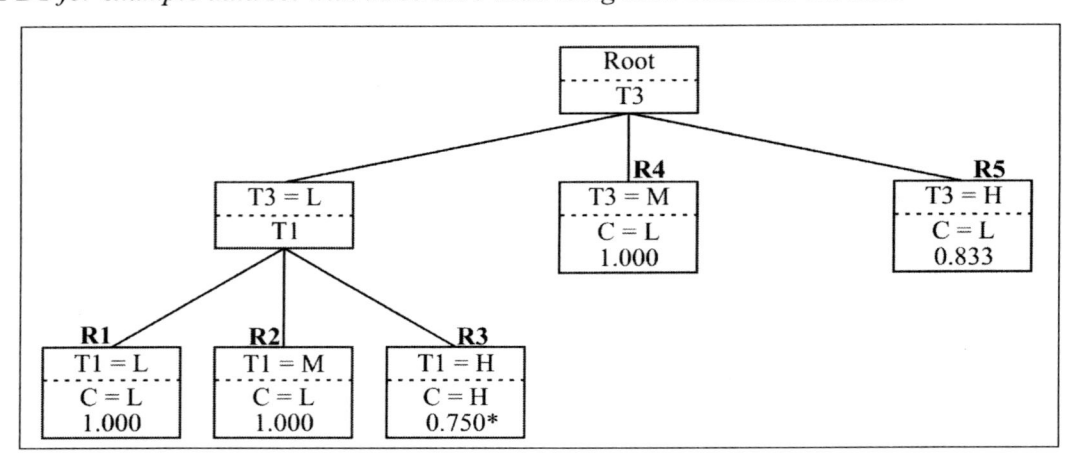

The MFs described in Figure 5 are each found from a series of defining values, in this case for; T1 - [[–∞,–∞, 6, 7, 9], [6, 7, 9, 11, 12], [9, 11, 12, ∞, ∞]], T2 - [[–∞,–∞, 9, 13, 14], [9, 13, 14, 19, 20] , [14, 19, 20, ∞, ∞]] and T2 - [[–∞,–∞, 13, 17, 20], [13, 17, 20, 26, 27], [20, 26, 27, ∞, ∞]]. Applying these MFs on the example data set achieves a fuzzy data set, see Table 3.

In Table 3, each condition attributes T1, T2, and T3, describing an object is itself described by three values associated with three fuzzy labels. A similar process is then undertaken to construct a FDT, as was performed for the previous fuzzy data set (in Table 2). The resultant FDT is shown in Figure 6.

The tree structure in Figure 6 shows two levels of the tree, use only the T3 and T1 condition attributes. There are five leaf nodes, which each have a defined decision rule associated with them. In R3, the *, along with $S(T3_L \cap T1_H) = 0.750 < 0.95$, indicates that there was insufficient improvement in classification ambiguity to warrant augmentation with the T2 attribute, not previously utilised.

FUTURE TRENDS

The future for fuzzy decision trees (FDTs) lies in its comprehensibility, in that it offers much that a decision maker desires from a decision support system. This comprehensibility includes the inductive nature of the general approach, and through the utilisaton of fuzzy set theory, the allowance for imprecision and uncertainty in the analysis. The fuzzy environment offers one crucial advantage, namely a linguistic interpretation to the fuzzy *'if .. then ..'* decision rules constructed from a FDT.

The readability of the decision support conclusions from a FDT makes it clearly accessible to analysts. Moreover, the results are in a form that can be used directly to manifest final decisions. Future trends need to make this appropriate. Within FDTs, this places emphasis on the *a priori* work required, such as deciding on what type and number of MFs should be employed, which directly affect the constructed FDT and set of concomitant fuzzy decision rules produced.

CONCLUSION

Decision trees, through their structure, demonstrate clearly the notion of inductive learning. Their reliance on samples of known objects (cases) is shown in the constructed paths through a tree, starting from the root node and ending at one of a number of leaf nodes. FDTs offer the additional feature of readability and the accommodation of possibly imprecise or vague data.

REFERENCES

Beynon, M. J., Peel, M. J., & Tang, Y.-C. (2004). The application of fuzzy decision tree analysis in an exposition of the antecedents of audit fees. *OMEGA—International Journal of Management Science, 32*(2), 231-244.

Chang, R. L. P., & Pavlidis, T. (1977). Fuzzy decision tree algorithms. *IEEE Transactions Systems Man and Cyrbernetics SMC, 7*(1), 28-35.

Chen, R. Y., Sheu, D. D., & Liu C. M. (2007). Vague knowledge search in the design for outsourcing using fuzzy decision tree. *Computers & Operations Research, 34*(12), 3628-3637.

Herrera, F., Herrera-Viedma, E., & Martinez, L. (2000). A fusion approach for managing multi-granularity linguistic term sets in decision making. *Fuzzy Sets and Systems, 114*(1), 43-58.

Hunt, E. B., Marin, J., & Stone, P. T. (1966). *Experiments in induction*. New York: Academic Press.

Ichihashi, H., Shirai, T., Nagasaka, K., & Miyoshi, T. (1996). Neuro-fuzzy ID3: a method of inducing fuzzy decision trees with linear programming for maximising entropy and an algebraic method for incremental learning. *Fuzzy Sets and Systems, 81*(1), 157-67.

Janikow, C. Z. (1998). Fuzzy decision trees: Issues and methods. *IEEE Transactions of Systems, Man and Cybernetics Part B, 28*(1), 1-14.

Kecman, V. (2001). *Learning and soft computing: Support vector machines, neural networks, and fuzzy logic*. London: MIT Press.

Li, M.-T., Zhao, F., & Chow L.-F. (2006). Assignment of seasonal factor categories to urban coverage count stations using a fuzzy decision tree. *Journal of Transportation Engineering, 132*(8), 654-662.

Li, Y., Deng, J-M., & Wei, M-Y. (2002). Meaning and precision of adaptive fuzzy systems with Gaussian-type membership functions. *Fuzzy Sets and Systems, 127*(1), 85-97.

Olaru, C., & Wehenkel, L. (2003). A complete fuzzy decision tree technique. *Fuzzy Sets and Systems, 138*, 221-254.

Pal, N. R., & Chakraborty, S. (2001). Fuzzy rule extraction from ID3-type decision trees for real data. *IEEE Transactions on Systems, Man, and Cybernetics Part B, 31*(5), 745-754.

Quinlan, J. R. (1979). Discovery rules from large examples: A case study. In D. Michie (Ed), *Expert systems in the micro electronic age*. Edinburgh, Scotland: Edinburgh University Press.

Wang, X., Chen, B., Qian, G., & Ye, F. (2000). On the optimization of fuzzy decision trees. *Fuzzy Sets and Systems, 112*, 117-125.

Yu, C-S., & Li, H-L. (2001). Method for solving quasi-concave and non-cave fuzzy multi-objective programming problems. *Fuzzy Sets and Systems, 122*(2), 205-227.

Yuan, Y., & Shaw, M. J. (1995). Induction of fuzzy decision trees. *Fuzzy Sets and Systems, 69*, 125-139.

Zadeh, L. A. (1965). Fuzzy sets. *Information and Control, 8*(3), 338-353.

Zadeh, L. A. (1978). Fuzzy sets as a basis for a theory of possibility. *Fuzzy Sets and Systems, 1*, 3-28.

KEY TERMS

Branch: Path down a decision tree from the root node to a leaf node.

Decision Tree: A tree-like way of representing a collection of hierarchical decision rules that lead to a class or value, starting from a root node ending in a series of leaf nodes.

Inductive Learning: The process of analysis through working with samples, which infers generalizations from the information in the data.

Leaf Node: Node at the end of a branch that discerns which decision class the associated branch classifies to.

Membership Function: Mathematical function to grade the association of a value to a set.

Root Node: First (top) node in a decision tree, from which all branches of the tree start from.

Subsethood: The degree to which the set A is a subset of the set B.

Fuzzy Thermal Alarm System for Venus Express

P. Serra
UNINOVA – CA3, Portugal

R. A. Ribeiro
UNINOVA – CA3, Portugal

R. Marques Pereira
Università degli Studi di Trento, Italy

R. Steel
VEGA IT, Germany

M. Niezette
VEGA IT, Germany

A. Donati
ESA/ESOC, Germany

INTRODUCTION

In the aerospace field, where satellites and spacecraft contain numerous components that require constant, yet indirect, surveillance of large amounts of data, monitoring tools give the operators constant access to the state of the machinery, facilitating prompt and appropriate responses to any problems that may arise.

The objective of developing a Venus Express alarm system (Steel, 2006) is to monitor the thermal characteristics of each spacecraft face with respect to spacecraft altitude relative to the sun's position. A thermal alarm monitoring tool assumes particular importance in the Venus Express mission as the spacecraft will be subject to high levels of solar radiation due to its proximity to the sun.

In the space context, in particular for mission-control purposes, fuzzy inference systems provide a suitable technique to build this type of alarm system because the knowledge is imprecise or partial, going beyond the use of traditional, that is, crisp, methods (Ribeiro, 2006). Furthermore, the fuzzy linguistic approach used (Mendel, 2001; Ross, 2004) allows for an effective complement to human operators by creating systems that can support their actions in case of any fault detected.

In this article, we discuss the design and development of a fuzzy thermal alarm system for the Venus Express spacecraft using a new inference scheme, the Choquet-TSK (Marques Pereira, Ribeiro, & Serra, in press; Marques Pereira, Serra, & Ribeiro, 2006). The new inference scheme is based on the integration of the Choquet integral (Grabisch, 1995, 1996, 1997) in a fuzzy inference system of the Takagi-Sugeno-Kang (TSK) type (Sugeno & Kang, 1986; Takagi & Sugeno, 1985). This integration allows expressing synergies between rules, and the necessary combined weights are obtained by using correlation matrices (Marques Pereira & Bortot, 2004; Marques Pereira, Ribeiro, & Serra). The new Choquet-TSK inference scheme together with a defined fuzzy-rule base is the basis of the thermal alarm system for the Venus Express spacecraft, developed within the context of a European Space Agency (ESA) project (AO/1-4635/04/N/ML). The main motivation behind this work was to show that expressing synergies between rules could improve the reliability of space monitoring alarm systems.

BACKGROUND

Fuzzy Inference Systems

Fuzzy inference systems (FISs), sometimes also called fuzzy expert systems or fuzzy knowledge-based systems (see, for example, Zimmerman, 1996), express their knowledge through fuzzy linguistic variables (Mendel, 2001; Ross, 2004; Zadeh, 1987), whose role is to define the semantics of the problem. Then, by means of the fuzzy linguistic variables formulation, the linguistic variables are characterized and quantified. FISs also include a set of rules that define the way knowledge is structured and an inference scheme that constitutes the reasoning process toward the result.

A typical FIS (Mendel, 2001; Ross, 2004; Wang, 1997) includes the following steps: (a) "fuzzification" of the input variables, (b) definition of the output variables, (c) definition of the rule base, and (d) selection of the inference scheme (operators, implication method, and aggregation process). In some inference schemes, for example, the Mamdani model (Mamdani, 1976), a "defuzzification" method is also required to transform the fuzzy output result into a crisp output. Here, because we follow the Takagi-Sugeno-Kang model (Sugeno & Kang, 1986; Takagi & Sugeno, 1985), which comprises fuzzy inputs but crisp outputs, we will not discuss defuzzification methods.

Fuzzification of the inputs implies their definition as fuzzy linguistic variables (Zadeh, 1987). Formally, a linguistic variable is characterized by the five-tuple (X,T,U,G,M), where X is the name of the linguistic variable; T is the set of linguistic terms, in which the linguistic variables X take values; U is the actual physical domain in which the linguistic variable X takes its crisp values; G is a syntactic rule that creates the terms in the term set; and M is a semantic rule that relates each label in T with a fuzzy set in U. For example, height={short, average, tall} is a linguistic variable with three terms, where each label is represented by a fuzzy set. A fuzzy set represents the membership degree of objects of a specific term or set (Zadeh).

The definition of the outputs depends on the FIS model selected and can be divided in two main classes (Mendel, 2001): the Mamdani type, which uses fuzzy inputs and fuzzy outputs, and the Takagi-Sugeno-Kang type, which uses fuzzy inputs but crisp outputs. The Mamdani consequents are usually represented by linguistic variables, while the TSK consequents are usually a function of the inputs. In our application, we only use constants for the output functions (TSK model).

The developer and domain expert in close collaboration usually define the rules for the inference system application. The domain expert is essential for the definition of the rule set because rules represent existing relations between input variables and the desired conclusion, and they have knowledge about those relations. A fuzzy rule is usually defined as:

IF X_1 is A_1 AND ... AND X_n is A_n THEN Y,

where X_k are the variables considered, A_k are the fuzzy terms of linguistic variables representing the variables considered, and Y is either a fuzzy term of a fuzzy output (Mamdani-type model) or a function (TSK-type model). For example, for a TSK model, the rule "IF Service is *excellent* THEN Tip=25" expresses that if the service in a restaurant is excellent (where excellent is defined by a fuzzy set), the tip should be 25% of the meal cost. For a Mamdani model, the rule "IF Service is *excellent* THEN Tip=*high*" expresses that if service is good, the tip should be high (where high is a fuzzy term of the linguistic output Tip).

The inference scheme process encompasses two phases for performing the inference (reasoning) of the application: the individual rule implication, which applies to all rules of the rule set, and the rule aggregation process, to reach a final result for a FIS. There are many implication operators to derive the conclusion for each rule (Lee, 1990; Wang, 1997; Zimmermann, 1996). However, the most used for FIS implication are, as mentioned before, the Mamdani one (minimum operator) and the TSK one (function of the inputs). The aggregation process, for all the rules implication values, depends, again, on the inference scheme selected. The Mamdani scheme proposes the max operator (many other operators could be used as can be seen in Wang; Zimmermann) while the TSK model uses a weighted average, where the weights are the normalized firing levels of each rule (Mendel, 2001; Ross, 2004).

New Choquet-TSK Inference Scheme

The Choquet integral (Grabisch, 1995, 1997) is an operator capable of aggregating discrete sets of classifications for decision-making variables, taking into account the relations (synergies) that exist between those variables. It is an extension of the simple average weighting method (Grabisch, 1995). In a FIS, the relations between variables can assume three different forms: complementarity between rules, redundancy (or a certain degree of overlapping) between rules, and an intermediate case or independence. In the Choquet-TSK approach (Marques-Pereira, Ribeiro, & Serra, in press; Marques-Pereira, Serra, & Ribeiro, 2006), the individual weights correspond to the firing levels of each rule, and relations are represented by a fuzzy measure (Murofushi & Sugeno, 1991), acting as a structure of relative weights. The basic rationale is that if the firing levels for two rules are systematically similar, then those rules encode the same information and thus have a degree of redundancy; the joint weight that they have in the aggregation (their firing levels) should decrease. If, on the other hand, the firing levels for two rules are systematically opposite, then those rules encode complementary information and are thus important; the joint weight that they have in the ag-

Fuzzy Thermal Alarm System for Venus Express

Figure 1. New Choquet-TSK inference scheme architecture

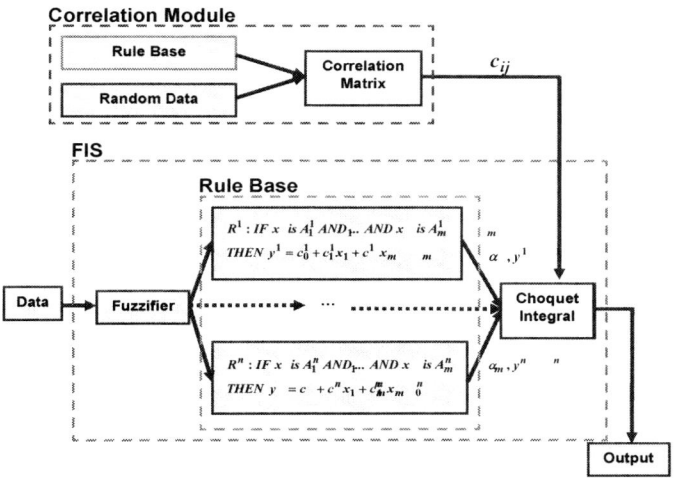

gregation (their firing levels) should increase. In the third case, independence, no change should be made to the joint weight of the rules as they are not related. To express the synergies between rules, the Choquet-TSK inference scheme uses correlation matrices (Marques-Pereira, Ribeiro, & Serra) to determine the combined weights (pair wise) necessary for defining the Choquet integral. In summary, this new inference scheme generalizes the classical weighted average of TSK FIS and enables handling synergies between rules in an FIS.

The general architecture (Figure 1) and respective reasoning process steps defined for the new inference scheme, Choquet-TSK, are presented next; details about the algorithm formulation and rationale can be seen in Marques-Pereira, Serra, and Ribeiro (2006) and Marques-Pereira, Ribeiro, and Serra (in press).

In Figure 1 α^i, y^i, c_{ij}, are, respectively, the firing level for rule i, the implication result for rule i, and the correlation value between rule i with rule j. These values are then used as parameters of the Choquet integral, which determines the crisp output for an FIS.

The new Choquet-TSK inference process includes the following steps:

1. Input vectors are randomly generated and the corresponding firing levels for each rule are computed.
2. The sample of firing levels is then used to obtain a correlation matrix associated with the set of rules.
3. For each input vector, the firing levels (consequents of rules) together with the correlation matrix values (combined weights) are used to create the setup parameters of the Choquet integral.
4. Finally, the defined parameters are aggregated, using the Choquet integral, to determine the crisp FIS output.

THE VENUS EXPRESS THERMAL MONITORING TOOL

Objectives

The objective of the Venus Express alarm system is to monitor the thermal characteristics of each face of the spacecraft with respect to the altitude of the spacecraft relative to the sun's position.

Each face of the Venus Express spacecraft contains thermistors (temperature sensors) that monitor temperature changes in a certain surface. The spacecraft, when illuminated by the sun, heats up. Excessive heat can cause unwanted effects in faces that contain sensitive equipment, and thus this situation requires monitoring (Steel, 2006). Only the sun side (the positive Y face) of the spacecraft is expected to heat up, with the opposite face remaining cool. If both sides are heated (or cooled)

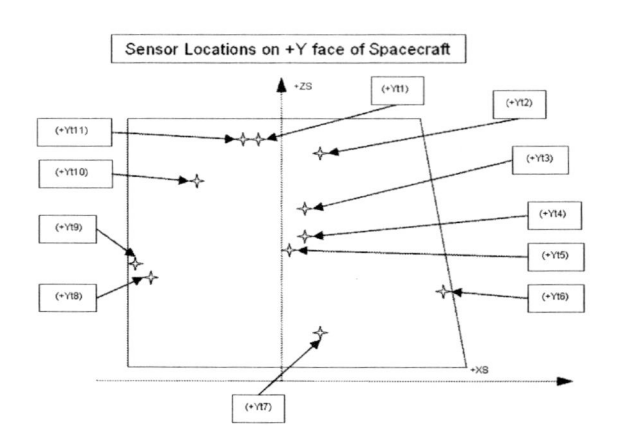

Figure 2. Location of the temperature sensors on the +Y face of the Venus Express spacecraft

then this could indicate a problem with the spacecraft or an environmental phenomenon (Steel). Information about the thermostatic sensors' status is important, in particular during operations, and is usually difficult to take into account. Figure 2 contains a schematic representation of the several existing sensors on the +Y face of the Venus Express spacecraft.

General System Description

The Venus thermal system includes 19 input variables (Steel, 2006) corresponding to thermistor status variables and incident solar energy flux. The developed alarm system is of the Choquet-TSK type, with the operator product representing the AND connector and a constant output function for the implication. The aggregation, inference reasoning, is done with the new inference scheme described above, Choquet-TSK. The descriptions of the variables considered for this alarm system are summarized in Table 1.

Input and Output Variable Representations

The fuzzification of the input variables representation was done together by the developer and domain expert. The domain-expert knowledge is essential to correctly determine the limits of each term of a fuzzy linguistic variable (Zadeh, 1987). Figure 3 depicts the generic plots considered for the input variable fuzzification, which correspond to the sensors and their status. +Yt_ is the generic fuzzy linguistic representation for thermistor variables, S_ corresponds to the ON or OFF status of the fuzzy linguistic variables, L_ corresponds to the fuzzy linguistic variable expressing the operational status, and SolarFlux is the fuzzy linguistic variable representing the different levels of sun energy considered.

Table 2, Table 4, and Table 5 summarize the parameters used for each fuzzy term of the input linguistic variables. Moreover, for +Yt_ variables, Table 3 shows auxiliary parameters used to obtain the actual parameters, as depicted in Figure 3.

Table 1. Description of the system's variables

Variables and their Descriptions	
Sensors for Temperature +Yt1 through +Yt11	Absolute value of the deviation from a nominal temperature for each of the +Y face thermistors
Status (ON/OFF) S1, S2, S8	Status variable indicating ON or OFF status; related only to thermistors 1, 2, and 8
Status (Operational) L3, L4, L7, L11	Status of the associated equipment (i.e., operating or not); related to thermistors 3, 4, 7, and 11
Solar Energy SolarFlux	Solar energy of the sun corresponding to an integration of the sine of the solar elevation angle over time with respect to the ZX plane of the spacecraft for nonzero values (positive angles toward the +Y axis). The integration is reset for negative angles.

Fuzzy Thermal Alarm System for Venus Express

Figure 3. Input linguistic variables

Input linguistic variable "+Yt_" corresponding to thermistors 1, 2, 3, 4, 7, 8 and 11.

Input linguistic variable "+Yt_" corresponding to thermistors 5, 6, 9 and 10.

Input linguistic variable "S_".

Input linguistic variable "L_".

Input linguistic variable "SolarFlux".

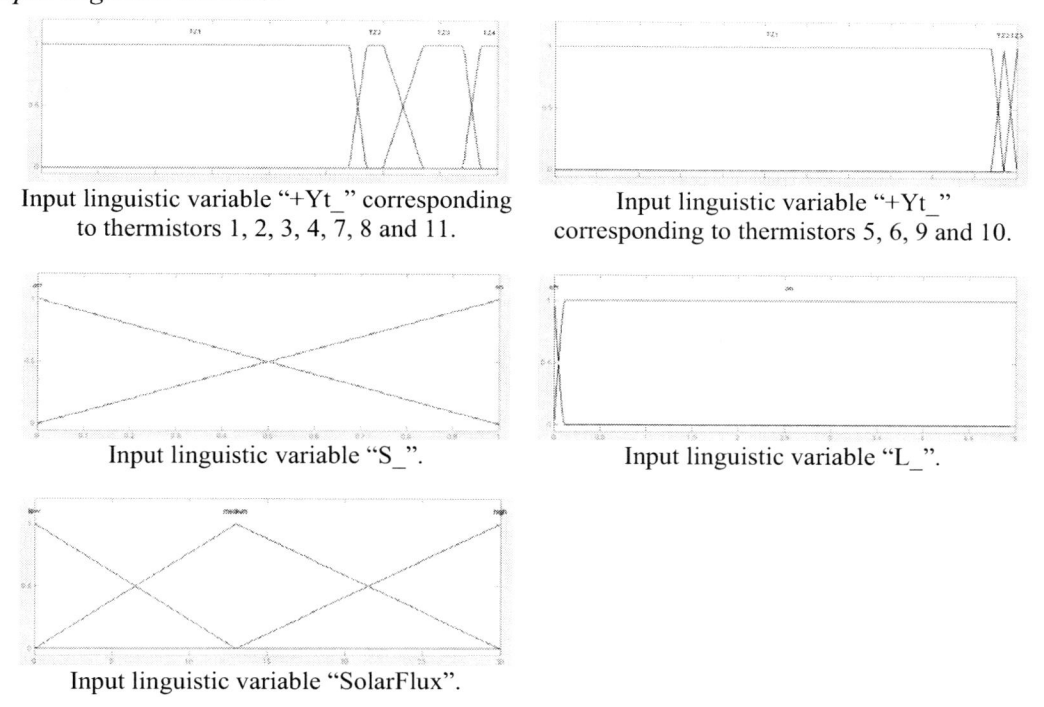

*Table 2. Formulas for fuzzy terms of variables +Yt_ and TZ_*

| Formulas for Terms of Fuzzy Variables TZ_ ||
+Yt1, +Yt2, +Yt3, +Yt4, +Yt7, +Yt8, +Yt11 Range: [0, T4]		+Yt5, +Yt6, +Yt9, +Yt10 Range: [0, T2]
TZ1	[0 0 T1 (T1+T2)/2] – Trapezoidal	[0 0 T1 (T1+T2)/2] – Trapezoidal
TZ2	[T1 (T1+T2)/2 T2 (T2+T3)/2] – Trapezoidal	[T1 (T1+T2)/2 T2] – Triangular
TZ3	[T2 (T2+T3)/2 T3 (T3+T4)/2] – Trapezoidal	[(T1+T2)/2 T2 T2] – Triangular
TZ4	[T3 (T3+T4)/2 T4 T4] – Trapezoidal	

Table 3. Auxiliary parameters for Table 2

Variables	T1	T2	T3	T4
+Yt1	52	55	62	65
+Yt2	37	40	47	50
+Yt3	27	30	37	40
+Yt4	27	30	37	40
+Yt5	72	75		
+Yt6	52	55		
+Yt7	27	30	37	40
+Yt8	39.5	42.5	49.5	52.5
+Yt9	72	75		
+Yt10	72	75		
+Yt11	47	50	67	70

Table 4. Fuzzy terms definitions for S_ and L_ variables

Variable	ON	OFF
S_ Range: [0 1]	[0 1 1] – Triangular	[0 0 1] – Triangular
L_ Range: [0 5]	[0 0.1 5 5] – Trapezoidal	[0 0 0.1] – Triangular

Table 5. *Fuzzy term definitions for SolarFlux variable*

Variable	Low	Medium	High
SolarFlux Range: [0, 30]	[0 0 13] – Triangular	[0 13 30] – Triangular	[13 30 30] – Triangular

Table 6. *Crisp output terms and membership values*

Output Variable	Good	Medium	Bad
Condition Range: [0, 1]	$y_{GOOD}(\underline{x}) = 0$	$y_{MEDIUM}(\underline{x}) = 0.5$	$y_{BAD}(\underline{x}) = 1$

Regarding the output variable of the fuzzy thermal alarm system, we defined, again with the help of the domain expert, three functions for the condition of the spacecraft. Since we are dealing with a TSK-type model (Mendel, 2001), we used first-order functions, which correspond to constants, as depicted in Table 6. The semantics for the condition output variable indicates a level of alarm for the thermal condition of the Venus spacecraft: good, medium, or bad.

System's Rule Base

The rule set necessary for this alarm system was, again, defined together by the developer and domain expert. Knowledge about the domain is essential to guarantee completeness and accuracy of all components that should be monitored (Ribeiro, 2006).

The rule base considered for this alarm system is composed of 141 rules divided into three groups: a first group relating to thermistors 1, 2, and 8 (3x15 rules in this group); the second group relating to thermistors 3, 4, 7, and 11 (4x15 rules in this group); and finally a third group relating to thermistors 5, 6, 9, and 10 (4x9 rules in this group). Since each group has similar rules, the generic rule set for each of the three groups is as follows (each group corresponds to one thermistor at a time).

Rules for First Group (Thermistors 1, 2, 8)

01. IF "+Yt_" is TZ1 AND "SolarFlux" is low THEN "condition" is good

02. IF "+Yt_" is TZ2 AND "S_" is off AND "SolarFlux" is low THEN "condition" is good

03. IF "+Yt_" is TZ2 AND "S_" is on AND "SolarFlux" is low THEN "condition" is medium

04. IF "+Yt_" is TZ3 AND "S_" is off AND "SolarFlux" is low THEN "condition" is medium

05. IF "+Yt_" is TZ3 AND "S_" is on AND "SolarFlux" is low THEN "condition" is bad

06. IF "+Yt_" is TZ4 AND "SolarFlux" is low THEN "condition" is bad

07. IF "+Yt_" is TZ1 AND "SolarFlux" is medium THEN "condition" is good

08. IF "+Yt_" is TZ2 AND "S_" is off AND "SolarFlux" is medium THEN "condition" is good

09. IF "+Yt_" is TZ2 AND "S_" is on AND "SolarFlux" is medium THEN "condition" is bad

10. IF "+Yt_" is TZ3 AND "SolarFlux" is medium THEN "condition" is bad

11. IF "+Yt_" is TZ4 AND "SolarFlux" is medium THEN "condition" is bad

12. IF "+Yt_" is TZ1 AND "SolarFlux" is high THEN "condition" is medium

13. IF "+Yt_" is TZ2 AND "SolarFlux" is high THEN "condition" is bad

14. IF "+Yt_" is TZ3 AND "SolarFlux" is high THEN "condition" is bad

15. IF "+Yt_" is TZ4 AND "SolarFlux" is high THEN "condition" is bad

Rules for Second Group (Thermistors 3, 4, 7, 11)

This set of rules is similar to the one from the first group but for the "L_" variables instead of the "S_" variables, hence we do not list them here.

Rules for Third Group (Thermistors 5, 6, 9, 10)

01. IF "+Yt_" is TZ1 AND "SolarFlux" is low THEN "condition" is good

02. IF "+Yt_" is TZ2 AND "SolarFlux" is low THEN "condition" is medium

03. IF "+Yt_" is TZ3 AND "SolarFlux" is low THEN "condition" is bad

04. IF "+Yt_" is TZ1 AND "SolarFlux" is medium THEN "condition" is good

Fuzzy Thermal Alarm System for Venus Express

05. IF "+Yt_" is TZ2 AND "SolarFlux" is medium THEN "condition" is bad
06. IF "+Yt_" is TZ3 AND "SolarFlux" is medium THEN "condition" is bad
07. IF "+Yt_" is TZ1 AND "SolarFlux" is high THEN "condition" is medium
08. IF "+Yt_" is TZ2 AND "SolarFlux" is high THEN "condition" is bad
09. IF "+Yt_" is TZ3 AND "SolarFlux" is high THEN "condition" is bad

Venus Express Choquet-TSK Inference Scheme

As mentioned in the background section, the inference scheme used in this case was first proposed by Marques Pereira, Serra, and Ribeiro (2006) and Marques-Pereira, Ribeiro, and Serra (in press) and is a generalization of the typical TSK FIS. Its novelty is the use of a more sophisticated aggregation operator, the Choquet integral, to substitute the weighted averaging generally used in FIS, as well as the use of correlation matrices to determine the interactions (synergies) between the rules.

Since the complete correlation matrix obtained for the Venus Express case is too large, here only some submatrices are shown (Figures 4, 5, 6). Each partial correlation matrix represents correlations among rules of the same group or between groups. Thus, the first

Figure 4. Correlations among rules in the first group

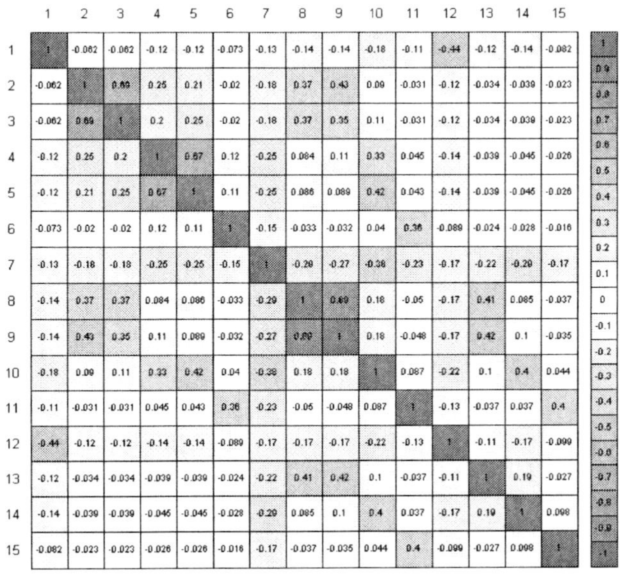

Figure 5. Correlations between rules of the first group and rules of the second group

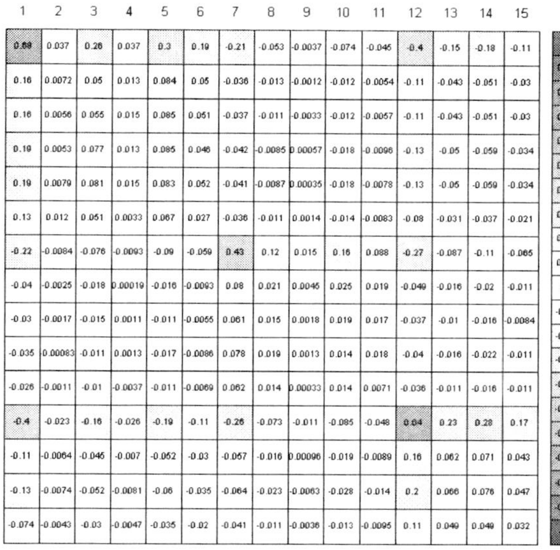

Figure 6. Correlations between rules of the first group and rules of the third group (Matrix C)

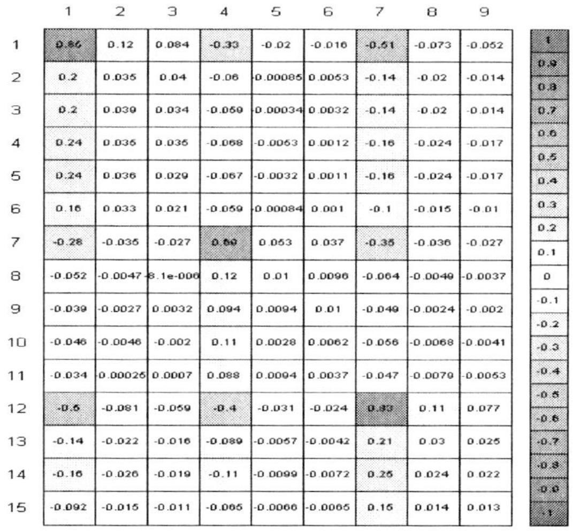

picture (Figure 4) represents the correlations among rules of the first group, the second picture (Figure 5) represents the correlations between the first group and the second group of rules, and the third picture (Figure 6) represents correlations between the rules of the first group and Group 3.

As can be observed in Figures 4, 5, and 6, each picture is divided into squares, each one corresponding to a correlation between a pair of rules; the squares contain the respective correlation value and a shading colour code that expresses the intensity of that correlation to help visualize the results: Darker shades of grey indicate correlations that are more intense.

In summary, the full, general correlation matrix has 141x141 elements, but, as mentioned before, for reasons of space, here we only showed partitions of 15x15 and 15x9 corresponding to different groups of rules.

Tests and Validation

Tests with real data, provided by ESA (for 20 days with two daily observations), were performed to validate the system. The real spacecraft telemetry data were transformed by scaling the values of the time series to facilitate the emission of alarms. Noise (normally distributed values) was added to the thermistors' data to further validate the system response. Figures 7 and Figure 8 show, respectively, the alarms produced with the Choquet-TSK inference and with the classical TSK inference.

Observing Figures 7 and 8, we see a first period (until January 15) where instability in the input data causes outputs with medium and high alarms, as follows: (a) the condition of the spacecraft reaches bad several times for the Choquet-TSK method and only sometimes for the classical TSK method, (b) both methods produce medium alarms during most of the period, although the Choquet-TSK produces higher values for the *medium* class, and (c) the TSK method produces four *good* alarms (i.e., thermal condition of the spacecraft is good) while the Choquet-TSK only considers the condition good three times. The comparison for this period clearly points out that the Choquet-TSK method provides higher values for alarms in the thermistor sensors' condition, thus warning the operator that something is wrong in a stronger way.

A second interesting period can be detected from the 15th to the 20th of January, where the alarms start showing some sudden drops, but mostly in the range of *medium* alarms. During this period, the main difference between the methods is that the Choquet-TSK clearly and strongly detects two *bad* alarms, while the TSK only detects one but with a very low value.

For the period of the 20th to the 30th, the system produces virtually no alarms (condition of sensors is good) for both methods.

In summary, the alarms obtained with the Choquet-TSK method, for the testing period, were considered correct by the client, ESA. The main difference between the two methods (Figures 7 and 8) is essentially in terms of the alarms' intensities. However, it is important to note that, for instance, the classical TSK FIS only triggers a low critical alarm value for both the 16th and 17th of January, while the Choquet-TSK triggers a high critical alarm. This fact can be very important for the operators to check what the problem is.

In order to better compare the results of the Choquet-TSK and classical TSK, we show a histogram (Figure 9) with the range of differences that were obtained with a randomly generated sample of inputs. Each bar in the histogram corresponds to a class (represented in the x-axis) and illustrates the percentage of input

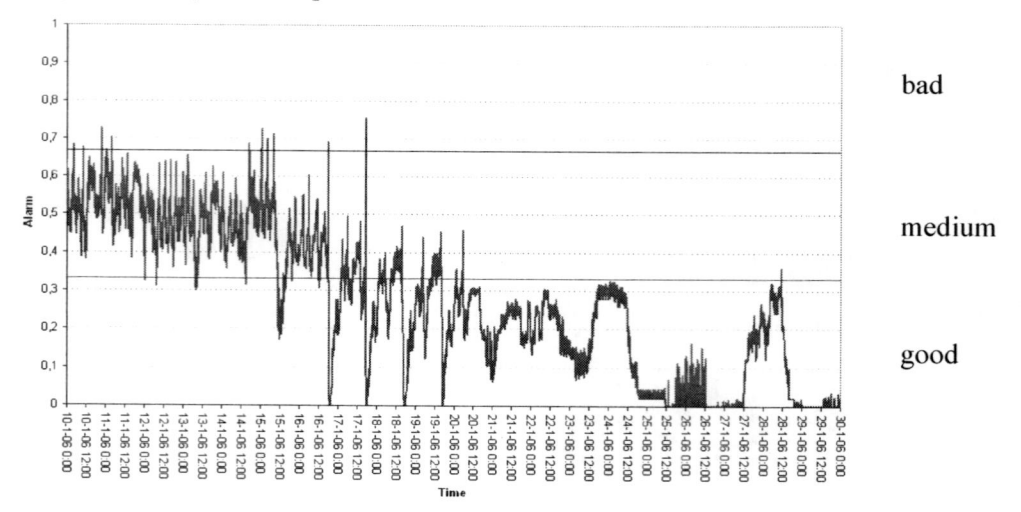

Figure 7. Alarms produced by the Choquet-TSK FIS

Fuzzy Thermal Alarm System for Venus Express

Figure 8. Alarms produced by the TSK FIS

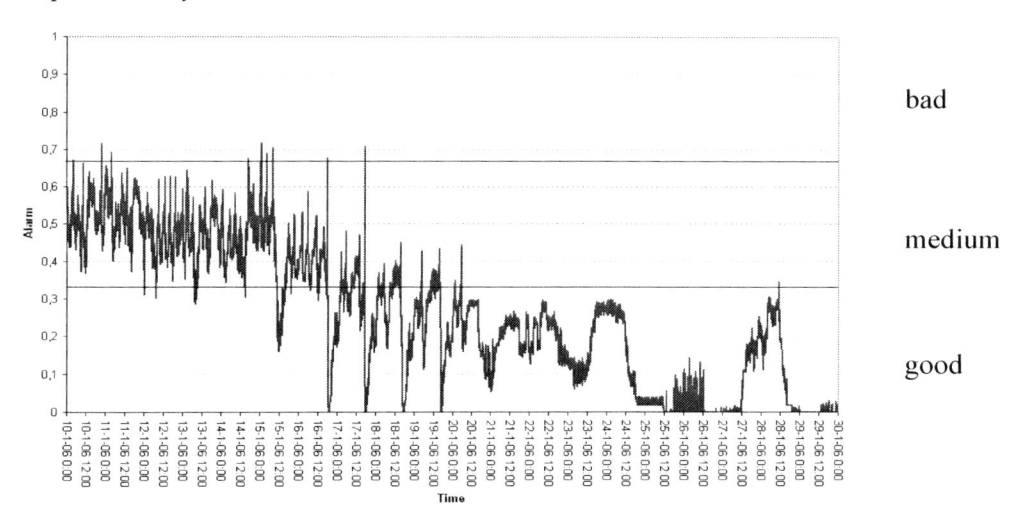

Figure 9. Distribution of the differences obtained between TSK FIS and Choquet-TSK FIS

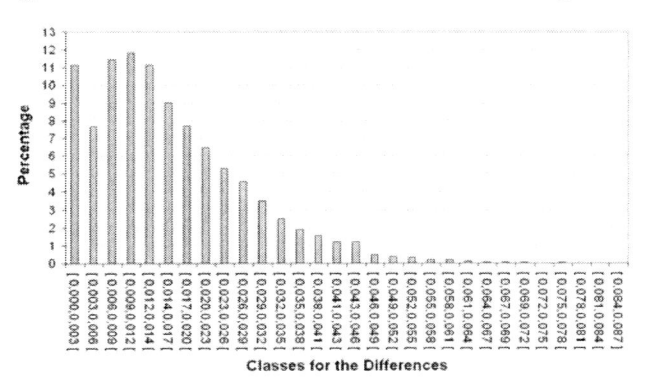

points that generated a difference (absolute value of the difference between Choquet-TSK FIS and TSK FIS) within that class.

Observing Figure 9, one can see that in approximately 2% of the cases, the absolute value of the difference falls within the interval [0.035, 0.038]. The interval with the greatest percentage of differences corresponds to the class [0.009, 0.012], and the class [0.012, 0.014] contains the median.

Even though the differences between the two methods were not that big for this problem, the Choquet-TSK clearly showed stronger intensities in the alarms provided. For problems where the synergies between rules (correlations) are big, the Choquet-TSK method will clearly perform better than the classical TSK method.

FUTURE TRENDS

The interesting results of the Choquet integral in the context of decision making and the increased usage of fuzzy inference systems as decision support tools make the integration of the two approaches a suitable method to deal with synergies between rules.

Further applications of the Choquet-TSK method will show its effectiveness in dealing with highly overlapping rules (i.e., synergies) and will unveil the way these redundancies bias the systems results.

Also, the use of fuzzy inference systems as alarm, monitoring, or decision support tools in the space domain is a good alternative to crisp methods, allowing, with greater simplicity, more flexibility and earlier warnings and alarms, enabling the operators to act before some serious problem happens.

CONCLUSION

The system built seems to accurately represent the situation of the Venus Express thermistors: It is able to issue alarms taking into account all thermistors' status and their individual characteristics.

The new Choquet-TSK method opens the door to improvements in the inference scheme of FIS because it generalizes the classical TSK FIS and uses important unused information about rule relations. The method seems appropriate for our application because the rules belonging to the same group showed some synergies, as can be observed in the correlation matrices.

REFERENCES

Grabisch, M. (1995). Fuzzy integral in multicriteria decision making. *Fuzzy Sets and Systems, 69*, 279-298.

Grabisch, M. (1996). The application of fuzzy integrals in multicriteria decision making. *European Journal of Operational Research, 89*, 445-456.

Grabisch, M. (1997). K-order additive discrete fuzzy measures and their representation. *Fuzzy Sets and Systems, 92*, 167-189.

Lee, C. C. (1990). Fuzzy logic in control systems: Fuzzy logic controller. Part II. *IEEE Transactions on Systems, Man and Cybernetics, 20*(2), 419-435.

Mamdani, E. H. (1976). Advances in linguistic synthesis of fuzzy controllers. *International Journal of Man-Machine Studies, 8*, 669-678.

Marques Pereira, R. A., & Bortot, S. (2004). Choquet measures, Shapley values, and inconsistent pairwise comparison matrices: An extension of Saaty's analytic hierarchy process A.H.P. In *Proceedings of 25th Linz Seminar on Fuzzy Set Theory*, Linz, Austria (pp. 130-135).

Marques Pereira, R. A., Ribeiro, R. A., & Serra, P. (in press). Rule correlation and Choquet integration in fuzzy inference systems. *International Journal of Uncertainty, Fuzziness and Knowledge-Based Systems*.

Marques Pereira, R. A., Serra, P., & Ribeiro, R. A. (2006). Choquet integration and correlation matrices in fuzzy inference systems. In B. Reusch (Ed.), *Computational intelligence, theory and applications* (pp. 15-18). Springer.

Mendel, J. (2001). *Uncertain rule-based fuzzy inference systems: Introduction and new directions*. Prentice-Hall.

Murofushi, T., & Sugeno, M. (1991). A theory of fuzzy measures: Representation, the Choquet integral and null sets. *Journal of Mathematical Analysis and Applications, 159*, 532-549.

Ribeiro, R. A. (2006). Fuzzy space monitoring and fault detection applications. *Journal of Decision Systems, 15*(2-3), 267-286.

Ross, T. (2004). *Fuzzy logic with engineering applications* (2nd ed.). Wiley.

Steel, R. (2006). *NOMDIS: Technical note* (Tech. Rep. No. NOMDIS-TN-002). VEGA IT, GmbH.

Sugeno, M., & Kang, G. T. (1986). Fuzzy modelling and control of multilayer incinerator. *Fuzzy Sets and Systems, 18*, 329-346.

Takagi, T., & Sugeno, M. (1985). Fuzzy identification of systems and its applications to modelling and control. *IEEE Transactions on Systems, Man, and Cybernetics, 15*(1), 116-132.

Wang, L.-X. (1997). *A course in fuzzy systems and control*. Prentice-Hall.

Zadeh, L. A. (1987). The concept of a linguistic variable and its application to approximate reasoning: I. In R. R. Yager, S. Ovchinnikiv, R. Tong, H.T. Nguyen (Eds.), *Fuzzy sets and applications: Selected papers by L. A. Zadeh* (pp. 219-269). New York: John Wiley & Sons.

Zimmerman, H.-J. (1996). *Fuzzy set theory and its applications*. Kluwer Academic Publisher.

KEY TERMS

Alarm System: It is a monitoring system that provides alarms in case of some faulty component.

Choquet Integral: The Choquet integral is a mathematical method for aggregating criteria that allows selecting an alternative that takes into account synergies between criteria.

Fuzzy Inference Systems: These are rule-based systems capable of drawing conclusions from given uncertain evidence to reach a decision using approximate reasoning.

Fuzzy Sets: Fuzzy sets is a set theory approach in which set membership is less precise than having objects strictly in or out of the set.

Linguistic Variable: It is a mathematical representation of semantic concepts that includes more than one term (fuzzy set)

Games of Strategy

Geraldine Ryan
University College Cork, Ireland

Seamus Coffey
University College Cork, Ireland

INTRODUCTION

We think strategically whenever there are interactions between our decisions and other people's decisions. In order to decide what we should do, we must first reason through how the other individuals are going to act or react. What are their aims? What options are open to them? In the light of our answers to these questions, we can decide what is the best way for us to act.

Most business situations are interactive in the sense that the outcome of each decision emerges from the synthesis of firm owners, managers, employees, suppliers, and customers. Good decisions require that each decision-maker anticipate the decisions of the others. Game theory offers a systematic way of analysing strategic decision-making in interactive situations. It is a technique used to analyse situations where for two or more individuals the outcome of an action by one of them depends not only on their own action but also on the actions taken by the others (Binmore, 1992; Carmichael, 2005; McMillan, 1992). In these circumstances, the plans or strategies of one individual depend on their expectations about what the others are doing. Such interdependent situations can be compared to games of strategy.

Games can be classified according to a variety of categories, including the timing of the play, the common or conflicting interests of the players, the number of times an interaction occurs, the amount of information available to the players, the type of rules, and the feasibility of coordinated action. Strategic moves manipulate the rules of the game to a player's advantage. There are three types of strategic moves: commitments, threats, and promises. Only a credible strategic move will have the desired effect.

In strategic games, the actions of one individual or group impact(s) on others and, crucially, the individuals involved are aware of this. By exposing the essential features of one situation we can find a hitherto hidden common core to many apparently diverse strategic situations. The aim of this article is to examine the key lessons, which these games can teach us.

BACKGROUND

Game theory began with the publication of *The Theory of Games and Economic Behaviour* by John Von Neumann and Oskar Morgenstern (first published in 1944, second and third editions in 1947 and 1953).[1] Von Neumann and Morgenstern (1944) defined a game as any interaction between agents that is governed by a set of rules specifying the possible moves for each participant and a set of outcomes for each possible combination of moves. They drew an analogy between games like chess, poker, backgammon, and tic-tac-toe with other situations in which participants make decisions that affect each other. Their book provided much of the basic terminology that is still in use today.

The next major contributor to this field was John Nash (1951, 1953). He demonstrated that finite games always have an equilibrium point, at which all players choose actions that are best for them given their opponents' choices. Another key contributor as Thomas Schelling (1960), whose book *The Strategy of Conflict* was among the first to apply the tools of game theory.[2]

In the 1970s, game theory, as a tool for analysing strategic situations, began to be applied to areas such as business, politics, international relations, sociology, psychology, evolution, and biology. In business, for example, the decision-maker must anticipate the reactions of others. Your competitor or employee or supervisor or customer makes decisions that both respond to yours and affect you in some way. The game-theoretic analysis of such actions and reactions is now at the centre of economic research.

Nobel prizes were awarded to John Nash, John Harsanyi, and Reinhard Selton in 1994 for their contributions to game theory and to Thomas Schelling and Robert Aumann in 2005 for their contributions to strategy. Now we are at a point where terms from game theory have become part of the language. As Paul Samuelson says, "to be literate in the modern age, you need to have a general understanding of game theory" (Dixit & Skeath, 1999).

WHAT IS GAME THEORY?

Game theory is not about "playing" as usually understood. It is about conflict among rational but distrusting beings. The nominal inspiration for game theory was poker, a game John von Neumann played occasionally and not especially well. In poker you have to consider what the other players are thinking. This distinguishes game theory from the theory of probability, which also applies to many games. Consider a poker player who naively tries to use probability theory alone to guide his play. The player computes the probability that his hand is better that the other players' hands, and wagers in direct proportion to the strength of the hand. After a number of hands, the other players will know that (say) his willingness to sink 12 chips in the pot means he has at least a three of a kind and will react accordingly. As poker players know, that kind of predictability is bad (a good "poker face" betrays nothing).

Good poker players do not simply play the odds. They take into account the conclusions other players will draw from their actions, and sometimes try to deceive other players. Von Neumann realised that this devious way of playing was both rational and amenable to rigorous analysis. Game theory is based on simple concepts and these are introduced and illustrated with the following example.

CAKE DIVISION

How can a parent divide a cake between two bold children? No matter how carefully a parent divides it, one child (or both!) feels he has been slighted with the smaller piece. The solution is to let one child divide the cake and let the other choose which piece she wants. Rationality and self interest ensures fair division. The first child cannot object that the cake was divided unevenly because he did it himself. The second child cannot complain since she has her choice of pieces.

This homely example is not only a game in von Neumann's sense, but it is also about the simplest illustration of the "minimax" principle upon which game theory is based. The cake problem is a conflict of interest. Both children want the same thing—as much of the cake as possible. The ultimate division of the cake depends both on how one child cuts the cake and which piece the other child chooses. It is important that each child anticipates what the other will do. This is what makes the situation a game.

Game theory searches for solutions—rational outcomes—of games. Dividing the cake evenly is the best strategy for the first child, since he anticipates that the other child's strategy will be to take the biggest piece. Equal division of the cake is therefore the solution to this game. This solution does not depend on a child's generosity or sense of fair play. It is enforced by both children's self interest. Game theory seeks solutions of precisely this sort.

GAMES AS TREES

Many games take place as a sequence of moves by the players. The point of decision can be represented diagrammatically as a square or node with each possible choice represented by a line emanating from that node. In the cake division game, the child cutting the cake faces two options: cut the cake as evenly as possible or make a non-even split. The second child face the options: take the larger piece or take the smaller piece. These give four possible outcomes. As the number of possible moves increases, the diagram branches out like a tree (see Figure 1).

Now that we have a complete picture of our simple game, we can determine the solution by looking for the "rational" choices by working backwards from the final outcomes. We know that the second child will always choose the larger piece so that eliminates outcomes 2 and 4. The first child then starts with a choice between outcome 1 and outcome 3. Clearly one is the preferred choice and the non-even split is eliminated. This process shows what the solution to this game will be for any pair of rational self interested players.

This can be done for almost any two-person game with no hidden information. The main restriction is that the game must be finite. It cannot go on forever,

Figure 1. Games as trees

		OUTCOMES	
		Child 1	Child 2
Even → 2 → Big	1.	Half less a crumb	Half plus a crumb
Even → 2 → Small	2.	Half plus a crumb	Half less a crumb
Non-even → 2 → Big	3.	Small piece	Big piece
Non-even → 2 → Small	4.	Big piece	Small piece

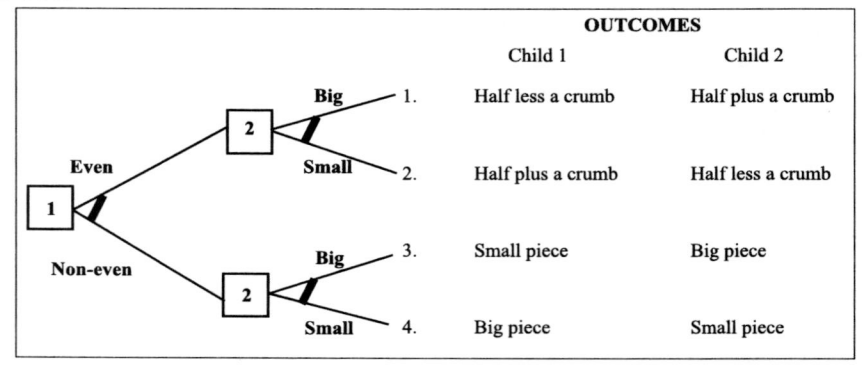

Table 1.

		Chooser's Strategies	
		Bigger Piece	**Smaller Piece**
Cutter's Strategies	Even Cut	Half minus a crumb, Half plus a crumb,	Half plus a crumb, Half minus a crumb,
	Non-even Cut	Small piece, Big piece	Big piece, Small piece

and the number of distinct choices at any move must also be finite. Otherwise we cannot determine the final outcomes to work back from.

GAMES AS TABLES

There is another way of looking at games, one far more useful in game theory. A game is equivalent to a table of possible outcomes for each possible strategy available to a player. The table must have as many rows as one player has strategies and a column for each of the other player's strategies. The trick is deciding which strategy to choose. The table gets all the facts out in the open, but this is not always enough. Neither player gets to choose the outcome he wants, only the column it appears in. The other player's choice makes an equal contribution. This puts the games beyond the scope of probability theory. The players would be wrong to assume that their opponent's choice is determined by chance. Chance has nothing to do with it. The players can be expected to do their very best to deduce the other's choice and prepare for it.

One of the few terms from game theory that has entered general parlance is "zero-sum game." This refers to a game where the total payoffs are fixed: one player's gain is another player's loss. The sum of the outcomes is zero. A two-person, zero-sum game is "total war" in which one player can win only if the other loses. No cooperation is possible.

The children in our cake division example are playing a zero-sum game. More cake for one means less for the other. A pay-off table of the outcomes looks like Table 1. The row players payoffs, the Cutter, are listed first followed by the column player, the Chooser.

We already know what to expect of this game. The cutter will split the cake evenly, or try as best he can. The chooser will pick the bigger piece. The result is the upper left cell.

If the cutter could have his pick of any of the four possible outcomes, he would want to end up with a big piece (lower right cell). He realises that this is not realistic as he knows what to expect from the chooser; namely, the worst—as small a piece as possible.

The cutter is empowered to decide only the row of the cake division outcome. He expects to end up with the least amount of cake in that row, for the chooser will act to minimise the cutter's piece. Therefore he acts to *maximise the minimum* the chooser will leave him. This amount, the maximum row minimum, is called the "maximin." This principle helps make sense of more difficult two-person zero-sum game.

What if the sequence in the cake division was reversed? What if the chooser had to announce her strategy first? Would this change the natural outcome? The solution to the cake division game is for each player to

Games of Strategy

have a "pure" strategy. The chooser will always pick the bigger piece and the cutter will always make an even cut. For some games the rational solution involves a random choice of each strategy or a "mixed" strategy. Again a simple example illustrates the point.

In "Matching Pennies" two players simultaneously place a penny on a table—heads up or tails up (see Nash, 1951). When the pennies match, the first player gets to keep both pennies. If the pennies do not match, the second player gets both (see Figure 2).

Is there a pure strategy that the players should follow? Obviously, it all depends on what the other player will do. If you knew what the other player was going to do, you would know what to do—and vice versa. The best way to play is to pick heads and tails randomly (with 50% probability each, if the payoff change these probabilities change accordingly). The payoff to the random mixed strategy in this game is zero. With this strategy the payoff table is shown in Table 3.

Using the maximin principle, we see that each player will choose the random strategy, even if each has to announce his strategy first. Heads and tails each have a minimum of minus one. The random strategy has an average payoff of zero, no matter what the other player does. Thus the random strategy has the maximum minimum. The lower right cell is the natural outcome. Both players adopt a mixed strategy.

Of course, this would appear to be only a confirmation of common knowledge. However, other games are not quite so simple, and for them game theory can crank out impeccably correct prescriptions that are by no means common sense. Using the maximin principle, von Neumann and Morgenstern (1944) proved that *every* finite, two-person, zero-sum game has a rational solution in the form of a pure or mixed strategy. It is a rational solution in that both parties can convince themselves that they cannot expect to do any better, given the nature of the conflict.

After von Neumann, the next major figure in game theory was John Nash. Nash's work was primarily concerned with non-zero sum games and games of three players or more. Nash proved that natural solutions also exist for non-zero-sum two-person games. It might seem that when two persons' interest are *not* completely opposed—where by their actions they can increase the common good—it would be even easier to come to a rational solution. In fact, it is often harder, and such solutions may be less satisfying.

Nash's approach emphasises "equilibrium points" (Nash, 1950). These are outcomes where the players have no regrets and would not change their strategy given how the other player played. If everybody is happy with the way they played, then that outcome is a Nash equilibrium point. We now turn to game theory's most famous noncooperative game.

THE ORIGINAL PRISONERS' DILEMMA

John and Liam have been arrested under the suspicion of having robbed the Bank of Arcadia and are placed in separate isolation cells. Both care much more about their personal freedom than about the welfare of their accomplice. The police have insufficient evidence for a conviction; visit each of the prisoners to offer them the same deal: You may choose to confess or remain

Table 2.

		Player 2	
		Heads	Tails
Player 1	Heads	Up a penny, Down a penny	Down a penny, Up a penny
	Tails	Down a penny, Up a penny	Up a penny, Down a penny

Table 3. Payoff table

		Player 2		
		Heads	Tails	Random
Player 1	Heads	Up a penny, down a penny	Down a penny, Up a penny	0,0
	Tails	Down a penny, Up a penny	Up a penny, Down a penny	0,0
	Random	0,0	0,0	0,0

Table 4.

	John Confesses	**John Denies**
Liam Confesses	Both serve 4 years	Liam goes free, John serves 10 years
Liam Denies	Liam serves 10 year, John goes free	Both serve 1 year

silent. If you confess and your accomplice remains silent I will drop all charges against you and use your testimony to ensure that your accomplice receives the full 10-year sentence. Likewise, if your accomplice confesses while you remain silent, he will go free while you do the time. If you both confess, I get two convictions, but I will see to it that you both get early releases after 4 years. If you both remain silent, I will have to settle for 1 year sentences on firearms possession charges.[3]

Each prisoner must make the choice of whether to betray the other or to remain silent. The dilemma resides in the fact that each prisoner has a choice between only two options, but cannot make a good decision without knowing what the other one will do. So the question this dilemma poses is: What will happen? How will the prisoners act? A one-shot, two-player prisoners' dilemma can be summarized as shown in Table 4.

The dilemma arises when one assumes that both prisoners only care about minimising their own jail terms. Each prisoner has two strategies: to cooperate with his accomplice and deny, or to betray his accomplice and confess. The outcome of each choice depends on the choice of the accomplice.

The problem with the prisoners' dilemma is that if both decision-makers were purely rational, they would never cooperate. Indeed, rational decision-making means that each prisoner makes the decision that is best for them, regardless of what the other prisoner decides. Let us assume that Liam is working out his best move. Liam's strategy will depend on John's actions. If John denies then Liam's best move is to confess as he then walks free instead of receiving the minor sentence. If, on the other hand, John confesses, then it is rational for Liam to confess, as this will ensure that he receives a relatively lesser sentence than he would have received had he stayed silent. As a result, Liam's pure or dominant strategy is to confess regardless of what John does. If John is rational, then his dominant strategy is also to confess. The Nash equilibrium is therefore for both prisoners to confess, thus leaving them with a suboptimal outcome, and each spending 2 years in jail.

If reasoned from the perspective of the optimal outcome, the correct choice would be for John and Liam to cooperate with each other and deny the allegations, as this would reduce the total jail time served. Any other decision would be worse for the two prisoners considered together. When the prisoners both confess, each prisoner achieves a worse outcome than if they had denied. This demonstrates that in a non-zero sum game the Pareto optimum and the Nash equilibrium can be opposite.

The only way to achieve the Pareto optimal solution in the one-shot Prisoners' Dilemma is if a prior agreement to deny is somehow enforceable. This would clearly be in the prisoner's joint interests. Unless the agreement to deny is enforced in some way, the incentive for both prisoners to confess is so strong that neither can trust the other to keep to any agreement. One possible way this enforcement could be achieved would be to punish confession after the event so as to make "Deny" the dominant strategy. However, this would change the payoffs of the game and it would no longer be a Prisoners' Dilemma.

Resolving the Prisoners' Dilemma

A significant amount of research on the Prisoners' Dilemma relates to evidence of collusion and cooperative behaviour. This type of behaviour contradicts the theoretical prediction. For example, large firms can and do collude. Camerer (2003) points out that people playing one-shot Prisoners' Dilemma games cooperate around 50% of the time.

How can such behaviour be explained? A number of possible answers have been suggested in the academic literature. First, it may be possible for the players to make an enforceable or binding agreement to secure the cooperative outcome. This would, in turn, lower the pay-offs from noncooperative behaviour or it could change the payoffs of the game so that it is no longer a prisoners' dilemma. The agreements could be enforced by the threat of punishment, either by a third party, the legal system, or through government imposed penalties (Carmichael, 2005).

Second, if a game is repeated (or iterated) then, intuitively, the players should have more of an incentive to cooperate, as the decisions taken by players in any period can now be related to decisions made by the other player in the previous iteration. Each player now has to consider what he stands to lose in the future if he defects now and if that defection causes the other player to defect in the future. Repetition means that players need to choose long-term strategies that take their future pay-offs into account. They also have time to learn about the game and about each other. In the Iterated Prisoners' Dilemma, players have an opportunity to "punish" the other player for noncooperative behaviour, thus, cooperation becomes a viable strategy. If there are enough repetitions of the game, then the possibility of higher pay-offs in the future as a result of earlier cooperative behaviour could outweigh the short-term gains from defection (see Kreps, Milgrom, Roberts, & Wilson, 1982; Rabin, 1993).

Prisoners' Dilemmas arise in a variety of contexts: policy setting, labour arbitration, international trade and investment, evolutionary biology, product pricing, and environmental decision-making. Take, for example, two rival companies trying to decide whether to set a high price or a low price for each of their products. The dilemma facing the companies is identical to the Prisoners' Dilemma. The best strategy is to set a high price. However, in the absence of enforcement mechanisms there is an incentive for one company to cheat. If companies both set either a high price or a low price then they will share the market with high and low profits, respectively. However, if one company sets a high price and the other a low price, then the company setting the low price will attract all of the consumers, thus stealing all of its' rivals profits.

In a once off game or a finitely repeated game, the only rational solution is for both companies to set a low price and share the consumers. In reality this is an infinitely repeated game and companies try to avoid these "price-war" type dilemmas. Instead they try to differentiate themselves from their rivals by branding their goods, targeting different customers, and using loyalty building schemes (McMillan, 1992).

The importance of reputation building and morality judgement has led to the development of theories of indirect reciprocity. These theories show how cooperation in larger groups can emerge when the cooperators can build a reputation (Nowak & Sigmund, 1998). These theories are very important in e-commerce applications where strangers interact online and exchange large amounts of resources. They highlight the importance of building trust and gaining a good reputation. This is especially important in growing online auction markets. For example, e-Bay recognised that Prisoners' Dilemma cooperation failures only apply in a one-shot transaction and so they instituted a reputation system so that the shadow of the future is cast on each transaction. Reputation systems like those from e-Bay are analysed in terms of their effect on the value of transactions in auctions. Among the transactions within e-Bay, less than 1% of the feedback is negative (Resnick, Zeckhauser, Swanson, & Lockwood, 2006).

CONCLUSION AND FUTURE RESEARCH

The Prisoners' Dilemma, over the past half century, has been both an inspiration to the development of new game theory ideas, and a paradox to critique it. The attraction of the Prisoners' Dilemma lies in its role as a simple, well studied mathematical game which models the key elements of a broad range of self interest vs. group interest scenarios. The repeated Prisoners' Dilemma captures the essence of a broad range of conflict and cooperation models where repeated interaction between the same agents plays a significant role.

One stream of current research is focusing on finding conventions of retaliation and reconciliation that allow the success of a strategy to depend on it being firm but forgiving (see Pattison, 2005). This is important for business, especially in tightly networked and highly interdependent areas such as the computer industry. Future research is likely to apply these or similar conventions to common distributed systems problems of network routing, congestion control, file sharing, peer to peer networking, and grind computing in the situations where the interests of the individual network user are in conflict with those of the group.

REFERENCES

Binmore, K. (1992). *Fun and games: A text on game theory*. Lexington, MA: D.C. Heath and Company.

Camerer, C. F. (2003). *Behavioural game theory: Experiments in strategic interaction*. Princeton, NJ: Princeton University Press.

Carmichael, F. (2005). *A guide to game theory*. Pearson Education Limited.

Dixit, A. K., & Skeath, S. (1999). *Games of strategy*. New York: Norton.

Flood, M. (1952). *Some experimental games*. Santa Monica, CA: Rand, RM-798, Rand Corporation.

Kreps, D.M., Milgrom, P., Roberts, J., & Wilson, R. (1982). Rational cooperation in the finitely repeated prisoners dilemma. *Journal of Economic Theory, 27*, 245-252.

McMillan, J. (1992). *Games, strategies and managers—how managers can use game theory to make better decisions*. Oxford University Press.

Nash, J. F. (1950). Equilibrium points in n-person games. In *Proceedings of the National Academy of Sciences of the United States of America*.

Nash, J. F. (1951). Non-cooperative games. *Annals of Mathematics, 54*, 286-295.

Nash, J. F. (1953). Two-person cooperative games. *Econometrica, 18*, 155-162.

Nowak, M. A., & Sigmund, K. (1998). Evolution of indirect reciprocity by image scoring. *Nature, 393*, 573-577.

Pattison, M. (2005) *An investigation of retaliation and reconciliation conventions in the repeated prisoner's dilemma, with implementation noise*. Unpublished manuscript, University of Melbourne, Melbourne, Australia.

Poundstone, W. (1992). *Prisoner's dilemma*. Sydney, Australia: Doubleday.

Rabin, M. (1993). Incorporating fairness into game theory and economics. *American Economic Review, 83*, 394-415.

Resnick, P., Zeckhauser, R., Swanson, J., & Lockwood, K. (2006). The value of reputation on e-bay: A controlled experiment. *Experimental Economics, 9*(2), 79-101.

Schelling, T. (1960). The strategy of conflict. Cambridge, MA: Harvard University Press

Von Neumann, J., & Morgenstern, O. (1944). *Theory of games and economic behaviour.* Princeton, NJ: Princeton University Press.

KEY TERMS

Common Knowledge: A fact is common knowledge if all players know it and know that they all know it, and so on. The structure of the game is often assumed to be common knowledge among the players.

Dominant Strategy: A strategy dominates another strategy of a player if it always gives a better payoff to that player, regardless of what the other players are doing. It weakly dominates the other strategy if it is always at least as good.

Game Theory: Game theory is the formal study of decision-making where several players must make choices that potentially affect the interests of the other players.

Maximin: Maximin is solely a one-person game strategy, that is, a principle which may be used when a person's "competition" is nature or chance. It involves choosing the best of the worst possible outcomes.

Mixed Strategy: A mixed strategy is an active randomisation with given probabilities that determine the player's decision.

Nash Equilibrium: A Nash Equilibrium, also called strategic equilibrium, is a list of strategies, one for each player, which has the property that no player can unilaterally change his strategy and get a better payoff.

Payoff: A payoff is a number, also called utility, that reflects the desirability of an outcome to a player, for whatever reason. When the outcome is random,

Games of Strategy

payoffs are usually weighted with their probabilities. The expected payoff incorporates the player's attitude towards risk.

Perfect Information: A game has perfect information when, at any point in time, only one player makes a move and knows all the actions that have been made until then.

Probability Theory: The use of statistics to analyze past predictable patterns and to reduce risk in future plans.

Rationality: A player is said to be rational if he seeks to play in a manner which maximises his own payoff. It is often assumed that the rationality of all players is common knowledge.

Zero-Sum Game: A game is said to be zero-sum if, for any outcome, the sum of the payoffs to all players is zero. In a two-player zero-sum game, one player's gain is the other player's loss, so their interests are diametrically opposed.

ENDNOTES

[1] Later on, after the creation of game theory, it became apparent that earlier economists, among them Cournot, Bertrand, Edgeworth and Stackelberg, had found solutions to games, too.

[2] It has been suggested Stanley Kubrick used John von Neumann as the basis for the Dr. Strangelove character in the 1964 Oscar nominated film of the same name. Nuemann attended several nuclear conflict conferences in a wheel chair. The film uses many commonly used game theory concepts in humorously exploring the Cold War. John Nash was the subject of the 2001 Oscar winning film A Beautiful Mind which was based on the novel of the same name by Sylvia Nasar.

[3] This situation is set up and described as a Prisoners' Dilemma in the 2002 film Murder by Numbers when two suspects are arrested and questioned on suspicion of murder.

Goal Programming and Its Variants

John Wang
Montclair State University, USA

Dajin Wang
Montclair State University, USA

Aihua Li
Montclair State University, USA

INTRODUCTION

Within the realm of multicriteria decision making (MCDM) exists a powerful method for solving problems with multiple objectives. Goal programming (GP) was the first multiple-objective technique presented in the literature (Dowlatshahi, 2001). The premise of GP traces its origin back to a linear programming study on executive compensation in 1955 by Charnes, Cooper, and Ferguson even though the specific name did not appear in publications until the 1961 textbook entitled *Management Models and Industrial Applications of Linear Programming*, also by Charnes and Cooper (Schniederjans, 1995). Initial applications of this new type of modeling technique demonstrated its potential for a variety of applications in numerous different areas. Until the middle of the 1970s, GP applications reported in the literature were few and far between. Since that time, primarily due to influential works by Lee and Ignizio, a noticeable increase of published GP applications and technical improvements has been recognized. The number of case studies, along with the range of fields, to which GP has been and still is being applied is impressive, as shown in surveys by Romero (1991) and Aouni and Kettani (2001). It can be said that GP has been, and still is, the "most widely used multi-criteria decision making technique" (Tamiz, Jones, & Romero, 1998, p. 570).

BACKGROUND

The GP model is a simple extension and modification of the linear programming technique that provides a simultaneous solution of a system of complex objectives rather than a single one (Munhoz & Morabito, 2002).

[It] is a technique used for optimizing problems that have multiple conflicting criteria. In goal programming, each objective is assigned a target level and a relative importance of achieving that target. It then finds an optimal solution that comes as close as possible to the target values. One significant difference between goal programming and other types of modeling is the use of goal constraints in addition to real constraints. A goal constraint is different from a real constraint in that the former is set equal to a target level that does not have to be achieved. With the introduction of deviational variables, the program can still reach a feasible solution without achieving the target level. (Nichols & Ravindran, 2004, p. 323)

GP provides a more satisfactory treatment of a problem where, in many cases, problems can still be solved using standard linear programming algorithms: "The overall objective of goal programming is to minimize the deviations between goal achievement and desired aspiration levels" (Henry & Ravindran, 2005, p. 112).

Two main types of models exist within GP: preemptive and weighted (nonpreemptive). Preemptive programming, also known as lexicographic GP, involves establishing goals in order of importance, from the most important to the least. Then, the objective function is optimized for each goal one at a time. According to Scott, Deckro, and Chrissis (2005, p. 96), "In 1965, Ijiri introduced preemptive priority factors as a way of ranking goals in the objective function of the linear goal programming model and established the assignment of relative weights to goals in the same priority level." Nichols and Ravindran (2004) argued that weighted GP is "similar to preemptive goal programming in that the objective is to minimize the amount of deviation from each specific goal. However, a weight (penalty) is used to quantify how important each goal is with respect to the other goals, instead of an established hierarchical priority level" (p. 324). Penalty functions were introduced in 1980 by Kvanli, using an interval target rather than a fixed target. These penalties are assessed when over- and/or underdeviations of goal achievement occurs. The objective then is to minimize the total penalties in satisfying the entire model. The idea of penalty functions makes the model more realistic and flexible, and has been applied to many real-world applications (Panda, Banerjee, & Basu, 2005).

After the model has been optimized and goal values have been met, sensitivity analysis can be used to evaluate its effectiveness and identify problem areas. Investigative areas include changes in the weighting of priority levels, changes of the weighting of deviation variables within a given priority level, changes in right-hand-side values, and reordering preemptive priorities.

MAIN FOCUS

Strengths and Weaknesses

Ease and flexibility, a wide variety of uses, and the compatibility of GP with subsequent analysis methods have all been identified as strengths of the modeling technique. GP is an extension of linear mathematical programming and, therefore, is easy to understand and easy to apply. It brings simplicity and ease of use by simultaneously handling a large number of variables, constraints, and objectives. Therefore, the model can be performed over and over again, adjusting the goals, objectives, and weights in order to obtain the decision maker's ideal solution. In this regard, it is a technique similar to both compromise programming and the reference-point methods of problem solving.

GP can also be applied to a large variety of uses from almost any industry and also for global applications. Some of the most common fields involved in the application of GP techniques include agriculture, engineering, financial investment planning, production, natural resources management, land-use planning, and human resources. Specific examples within these fields involve bank asset allocation, employee scheduling, and component production within a supply chain. GP can also be used in combination with other decision-making applications. Also, the two main types of GP themselves can be used in combination. For example, the user can begin with weighted GP and then double-check the conclusions by running the preemptive GP approach as well.

With all the clear benefits and efficiencies that GP brings, it does not come without some surrounding criticism. The main weakness of GP is the tendency for the solution obtained to be Pareto inefficient. Pareto inefficiencies occur when the achieved level of any one objective can be improved without negatively impacting the achieved level of any other objective. However, this is only a problem if alternative optimum solutions are presented (Caballero & Hernández, 2006). In order to change the inefficient solution to an efficient result, one must first safeguard each objective against degradation by placing upper and lower bounds on the deviational variables. These inefficiencies can be resolved by applying efficiency detection and restoration techniques.

There are three common restoration methods to resolve the issue of Pareto inefficient results when using GP. The first method, straight restoration, simply finds the maximization of the sum of the unweighted deviation variables of the inefficient objectives. The second method, preference-based restoration, finds the sum of the unwanted deviational variables and penalizes these a second time. The third method, interactive restoration, involves the decision maker at this stage, hence the name. He or she chooses the one single inefficient objective that they would like to see become the most improved (Tamiz et al., 1998).

Another criticism or weakness of GP is the challenge of assigning appropriate weights to the objectives. Weights are assigned to the objectives for two purposes. It is often difficult for the decision maker to determine a goal for each objective, causing inaccuracies in the input and therefore in the results. The first purpose is to normalize the goals and the second one is to indicate the decision makers' preferences with respect to each goal. One way this can be controlled is by using the analytic hierarchy principle (AHP) or analytic network principle (ANP). This method determines weights by a pair-wise comparison. Another method of assigning appropriate weights is that of a totally interactive approach by the decision maker. This reflects back to one of the strengths of GP. One of the benefits is ease of use, which enables the user to run the model repeatedly, making adjustments to the goals, objectives, weights, and so forth as he or she goes along. This is where the decision maker would be involved. The user can run the application, review the results, make any adjustments, and complete the model as many times as is necessary to obtain the optimal result.

Yet another method of assigning appropriate weights is called a naive prioritization approach. This approach can be used to assign weights, after which redundancy checking can be performed. Those goals that prove redundant can be due to an excessive number of priority levels, targets set equal or close to the ideal variables, or a goal where both the deviational variables are penalized (two-sided goal). Identifying redundancy is much easier than resolving it.

A final weakness of GP is the tendency to have incommensurable results, a common and frequent occurrence. Many times the necessary inputs do not have a common unit of measurement. Incommensurable results occur when objectives with deviational variables measured in different units are summed directly. This causes bias toward objectives with larger magnitudes and, therefore, misleading results.

There are five main methods to resolve the tendency of incommensurable results. The first is to simply divide each objective by a normalization constraint. A second method that can achieve normalization or correction of incommensurable results is percentage normalization. Percentage normalization ensures that all deviations are measured on a percentage scale. A third normalization method uses a Euclidean norm coefficient. However, this does not restore the original significance to the final achievement function value. A fourth method is the summation normalization method. This method is better than the Euclidean method when scaling a badly incommensurable problem. However, like the Euclidean method, it does not restore original significance to the final achievement function value. In the fifth method, the zero-one normalization method, the constant "is equal to the distance between the target value and the worst possible value for the relevant deviation variable within the feasible set defined by the hard constraints in the model" (Tamiz et al., 1998, p. 573).

Mathematical Descriptions for Two Basic GPs

Consistent with Schniederjans (1984, 2001), the GP objective function is commonly expressed in minimization form as:

$$\text{minimize } Z = \sum_{i=1}^{T} w_{kl} P_k (d_i^- + d_i^+)$$
$$\text{for } k = 1,..,K; l = 1,...,L,$$

where i is the goal constraint index, k is the priority rank index, and l is the index of the deviation variables within priority rank. In the objective function, Z is the summation of all deviations, the w_{kl} are optional mathematical weights used to differentiate deviation variables within a kth priority level, the P_k are optional rankings of deviation variables within goal constraints, the d_i^- values are the negative deviational variables, and the d_i^+ values are the positive deviational variables. The P_k rankings are called preemptive priorities because they establish an ordinal priority ranking (where $P_1 > P_2 > P_3 >$...etc.) that orders the systematic optimization of the deviation variables.

The fact that the optimization of the variables in the objective function is ordered by the preemptive priority ranking has given rise to the use of the term satisficing. This term results from the fact that a solution in a GP model satisfies the ranking structure while minimizing deviation from goals. One of the best features of GP is that the P_k permit the decision makers to rank goals in accordance with their personal preferences, and even weight the importance of those preferences within goals using w_{kl}. The greater the w_{kl} mathematical weighting, the greater the importance attached to its related deviation variable.

The goal constraints in a GP model can be expressed as:

$$\sum^{T} a_{ij} x_j + d_i^- - d_i^+ = b_i \quad \text{for all i.}$$

Here, the a_{ij} values are the resource utilization rates representing the per-unit usage of the related resource b_i, and the x_j are decision variables we seek to determine. The goal constraints in a GP model are used to express goals that we seek to achieve by minimizing deviation (in the form of deviation variables) from their right-hand-side b_i goal targets. In essence, this use of deviation variables minimizes the absolute difference between the right- and left-hand sides of each constraint. The d_i^- are termed underachievement variables, and the d_i^+ are overachievement variables. The nonnegativity requirements in a GP model are usually expressed as

$$(x_j, d_i^-, d_i^+) \geq 0 \quad \text{for all } i,j.$$

When preemptive priorities are not established, the GP model takes on the form

minimize $z = \sum (w_i^- d_i^- + w_i^+ d_i^+)$

subject to: $\sum a_{ij} x_j + d_i^- - d_i^+ = b_i$ for all i

$(x_j, d_i^-, d_i^+) \geq 0$ for all i,j.

The w_i^+ and w_i^- are positive, negative, or zero weights. A constraint may not be a goal constraint in that we can let $d_i^- = d_i^+ = 0$ if the condition must be met exactly, as, for example, a fixed-budget condition.

Golokolosova and Meshechkin (2007) introduced a basic weighted model of GP. Their methods of goal programming included groups of methods for the decision of a vector problem of mathematical programming that assume the presence of a definite purpose $\overline{F} = \{\overline{f}_k, k = \overline{1,K}\}$ for each criterion. Using values of the purposes $\overline{f}_k, k = \overline{1,K}$, it will be transformed into a problem of goal programming that can be represented as the minimization of the sum of deviations with normalized weights:

$$\min d(F(X)\ \overline{F}) = (\sum_{k=1}^{K} w_k |f_k(X) - \overline{f}_k|^p)^{1/p},$$
$$X \in S,$$

where $\overline{F} = \{\overline{f}_k, k = \overline{1,K}\}$ is a vector of the purposes; $W = \{w_k, k = \overline{1,K}\}$ is a vector of weights by $k \in K$ criterion, usually $\sum_{k=1}^{K} w_k = 1$, $w_k \geq 0$, $k = \overline{1,K}$;

factors p lay within the limits of $1 \leq p \leq \infty$; and $d(\cdot)$ represents the distance between $F(X)$ and $\overline{F}$. Vectors of the purposes $\overline{F}$ and weights W are set, and depending on the change of value $1 \leq p \leq \infty$, there are various cases of use of goal programming.

The shortcomings of the considered methods are as follows:

1. For each criterion, values $|f_k(X) - \overline{f}_k|$, $\forall\ k \in K$ are not commensurable among themselves.

2. The problem of weights w^k, $k = \overline{1,K}$ is not solved.

Variants of GP and New Theoretical Breakthrough

In line with the Committee on Stochastic Programming (COSP, 2006), stochastic GP is a framework for modeling optimization problems that involve uncertainty, as the definition of the word stochastic means involving randomness or probability. Real-world problems almost invariably include some unknown parameters. Stochastic programming models are similar in style but take advantage of the fact that probability distributions governing the data are known or can be estimated. The goal here is to find some policy that is feasible for all (or almost all) the possible data instances and that maximizes the expectation of some function of the decisions and the random variables. More generally, such models are formulated, solved analytically or numerically, and analyzed in order to provide useful information to a decision maker.

The most widely applied and studied stochastic programming models are two-stage linear programs. Here the decision maker takes some action in the first stage, after which a random event occurs affecting the outcome of the first-stage decision. A recourse decision can then be made in the second stage that compensates for any bad effects that might have been experienced as a result of the first-stage decision. The optimal policy from such a model is a single first-stage policy and a collection of recourse decisions (a decision rule) defining which second-stage action should be taken in response to each random outcome. An alternative modeling approach uses so-called chance constraints. These do not require that decisions are feasible for (almost) every outcome of the random parameters, but require feasibility with at least some specified probability. Stochastic models are applied most often to portfolio management and asset allocation problems.

Fuzzy GP is another method that can be used to compute an optimal portfolio. According to Faheem, Konkati, and Kumar (2006, p.1),

The fuzzy goal programming model incorporates aspiration levels, and intervals in the decision making process to optimize multiple objectives. The linear and continuous membership functions quantify the aspiration levels and the solution does not change from one decision maker to another. In addition, the model yields an efficient compromise solution for overall degree of satisfaction with multiple fuzzy goals.

This model is useful when imprecision exists in the selected variables as opposed to true randomness. The decision maker can interact with the system and modify the fuzzy data and model parameters until a satisfactory solution is obtained.

Min-max GP is similar to the weighted GP approach, but instead of minimizing the weighted sum of deviations from targets, the maximum deviation of any goal from target is minimized (Deb, 2001). Another complex variant of GP involves linear fractional functions; however, it is not widely reported on in the literature (Caballero & Hernández, 2006). Interactive GP involves decisions to be made amongst the goal achievement optimization process. This variant method has relevant applications in airline scheduling, supply chain management, and call center operations (Golany, Xia, Yang, & Yu, 2002).

Khorramshahgol and Steiner (1988) were able to integrate GP with the Delphi method through a decision support system to attain estimates of preferential weights. By merging GP with other commonly used and proven techniques in the mix, it is obvious that a better solution will arise. This will especially appeal to decision makers who cannot settle for any solution less than the best. This combination of methods will improve the chances of the end result being the optimal solution because it was derived using an application stronger than goal programming alone. This should also attract decision makers because their preferred solution will be based on more than just the tried and true success of one method on its own.

The use of nonlinear GP is also a theoretical application for this procedure. Although GP is mainly used with linear achievement functions, goals, and constraints in linear cases, this method can also be applied to nonlinear cases as well. A particular type of nonlinear GP is fractional GP, in which the objective value that is attained from a linear function is divided by another linear function (Tamiz et al., 1998). Broadening the types of cases where GP can be applied helps to add to the flexibility that the method is widely known and praised for. This serves to increase the validity of GP because it shows that the process can be used over a wide variety of applications. It also illustrates that GP is even reliable in uses other than for which it was intentionally developed. A method such as this that can extend itself over time to many different situations proves to be a worthy application that will continually be examined for prospective uses.

One such especially appealing future application of GP is employing it as a statistical tool in the estimation process. Recent studies have shown that GP would be a suitable alternative to standard statistical applications because of its flexibility. These flexible modeling procedures allow the decision maker to incorporate his or her knowledge and experience into the model's parameters (Aouni & Kettani, 2001). This likely future use of GP is important because it shows that this method is as valuable and effective as other major applications within statistics.

A new GP method that utilizes partitioning as an application to solve the problem is the partitioning Nelder-Mead complex. By using this method, the first objective is to solve for the first goal. Then, if the value that was targeted for the first goal is reached, the problem continues on to the second goal. However, if the first goal's target value is not reached, then the problem will stop. If the desired value is attained, then the first goal now becomes a real constraint. At this point, the problem is solved again using the complex search method, however, this time solving only for the second goal. Once again, if the targeted value for the second goal is reached, then this goal will become another constraint in the problem. This process of solving for the specified goal in order to attain the desired target level will continue until it becomes impossible to solve for a specific goal without violating one of the previous constraints (Kuriger & Ravindran, 2005). This method's ability to solve for a goal and then use the goal as a constraint after the target value has been attained allows for the constraints to be much more accurately derived. In addition, since the problem is stopped, if the targeted value of the current goal is not met, then this allows for a more rigid quality structure to be in practice in regard to the use of the method.

Main Applications of GP

In 1977, Charnes and Cooper claimed GP to be "the most powerful and easy to use 'workhorse'" (as cited in Aouni & Kettani, 2001). As evidenced by the bulk of literature on theory and applications in the field, GP has become, by far, the most popular technique for addressing linear multiobjective problems (MOPs; Carrizosa & Fliege, 2001). Romero (1991) has categorized a bibliography of over 355 papers just on applications alone. Schniederjans (1995) developed a comprehensive bibliography of 979 GP journal research publications, which represents nearly all of the population of GP articles published in the English language between 1961 and 1993. However, he has also determined a life cycle for research on the topic and detected a decline in the early '90s with regard to theoretical developments. The turn of the century has brought a revival of literature again, with numerous published papers dealing with variants of GP and an impressive range of real-world applications. Aouni and Kettani reported that the field of GP is "alive more than ever, supported by a network of researchers and practitioners continually feeding it with theoretical developments and applications, all with resounding success" (p. 225).

From a stochastic GP program for employee scheduling (Easton & Rossin, 1996) to land use planning in agricultural system (Biswas & Pal, 2004), to nonlinear goal programming models quantifying the bullwhip effect in a supply chain based on autoregressive integrated moving average (ARIMA) parameters (Dhahri & Chabchoub, 2007); from forest management optimization models and habitat diversity (Bertomeu & Romero, 2002) to a 0-1 GP model for nurse scheduling (Azaiez & Al Sharif, 2005), to a fuzzy multiobjective covering-based vehicle location model for emergency services (Araz, Selim, & Ozkarahan, 2007), to a robust optimization model for production planning of perishable products (*Leung*, Lai, *Ng*, & *Wu*, 2007), GP has

been applied everywhere. Tamiz et al. (1998) showed that around 21% of GP applications reported in the literature used weighted GP and 64% used nonpreemptive GP. Other variants of the GP method, accounting for the remaining 15% reported in the literature, included stochastic GP, fuzzy GP, and min-max GP, which is also known as the Chebyshev model. Ignizio suggests that "any problem that is a candidate for mathematical programming (optimization) is suitable for GP" (as cited in Scott et al., 2005, p. 96). The first MOP/GP research conference took place in 1994 with 34 papers, and it has continued biannually since then.

FUTURE TRENDS

Based on its wide variety of uses and methods, GP promises to have an interesting future. One such new advancement in the topic is interactive GP. This area uses interactive algorithms because they greatly aid in improving the flexibility of the GP model. By utilizing this method, decision makers are able to use a set of target values and penalty weights that best suits their needs, thus allowing them to become more instrumental in finding an optimal solution. Due to its nature, it becomes clear to see why decision makers would think of interactive GP as a major helper. By allowing an organization's most critical employees to become an integral part in the key decisions to be made, there is an increased likelihood that the solution they agree upon will be the most favorable. The increased flexibility that interactive GP brings along with it enables the key decision makers to assign a set of weights and target values that conform to specific and required desires.

Aouni and Kettani (2001) claimed that another future event that will certainly impact the topic of GP is the use of appropriate software. With only a few exceptions, GP and its many applications do not have the proper software and tools needed to aid in the process of decision making. The lack of suitable software programs that fully support the model indeed restricts the usage of GP. By limiting the software access to GP, this adversely impacts both researchers and general decision makers who would have liked to explore the optimal solution to their proposed problem as well as engaging perhaps in some further applications of GP.

CONCLUSION

GP is a very useful management science technique that can be applied to a variety of real-world situations. Its far-reaching popularity is primarily due to its flexibility and ease of use. While mathematical modeling can be complex, GP is rather logical and sequential. This helps to simplify the process for use either by researchers in academia or by the business community alike.

The advances of the 21st century have produced new challenges involving decision-making systems for managers and researchers. Globalization of the economy exposes an entity to new political, economic, and social systems throughout the world. Advances in networking technology now lead to involvement and input within the decision-making process integrated by more people and groups than ever before. Increased competitiveness and threats of outsourcing now render the need for quick and comprehensive solutions to problems. Now, more than ever, the business world needs models and tools such as GP that can encompass collective decision-making and consensus-based approaches.

REFERENCES

Aouni, B., & Kettani, O. (2001). Goal programming model: A glorious history and a promising future. *European Journal of Operational Research, 133*(2), 225-231.

Araz, C., Selim, H., & Ozkarahan, I. (2007). A fuzzy multi-objective covering-based vehicle location model for emergency services. *Computers & Operations Research, 34*(3), 705-726.

Azaiez, M. N., & Al Sharif, S. S. (2005). A 0-1 goal programming model for nurse scheduling. *Computers & Operations Research, 32*(3), 491-507.

Bertomeu, M. & Romero, C. (2002). Forest management optimization models and habitat diversity: A goal programming approach. *Journal of the Operational Research Society, 53*(11), 1175-1184.

Biswas, A., & Pal, B. B. (2004). Application of fuzzy goal programming technique to land use planning in agricultural system. *Omega: The International Journal of Management Science, 33*(5), 391-398.

Caballero, R., & Hernández, M. (2006). Restoration of efficiency in a goal programming problem with linear fractional criteria. *European Journal of Operational Research, 172*(1), 31-39.

Caballero, R., Luque, M., & Ruiz, F. (2005). MOPEN: A computational package for linear multiobjective and goal programming problems. *Decision Support Systems, 41*(1), 160-175.

Carrizosa, E., & Fliege, J. (2001). Generalized goal programming: Polynomial methods and applications. *Mathematical Programming, 93*(2), 281-303.

Committee on Stochastic Programming (COSP). (2006). *Stochastic programming introduction.* Retrieved July 29, 2007, from http://stoprog.org/index.html

Deb, K. (2001). Nonlinear goal programming using multi-objective genetic algorithms. *Journal of the Operational Research Society, 52*(3), 291-302.

Dhahri, I., & Chabchoub, H. (2007). Nonlinear goal programming models quantifying the bullwhip effect in supply chain based on ARIMA parameters. *European Journal of Operational Research, 177*(3), 1800-1810.

Dowlatshahi, S. (2001). Product life cycle analysis: A goal programming approach. *Journal of the Operational Research Society, 52*(11), 1201-1214.

Easton, F., & Rossin, D. F. (1996). A stochastic goal program for employee scheduling. *Decision Sciences, 27*(3), 541-568.

Faheem, M. I., Konkati, E., & Kumar, V. S. S. (2006). *Multiple fuzzy goal programming approach for optimizing project cost and duration in the construction industry.* Retrieved July 29, 2007, from http://www.itcon.org/cgi-bin/submissions/

Golany, B., Xia, Y., Yang, J., & Yu, G. (2002). An interactive goal programming procedure for operational recovery problems. *Optimization and Engineering, 3*(2), 109-127.

Golokolosova, T. V., & Meshechkin, V. V. (2007). *Operations research.* Retrieved July 29, 2007, from http://www.math.kemsu.ru/faculty/kmc/book/io/4_2_3.doc

Henry, T. M., & Ravindran, A. R. (2005). A goal programming application for army officer accession planning. *INFOR, 43*(2), 111-119.

Khorramshahgol, R., & Steiner, H.M. (1988). Resource analysis in project evaluation: A multicriteria approach. *Journal of Operations Research Society, 39*(9), 795-803.

Kuriger, G., & Ravindran, A. R. (2005). Intelligent search methods for nonlinear goal programming problems. *INFOR, 43*(2), 79-92.

Leung, S. C. H, Lai, K. K., Ng, W.-L., & Wu, Y. (2007). A robust optimization model for production planning of perishable products. *The Journal of the Operational Research Society, 58*(4), 413-422.

Munhoz, J. R., & Morabito, R. (2002). A goal programming model for the analysis of a frozen concentrated orange juice production and distribution systems. *OPSEARCH, 38/39*(6/1), 630-646.

Nichols, T. W., & Ravindran, A. R. (2004, November). Asset allocation using goal programming. In *34th International Conference on Computers & Industrial Engineering*, San Francisco (pp. 321-326).

Panda, S., Banerjee, K., & Basu, M. (2005). Determination of EOQ of multi-item inventory problems through nonlinear goal programming with penalty function. *Asia-Pacific Journal of Operational Research, 22*(4), 539-553.

Romero, C. (1991). *Handbook of critical issues in goal programming*. Oxford: Pergamon Press.

Schniederjans, M. J. (1984). *Linear goal programming*. Princeton, NJ: Petrocelli Books.

Schniederjans, M. J. (1995). The life cycle of goal programming research as recorded in journal articles. *Operations Research, 43*(4), 551-557.

Schniederjans, M. J. (2001). Goal programming. In S. I. Gass & C. M. Harris (Eds.), *Encyclopedia of operations research and management science* (2nd ed.). Kluwer Academic Publishers.

Scott, M. A., Deckro, R. F., & Chrissis, J. W. (2005). Modeling and analysis of multicommodity network flows via goal programming. *INFOR, 43*(2), 93-110.

Tamiz, M., Jones, D., & Romero, C. (1998). Goal programming for decision making: An overview of the current state-of-the-art. *European Journal of Operational Research, 111*(3), 569-581.

KEY TERMS

Deviation Variable: A deviation variable represents the difference in distance between the desired target level and the actual achieved target level.

Goal: This is the specified and definite target level of the objectives.

Goal Programming: It is an extension of linear programming that is capable of handling multiple and conflicting objectives.

Linear Programming: It is a branch of mathematics that uses linear inequalities to solve decision-making problems involving maximums and minimums.

Objective: An objective is an issue of importance that the model should address such as cost, profit, quality, and so forth.

Objective Function: This is the function to be minimized or maximized, representing cost or profit, and so forth.

Pareto Efficient: It is the achieved value of the objective that cannot be improved without negatively affecting the level of another objective.

Penalty Weights: These are the values in weighted GP that measure how critical it is to the model that these values do not contain deviations.

Preemptive or Lexicographic GP: This is a form of GP that ranks each goal according to its specified importance in the overall model.

Priority Level: Priority levels separate the objectives of the model into categories that must be achieved in a particular order.

Weighted GP: A weighted GP is a form of GP that uses penalty weights to find the optimal solution that minimizes the sum of the weights.

Group Verbal Decision Analysis

Alexey Petrovsky
Institute for Systems Analysis – Russian Academy of Sciences, Russia

INTRODUCTION

Ordering and classification of objects by their properties are among the typical problems in multiple criteria decision aiding (MCDA). The difficulties of choice problems increase when the same object may exist in several copies with different attributes' values, and values of different attributes may be repeated within the object description. For example, such situation arises when several experts estimate alternatives upon multiple criteria. In this case, individual expert assessments may be similar, diverse, or contradictory. Various techniques for classification of alternatives or their ranking have been developed. But most of the methods do not pay a serious consideration to contradictions and inconsistencies in decision makers' (DM) preferences and a problem description.

Group verbal decision analysis (GroupVDA) is a new methodological approach in the MCDA area, which enlarges verbal decision analysis (VDA) approach to a group decision. GroupVDA deals with choice problems where preferences of several decision makers may be discordant, and alternatives are described with manifold repeating quantitative and qualitative attributes. New GroupVDA methods are based on the theory of multisets or sets with repeating elements, and represent multi-attribute objects as points in multiset metric spaces.

The main goal of this article is to consider the state-of-the-art methods and models for collective choice of several independent actors. We start with an overview of existing MCDA approaches to collective choice. Then we motivate our respect of group decision method under VDA. In next section we describe a multiset model for representation of multi-attribute objects. It is shown that the theoretical model of multisets is well appropriated for representing and analyzing a collection of objects that are described with many inconsistent quantitative and qualitative attributes and may exist in several copies. Then we introduce GroupVDA methods for searching solution of ordering and classification problems of multi-attribute objects as points in multiset metric spaces. Objects are arranged by closeness with regard to any "ideal" object in any multiset metric space. An objects' classification is built in any multiset metric space in accordance with the generalized classification rule that approximates diverse (and may be contradictory) individual sorting rules of several actors. Finally, we give the short examples of case studies and analyze some perspective of GroupVDA methods.

BACKGROUND

A DM's preference is one of the milestones in the MCDA area. The person expresses his/her preferences when he/she describes properties and characteristics of a problem under analysis, compares decision alternatives, and estimates the quality of choice. Preferences may be represented as decision rules of a mathematical, logical, and/or verbal nature and explained with any language. While solving the problem, a person may behave inconsistently, make errors and contradictions. In the case of individual choice, the consistency of subjective preferences is postulated.

A collective choice of several independent actors is more complicated and principally different due to variety and inconsistency of many subjective preferences. Each of the DMs has his/her own personal goals, interests, valuations, and information sources. As a result, individual subjective judgments of several persons may be similar, concordant, or discordant. Usually, in MCDA techniques, one tries to avoid possible inconsistencies and contradictions between judgments of several persons and replace a number of opposite opinions with a single so-called common preference that is the mostly agreed with all points of view. Nevertheless, individual preferences may be coordinated not always.

Let us discuss some ranking and classifying methods. Direct sorting objects is very popular due to its simplicity for a person. Every object, which is estimated under a numerical criterion, is assigned to one of the given classes immediately. In the case of several persons, the final ordering of objects may be constructed, for instance, as weighted averages or as the Kemeny median, if a concordance of estimates is acceptable (Kemeny & Snell, 1972).

In the pairwise comparisons, the final ordering objects will be complete if all pairs of objects are comparable, and DMs' preferences are transitive. If objects are incomparable, then ordering will be partial. In the case of multiple criteria and/or several persons, for example, in MAUT (multi-attribute utility theory) and TOPSIS (technique for order preference by similarity to ideal solution) (Hwang & Lin, 1987), the final arrangement of objects by comparing many matrixes is cumbrous. Objects may be arranged also by their ranks, which are calculated or evaluated by a decision maker.

In AHP (analytic hierarchy process) techniques (Saaty, 1990), priorities for the alternatives and criteria are derived by hierarchical paired comparisons with respect to a contribution to the problem goal. In ELECTRE methods (Roy, 1996, Vincke, 1992), multicriterial alternatives are compared and arranged by the outranking relation based on the special indexes of concordance and discordance. In ZAPROS methods (Larichev & Moshkovich, 1997; Moshkovich, Mechitov, & Olson, 2002), the so-called joint ordinal scales are to be constructed for ranking multicriteria alternatives. (Note that rearrangement of rank vectors in an ascending order, which is used in ZAPROS methods for alternatives comparison, generally, is mathematical incorrect.) In all of the mentioned techniques, the final results imply any coordination of individual judgments.

In the case of one criterion and a small collection of objects, an arrangement/classification of objects is not so difficult for a DM. The more number of objects, criteria, and/or actors, the more complicated and difficult a procedure is due to persons' errors, inconsistencies, and contradictions. Multiplicity and redundancy of attributes, which describe the choice problem, produce an additional difficulty of problem solving because manifold data are to be processed simultaneously without non-numerical transformations such as data "averaging," "mixing," "weighting," and so on. So, new methods are needed, which do not exclude discordant information and provide for a reasonable decision.

VDA emphasizes ill-structured discrete choice problems represented with quantitative and qualitative attributes. The most important features of VDA are as follows: (1) the problem description with a professional language, which is natural and habitual for a decision maker; (2) a usage of verbal (nominative, ordinal) data on all stages of the problem analysis and solution without transformation into a numerical form; (3) an examination of the DM's judgments consistency; (4) a logical and psychological validity of decision rules; and (5) an explanation of intermediate and final results. These VDA peculiarities are almost the same as mentioned (Larichev & Moshkovich, 1997).

In the case of individual rational choice, when decision rules are based on judgments of the only DM, the consistency of DM's subjective preferences is postulated as preference transitivity in many MCDA techniques. So, special facilities for discovering and removing possible inconsistencies and contradictions within single DM's judgments are included in VDA-based methods. A situation, where decision rules are based on judgments of several independent DMs, is principally different due to variety and inconsistency of DM's subjective preferences. As a result, individual decision rules may be similar, diverse, or contradictory. Such kinds of peculiarities would not be agreed or excluded but have to be included into GroupVDA procedures.

MULTISET MODEL FOR REPRESENTATION OF MULTI-ATTRIBUTE OBJECTS

Let $A=\{A_1,...,A_n\}$ be a collection of n objects evaluated upon m criteria $Q_1,Q_2,...,Q_m$. A criteria list depends on the aim of analysis. Different criteria may have a different relative importance (weight) for various cases. Each criterion has a nominal or ordinal scale of verbal estimates $Q_s=\{q_s^{es}\}, e_s=1,...,h_s, s=1,...,m$. Ordinal estimates are ordered from the best to the worst as $q_s^1 \succ q_s^2 \succ ... \succ q_s^{h_s}$. Criterion estimates q_s^{es} may be either quantitative or qualitative. Sometimes it is useful to transform a quantitative continuous scale into a qualitative discrete scale with a reasonably small number of grades. For instance, scales of criteria Q_1-Q_7 may be the following: q_s^1 – very large; q_s^2 – large; q_s^3 – medium; q_s^4 – small. On the other hand, verbal estimates are never converted into numerical ones.

Usually a multi-attribute object A_i is represented as a vector or cortege $q_i=(q_{i1}^{e1},...,q_{im}^{em})$ in the Cartesian m-space of attributes $Q=Q_1 \times ... \times Q_m$. When an object A_i is evaluated by k several individuals upon m criteria independently, multi-attribute description of object consists of many repeating quantitative and/or qualitative estimations $q_s^{es} \in Q_s$, which may be diverse, inconsistent and even contradictory. One and the same object A_i is represented now as a collection of k corteges $\{q_i^{(1)},\ldots,q_i^{(k)}\}$ where $q_i^{(j)}=(q_{i1}^{e1(j)},\ldots,q_{im}^{em(j)})$, $j=1,\ldots,k$ because k actors evaluate this object. And this group of corteges is to be considered as a whole in spite of a possible incomparability of separate corteges $q_i^{(j)}$. A collection of such multi-attribute objects has an overcomplicated structure that is very difficult for analysis. For instance, in group decisions (see Hwang & Lin, 1987), a collection of k vectors $\{q_i^{(1)},\ldots,q_i^{(k)}\}$ is replaced usually by one vector that is to be the mostly closed to all vectors within the group. Thus properties of all initial vectors $q_i^{(1)},\ldots,q_i^{(k)}$ could be lost.

So, instead of m-space $Q=Q_1\times\ldots\times Q_m$, let us now define the combined attribute scale or the hyperscale—a set $G=Q_1\cup\ldots\cup Q_m$ that consists of m attribute (criteria) groups $Q_s=\{q_s^{es}\}$, and represent an object A_i as the following set of repeating attributes:

$$A_i = \{k_{Ai}(q_1^1)\circ q_1^1,\ldots,k_{Ai}(q_1^{h1})\circ q_1^{h1},\ldots, k_{Ai}(q_m^1)\circ q_m^1,\ldots, k_{Ai}(q_m^{hm})\circ q_m^{hm}\}. \quad (1)$$

Here $k_{Ai}(q_s^{es})$ is a number of attribute q_s^{es}, which is equal to a number of experts evaluated the object A_i with the criterion estimate $q_s^{es}\in Q_s$; the sign $\circ$ denotes that there are $k_{Ai}(q_s^{es})$ copies of attribute q_s^{es} within the description of object A_i.

Thus, the object A_i is represented now as a set of many repeating elements (criteria estimates q_s^{es}) or as a multiset A_i over the domain G that is defined by a counting function $k_{Ai}:G\to\mathbf{Z}_+=\{0,1,2,3,\ldots\}$. A multiset A_i is said to be finite when all $k_{Ai}(q_s^{es})$ are finite. Multisets A and B are said to be equal ($A=B$), if $k_A(q_s^{es})=k_B(q_s^{es})$. A multiset B is said to be contained or included in a multiset A ($B\subseteq A$), if $k_B(q_s^{es})\leq k_A(q_s^{es})$, $\forall q_s^{es}\in G$.

There are defined the following operations with multisets: union $A\cup B$, intersection $A\cap B$, arithmetic addition $A+B$, arithmetic subtraction $A-B$, symmetric difference $A\Delta B$, complement $\overline{A}=Z-A$, multiplication by a scalar (reproduction) $c\cdot A$, arithmetic multiplication $A\cdot B$, arithmetic power A^n, direct product $A\times B$, direct power $(\times A)^n$. Z is the maximum multiset with $k_Z(q_s^{es})=\max_{A\in\mathcal{A}}k_A(q_s^{es})$. Many properties of operations under multisets are analogues to properties of operations under sets. These are an idempotency, involution, identity, commutativity, associativity, and distributivity.

As well as for sets not all operations under multisets are mutually commutative, associative and distributive. Some properties of any operations under sets and multisets are not always the same. Some properties of operations, which exist for sets, are absent for multisets. And at the same time new properties of operations appear that has no analogues for sets. In general, the operations of arithmetic addition, multiplication by a scalar, arithmetic multiplication, and raising to an arithmetic power are not defined in the set theory. When multisets are reduced to sets, the operations of arithmetic multiplication and raising to an arithmetic power degenerate into a set intersection, but the operations of set arithmetic addition and set multiplication by a scalar will be impracticable.

A collection $A=\{A_1,\ldots,A_n\}$ of n multi-attribute objects may be considered as points in the multiset metric space (A,d). Different multiset metric spaces (A,d) are defined by the following types of distances between multisets:

$$d_{1p}(A,B)=[m(A\Delta B)]^{1/p}; \quad d_{2p}(A,B)=[m(A\Delta B)/m(Z)]^{1/p};$$
$$d_{3p}(A,B)=[m(A\Delta B)/m(A\cup B)]^{1/p}, \quad (2)$$

where $p\geq 0$ is an integer, and $m(A)$ is a measure of multiset A. Multiset measure m is a real-valued non-negative function defined on the algebra of multisets $L(Z)$. The measure $m(A)$ of multiset A may be determined in the various ways, for instance, as a linear combination of counting functions: $m(A)=\sum_s w_s k_A(q_s^{es})$, $w_s>0$. The distances $d_{2p}(A,B)$ and $d_{3p}(A,B)$ satisfy the normalization condition $0\leq d(A,B)\leq 1$. For any fixed p, the metrics d_{1p} and d_{2p} are the continuous and uniformly continuous functions, the metric d_{3p} is the piecewise continuous function almost everywhere on the metric space for any fixed p. Note, that the distance $d_{3p}(A,B)$ is undefined for $A=B=\emptyset$. So, $d_{3p}(\emptyset,\emptyset)=0$ by the definition.

The proposed metric spaces are new types of spaces that differ from the well-known ones. The distance $d_{1p}(A,B)$ is analogues of the Hamming-type distance between objects, which is traditional for many applications. The distance $d_{2p}(A,B)$ characterizes a difference between two objects related to common properties of all objects as a whole. And the distance $d_{3p}(A,B)$ reflects a difference related to properties of only a pair of objects. In the case of sets for $p=1$, $d_{11}(A,B)=m(A\Delta B)$ is called the Fréchet distance, $d_{31}(A,B)=m(A\Delta B)/m(A\cup B)$ is called the Steinhaus distance (Deza & Laurent, 1997). For more details on multisets and multiset metric spaces see Knuth (1998), Yager (1986), Blizard (1989), and Petrovsky (1994, 2001, 2003ab, 2006a, 2006b).

The theoretical model of multisets is well appropriated for representing and analyzing a collection of objects that are described with many inconsistent quantitative and qualitative attributes and may exist in several copies. Variety of operations with multisets allows us to use different ways for combining multi-attribute objects into classes. For instance, a class X_t of objects A_i may be aggregated as an addition $X_t=\sum_i A_i$, union $X_t=\cup_i A_i$ or intersection $X_t=\cap_i A_i$ of multisets, which represent the objects considered. A class X_t of objects may be also formed as a linear combination of corresponding multisets $X_t=\sum_i c_i \cdot A_i$, $X_t=\cup_i c_i \cdot A_i$ or $X_t=\cap_i c_i \cdot A_i$, $c_i>0$. When an object class X_t is formed as a multiset addition, all properties of all objects in the group X_t (all values of all attributes) are combined. In the case of union or intersection of multisets, the best properties (maximal values of all attributes) or the worth properties (minimal values of all attributes) of individual objects in the group X_t are intensified.

ORDERING MULTI-ATTRIBUTE OBJECTS

New method *aggregation and ranking alternatives nearby the multi-attribute ideal situations* (ARAMIS) is developed for group ordering multi-attribute objects. Let us represent an object A_i that is described by many repeated quantitative and qualitative attributes as a multiset (1). So, the problem of ordering multi-attribute objects is transformed into ordering multisets. Consider now multi-attribute objects as points of multiset metric space (A,d). There are two multisets

$$A_{max} = \{k \circ q_1^1, 0, \ldots, 0, k \circ q_2^1, 0, \ldots, 0, \ldots, k \circ q_m^1, 0, \ldots, 0\},$$
(3)
$$A_{min} = \{0, \ldots, 0, k \circ q_1^{h1}, 0, \ldots, 0, k \circ q_2^{h2}, \ldots, 0, \ldots, 0, k \circ q_m^{hm}\},$$
(3)

which correspond to the best A_{max} and the worst A_{min} objects, k is a number of experts. These objects may not exist in real life and are called also as the ideal and anti-ideal situations or referent points. So, all objects may be arranged with respect to closeness to the best object A_{max} or the worst object A_{min} in the multiset metric space (A,d). The objects closeness may be defined using the the Hamming-type distance (3) $d_{11}(A,B)$ in the following form:

$$d_{11}(A,B)=m(A\Delta B)=\sum_{s=1}^{m} w_s \sum_{e_s=1}^{h_s} |k_A(q_s^{es})-k_B(q_s^{es})|,$$
(4)

where $w_s>0$ is a relative importance of the criterion Q_s. If all criteria are equally important, then all $w_s=1$ or $w_s=1/m$.

An object A_i is said to be more preferable than an object A_j ($A_i \succ A_j$), if a multiset A_i is closer than a multiset A_j to the multiset A_{max}, that is $d(A_{max},A_i)<d(A_{max},A_j)$. All objects are ordered by the values of distances from the best object A_{max}. If the distance values $d(A_{max},A_i)$ and $d(A_{max},A_j)$ are equal for certain objects A_i and A_j, then these objects are equivalent or incomparable. Therefore, the obtained descending ranking will be non-strict and partial. In order to arrange equivalent or incomparable objects from the best to the worst one, one may find the weighted sums of the first, second, third, and so forth objects' estimates by all criteria Q_s. Some objects within the subgroup could be ranked from the best to the worst one according to the values of corresponding weighted sums. This procedure is being repeated until all objects of the collection $A=\{A_1,\ldots,A_n\}$ is ordered.

Ascending ordering multi-attribute objects with respect to closeness to the worst object A_{min} is constructed analogously. An object A_i is said to be more preferable than an object A_j ($A_i \succ A_j$), if a multiset A_i is more far than a multiset A_j from the multiset A_{min} in the multiset metric space (A,d), that is if $d(A_{min},A_i)>d(A_{min},A_j)$. The final ranking could be constructed as a combination of the descending and ascending arrangements.

CLASSIFICATION OF MULTI-ATTRIBUTE OBJECTS

Consider a problem of multi-attribute objects' classification. Several experts evaluate each object with all criteria $Q_1,\ldots,Q_m$ and make a recommendation r_t for sorting object into one of the classes X_t. The individual sorting rule of expert is a production

IF ⟨conditions⟩, THEN ⟨decision⟩.

(5)

The antecedent term ⟨conditions⟩ corresponds to various attribute values q_s^{es}. The consequent term ⟨decision⟩ is an expert recommendation r_t. Obviously, different experts can evaluate one and the same project differently. And there are a lot of discordant individual rules for sorting objects. The inconsistencies of rules may be caused, for instance, by errors in the expert classification of objects, the incoherence between experts' estimates of objects and decision classes, the intransitivity of expert judgments, and other reasons. Need to find a simple general rule, which approximates maximally a large family of inconsistent individual expert-sorting rules and assigns objects to the given classes with the accuracy admitted. So, for solving the choice problem, one needs to aggregate all individual (and may be contradictory) preferences of several decision makers into a joint collective preference without rejecting inconsistent opinions.

The method MASKA (Russian abbreviation of Multi-Attribute Consistent Classification of Alternatives) is used for group classifying multi-attribute objects. An object A_i with a multiple criteria estimates may be represented as the following multiset of the type (1):

$$A_i = \{k_{Ai}(q_1^1)\circ q_1^1,\ldots,k_{Ai}(q_1^{h1})\circ q_1^{h1},\ldots, k_{Ai}(q_m^1)\circ q_m^1,\ldots,k_{Ai}(q_m^{hm})\circ q_m^{hm}, k_{Ai}(r_1)\circ r_1,\ldots,k_{Ai}(r_f)\circ r_f\}, \quad (6)$$

which is drawn from another domain $P=Q_1\cup\ldots\cup Q_m\cup R$. Here $k_{Ai}(q_s^{es})$ and $k_{Ai}(r_t)$ are equal to numbers of experts who estimates the object A_i with the attribute q_s^{es} and gives the recommendation r_t. Each group of criteria estimates $Q_s=\{q_s^{es}\}$, $s=1,\ldots,m$ is the family of the object properties. The group of sorting attributes $R=\{r_t\}$, $t=1,\ldots,f$ is the set of expert recommendations (may be discordant) for assignment of each object the specific class X_t.

We consider now the representation (6) of object A_i as a collective expert-sorting rule of the type (5), which is associated with arguments in the formula (6) as follows. The antecedent term ⟨conditions⟩ includes the various combinations of criteria estimates q_s^{es}, which describes the object properties. The consequent term ⟨decision⟩ denotes that the object A_i is assigned the class X_t, if some conditions are fulfilled. For instance, the object A_i is said to belong to the class X_t if $k_{Ai}(r_t)>k_{Ai}(r_p)$ for all $p\ne t$, or if $k_{Ai}(r_t)>\sum_{p\ne t}k_{Ai}(r_p)$.

In order to simplify the problem, let us assume that the collection of objects $A=\{A_1,\ldots,A_n\}$ is to be sorted beforehand only in two classes X_a and X_b, and these classes are formed as sums of multisets. The demand to sort objects out of two classes is not the principle restriction. In this case, the object classes X_a and X_b are represented as multisets

$$X_t = \{k_{Xt}(q_1^1)\circ q_1^1,\ldots,k_{Xt}(q_1^{h1})\circ q_1^{h1},\ldots, k_{Xt}(q_m^1)\circ q_m^1,\ldots,k_{Xt}(q_m^{hm})\circ q_m^{hm}, k_{Xt}(r_a)\circ r_a, k_{Xt}(r_b)\circ r_b\}$$
$$(t=a,b),$$

and may be aggregated as a sum of the following multisets:

$$X_t = \sum_{s=1}^m X_{ts} + X_{tr}, \quad X_{ts}=\sum_{i\in I_t} A_{is}, \quad X_{tr}=\sum_{i\in I_t} A_{ir}$$

where $A_{is}=\{k_{Ai}(q_s^1)\circ q_s^1,\ldots,k_{Ai}(q_s^{hs})\circ q_s^{hs}\}$, $A_{ir}=\{k_{Ai}(r_a)\circ r_a, k_{Ai}(r_b)\circ r_b\}$, $k_{Xt}(x_p)=\sum_{i\in I_t} k_{Ai}(x_p)$, $\forall x_p \in P$, $x_p=q_s^{es}$, r_a or r_b. Here I_a and I_b are the subsets of indexes for the classes X_a and X_b, $I_a\cup I_b=\{1,\ldots,n\}$, $I_a\cap I_b=\varnothing$.

Let us represent now the problem of object selection as the problem of multiset classification in a metric space (A,d). The main idea of approximating a large family of discordant sorting rules with a compact decision algorithm or a simple classification rule may be formulated as follows. For every group of attributes $Q_1,\ldots,Q_m,R$, the pairs of new multisets would be generated so that the multisets within each pair are the mostly coincident with the initial sorting objects out of the classes X_a and X_b. A combination of the attributes, that define the pairs of the new generated multisets, produces the generalized decision rule for objects classification.

Form new multisets over the same domain P, which are categorical multisets

$$R_a=\{k_{Xa}(r_a)\circ r_a, k_{Xb}(r_a)\circ r_a\}, \quad R_b=\{k_{Xa}(r_b)\circ r_b, k_{Xb}(r_b)\circ r_b\},$$

and substantial multisets

$$Q_{as}=\sum_{j\in J_a} Q_j, \quad Q_{bs}=\sum_{j\in J_b} Q_j$$

where $Q_j=\{k_{Xa}(q_s^j)\circ q_s^j, k_{Xb}(q_s^j)\circ q_s^j\}$. Here the index subsets $J_{as}\cup J_{bs}=\{1,\ldots,h_s\}$, $J_{as}\cap J_{bs}=\varnothing$.

It is easy to show that the binary decomposition of the categorical multisets R_a, R_b is equivalent to the potentially best partition X_{ar}, X_{br} of the object collection $A=\{A_1,\ldots,A_n\}$. Indeed, the distances $d(R_a,R_b)$ and $d(X_{ar},X_{br})$ are equal. So, in a metric space (A,d) the distance $d(R_a,R_b)=d^*$ is the maximal of all possible distances with regard to all attribute groups for the given family of expert-sorting rules. In the case of the ideal object classification without inconsistencies of individual judgements, the maximal distance is equal correspondingly to $d_{11}^*=kn$, $d_{21}^*=1/(h_1+...+h_m+2)$, $d_{31}^*=1$.

Thus, in every s-th attribute group Q_s, we need to find the best binary decomposition of new substantial multisets $\boldsymbol{Q}_{as}$ and $\boldsymbol{Q}_{bs}$ such that new submultisets are placed at the maximal distance from each other in the multiset metric space (A,d). Now the problem of multi-attribute objects' classification is transformed into the m optimization problems:

$$d(\boldsymbol{Q}_{as}, \boldsymbol{Q}_{bs}) \rightarrow \max d(\boldsymbol{Q}_{as}, \boldsymbol{Q}_{bs}) = d(\boldsymbol{Q}_{as}^*, \boldsymbol{Q}_{bs}^*).$$

The solution of every previous problem gives us a set of attributes within s-th group, which combination forms the generalized decision rule for the objects' categorization in the form (5) as follows:

$$\text{IF} \langle (q_{iu} \in Q_{tu}^*) \text{AND} (q_{iv} \in Q_{tv}^*) \text{AND}...\text{AND} (q_{iw} \in Q_{tw}^*) \rangle,$$
$$\text{THEN} \langle \text{Object } A_i \in X_l \rangle. \tag{7}$$

Attributes $q_{is} \in Q_{ts}^*$ for various attribute groups can be ordered in accordance with the values of distances $d(\boldsymbol{Q}_{as}^*, \boldsymbol{Q}_{bs}^*)$. The attribute q_{is} that provides the demanded level of approximation rate $L_s \geq L_0$, $L_s = d(\boldsymbol{Q}_{as}^*, \boldsymbol{Q}_{bs}^*)/d^*$, is to be included in the final classification rule. Note that the value of approximation rate L_s characterizes, in other words, a relative significance of the s-th property Q_s within the general decision rule. Remark also that the decision rules (7) for classifying objects into diverse categories X_a and X_b, generally, are quite different.

CONCLUSION AND FURTHER RESEARCH

The new GroupVDA tools for ordering and classifying a collection of objects described by many quantitative and qualitative attributes, when several copies of an object may exist, are based on the theory of multiset metric spaces. The GroupVDA approach allows us to solve traditional MCDA problems in a more simple and constructive manner, and to discover new types of problems never being sold earlier, while taking into account inconsistencies of objects' properties and contradictions of group actors' preferences. The techniques proposed were applied to real-life MCDA cases where several experts estimated alternatives upon many criteria.

Ranking about 50 Russian companies on information and telecommunication technologies (Petrovsky, 2006a) was prepared with the ARAMIS method. Fifty experts estimated the company activity in any market sector upon dozen qualitative criteria such as follows: Q_1: "Business activity"; Q_2: "Total profit"; Q_3: "Gross sales"; Q_4: "Net sales"; Q_5: "Number of projects"; Q_6: "Number of employees"; Q_7: "Professional skills of the staff"; and so on. Thirty companies were selected as leading high-tech companies, 10 companies as leading developers of software, and 10 as the mostly dynamic developers.

The ARAMIS technique arranges multi-attribute objects represented as multisets by their closeness to any «ideal» objects in a multiset metric space. This method is simpler than the well-known approaches, for instance, the TOPSIS method. The ranking of all objects is found without building many different expert arrangements by many criteria, and without an aggregation them into a common ranking. The object arrangement takes into account various inconsistent and contradictory expert estimates without forcing one to find a compromise among them.

The MASKA method was tested on multiple criteria expert conclusions related to the USSR State Scientific and Technological Program on High-Temperature Superconductivity (Petrovsky, 2001). Five expert groups considered more than 250 applications and approved about 170 projects. Three experts estimated every application upon six criteria Q_s with verbal scales. The questionnaire for the estimation of applications includes the following criteria: Q_1: "The project contribution to the program goals"; Q_2: "Long-range value of the project"; Q_3: "Novelty of the approach to solve the task"; Q_4: "Qualification level of the team"; Q_5: "Resources available for the project realization"; and Q_6: "Peculiarity of the project results." Several generalized decision rules in the form (7) that approximates many contradictory sorting rules had been found for a selection of the approved projects. One of these classification rules completely coincided with the real empirical rule (Larichev, Prokhorov, Petrovsky, Sternin, & Shepelev, 1989). Note that such group decision rules are based on many contradictory individual decision rules and could not been found with any other known MCDA techniques.

The multiset approach to an operation with multi-attribute objects is useful not only in MCDA area but also in the pattern recognition (Arlazarov, Loginov, & Slavin, 2002), data mining and cluster analysis (Petrovsky, 2003b), text processing, and other areas. One of the promising applications of GroupVDA may be *multimedia information analysis* and *content-based image retrieval*. Instead of searching for images by using different characteristics such as color, brightness, and so on, GroupVDA approach allows us to apply semantic for description, retrieval, arrangement, and classification of multimedia information. We underline once more that available information, which is contained in the object descriptions, is used only in the native form without any transformation of non-numerical data into numbers.

REFERENCES

Arlazarov, V. L., Loginov, A. S., & Slavin, O. L. (2002). Characteristics of programs for optic recognition of texts [in Russian]. *Programming, 3,* 45-63.

Blizard, W. (1989). Multiset theory. *Notre Dame Journal of Formal Logic, 30*(1), 36-66.

Deza, M. M., & Laurent, M. (1997). *Geometry of cuts and metrics.* Berlin, Germany: Springer-Verlag.

Hwang, C. L., & Lin, M. J. (1987). *Group decision making under multiple criteria.* Berlin, Germany: Springer-Verlag.

Kemeny, J. G., & Snell, J. L. (1972). *Mathematical models in the social sciences.* Cambridge, MA: MIT Press.

Knuth, D. E. (1998). *The art of computer programming. Vol. 2: Seminumerical algorithms.* Reading, PA: Addison-Wesley.

Larichev, O. I., & Moshkovich, E. M. (1997). *Verbal decision analysis for unstructured problems.* Boston: Kluwer Academic.

Larichev, O. I., Prokhorov, A. S., Petrovsky, A. B., Sternin, M. Yu., & Shepelev, G. I. (1989). The experience of planning of the basic research on the competitive base [in Russian]. *Vestnik of the USSR Academy of Sciences, 7,* 51-61.

Moshkovich, E. M., Mechitov, A., & Olson, D. L. (2002). Ordinal judgments for comparison of multiattribute alternatives. *European Journal of Operational Research, 137,* 625-641.

Petrovsky, A. B. (1994). An axiomatic approach to metrization of multiset space. In G. H. Tzeng, H. F. Wang, U. P. Wen, & P. L. Yu (Eds.), *Multiple criteria decision making* (pp. 129-140). New York: Springer-Verlag.

Petrovsky, A. B. (2001) Multiple criteria project selection based on contradictory sorting rules. In M. Godlevsky & H. Mayr (Eds.), *Information systems technology and its applications* (pp. 199-206). Bonn, Germany: Gesellschaft für Informatik.

Petrovsky, A. B. (2003a). *Spaces of sets and multisets* [in Russian]. Moscow: Editorial URSS.

Petrovsky, A. B. (2003b). Cluster analysis in multiset spaces. In M. Godlevsky, S. Liddle, & H. Mayr (Eds.), *Information systems technology and its applications* (pp. 109-119). Bonn, Germany: Gesellschaft für Informatik.

Petrovsky, A. B. (2006a). Multiple criteria ranking enterprises based on inconsistent estimations. In D. Karagiannis & H. Mayr (Eds.), *Information systems technology and its applications* (pp. 143-151). Bonn, Germany: Gesellschaft für Informatik.

Petrovsky, A. B. (2006b, June 28-July 1). Inconsistent preferences in verbal decision analysis. *Papers from IFIP WG8.3 International Conference on Creativity and Innovation in Decision Making and Decision Support,* London, UK (Vol. 2., pp. 773-789). London: Ludic Publishing Ltd.

Roy, B. (1996). *Multicriteria methodology for decision aiding.* Dordrecht, The Netherlands: Kluwer Academic.

Saaty, T. (1990). *Multicriteria decision making: The analytic hierarchy process.* Pittsburgh, PA: RWS Publications.

Vincke, Ph. (1992). *Multicriteria decision aid.* Chichester, UK: Wiley.

Yager, R. R. (1986). On the theory of bags. *International Journal of General Systems, 13,* 23-37.

KEY TERMS

Aggregation and Ranking Alternatives nearby the Multi-Attribute Ideal Situations (ARAMIS): ARAMIS is the method for group ordering multi-attribute objects represented as multisets by their closeness to any "ideal" objects in a multiset metric space. The ranking of all objects is found without building many different expert arrangements by many criteria, and without an aggregation them into a common ranking. The object arrangement takes into account various inconsistent and contradictory expert estimates without forcing one to find a compromise among them.

Decision Maker (DM): The DM is a person who is responsible for solution of choice problem.

Group Verbal Decision Analysis (GroupVDA): Group VDA is a new methodological approach in the MCDA area, which enlarges VDA approach to a group decision. GroupVDA deals with choice problems where preferences of several decision makers may be discordant, alternatives are described with manifold repeating quantitative and qualitative attributes, and may exist in several copies.

Measure of Multiset m: Measure of multiset m is a real-valued non-negative function defined on the algebra of multisets $L(Z)$.

MASKA (Russian abbreviation for the name: Multi-Attribute Consistent Classification of Alternatives): MASKA is the method for group classifying multi-attribute objects, which are represented as multisets. The method allows us to construct some generalized decision rules for a selection of "good" and "bad" objects from a set of contenders that approximates many inconsistent and contradictory individual sorting rules of several actors with the demanded level of approximation rate.

Multiset (a set with repeating elements or a bag): Multiset is a collection of elements' groups

$$A = \{k_A(x_1) \circ x_1, \; k_A(x_2) \circ x_2, \ldots, k_A(x_j) \circ x_j, \ldots\} = \{(k_A(x) \circ x) | x \in X\}$$

drawn from an ordinary set $X = \{x_1, x_2, \ldots, x_j, \ldots\}$. Here $k_A : X \to Z_+ = \{0, 1, 2, 3, \ldots\}$ is called a counting or multiplicity function of multiset, which defines the number of times that the element $x_j \in X$ occurs in the multiset A, and this is indicated with the symbol $\circ$. A multiset A becomes a crisp (ordinary) set when $k_A(x) = \chi_A(x)$, where $\chi_A(x) = 1$ if $x \in A$, and $\chi_A(x) = 0$ if $x \notin A$.

Multiset Metric Space (A,d): Multiset metric space (A,d) is a collection $A = \{A_1, \ldots, A_n\}$ of multisets with any distance d between multisets.

Operations with Multisets: Union $A \cup B$, intersection $A \cap B$, arithmetic addition $A+B$, arithmetic subtraction $A-B$, symmetric difference $A \Delta B$, complement $\overline{A} = Z - A$, multiplication by a scalar (reproduction) $c \bullet A$, arithmetic multiplication $A \bullet B$, arithmetic power A^n, direct product $A \times B$, direct power $(\times A)^n$. In general, arithmetic addition, multiplication by a scalar, arithmetic multiplication, and raising to an arithmetic power are not defined in the set theory.

Verbal Decision Analysis (VDA): VDA emphasizes ill-structured discrete choice problems, which are represented with quantitative and qualitative attributes. The most important features of VDA are as follows: (1) the problem description with a professional language, which is natural and habitual for a decision maker; (2) a usage of verbal (nominative, ordinal) data on all stages of the problem analysis and solution without transformation into a numerical form; (3) an examination of decision maker's judgments consistency; (4) a logical and psychological validity of decision rules; and (5) an explanation of intermediate and final results.

How Groupware Systems Can Change How an Organisation Makes Decisions: A Case Study in the Publishing Industry[1]

Frédéric Adam
University College Cork, Ireland

Jean-Charles Pomerol
Université Pierre et Marie Curie, France

Patrick Brézillon
University Paris 6, France
Université Pierre et Marie Curie, France

INTRODUCTION

In this article, a newspaper company which has implemented a computerised editorial system is studied in an attempt to understand the impact that groupware systems can have on the decision making processes of an organisation. First, the case study protocol is presented, and the findings of the case are described in detail. Conclusions are then presented which pertain both to this case and to the implementation of decision support systems that have a groupware dimension.

BACKGROUND TO THE CASE

XYZ Publications Ltd (XYZ) is a news organisation which has published two newspapers: a national morning newspaper and a local afternoon newspaper, since the 19th Century. The publishing industry is one which has faced many challenges over the last 20 years and XYZ has undergone considerable change of both structural and commercial nature consistent with what has happened in the rest of this industry.

In XYZ, the researchers interviewed key actors in an attempt to understand the nature of the changes undergone by the firm and their implications for the decision making routines of the firm. One of the key changes was the implementation, at the end of a long process of analysis, of a collaborative computer system to support the creation of the newspapers.

A case study protocol was put together which focused on understanding in detail how editorial and commercial decisions are made, that is, how knowledge is collected, stored, selected, organised, and circulated.

We also analysed the impact which the implementation of the groupware editorial system has had on decision making processes. Our interest in this case was motivated by the observation that XYZ has a very open decision making style, a highly developed circulation of information, and very quick decision making cycles reflecting the nature of the industry in which XYZ operates. This gave the opportunity to observe many repetitions of editorial decision making cycles within a short timeframe.

MAIN FOCUS: THE STUDY AT XYZ

Management and decision making at XYZ is overwhelmingly characterised by the nature of the firm's activity, whereby the publication of two daily newspaper titles dictates the pace of every aspect of operational decision making. One interviewee likened this situation to working for a company which must produce two new products every day; each of these products having a life span of 6 hours maximum! This cyclical process has implications for every aspect of XYZ's business as key decisions related to the information content of the papers and the key steps that lead to them are repeated every few hours following highly informal processes nevertheless routinised by usage.

Thus, whatever happens, the national title must be ready for 2:00 a.m. while the local title must be ready by 12:00 p.m. and all the work is organised around these two daily deadlines. The natural leaders of the organisation are the editor-in-chief, the sales manager (in charge of selling the advertising space without which no newspaper can exist) and the Managing

Director (MD). The finance department plays more of an arbitration role, reminding actors that maximising revenues is also critical to XYZ's success (even good newspapers can go bankrupt) as some editorial decisions are sometimes very costly and have an uncertain impact on the short term and long term success of the paper. This dichotomy between editorial decision making and editorial expenditure on the one hand, and the financial success of the newspaper on the other hand, is a fundamental feature of this case study.

CHARACTERISING DECISION MAKING AT XYZ

Decision making in XYZ is characterised by two dominant types of problems. These are: editorial decisions and decision about the sales of advertising space, which overall must "balance the books." In these two areas, XYZ's managers display different styles and use different routines as explained in the next sections.

Editorial Decision Making

The core decision making process at XYZ is concerned with the creation of the two newspaper titles, twice a day. It is characterised by an abundance of routine, unstructured decisions made by the editorial team from its core position at the centre of a complex network of information-rich relationships with a large number of actors inside and outside the firm. The production of a newspaper necessitates the availability of news and its selection and organisation in order to create an interesting and relevant end product. Access to information and information sharing are, therefore, fundamental factors in enabling an editorial team to perform its task. There are also key internal linkages between the editors and the manager for sales of advertising space (because the news can be used as an incentive for certain organisations to advertise) and the finance manager (to establish whether the newspaper can afford certain high profile reports).

Sourcing Information

The Editor-in-Chief explained that XYZ's sources of information are plentiful, which is required in order to guarantee the continuous flow of news, pictures, and opinion pieces that make up a daily newspaper. Thus, even though the newspaper employs around 300 people, XYZ is connected to dozens of free lance journalists from whom material is purchased. Similarly, foreign reports are purchased from international agencies or exchanged or purchased from local newspapers. This highlights a fundamental aspect of the newspaper business: newspapers sell as much information as they buy. Thus, networking, that is, creating webs of contacts in order to trade information, is the most fundamental aspect of the work of senior managers at XYZ. This applies in particular to the MD, the two full time editors, the five assistant editors, and the many subeditors.

This aspect of XYZ's business is illustrated by the area of dense information exchange between internal actors and the external sources of information represented in Figure 1 (production process at XYZ). Figure 1 shows one of the dense clusters of relationships that exist in XYZ and highlights the density of relationships with the outside. This illustrates XYZ's information web and the two dense clusters structured around the editorial and ad sales functions. However, our observations revealed that the networking aspect of XYZ's business is primarily an individual activity. Contacts provide information to their usual source, not to anyone indiscriminately. Much collaboration is required to create a newspaper, but the "address book" of editors and assistant editors is their private asset and the management of this key organisational knowledge escapes any form of central control. In this case, the only way to manage the overall company's address book is to get (and keep) the proper mix of people.

Figure 1. Production process at XYZ

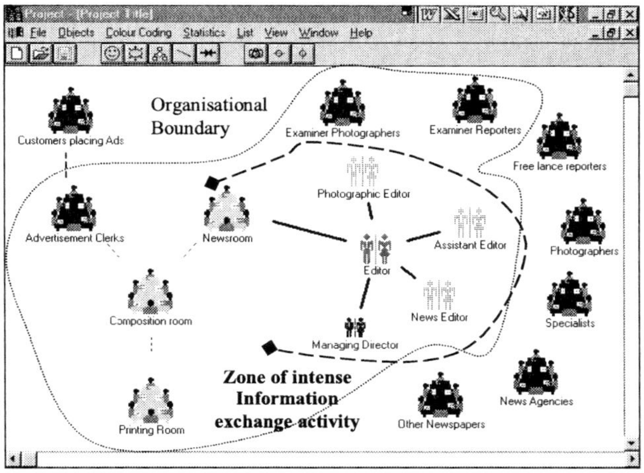

This type of decision making characterises XYZ in that the nature of this organisation is to make decisions as to how to produce a newspaper that is profitable and can sustain its success by maintaining the loyalty of a large customer base, within budgetary constraints (the editorial budget represents more than 75% of XYZ's total expenditure). Thus, editorial decisions and the process whereby the personality and appearance of the newspapers is debated, negotiated, and created by actors are highly complex in their outcome as well as their occurrence over time. As such, the management of XYZ provides illustrations of highly unstructured decision problem, but elements of the process have also become highly structured.

Making the Newspaper

Talking to the MD and the Editor, it appears that, contrary to common perceptions about newspapers, the editorial policy is not a topic of regular discussion at XYZ. The decision making that applies to the contents of the paper is not about editorial policy *per se*, it is about strings of daily unstructured decisions that must be made regarding which items of news go in the paper and which do not. These decisions are made by the people who are responsible for the newspaper's personality: the editors and subeditors, free from interference from top management or the shareholders—and apart from the computerised template that prescribes the general layout of the paper, there is no visible model of what the newspapers should look like. The know-how of the team is best observed in the smooth and efficient process that runs twice daily. This highlights that even though decision making at XYZ is the results of a multitude of actions taken by individual actors, there is an element of quick thinking and routine to the whole process, which is very reminiscent of Winter's (1985) *mechanistic decision making*, whereby a firm does not need to *think* in order to quickly tackle known decision problems.

This mechanistic decision making revolves around a smooth process of consultation, access to news, discussion, and decision that is going on around the clock and has the duty editor at its core. From 8:00 a.m. to 1:00 a.m. the following morning, he is in charge of collecting the news and interfacing with all potential sources of information. This collaborative process is enabled by the use of a "groupware" news agenda, which is an electronic content management system that can be accessed and updated by everyone in the team and contains every event on the diary. This agenda is used to focus people's attention on what is going on and helps them get ideas for the contents of the paper. The events in the diary are then used as "hooks" on which to hang news items. This document and the computer system on which it is held are really at the core of the editorial decision making process at XYZ and every evening before leaving the company, the Editor spends some time studying the agenda, adding comments, and allocating tasks to carry out, such as photos to obtain for the morning, requests to send a reporter to follow up on a radio interview heard during the day, and so forth. The editor on duty will supervise the execution of these tasks. He will also send reporters out, buy information from Reuter, and make contact with the foreign correspondents. Other reporters will contact him to provide interesting leads. This system constitutes a striking example of Group Decision Support System even though it bears no such label in the company. Given the electronic nature of much of the news that reaches modern newspapers, it is particularly well integrated with XYZ's network of information flows. It is also integrated downstream with the activities involved in producing the newspaper, as explained further.

Much unsolicited information also reaches the newsroom. Public relations organisations lobby the newspaper on an on-going basis either by phoning the executives of the company or by ringing reporters and editors they know to ask them to send someone to attend a seminar or a press conference. This overall process is reminiscent of the garbage can model of decision making put forward by Cohen, March, and Olsen (1972) where organisations are characterised by collections of ideas looking for problems, just as items of news are being presented for inclusion into the newspaper.

At the end of the process of production of the paper, the final decisions are made in a series of meetings taking place throughout the day. The first of these meetings takes place at 12:00 p.m. and aims to ascertain the volume of ads that must be accommodated. A first round-up of the stories of the day is also done. The second meeting takes place at 2:30 p.m. and involves selecting the cover story and the rest of items to go in each section of the newspaper. The news agenda mentioned previously is at the core of this process of decision making where the editor attempt to guess what will be of most interest to the public. The final meeting, at 5:30 p.m., is used to confirm decisions made earlier based on whether the pictures requested have arrived and whether reporters were successful in securing interviews. Occasionally, the news requires that the plan is changed totally, but generally, decisions made at 2:30 p.m. stand.

The last important task in the production process is accomplished by the subeditors who, under the supervision of the chief subeditor, design each of the features that make up the newspaper, add and crop the pictures, and integrate all the material presented into a coherent and attractive whole. Again, the job carried out by this small group of people is fundamental in giving the national title its identity and its appearance. From a decision making point of view though, it must be observed that editorial decision making does not rely on any high level set of criteria and that it relies solely on a string of operational decisions. This illustrates that the managerial culture of editors is essentially technical. Their primary concern is to produce a good newspaper and they find it difficult to integrate financial considerations in their mental models. The regular meetings with the finance director do not have a significant bearing on the process of production of the newspaper.

SELLING ADS: THE OTHER AREA OF DECISION MAKING

Another key feature of XYZ's business resides in the nature of the relationship between XYZ and its customers. The interviews revealed that XYZ has two very distinct categories of customers: purchasers of advertising space and readers. Both categories of customers are equally important financially (the street price of the newspapers covers only 70% of the expenditure of the company—the rest and the profit margin are provided by advertising revenues), but dealing with these two categories of customers is quite different and two separate areas of the organisation are specifically in charge of each category. The linkage with corporate customers, who pay large sums of money to place their ads and constitute a vast source of revenue, is handled by a group of sales representatives. Direct telephone interaction also takes place between individuals placing ads and XYZs' telesales operators. There are some tenuous linkages with the editorial policy as some advertisers may be convinced to purchase space in a newspaper issue because certain news is covered or because a special topical report is presented. However, these linkages are not well organised and there is no direct communication between sales representatives and editors. In specific cases, special advertising features reporting the progress of a company may be negotiated by sales representatives, which requires detailed communication of the proposed contents and size to the editorial team.

The process of collection and presentation of ads is partly automated. Tele-ads operators feed a continuous flow of ads into a Windows-based system. These ads come from a variety of sources including phone, fax, and electronic mail. In addition, display ads (those that contain pictures) are brought in by a group of sales representatives who actively seek large advertisements from local businesses. All ads are automatically saved in a database which then organises them in pages. This important process used to be extremely time consuming as it involved a set of large pin-boards where ads were provisionally booked. The database now organises all ads in a matter of minutes. This basic automation cannot hide the fact that this aspect of XYZ's business is carried out in an essentially ad-hoc fashion. On the one hand, the newspaper cannot exist without selling ads. On the other hand, this is not an aspect of the business that motivates top managers as much as the production of the paper and less energy goes into increasing the ad sales side of the business, especially at top management level. At an operational level, actors actively try to sell space to local business (the currently buoyant economic climate helps greatly), but at a strategic level, this area of the business is more characterised by an absence of creative decision making than by pro-active development of the business.

IMPLEMENTING A GROUPWARE SYSTEM FOR EDITORIAL ACTIVITIES

XYZ's managers insisted on the importance of the decision made to purchase a leading edge computerised production system for the newspapers and it appeared that there were many different aspects to the decision. The major benefits expected from the implementation of the system included better usage of materials, better workflow, reduced staff, reduced skills requirement, better quality output, substantial time savings, better sales information, and elimination of out-dated production equipment.

This extensive list of potential benefits illustrates why managers at XYZ were committed to the large spending this investment represented. All these potential benefits added up to an overwhelming case for the investment even before a preliminary study was undertaken to establish what systems had been implemented in other newspapers. Thus, there was a consensus that a substantial investment was required, but no one in the organisation had a clear picture of what was required, what was available or how to get it. Naturally, this was not sufficient to call in a supplier and buy a new system. Thus, much research went into selecting a combination of systems that would meet XYZ's requirements. The research process that followed took more than 5 years. This decision process was long by any standard (Eisenhardt, 1989), which is a consequence of the types of problems managers were faced with. This decision involved a radically new problem, never faced before and for which there was no model available whatever. Also, because of the size of the investment, managers perceived that their decision would not be reversible. These parameters explain why XYZ took so long to commit to a solution (Adam, 1996).

The interviews revealed that the implementation of the system has shifted the attention of staff away from trivial production issues and blind respect of the deadlines onto new issues such as providing better customer service in the ads sales department and providing a better quality news product. Production issues used to dominate the agenda and the limited attention of staff meant that there was little room for debate. The implementation of new solutions to the production problems means that managers and staff can now concentrate on the provision of better and new products for their readers. The computer system in which the papers are created acts as a formative mechanism and help the editorial team give a more consistent look to the paper. The impact of decisions made in relation to the contents and layout of the paper can be visualised before being committed to paper and this provides a much stronger basis for decision making. The decision to buy this system has been very extremely important for XYZ, maybe more important than managers realised at the time it was initiated. The new system has contributed to turning XYZ into a profitable organisation with a national distribution instead of simply a local presence, using differentiated issues of the newspaper designed specifically for the newspaper's home town, for Dublin and for other areas (which the previous production system never allowed). The increase in printing quality enabled the development of new, very profitable commercial activities involving printing other titles on behalf of UK-based newspapers. The high-tech nature of the system also allowed the organisation to shed close to 50 jobs.

Another key consequence of the implementation of the new system has been the shift in power and control over the process of production of the newspapers. Up until 1994, a group of 80 individuals—the compositors—possessed such a unique expertise that they could decide on a daily basis whether the newspaper would be in the streets or not (see Figure 1). This situation is reminiscent of Crozier's (1964) analysis of how a group possessing a unique and crucial expertise can create uncertainty for the people both below and above it in the hierarchy (see also Crozier & Friedberg, 1977). In XYZ, the compositors were a strong, heavily unionised clique which negotiated fiercely its terms and conditions of employment. This resulted in high levels of pay and short promotion paths. The rift between compositors and other organisational actors was accentuated by the physical layout of the plant because this group was isolated from the other stages in the production process in one "composition" room.

The power of the compositors stemmed from their being in a position to decide when the paper would be ready for publication and whether it would be quality product or just thrown together. This weakened the editorial group and created uncertainty for top management. The change brought about by the new computerised system was simple: it eliminated the composition room. The newspaper can be composed directly in the computer package by the editorial team and, when ready, merely sent to the presses in electronic format. This eliminated the compositors, 40 of whom left voluntarily while the others where transferred in other areas. Thus, the decision making power swung back to the editorial team and the focus shifted entirely to the creation of the product rather than its production. The Editor, who operated under both systems, explained that his control over the production process has increased drastically as a result of the smaller number of people involved. He stated, "Now, there are no middlemen involved in the process. All the people who work on the production of the paper work directly for me."

Thus, the computerisation of the production process has radically changed the way the products are created and has introduced some formalisation in the whole procedure. At the same time, it has re-enforced the power of the Editorial group, now more powerful than ever in the management and distribution of knowledge at XYZ and at the core of the decision making process.

The editorial system that has been implemented after 5 years of research has reduced the time required to produce the newspapers by several hours and the time freed can now be used to concentrate on the content of the newspaper. Staff in the newsroom can type in articles and save them in electronic spaces corresponding to the different areas of the paper and for the various issues in a given week. This constitutes a pool of material that can be used by the Editor once his mind is made up.

CONCLUSION

A core finding of this case is that the newspaper industry has many unique characteristics, inherited from the technical culture of Editorial decision making. This is strong culture rooted in 19th Century operational concerns with using a long established technology to produce a newspaper. One interest of this research project was to show how the emergence of radically new technology affected this culture in a subtle way. At a basic level, the case at XYZ shows the great potential of technology in supporting the process of gathering, selecting and organising new knowledge and in improving the financial robustness of the newspaper industry. The story presented in XYZ is not unique in this respect. Many other newspapers in the UK have undergone similar transformations, with similar benefits. Nowadays, most newspapers have implemented computerised production systems, as this is the only way to sell newspapers at a cost which customers are willing to pay.

However, the most significant findings of this case relate to decision making and the role of IT in supporting it. One of XYZ's greatest assets resides in the complex decision making process whereby a large number of individuals collaborate in the creation of the newspapers. This process, while essentially *ad-hoc* and informal has the mechanistic efficiency of a well-established managerial process. It is in contrast with some other areas of decision making at XYZ which are characterised by an absence of pro-active decision making from the part of the managers involved.

More specifically, there is a striking lack of curiosity in looking at some of the key indicators of the business which could now be examined in detail with the support of the recently-introduced computer systems. There seems to be no interest in pursuing new avenues which Hall (1984) also noted in another newspaper. He stated:

It is a perpetual enigma that a complex organisation (…) can coordinate such a wide array of highly specialised activities (from editing to printing) and yet formulate major policy decisions on out-of-date maps of causality containing untested beliefs and the simplest arguments. Furthermore, it seems that once these maps become established, they are difficult to change and require a crisis or a substantial turnover of senior managers to effect any radical revision. (p. 923)

With regards to Hall's (1984) last sentence, one of the conclusions of this study is that computerisation and even an IT revolution are not always sufficient to affect the way high level managerial decisions are made.

Thus, the crucial role that IT is coming to play in the management of XYZ is significant in this case study. Interestingly though, the extent of this role is commensurate to managers' confidence in what they think should be done in the different areas of the business. In areas where managers are comfortable, IT has been able to provide a high level of support, as the IT-based revolution of editorial decision making illustrates. In other areas where managers are not so confident that they know where XYZ should go and lack a model of how decision problems should be tackled, IT has only been able to provide an operational support, as illustrated by the basic automation of the ad sales process. Both areas of the business are equally complex and involve a certain level of idiosyncrasy which indicates that the difficulty in developing effective decision support systems may come far more from the lack of vision of managers than from the complexity of the problems. These two factors are obviously linked in that managers are more likely to run out of ideas in complex situations, but the case data at XYZ proves that managers can have a vision of how to best tackle a problem, at least at a high representation level (Humphreys, 1989), even when the situation they face is quite complex, as long as it corresponds to their area of technical expertise, here the production of the newspaper. Outside their area of expertise, managers appear more tentative and use proven routines rather than accurate information that may challenge their views when they make their decisions.

REFERENCES

Adam, F. (1996). Experimentation with organisation analyser, a tool for the study of decision making networks in organisations. In Humphreys, Bannon, McCosh, Migliarese & Pomerol (Eds.), *Implementing systems for supporting management decisions—concepts, methods and experiences* (pp. 1-20). London: Chapman and Hall.

Carlsson, S.A. (1994). Continuous development of decision tasks vs. redesign of decision processes. In Mayon-White et al. (Eds.), *Proceedings of IFIP WG 8.3 Working Conference,* San Sebastian (pp. 137-154).

Cohen, D., March, J.G., & Olsen, J.P. (1972). A garbage can model of organisational choice. *Administrative Science Quarterly, 17,* 1-25.

Crozier, M. (1964). *The bureaucratic phenomenon.* Chicago: University of Chicago Press.

Crozier, M., & Friedberg, E. (1977). L'acteur et le système, Edition du Seuil, Paris.

Eisenhardt, K.M. (1989). Making fast decisions in high velocity environments. *Academy of Management Journal, 32*(3), 543-576.

Hall, R.I. (1984). The natural logic of management policy making: its implications for the survival of an organization. *Management Science, 30,* 905-927.

Humphreys, P. (1989). Intelligence in decision making—a process model. In G. Doukidis, F. Land and G. Miller (Eds.), *Knowledge-based management systems.* Hellis, Hovwood, Chichester.

Knoke, D., & Kuklinski, J. (1982). *Network analysis.* Beverly Hills, CA: Sage Publications.

Laumann, E.O. (1994). Network analysis in large social systems: Some theoretical and methodological problems. In P. Holland and S. Leinhart (Eds.), *Perspectives on social network research* (pp. 379-402). New York: Academic Press.

March, J.G. (1987). Ambiguity and accounting: The elusive link between information and decision making. *Accounting, Organisations and Society, 12*(2), 153-168.

March, J.G. (1988). Mundane organisations and heroic leaders. In L.B. Mayhew & F. Leon-Garcia (Eds.), *Seminarios sobre administracion universiteria,* Mexicali.

Miles, M., & Huberman, A. (1994). Qualitative data analysis: An expanded sourcebook. CA: Sage Publications.

Murphy, C. (1994, September). Decision support systems—putting emphasis on personnel rather than technology. In Mayon-White, W.M., S. Ayestaran, P. Humphreys (Eds.), *Proceedings of IFIP WG 8.3 Conference* (pp. 106-120). San Sebastian.

Nohria, N. (1992). Introduction: Is a network perspective a useful way to studying organisations. In Nohria, N. and Eccles, R.G. (Eds.), *Networks and organisations: Structure form and action.* Boston, MA: Harvard Business School Press.

Perrow, C. (1970). *Organisational analysis—a sociological view.* Tavistock Publications.

Roethlisberger, F., & Dickson, W.J. (1939). *Management and the worker.* Cambridge: Harvard University Press.

Simon, H. (1977). *The new science of management decisions.* Englewood Cliff, NJ: Prentice Hall.

Stake, R.E. (1994). Case studies. In Denzin, N.K., and Lincoln, Y. S. (Eds.), *Handbook of qualitative research.* London: Sage Publications.

Wasserman, S., & Faust, K. (1994). *Social network analysis: Methods and applications.* Cambridge, England: Cambridge University Press.

Winter, S.G. (1985). The case for mechanistic decision making. In Pennings & Associates (Eds.), *Organisational strategy and change.* London: Jossey-Bass Publishers.

Yin, R. (1994). *Case study research—design and methods, applied social research methods series.* London: Sage Publications.

KEY TERMS

Groupware: The category of software which is destined to support the work of groups working on collective tasks. Groupware applications can be very simple, such as e-mail, or very complex, such as workflow modeling systems.

Mechanistic Decision Making: Refers to Winter's (1985) notion that organizations are actually quicker when they do not spent too much time reinventing the wheel. In mechanistic decision making, the reliance on well charted routines and procedures can allow for a rapid reaction to known situations as well as to situations that are nearly like known situations.

Routinisation: The process whereby a certain procedure or process become ingrained in the fabric of an organisation such that actors no longer question its use. If the procedure or process is well understood and its use is correct, then routinisation allows firms to become very adept at solving certain types of problems. In other circumstances, routinisation can also lead to loss of adaptability and poor reaction to certain infrequent events.

Structured and Unstructured Decisions: The degree of structuredness of a decision is analogous to Simon's (1977) notion of programmable vs. to non-programmable decision, which describes the extent to which a complete model can be proposed for the decision in all its aspects—it is all the variables it involves and the relationships amongst them.

ENDNOTE

[1] An earlier version of this case study was published as part of Brézillon, P., Adam, F. and Pomerol, J.-Ch. (2004) Supporting complex decision making processes in organizations with collaborative applications - A case study. In: Favela, J. & Decouchant, D. (Eds.) Groupware: Design, Implementation, and Use. LNCS 2806, Springer Verlag, pp. 261-276.

Identifying Resilient Actions in Decision Making During Emergencies

Marcelo Índio dos Reis
Federal University of Rio de Janeiro, Brazil

Marcos R. S. Borges
Federal University of Rio de Janeiro, Brazil

José Orlando Gomes
Federal University of Rio de Janeiro, Brazil

INTRODUCTION

All emergency management phases demands knowledge that is embedded in procedures and also in the minds of people who handle them. Specifically in emergency response, a great amount of contextual information is generated which results from the development of the event, including the unplanned remedial actions carried out by the teams. Part of these remedial actions and decisions are made on the fly because they are not part of the formal procedures. After the event, the understanding and the analysis of these situations are important to refine the emergency plans. Many emergency investigations do this, but they usually concentrate on failures. Our approach is to concentrate on those actions that resulted in success.

Telling stories is a natural way of transmitting tacit knowledge among individuals and groups. Stories are great vehicles for wrapping together elements of knowledge such as tacit knowledge, emotion, the core, and the context. They are a very powerful way to represent complex, multidimensional concepts. While a certain amount of knowledge can be reflected as information, stories hold the key to unlocking vital knowledge, which remains beyond the reach of codified information (Ruggles, 2004).

This article shows how collective stories (Valle, Prinz, & Borges, 2002) could be used for identifying resilient actions during an emergency response. The approach used to analyze the incident reports is based on resilience engineering. This approach is challenging, but the benefits are very useful to the design of response procedures. Among these benefits we can mention the initial understanding of how emergency workers adapt their actions in response to unpredicted situations, the identification of the security boundaries, and the possibility of incorporating new successful procedures in the emergency plans. As pointed out by Cook and Woods (2006), "an important question for resilience management is a better understanding of how the window of opportunity for learning can be extended or enhanced following accidents" (p. 317).

The article also reports a case study where we used the method and the tool (Carminatti, 2006) to recall stories during a large fire in a supermarket in Rio de Janeiro. The stories were told by firefighters who participated in the response to this incident.

The article is divided as follows: the second section reviews the background of collective knowledge recall and the characteristics of the knowledge generated during emergency response situations. The next section explains a method for identifying resilient actions from stories and the group dynamics associated with this process. It also reports an experiment performed by firefighters who used group storytelling to report their decisions and actions during a fire in a supermarket in Rio de Janeiro, Brazil. The following section examines the future trends in the use of the resilience engineering approach in emergency situations and we then conclude the article.

BACKGROUND

The importance of knowledge has motivated companies to develop practices to facilitate its management. Many organizations assign high priority to documentation, but not all knowledge is stored in documents (Desouza, 2003). The experience of its members, their ideas and decisions are also part of the organization's knowledge.

Nonaka and Takeuchi (1995) define these elements as tacit knowledge. It consists of technical abilities: mental models, beliefs, and ingrained perspectives not easily manifested.

When we want to recall an episode that has occurred in the past and which has been witnessed by a group of people, we should count on their collective testimony to try to reconstitute the episode. It usually happens, however, that any individual participant is unable to tell the full story because the individual knows only part of the full event. Only when grouped together do the events make sense. This state is achieved through knowledge exchange and combination. Although this is not enough to guarantee the full reconstitution of the episode, as some events may not have been witnessed or some witness may not be available, the collective knowledge recall is more complete than individual recall reports.

The reporting of an episode can have four versions: the version stored in the minds of the people who witnessed or participated in all or some of the events (the stored version); the version reported by these people, that is, the externalization of their tacit knowledge (the recounted version); the version known by these people, that is, the set of knowledge the participants possess (the tacit version); and the real or true description of the events, which is probably nonexistent (Carminatti, Borges, & Gomes, 2006) (the faithful version). The distinction between the stored and the tacit versions bears explanation.

The reported version is generated when the participants externalize their knowledge about the events they have witnessed. However, during this process they can forget and disregard events they think are not relevant, making the reported version different from the known version. There are also cases where faulty memory, subjective perception, and partial or erroneous knowledge may distort the report. The goal of the tuning/recalling process is to approximate the reported version to the known version. The closer the reported version is to the known one, the better the recalling process is. Thus, the first goal of our method is to reconstruct the story as closely as possible to the collectively known story. In our work we used a group storytelling technique, instead of the more traditional approach, based on interviews.

Before an emergency response story can serve as knowledge transfer, it must be constructed. The assembly of a real story is the process of recalling knowledge from past events that have occurred. This can be an individual or a group task depending on whether the story fragments are remembered by one or more individuals. In the latter case, members of a group contribute to creating a story collectively. This technique is called group storytelling. The knowledge generated by a group storytelling process is usually richer than that generated by individuals interviewed individually (Shen, Lesh, Vernier, Forlines, & Frost, 2002). A group storytelling process develops on and explores possible differences in points of view, is stimulating and dynamic, and promotes synergy among participants.

The idea of using a group storytelling mechanism is simple, but its execution or implementation is not. It depends on the existence of a knowledge management culture as well as that of a collaborative culture. A collective story is more difficult to obtain but in many cases is also richer.

The group storytelling approach has been used in some works. Valle et al. (2002) reported its use for recalling decision processes. Carminatti et al. (2006) compared the group storytelling approach against the interview and the group dynamics techniques, demonstrating the advantages of the first. Schäfer, Valle, and Prinz (2004) applied group storytelling to create team awareness. Acosta, Collaxos, Guerrero, Pino, Neyem, and Motelet (2004) used the group storytelling approach to support the externalization of tacit knowledge.

According to Bertlanffy, as mentioned by Sundström and Hollnagel (2006), a system is "a complex set of elements in [dynamic] interaction" (p. 221). We can consider that the composition of one or more teams of workers responding to an emergency, or even the occurrence of the emergency itself, is a system, inasmuch as it is possible to define the elements that compose it and the objectives of its existence. Therefore, a unit of the fire department fighting a fire or a police unit responding to a hijack event can also be considered a system.

It is possible to define a system's working states and the transitions among them (Hollnagel & Sundström, 2006; Sundström & Hollnagel, 2006). These states are established considering how close the system is to its safety limits and how effectively it reaches the objectives for which it was created. Thus, we consider resilient those decisions that are successful, adopted to guarantee a system's dynamic equilibrium, so as to correct, minimize, or even avoid the effects of an unforeseen event. This event can act on the system and drive its transition from a more stable functioning state to a less stable one, or even to a state of inadequate functioning. These decisions generate plans composed of one or more actions and are defined based on the results of the interaction among the members of the teams that participate in the response to an emergency.

Among the various resilience characteristics in making a decision, we consider fundamental:

- The recovery or maintenance of system stability in the system on which the decision acted, which can be assessed through the analysis of the system's prior and following states, after the occurrence of some event.
- Anticipation, achieved through recognizing the warning signs of the imminent occurrence of unforeseen events. The greater the anticipation relative to the occurrence of the event, the more resilient it is. Making decisions ever more pro-active should be a constant goal of organizations.

For a decision to be successful it needs a correct analysis of the situation at hand, which requires current and contextualized information. The anticipation which characterizes a decision's degree of resilience is made possible by the decision maker's ability to recognize the warning signs of undesired and unforeseen events. This is achieved through the integration of prior formal knowledge obtained through training and previous experience, and contextual knowledge available about the current emergency, that the decision maker brings to bear on the threat faced (Diniz, Borges, Gomes, & Canós, 2005).

Incorporating resilient decisions into emergency plans favors this inasmuch as it spreads the knowledge to the rest of the organization. This can improve access to knowledge that was collectively produced by the teams that partook in the response to an emergency and help increase professionals' perception when making future decisions.

The model in Figure 1 presents, on the left, the barriers that attempt to stop the threat propagation and concatenation that can provoke a damaging event, and on the right, barriers that attempt to mitigate the consequences of such event (Hale & Heijer, 2006).

These barriers are defined during the system's design stage, in response to threats identified during its conception. Due to the variability to which the system

Figure 1. Bowtie model (Hale & Heijer, 2006)

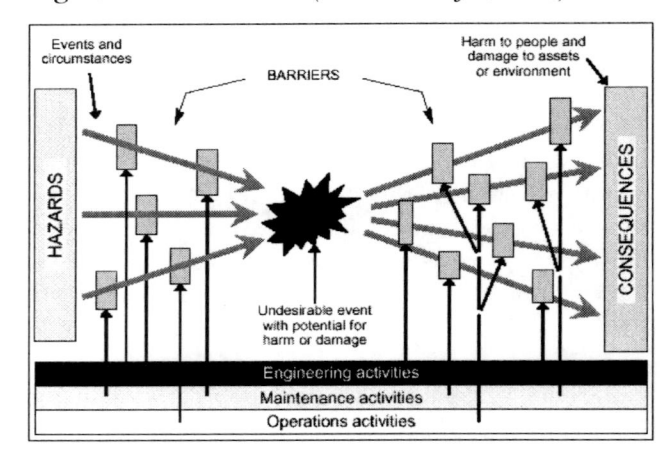

is subjected during operation, unforeseen threats appear which may or may not be perceived beforehand. These will require the decision-maker to develop action plans from the decisions made and implemented to attempt to somehow maintain the system's stability.

A resilient decision needs to be based on information from the context in which the decision occurs, to allow the decision-maker a correct understanding of the threats jeopardizing the system's stability. Diniz (2006) presented a framework of the snapshot information that supports decision-making by the system's manager.

On the other hand, it is possible that some decisions have no effect on the system, or it may even be prejudicial to the system's stability. This may make evident that the decision was made based on a false perception of the existing threats, where the model adopted to analyze the situation did not match the real possibilities of the emergency's development. Another possibility is that, in spite of the information available to him reflecting the real situation, the decision-maker did not make and implement decisions capable to maintain the system's stability.

An issue particularly relevant to organizations is identifying, capturing, and structuring resilient decisions made by their personnel during actions on a given system. Eliciting and incorporating this knowledge into the organization's memory can favor the improvement of system safety inasmuch as it allows the collective appropriation of the decisions made and allows that they subsidize new decisions in similar contexts.

MAIN FOCUS

To enable the identification of resilient decisions made during emergency responses and their incorporation into the organization's emergency plans, we propose a method based on the resilient action identification method (Reis, Borges, & Gomes, 2007), consisting of the six phases listed in Table 1.

The first phase includes the definition of the system being analysed, its objectives and components, as well as a system state model which enables its characterization relative to its functioning health, or the fluency with which it reaches its objectives. This task is executed by one or more domain specialists with a broad system knowledge relative to the analysed emergency response.

Figure 2 presents the system states model proposed to characterize business systems in general and those focused on financial services in particular (Sundström & Hollnagel, 2006).

The second phase deals with the recovery of the history of events in the emergency response. The group storytelling technique, a way to create a story through the collaboration of people who participated or witnessed the response to some emergency, is used for this; in this case, with the workers of the organizations that responded to the emergency and witnesses.

In the third phase, as presented in Figure 3, one or more time-lines that link the various events in the emergency response story chronologically are created, in a manner similar to that proposed by Crandall, Klein, and Hoffman (2005). They are necessary to characterize the system states before and after a decision to allow its degree of resilience to be established.

The fourth phase refers to the identification of the resilience characteristics in the decisions made during the emergency. This is done by a resilience analyst so as to reduce the number of decisions required of the domain specialist in the next phase.

In the fifth phase, the domain specialist, or group of specialists, assesses the states the system was in before and after an analysed decision and its implementation. If the decision contributed to maintaining the system's dynamic equilibrium, it is deemed resilient. Figure 4 presents the possible state transitions resulting from a decision made in an attempt to maintain system stability.

In this same phase, the domain specialist(s) assesses the decision's degree of anticipation, checking to see if it avoided an event or minimized its consequences. A system equilibrium maintaining decision is more resilient the greater its anticipation is.

In the sixth phase, the domain specialist will check to see whether the decision is already part of the organization's emergency plans, and if not, will require that the convenience of including it in those plans be analysed.

The resilient decisions identification and analysis using the proposed method will allow them to be incorporated into the organization's memory, where

Table 1. The six phases of the resilient action identification method

1.	Characterization of the system and its possible working states;
2.	Collective recounting of the emergency response story;
3.	Construction of a time-line of events described in the emergency response story;
4.	Identification of possibly resilient decisions;
5.	Analysis of identified decisions;
6.	Selection and incorporation of the resilient decisions into the emergency plans.

Figure 2. Three key business system states transition behaviours (Sundström & Hollnagel, 2006)

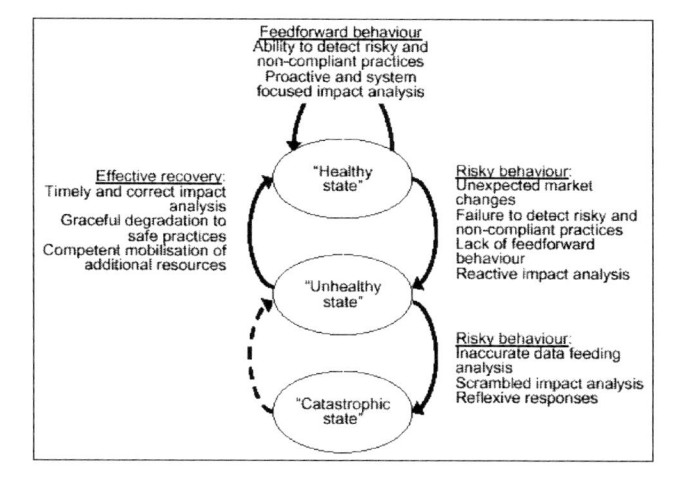

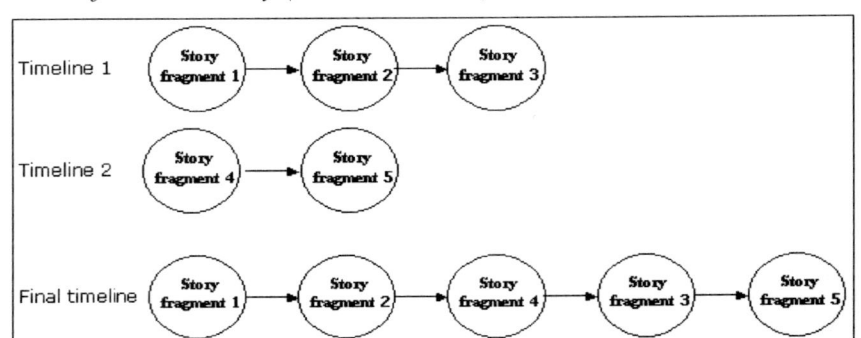

Figure 3. Time-lines identified in the story (Reis et al., 2007)

Figure 4. Predecessor and successor states of the system upon execution of a decision

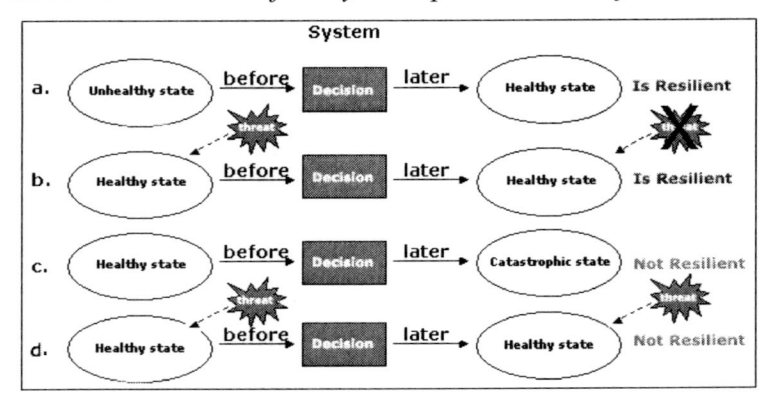

they can increment its emergency plans as well as aid in training decision makers.

The case studied to assess the proposed method was the Rio de Janeiro State Fire Department's emergency response to a fire in a supermarket in a medium sized commercial building in November 2005. The fire began on the building's upper floor in the storeroom, and, due to the high inventory level held for the oncoming holiday season, it spread rapidly, hindering the firemen's work.

The story of the emergency response was recounted by the fire-fighting officers who participated in the incident, using the TellStory tool. The decision analysis phase was conducted by a high ranking officer with 25 years experience in the fire corps, including 6 years in a command position.

The domain specialist was also active in the method's first phase, defining the system, its objectives, components, and functioning states using the state-space diagram presented in Figure 2. Although the diagram was originally developed to characterize business systems in general, and those focused on financial services in particular, it was considered capable of confirming the hypothesis put forth in this work. This is shown in Table 2.

During the analysis of the decisions recounted in the story of the response to the emergency the resilience analyst identified resilience characteristics in one of them, the decision to relieve the load on the structure due to water accumulation within it. This decision has resilience characteristics, such as the ability to anticipate threats and their consequences (Westrum, 2006), the ability to react rapidly and even reorganize the system when faced with problems, flexibility (Reis, 2007), and perception (Wreathall, 2006).

Upon noticing that the building had not been designed to hold the weight of the full storeroom with drenched inventory, besides the water which was accumulating undrained, the system manager made and implemented the decision to relieve the weight

Identifying Resilient Actions in Decision Making During Emergencies

Table 2. Summary of the analyzed system's characterization

Title: Small and medium size commercial building fire-fighting system	
Objective: Extinguish fire in commercial buildings with up to three floors of space, without dangerous chemical or radioactive material storage	
Components: Water source and supply, team of fire-fighting professionals	
System working states and their characterization	
State	**Characteristics**
Healthy	The fire-fighting team is able to control the situation, gradually quelling the flames until their total extinction. The team members do not face risks of death, although accidents that may take them out of action are possible.
Unhealthy	The fire-fighting team is unable to control the situation, and the flames threaten to destroy the building and spread to neighboring buildings. The team members face risk of death, which make continued operations untenable in the present operating mode.
Catastrophic	The building is totally destroyed and collapses, several neighboring buildings are affected by the flames, and the intervention of additional fire units beyond the first one is necessary. Team members die due to accidents during the fire-fighting operations.

Figure 5. Adaptation of the conceptual map of knowledge support during an emergency response phase (Diniz, 2005)

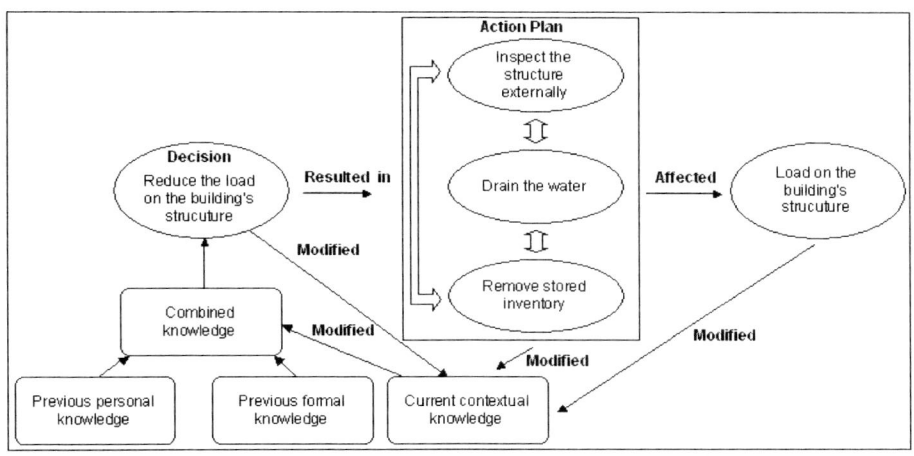

on the structure. This decision shows anticipation in recognizing a threat, and lead to maintenance of the system's stable state.

The action plan, which resulted from the decision to relieve the weight on the structure, produced three actions, as we can see in the diagram in Figure 5, adapted from the conceptual of knowledge support during an emergency response phase (Diniz, 2005).

In Table 3 we can see that, prior to the adoption of the decision, the system's state was healthy according to the domain specialist's analysis, with a possible transition to unhealthy due to the threat of structure collapse due to excess weight, which could even cause the death of the fire-fighters that were in the building should it collapse.

FUTURE TRENDS

The resilience engineering approach has been suggested as a way to create foresight and manage risk proactively. There will always be finite resources and uncertainty when dealing with emergencies. The traditional approach prescribed to most risky situations is to create new barriers when a potential threat is revealed. As systems become increasingly complex, alternatives have

Table 3. Summary of the analysis of the decision

Incident: Supermarket fire in Ilha do Governador, Rio de Janeiro, Brazil	
Contextual knowledge:	The operation commander noticed the large amount of inventory in the supermarkets storeroom. The availability of numerous fire-fighting vehicles at the scene prompted an attempt to quell the fire through the use of a large quantity of water. The weight of undrained water absorbed by the inventory increased the load on the structure.
Risks:	Bodily harm to the members of the fire-fighting team that were in the building and material losses, due to a possible collapse of the building.
Decision:	Relieve the structure of the increasing weight.
Action plan:	(a) Analyze the building structure to verify the imminence of structure collapse. (b) Drain the water by opening a path between the shelves in the storeroom. (c) Discard the inventory through an existing window on the building's side wall.
Action consequences:	(a) The analysis did not indicate imminent collapse, allowing the fire-fighting teams to remain in the building. (b) Opening the drainage passage was not successful due to some shelves falling over and blocking the way. (c) Dumping much of the inventory assured the relief of the weight on the structure.
State prior to the decision's implementation:	Although healthy, it was unstable due to the existing threat of collapse of the building's structure.
State after the decision's implementation:	Healthy without the threat, due to the reduction of the load on the structure.
Decision classification:	Resilient, even though not all of the planned actions were successful.

been researched. The resilience engineering represents a paradigm shift towards safety systems.

To achieve resilience organizations need support for decisions about safety tradeoffs—how to help organizations decide when to relax production pressure to reduce risk. Woods (2006) and Wreathall (2006) refer to these tradeoff decisions as sacrifice judgments because acute production or efficiency related goals are temporarily sacrificed, or the pressure to achieve these goals relaxed, in order to reduce risks of approaching too near safety boundary conditions. We need to improve our knowledge about these situations and develop models to deal with these tradeoffs. Unfortunately, most of this knowledge remains tacit in the minds of experienced workers.

A possible way to deal with tacit knowledge used in emergency response situations is trying to recall the decisions made during the event using collaborative tools. The collaboration is justified because most incidents and decisions have different facets that can only be collectively recalled. In most emergencies, unanticipated events occur and require decisions and actions not prescribed in emergency plans (French & Turoff, 2007).

We believe that the collective knowledge recall supported by the group storytelling technique associated with the resilience engineering approach is very promising. We have been able to recover events that are not part of the official reports and up to the time of this group storytelling exercise only existed in the minds of the participants. The discovery of resilient actions has the potential of improving the response procedures, that is, they can promote the processes of knowledge acquisition and transfer, especially the knowledge that remains tacit in the minds of experienced workers. This is particularly important for new technologies, such as mobile artifacts.

CONCLUSION

In this article we have presented a method for identifying resilient actions during emergency responses. The method consists of six phases and uses the stories told by the participants in the event and the knowledge of specialists to select actions for a comprehensive analysis of their implications in the event states. The resilience engineering approach concentrates on the actions that were considered successful, that is, brought the emergency from an unstable state to a stable or less unstable state. The method was applied in the analysis of a real event, although only a simple illustration was presented in this article. The complete study is under construction (Reis, 2007).

The proposed method is under evaluation and still has many uncertainties and limitations. Although we have successfully applied the group storytelling approach in other contexts, we are not sure yet how cooperative the participants would be in emergency reports. The results obtained so far are not enough to confirm our assumptions. The method is also very dependent on the set of states defined by the emergency specialists. An incorrect definition can result from erroneous recommendations. The method will need to be refined and more case studies carried out before we can ascertain its benefits.

ACKNOWLEDGMENT

Marcelo Indio dos Reis is supported by a grant from the Fire-Fighting Department of the Military Police of Bahia State (Corpo de Bombeiros da Polícia Militar da Bahia - Brazil). Marcos R. S. Borges and Jose Orlando Gomes were partially supported by grants from Conselho Nacional de Desenvolvimento Científico e Tecnológico – CNPq (Brazil), 305900/2005-6 and 484981/2006-4, respectively.

REFERENCES

Acosta, C. E., Collazos, C. A., Guerrero, L. A., Pino, J. A., Neyem, H. A., & Motelet, O. (2004). StoryMapper: A multimedia tool to externalize knowledge. In *Proceedings of the 24th International Conference of the Chilean Computer Science Society*, Chile (pp. 133-140).

Carminatti, N. (2006). *Group storytelling applied to collective knowledge recall*. M.Sc. dissertation, Graduate Program in Informatics, Federal University of Rio de Janeiro (in Portuguese).

Carminatti, N., Borges, M. R. S., & Gomes, J.O. (2006). Analyzing approaches to collective knowledge recall. *Computing and Informatics, 25*(6), 1001-1024.

Cook, R.I., & Woods, D. D. (2006). Distancing through differencing: An obstacle to organizational learning following accidents. In E. Hollnagel, D. D. Woods & N. Leveson (Eds.), *Resilience engineering: Concepts and precepts* (pp. 329-338). Williston, VT: Ashgate.

Crandall, B., Klein, G., & Hoffman, R. R. (2006). *Working minds a practitioner's guide to cognitive task analysis*. The MIT Press, 76-77.

Desouza, K. C. (2003). Facilitating tacit knowledge exchange. *Communications of the ACM, 46*(6), 85-88.

Diniz, V. B. (2006). An approach for designing knowledge management systems in emergency response domain. M.Sc. dissertation, Graduate Program in Informatics, Federal University of Rio de Janeiro (in Portuguese).

Diniz, V. B., Borges, M. R. S., Gomes, J. O., & Canós, J.H. (2005). Knowledge management support for collaborative emergency response. In *Proceedings of the Conference on Computer Supported Cooperative Work in Design*, Coventry, UK (Vol. 2, pp. 1188-1193).

French, S., & Turoff, M. (2007). Decision support systems. *Communications of the ACM, 50*(3), 39-40.

Hale, A., & Heijer, T. (2006). Defining resilience. In E. Hollnagel, D. D. Woods & N. Leveson (Eds.), *Resilience engineering: Concepts and precepts* (pp. 31-36). Williston, VT: Ashgate.

Hollnagel, E., & Sundström, G. (2006). States of resilience. In E. Hollnagel, D. D. Woods & N. Leveson (Eds.), *Resilience engineering: Concepts and precepts* (pp. 339-346). Williston, VT: Ashgate.

Nonaka, I., & Takeuchi, H. (1995). *The knowledge-creating company: How Japanese companies create the dynamics of innovation* (pp. 21-45). Oxford, England: Oxford University Press.

Reis, M. (2007). *Recalling resilient actions during emergency response*. M.Sc. dissertation, Graduate Program in Informatics, Federal University of Rio de Janeiro (in Portuguese, under development).

Reis, M. I., Borges, M. R. S., & Gomes, J.O. (2007). Recalling resilient actions during emergency response. In J. Löffler & M. Klann (Eds.), Mobile response 2007. *Lecture Notes in Computer Science, 4458*, 153-162.

Ruggles, R. (2004). *The role of stories in knowledge management*. Storytelling Foundation. Retrieved December 11, 2007, from http://www.providersedge.com/docs/km_articles/The_Role_of_Stories_in_KM.pdf

Schäfer, L., Valle, C., & Prinz, W. (2004). Group storytelling for team awareness and entertainment. In *Proceedings of the 3rd Nordic Conference on Human-computer Interaction*, Tampere, Finland (pp. 441-444).

Shen, C., Lesh, N. B., Vernier, F., Forlines, C., & Frost, J. (2002). Building and sharing digital group histories. In *Proceedings of the 2002 ACM Conference on Computer Supported Cooperative Work (CSCW)*, New Orleans, Louisiana (pp. 324-333).

Sundström, G., & Hollnagel, E. (2006). Learning how to create resilience in business systems. In E. Hollnagel, D. D. Woods & N. Leveson (Eds.), *Resilience engineering: Concepts and precepts* (pp. 220-237). Williston, VT: Ashgate.

Valle, C., Prinz, W., & Borges, M. R. S. (2002). Generation of group storytelling in post-decision implementation process. In *Proceedings of the 7th International Conference on Computer Supported Cooperative Work in Design*, Rio de Janeiro, Brazil (pp. 361-367).

Westrum, R. (2006). A typology of resilience situations. In E. Hollnagel, D. D. Woods & N. Leveson (Eds.), *Resilience engineering: Concepts and precepts* (pp. 55-65). Williston, VT: Ashgate.

Wreathall, J. (2006). Properties of resilient organizations: An initial view. In E. Hollnagel, D. D. Woods & N. Leveson (Eds.), *Resilience engineering: Concepts and precepts* (pp. 258-268). Williston, VT: Ashgate.

Woods, D. D. (2006). How to design a safety organization: Test case for resilience engineering. In E. Hollnagel, D. D. Woods & N. Leveson (Eds.), *Resilience engineering: Concepts and precepts* (pp. 315-326). Williston, VT: Ashgate.

KEY TERMS

Emergency: A serious situation triggered by one or more events that poses a risk to life, property, or environment.

Emergency Plan: A set of predefined procedures to be adopted during the occurrence of an emergency.

Emergency Response: An articulated response to an emergency.

Group Storytelling: A technique for acquiring tacit knowledge retained by a group of people.

Resilient Decisions: Well succeeded decisions adopted to guarantee a system's dynamic equilibrium, so as to correct, minimize, or even avoid the effects of an unforeseen event.

The Impact on Decision Making of Centralisation in a Multinational Manufacturing Company: The Materials Purchasing Function

Fergal Carton
University College Cork, Ireland

INTRODUCTION

Multinational companies faced with an uncertain world are notorious for centralising control of their far flung empires to the extent that local decision making becomes a matter of managers merely executing orders rather than showing creativity or initiative in solving issues. Control can be best exerted by *standardising* processes and centralising responsibility for decision making. Enterprise resource planning (ERP) systems are a perfect vehicle for such centralising forces, imposing a common way of doing business across the organisation, and simultaneously providing a head office with centralised control of those practices. On the other hand, these *highly integrated systems* exacerbate rather than resolve the managers' information deficit problems. Though providing a high level of granularity of transactional data, they fail to assist managers in controlling business *performance* to predefined targets. Taking the material purchasing department of a manufacturing multinational as an example, this article studies the impact of ERP-enabled centralisation on day to day decision making of managers both at a local plant and at corporate head office (HQ). Although huge improvements in *data integrity* at an operational level (inventory, procurement, *standardisation* of codes, prices, and so forth) have made local *cost control* much more robust, local managers have sacrificed the ability to investigate these costs. As prices are set centrally by commodity teams, local managers have been disempowered with respect to leveraging purchase price variance (PPV) and quality in their relationships with suppliers. Furthermore, they are asked to implement radical *cost saving programmes* without disturbing the availability of raw materials for production. From a local point of view, managers do not have a say in the setting of targets, and do not have the tools (or know how) to work with the detailed transactional data in the ERP system to be able to understand *cost drivers*. HQ, on the other hand, gain in visibility of local *costs*, and typically make no change to *integrate* their own planning applications, retaining legacy tools and interfaces. This article examines the apparent imbalance between the price paid by local materials buyers, namely a huge bureaucratic overhead, and the benefit derived by corporate purchasing.

BACKGROUND

ERP could be classified as one of Thompson's (1967, p. 17) "mediating" technologies, requiring the *extensive* operation of activities in *standardised* ways. The benefits of standardisation have been compared with utilities/ banks/ employment agencies, where the benefits do not accrue until all subscribers are incorporated into the network.

The problem of organisation design is to create mechanisms that permit coordinated action across large numbers of interdependent roles (Galbraith, 1974). Furthermore, the greater the task uncertainty, the greater the amount of information that must be processed among decision makers during task execution in order to achieve a given level of performance (Galbraith, 1974). So the organisation adopts integrating mechanisms which increase its information processing capabilities.

Davenport (1998) showed the paradoxical impact of ERP on companies' organisation and culture. On the one hand, by providing universal, *real-time* access to operating and financial data, ERPs allow companies to streamline their management structures, creating flatter, more flexible, and more democratic organisations. On the other hand they also involve the centralisation of control over information and the *standardisation* of processes, which are qualities more consistent with hierarchical, command and control organisations with uniform cultures.

Thus, multinationals face a choice between using their ERP as a *standardisation* tool or preserving some degree of local independence in software and business processes (Davenport, 1998). Most local subsidiaries do not have a say in the decision to implement ERP, so it is usual that the global solution lacks some capability to deal with the local requirements, though some local sites with better political connections or more influence on key processes typically get better treatment than others.

In the case of the purchasing (materials) department, many ERP implementations derive much of their justification from the rationalisation of the supply base. Adam (2004) describes how businesses can succumb to the "ERP steamroller" of integration in the area of procurement. *Cost savings* are realised through a rationalisation of local suppliers and purchasing patterns and the elimination of redundant suppliers. Advantageous volume purchase agreements may be negotiated at a global level, therefore leveraging the buying power of the corporation as a whole. At the same time, key local relationships and more flexible person-to-person arrangements are sacrificed without a possible measure of how critical they are in operational terms.

These benefits can of course be obtained without the attendant implementation of centralised data and processes (as exemplified by single instance ERP applications) but typically the savings are realised through the roll out of a system to manage the newly structured master data and procedures throughout the dispersed multinational.

To understand the role of ERP in procurement, it is useful to look briefly at the history of these applications, and, in particular, to consider the evolution of *material requirements planning* (MRP) through to present day ERP.

MRP: THE FIRST STEP ON THE ROAD TO BUSINESS INTEGRATION

MRP originated in the early 1960s as a computerised approach for the planning of materials acquisition and production for more complex manufacturing processes where interdependencies between components existed. Orlicky (1975) realised that a computer enabled the detailed application of the technique, making it effective in managing manufacturing inventories.

Based around the Bill of Materials (BOM), early applications exploded a production plan for a top level parent item into a plan of production and purchasing for component items. These systems were implemented on large mainframe computers run in centralised material planning departments for large companies.

Closed loop MRP, which provided for the feedback from the execution to the planning cycle, together with some financial modules, developed into an *integrated* approach to the management of manufacturing resources known as Manufacturing Resource Planning or MRP II. From the 1980s onwards, MRP II applications became available at lower cost on minicomputers and then microcomputers.

Extending the integration into other functional areas such as finance, distribution, and human resources, ERP systems can be linked to an increasing business trend towards globalization. To be successful, a global company must be able to control and coordinate their various remote operating units. Accurate, *real-time information* provided by an ERP system has the ability to *integrate* the more remote subsidiaries into corporate practice because an ERP system allows the sharing of information in *standard* format across departments, currencies, languages, and national borders. Thus, ERP systems can be used to provide a "common language" between units (Bingi, Sharma, & Godla, 1999; Horwitt, 1998).

Multinational manufacturing companies can clearly benefit from this centralising effect of ERP implementations. However, it is unclear whether these benefits accrue to all levels in the organisation. Furthermore, research would suggest that the benefits that do accrue tend to accumulate around the finance department, which has the greatest need of *real time information* on expenditure and revenues for planning and control purposes.

CENTRALISATION AND MATERIALS PLANNING

In this article we focus on two aspects of the centralisation of decision making associated with ERP implementations: first how it affects the materials purchasing department of a large multinational manufacturing organisation and second how its impact is perceived across the organisational divide between head office and the local site.

There are a number of reasons why the *materials department* is suitable as an example to illustrate the impact of centralisation on management decision making. As it is where demand meets supply, it is a critical survival process for any business. On the one hand, material must at all costs be available for manufacturing goods so as to fulfil customer demands, no matter what the circumstances; thus this function is highly dependent on the accuracy of sales forecast. On the other hand, finishing the quarter with excess inventory in most manufacturing companies is unacceptable because, as well as incurring a *cost* for carrying the inventory, the resources and capacity used in producing that unsold inventory might have gone toward revenue generating products.

In manufacturing companies with long lead times this is doubly constraining, as planning horizons are, because of the complexity of the production process, too long to allow planners to await the final confirmed orders before beginning production. So planners are working in a twilight zone where key planning decisions must be made in the absence of actual orders.

As the quarter progresses, buyers must deal with a number of issues that may distort the parameters of the original decisions earlier in the quarter:

- Changes in actual production yields (which may arise due to issues with suppliers, component quality, manufacturing capacity, labour shortage, and so forth)
- Changes in sales targets arising from new market conditions or customer reaction to products
- Changes in inventory management targets related to the financial *performance* of the company.

It is how a company deals with these changes that is most telling in terms of the maturity of management decision processes. For large manufacturing multinationals, it is likely that a lot of the information involved is held in centralised systems, although the extent to which ERP systems are *integrated* in this function varies greatly.

The information required by planners is highly structured (customer demand, on-hand inventory, supplier lead times, etc.). The volume of information required is high, and the timeliness of the information is critical. Information of different types (currency, units, date, etc.) needs to be managed.

The scope of the decisions taken will span over more than one geographic location. This has an important technical and organisational connotation: managers must have access to the required information in a format and timescale commensurate with the urgency of the decision being made.

RESEARCH OBJECTIVE

The research objective is operationalised into three aspects of the impact of centralisation, organisational, decisional, and informational. The *organisational* aspect is explored in the centralisation of supplier relationship management to a corporate function, divesting the local site of all but the execution elements of the procurement cycle. Crucially, we will look at how this affects the local material department's ability to achieve *cost* targets in the light of an ever changing demand pattern.

The *decisional* impact is analysed from the point of view of the types of decisions that need to be made, their frequency and efficiency. Of particular interest here are areas where the centralisation of the purchasing function has resulted in a net deterioration of visibility for buyers due to the latency in the planning process itself.

The *informational* impact is considered from the point of view of the granularity of the data required by managers, and particularly of the capability of local management to exploit the highly detailed information contained within the database of production information contained within the ERP system.

These themes were used subsequently in the coding of observations, using the MD_03 code as described below.

THE RESEARCH METHOD

As already indicated, our study focused on the decisions made by materials purchasing managers from a large multinational company in the high tech manufacturing sector. The company studied for this research is presented in Table 1.

Interviews were carried out using a semistructured format, and each interview lasted at least an hour. All interviews were transcribed, and each transcript is coded at three levels, the header level, the seed category level, and the decision level. The header level identified the interviewee, the function to which they were affiliated, and the role within that function.

The seed categories, derived from the research objective described above, allowed the isolation of the observations related to this research (management decisions) from other observation categories used in this field work.

The decisional level coding (MD_01 to MD_04) allowed the observations relating to management decisions to be further classified according to their content (abstracting a higher level of meaning from the initial observation as transcribed).

MD_01 involved "decontextualising" the observation, extracting one level of meaning beyond the immediate organizational context of the interview transcript, that is, creating labels for each management decision in a way that could be understood outside the case study itself. This allowed a certain level of reduction of the overall count of management decision observations (23%).

MD_02 classified the observations by the business process area being commented on, independently of the interviewee's own affiliation. These processes covered manufacturing processes (Plan, Buy, Make, Deliver), finance processes (Forecast, Approve & Pay, Order entry, Report), and Sales processes (Sell, Service). For the purposes of this research, observations concerning "Buy" decisions were isolated from the other process areas. Table 1 gives the breakdown of observations by process area and by functional background of the interviewee.

The 45 decision observations referring to the Buy process are the subject of this article. They came from eight interviewees, comprising three managers, three directors, and two vice presidents. They came in the main from the Materials function, but with a small number coming from the related functions of Finance, Manufacturing, and Information Systems.

The Buy process observations were also coded according to the three themes identified in the research objective section, that is, observations were classified according to whether they referred to organisational, decisional or informational dimensions (MD_03). Table 3 shows the count of observations by theme in the sample.

Finally the decision data was coded according to the nature of the observation, that is, what characteristic of the decision making process was referred to in the observation. Table 4 shows the count of observations by decision characteristic (MD_04).

Note that characteristics with only one observation were excluded, resulting in the reduction in number of observations included. The decision characteristics thus eliminated were Commercial leverage, Flexibility, Lean, and Speed.

Of those characteristics remaining, Centralisation, Goals, and Hard vs. Soft target are decision charac-

Table 1. Presentation of the case study company

	Store-It Technologies (SIT)[1]
Industry	Data management
Turnover 06 ($bn)	11.2
Employees	26,500
WW operations	52
Manufacturing sites	3
Head Office	Boston, USA
ERP System	Oracle 11.03
Architecture	Single instance
Server location	Boston, USA
Go-live	Big-bang 2001

Table 2. Breakdown of observations by process area and functional background of interviewee

MD_02: Business Process	Customer service	Distribution	Finance	HR	IS	Manufacturing	Materials	Sales	Grand Total
Approve & Pay			11		1				12
Buy			3		1	1	40		45
Deliver		25	32	2	20	24	2		105
Forecast			5		4				9
Make			1		8	5	37		51
Order entry			9						9
Plan			21	1		11	3		36
Report		3	38		21				62
Rev report			37						37
Sell			28		1	1		13	43
Service	4				2				6
Grand Total	7	25	185	11	55	74	45	13	415

Table 3. Breakdown of sampled observations according to research theme

MD_03: Research theme	Buy
Decisional	22
Informational	9
Organisational	14
Grand Total	**45**

Table 4. Breakdown of sampled observations according to decision characteristic

MD_04: Decision characteristic	Buy
Centralisation	2
Goals	7
Granularity	7
Hard vs. soft target	2
Latency	5
Manual	13
Uncertainty	5
Grand Total	**41**

teristics that relate to the strategic and planning level of the business activity, that is, how are organisational goals are defined, communicated, and operationalised. These are design choices made by the organisation in the way it utilises resources to achieve its aims.

Managers are charged with the execution of these goals, and, as will be discussed in the Findings section, all management decisions involve the juxtaposition of a plan or a goal against actual progress.

On the other hand, Granularity is a characteristic which is related to the level of detail of the information itself, not of the organisation. As such it can be considered an element of technical design, and, unsurprisingly, finds embodiment in the information systems implemented in the organisation. It is a contention of this research, as discussed in the Conclusions, that information granularity is "imposed" as a consequence of how information systems are delivered, rather than a deliberate design choice related to an understanding of managerial decision making processes.

Finally, the Latency, Manual, and Uncertainty characteristics refer to the decisions made by managers, and, interestingly, stem predominantly from Site level (only 3 of the 23 observations come from HQ). These clearly reflect the difficulty managers experience in being at the sharp end of goal execution.

Uncertainty comes from the business environment, cannot be avoided, and, in all likelihood, will probably worsen as competition for market share inevitably increases. Businesses do not stand still, so it is up to the manager to do his or her best to interpret the signals coming from both internal resources and external partners (customers and suppliers) in the efficient execution of the organisation's goals.

The case demonstrates that Uncertainty leads to a proliferation of Manual methods of processing information, typically involving downloading information from a central repository and manipulating it off-line using a data warehouse application or inevitably, a spreadsheet. In itself, off-line manipulation is no bad thing, as long as it leads to good business decisions, but it can be observed in this case that the extent of interfaces and data manipulation can introduce unacceptable delays in the decision process.

Latency in decision making can be attributable both to technical aspects of the organisation (for example, an ERP system begins to fall behind as quarter end approaches because of the sheer volume of data and workload being demanded), but also can be the result of poor decision process design. Indeed, how managers make decisions appears to receive a lot less focus than how operators process basic transactions. The notion of managers intuitively "knowing" how to make decisions appears to still have currency today, despite an enormous increase in the complexity of the demands placed on them.

These decision criteria together provided the basis for the analysis of the data as presented in the Findings section. In addition, by crossing these dimensions using pivot tables, the underlying interdependencies were exploited for the Conclusions section.

PRESENTATION OF THE CASE STUDY

The market leader in data management solutions, SIT's mission is to help its customers get maximum value from its information. Although originally a "large systems" company with an engineering culture, SIT has been diversifying into mid tier and lower end systems, as well as consolidating its position in the software and services market.

SIT's growth has shadowed the commoditization of computer hardware over the last three decades, as advances in integration allow desktop machines to handle ever greater amounts of information. The advent of the Internet, increasingly media-rich applications and the growth in use of e-mail to distribute content has exploded the demand for data storage capacity. Enterprise applications such as ERP have in turn increased the appetite of business users for access to in-depth transactional history.

As the complexity of data management increases for its customers, SIT has evolved from being a hardware company to a full service company, creating value for customers by delivering software tools and consulting services that address the efficient management of corporate information.

Market conditions have rebounded following the dot com bust of 2001/2002, and the company is again following an aggressive growth pattern, with 17% growth in consolidated revenue in 2005, which was the year in which the case study was carried out. Revenues have since then continued their upward growth trend, topping $11.2 billion in 2006.

SIT implemented a single instance global ERP system in 2001. This big bang implementation addressed user requirements for transaction processing in back office activities such as sales order processing, manufacturing, materials, distribution and finance. Covering over 43 geographies, the Oracle based system supports over 4,500 users worldwide.

The ERP system is one of several systems used by planning and manufacturing, the others being concerned with production planning, process control, allocation of finished goods to orders, spend analysis, and business intelligence. It is the objective of this article to demonstrate the footprint of ERP in this multi-application environment, not in terms of its interfaces with these other systems, but rather in the landscape of decision making processes.

MATERIAL PLANNING PROCESSES AT SIT

SIT has recently re-organised its supply chain, entering into strategic arrangements with global suppliers of components, subassemblies, and, in some cases, entire products. New relationships have also been forged with third party logistics suppliers (3PLs), opening up the door to "merge in transit" operations. In this scenario, unthinkable in the traditional business model where SIT physically "touched" anything shipped to customers, product from a factory meets contract manufactured product stored off-site, at an intermediate location, where it is merged to a single sales order, and from there is shipped to the customer.

There are other examples of how changes in the business model have had a huge impact on the way that inventory is managed. For example, an increase in the sale of "in-place" upgrades, as distinct from entire systems, has meant that forecasting needs to be carried out at a component level, for certain products, rather than at a final product level. The diversification into mid-tier and lower end systems has increased transactional volumes tenfold.

This transactional stress is experienced most acutely at quarter end, as the company experiences the rhythmic pressure of the "hockey stick" effect: 80% of revenue is realised in last 2 weeks of the quarter. With a singular focus on target achievement, customers and sales reps are inexorably drawn into a pattern of "reverse auction" that intensifies as quarter end approaches, where the customers strives for the best possible deal on a rapidly diminishing lot of available products.

The effect of this hockey stick, traditionally felt on high margin product, appears to be spreading into other product domains, which, coupled with the higher unit volumes, has a mushrooming effect on quarter end. It is also the case that there is not just one quarter end. Channel partners shipping high volumes can themselves provoke their own mini-hockey stick effects. Additionally, geographic remoteness can mean that a European plant feels a hockey stick effect for all Asian sales where the cut-off date for delivery is several weeks before the actual end of quarter.

Thus at quarter end there is a build up on both sides of the equation: manufacturing push product into finished goods to meet the build plan, and sales push orders through bookings and into backlog to meet the revenue goal. From a procurement perspective this means that if the demand pattern takes a shape that is materially different from the build plan, last minute arrangements are required to procurement schedules. It is this type of local flexibility that conflicts with the notion of centralized goal setting in terms of *costs savings*, which conveniently ignores the "premium" costs of last minute changes to the plan.

These changes bring new challenges to the application of legacy information systems to support management decisions. Currently, despite the investment in enterprise systems to centralize business processes, planning is still carried out in a relatively "manual" fashion at each manufacturing site.

Business *performance targets* are communicated downwards through the organisation from a quarterly sales review meeting (in dollars by product). A custom built materials management tool (MMT), picks up these demand figures, and via an interface to the ERP system, compares them to a snapshot of on-hand inventory balances.

Recent shipments are "netted off" in MMT to allow for inventory that has already been consumed. MMT also takes into account various other SIT specific inventory management policies (netting logic), such as part substitution, alternate sources of supply and field spares. It was principally because of the flexibility required by these business policies that a custom built planning tool had to be implemented alongside ERP.

The net demand derived in MMT is fed back into the ERP system, and an MRP cycle is kicked off. Unfortunately, because of the time delay between the snapshot of on-hand inventory and the output from the MRP cycle, which typically runs to 4 working days, planners take the output from MRP and manually *integrate* it into their own planning spreadsheets. It is these Excel-based procurement schedules which drive purchasing activities with suppliers.

The value of MRP in this scenario is extremely limited: the only reason net demand is fed into ERP is that the parts master, supplier file, and bill of materials allows the blowing out of net demand at a product level down to the component level. But the order levels at the component level are managed off-line in spreadsheets. ERP is being used as a (rather expensive) repository for master data, with important logic being executed in MMT and off-line.

MRP is typically used to model supplier lead times against a forecast build plan to evaluate the feasibility of that build plan. SIT production planning, on the other hand, is based on a "load and chase" culture, where component requirements are input based on estimated demand, and then planners do whatever is necessary to make it happen, even if that is inside *standard* lead times.

It is in this context of manual planning processes that our analysis of the footprint of ERP took place.

FINDINGS

As described in the research objective, the centralisation of management decisions is classified according to organisation, decisional or informational dimensions.

Organisational Dimension of Centralisation

The centralisation of purchasing activity into commodity teams and subsequent focus on continual product *cost* improvements has effectively separated the more strategic element of the management of the supplier relationship from the transactional aspect. How interviewees perceive this change to their work practices is presented in Table 5. (Note: the observations shown are hyperlinks to the original transcripts).

A key leverage point in working with suppliers is unit price. Most other attributes of the relationship (lead time, quality, responsiveness in emergencies, etc.) can be manipulated if the price is negotiable. However, the centralisation of supplier relationship management has usurped the local buyers of their influence on price in this vital discussion.

This price is negotiated at a global level and based on an ideal "picture" of how demand will actually pan out over the quarter. As one local purchasing manager described it, "And then it's based on an ideal level load, the whole lot of the pricing based on, in a perfect world, what should a [component] be costing."

The price could be considered a "soft" target, in that it is set outside the constraints of the real world, and assumes certain volume and periodicity in demand. In turn, the global nature of these negotiations has empowered corporate commodity teams to pursue aggressive cost reduction programmes. In SIT's case, this has gone as far as suppliers being told what their products "should" cost, and this being the basis for a supply contract.

The tendency to outsource supply to lower *cost* geographies means that commodity teams can achieve step changes in cost reduction, but inevitably at the expense of proximity (assuming the manufacturing plants stay in their current European and US locations).

However, local buyers need to work with suppliers in "hard" numbers to ensure component availability

Table 5. "Buy process" decisions filtered for oganisational dimension

Management decisions	MD_04
buyers solely responsible for availability, but take CM flak for price changes	Centralisation
pricing was local, but post McKinsey, pricing and contractual stuff was done at a global point of view	Centralisation
how much we buy from them, they also know how much we sell to them	Commercial leverage
re-negotiating contracts so purchasing plans are staggered to new demand picture	Flexibility
buyers don't get involved in costs, that's the commodity angle (downstairs)	Goals
I'm not a fan of on-time delivery	Goals
on-time delivery is 99%, but one part could hold up the whole plant	Goals
most key measurement for our group is how the floor is keeping up with the MPS	Goals
What is TCO, including failure and returns	Goals
Total landed cost	Goals
eg. boards from Thailand, bring at normal service (7 days) or premium service (2 days): impact on TLC goal!	Goals
2 weeks to quarter end, we've only pulled 30% of the build plan, vendor will say, OK, use it or lose it	Hard vs. soft target
if forecast is wrong, factories take into account total landed cost from suppliers, including premium cost	Hard vs. soft target
left money on the table because we didn't get aggressive enough on inbound logistics	Lean

for manufacturing, including responding to production yield issues, component quality issues, recalls, and plain old fashioned changes to the build plan. This implies that buyers risk incurring higher premium costs if a contingency arrangement has to be made: We're bringing in [components] from Thailand, do we bring them in at normal service (get here in 7 days) or premium service (get here in 2 days)?

So buyers are closer to the real pattern of actual customer demand and production contingency, as distinct from a "level loaded" picture as is assumed by corporate commodity teams.

It is also evident from the observations that the use of *Key Performance Indicators* (KPIs) is a double edged sword. Commodity teams drive deals with global suppliers independently of buyer negotiations for operational supply, and the performance of one can negatively impact the other. As one site level Director of materials put it, in describing an overly zealous pursuit of one particular KPI, on-time delivery, "It's kind of old school, my on-time delivery is 99%, but what if that one part, that you're not getting in, is holding up the whole plant."

The separation of price negotiations from purchasing deals implies that suppliers have two points of contact in the organisation, which can generate a certain degree of tension between buyers and colleagues in the commodity teams. A director at one plant described this as "interesting": It's very interesting, to listen to some of the conversations when the new pricing comes out, we actually hear people, what are you doing? Hey, that's the price they told us to get and the price that you agreed. You're crazy!

The impact of centralised goal setting on local decision making is best illustrated by looking at how buyers perceive the choices facing them in exercising their roles.

Decisional Dimension of Centralisation

MRP works well in an environment that is predictable and where lead times drive purchasing and production schedules. At SIT, supplier lead time is considered another variable to be played with in order to meet the material availability plan. It is almost a point of honour as expressed by the materials director at one plant, "and, trust me, the procurement group that's set up, our core competency is figuring out how to get the stuff with no lead times."

The key difficulty of a centralised planning process for procurement is that uncertainty in demand, experienced as frequent changes to the forecast, forces local buyers into a manual process. Their *performance* will ultimately be judged on their ability to achieve the plan, regardless of the number of changes to that plan. The difficulties for decision making as expressed in interviews with the local material procurement managers are summarised in Table 6.

Demand uncertainty makes decision making frustrating for buyers at both sides of the quarter end, where most shipments are made. As quarter end approaches, buyers who have committed to a certain level of product from suppliers, but who have only "pulled" a fraction of that volume to date, are faced with a situation in which suppliers themselves are capacity constrained, and the decision to commit to that remaining volume

Table 6. Observations of by "process" filtered for decisional dimension

Management decisions	MD_04
then at end Q2, ERP or no ERP, sales didn't happen, we had a lot of finished goods	Uncertainty
our next MRP run showed we were netting all this in finished goods	Uncertainty
with a good forecast, I could put capacity in place without incurring huge cost	Uncertainty
there's still a lot of hockey stick for everything, it's not just Dell	Uncertainty
are you going to make the BRM, or are you going to second guess it	Uncertainty
we hadn't done numbers in Q1, Q2 had also reduced were bringing that number back down	Manual
before you get an SO, you have to make an intellectual decision, yes, go and build it	Manual
it'll take me probably a good 4 days probably for me to get everything out to my vendors	Manual
if we had just one product change, we would do a manual change, we wouldn't re-do MRP	Manual
then I have to re-capture all my receipts from the time that he took his snapshot	Manual
that's for us to prove, the goal will be there, we've to justify higher TLC	Manual
if we see that BRM is off, we will re-run MRP again, we can run MRPas often as we want	Manual
we got to check the checks	Manual
so you're going to have to give me a false pull, to make it	Manual
planning would do a simple blow down thing on a spreadsheet for us	Manual
once MRP is released to us, we run planning detail reports, netting the receipts manually	Manual
CM's don't see old plan and therefore deltas, but they work it out anyway	Manual
from the time that we get a BRM feed to the time that I'll get an MRP, it takes 4 to 5 days	Latency
then they'll have to wait a day or 2 days or 4 days, to run their MRP's	Latency
my clock is stopped basically, because they'll have to come back to me with their commit	Latency
before I could come back with a committed MRP it could take me 10 working days	Latency
because we're sub-contracting so much, that 10 days is being very optimistic	Latency

must be made, often in the absence of actual demand. A site based materials manager described this decision constraint as, "Your vendor is coming to within 2 or 3 weeks of quarter end, and we have only pulled 30% of the build plan, he is going to say, OK, use it or lose it, now."

This leaves buyers in the unenviable position of having to make a "judgement call" on whether actual demand will be realised or not. For this manager it is a no-win situation: "so therefore, at a point in time, which comes before you actually get a sales order, you are going to have to make an intellectual decision, to say, yes, go and build it."

Thus buyers are forced down a route of creating a "false pull" in order to reserve the supplier capacity to meet the build plan, without the sure knowledge that actual demand will follow the build plan. This is, in essence, where actual demand and "virtual" demand, as represented by the information recorded in the system, begin to diverge. The decision scenario is described by one materials manager: "are you going to make the [build plan], or are you going to second guess it."

The penalty for missing this goal is severe, according to a materials manager, "but if that 1000 happens, on day 30 of month 3, and you don't have the 1000 there, you could get fired."

After quarter end, on the other hand, because of forecast inaccuracy, product can be left over in finished goods. This, in turn, perturbs the procurement plan for the next quarter. So many manual updates are required to procurement plans, which explains the use of manual tools (spreadsheets) instead of MRP driven decision making.

This manual manipulation of procurement plans, alongside the complexity of the different systems involved in planning and procurement, introduces a latency in the decision making process that pushes a net change calculation into a 10 day horizon, instead of being a question of simply running MRP again.

This *process* latency has little to do with the information systems, per se, that are used by buyers to manage their work, but has much to do with the nature of the information itself. Driving soft forecast demand targets into hard time-bound procurement plans is a strategy chosen by the organisation to achieve its manufacturing build plan efficiently. In the next section we explore the informational aspects of centralisation, focusing to a large extent on the granularity of the information used.

Informational Dimension of Centralisation

Information visibility is vital in the buying activity of any firm, and especially one where global agreements have been signed with suppliers. As raw materials arrive at the local plant for manufacturing, the capture of the transactional level detail is crucial in order for the firm to be able to track overall supplier *performance* criteria (such as quality, lead time, purchase price variance, etc.).

Indeed, the need for integration is most evident here in that individual Goods Received Notes (GRN's) need to be re-united with the other elements of the transaction (purchase requisition, cost center, purchase order, invoice, etc.) in order for a complete purchase cycle to be possible. This is precisely the strong point of *integrated systems* such as ERP, which enforce *data integrity* at the point of data capture (e.g., correct material code required to receive goods on system).

Table 7 shows the sampled observations filtered for the informational dimension of the decisions sampled.

Planning at a global level takes place in an off-line manner, in the sense that the setting of global supply contracts is not *integrated* with the processing of transactional information on a day to day basis. However, the ability to judge actual *performance* of suppliers relies heavily on the granularity of the information recorded about each and every delivery.

An ERP system is a repository for the transactional detail, therefore provides precisely this type of granularity. However, in SIT's case, it is not used for the planning level information, thus any *performance* reporting is by definition off-line and manual.

The desire to understand *cost* drivers in order to continually seek economies can be felt at the corporate level, but the lack of integration of planning tools and transactional tools has hampered buyers' abilities to carry out such analysis. Much work is done off-line on spreadsheets, starting with a download from the ERP system, with the attendant duplication of effort, *standardisation,* and tracability issues.

Cognizant of this gap, the firm has invested in a separate system at the global level to analyse spend for global commodity teams, and it is thought that the same tool will be rolled out to local manufacturing buyers to give them the same analytical capability.

The initial analysis of the case study has allowed the researchers to cut the observations in terms of the three research dimensions identified, and this has shone a spotlight on several themes that will be re-visited in the next section.

CONCLUSION

This sample of observations for the purchasing process has been viewed in the previous section according to organisational, decisional, and informational themes. This has helped focus on particular impacts of centralisation, without attempting to derive the relationship between these impacts. In this final section, we look for dependencies across these findings which allow us to draw some conclusions about the causality involved.

Table 8 shows how the decision characteristics (MD_04) map across the research themes (MD_03) in terms of number of observations.

"Soft" goals are set at a high level in the centralised organisation, derived in *unintegrated systems* because flexibility and scenario testing is required. At the same time, management decision making inevitably compares data from this nonintegrated source to operational *performance* (hard data from ERP system).

Managers provide the link between goal setting and goal execution in organisations, and therefore the clear communication of goals and *performance* targets is vital for optimal execution results, if not managerial sanity. The relationship between the soft information used to drive *performance* at the corporate level and

Table 7. Observations of buy "process" filtered for informational dimension

Management decisions	MD_04
people want to know they have the best plan, they are more informed	Granularity
controllers don't have visibility, and only look at their cost centers	Granularity
Finance look at Essbase, they got no detail, nothing to make a decision on	Granularity
exception reporting, why is this in here, why are we miscoding?	Granularity
PC's: lease or buy, you have visibility to spend on computer equipment	Granularity
Should cost / clean sheeting	Granularity
understanding capital spend	Granularity
I can just go to the starts plan (spreadsheet) and see where we are	Manual
the speed with which we have to deliver the information is getting greater	Speed

the underlying transactional nature of systems available to operational managers (as studied in this case) raises interesting questions about the skills and expectations of the organisation with respect to its management.

The gap in a common language between HQ and site seems to be expressed in the management perception of decision making being hampered by uncertainty, leading to more manual methods of processing, which in turn creates an unacceptable level of latency in the process.

The impact of this uncertainty seems to be felt strongest at the local purchasing level, where supplier relationships are strained by the frequent late changes to the forecast. Buyers seem to have to depart from any systematic method and rely on a gut feel instinct about the way sales demand will fall each quarter.

These tacit processes can subvert the *integrity* of overly literal systems such as ERP. Creating false demand to keep a steady pull on suppliers is an example of how the virtual picture can diverge from reality. For example, the only way to create false demand is to create sales orders, and once a sales order is created in an ERP system, *relational integrity* at the database level ensures that it cannot easily be deleted. In highly *integrated* environments such as these, workarounds have ripple effects, the clean up of which often end up consuming more resource than the process merits.

All of this comes to a head in periods of high stress in the business cycle, where managers try to cope with HQ changing the goal posts in response to external stakeholder pressures, all the while trying to understand basic execution challenges through a haze of transactional data being dutifully generated by operational systems.

The granularity of the information being recorded is not in itself the problem, on the contrary, the need for information processing increases as uncertainty increases, as managers try to understand what is happening. However, information granularity creates a need for analytical skills, query tools and data access. This may not be recognised in the centralised organisation, where such resources tend to be more easily obtained at HQ than at the operating plant level.

From the point of view of management decision making, there is also a (not uncommon) phenomenon exhibited in this case of inundating managers with detailed transactional data without regard to the level of granularity that a particular decision process might require. ERP systems are transactional in focus, but decisions relating to the achievement of goals may require several levels of aggregation in order to be meaningful for managers. It may even be that managers themselves should be free to change the parameters of this aggregation, depending on the decision at hand.

In the final section we will suggest some preliminary conclusions for extending this line of research in the future.

FUTURE DIRECTIONS

There are several interesting themes for further research raised in this study, and these articulate around the framework, tools, and resources that are put in place post-ERP to account for the gap between the operational information gathered at the transactional level and the planning information required at the managerial level.

As we have seen in this research, there are latency issues associated with the collection of data in highly *integrated systems* that limit their usefulness in a decision making context.

The authors believe that there is much value to be gained from the development of a framework to model the gap between organisational goals on the one hand, and the physical transactions that make-up the administration of business processes, such that managers have a vocabulary to discuss, recognize, and measure this gap.

Table 8. Decision impact categories viewed by research theme

MD_04 Decision characeristics	Decisional	Informational	Organisational	Grand Total
Centralisation			2	2
Commercial leverage			1	1
Flexibility			1	1
Goals			7	7
Granularity		7		7
Hard vs. soft target			2	2
Latency	5			5
Lean			1	1
Manual	12	1		13
Speed		1		1
Uncertainty	5			5
Grand Total	22	9	14	45

It is often said that ERP systems provide a common grammar for the business, but this grammar needs to be extended to cover explicit, dynamic departures from template ERP processes. It also needs to incorporate the decisions that are typically made by managers, such that the underlying transactional information can be mapped at some point to the decisional layer most used by managers.

An obvious starting point here would be to research the integration of forward looking *performance* parameters (such as budgets, forecasts, and targets) into the ERP data model such that comparison to actual figures is automatic and *real-time*. The design implications of this type of automatic KPI generator (or dashboard) could best be explored through combined field research and laboratory prototype development.

REFERENCES

Adam, F., & Sammon, D. (2004). The enterprise resource planning decade: Lessons learned and issues for the future. Hershey, PA: Idea Publishing Group.

Bingi, P., Sharma, M., & Godla, J. (1999, Summer). Critical issues affecting an ERP implementation. *Information Systems Management, 16*(3), 7-14.

Davenport, T. (1998, July/August). Putting the enterprise into the enterprise system. *Harvard Business Review,* 131-131.

Galbraith, J. (1974). Organisation design: An information processing view. *Interfaces, 4*(3), 28-37.

Horwitt, E. (1998, March). Enduring a global rollout — and living to tell about it. *Computerworld 32*(14), 8-12.

Orlicky, J. (1975). *Materials requirements planning : The new way of life in production and inventory management.* New York: McGraw Hill.

Thompson, J.D. (1967). Organizations in action: Social science bases of administrative theory. New York: McGraw-Hill.

KEY TERMS

Centralisation: The localisation of decision making responsibility to a central location, usually a head office, leaving the local operation with the responsibility for execution.

Enterprise Resource Planning (ERP): A suite of software modules which manage the administration of a firm's business processes, including inventory and cash transactions related to sales orders, work orders, purchase orders, financial and management accounting.

Granularity: The level of detail recorded regarding business transactions, usually down to the level of individual items of inventory and their value. The aggregation capability is defined by the amount of detail held on each line item.

Latency: Slowness or lack of responsiveness in decision making induced by structural complexity, in this context relating to either organisational, technical, or uncertainty factors.

Material Requirements Planning (MRP): The generic term used to describe the process of decomposing customer demand for finished goods into its stock item requirements, and used to drive procurement and production planning.

Uncertainty: The variability introduced into business decision making by fluctuations in factors external to, and beyond the control of, the organisation. Generally caused by aspects of customer behaviour, market dynamics, and competitive forces.

ENDNOTE

[1] Not the company's real name.

The Implementation of Large-Scale Decision-Making Support Systems: Problems, Findings, and Challenges

Manual Mora
Autonomous University of Aguascalientes, Mexico

Ovsei Gelman
Universidad Nacional Autónoma de México, Mexico

Guisseppi Forgionne
University of Maryland – Baltimore County, USA

Francisco Cervantes
Universidad Nacional Autónoma de México, Mexico

ABSTRACT

This article reviews the literature-based issues involved in implementing large-scale decision-making support systems (DMSSs). Unlike previous studies, this review studies holistically three types of DMSSs (model-based decision support systems, executive-oriented decision support systems, and knowledge-based decision support systems) and incorporates recent studies on the simulation of the implementations process. Such an article contributes to the literature by organizing the fragmented knowledge on the DMSS implementation phenomenon and by communicating the factors and stages involved in successful or failed large-scale DMSS implementations to practitioners.

INTRODUCTION

This article reviews the literature-based issues involved in implementing large-scale decision-making support systems (DMSSs). Unlike previous studies, this review studies holistically three types of DMSSs (model-based decision support systems, executive-oriented decision support systems, and knowledge-based decision support systems) and incorporates recent studies on the simulation of the implementations process. The article ends with a brief discussion of the practical and research challenges for the implementation process. Such a study contributes to the literature by organizing the fragmented knowledge on the DMSS implementation phenomenon and by communicating the factors and stages involved in successful or failed DMSS implementations to practitioners.

A large-scale DMSS can be defined as a specialized computer-based information system designed to support some, several, or all phases of a decision-making process that requires substantive financial, organizational, human, technical, and knowledge resources for being deployed in organizations (Forgionne, 1991; Forgionne, Mora, Cervantes, & Kohli, 2000; Turban, 1995). From its initial theoretical conceptualization (in the early 1970s by Scott Morton, 1971) until now (Forgionne, Mora, Gupta, & Gelman, 2005), these systems have been designed with different architectures. Consequently, these systems have also provided distinctive decision support. Such systems can be grouped into four main categories: model-based decision support systems (Sprague & Carlson, 1982), executive-oriented decision support systems (Rockart, 1979), knowledge-based decision support systems (Feigenbaum, McCorduck, & Nii, 1988), and general decision-making support systems (Forgionne et al., 2000). Table 1 summarizes the main support provided by each type of DMSS.

Table 1. Decisional support of main types of DMSSs

PHASE/ ACTIVITY	Model-Based DSS	Executive-Oriented DSS	Knowledge-Based DSS	General DMSS
INTELLIGENCE • Identify objectives • Recognize problem • Gather data	Few explored	• Drill-down analysis • Data query • Graph & tabular data access • DM/KD analysis	• Qualitative reasoning • Problem solving • Intelligent advice	• Decisional support from executive and knowledge-based DSS modules
DESIGN • Formulate model • Establish criteria • Generate alternatives	Few explored	Few explored	• Qualitative reasoning • Problem solving • Intelligent advice	• Decisional support from knowledge-based DSS modules
CHOICE • Evaluate alternatives • Select best alternative	• What-if analysis • Goal-seeking analysis • Sensitivity analysis • Value/utility analysis	Few explored	• Qualitative reasoning • Problem solving • Intelligent advice	• Decisional support from model-and knowledge-based DSS modules
IMPLEMENTATION • Decision confidence • System effectiveness • Implement decision	Few explored	• Drill-down analysis • Data query • Graph & tabular data access	Few explored	• Decisional support from executive-based DSS module
LEARNING • Analysis • Synthesis	Few explored	Few explored	• Automated learning (CBR, NN, etc.)	• Decisional support from related tools like knowledge management system (KMS)

Large-scale DMSSs are highly appreciated and required in large organizations because relevant benefits can be achieved after a successful implementation. Among the main benefits reported are better decision quality, enhancement of decision makers' mental models, improved analytical skills, better communication, and a reduction in decision time (Eom, Lee, Kim, & Somarajan, 1998; Feigenbaum et al., 1988; Leidner, 1996; Liebowitz, 1990; Rockart & DeLong, 1988; Turban, 1995; Tyran & George, 1993; Udo & Guimaraes, 1994; Watson, Rainer, & Koh, 1991). Still, failures in DMSS implementation are not scarce and are economically significant (Alavi & Joachiminsthaler, 1992; Gill, 1995; Glover & Watson, 1992). The main reported causes of failure (Mora, Cervantes, Gelman, Forgionne, Mejia, & Weitzenfeld, 2002; Mora, Forgionne, Gelman, Cervantes, Weitzenfeld, & Raczyinski, 2003) are the inherent high complexity of the overall process, where multiple financial, organizational, human, technological, sociocultural, and political issues interact, and the nature of the organizational environment. Consequently, the number of current DMSSs in organizations is less than expected, and benefits are only reached by organizations that are aware of the complexity of this process and pursue these projects with managerial, technical, and organizational adequacy.

THE BARRIERS TO ACHIEVING SUCCESSFUL DMSS IMPLEMENTATIONS

The concept of implementation has two meanings in the information systems literature: (a) a reduced view that refers to a stage of the systems development life cycle, which starts with the business modeling activity and ends with the system delivering activity in the organization (Satzinger, Jackson, & Burd, 2000), or (b) an extended view that starts with the acknowledgement or discovering of a new need-technology pair and ends with the entire institutionalization of the system deployed using such technology (Finlay & Forghani, 1998; Tyran & George, 1994). Figure 1 exhibits the difference between these two concepts.

The Implementation of Large-Scale Decision-Making Support Systems

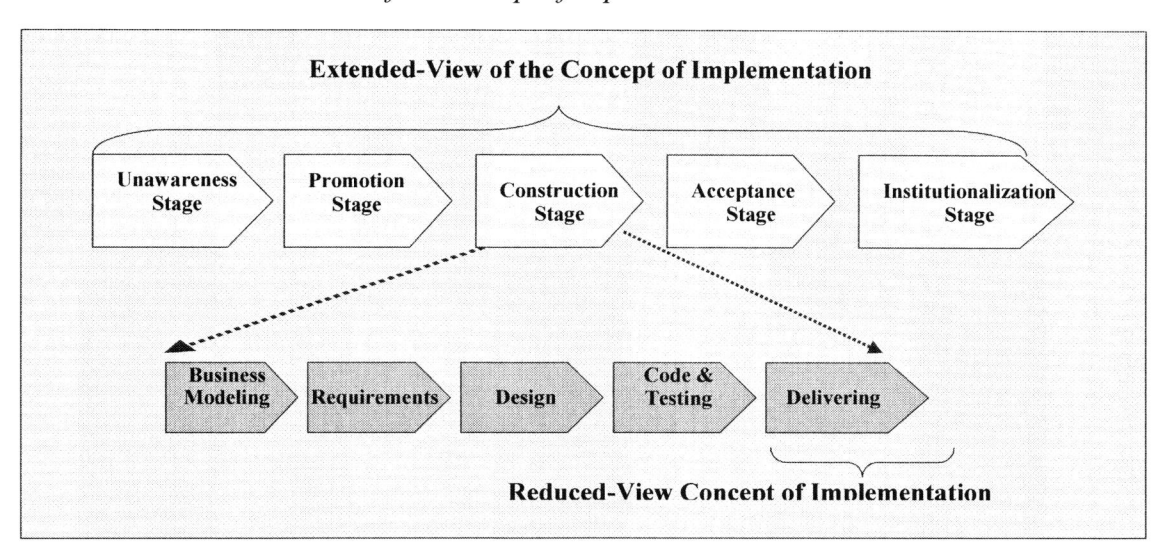

Figure 1. Extended vs. reduced views of the concept of implementation

This article utilizes the extended view for the analysis of DMSS implementations. According to Mora et al. (2002, p. 334),

Researchers and practitioners are interested in the topic because of the high financial and organizational efforts dedicated to implement an IS. Failures in the process can cause the project to be cancelled during development, under utilization of the developed system, or eventual discarding of the developed system. These negative implementation results have adverse impacts on the organization. There could be a loss of financial resources, wasted organizational efforts, and organizational distrust in the system development process (Mohan & Bean, 1979 quoted by Hardaway & Will (1990); Poulymenakou & Holmes, 1996; Ewusi-Mensah, 1997).

Table 2 (adapted from Mora, Gelman, Cervantes, Mejia, & Weitzenfeld, 2003) summarizes the particular implementation problems and symptoms identified in the relevant DMSS literature from empirical survey-based or case studies. These problems and symptoms involve technically oriented issues as well as managerial, financial, and environmental influences. Hence, the implementation of a large-scale DMSS should consider a very complex set of interrelated financial, organizational, and technical tasks that affect several critical stakeholders (top management, sponsors, users, IS people, IT consultants, IT suppliers) and consumes substantial financial, technological, and organizational resources.

MAIN FINDINGS ON LARGE-SCALE DMSS IMPLEMENTATIONS

Two main approaches have emerged to study the phenomenon of implementing a new and advanced information system or technology (like a large-scale DMSS): the factor-based and the stage-based approaches (Kwon & Zmud, 1987). According to Mora et al. (2002), there have been five integrative studies for the factor-based approach (Eierman et al., 1995; Kwon & Zmud, 1987; Mora, Cervantes-Perez, & Forgionne, 2000; Turban & Aronson, 1998; Watson et al., 1991), and five studies for the stage-based approach (Cooper & Zmud, 1990; Lewin-Schein (Lewin, 1952); Mora et al., 2000; Rogers, 1983, 1995).

The existence of several frameworks reveals that there is no standard for modeling and analyzing the DMSS implementation process. Adapted from Mora et al. (2002) and Mora, Forgionne, et al. (2003), Tables 3 and 4 present a summary of the main reported findings. Results reported in Table 3 account for practically all the factors that are potentially associated with the success or failure of large-scale DMSS implementations. In turn, Table 4 presents an integrator framework of the *stage-based approach* updated from Mora, Forgionne, et al.

Table 2. Symptoms and influences in large-scale DMSS implementation failures

Type of Symptoms and Influences	Symptoms and Influences of Large-Scale DMSS Implementation Failures	Sources of Evidences
Financial Issues	Low project ROI (return on investment) from underutilized systems due to voluntary usage; inadequate cost-benefits justification process	Alavi and Joachiminsthaler (1992); Glover and Watson (1992)
	Financial losses by projects abandoned despite high technical quality	Gill (1995); Duchessi and O'Keefe (1995)
	Insufficient budget for excess of current IS projects that compete with the DMSS project	Glover and Watson (1992)
Environmental and Organizational Issues	Low number of successful cases of EISs (expert information systems) and ES/KBSs (expert and knowledge-based systems) reported	Rai and Bajwa (1997); Tyran and George (1993)
	Organizational disturbances and dissatisfaction in future potential users by ES/KBS implementation failures; lack of organizational support	Duchessi and O'Keefe (1995); Udo and Guimaraes (1994)
	Unready corporate culture or environment for EIS; organizational resistance; nonintegration of the system in the management process; political resistance; inadequate organizational climate	Glover and Watson (1992); Rainer and Watson (1995); Young and Watson (1995); Tyran and George (1994); Turban (1992)
	EIS implementations are considered projects of high risk; ES/KBS special characteristics are ignored	Rainer and Watson (1995); Turban (1992)
Managerial and Behavioral Issues	Political and organizational issues are underestimated; inadequate implementation procedures by ignoring that EISs are complex technological innovations	Finlay and Forghani (1998)
	Lack of top-management support; lack of executive sponsorship	Rainer and Watson (1995); Guimaraes, Igbaria, and Lu (1992); Barsanti (1990); Yoon and Watson (1995); Duchessi and O'Keefe (1995)
	Lack of a well-defined purpose of the EIS; unclear links to business objectives; system not aligned with business strategy	DeLong and Rockart (1986); Guiden and Ewers (1988)
	Lack of user participation and involvement; lack of management commitment	Rainer and Watson (1995); Glover and Watson (1992); Guimaraes et al. (1992)
Implementation, Technical, and System Issues	Usage of inadequate technology (software and hardware); usage of inadequate system development approach; management project techniques underestimated	Glover and Watson (1992); Rainer and Watson (1995); Young and Watson (1995); Eierman, Niederman, and Adams (1995); Turban (1992)
	Lack of business skills of project leader; inadequate development team; lack of technical capabilities; lack of a core support group	Rainer and Watson (1995); Finlay and Forghani (1998); Barsanti (1990); Tyran and George (1994); Guimaraes, Yoon, and Clevenson (1996)
	Low value perceived of system output despite high technical quality; system does not meet organizational objectives; low general system quality; inadequate project selection	Watson et al. (1991); Glover and Watson (1992); Rainer and Watson (1995); Barsanti (1990)
	High-complexity and nonintuitive system; lack of adequate user training	Watson et al. (1991); Young and Watson (1995); Guimaraes et al. (1992); Alavi and Joachiminsthaler (1992)
	Data accessibility problems; data integrity problems; data management problems; lack of understanding and control of data	DeLong and Rockart (1986); Glover Watson (1992); Rainer and Watson (1995); Young and Watson (1995); Duchessi and O'Keefe (1995)

Table 3. Integrated framework of large-scale DMSS implementations factors

	CATEGORY	FACTORS
1.	User's characteristics	1.1 User's aptitude; 1.2 Normative motivation; 1.3 Cognitive style; 1.4 Realistic user expectations
2.	Task's characteristics	2.1 Task difficulty and newness; 2.2 Task uncertainty degree; 2.3 Task organizational alignment (priority); 2.4 Adequate task domain and complexity
3.	Development team's characteristics	3.1 Project champion; 3.2 Leader's business skills; 3.3 Leader's technical skills; 3.4 Developer's technical skills
4.	Core process of implementation	4.1 User's training; 4.2 User's involvement; 4.3 Development methodology; 4.4 Development time frame; 4.5 Cost-benefit analysis; 4.6 Data accessibility; 4.7 Change and resistance management; 4.8 Support for evolution and diffusion; 4.9 Support of IS department; 4.10 Commitment of maintenance
5.	Technological characteristics	5.1 Software tools; 5.2 Hardware tools
6.	Organizational characteristics	6.1 Top-management support; 6.2 Top sponsors; 6.3 Organizational climate
7.	Environmental characteristics	7.1 Hostile and uncertain environment; 7.2 Relationships with IT suppliers; 7.3 Relationships with research centers
8.	System (DMSS) characteristics	8.1 Accuracy and format of results; 8.2 Management level supported; 8.3 Decisional phase supported; 8.4 Relevance of results; 8.5 Degree of system sophistication; 8.6 Timeless information; 8.7 Ease of usage; 8.8 Impact on user's work; 8.9 Legal and ethical issues

Table 4. Integrated framework of DMSS implementation stages

Lewin-Schein's Model	Roger's Model	Kwon-Zmud and Cooper-Zmud's Model	Mora, Cervantes-Perez, and Forgionne's Model
	Phase of Knowledge Acquisition		Phase of Organizational Unawareness
Phase of Unfreezing	Phase of Persuasion	Phase of Initiation	Phase of Promotion
	Phase of Decision	Phase of Adoption	
Phase of Moving	Phase of Implementation	Phase of Adaptation	Phase of Construction
Phase of Refreezing	Phase of Confirmation	Phase of Acceptation	Phase of Acceptance
		Phase of Routinization	Phase of Institutionalization
		Phase of Infusion	

The exhibited findings offer a rich picture of the complexity of the implementation process of large-scale DMSSs. These literature-based findings indicate that this corpus of knowledge seems sufficient to describe, explain, and control the implementation process. However, while the main components (factors or stages) are known, their influences and interactions are partially known at present. Mora et al. (2002) and Mora, Forgionne, et al. (2003) have suggested simulation-based systemic methods based on the systems approach (Mora et al., 2002) to explicitly represent and analyze the relevant relationships.

From the *factor-based-approach* research stream (Table 3) it can be inferred that the successful implementation of a large-scale DMSS will demand the coexistence of multiple factors. Table 3 does not imply that each factor is equally appropriate for a successful DMSS implementation. Rather, Table 3 indicates that the coexistence of some factors increases the likelihood that a DMSS implementation will be successful. For example, user participation as well as top-management support is not associated with the successful implementation of model-oriented DMSS (Fuerst & Cheney, 1982). However, in subsequent related studies (Guimaraes et al., 1992; Kivijarvi & Zmud 1993), these factors have been found to be relevant (see final framework of Table 3[1]). Hence, the main knowledge generated by the DMSS factor-based research stream can be synthesized in the following findings: (a) the discovery of the most usual factors found in successful implementations, (b) the development of valid and reliable conceptual instruments to measure such factors, and (c) the formulation of several frameworks to organize the factors. These findings have been useful to establish the theoretical basis for subsequent studies.

Using the four frameworks reported in Mora et al. (2002), it can be inferred that the stage-based approach has also generated relevant findings on the DMSS implementation phenomenon. The main assertion is that the implementation process is a dynamic flux of factor-related events and activities associated with final success. This type of research, then, has helped to determine how and why some factors influence the final result. Due to the greater cost, time, financial, and organizational resources required for conducting stage-oriented research, few such studies have been reported for large-scale DMSS implementations (Finlay & Forghani, 1998; Palvia & Chervany, 1995; Welsch, 1986). Such studies have used the first conceptual framework (Lewin-Schein (Lewin, 1952)). Other frameworks have been used in information systems or general innovations research (Alanis, 1990; Rogers, 1995), or only in theoretical formulations (Mora et al., 2002; Mora et al., 2000; Turban & Aronson, 1998).

According to Mora et al. (2002, p. 344) from the Lewin-Schein model,

early start with technical activities, i.e. the moving phase, is highly risky and involves potential negative consequences for user acceptance. [Then] the first stage, i.e. "unfreezing," is useful to gain the trust of future users about the positive impacts of the system. Also, the last stage, i.e. "refreezing," is necessary to formalize the new user and organizational behavioral patterns and to get the institutionalization of the system (Welsch, 1986; Palvia & Chervany, 1995; Finlay & Forghani, 1998; Marakas, 2000).

Based on Rogers' framework (1983, 1995), Mora et al. (2002, p. 344) note that the conceptualization of a DMSS implementation can be considered as an innovation (DeLong & Rockart, 1986; Dologite & Mockler, 1989; Keen & Scott-Morton, 1978). In this view,

the final acceptance of an innovation, i.e. in this case a DMSS, does not occur randomly, but it follows a process...then, the first two phases, i.e. "knowledge" and "persuasion" are critical phases to create realistic expectations about the system and to create the awareness of these systems. Internal or external organizational sources are used to create the knowledge and persuasion. In a similar way, the last phase is required to reinforce the positive, and manage the negative, impacts of the system (Mora et al., 2002).

Cooper and Zmud's (1990) and Kwon and Zmud's (1987) stage-oriented framework incorporates postadoption activities (Zmud & Apple, 1989). These researchers suggest that without these activities, the organizational postadoption behaviors, the refreezing stage, would be a weak stage likely resulting in a failed implementation (Mora et al., 2002). This model, then, emphasizes the relevance of the last stage. Mora et al. (2002, p. 345) also indicate that,

by highlighting the importance of the last stages of the implementation cycle, the Zmud's model provides a prescription for maintaining an adequate atmosphere in the organization for the introduction of future innovations. In addition, the model identifies the need to relate stages and factors when studying the implementation phenomenon.

Mora et al.'s (2002) analysis indicates that Roger's and Zmud's models are unbalanced in the relevance assigned to each stage. Mora et al.'s model reinterprets Rogers's first stage by highlighting the need to overcome organizational knowledge deficiencies through the availability of the innovation during the extended implementation process. As Mora et al (idem, p. 346) report,

previous models assume that innovations arrive automatically to organizations through an external or internal source, or are already under consideration. Yet, advanced IT, such as DMSS, can be available for some time before they are recognized and adopted by organizations. For example, Fichman & Keremer (1999), in a study about diffusion of IT innovations, point out that the existence of knowledge barriers can cause organizations to defer the acquisition of an IT innovation. Nambisan, Agarwal & Tanniru (1999), in turn, in a study about the role of users as sources of organizational IT innovations, point out the relevance of the organizational knowledge creation process to initiate the introduction of an advanced IT.

Thus, Mora et al. (2002) suggest that initial stage inertia can create opportunity costs and other organizational losses.

According to Mora et al. (2002), Mora et al. (2000), Mora, Forgionne, et al. (2003), the stage-oriented approach has contributed to the DMSS implementation knowledge because (a) it has provided a high-level conceptual dynamic view of the phenomenon, (b) it has confirmed some findings from factor-based research, (c) it has offered explanations based on qualitative case studies of how and why an implementation process fails, (d) it has developed a more holistic framework than the factor-based approach, and (e) it has generated implementation guidelines and recommendations for practitioners.

CHALLENGES AND TRENDS OF LARGE-SCALE DMSS IMPLEMENTATIONS

The factor- and stage-oriented research streams suggest that both approaches are complementary (Duchessi & O'Keefe, 1995), and together these approaches can fully describe and explain the DMSS implementation phenomenon. Each approach separately, however, is methodologically incomplete (Kwon & Zmud, 1987; Mora et al., 2002; Nandhakumar, 1996; Rogers, 1995; Williams & Ramaprasad, 1995).

Mora et al. (2002, p. 348) report that the main identified limitations for the *factor-based approach* are:

(a) consideration of a reduced set of variables of study by practical considerations that study subjects fulfill long questionnaires; (b) statistical restrictions usually are not realized and thus only the lowest level of criticality of factors are established; (c) quantitative analysis per se hides "how" and "why" deep explanations of the phenomenon; (d) a "snapshot" of the phenomenon can only be studied through the "variance research methods" that concentrate on a fixed point of time and on the covariance of the study variables (Rogers, 1983); and (e) experimental procedures are not feasible since the subject or units of study are usually large organizations.

According to these Mora et al (2002, p. 349), the *stage-based approach* also has methodological research limitations:

a. The findings offer a very high conceptual perspective of the phenomenon and thereby rely on an open interpretation by new researchers and practitioners;
b. It is based on a qualitative research approach that usually demands more resources and time to develop, thereby financially precluding deep and complete views of the whole phenomenon;
c. It fails to include the full set of factors provided by the Factor-Based approach and only a few of them are studied in some stages;
d. It fails to help researchers forecast correctly the dynamic behavior of a complex phenomenon (Forrester, 1991, pp. 13), and
e. It is not feasible to conduct experimental studies by operational restrictions of the units of study, i.e. large organizations.

A successful implementation of a large-scale DMSS, then, is a complex task where multiple organizational, financial, technical, and human-based factors interact during a sequence of activities over a long time. Such complexity and the main approach limitations have motivated researchers to analyze how similar complex and dynamic processes are studied in other disciplines. A novel research stream in DMSS implementation (Mora, Cervantes, Gelman, & Forgionne, 2004; Mora et al., 2002; Mora, Forgionne, et al., 2003; Mora, Gelman, Forgionne, & Cervantes, 2004) is based on the systems approach (Gelman & Garcia, 1989; Gelman, Mora, Forgionne, & Cervantes, 2005a, 2005b; Mora, Gelman, Cano, Cervantes, & Forgionne, 2006; Mora, Gelman, et al. 2003). The main premise of such studies is that the systems approach can offer a rich methodological tool set and robust philosophical foundation to study DMSS implementations.

Based on this literature-based analysis, we can identify the following challenges and trends for a better understanding of this rich and complex phenomenon: (a) Factor- and stage-oriented research streams have methodological limitations that can be alleviated with the integration of a broader methodological research tool set like the systems approach, (b) DMSS implementation researchers would benefit from simulation-based analysis, (c) further research is required to develop the theoretical basis of such methodological integrations, and (d) new variations of DMSS, such as data warehouse DMSS, ERP- (enterprise resource planning) like DMSS, and KMS, will require similar integrated studies.

CONCLUSION

In this article, we have provided a broad review of the issues involved in achieving successful implementations of large-scale DMSS. This review has reported the main findings from the factor- and stage-oriented research streams that have dominated the DMSS implementation literature. A final conclusion can be posed that the implementation of a large-scale DMSS is a complex task where multiple organizational, financial, technical, and human-based factors coexist and interact during the execution of a sequence of ongoing activities over a long time period (several years). While the main factors and stages are well-known issues, the entire consequences from the factor and stage interactions are only partially known. However, inherent methodological limitations from empirical studies (survey, experimental, and case-study approaches) demand further research with a complementary and holistic approach. The systems approach is suggested by the authors for helping to address the unresolved issues of this rich and relevant phenomenon.

REFERENCES

Alanis, M. (1990). Controlling the introduction of strategic information technologies. In E. Szewczak, C. Snodgrass and M. Khosrow-Pour (Eds.), *Management impacts of information technology: Perspectives on organizational change and growth* (pp. 421-437). Hershey, PA: Idea Group.

Alavi, M., & Joachiminsthaler, E. A. (1992). Revisiting DSS implementation research: A meta-analysis of the literature and suggestions for research. *MIS Quarterly, 16*(1), 95-116.

Barsanti, J. B. (1990). Expert systems: Critical success factors for their implementation. *Information Executive, 3*(1), 30-35.

Cooper, R. B., & Zmud, R. W. (1990). Information technology implementation research: A technological diffusion approach. *Management Science, 36*(2), 123-139.

DeLong, D. W., & Rockart, J. F. (1986). Identifying the attributes of successful executive support system implementation. In *Transactions of the 6th International Conference on Decision Support Systems*, Washington, DC (pp. 41-54).

Dologite, D. G., & Mockler, R. J. (1989). Developing effective knowledge-based systems: Overcoming organizational and individual behavioral barriers. *Information Resource Management Journal, 2*(1), Winter, 27-39.

Duchessi, P., & O'Keefe, R. M. (1995). Understanding expert systems success and failure. *Expert Systems with Applications, 9*(2), 123-133.

Eierman, M., Niederman, F., & Adams, C. (1995). DSS theory: A model of constructs and relationships. *Decision Support Systems, 14*, 1-26.

Eom, S., Lee, S., Kim, E., & Somarajan, C. (1998). A survey of decision support systems applications (1998-1994). *Journal of Operational Research Society, 49*, 109-120.

Ewusi-Mensah, K. (1997). Critical issues in abandoned information systems development projects. *Communications of the ACM, 40*(9), 74-80.

Feigenbaum, E., McCorduck, P., & Nii, H. P. (1988). *The rise of the expert company.* Time Books.

Fichman, R., & Keremer, C. (1999). The illusory diffusion of innovation: An examination of assimilation gap. *Information Systems Research, 10*(3), 255-275.

Finlay, P. N., & Forghani, M. (1998). A classification of success factors for decision support systems. *Journal of Strategic Information Systems, 7*, 53-70.

Forgionne, G. A. (1991). Decision technology systems: A vehicle to consolidate decision making support. *Information Processing and Management, 27*(6), 679-797.

Forgionne, G. A., Mora, M., Cervantes, F., & Kohli, R. (2000, August 10-13). Development of integrated decision making support systems: A practical approach. In *Proceedings of the AMCIS Conference*, Long Beach, CA (2132-2134).

Forgionne, G. A., Mora, M., Gupta, J., & Gelman, O. (2005). Decision-making support systems. In *Encyclopedia of Information Science and Technology* (pp. 759-765). Hershey, PA: Idea Group.

Fuerst, W. L., & Cheney, P. H. (1982). Factors affecting the perceived utilization of computer-based decision support systems in the oil industry. *Decision Sciences, 13*, 564-569.

Gelman, O., & Garcia, J. (1989). Formulation and axiomatization of the concept of general system. *Outlet IMPOS (Mexican Institute of Planning and Systems Operation), 19*(92), 1-81.

Gelman, O., Mora, M., Forgionne, G., & Cervantes, F. (2005a). Information systems: A formal view. *ACTA SYSTEMICA, 5*(2), 37-42.

Gelman, O., Mora, M., Forgionne, G., & Cervantes, F. (2005b). Information systems and systems theory. In *Encyclopedia of information science and technology* (pp. 1491-1496). Hershey, PA: Idea Group.

Gill, G. T. (1995). Early expert systems: Where are they now? *MIS Quarterly, 19*(1), 51-81.

Glover, H., & Watson, H. T. (1992). 20 ways to waste an EIS investment. *The Executive's Journal, 8*(2), 11-18.

Guiden, G., & Ewers, D. E. (1988). The keys to successful executive support systems. *Indications, 5*(5), 1-5.

Guimaraes, T., Igbaria, M., & Lu, M. (1992). The determinants of DSS success: An integrated model. *Decision Sciences, 23*(2), 409-430.

Guimaraes, T., Yoon, Y., & Clevenson, A. (1996). Factors important to expert systems success: A field test. *Information and Management, 30*(3), 119-130.

Hardaway, D. E., & Will, R. P. (1990). *A review of barriers to expert systems diffusion*. Paper presented at the 1990 ACM SIGBDP conference on Trends and directions in expert systems. Orlando, FL, (pp. 619-639).

Keen, P., & Scott-Morton, M. S. (1978). *Decision support systems: An organizational perspective*. MA: Addison-Wesley.

Kivijarvi, H., & Zmud, R. W. (1993). DSS implementation activities, problem domain characteristics and DSS success. *European Journal of Information Systems, 2*(3), 159-168.

Kwon, T. H., & Zmud, R. W. (1987). Unifying the fragmented models of information systems implementation. In R. J. Boland & R. A. Hirschheim (Eds.), *Critical issues in information systems research* (pp. 227-251). Boston: Wiley.

Leidner, D. (1996, December 16-18). *Modern management in the developing world: The success of EIS in Mexican organizations*. Paper presented at the International Conference on Information Systems, Cleveland, OH.

Lewin, K. (1952). Group decision and social change. In T. M. Newcomb & E. L. Harley (Eds.), *Readings in social psychology* (pp. 459-473). New York: Holt.

Liebowitz, J. (1990). *Expert systems for business and management*. Englewood Cliffs, NJ: Yourdon Press.

Marakas, G. (1998). *Decision support systems in the twenty-first century* (pp. 412-436). Saddle River: Prentice-Hall.

Mohan, L., & Bean, A. S. (1979). Introducing OR/MS into organizations: Normative implications of selected Indian experience. *Decision Sciences, 10*(1), 136-150.

Mora, M., Cervantes, F., Gelman, O., & Forgionne, G. (2004, July 1-3). *Understanding the strategic process of implementing decision-making support systems: A systems approach*. Paper presented at the 2004 IFIP International Conference on Decision Support Systems (DSS2004), Prato, Tuscany, Italy.

Mora, M., Cervantes, F., Gelman, O., Forgionne, G., Mejia, M., & Weitzenfeld, A. (2002). DMSSs implementation research: A conceptual analysis of the contributions and limitations of the factor-based and stage-based streams. In M. Mora, G. Forgionne, & J. Gupta (Eds.), *Decision making support systems: Achievements, challenges and trends* (pp. 331-356). Hershey, PA: Idea Group.

Mora, M., Cervantes-Perez, F., & Forgionne, G. (2000, June 1-3). *Understanding the process of successful implementations of management support systems: A review of critical factors and theories about adoption of new information technology*. Paper presented at the Third BITWorld Conference, Mexico.

Mora, M., Forgionne, G., Gelman, O., Cervantes, F., Weitzenfeld, A., & Raczyinski, S. (2003). Implementation of DMSS: A systemic approach. In G. Tonfoni & L. Jain (Eds.), *Innovations in decision support systems* (pp. 17-84). Magill, Australia: Advance Knowledge International.

Mora, M., Gelman, O., Cano, J., Cervantes, F., & Forgionne, G. (2006, July 9-14). Theory of systems and information systems research frameworks. In J. Wilby, J. Allen, & C. Loureiro (Eds.), *Electronic Proceedings of the Sonoma 2006: 50th Annual Meeting of the International Society for the Systems Sciences*, Rohnert Park, CA (pp. 1-7).

Mora, M., Gelman, O., Cervantes, F., Mejia, M., & Weitzenfeld, A. (2003). A systemic approach for the formalization of the information system concept: Why information systems are systems. In J. Cano (Ed.), *Critical reflections of information systems: A systemic approach* (pp. 1-29). Hershey, PA: Idea Group.

Mora, M., Gelman, O., Forgionne, G., & Cervantes, F. (2004, May 19-21). *Integrating the soft and the hard systems approaches: A critical realism based methodology for studying soft systems dynamics (CRM-SSD)*. Paper presented at the Third International Conference on Systems Thinking in Management (ICSTM 2004), Philadelphia.

Nambisan, S., Agarwal, R., & Tanniru, M. (1999). Organizational mechanisms for enhancing user innovation in information technology. *MIS Quarterly, 23*(3), 365-395.

Nandhakumar, J. (1996). Design for success?: Critical success factors in executive information systems development. *European Journal of Information Systems, 5*, 62-72.

Palvia, S. C., & Chervany, N. L. (1995). An experimental investigation of factors influencing predicted success in DSS implementation. *Information & Management, 29*, 43-53.

Poulymenakou, A., & Holmes, A. (1996). A contingency framework for the investigation of information systems failure. *European Journal of Information Systems, 5*(1), 34-46.

Rai, A., & Bajwa, D. S. (1997). An empirical investigation into factors relating to the adoption of executive information systems: An analysis of EIS collaboration and decision support. *Decision Sciences, 28*(4), 939-974.

Rainer, R. K., & Watson, H. J. (1995). What does it take for successful executive information systems? *Decision Support Systems, 14*(2), 147-156.

Rockart, J. F. (1979). Chief executives define their own data needs. *Harvard Business Review, 57*(2), 81-93.

Rockart, J. F., & DeLong, D. W. (1988). *Executive support systems*. Homewood, AL: Dow Jones-Irwin.

Rogers, E. M. (1983). *The diffusion of innovations* (3rd ed.). New York: Free Press.

Rogers, E. M. (1995). *The diffusion of innovations* (4th ed.). New York: Free Press.

Satzinger, J. W., Jackson, R. B., & Burd, S. D. (2000). *Systems analysis and design in a changing world*. Thompson Learning Course.

Scott Morton, M. S. (1971). *Management decision systems*. Boston: Harvard University, Graduate School of Business Administration.

Sprague, R. H., & Carlson, E. D. (1982). *Building effective decision support systems*. New Jersey: Prentice Hall.

Turban, E. (1992). Why expert systems succeed and why they fail. In E. Turban & J. Liebowitz (Eds.), *Managing expert systems* (pp. 2-13). Harrisburg, PA: Idea-Group.

Turban, E. (1995). *Decision support systems and expert systems (Management support systems)* (4th ed.). Prentice-Hall.

Turban, E. & Aronson, J. (1998). *Decision Support Systems and Intelligent Systems*. New Jersey: Prentice Hall.

Tyran, C. K., & George, J. F. (1993). The implementation of expert systems: A survey of successful implementations. *Data Base, 24*(4), 5-15.

Tyran, C. K., & George, J. F. (1994). Expert systems implementation and impacts: A managerial perspective. *Journal of Information Technology Management, 5*(1), 27-36.

Udo, G. J., & Guimaraes, T. (1994). Empirically assessing factors related to DSS benefits. *European Journal of Information Systems, 3*(3), 218-227.

Watson, H. J., Rainer, K., & Koh, K. (1991). Executive information systems: A framework for guiding EIS development and a survey of current practices. *MIS Quarterly, 15*(1), 13-30.

Welsch, G. (1986). The information transfer specialist in successful implementation of decision support systems. *ACM SIGMIS Data Base, 18*(1), 32-40.

Williams, J. & Ramaprasad, A. (1996). A taxonomy of critical success factors. *European Journal of Information Systems, 5*(4), 250-260.

Young, D., & Watson, H. J. (1995). Determinates of EIS acceptance. *Information and Management, 29*(3), 153-164.

Zmud, R. W., & Apple, L. (1989). *Measuring information technology infusion.* Unpublished manuscript.

KEY TERMS

Executive-Based Decision Support System: This is "a computer based system composed of a user-dialog system, a graph system, a multidimensional database query system and an external communication system, which enables decision makers to access a common core of data covering key internal and external business variables by a variety of dimensions (such as time and business unit)" (Forgionne et al., 2005, p. 765).

Implementation Failure: It is an implementation project that is cancelled during its development, is ended with a system underutilized, or is removed early with relevant financial and organizational losses.

Implementation Process: This is the complex and long-term process where multiple organizational, financial, technical, and human-based factors interact since the acknowledgement or discovering of a new technology until the total institutionalization of the system.

Knowledge-Based Decision Support System: This is "a computer based system composed of a user-dialog system, an inference engine, one or several intelligent modules, a knowledge base and a work memory, which emulates the problem-solving capabilities of a human expert in a specific domain of knowledge" (Forgionne et al., 2005, p. 765).

Large-Scale Decision-Making Support System (DMSS): A DMSS is an information system designed to support some, several, or all phases of the decision-making process that demands substantive financial, organizational, human, technical, and knowledge resources for being deployed in organizations.

Model-Based Decision Support System (DSS): A model-based DSS is "an interactive computer-based system composed of a user-dialog system, a model processor and a data management system, which helps decision makers utilize data and quantitative models to solve semi-structured problems" (Forgionne et al., 2005, p. 765).

ENDNOTE

[1] Actually, in the final Eierman et al. (1995) framework, user participation and top-management support are reported as factors useful in the analysis of a model-oriented DMSS.

Index

A

ABC implementation, methods of appraising 630
ABC implementation 15
ABC model 4
Abilene Paradox 468, 469, 470, 473
absolute percentage error (APE) 136
accommodating decision making 618
activity-based costing, definition of 3
activity-based costing (ABC) 1, 628
activity-based information system (ABIS) 4
added value 724, 730
adoption decision 470
adverse selection 777, 780, 782
affect infusion model (AIM) 482
agent-based exploratory simulation 718
agent-based simulation (ABS) 555, 556, 560, 561, 562, 645, 646, 647, 651
aggregation and ranking alternatives nearby the multi-attribute ideal situations (ARAMIS) 421
agile manifesto 466, 471
AHP, rank reversal 31
AHP, subjectivity and time consumption 31
AHP and farm-level decisions 35
AHP and health care system 35
alarm system 532
algorithm 296
American Association of Petroleum Geologists (AAPG) 733
analysis of variance (ANOVA) 663, 664, 665, 667
analytic hierarchy principle (AHP) 29, 411
analytic hierarchy process (AHP) 816, 873
analytic network principle (ANP) 411

analytic network process (ANP) 35, 254, 259, 260, 261, 262, 263, 264
analytical hierarchy process (AHP) 212, 320
analytical model (AM) 640
analytic-holistic model 761, 762
Answer Set Semantics 593
ant colony optimization (ACO) 604, 606
application service provider (ASP) 50
architectural capability level 324
ArcXML 703, 708
artifact selection 618-627
artificial intelligence (AI) 135, 329
asymmetric information 725, 726, 730, 776, 777, 778, 779, 780, 782
asynchronous collaboration media (ACM 791, 792, 797
asynchronous creativity theory (ACT) 797
attention-based view 38-45
Australian Technology Park (ATP) 860
auto lifecycle 671-674
automarketism 674-676
automated argumentation 489
automating 135
automation of information distribution, push mode 489

B

balanced scorecard (BSC), in a decision support system 50
balanced scorecard (BSC) 46
Barnard, Chester 20
Bayes, Thomas 653
Bayesian mathematicians 653

benchmark 710
Bernoulli, Daniel 653
Bill of Materials (BOM) 444
biproduct data suppliers 850
Black Scholes method 769
body of evidence 278, 285
Boston Public 877
bounded rationality 932
building assessment 958, 959, 968
business activity monitoring (BAM) 62
business intelligence (BI) 5, 49, 811
business intelligence (BI) systems 232
business intelligence analytics (BIA) 668, 670, 677, 679
business intelligence analytics framework 669-671
business model innovation 891
business process 497, 498, 500
business process analysis (BPA) 62
business process improvement 792, 794
Business process management (BPM) 61
business process modeling 245
business processes 496

C

cake division 403
case-based reasoning (CBR) 325
causal loop diagram (CLD) 247, 496, 501
causality 751, 753, 754, 755, 756
changing organisational context 924
characteristic parameters 368
characterizing extreme events 69-70
chief executive officer (CEO) 20
Choquet integral 392
Choquet-TSK 391
CLEHES© 613, 617
climate change 253
closed world assumption (CWA) 579
clustering-classification types 297
clusters 296
coaching 613, 614, 615
cognitive map 830
collective decision-making process 110
collectivism 316
Common Criteria (CC) 213
common gateway interface (CGI) 274
communication support 72
communications-driven DSS 232
community colleges 339
complex adaptive system (CAS) 675, 679
complex problem 289, 293
compromise revision (CR) 376

compromise solution 553
computational symbol-program level 324
computer aided facility management (CAFM) software 84
computer supported cooperative work (CSCW) 63
computer-supported collaborative work (CSCW) 196
concept map 830
condition class 784, 789
confidence value 76, 79
conjectures (C) 719
consistency ratio (CR) 30
contextual cues 102
contextual elements 103
contextual graph 103, 104, 106
contextual knowledge 102, 103
continuous event simulation 308-309
contracts 724, 725, 726, 728, 729
contribution margin (CM) 1
contribution margin I 12
contribution margin II 12
cooperative decision support system 109-115
core competence 724
corporate culture 933
cost calculation, five stages of 6
cost calculation 6
creative decision-making 151
criterion flow values 749
critical success factors (CSFs) 48, 350
cues 790, 791, 793, 797
culture and ethical decision making 315
current contextual knowledge (CCK) 186
customer order management cycle (COM) 496
customer relationship management (CRM) 50, 124

D

dashboard system applications 116
dashboards, characteristics of 117
dashboards, risks and problems 119
data, selling and delivering 852
data and knowledge (DK) 325
data envelopment analysis (DEA) 709-715
data flow diagrams (DFDs) 64, 807
data mining capabilities 196
data quality verifiers 850
data warehouse (DW) 848
data warehouse life cycle management (DWLM) 128
data warehousing 124
data warehousing methodologies 128
database (DB) 640

Index

data-driven DSS 232, 934
dataset, visualization of 296
datasets 296
decentralization through objectives 933
decision analysis (DA) 654
decision biases 134
decision class 565, 566, 567, 573, 784, 785, 789
decision hedgehog 149
decision maker (DM) 320, 514, 653, 732
decision makersÕ (DM) 418
decision making, nature of 653
decision making (DM) 102, 374
decision making units (DMU) 709-715
decision modeling 496
decision modeling diagrammatic tools 245
decision modeling diagrams 496
decision module 503
decision processes 141
decision rules 783, 784, 785, 788, 789
decision set, ordered mode 177
decision set, unordered mode 177
decision support 503, 716
decision support 54, 57, 59
decision support portals 38, 43
decision support system (DSS) 26, 50, 65, 84, 93, 116, 124, 165, 192, 211, 212, 218-224, 272, 296, 320, 329, 474, 584-592, 593, 604, 653, 680, 699, 708, 823, 838, 872, 969, 970
decision theory 568, 766
decision tree (DT) 247, 382, 476, 501
decision tree diagram 249
decision tree methodology 250
decision variable space, definition of 246
decisional methods 953
decisional service-task level 322
decision-enabled process modeling diagram 496
decision-makers 38, 39, 40, 41, 43
decision-making 225
decision-making activities 246
decision-making as choice 38-39
decision-making level 322
decision-making model 245
decision-making process (DMP) 218-224, 680, 681
decision-making situation (DMS) 682
decision-making support systems (DMSS) 320, 455, 680, 939
decision variables 502
DecisionNet 274
decisions, emotional consequences 482
deductive databases 594

default reasoning 578
defeasible argumentation 490
defeasible logic programming (DeLP) 490
defeaters 490
degree of satisfaction 548, 549
Dempster-Shafer (DS) structure 733
Dempster-Shafer Theory 278, 284, 285
dendrogram 298
descriptive theories 764
devilÕs advocate 350, 469, 470
diagnosis 565, 570, 571, 572, 574
dialectic inquiry 469, 470
dimensional model 237, 240, 242, 244
dimensions 237, 238, 244
discourses of truth 227
discrete event simulation 306, 307
Discrete Event Simulation (DES) 555, 556
discriminant function analysis 298
disjunctive logic programs 599
distributed artificial intelligence 798, 805
distributed decision making 800
D-model 162
DMSS implementation, failures in 456
DMSS implementations, analysis of 457
document-driven DSS 934
drivers, identification of 828
DSS community 94
DSS components 232
DSS framework 232
DSS matrix 296
DSS possibility matrix 844, 845
dual process 757-765
dual set theory 903
dynamic system simulation 306-312

E

e-business 692
e-business model 883, 888, 890, 891
economic added value 47
economic control 884, 885, 886, 887, 890
economies of scale 727
e-democracy 692, 697
efficient DMU 710, 715
efficient solution 53
e-government 691, 692, 695, 696, 697, 698
ELECTRE methods 419
electronic data interchange (EDI) 362, 768
electronic response systems (ERS) 865, 866, 867, 871
emergency management 69-75
emergency management systems (EMS) 186

emergency plans 184
emergency response 184
emergency response phase 184, 185
emergency response story 435
emergent behavior 677
emergent behaviour 556
emotions,influence of 484
emotions, study of 482
enterprise resource planning (ERP) 49, 86, 245, 348, 443
entity relationship diagrams (ERDs) 807
entity-relationship data model 244
environmental information system 697, 698
epistemic specifications 600
equivalence class 78
equivalence class 784, 789
e-services 638
European Space Agency (ESA) 391, 528
event complexity 70
event-driven process chain (EPC) 496
evolutionary algorithms (EA) 83, 604, 607
executive information system (EIS) 116, 124, 232, 329, 680, 807, 946
ExoMars rover 528
expected utility theory 653, 757, 758, 759
expected value theory 757, 758, 759, 762
expert knowledge acquisition (EKA) 519
expert or knowledge-based systems (ES/KBS) 680
expert system (ES) 219, 220, 329, 946
explanation facility module 529
explanations (E) 719
explicit structuring mode 520
extended EPC (eEPC) 497
extended network 925
extensible markup Language (XML) 274
external knowledge 102
external validity 663
extract, transfer, and load (ETL) 125
extraction, transformation, and loading (ETL) 811

F

facility management (FM) 84
fact table 237, 238, 244
factor analysis 298
factor-based-approach 459
fast-moving consumer goods (FMCG) 1
Federal Emergency Management Agency (FEMA) 185, 340
Federative Decision Support System (DSS) 368-373
focal element 76, 83, 278, 280, 282, 285

forecast 661, 662, 663, 664
FORTRAN 192
frame of discernment 278, 280, 281
framing discourse 228
functional integration 884, 885, 886, 888, 890
fuzziness, concept of 901
fuzzy band 551, 553
fuzzy decision tree (FDT) 382-390
fuzzy GP 414
fuzzy inference systems (FISs) 391
fuzzy knowledge-based systems (FKBS) 528
fuzzy linear programming (FLP) 539-553
fuzzy logic (FL) 325, 539-553, 904
fuzzy logic models 528
fuzzy membership functions (MFs) 382-389
fuzzy set 539-553
fuzzy set theory 902
fuzzy sets, and probability 904

G

game theory 403
games 402
games as tables 404
games as trees 403
general algebraic modeling systems (GAMS) 273
General Motors 35
generalised criterion preference functions 750
generalized probability box (GPB) 736
genetic algorithm (GA) 325
geographic information system (GIS) 370, 373, 699, 700, 701, 703, 704, 707, 708, 958, 959, 960, 964, 965, 966, 968
geographical information systems (GIS) 188
geometrical analysis for interactive assistance (GAIA) 743, 750
GIE arithmetic 735
GIE trace 735
global sourcing 816
goal programming (GP) 410
governance 340
governmental agencies 850
greedy randomized adaptive search procedure (GRASP) 604, 606
gross domestic product (GDP) 84
group communication and decision support (GDACS) 229
group decision and negotiation system (GDNS) 584, 586, 587, 589, 591
group decision making learning task (GDMLT) 874
group decision support software (GDSS) 656

G (cont.)

group decision support system (GDSS), computer based 872
group decision support systems (GDSS) 63, 148, 196, 229, 232, 857, 872, 922
group storytelling approach 435
group support systems (GSS) 65, 286, 287, 291, 823
group verbal decision analysis (GroupVDA) 418
groupthink 468, 469, 470

H

hard decision, concept of 484
Hazard Avoidance and Critical Control Point (HACCP) 360
hemispheric assumption 762
hidden action 724, 726
hidden information 726
hierarchical clustering methods 297
holistic model 761, 762, 763, 764
HTML 703, 708
human activity systems (HAS) 655
human-computer interaction (HCI) 94
hypotheses (H) 719

I

immediacy 790, 791, 797
imputation 83
incentive theory 730
Incident Command System (ICS) 185
indiscernibility relation 783, 784, 785, 789
inductive learning 389
inefficient DMU 715
inference engine module 529
influence diagram (ID) 496,, 500
influence diagram tools 501
influence diagrams, and spreadsheets 478
influence diagrams, for decision support systems 477
influence diagrams (IDs) 247, 248, 475,
informating 135
information 724, 725, 726, 727, 728, 730, 731
information and communications technology (ICT) 84, 134, 856
information and knowledge (IK) 489
information requirements determination (IRD) 807
information support 72-73
information systems (IS) 211, 356
information systems development (ISD) 807
information technology (IT) 61
information webs 923

inherence dominance relations 520
integrated decision making 618
intellectual property 778
intelligent agent (IA) 325, 505, 508, 509, 510, 512
intelligent building 961, 962, 963, 964, 967, 968
intelligent decision support system (IDSS) 506, 507, 508, 509, 510, 513, 515, 943
intelligent DMSS (i-DMSS) 680
interactive Internet map server 969
interface 567, 568, 569, 571, 572, 573
interface agent 800, 803
interface-dialog module 529
internal return rate (IRR) 628
International Facility Management Association (IFMA) 85
International Organization for Standardization (ISO) 528
Internet map server 703
Internet technology 272
interrelationship digraph 342
intuition gap 21
intuitions (I) 719
investments for productivity improvement 200
irrelevant consequences problem 378

J

joint application development (JAD) 807
Jung, Carl 20

K

key processing (or performance) indicators (KPI) 117
knowledge, definition of 839
knowledge acquisition module 529
knowledge base module 529
knowledge bases (KB) 374
knowledge chain 843, 846
knowledge discovery from databases (KDD) 176
knowledge discovery in databases (KDD) 236, 242, 244
knowledge harvesting 867
knowledge management (KM) 134, 374, 837
knowledge management influences 841
knowledge management system (KMS) 134, 196, 374
knowledge manipulation 840
knowledge representation 576
knowledge system (KS) 569-570
knowledge visualization 966, 968

knowledge worker desktopÕs model (KWDM) 584-592
knowledge-based systems (KBS) 135, 329
knowledge-driven DSS 934
Kolmogorov axioms 902

L

large group decision support system (LGDSS) 865-871
large-scale DMSSs 456
leaf node 384, 386, 387, 390
lean media 790, 792, 793, 794, 797
Learning Teams Adventure Game (L-TAG) 878
least squares Monto Carlo (LSM) 771
left-brain style decision making 618
legacy information systems (LIS) 94
Liebnitzian system 193
linear programming (LP) 542
linguistic variables 903
local decision making (improvisation) 71
local e-government 970, 975
local search algorithms 605
location problems 53-60
logic programming languages, family of five 594
logical layout 156, 158, 160, 161, 162, 163, 164
lower unit costs 47

M

main-stream data 584, 585, 591
maintenance of system stability 436
major ethical decision models 314
Malaysia 316
Mamdani model 392
management and organizational theories 654
management information systems (MISs) 116
management practices 645, 646, 651, 652
managerial decision making 200
market failure 777
masculinity 316
Maslow, Abraham 20
mass values 76, 77, 79, 80, 81
material requirements planning (MRP) 444
materialized view 236, 241
MATLAB 548, 553
mean absolute percentage area (MAPE) 664, 665, 667
media richness theory (MRT) 790-794
media synchronicity theory (MST) 790-794
MegaPascale (MPa) 532
membership function (MF) 541, 543, 547, 548, 552, 553

metadata 126
metaheuristic applications 604
metaheuristic methods 604
meta-interpreter, for logic programs 578
metaphors (M) 719
metric-drive design 244
min-max GP 414
Mobile DSS 641
model management 273
model management systems (MMS) 273
model schema 272
model-driven DSS 619, 620
modeling lifecycle 272
MODI-Monitoring 528
monitoring and diagnosis for Mars driller (MODI) 531
monopoly SDSs 851
Monte Carlo simulation 306, 307
moral hazard 777, 780
multi-agent model 652
multi-agent simulation 554-564, 645-652
multi-agent system (MAS) 506, 509, 556-558, 679, 800, 806
multi-agent system (MAS) design 558-560
multi-agent-based simulation (MABS) 718
multi-algorithm DSS 299
multi-attribute classification problem (MAC) 518
multi-attribute utility theory (MAUT) 212, 865, 866, 867, 868, 870, 871, 872
multi-criteria decision making (MCDM) 410, 514
Multicriteria Model 321
multiple criteria decision aiding (MCDA) 418
multiple objective linear programming (MOLP) 709-715
multiple sourcing 816
multiple-rule decision-making 177

N

National Aeronautic and Space Administration (NASA) 34, 339
natural disaster 255, 256, 257, 261, 263
necessity 751, 755
necessity investments 200
negation-as-failure 577
Nelder-Mead complex 414
net flow values 750
net present value (NPV) 628, 768
netcasting 489
network analysis 923
network boundaries, setting 952
network perspective 951

network representation and visualisation 952
neural network (NN) 325, 661-667
non-decision making (NDM) 910
non-dominated solution 709, 712, 713
nonlinear GP 414
non-uniqueness problem 378

O

objective function 77, 78, 79, 81, 82, 662, 663
obligatory passage points (OPP) 952
observations (O) 719
online analytical processing (OLAP) 5, 125, 232, 811
online environmental information systems 691-698
online transaction processing (OLTP) 125
operational control center (PC OPS's) 589
operational performance management (OPM) 584, 586, 588, 591
operations research (OR) 654
opponent, oddly indexed arguments 490
organisational prerequisites 884
organisational structure 815
organizational decision making 69, 71, 72
organizational decision support system (ODSS) 61
organizational observer 612-617
organizational transformation 612-617
outsourcing 724, 727, 729, 816

P

parallel action grouping 106
parallel processing 236, 241
parallelism 791, 792, 793, 794, 795
paranoid discourse 227
Pareto inefficient results 411
personal assistant 799, 800
personal decision analysis (PDA) 141
personal knowledge (PK) 186
personal transformation 617
personality assumption 762
perspectives 286-295
physical layout 158
pignistic probability 278, 280, 283
planning support systems (PSS) 699, 708, 969, 970
plausibility 278, 280, 283, 285
policy decision support 720
poly-interval estimation (PIE) 734
pooled interdependent decision-making 219
positional method 953
possibility theory 904
power distance 316

power transmission system, components of 165
previous formal knowledge (PFK) 185
previous personal knowledge (PPK) 185, 187
prime implicants 753
principal-agent 724, 725, 726, 729, 730
prisoners' dilemma 405
probability, concepts of 902
probability theory 902
problem formulation 292, 294
problem representation, levels of 226
problem-based learning (PBL) 875
problem-expressing discourse 227
problem-solving approach, analytical 23
problem-solving approach, intuitive 23
procedural rationality 932
proceduralized context 103, 104
process modeling 157-160, 245, 496
process models 500
process planning 155, 163, 164
processing (P) 325
product modeling 157-160
production system 253, 254, 256, 259, 264, 269
profitability analysis 3
PROMETHEE 253, 258, 259, 268, 269, 270, 743-750
proponent, evenly indexed arguments 490
prospect theory 759, 760, 763
public interest 780, 782
public policies 716
pull systems 489
purchase price variance (PPV) 443
push technologies 489

Q

qualitative comparative analysis 751-756
quality of classification 784, 785, 786, 787, 789
quality of data (QoD) 639

R

ranking 750
rapid application development (RAD) 807
rational view, challenges on 654
rational/intuitive orientation 22
real options analysis 766
real options reasoning 766
recency 661, 662, 663, 664, 665, 666
recognition 565
recognition-primed decision (RCP) 351
reduct 785, 787, 789
reference buildings 963, 964, 965, 966, 968

regulation 776, 779, 780, 781, 782
regulatory boards 850
rehearsability 791, 792
relational methods 953
relevance assumption 762
reported version 435
reprocessability 791, 792, 793
reputational methods 953
request for attention (RFA) 188
requests for information (RFI) 188
required decisions 29
retailing SDSs 851
return on capital 47
return on investment (ROI) 47
revenue growth 47
revisited cognitive decision making process 110
right-brain style decision making 618, 621
risk 725, 726, 727, 728
risk equalisation 780
root node 382, 386, 389, 390
rough set theory, variations of 907
rough sets 905
roughness 901
rule qualities, combining 179
rule quality 177

S

sales decay navigation 671-674
satisfactory solution 544, 552
satisficing decision making 627
scatter search (SS) 604, 608
scenario process 832
security decision support system (SDSS) 211, 212
self-organization maps (SOM) 299
Semantic Web 66
semi-obnoxious facilities 54, 55, 60
semi-structured decision 506
semi-structured problem 220
sense-making process 917
Sense-Making Theory, impact of 919
Sense-Making theory 916
sensitivity analysis (SA) 638
service oriented architectures (SOA) 274
shared conceptual space 857
shared data 585
shareholder value 47
signalling 777, 781
Simon, Herbert 22
simple object access protocol (SOAP) 274
simplex plot 76, 77, 78, 80, 81, 82
simulated annealing (SA) 604, 606

single display groupware (SDG) 875
single sourcing 816
small to medium enterprises (SMEs) 356
snowflake schema 237, 238, 241, 243
social cohesion 952
social network analysis (SNA) 950
Society of Petroleum Engineers (SPE) 733
soft systems methodology (SSM) 655
software agents 798-806
software assistant 800
software development methodology 466, 467
Software Engineering Institute (SEI) 339
software risk evaluation (SRE) 341
source-of-knowledge data 585, 586, 591
Space monitoring systems 528
spatial DSSs (SDSSs) 232
specificity 490
spindle head 156, 159, 160, 161, 162, 163, 164
spontaneous habitat 368
SRE method description tools 341
star schema 237, 238, 239, 241, 244
starflake schema 237, 238, 239
statistical institutes 849
stock 307, 309
strategic choice approach 704, 707
strategic decisions 20
strategic games 402
strategic investments 200
strategic partnership 730
strength optimization, refined 173
strong negation 577
structured decision 505
structured problem 219, 223
structured query language (SQL) 124
structuring 565
subsethood 384, 386, 387
suggestion models 620
supply chain, definition of 245
supply chain, structure of 815
Supply Chain Council 815
supply chain information systems 815
supply chain management (SCM) 245, 356, 357, 814
Supply Chain Operations Reference (SCOR) model 815
supply chain structure 816
supply chains 814
Sweater Game 876
syndicate data suppliers (SDSs) 848
system dynamics (SD) 307, 310, 311, 554, 555

Index

T

tabu search (TS) 604, 605
Takagi-Sugeno-Kang (TSK) 391
target 710
task acquired knowledge potential (TAKP) 875
task acquired skill potential (TASP) 875
task energy potential (TEP) 874
task interdependency potential (TIP) 874
team learning system (TLS) 856
technical, personal and organizational (T, P and O) perspectives 289-293
terrain-hardness detection 533
Tetris blocks 296
The KIV model 959-960
theory (T) 719
theory of need 873
theory of personal probability 653
ThinkClick 865-871
ThinkTeam 875, 878, 879
time pressure 70
time series forecasting 661-667
time-critical decision making problems 638
time-critical situations 638
TLS, etiquette 857
TLS facilitator 857
top-down induction of decision trees (TDIDT) 176
TOPSIS method 423
transfer machine 155, 156, 158, 160, 162, 163
transmission system design 165
transmission systems 165, 166
triangulation paradigm 496, 500

TRIMAP 709, 712-715

U

uncertain reasoning 76, 82, 83
uncertainty, degrees of 902
uncertainty avoidance 316
uncertainty quantification 733
UniComBOS 515
unified modeling language (UML) 64
universal description, discovery, and integration (UDDI) 274

unstructured decision 505
unstructured problem 220
urban cluster 254, 255, 270
urban planning and development 368-373
usability, in interfaces 530
user interface (UI) 325, 640

V

vagueness 901
value-based software engineering 94
variable precision rough sets model (VPRS) 784, 789
vehicle routing problem (VRP) 604
Venus Express alarm system 391
verbal decision analysis (VDA) 418, 514
Virtual Information Centre (VIC) 188
virtual teams 790, 791, 794, 795, 796
visual interactive modeling DSS 627
vote error (VE), squared 300
vote matrix 299

W

Web-based public participatory GIS 969-976
Web services description language (WSDL) 274
Webcasting 489
WebGIS 699, 700, 703, 705, 706, 707, 708
wireless devices 638
Workflow Management Coalition (WfMC) 62
workflow management systems (WfMS) 188
World Petroleum Congresses (WPC) 733

X

Xerox Corporation 35

Z

ZAPROS methods 419
Zing team learning system (TLS) 856
Zing Technologies 857
zone of proximal development (ZPD) 856

```
HD          Encyclopedia of
30.213        decision making and
.E527         decision support
2008          technologies.
```

35019000025790

DATE			

BAKER & TAYLOR